Multimedia Power Tools®

Multimedia Power Tools®

Peter Jerram and Michael Gosney

with
Scott Billups
David Poole
Terry Schussler
Christopher Yavelow

and the editors of *Verbum* Magazine

Illustrations by Jennifer Gill

RANDOM HOUSE
ELECTRONIC PUBLISHING

Multimedia Power Tools®

Published in the United States by Random House, Inc., New York, and simultaneously in Canada by Random House of Canada, Limited.

Produced by Verbum, Inc. and The Gosney Company, Inc., P.O. Box 189, Cardiff, CA 92007-0189, 619/944.9977, fax 9995

Manufactured in the United States of America

First Edition

0 9 8 7 6 5 4 3 2 1

ISBN 0-679-79118-3

For additional copyright information on previously published material appearing in this book-software package, see Appendix D.

New York Toronto London Sydney Auckland

CHIEF WRITER
Peter Jerram

PRODUCER
Michael Gosney

ASSOCIATE PRODUCER
Elizabeth Tilles

PROGRAMMING
Terry Schussler, Don Brenner

BOOK ILLUSTRATOR
Jennifer Gill

MUSICAL SCORE
Christopher Yavelow

DISC PROJECT COORDINATOR
Bruce Powell

TECHNICAL EDITOR
Goopy Rossi

INTERFACE GRAPHICS
Mark Lyon, Danielle Foster

DISC TEXT EDITOR
Susan Lyon

BOOK PRODUCTION
Danielle Foster

DISC PRODUCTION
Don Doerfler, Mike Soloman, Steve Downs, Frank Tycer
Don Brenner, Henri Poole, Elizabeth Tilles

CONTRIBUTING EDITORS
IMAGING AND ANIMATION: Farshid Almassizadeh, Mark Crosten (Imaging Tools Chapter), Jack Davis, John Odam, Goopy Rossi, Lynda Weinman
AUTHORING/INTERACTIVITY: Paul Burgess, Matthew Fass, Helene Hoffman, Ann Irwin, David Poole (Authoring Chapters) , Karen Rall (Production Chapters)
SOUND: Mike Salomon, Steve Rappaport, Christopher Yavelow (Sound Chapters)
VIDEO: Stephen Axelrad (Video Chapters), Scott Billups, Don Doerfler, David Fox (Video Chapters), Harry Mott, Greg Roach, Mike Salomon

SPECIAL THANKS TO
Bill Gladstone, Elizabeth Schimel, Curtis Wong, Vivid Publishing, Valerie Bayla, Reegan Ray, Peter Kreklow, Jack Davis, Michel Kripalani, John Laney, Craig McClain, Sharon Powell, John Najera, Jean Davis Taft

EDITOR/PROJECT MANAGER
Michael Roney

PUBLISHER
Kenzi Sugihara

Book Overview

Contents

Introduction

Multimedia Power Tools is more than just another book on multimedia. It is a book about producing multimedia on the Macintosh, written in collaboration with many of the top hands-on authorities in the field. And it's more than a book. It's interactive—a working example of new media—with a companion multimedia CD-ROM.

We're not being self-serving when we state that the Macintosh is by far and away the most robust multimedia development platform going. It *is*. Why? First of all, because the Mac was destined, from the very beginning, to change the way people work with media. Even in its original incarnation, this little "computing machine" had the seeds of today's new media revolution: a graphical user interface, built in sound and graphics capabilities and a knack for combining media forms, as expressed in the early programs MacPaint, VideoWorks, Thunderscan and Pagemaker. Those of us who had the pleasure of knowing Macintosh in its youth remember working with digital painting, vector graphics, scanned imagery, music and even animation. As the Mac established itself as the creative computer and the computer favored by creative people, these applications evolved. Today, it all adds up to a multimedia tour-de-force: the Macintosh family of computers, a plethora of advanced software, and powerful peripheral devices for scanning, printing and video capture. But perhaps the Mac's most important asset is the community of creative professionals who use it in countless ways. Graphic designers, musicians, animators, photographers and videographers—and the programmers who work with them—have evolved their own ingenious ways of doing things in the digital domain. Each field has been revolutionized. And thanks to the Mac's media integration and "cut and paste" interface standards, the convergence of these fields in the new craft that is interactive multimedia is happening almost organically.

About Verbum

Since 1986, the Verbum team based here in San Diego, along with our network of friends and associates around the world, has been producing publications and events to bridge the worlds of art and digital media. Our publications include *Verbum* magazine, the Verbum Book series, and the first true multimedia magazine on CD-ROM, *Verbum Interactive.* Our events have included the Imagine exhibit of Personal Computer Art held in Boston, Tokyo, and other cities, CyberArts International, produced with *Keyboard* magazine and held in Los Angeles, and The Digital Art Be-In, held annually in San Francisco during the January Macworld Expo.

How Power Tools Came to Be

Over the years, we have really enjoyed working with developers in the evolution of digital art tools, and, most of all, in helping to introduce these tools to creative people. Digital tools—whether for writing, music, graphics, animation, video, or interactive authoring—have something to offer everyone.

Verbum's philosophy has been one of experimentation, emphasizing the voice of hands-on artists and producers speaking from the trenches. Our magazine, books, and the Verbum Interactive CD-ROM all followed this approach. Verbum Interactive (VI) proved to be very instructional for multimedia producers, but its content was really oriented to a broader audience. We thought it would be great to combine the approach of our book series, which featured step-by-step projects, with the multimedia resources introduced on VI. In addition, we planned to include actual *tools,* usable files and programs, as well as demo programs. When Peter Jerram got involved and we began envisioning the book with Mike Roney at Random House, it grew. The disc concept was already pretty well defined, but the book evolved beyond its original conception into an extremely comprehensive resource covering all aspects of multimedia technology, tools, and processes. The *Multimedia Power Tools* interactive book was born.

As you might imagine, this project has been far from easy. For one thing, the multimedia field is growing and changing rapidly, still really defining itself. (Try asking 10 people their definitions of multimedia.) Also, the book and the CD-ROM are both very ambitious projects, with (as always) a somewhat constrained budget. But it has been extremely rewarding for all of us involved, and we are pleased to send it out into the world, hoping that it will help many in their work.

I would like to express my sincere thanks to each person who contributed to this challenging project—it resonates with your spirit. And I'd like to thank *you*—our treasured reader/user—for buying it. *Change the world now!*

—Michael Gosney

Preface

This integrated book/CD-ROM package is a complete information and resource kit for creating professional multimedia presentations and publications on the Macintosh. It covers the component elements of multimedia as well as the overall production process.

If you're looking to put together an effective business presentation, you'll find ample information herein about animated presentation techniques and packages. Or, you may have wanted to try your hand at animation ever since you first saw Elmer Fudd take a shot at that Wascally Wabbit. Check out our chapters on desktop animation tools, utilities, and techniques.

Fancy yourself as the next Spielberg? You'll find a full exposition on QuickTime, Apple's seminal digital video standard, as well as complete descriptions on the digital video production process, and the new video tools.

Likewise, chapters on digital sound and music give exhaustive summaries of recording, synthesis, processing, and capture tools and techniques. Interactivity, the force that anchors and connects this panoply of new media, also merits its own chapters, which cover interface design, programming, and assembly of components.

Book Organization

The book is logically divided into three parts:

Part One: Multimedia Tools and Technology covers what multimedia is and what tools are used to produce it. It begins by defining multimedia and surveying the multimedia development process, and then moves on to cover Macintosh system software and hardware, as well as peripherals pertinent to multimedia production. It concludes with detailed overviews and comparisons of multimedia creation software in the major categories: imaging, sound, animation, video, and authoring.

Part Two: Creating Multimedia on the Macintosh begins with chapters on planning and design and cross platform development, and continues with detailed looks at the multimedia creation process for sound, animation, video, and interactive presentations. Companion chapters provide background for the critically acclaimed projects featured on the Power Tools CD-ROM.

Part Three: The Power Tools CD describes the organization and contents of the Power Tools CD-ROM.

Here's a more detailed peek at the entire contents of the book:

Part One: Multimedia Tools and Technology

Chapter 1: Multimedia Defined is a broad overview of multimedia, what it is, what it means, and where it comes from.

Chapter 2: The Desktop Multimedia Process outlines the entire multimedia production process, from pre-production through final presentation.

Chapter 3: Macintosh System Software and Hardware tells you all you need to know about the Mac—its system software and extensions, memory management, and the range of Mac models and their capabilities.

Chapter 4: Hardware Components examines the full scope of hardware peripherals, from scanners to cameras, monitors to disk drives.

Chapter 5: Imaging Tools covers image processing software, which is at the core of any multimedia production.

Chapter 6: Sound Tools explains sampling and sound capture, sequencing and synchronization, before launching into a review of audio software.

Chapter 7: 3-D and Animation Tools explores the kaleidoscope of animation tools, from animated presentation software and utility programs, to modeling, rendering, and animation packages.

Chapter 8: Video Tools discusses video capture, compression, and processing, as well as available video editing and production tools.

Chapter 9: Authoring Tools covers authoring, interactive, and media integration software.

Chapter 10: Outside Resources is a directory of sources for multimedia content: art, photography, music, video, and animation clip art.

Part Two: Creating Multimedia on the Macintosh

Chapter 11: Project Planning and Design describes the planning process that is essential to any multimedia presentation or production.

Chapter 12 Working Cross Platform gives advice and tips for developing multimedia for delivery on other platforms.

Chapter 13: Producing Sound explores digital sound, from capture, to processing and editing.

Chapter 14: Sound Projects includes background on the sound projects on the Power Tools CD, as well as interviews with he developers themselves.

Chapter 15: Creating Animation is a comprehensive look at the digital animation process.

Chapter 16: Animation Projects provides a backdrop for the animation projects on the CD, along with insights of the project creators.

Chapter 17: Creating Video explores digital video, from pre-production through production itself.

Chapter 18: Video Projects is an introduction to this group of Power Tools CD projects, complete with advice and tips by the experts who created them.

Chapter 19: Creating Interactive Multimedia gives you professional perspectives for putting it all together: assembling your multimedia components, creating an interface, and setting up interactivity.

Chapter 20: Interactive Multimedia Projects describes this group of Power Tools projects, and includes a behind-the-scenes look at the creative process.

Part Three: The Power Tools CD

Chapter 21: Using the CD-ROM tells you how to install and use the Power Tools CD-ROM, and gives you an overview of the elegant interface that makes this product a multimedia "title" itself.

Chapter 22: Projects and Power Tools on the CD-ROM describes the valuable software on the disk, including the interactive Sample Projects and the scores of clip media collections, valuable utilities and applications demos.

Finally, the book closes with appendices that will aid you even more in producing your own multimedia:

Appendix A: Resources lists all the products and companies featured in the book and on the CD-ROM, complete with addresses and phone numbers.

Appendix B: Power Tools lists every Sample Project, clip media collection, application and utility on the disc, along with the Power Code for each.

Appendix C: Copyright Act of 1976 will provide you with legal guidance in acquiring and publishing multimedia material.

The book ends with an extensive multimedia glossary compiled by Steve Rosenthal, and, of course, an index.

CD-ROM Features

The CD-ROM is packed with 650 Mb of interactive tutorials, clip media, utilities and applications. It includes fifteen producer-guided tours of *So You Want to Be a Rock and Roll Star*, the *Robot from the Journeyman Project*, the *Lawnmower Man* logo, *The Madness of Roland,* Linda Weinman's *Video Quilt,* and many more critically acclaimed projects. It also features over 200 megabytes of Power Tools: valuable applications, utilities, demos, photographs, background textures, video clips, animations, sounds and more—from companies such as Apple Computer, Macromedia, Adobe Systems, Strata, DiVA, Passport Designs and CoSA. For a complete rundown of the disc contents, see Chapter 22, "Projects and Power Tools on the CD-ROM," and Appendix B.

Power Codes

This is truly an interactive book-disc, thanks to a unique feature called *Power Codes.* Anytime the book mentions an application or utility included on the disc, you'll be able to zip right to it by typing a Command-key combination. The book pages display Power Code icons, along with the appropriate key commands, in the page margins opposite each *first mention* of a tool or project in a chapter, or when a tool or project is related to a particular subject. As mentioned above, a complete listing of disc contents and their Power Codes is given in Appendix B.

Taking Aim at a Moving Target

Advances in multimedia technology are happening so incredibly fast! There are usually at least a few new product announcements with every passing week. Indeed, even as we are going to press we are learning about additional hardware advances and software upgrades. Keeping up with this constant evolution is an unrealistic mission for a book; it's a pursuit much better suited to magazines and newsletters.

In these pages we provide you with solid, critical information on the capabilities and interfaces of hardware peripherals and software applications, along with informed projections on the directions in which these technologies are evolving. By looking at the basic concepts of multimedia tools and technology, by showing how they interrelate, and by providing expert perspectives and examples for creating multimedia, we'll give you a knowledge base that no magazine can match.

Nevertheless, you still need to stay current with the exciting product revisions that are constantly coming to market! We recommend that you check out periodicals such as *Macweek, New Media, Morph's Outpost,* Seybold's *Digital Media,* and Hypermedia's *Inside Report on New Media* newsletters to keep track of the latest revisions to the hardware and software products we cover here.

Bon Voyage

Whether you're a professional communicator, an artist, or simply someone interested in the magic of multimedia, this book's for you. Its tapestry is as rich as the promise of multimedia itself. Learn. Enjoy. Create!

Acknowledgments

For Guy and Elise
who read to me

Peter Jerram

When I first decided to write about multimedia, in 1991, I had no idea what I was getting into. I'd envisioned a modest little book about emerging trends and technologies that I found interesting. I owe it to Bill Gladstone, my agent, for putting me in touch with the folks at Verbum and Random House, who had something bigger in mind.

Mike Roney, my editor and friend, deserves special thanks. Going far beyond the customary editorial stewardship, Mike often worked late into the night on rewrites, and even wrote some parts himself. I'd also like to thank Mike Gosney at Verbum, for coming up with a great concept, and being so easy to work with.

Also at Random House, thanks go to Kenzi Sugihara, Jean Davis Taft, and Niki DiSilvestro for their support. Likewise to the Verbum staff for their gracious help and hard work.

Many people submitted to interviews, trying with varying degrees of success to educate me on the intricacies of multimedia production. Though I can't mention them all, in particular I'd like to thank Barry Grimes, Donald Grahame, Joe Sparks, Paul Pillitteri, Lynda Weinman, Harry Marks, Jonathan Seybold, Drew Huffman, Vinny Carrella, Adam Lavine, James A. Collins, Robert May, Britt Peddie, David Arnowitz, Syd Mead, Lee Gomes, Frank Dutro, Darlene Yaplee, Kathleen M. Nilles, Kim Orumchian, Dave Larson, Dr. Allan Shelton, and Craig Weiss.

Thanks also to the many companies and people who provided software, equipment, and their valuable time, especially Teri Chadbourne at Adobe, Rix Kramlich and Alane Bowling of Macromedia, Kathy Englar of Ray Dream, Flora W. Perskie of Imergy, Mark O'Hara of CKS Partners, William W. Liu of CD Technology, Shelly Watson of Strata, Michelle De La Rosa of AT&T Graphics Software Labs, Damian Rosskill of Specular International, Karen Allen of Toshiba, Carrie L. Coppe of RasterOps, Laurie McLean and Kim Haas of McLean Public Relations, and Mary Hill and Cathy Galvin at SuperMac.

Finally, honorable mention to my friends and family who withstood endless rantings on multimedia: my sister Maria Jerram; Dr. Werner Feibel, Philip Garfield, and Art O'Sullivan, who gave professional advice and friendly sympathy; colleagues and friends Rose Kearsley and Logan Harbaugh; and my boss at Novell, Sue Szymanski, who gave her blessing. And last, Simon Bryant, and especially Tina, for just being there.

Michael Gosney

This project has involved so many talented and enjoyable people that I would have a hard time thanking each of them in appropriate fashion. I will, however, single out those few who played crucial roles in the project's genesis. William Gladstone, cyber-agent, put together the practical resources to make the idea a reality. Editors Mike Roney and Liz Schimel believed in the project—and Mike rode the bucking bronco all the way through. Peter Jerram was a joy to work with, showing that it takes more than talent (and his is substantial) to follow through and produce. Elizabeth Tilles deserves special recognition for her diligent management of, and work on, the CD-ROM. She also helped in the book and oversaw the Power Codes implementation. Bruce Powell of Synergy was patient and methodical in his essential contributions to the disc production. Danielle Foster kept her cool and met her deadlines on the book production. Don Doerffler, Mike Soloman, Steve Downs, and Mark and Susan Lyon contributed important technical and artistic resources to the disc. Don Brenner powered out the final code and handled the disc mastering under pressure from everyone else involved.

I would also like to acknowledge the Verbum team(s), contributors and readers who have catalyzed our vision of creative work with digital media over the years. In particular, I'd like to thank Jack Davis, Michel Kripalani, Ed Coderre and Steve Lomas, whose work on Verbum Interactive 1.0 planted the seeds for this and many other multimedia projects.

Finally, I'd like to thank Susan, who inspires my days.

Part One

MULTIMEDIA TOOLS AND TECHNOLOGY

1

Multimedia Defined

"Multimedia stutters on the brink of something really incredible. But what?"

— Floyd Wray, multimedia consultant.

Movies are popping up in strange places—in your E-mail, in your spreadsheets. Your Mac squawks when you insert a floppy disk. An animated tour guide explains your new program to you. These are the early warning signs of a digital and communications revolution that is sweeping the desktop.

The world is going digital, and there's no turning back. Sound, music, graphics, animation, photography, and video can now be fed into an ordinary computer, where they can be sliced, diced, combined, and reconstituted into arresting works of the imagination. Perhaps no other development of the modern age has held equal power to free the mind and the spirit of humans; perhaps the ultimate destiny of the computer has been realized. And maybe we can all make a few bucks on the side.

Welcome to the Bitstream

"Multimedia" is hard to define because both its scope and applications are so broad that it defies a simple explanation. At its most basic, "multimedia" refers to the personal computer's growing ability to process not just text, but all sorts of visual and sonic information.

Thus, at the simplest level, you can spruce up a corporate presentation with video clips, read about a composer's life while listening to his symphony, or use 3-D animation to visualize your new kitchen addition—all on the desktop, and all with your Mac. (Of course, you'll also need a few items of hardware, some clever pieces of software, and a whole lot of time to burn. Otherwise, we'd have nothing to explain, and no reason to write this book.)

PROJECTS Video Quilt 020

But even this isn't the whole story. Multimedia is a lot more than chucking a few video frames into your slide show. In California, the Tulare county department of social services uses interactive touch screens to help people apply for Medicaid and other social programs. It's estimated that the system will save the county over $18 million per year in improved efficiency and reduced errors.

In early 1993, an entrepreneur began broadcasting a talk radio show over Internet, a rapidly growing worldwide computer network.

This is multimedia.

And consider a trip to the Louvre without actually flying to Paris. In The Voyager Company's *The Louvre, Volumes I–III,* you can scan hundreds of reproductions of the museum's works, while being guided by narrative tracks in French or English. An understanding of the museum's rich treasures is deepened by interactive maps, timelines, glossaries, and essays.

This is multimedia, too.

Rock and Roll 013

Or, you may want to pick up a musical instrument, but don't have the patience for lessons. Using Interactive Records' *So You Want to Be a Rock and Roll Star* CD, you can watch multimedia animation and artwork set to pop songs. Then, display the sheet music for songs, each measure of which is highlighted as it is played. Learn music theory with the help of voice annotation, and chords explained with color coding.

You guessed it, multimedia again. (By the way, *So You Want to Be a Rock and Roll Star* is one of the featured projects on our CD—check it out.)

EcoSpies 033

Multimedia is even reinventing entire industries. Consider the world of professional video production, which traditionally has been dominated by high-priced equipment and a professional staff of overpaid, coffee-drinking specialists. Now, *desktop* editing systems based on Apple's QuickTime video standard are being released at prices that are spiraling downward even as features and quality are matching systems in the traditional "post houses."

Clearly, multimedia is a broad-based phenomenon that already has a far-reaching impact in business, education, entertainment, and personal creativity. Its emerging influence on the desktop is being driven by increasingly sophisticated personal computers and by the metamorphosis of information into digital form.

The Computer That Ate *Leave It to Beaver*

Multimedia is being brought to your desktop by an unprecedented digital information convergence (Figure 1.1). All of a sudden, computers can be equipped with different flavors of low-cost *digitizers,* which convert everyday media (artwork, photographs, music) into binary format.

Flat-bed scanners convert type, artwork, or whatever else you can heave onto the scanning bed (paving stones? peacocks?); sound digitizers capture sound and music with stunning fidelity; video capture boards pluck and convert individual frames in real time, and will play them back at full speed, full-screen; slide scanners will do the same with photographs, and Kodak's Photo CD provides you with near-film resolution versions of your own snapshots.

Once all of this stuff is in the computer, there is a wondrous assortment of applications to help you manipulate, combine, and shape your sound and imagery. And the personal computer itself is undergoing a metamorphosis to adjust to this CPU-numbing assault of information.

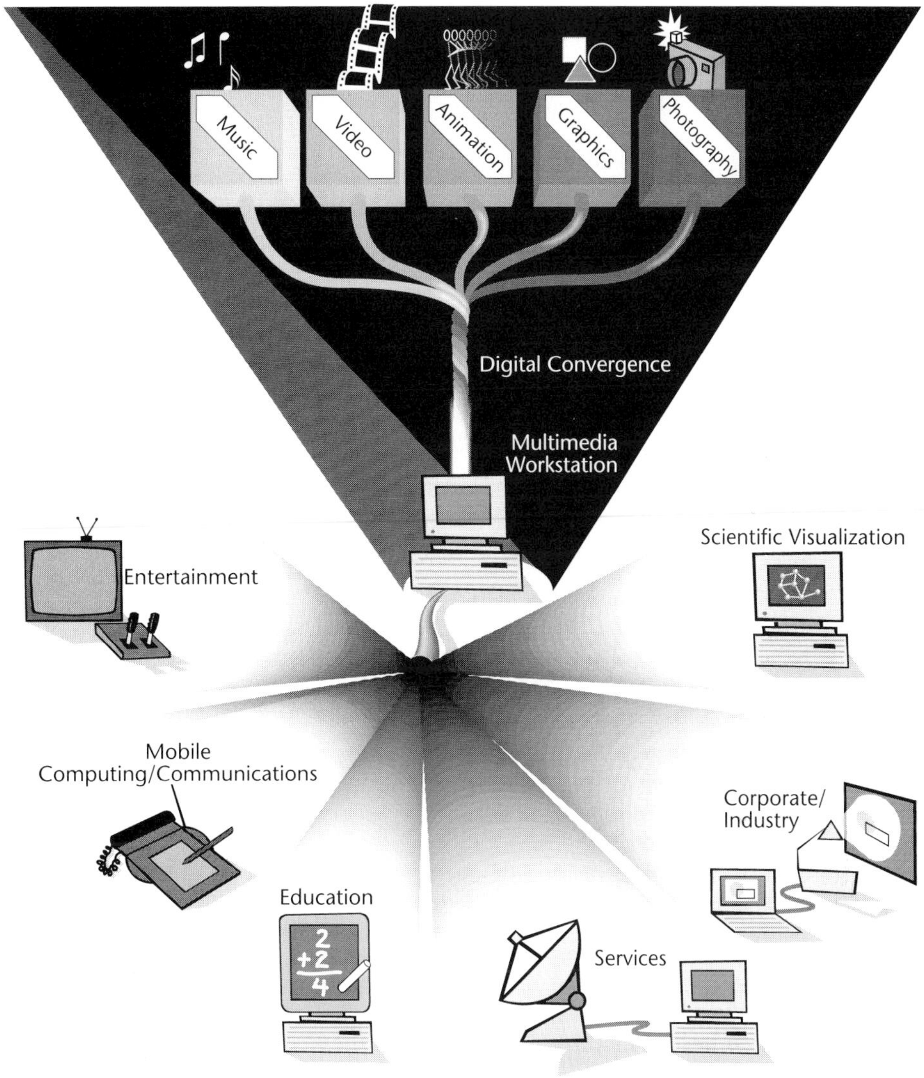

Figure 1.1 The desktop computer as center of the multimedia universe

You can now buy Macs with CD-ROM drives, built-in support for big-screen color, accelerated buses that speed data transfer, system software in ROM to quicken access times, and more *base* RAM than you could shoehorn into the average machine just a few years ago (see Chapter 3, "Mac Software and Hardware").

Harmonic Convergence

We've limited the scope of this book to an exploration of personal computer-based, or *desktop* , multimedia. But the formerly distinct spheres of computing, communications, entertainment, and consumer gadgetry are colliding, and you can bet multimedia will be there when the smoke clears. So, we'll begin by taking this little side trip into the jangling world of technological symbiosis.

Mobile Computing and Communications

The tiny box on your hip squeals—voice mail has tracked you down: E.T.—PHONE HOME. No phone? No problem. The little device is also a cellular phone, and you check in. Uh-oh, Mr. Big wants the numbers for that commercial you're working on. Naturally, the box is also a computer (with modem), so you send the file—uplink or fax, your choice. Next year, you'll just send the entire commercial.

Fueling the growth of desktop multimedia is a communications and consumer electronics cataclysm. While they are not themselves "multimedia," the twin dynamos of communications and consumer electronics are helping to propel the M word into the mainstream.

The cellular telephone business is currently in a growth cycle of truly appalling proportions. In fact, the changes are so profound that they could revolutionize communications. At the end of 1992, cellular phones were already a $7 billion industry, and some 7000 cellular phones were being sold *per day*. This breakneck growth was achieved in spite of high equipment and usage fees that have kept many waiting for costs to drop. And sure enough, the emergence of so-called PCS (personal communications services) will send both equipment and line use fees plummeting, turning cellular phones into a $30 billion business by 1995. More important, the line between communications and computing will begin to blur as PCS devices become indistinguishable from their computer-based cousins, PDAs (personal digital assistants—see Figure 1.2). While PCSs are telephones with

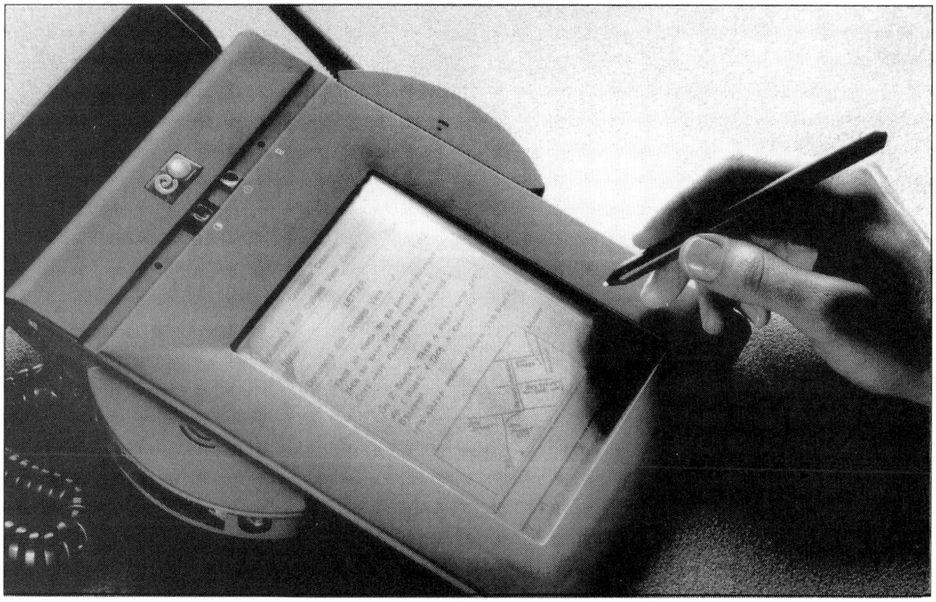

Figure 1.2
The EO personal digital assistant

computing features, PDAs are computers with built-in communications; go figure.

Meanwhile, two industry giants, AT&T and McCaw Cellular, are teaming up to form a nationwide wireless telephone network that could change the whole concept of communications. In the near future, for example, you may be issued a single telephone number, and sophisticated computers will hunt you down and transfer incoming calls to your PCS/PDA or nearest conventional phone.

The idea of computers out there "looking" for you may not sound particularly appealing, but this synthesis of mobile computing/communications is not some weird science fiction scenario. Just as price wars have turned desktop computers into commodities over the last few years, portable computing devices have been selling in giant quantities, all but leaving the desktop market for dead. Apple alone sold an estimated $1 billion worth of PowerBooks their first year out.

The point is that PCS and PDA devices could play an important role in the development of multimedia. Like their desk-bound counterparts, they'll be able to send, receive, and process all kinds of digital information, from faxes and voice mail to music and video. Look at it as a few more venues (a hundred million or so) for your latest QuickTime concoction.

Consumer Electronics

Not surprisingly, consumer electronics giants are joining communications and computer manufacturers in the rush to define the multimedia devices of the not-too-distant future. No need to impress upon companies like Sony the potential for handheld devices that will, say, download full-length digital movies for playback on the commuter train home from work.

Already, there are a variety of multimedia players that plug into an ordinary television set (Figure 1.3). These machines are really computers, but manufacturers don't want to say that too loudly—they might frighten the couch potatoes whose wallets they're after. Tandy, Commodore, Kodak, and Phillips (and soon, 3DO) have various boxes that will play interactive games, multimedia references, music, and photographs. (See Chapter 4, "Hardware Peripherals" for more information on 3DO.)

Apple sees itself as uniquely positioned to profit from convergent technologies. The company has even formed a whole division called Personal Interactive Electronics (Apple PIE—get it?) Its first PDA has been dubbed "Newton." Apple Chairman John Sculley, who recently stepped down as CEO, has been in his element trying to engineer Apple's role in this shifting landscape. Indeed, Sculley claims that Apple will be unrecognizable in a few years as it transforms itself from a personal computer company into a cross-bred multimedia monolith. As further evidence of Apple's determination to reinvent itself, Sculley himself has been seen lurking around Hollywood, indulging in power lunches and seeking entertainment content for his new toys.

Everybody's favorite company, Microsoft, has been right in there from the beginning. Like Apple, Microsoft has a new division, Consumer Systems Group,

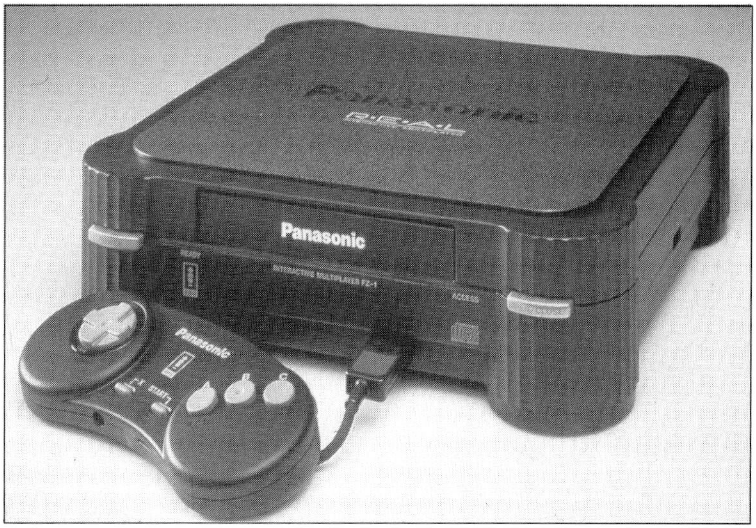

Figure 1.3
3DO's hot new system brings computer-based entertainment to the TV set.

devoted to consumer products. For years, Bill Gates has been buying up the electronic rights to books and artworks as fast as he can (which is pretty darn quick). Gates is hoping that consumers will take to computers disguised as home playback devices that just happen to be running the Trojan Horse version of his Windows operating system (actually called Modular Windows). Then he can inundate the home market with all the multimedia content he's been acquiring (not to mention collecting royalties for Windows on all of those boxes).

That's Entertainment

While the computer captains are going after entertainment markets with a vengeance, telephone and cable-TV companies have been positioning themselves to deliver multimedia entertainment their own way. These companies have a crucial lock on a very valuable infrastructure network of phone lines, TV cable, and satellite links. And you can bet they're not going to be happy to just rent out these data pipelines to the other guys.

For example, crack AT&T research arm Bellcore has figured out a way to send movies into homes over phone lines, in the process potentially depriving the cable-TV and video rental industries of their combined $33 billion annual revenue. ADSL (asymmetric digital subscriber line) acts like a "video server," downloading high-quality video signals over existing phone lines. It's only a matter of time before those digital movies will be oozing from the ether—and into your computer or PDA.

Cable-TV companies are scrambling to offer similar services, and they have something of an advantage, since they already have cable running into tens of millions of homes. The coaxial TV cable has a much higher bandwidth than phone lines, perfect for sending loads of digital multimedia entertainment into residences.

In late 1992, Tele-Communications, Inc., the nation's largest cable company,

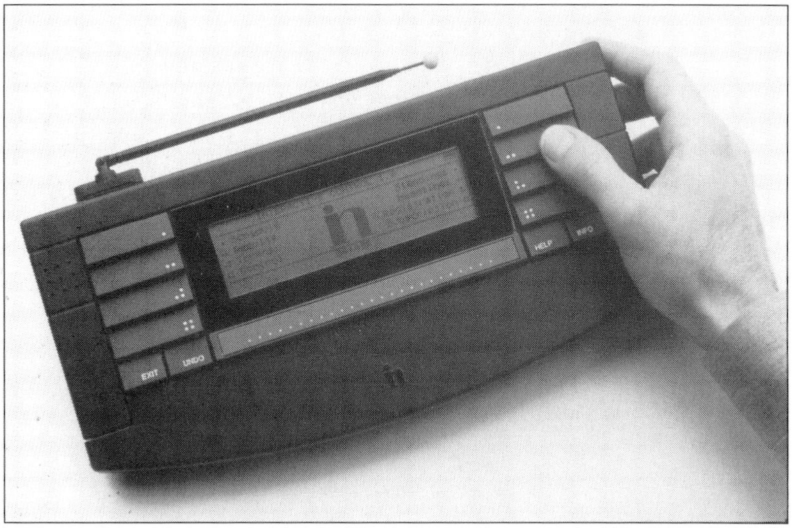

Figure 1.4
With IN's device, you can bet on professional sports without going to Vegas.

announced the development of a digital transmission technology that can deliver up to 500 TV channels. While this is an appalling idea, it also means that there will be an incredible source of content that can be fed directly into computers. (TV viewers will have to use a small appliance to decode the digital signal for viewing, at least until high-definition digital TV (HDTV) sets are widely available.)

In a move that signals the serious intentions of the big boys, Baby Bell US West invested $2.5 billion in media giant Time Warner's entertainment division. The alliance is expected to deliver a host of computing and communications services directly to homes.

Other companies, such as Interactive Network and NTN Entertainment Network, are setting up so-called interactive TV networks (see Figure 1.4). Viewers have the illusion of participating by playing along with, say, a game show. Results can be sent by modem to the network, which will broadcast the names of winners.

All of this is interactive in the sense that viewers can send and receive customized information, but none of it really affects programming. It's a level of participation Denise Caruso, editor of *Digital Media,* calls "fake interactive." However, the industry is moving towards a two-way cable or fiber optic link that will allow true instantaneous interactivity. Then viewers can do things like affect sitcom plot lines (which will no doubt be an improvement over network television's efforts).

Playing the Game

Multimedia's effect on entertainment is not limited to the not-too-distant future. Game kingpins such as Nintendo and Sega have been churning out popular, if uninspired, game cartridges for years. A more recent development is the interactive CD-ROM–based game. Many of these feature 3-D graphic, digital music, and sound effects. Prime examples include Reactor's Spaceship Warlock,

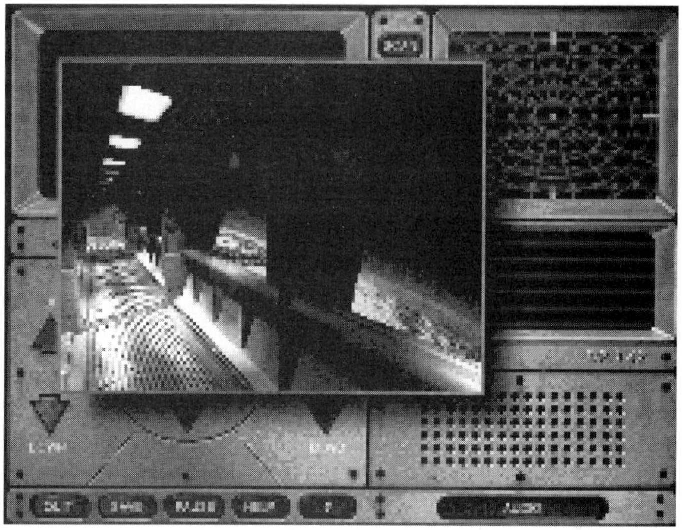

Figure 1.5 Iron Helix is a CD game that features skillfully rendered animation.

PROJECTS

Journeyman 024

Pop Rocket's Total Distortion, Presto's *Journeyman* project, and Iron Helix by Drew Pictures (Figure 1.5).

The most significant multimedia toys may come from The 3DO Company, a start-up that has the distinction of the first company in history to go public without a product. 3DO, backed by Time Warner, Matsushita Electric, and fronted by game designer Trip Hawkins, founder of Electronic Arts, calls its new CD device an "interactive multiplayer." The box is a 3-D animation powerhouse, capable of manipulation 3-D images and displaying them on an ordinary TV.

Multimedia's Roots

The concept of mixed media or multimedia has been around for some time, the form and its impact having been registered well before the advent of the computer, personal or otherwise.

By Any Means Necessary

Artists have long used every means at their disposal to describe and enrich the world around them. At the dawn of the modern age, pioneering cubists like Pablo Picasso, Georges Braque, and Juan Gris stretched the bounds of painting by creating works of *collage*. These artworks incorporated newsprint, mirror glass, photographs, and other found objects. The collage method of the cubists was soon extended to works known as *assemblages* (French for "multimedia"). An assemblage was a work that might contain newspaper clippings, wood, metal, parts of dolls, seashells, stones, or almost anything. Later artists, such the Italian futurists, dadaists, and surrealists, also experimented with mixed media.

In the '60s, Pop Art often coopted imagery from television, photography, and the movies. The giant images of Roy Lichenstein drew on pop icons like comic

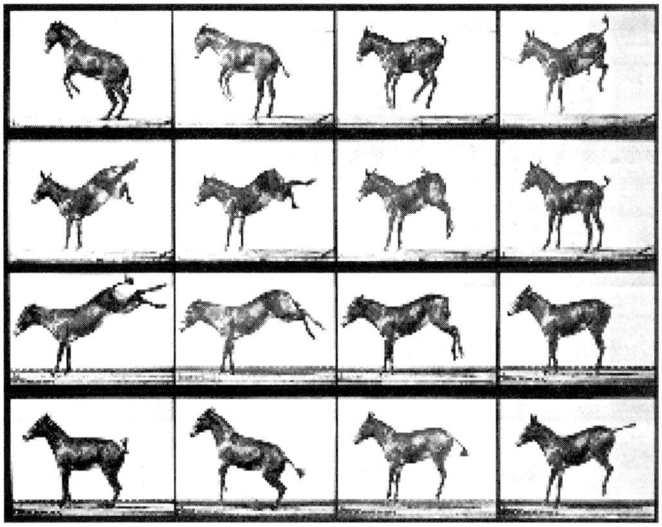

Figure 1.6 Eadweard Muybridge's "The Buck and Kick"

books, and Andy Warhol's repeated sequential images recalled the motions series of Eadweard Muybridge, a pioneering nineteenth-century photographer who used the medium to describe motion (Figure 1.6).

Some '60s survivors might also remember the psychedelic "be-ins" and "happenings," colorful multimedia sound and light shows that stretched the mind and imagination.

Today, multimedia performance art, complete with towering holograms and animations, is enjoying something of a renaissance. And "installation art," touted by *The New York Times* as "that most multimedia of art forms," incorporates mixed media elements such as gigantic lightning storms into room-sized exhibits.

Spitballs and Science

Baby boomers in particular may well recall grade school days "enlivened" by an earlier form of multimedia still called AV, or audiovisual presentations. In the 1950s, the teaching profession underwent a change as it struggled to cope with students who had been conditioned by modern communications. Teachers realized that they had to somehow compete with TV, radio, movies, magazines, and comic books. Filmstrips that projected photographs and artwork, movies that drove home the virtues of personal hygiene, and tape recordings of great performances all struggled to capture the minds and senses of young people newly tuned to the power of audio and visual communications. As Michael Goudket warned in *An Audio Visual Primer*, "we must do more than talk or nobody listens."

The Corporate AV Market

The business world has also used AV for some time to brighten drab sales presentations, to supplement technical lectures, and to communicate corporate messages. Corporate multimedia, even up to the present day, has generally taken the form of prosaic overheads or slightly more engaging slide shows. Naturally, the entertainment industry raised even lowly slide shows to multimedia extravaganzas mind-boggling in their glitzy indulgence.

Barry Grimes, who now heads his own design firm, remembers working in the mid-'80s on affiliate shows, annual junkets hosted by the networks, who fly in local TV franchise executives and their families for week-long pep rallies designed to whip up enthusiasm for the company and the new season lineup. (Networks still do these shows, but they're not as opulent as they were in the go-go '80s.)

Grimes would spend weeks accumulating up to $100,000 worth of 35mm slides for a given show, while an engineer programmed a small computer to control banks of xenon slide projectors. Although this was largely a mechanical process, much ingenuity went into the carefully arranged slide sequences, which were set up for quick dissolves, pixelation effects that would provide rippling transitions, and rapid-fire projection that would give a cinematic or animated effect.

Grimes gives a lot of credit for the development of corporate multimedia shows to Image Stream, a company that "made the whole multi-screen show into a beautiful art form" for such companies as Apple. Image Stream took early Mac bitmap graphics and animated them into myriad shifting multi-screen projections.

The advent of desktop multimedia has made it possible for the corporate shows of the '90s to use computer-based animation and presentations instead of slides, and the technology applies equally well to day-to-day corporate presentations utilizing notebook computers running presentation software like Action or Cinemation.

Clearly, pre-digital multimedia applications have been around for some time. Likewise, the prototypes of today's multimedia processors and players also got their start decades ago.

Hardware Roots

Though many people even today think of the computer mainly as a number cruncher, early visionaries saw its future role as an information and media processing powerhouse. America's chief scientist in the Roosevelt administration, a man named Vannevar Bush, envisioned a device he called "memex" or the Rapid Selector. Bush described memex as a scheme for indexing and retrieval of the immense store of information and knowledge that the world already had and was yet to produce. The machine itself was a Rube Goldberg gadget that combined microfilm storage, automatic indexing, and photocopying.

Though memex was never built, Bush himself was no rube, having designed and built giant pre–World War II calculators that presaged the development of modern computers. And the idea of memex captured and held the attention of many influential computer visionaries to come.

In the '50s, after reading about memex, Douglas Englebart envisioned the basic concept of the personal computer; J.C. Licklider, a scientist at the Pentagon's Advanced Research Projects Agency (ARPA), conceived of "interactive computing;" and still others, such as Alan Kay, were at Xerox PARC in the '60s developing the Alto, on which the Macintosh was based (see Chapter 3, "Mac System Software and Hardware," for more on this).

Motivations

Why use multimedia? *Because everyone else is using it!* No, but seriously, there are a some basic underlying reasons why multimedia is such a compelling idea.

The Power of Pictures

The undeniable force and appeal of multimedia stem directly from the power of the visual image itself, a power that has only recently been tapped in the world of computers, although it is readily apparent in everyday life.

In 1989, for example, the world was stunned by the democratic uprisings in China, which were centered in Beijing's Tiananmen Square. The television networks arrived quickly and prepared to record and transmit events as they unfolded, but were thwarted when China shut down the normal satellite trans-mission links. Undaunted, the newshawks used still-video cameras and transmitted the photos over standard phone lines. Even though these pictures were motion-less and without sound, viewers watched in wonder, transfixed by the stirring images, which were seen worldwide less than 20 minutes after they were taken.

Pictures simply have an inherent power to stir interest and emotion—a power that is far beyond that of the written or spoken word; at least, in its popular appeal.

The Power of Interactivity

The concept of *hypertext* is especially relevant to multimedia. Through the ages, information has been presented and absorbed in a linear fashion. You read a book from cover to cover, watch a movie from beginning to end. Even so, people have long recognized that this may not be the best means of communicating all types of information.

You might in fact want to hop around in a book as the whim takes you, or to read more about a topic of interest before continuing on with the linear narrative (as you would using a cross-reference in a book). Of course, the computer is a natural for this sort of thing, and somebody sooner or later had to think of the idea of hypertext. That someone is generally agreed to be Ted Nelson, a computer visionary whose seminal 1974 book *Computer Lib* is still in print and still worth a read.

In the late '80s, Apple introduced HyperCard, which is based on the hypertext concept. Using HyperCard, you create links in a given work, which can be an electronic book, multimedia presentation, anything that might best be explored in a nonlinear way. Then, when a user is reading or exploring, he or she can click on icons to zoom to related topics, which may be in the same file or in another one altogether.

This simple idea has great impact on multimedia because it enables the interactivity that is so important to its basic allure. Robert Abel, an early multimedia research pioneer, has created a number of important works. Abel's unreleased version of

Picasso's *Guernica* is a work often cited as a premier example of interactive multimedia at its most seductive. Using an interactive program, one can explore a reproduction of the great artwork while clicking on icons linking preliminary sketches that Picasso used. Video interviews with Picasso himself and with survivors of the actual Spanish Civil War bombing at Guernica, the inspiration for the painting, further deepen an understanding of the work.

Such skillfully rendered interactivity offers insights into the mind of the artist, and helps to fix his work in its historical and cultural contexts. It's a wonderful illustration of multimedia in the service of a great work of art, rather than art subverted by the medium.

Costs of Multimedia versus Traditional Technologies

The impact of the personal computer and desktop multimedia tools on such professions as video production, animation, and sound and music recording is becoming widely felt. Not only is professional-quality work now possible on the desktop, but it is possible with far less investment in time and money.

In film and broadcast production, post-production suites that used to cost millions of dollars can now be fully outfitted for less than $50,000. And this is for top-quality professional work, not for those of us just noodling around with QuickTime. Commercials that would have cost $50,000 to $100,000 and taken days to prepare and shoot can now be put together for a fraction of that and assembled over a weekend using computer-generated imagery for the sets. Such high-profile films as *Terminator 2* and *The Lawnmower Man* have made extensive use of 3-D computer graphics.

PROJECTS

Lawnmower Man 022

The Disney studio, known for its exquisitely detailed animation, is getting into the act too, although keeping a low profile. A recent full-length feature, *Beauty and the Beast*, had over a million drawings with nearly 600 laboring artists and technicians, but the ballroom scene background was rendered by a handful of 3-D specialists in Disney's Computer Generated Imagery (CGI) department.

Multimedia in business, advertising, and marketing is also bringing costs down. Ads and colateral marketing created with image-editing software allow businesses to create materials in-house and make changes on-the-fly, greatly reducing costs. Interactive advertising can draw people in more effectively than print ads, and can be produced for less.

PROJECTS

Power Tools Theme 012

In professional music recording and production, the story is much the same. MIDI (musical instrument digital interface) allows you to create and play back music and other sound with great fidelity. Using MIDI sound clip libraries, you can add high-quality sounds to your latest music video for pennies (see Chapter 13, "Producing Sound," for more details). By contrast, getting sound clips (so-called "needle-drop" music) from a music studio or production house can cost $100 per minute.

Applications

Multimedia has broad applications in everyday life. Education, business, and publishing are just a few of the areas that are changing under multimedia's colorful and exuberant assault.

Business

Most corporate presentations still use the tried and true handouts and overheads. But as the yawns get louder and audiences become more jaded, many companies are turning to whizz-bang multimedia presentations with animation, video, and eye-catching graphics.

The rise of multimedia in the boardroom has been driven primarily by new easy-to-use presentation software such as Magic, Special Delivery, and Cinemation (Figure 1.7). The programs are not as sophisticated as multimedia mainstays like Macromedia Director, but are much easier to use.

TOOLS
Director 210

New hardware developments also have helped speed the use of sophisticated multimedia presentations. A primary innovation has been the LCD display panel. About the size of an inch-thick file folder, this device is plugged into a computer and placed on an overhead projector. Anything that is displayed by the computer monitor is projected in this manner, where it can be viewed during group presentations.

Most companies willing to experiment with the new media limit their multimedia forays to high-impact, critical applications such as speaker support materials for important product rollouts, annual shareholder meetings, and important customer briefings. Others with greater commitment or interest have formed in-

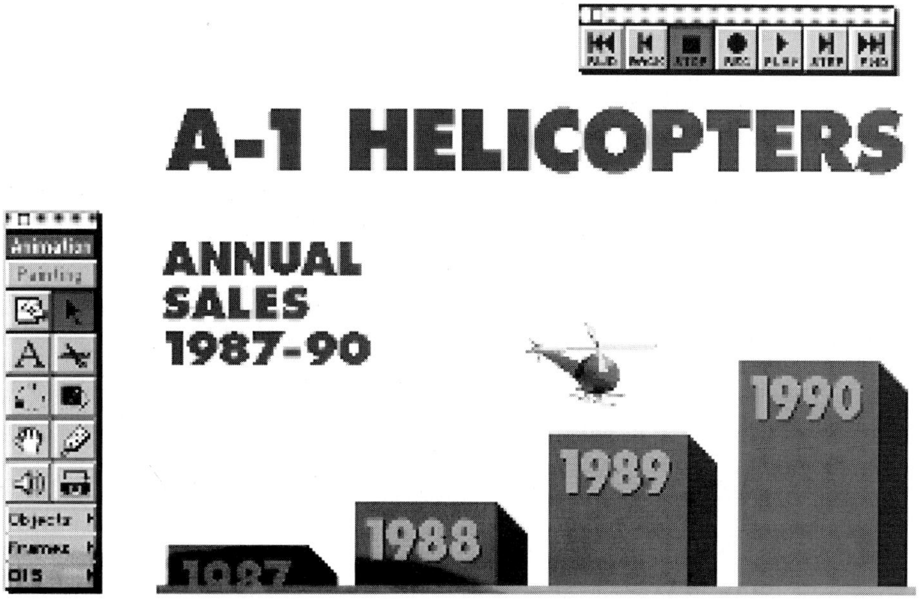

Figure 1.7 With a presentation program like Cinemation, businesses can use canned elements to rapidly assemble multimedia presentations.

house multimedia development groups whose work rivals the complexity and richness found in the best presentations created by outside experts.

Marketing and Sales

Advertising is also taking its cue from multimedia. Companies like Amazing Media and the Interactive Marketing Group develop interactive ads on floppy disks. For roughly the same price as a print ad, their clients get a state-of-the-art interad, and potential customers get something less obnoxious that the usual screaming headlines and seductive sales pitches.

Interads on floppies can be bound right into a magazine, which is less expensive than sending them to customers as part of direct mail campaigns. Viewers can interact in various ways—for example, by playing little games, or using a calculator to decide how to invest in mutual funds.

PROJECTS
Health Care Kiosk 042

Electronic *Kiosks* are also being heavily used in "electronic retailing." Scattered through shopping malls, airports, and trade shows, kiosks handle everything from film processing to clothing sales. In the latter instance, buyers look at videos of models wearing clothing articles, which can be ordered by specifying size, color, and credit card information. Well aware that many buying decisions are made while in the store, retailers use kiosks to dispense information at point-of-sale locations, where customers find out about new products. While they're at it, kiosks can also get customers to answer questions, and the resulting demographics are tabulated for retailers on the spot—instant market research surveys.

Kiosks are becoming a familiar sight at trade shows, where they give out directions and recommend restaurants and shopping areas to out-of-towners. To

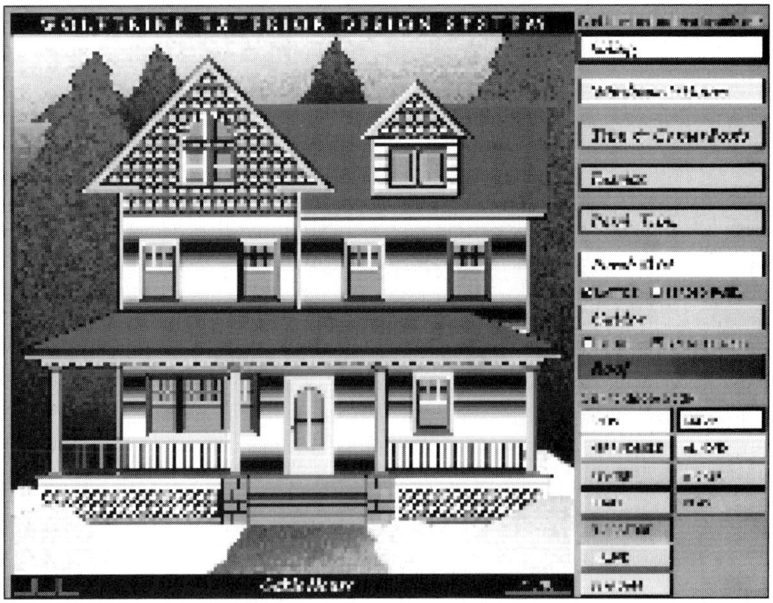

Figure 1.8 Using Clement Mok Design's Wolverine Exterior Design System, customers can simulate various exterior design elements.

Figure 1.9
Billboard's CD Listening Station

appear unintimidating, kiosks often substitute touch screens for keyboards. Many trade show vendors feature splashy multimedia product demos that give browsers a chance to take a look without the need for a live demo person.

The home improvement industry is making effective use of interactive multimedia. Customers can look at tile, carpet, or wallpaper samples, then apply their choices to model rooms using visualization software (Figure 1.8). In fact, even building remodeling projects can be simulated this way, allowing homeowners to create model floor plans and then "walk" through them using sophisticated animation software.

Donald Grahame, a San Francisco–based animator, has created an animated music listening station for a record store. Using the interactive software, listeners can hear music before buying it (Figure 1.9).

Education

One of the truisms in the learning business is that people absorb and retain new information in different ways and at varying rates. To some, the linear flow of a book or TV program works just fine, but to many others this ancient mode of learning is uncomfortably confining.

One of the reasons computer "gurus" are popular people is because it's easier to ask someone to decipher an error message than to read the manual yourself. But consulting with a real person is also interactive—answers may lead to other questions or points of interest. You go through a similar process when you look up an entry in an encyclopedia, only to find other things to look up, which lead to still other topics, until you're hopping all over.

Interactive multimedia brings the freedom to explore the unknown with lightning-fast links to related topics. It is this interactivity, along with dynamic elements such as video and music, that makes multimedia such an exemplary learning tool—especially for children, since multimedia resembles the TV and video games that have become imbedded in youth culture.

For these reasons, training and education are often cited as ideal multimedia applications. Next to business applications, market analysts rank training and education as the largest multimedia market. In fact, some of the most effective multimedia projects have been those associated with learning and teaching.

Examples abound. Apple's Multimedia Lab (now defunct) experimented with many interesting projects. One piece, Moss Landing, is an interactive videodisc that describes daily life in a small seacoast town. You can click on different "hot" areas of the digital video images and be whisked away to different scenes. Click on a waterfront video screen showing fishing boats, for instance, and you're suddenly you're at sea, jetting through the ocean spray.

In another use of multimedia, students and teachers at San Francisco's Lowell High School created "Grapevine: The Steinbeck Story," with the help of Apple's Education Research Group. The interactive CD helps students feel both the impact of the Great Depression and a deeper understanding of Steinbeck's seminal novel about the period, *The Grapes of Wrath*. The project began as a classroom presentation, but was so successful that it was made into a CD-ROM and videodisc incorporating sound, video, and photographs.

While there are many anecdotal examples of the fledgling influence of multimedia on education, it will probably not register significantly until the issues of equipment, development costs, and teacher training are resolved. This last is crucial, since many teachers are put off or intimidated by the technology. In answer, programs to help ease the transition are springing up.

The Teacher Explorer Center in East Lansing, Michigan teaches educators how to develop basic multimedia documents. The center also advises teachers how to combat tight budgets by scrounging for forgotten equipment that may be buried in school basements. The College of Education and Human Service Professions, at the University of Minnesota at Duluth, has developed methods and instructional designs for teaching with multimedia. Universities and colleges are also adopting multimedia curricula, and some even offer degree programs (for a list of programs, see Chapter 10, "Outside Resources").

At the Teacher's Living Resource Center at the St. Louis Zoo, educators use courseware design software to create interactive classes for studying animals in the zoo (see Figure 1.10). The project, created by Arnowitz Productions Inc. of Mill Valley, California, uses sophisticated software to help teachers assemble courses that include video and animation clips, as well as textual information.

The Big Boys Step In

Some of the most visible educational titles are being produced by large corporations like IBM. These products range from simple electronic books to extremely detailed and lengthy courses. Perhaps the best known is IBM's *Columbus: Encounter, Discovery and Beyond*, a $2000 set of videodiscs and CDs.

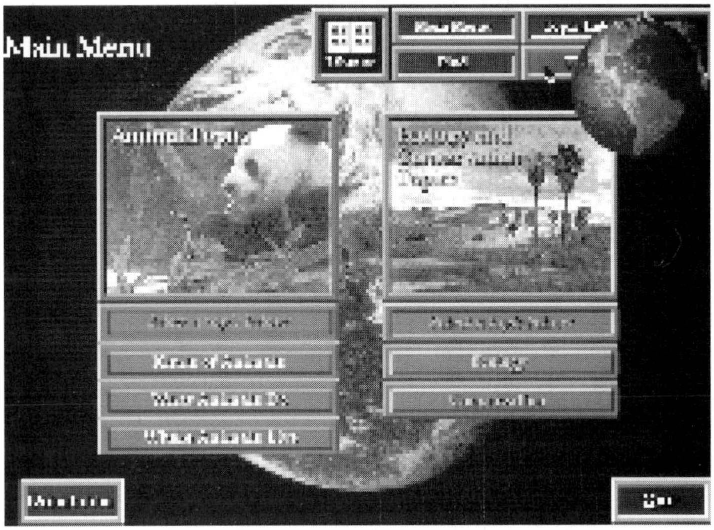

Figure 1.10 Teacher's Living World helps educators develop multimedia course materials.

The product, which IBM calls a "knowledge system," took $6–8 million to produce, and contains 180 hours of documents, images, and sounds.

Microsoft recently spent $5 million and over five years developing an intriguing multimedia encyclopedia called Encarta. Electronic references, although teeming with potential, have so far been disappointing, as vendors have thrown them together on CDs mainly as a way to push their CD drive hardware. But Encarta is different; the encyclopedia has 21,000 articles, over seven hours of sound and music, 100 animations, and over 10,000 graphics.

On a smaller scale, but no less intriguing, are the CDs and videodiscs offered by The Voyager Company. Justly acclaimed, these titles include some wonderful children's stories and exploratory games. In *A Silly Noisy House,* children can amuse themselves by exploring the mysteries of an old house. The disc includes kinetic surprises, such as a pop-up jack-in-the-box and a flock of honking geese flapping by an open window.

Broderbund Software's Living Books series also has some interactive titles that small children find delightful. Kid Pix is the sort of clever and absorbing program that makes you wonder why it wasn't invented years ago. Intended as a paint program for children, it has lured many adults into its wacky world. Kid Pix eliminates the scroll bars and hidden tool palettes that might confuse small children. A small face called the Undo Guy reverses any unwanted effects. Sound plays a big role in Kid Pix, and most actions provoke some sort of funny noise. Each letter of an alphabet along the bottom of the screen sounds its name when clicked on.

Training

Corporations spend billions on employee training, and the immediacy and appealingly low long-term costs of multimedia-based training have given multimedia its first major market conquest. Companies are finding that they can train their staffs less expensively and more effectively using computer-based training (CBT) than with traditional classroom methods.

Employees also like multimedia courses better: the interactivity keeps them awake and engaged. Many large companies have teaching labs and centers, where they set up computers equipped with multimedia and peripheral equipment such as laserdiscs and CD-ROM drives.

PROJECTS Training 040-041

Soon, with wider adoption of multimedia-ready computers, employees will be able to take courses right at their desks. Microsoft is already offering a CD version of Multimedia Works, a suite of basic productivity software. On the CD along with the program itself is a 50-minute multimedia tutorial that uses animation and audio annotation.

Apple has developed a multimedia-produced training video that explains basic computer networking concepts. In the production, live "actors" (Apple technical support staff) were superimposed over an animated "studio" inspired by the bridge of the *Starship Enterprise*. The video cost $40,000 to produce, a fraction of the expense for a traditionally produced video. Figure 1.11 shows a similar computer-based guide to networking produced by networking giant Novell.

Significantly, multimedia CBT techniques are not limited to the high-tech industry alone, but are being used across a broad sector of American business. Bethlehem Steel uses interactive video to teach workers about a variety of steel production methods. Federal Express has implemented Interactive Videodisc Instruction (IVI), a program that teaches employees about a wide range of skills,

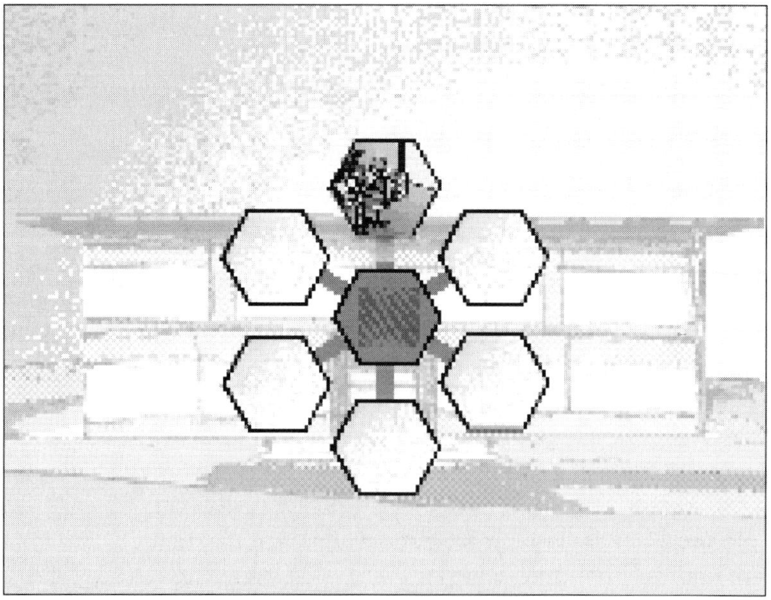

Figure 1.11 Novell's basic introduction to networking includes an animated guide.

from driver training to phone and counter service. IVI is made up of 25 CDs, which are updated monthly. Federal Express estimates that IVI cuts training time by two-thirds, and random tests show that employees retain information better than with classroom training.

The 1992 U.S. Olympic wrestling team was trained in part by an interactive program that integrates 35 hours of video from 350 sample matches, analysis of selected matches, and bios of competitors.

Opportunities and Challenges

Because the major costs of corporate training are in the time it takes employees and instructors to participate in classes, CBT is a big draw for companies. There are, however, still considerable costs associated with the development of CBT. Software must be bought and mastered, and equipment must be purchased and installed.

Since the payoff is substantial, many companies are willing to invest the up-front money and development time. While some companies hire full-time staffs, many more rely on outside experts to develop CBT; either way, CBT creates significant career opportunities.

Skills necessary for the development of interactive training programs include a strong familiarity with authoring tools such as Authorware Professional, IconAuthor, and Director. For a description of these tools, see Chapter 9, "Authoring Tools." Also, take a look at the interactive projects on the accompanying CD for a good introduction to the techniques used by professionals.

Publishing

Electronic books and magazines predate the concept of multimedia. After all, getting plain text on the computer is no big deal. Computer Library, for example, offers an electronic magazine article service. Each month, subscribers get a new CD that contains over 70,000 articles from computer industry publications.

Voyager's Expanded Books series includes electronic versions of old favorites like *Alice in Wonderland,* as well as contemporary novels. You can add your own margin notes, highlight passages, and mark your place.

As interesting as these products are, the basic challenge of electronic publishing is getting people to read the things in the first place. Most people simply don't like to sit and read text on the screen (although Voyager takes an important step by tailoring its Expanded Books specifically for notebook computers).

Enter multimedia. By reproducing the graphics and photographs of original works, and by adding multimedia elements like sound and video, electronic publishing is transformed into a much more intriguing option.

Sumeria is a spin-off of popular *Macworld* magazine, and is run by a former Macworld editor-in-chief. The same company publishes *Macworld Interactive,* complete with full color graphics and photos (Figure 1.12).

Verbum, developer of the CD-ROM included with this book, was an early pioneer of multimedia magazines, issuing Verbum Interactive in 1991. The interactive CD-ROM features interactive articles, a wide-ranging multimedia

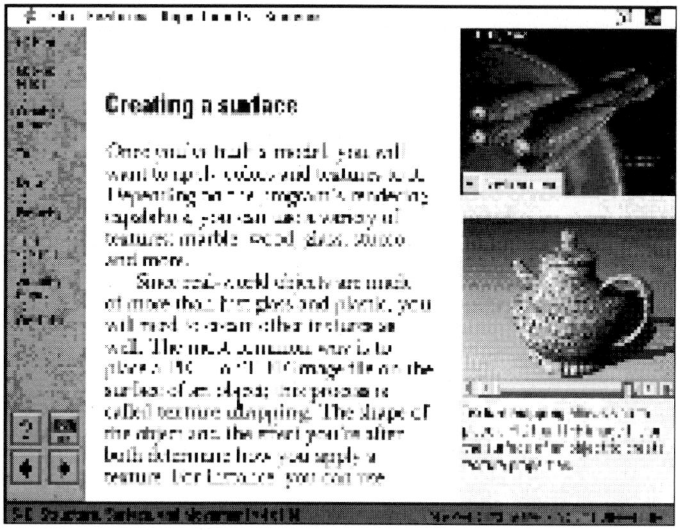

Figure 1.12 ***Macworld Interactive*** **features interactive versions of the print magazine's articles.**

gallery, a pre-QuickTime video roundtable discussion featuring industry luminaries, and music (playable on regular audio CD players) from artists such as Graham Nash, Todd Rundgren, and Pauline Oliveros. The disc makes extensive use of animated sequences, including 3-D animation and talking agents.

More recently, photographer Rick Smolan published *From Alice to Ocean: Alone Across the Outback.* This book/disc package is a fascinating example of multimedia's power to fuse visual and sound imagery with computer-driven interactivity (Figure 1.13). The project is the story of Robyn Davidson's journey by camel across Australia's remotest territories. The printed book contains the story illustrated by the handsome photographs of Smolan, best known as the creator of the popular *Day in the Life* books.

One of the two discs in the package is in Kodak's new Photo CD format, which allows photos to be viewed on an ordinary television, as well as on a computer, where they can be manipulated like any other digital information. (Although the discs will display photos on any TV or color computer, you do need a special Photo CD player—see Chapter 4, "Hardware Components", for more details.) Both the Photo CD disc and the other disk, which plays on standard Mac-compatible drives, are interactive, and you can hop around the narrative at will, looking at maps, viewing snippets of video, or listening to the eerie aboriginal *didgiridoo* soundtrack.

The core of the material was previously published in other forms. Davidson's *Tracks*, an account of her trip, was published in 1980, and most of Smolan's photographs were originally published in a 1977 issue of *National Geographic*. *From Alice to Ocean* graphically illustrates what can be done with the world's vast store of existing information—and it explains why forward thinkers like Mr. Gates are snapping up electronic publishing rights to so many works.

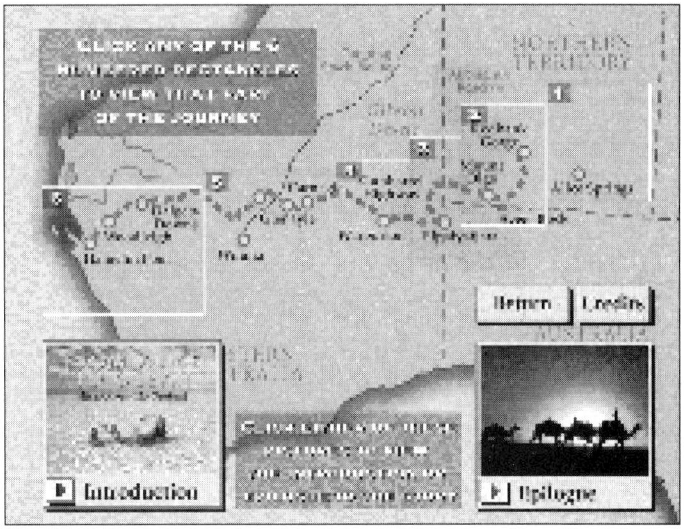

Figure 1.13
***From Alice to Ocean* fuses photography, travelogue, and interactivity.**

The Challenges

For creators of multimedia, there are a few challenges. The biggest one is the time, skill, and effort it takes to design, create, and link the complex visual and sonic landscapes of multimedia.

System Costs

The equipment you're going to need depends a lot on your level of involvement. If you just want to explore what's out there, a basic color Mac in the II series will do just fine. You'll also need a CD-ROM drive and at least 8Mb of RAM. Add a basic presentation package and an image-editing or paint program, and you'll be able to create simple multimedia presentations. If you're starting from scratch, such a system can be had for around $2500.

If you want to develop QuickTime videos, interactive presentations, or electronic music, you'll need to add a video digitizer, a media integration program like Director, and sound equipment such as a MIDI interface and sound digitizer. Because the files you're working with will be very large, you may also want to add more RAM, and a removable disk drive for file storage. A faster Mac such as a IIci, IIvx, or Quadra would be ideal. Figure on up to $10,000 for this system.

Finally, if you're going to go all out and work with digital video or create professional quality interactive presentations, you'll need some additional video equipment such as a second monitor, a video recorder, and perhaps some specialized equipment like an editing controller and audio mixer. You'll also want the fastest Mac you can get—a Quadra, or at least a IIfx; the sky's the limit here—you could assemble such a system for as little as $20,000, but could easily spend several times that.

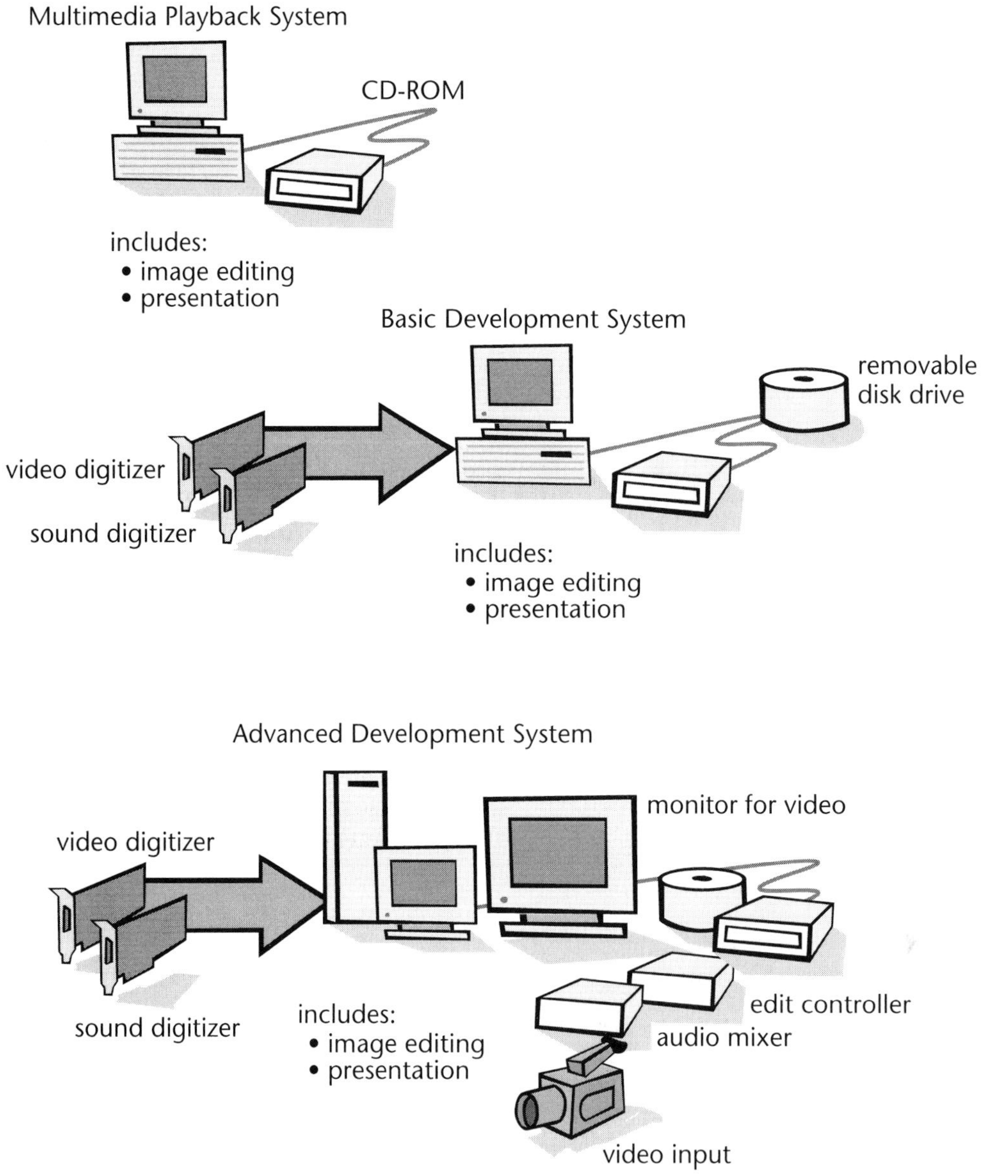

Figure 1.14 System configurations

Unless you get really hooked, or work for a corporation with deep pockets and big ambitions, you shouldn't have to spend much at all to explore and even create irresistible multimedia. For a complete rundown on the Mac and peripheral equipment, see Chapters 3 and 4. Software packages are listed and described in the "Tools" chapters throughout the book.

Cross-Platform Delivery

If you plan to create multimedia for viewing on more than one platform, you've got your work cut out for you. There are really no multimedia standards to speak of, and Apple and IBM's efforts to create some through Kaleida haven't yet borne fruit.

The situation is improving, but still dicey. If you're creating QuickTime movies on the Mac, they'll play back under Windows and on some Unix workstations, such as those made by Silicon Graphics. But full-fledged multimedia presentations are not too portable, and such key elements as graphics file formats are only sometimes compatible.

For a complete look at the situation, see Chapter 12 "Working Cross-Platform."

Technical Expertise

TOOLS
Swivel 3D Demo 220
Photoshop Demo 222

For the most part, you do not have to be a rocket scientist to create multimedia, but you do have to have a lot of time and patience. Multimedia applications are getting easier and easier to use, so that you can often surprise yourself by producing impressive work fairly quickly.

However, specialized programs such as 3-D animation, media integration, and image editing software can be tricky and a little difficult to master. To avoid initial frustration, we recommend taking a class or seminar (after you read this book, and view the disc, of course). Many are now available, with local colleges and universities offering low-cost courses taught by experts. For a list, see Chapter 10 "Outside Resources."

Hardware, especially getting different pieces of equipment to coexist, can be trying, too. Generally, though, all you have to do is install hardware and any accompanying software to get up and running in a short time. At least a passing familiarity with the Mac's system software is very helpful in this regard. A good book on the Mac (and perusal of Chapter 3 of this book) will be very useful in troubleshooting INIT conflicts and other bugaboos of desktop computing.

Content Development

Developing high-quality, entertaining, and beautiful multimedia takes skill and experience. There. We said it. This is the dirty little secret of multimedia. No hype here, folks, all the digitizers and Quadras and graphic gewgaws in the world cannot make you an artist (sorry). Stan Cornyn, former president of Warner New Media, agrees: "I don't care if you can store 300 million pages, that is not multimedia."

"Multimedia has too often fallen into the hands of 'code writers,' those who can keep the computers from clutching up. The sooner we fix this, the sooner the public will give us their business." In comparing multimedia to the recording industry, Cornyn says: "Why do you think recording engineers are kept behind thick glass, away from the talent?"

The tools of multimedia are exactly that: tools. Creation of art, electronic or otherwise, takes talent and an aesthetic sensibility. And lots of time. That's why the heart of this book and the accompanying disc are devoted to the development of excellent multimedia content. Through an explanation of the processes, interviews with developers, and step-by-step explication of project development, you'll see how the pros do it.

But even if you can't draw a box with parallel sides, don't despair. You can still have a lot of fun with multimedia; just don't expect to bang out *StarTrek* and you'll be fine. There's no question that the power of the computer and the sophistication of multimedia software make it easier than ever to create inventive and inviting works of the imagination.

2

The Multimedia Development Process

Multimedia development methods are as varied and colorful as the medium itself. How you go about developing multimedia depends on the nature of your project and how it will be viewed and heard. A HyperCard presentation made for display on a small black and white screen will be assembled much differently than a digital music video played back on a wall of million-color monitors. Likewise, sound can dominate a presentation, or may be a discreet addition that enhances the larger message. For all of these reasons, there is no multimedia development formula.

Still, there are some general, universal patterns and processes for developing multimedia—and we'll give you the 30,000-foot overview in this chapter. As the overall process becomes clearer, you can refer to other chapters for advice and suggestions on more specific topics. For example, Chapter 3, "Mac System Software," covers computer choices and configurations. Similarly, Chapter 4, "Hardware Peripherals," offers a rundown of the many additional hardware devices—keyboards and mice, scanners, monitors, accelerators, and more—that can help you manage your multimedia menagerie. The subsequent "Tools" chapters in the first section of the book compare and contrast multimedia software in many different categories, while the "Creating" chapters in Part II focus on the details of producing different multimedia elements. Finally, the Power Tools CD further illuminates the production process with behind the scenes, step by step analysis of several exemplary multimedia projects, demo programs for you to test drive, and scores of *very* usable software tools—utility programs and clip media—that will help your multimedia projects fly.

Throughout the book and disc you'll find insights and anecdotes from multimedia experts. These will help you refine your skills, and will save you countless hours as you read about the experiences of those who have "been there before." Of course, as you gain experience in multimedia production, you'll develop your own methods and styles. (We are reminded of a junior high school English class studying the novels of William Faulkner, whose language and syntax are notoriously idiosyncratic. During class a student piped up, " How come *Faulkner* doesn' t have to follow the rules?" To which the teacher replied, " Because *he* knows what they are").

Development Overview

The process of creating a multimedia project can be broken down into a series of basic steps covering both interface/architecture development and content development (illustrated in Figure 2.1). These steps can be summarized as follows:

- Conceiving an idea
- Planning the development process
- Outlining and Prototyping
- Designing the architecture and interface
- Creating interface elements
- Acquiring and producing content
- Preparing content
- Assembling the elements into a cohesive production
- Testing and making adjustments
- Duplicating and distributing the final product

This represents an idealized scenario, though there are many intermediate steps. In the sections that follow, we'll look at each one in a bit more detail.

Conceiving an Idea

Inspiration is the first thing one needs to get going, and an idea for a multimedia project can come from many sources. It can be based on a hobby or area of personal or academic interest; it can come from a film or a record album—or even a dream. Corporate in-house development teams are often assigned specific projects and budgets from other areas of the company, or an organization may approach a multimedia contractor with a concept they will pay to have developed.

Whatever the source, the idea is usually brief and vague at first. It can be a statement or paragraph, with little or no reference to how the project will eventually look or sound. Even the machine it will run on might be irrelevant at this point. There may be some thoughts about bits and pieces of animation, sounds, or content. This original germ of an idea needs to be scrutinized and expanded into a realistic starting point for the project.

Planning the Development Process

It would be nice if someone walked up to you and said "Hey, you' re good with computers! Could you make me an interactive, multimedia version of the life and

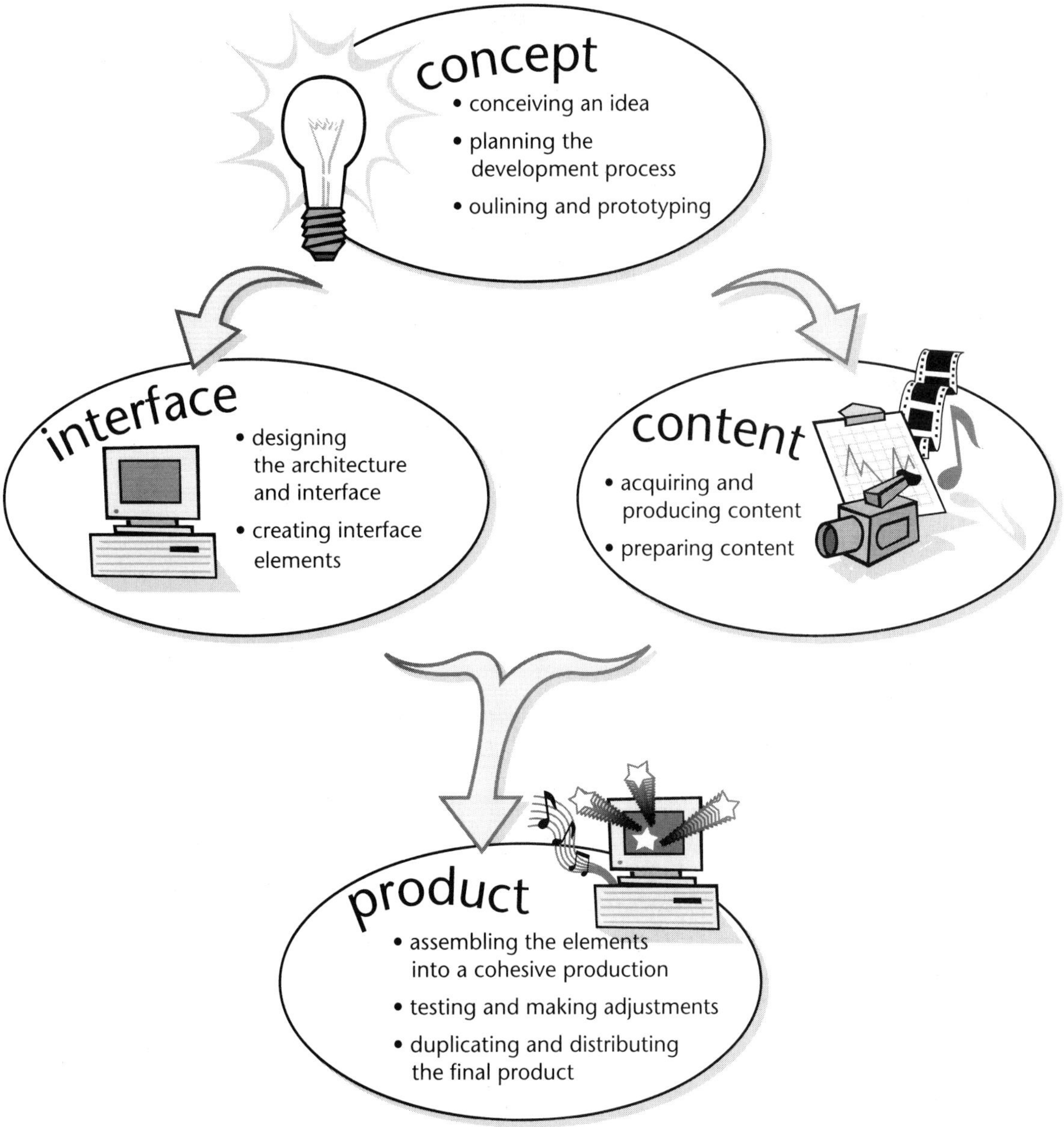
concept
• conceiving an idea
• planning the development process
• oulining and prototyping
interface
• designing the architecture and interface
• creating interface elements
content
• acquiring and producing content
• preparing content
product
• assembling the elements into a cohesive production
• testing and making adjustments
• duplicating and distributing the final product

Figure 2.1 The desktop multimedia design process

times of John Lennon?" It would be even nicer if that person then provided you with all the equipment you would need; gave you unlimited access to writers, artists, and programmers; made available photographs, video, and music (with all required permissions, of course), and threw in a blank check. You could make some key decisions that defined the project in detail, get the right people to do the work, then turn out thousands of CD-ROMs to fill the orders that would undoubtedly pour in. Poof! In a matter of months your project would make headlines in all the industry papers.

Millions Line Up for Lennon CD
NEW YORK—Echoes of Beatlemania reverberated today, as throngs cued up in driving rain to buy a hot new CD on the life of martyred Beatle John Lennon. The disc, created seemingly overnight, has charmed both fans and critics alike.

Every multimedia producer dreams of a project like that—a focused topic, unlimited resources, an enthralled audience and someone else to foot the bill for development (not to mention great publicity and fawning critics). In reality, however, there is no such thing as unlimited resources. This is why planning is essential. This planning phase gives a producer the chance to decide what is important for a project based on the available resources. This requires numerous decisions based on message, audience, and budget.

These factors help a producer shape and focus the original idea. The planning can then progress to deciding which elements will be needed to express an idea, as well as which talents and resources will be required to execute it. The decisions agreed upon during this preproduction phase will save immense amounts of time later. Defining the project's scope, limits, and resources early on will give it discrete boundaries that simplify production decisions further down the road.

Preproduction is an art form that requires a good imagination and logical frame of mind in order to visualize a non-existent project at various stages of development. It gets easier with experience.

Some individuals have a hard time with the logical processes of preproduction. They prefer to go with the flow and make these decisions as their project evolves. Usually, when a successful multimedia producer claims to have worked without a plan, the preproduction has been done, just in a less conventional way. The scope of today' s multimedia projects generally requires a standard organizational approach to preproduction.

Project Definition

Answering a few simple questions helps a multimedia producer to more fully define the original concept for the project:

Who is the audience?

What is the delivery platform?

What is the budget?

What multimedia elements will the project include?

What development software and hardware is required?

When does it have to be finished?

Once the producer defines the audience, he or she is able to determine the style and form of the message, as well as the criteria for distribution and playback. The delivery platform—the system on which the project will ultimately be viewed—affects the project's technical parameters, as well as its market and accessibility. Once the budget is set, the producer can make decisions about the project's size and scope. Last (but certainly not least) is the project's target completion date: Making the final deadline can have a large effect on its ultimate success and the producer's credibility.

After addressing each of these issues, the producer has a firm criteria which not only help define the remaining facets of preproduction, but also aid in dealing with the multitude of small issues that inevitably crop up during production.

Audience and Delivery Platform

The intended audience is probably the most critical factor in planning a project. It determines not only the style of the presentation, but also the method by which the project will ultimately be developed and distributed. If the audience is a relatively small group of business people, museum visitors or a trade show crowd, the project might be most efficiently presented on a single custom-designed system. If the project is meant for mass distribution, it would probably be distributed on a CD-ROM and played on a relatively wide assortment of machines, resulting in an entirely different set of development considerations.

Budget

The amount of money available for a project has a direct effect on its scope and the amount of time needed to complete development. Producing multimedia can be a very expensive proposition. At minimum, it includes the cost of a suitably powerful Mac with some kind of authoring software. At maximum, it can run into the hundreds of thousands of dollars required to fund a diverse coalition of talented artists, programmers, and production services; not to mention additional costs for licensing content.

There is hope for the solo multimedia producer; there are many tools available that help non-artists create graphics, and there is a "homemade" way to produce nearly anything. The lowest budget project can be successful, even if it is done by one person in black and white in HyperCard on a Macintosh Classic. There are also many sources of clip art, sound libraries, and other elements usually available for a price lower than hiring someone to create the element exclusively for a particular project. (Beware, however, the same kind of fate that befell early desktop publishers intoxicated with the power at their command: after enduring several issues of the company newsletter with its 26 typefaces and too-cute clip art, the boss finally made our sobered desktop hero hire a graphic artist to "make it professional.")

With a bigger budget the producer can put together a team, or contract out portions of the production. Under this plan, the producer needs to carefully break down the jobs into manageable portions. A considerable trade-off in this approach is that project management and coordination become major issues. Regardless of the size of the team, someone must coordinate each area of development, ensuring that each element will integrate easily into the final product at the required time. The larger the project team, the more time the producer spends supervising and directing.

Content

Content is a project's heart and soul, encompassing its main message or theme, and the media that will be used to communicate it. When planning content—amd ots [resemtatopm—the producer considers the types of media components the project will require, addressing a wide array of critical questions and choices: What kinds of still images will be used, and what will be their relationship to text and other elements? How will text be used? Will the project require animation, and if so, what kind? Will there be major animation sequences or just small amounts now and then? What types of sounds will enhance the user's experience and retention of the project's content? Does the project require a soundtrack or just intermittent sound effects? How good does the sound quality have to be? In the case of a CD-ROM project distributed to a large audience, will users need to have external speakers, or will the built-in Macintosh speaker be adequate?

And how about video? Will the added impact of video sequences be worth the cost in disk storage and processing requirements? How much or how little should be used?

Of course, the producer also needs to consider sources of content. Will the budget allow an original soundtrack or licensed music? Will it require original animation and video footage, or will clip media suffice? What permissions will be required? Will royalties be paid to contributors?

Interface and Interactivity

Interface is another critical facet of a multimedia project. Here's where a skilled producer can create a delightful and powerful synergy among its various content elements, forging new ways for the audience to learn, experience, and understand. This is what puts the "multi" into multimedia. And, on many levels, this is what sells.

Interface also happens to be one of the greatest challenges of multimedia, for a successful producer can't just settle for the prettiest icons, the coolest music or the most impressive special effects. As with content, he or she has to balance purely esthetic wishes with the realities and logic of multimedia architecture. How is the data going to be organized on the disk? How will it be indexed, searched, and interconnected? How will external video equipment, other software applications, or database access be handled? Will there be enough room for everything?

And then there's the interactive element. Should users navigate through menus or a palette of icons, or should they get around by clicking and exploring the screen? How far can the user wander before getting lost? Is a highly animated interface too sluggish in it's performance? How much information will be in the main narrative and how much is tangential and may be best tapped into via hyperlinks? It's a real left-brain, right-brain balancing act, and a producer's skills at pulling it off in an elegant, exciting, and logical manner could make all the difference in the project's ultimate success or slide into digital oblivion.

Development Software and Hardware

Of course, the project's proposed content and interface, along with the production money available, will determine the software and hardware required for development. Chapter 3, "Mac Software and Hardware," and Chapter 4, "Hardware Peripherals" feature an in-depth look at the types of equipment available for multimedia and what might be required for different types of desktop multimedia projects, while the subsequent "Tools" chapters focus on software.

In general, the more powerful the authoring equipment, the faster and easier development will be. However, a producer needs to be aware of the target delivery platform. A project intended for retail distribution must be designed to run on a large number of machines, many of which will probably be less powerful than those on which it was developed. Many experienced producers create their projects on fast machines to save time, but continuously test on less-powerful systems that approximate those used by their intended audience.

Disc Duplication

If the project will be distributed on compact disc and or videodisc, the producer will need to locate manufacturers. The pricing for manufacturing a CD or videodisc needs to be included in the budget. There is more on this later in this chapter and in Chapter 10, "Outside Resources."

Outlining and Prototyping

The real production phase of the project begins with the creation of an outline or flowchart that will aid in defining its organization, flow, and internal architecture, as well as the technical and esthetic requirements for the content elements. This basic plan can then be tested with a working prototype.

Outlining

Film production often starts with a script, which describes what the actors say, as well as essential visual and aural information. In multimedia production, the producer generally begins the serious planning stage by creating an outline or flowchart that provides an overview of the project's interface design, including proposed content elements, user navigation options, and interactivity. This gives the producer a feel for what content and interface design materials will be needed, what jobs need to be done, in what order they need to be finished, and how everything will integrate into a single entity.

Designing interactivity requires visualizing a project in three dimensions, which may not always be easy with a two-dimensional chart. The third dimension can be better represented by mocking up a sample routine with a program like HyperCard. It can then be tested further in an early project prototype.

Prototyping

The interactive "shell" of a multimedia project is the most critical component, the foundation upon which the content organization and delivery will be built. The design and technical specifications of this shell—which contains the interface and programming—must be established before content production begins.

This prototype provides a chance to test and see if all the ideas can indeed be translated into reality. The prototype is ideally created in the actual authoring system, but may be produced in another environment. For complex projects, creation of the prototype becomes, of necessity, the primary design and programming task, requiring the most advanced skills, up front. It becomes the *actual* shell of the project.

Using the prototype, the producer can finalize decisions on a broad range of project specs, including overall screen design and geometry, the placement of buttons and windows, the required number and types of still images and interface graphics, the required types and lengths of video and audio clips, color depth, sound content and quality, types of animation, interactivity options, and much more. The prototype also provides a foundation for estimating the project's final size and complexity.

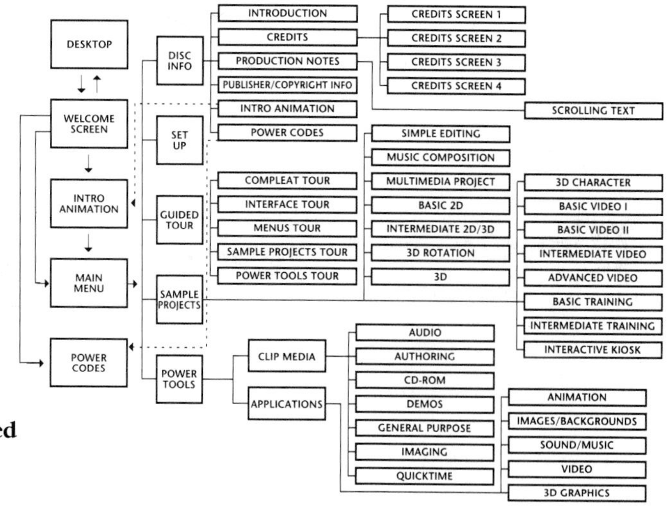

Figure 2.2 Early outline used for the Power Tools CD

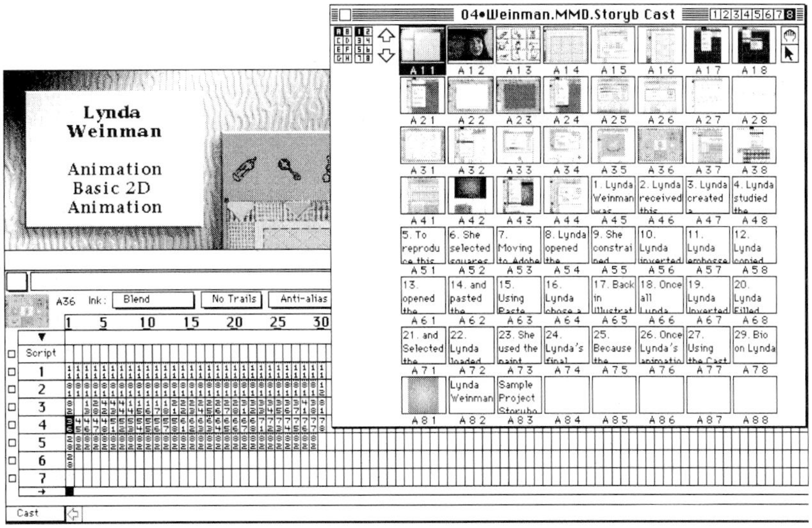

Figure 2.3
A typical multi-media storyboard

Storyboards

Once the outline has been created and refined, and the functional specifications established with the prototype design, a producer may map out the content exactly how each element is going to work, planning screen-by-screen what is accessible to the user. Storyboards can be created on paper or on the computer using a "slide show" presentation program, such as Aldus Persuasion or Microsoft's PowerPoint. They also may be created in rough form using the prototype shell. They usually show a still representation of each screen—often using early versions of (or actual) content images and interface graphics that will be included in the finished project—along with screen instructions and important information on user input and linking options (see Figure 2.3).

Storyboards save a producer lots of wasted effort by forcing a solid plan at the outset and clarifying the resources required for the project. They become more crucial with bigger projects and with more people involved. It is often hard to write a storyboard if you don't know what is feasible, or if a project requires extensive programming or creative input that builds as it progresses. A project will naturally evolve as it unfolds, but it's most efficient to get a sense of requirements and anticipated changes in its early stages.

Producing Project Elements

The next (and often longest) stage in the development process is acquiring and/or preparing the actual materials needed for the project, based on initial planning and prototyping. This stage follows two separate but interrelated tracks: one focusing on the development of the project's interface and architecture; the other on content development.

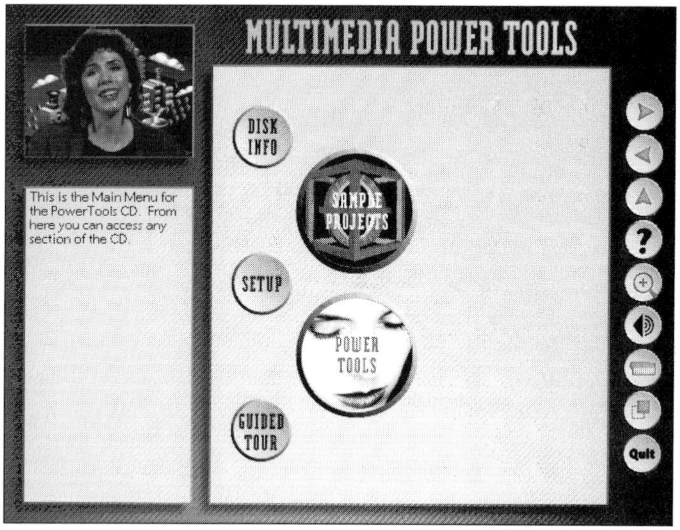

Figure 2.4
The main screen design for the Power Tools CD.

Producing the Interface

Once a project prototype is tested and refined, work can proceed on creating final interface screens and the underlying project architecture to which the various content elements will be linked. Interface production usually involves creating artwork for screens and buttons using a drawing or painting package, while making sure that all the interface elements fit into the overall project specifications and limitations revealed in the design and protoyping phase.

The interface is an extremely critical facet of a multimedia project, so screen design must be well thought-out from the perspectives of good graphic design, user-friendliness, and appropriateness to the content, user pathways, and general architecture of the project. This is a situation where the producer, graphic designer, and programmer will work closely to develop a design that is esthetically pleasing and serves the more technical aspects of the program. Chapter 19, "Interface and Interactivity" offers important advice and guidance for successfully executing this stage of the process.

Producing Content Materials

While work is proceeding on the interface, the the producer or development team must focus on gathering and preparing content material. There are basically two ways to create content for a project: produce it yourself or get it from elsewhere. Usually the method chosen will depend on the nature of the project: a corporate presentation will often require a good deal of original material—for example, photographs or video clips of the company's operations—while a project covering science, history, or current events would often use stock photography or film footage. The *preparation* of content materials will be determined by the specifications established in the prototype design: Bit-depth, size and color of graphics, sound file types, video formats, etc.

The first scenario may involve hiring artists, recording engineers, or videographers to create and produce original material, a situation that could rapidly eat up a budget, but may be necessary for a first-class, quality production. On the other hand, a lot of original material can be self-produced on a shoestring, if the producer has the right tools and a touch of artistic know-how. The "Creating" chapters in Part II of the book offer numerous tips and techniques for low-budget, "in-house" productions. Either way, traveling this route often consumes a lot of time, whether it's from waiting for the artists/experts to do what they do best, or from the steep learning curve of "doing it yourself."

Acquiring stock graphics and media clips from elsewhere is another option that almost every producer uses to some extent. Some multimedia projects may rely almost entirely on "pick up" media, and even high-budget extravaganzas use some stock art. Often, useful content is in the public domain, and can be acquired for free from libraries, television stations or elsewhere.

TOOLS Clip Media 500-990

Often, a producer can acquire media for a very reasonable price. A great deal of clip media can be obtained from companies that specialize in selling collections. The Power Tools CD features numerous license-free collection samples that are free for you to use.

Often, a producer will need to pay a licensing fee in order to use specific music, animation, photographs, or video clips. Whatever the source, a producer always needs to be careful to assure that permission is obtained for any pre-produced material.

Chapter 10, "Outside Resources," covers clip media in detail.

Assembling Elements into a Cohesive Production

TOOLS Director 210

When the development team has created and collected the various interface and content elements, they're assembled into a final product using an authoring program such as Macromedia Director, HyperCard, and others (see Chapter 9, "Authoring Tools"). These systems are in large part *object oriented,* allowing a producer to link multimedia elements simply by moving icons on a screen. However they also feature advanced interactive capabilities accessible through their own scripting languages . Most scripting languages are similar and are *high level*—meaning they're more like English than traditional programming languages such as Pascal or C.

Graphics and sound can be imported directly from other programs, or they can be created using graphic tools that are a part of the authoring system. Some authoring systems have tools that can help create graphics and 2-D animations. Sounds and video need to be pre-recorded and put into a form that can be handled by the authoring system.

Before project assembly begins, it is essential to have all the pieces ready for the programmer. Usually the graphic interface elements are put into place first.

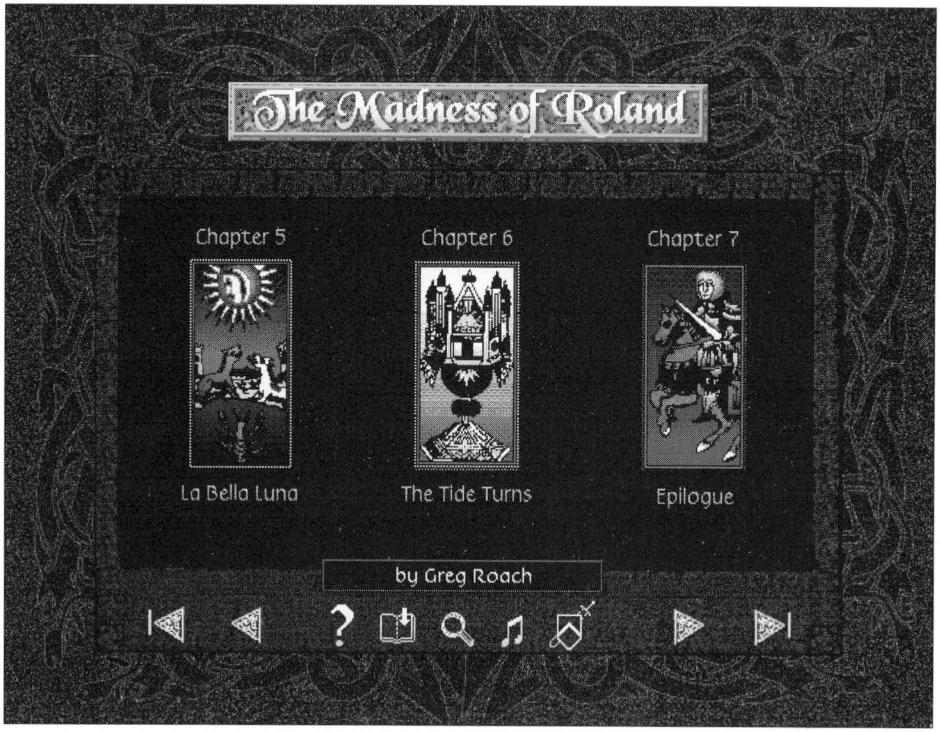

Figure 2.5
In *The Madness of Roland*, the user leaves a "trail" of where her he or she has been.

The programmer writes a script for each button and menu to make something happen when the user clicks on it.

Madness of Roland 032

Additional programming coordinates animation and sound. Sometimes additional code assures that everything on the screen is set properly when it is displayed. Other times the programmer needs to have code to keep track of what the user has been doing. *The Madness of Roland*, on the Power Tools CD, keeps track of exactly who the user has interacted with. The programmer created a screen that allows the user to see whether or not he has spoken to all the characters. This type of technique is often used to help users remember what they have done within the program.

Assembling a program in an authoring system is the last big job in putting together a multimedia project. During this stage, each element becomes a part of the whole. The programmer uses the script, the outline, the prototypes and storyboards, to transform the static pieces into a multidimensional entity.

Testing and Making Adjustments

Once a working version of the project is assembled, it is thoroughly tested—preferably by a number of people who have not been involved in production. Of course, the production team will test the product, but the most important

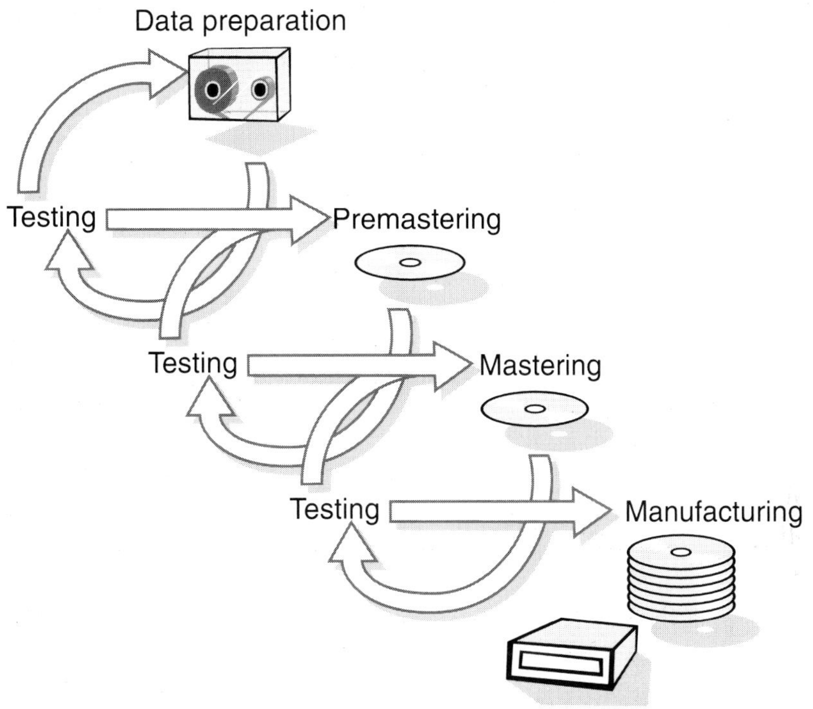

Figure 2.6
The process of preparing data to make a compact disc.

findings will probably come from others who don't know what to expect, and will try things that the developers may never have thought of.

Testing takes time and effort (a typical testing period can last anywhere from a few days to several months), but an error on a compact disc is there forever. Users will do things you cannot possibly imagine. It's better to find the bugs before the project "goes public."

Final Form: Presentations to CD-ROMs

A small multimedia production, such as one used a single time for a short presentation to a group, usually ends up either on a floppy disk, cartridge drive, or a portable hard drive. A HyperCard stack with a few sounds and bit-mapped graphics will fit on a floppy disk; a lecturer can use a stack of this sort to link quickly to bullet charts or extra information as it is needed and never lose his or her place in the presentation. However most multimedia projects utilizing extensive graphics, sounds, animation and video are distributed on high-capicity media such as removable cartridges, CD-ROMs and videodiscs.

Floppy Disks

A small project, such as a software demo or short presentation, can fit on a floppy disk distribution, which is economical and guarantees a wide audience for the work. Disks can be duplicated by companies with mass duplication equipment.

These duplication machines are not terribly expensive compared to the cost of sending many disks out for duplication, so a producer might consider purchasing a disk duplication machine for regularly produced, small projects.

Removable Cartridge Drives

The cartridge is portable, slightly bigger than a compact disc, and is good for presentations or a situation where a single cartridge can be routed to various people. They are relatively expensive (about $80 per cartridge), and hold up to 44Mb of data (some hold 88Mb, but aren't as common). A 44Mb cartridge will hold several applications and 20 to 30 moderately-sized 256-color or gray-scale images. This is good for one-time, "slide show" presentations of up to an hour or so. The more complex the presentation, the more space is required. Projects displayed on kiosks or single computers at trade shows generally work better on a hard drive, which boast better access speeds.

Optical Disks

In recent months removable media has taken another step ahead with the introduction of high-density, small-size magneto-optical discs. Initially too slow for practical use, "MO" discs now feature fast access times and very large storage capacities (300 Mb for the 5.25-inch size;—128 Mb for the 3.5-inch versions).

Compact Discs

Most large-scale retail multimedia projects are distributed on CD-ROM, due to that medium's high data capacity, economy, and convenience. Data preparation for making a 650Mb compact disc is virtually the same as for making a master floppy disk, and doesn't cost much more. Mastering runs about $1000, but duplication often only costs about $1/unit. Testing for a compact disc must be done meticulously, since once pressed, the disc will be that way for the next 50 years or so.

The process of mastering disks is actually pretty straightforward, and the appearance of inexpensive CD recorders has made the process very economical as well.

Videodiscs

Videodiscs are perfect for high-quality storage and playback of still images or moving pictures and sound, especially when that media is part of a single exhibit or kiosk. The source material may be from videotape, film, or digitized still images. The sound may be come with the original video or from another source, usually stored on DAT tape.

Creating a videodisc is not extremely different from the steps involved in making a compact disc. The premastering is usually done by experienced professionals at a postproduction house. The producer provides the source material and the order in which the clips should be physically placed on the disc. (For interactive products, the order is not terribly important, as long as each element can be accessed later.) Materials are assembled onto one inch videotape or onto D2 (digital composite video) tape. The D2 tape uses newer technology and is currently used more often than the one-inch video tape.

The post production house can then provide the producer with a VHS cassette copy of the D2 tape that has timecodes on it. This copy can be used to check that all the information made it onto the D2 tape and that it is in the specified order. Once the D2 master is approved, it is sent to the videodisc manufacturer, who turns it into a videodisc.

Getting Started

Multimedia clearly requires a multitude of tools, skills and planning. And, although it can be created on the desktop, it requires much thought, patience and hard work. The development process seems long and involved when you read about it, and (frankly) can seem even longer and more involved while you are doing it! On the other hand, each segment can be both challenging and fun to produce. There are tools that make it possible for you to do anything you want on the computer without extensive knowledge of programming or mathematics. You can see an idea become a full-fledged product in a matter of days for a presentation, or a matter of weeks or months for a more involved, in-depth project.

When you begin your first multimedia project, start with something small that you can finish quickly. You will get a feel for the process and learn techniques for working in an interactive, multifaceted environment. It gets easier as you go along. Remember to experiment and play the tools that interest you. Later, what you learned will pop back into your mind as a brilliant solution to a creative problem you are facing. Enjoy what you are doing, and your users will be more likely to enjoy their experience with your project.

3

Mac Software and Hardware

"The only computer worth criticizing."

Alan Kay on the Macintosh

In the late 1960s, when antiwar protests and whisperings of revolution swept through streets and college campuses nationwide, another sort of revolution was unfolding in the rolling hills near Stanford University. Here, at Xerox Corporation's Palo Alto Research Center (PARC), the personal computer was being born.

Xerox had managed to attract the best and brightest computer scientists from around the country and throughout the world. By 1974, they had a working prototype of a desktop personal computer, which they dubbed Alto. The Alto had a "bitmapped" display lit up by 500,000 pixels. Bitmapping allowed the pixels to be turned off and on independently, which for the first time enabled the simultaneous display of graphics and text. The graphical user interface (GUI) employed overlapping windows, icons instead of complex commands, and pull-down menus. The whole thing was designed to look like a desktop, and you navigated your way through it by pointing and clicking with a mouse.

If all this sounds familiar, it's because the GUI, desktop metaphor, bitmap display, and mouse are in wide use today, most notably in Apple Macintoshes and in Microsoft's Windows user interface. Xerox, however, gravely underestimated the power of these concepts, and never successfully marketed the Alto or its better known successor, the Star. (This failure is particularly ironic, since Xerox owed its overall success to marketing of photocopy technology developed by IBM in the 1950s, but subsequently ignored by Big Blue.)

Xerox executives decided that the real action was in the home computing market—at the time, the turf of Apple Computer—so rather than develop the Alto technology for the business world, they contacted Apple with the idea of buying in. But even as early as this date, 1979, Apple stock was hot property. Xerox would have to give something in exchange for being allowed to buy stock; what they gave up was the Alto technology.

In return for being allowed to buy 100,000 shares of Apple stock, Xerox gave a PARC tour to Apple's vice-president for research and development, Steve Jobs. When he got a demo of the Alto, Jobs immediately grasped what Xerox had not: the machine's enormous commercial potential. He soon thereafter began work on what was to become the Lisa and, later, the Macintosh.

PARC is still around, developing what it is calling invisible or "ubiquitous" computing. And technology isn't all PARC is exporting. PARC alumni include Microsoft chief scientist Charles Simonyi, Apple Fellow Alan Kay, Macromedia CEO Tim Mott, Adobe Systems founder John Warnock, Ethernet inventor Robert Metcalf, and Alvy Ray Smith, cofounder of Pixar. But perhaps none of PARC's inspirations has been as influential as its personal computing innovations, which are best and most clearly embodied in the Macintosh.

In this chapter, we'll take a look at the Mac's System software, which has been heavily influenced by PARC's original concepts. We'll also help you sort through the Apple orchard itself, to help you pick the best of the multimedia Macs.

Computer Presentation and Media Environments

Today, personal computer operating environments, or user interfaces, are nearly all graphical in nature. Sun and SGI machines have Open Look and Motif, the Amiga has Workbench and New Look, PCs have Windows, and Macs have the Finder.

These systems all share basic attributes—files and programs are represented by little icons, which you select or activate using a mouse; you can manipulate files by "dragging and dropping" them into "folders," or delete them by "throwing" them into a trash can or recycler icon; overlapping windows resemble papers on a desk, and you can hop between them with the mouse, even if the windows represent files from different applications.

The fact that so many different kinds of desktop computers have settled on the same set of visual metaphors confirms the basic common sense of the approach, and is a testament to PARC's original ideas.

Because these operating environments are so natural and intuitive, they are well suited to nearly all computer applications, but their visual dynamism holds special appeal for the multimedia adventurer.

The Macintosh World

In 1991, Apple released its a long awaited—and long overdue—System 7 software. It was the biggest change to the Mac's operating environment and "personality" since the machine itself was introduced in 1984.

System 7 has been out for over two years, yet some people haven't yet made the switch. A few years ago, there were good reasons for this—many applications did not work properly with the new system, and it is much larger than System 6, taking up precious space on smaller machines.

But System 7 offers many serious advantages over previous versions of the Mac OS—particularly for multimedia developers—and application incompatibilities have all but disappeared.

Advantages of System 7

System 7 is no less than a complete make-over of the Mac, and its many improvements are too numerous to list here, so we'll just summarize the ones that are the most important to multimedia.

32-bit addressing allows the Mac to use more than 8Mb of RAM. With the large size of such multimedia components as digital video, animation, and scanned imagery, this is a critical enhancement. See "Managing Memory," below for a more complete description of 32-bit addressing.

File sharing lets you link several Macs and share your files with anyone to whom you give access. This is particularly useful for collaborative multimedia projects, in which several people are working on different pieces of a large project. File sharing allows them to quickly view, share, and transfer different components. Animators have found file sharing indispensable, because they can use it to send files to other machines for rendering. In rendering, the computer is used to perform the immense number of calculations necessary to give a 3-D image realistic effects like lighting, shadow, and color. File sharing makes it easier to manage this process, which is very slow, often taking hours or even days.

Virtual memory is a technique that allows you to make up for a lack of RAM by designating part of your hard disk as "virtual" RAM. Although slower than physical RAM, virtual memory can be a great help in a pinch. This feature is also more fully described in the section "Managing Memory."

Interapplication Communication (IAC) is a set of protocols that allows Mac applications to communicate directly with one another. Apple Events is the IAC component that actually sends the messages, which it can even forward to other Macs across a network. IAC will have a broad impact once applications have been revised to take advantage of its considerable power. In fact, it has already made possible *network rendering*, an important development in the animation field. If you are an animator working in an environment with more than one Mac, you can use network rendering to spread rendering tasks among multiple Macs, which can drastically reduce rendering time. See Chapter 6, "Animation Tools," for a description of this process and the products that do it.

Also part of IAC, the *Edition Manager* controls **Publish and Subscribe,** another major System 7 innovation. Publish and subscribe supports dynamic links between files. For example, you can imbed a sound or graphics file in a presentation; if you were to subsequently change the imbedded files, the presentation would automatically be updated.This works across networks and will even update multiple versions of the original file.

TrueType is a font technology that provides scalable screen fonts in any size. See the section below on "Adobe Type Manager and "TrueType."

Aside from these major features, System 7 provides many niceties, including:

- *Aliases*, which allow you to place "copies" of often-used files and programs on the desktop. (Aliases are not actually copies, but small 1K to 3K files that direct the computer to the real file or program.) They also allow you to simplify access to file servers.
- Improved Finder windows that make it much easier to organize files.
- A powerful Find command for locating files and programs.
- An improved System file that organizes files by category, eliminating clutter.
- The ability to capture screen contents as a color PICT file.

In the discussion of the Mac desktop and system software that follows, we have used System 7 in all examples.

The Macintosh Desktop and System Software

The Mac desktop, also referred to as the *Finder*, is your interface with the computer. It is an electronic work surface that gives you access to system services, applications, file management utilities, and all user-accessible areas of the machine (Figure 3.1).

Macintosh system software and utilities that allow you to control your Mac environment are located in the *System folder* (Figure 3.2). Following is a list of some of its more important components.

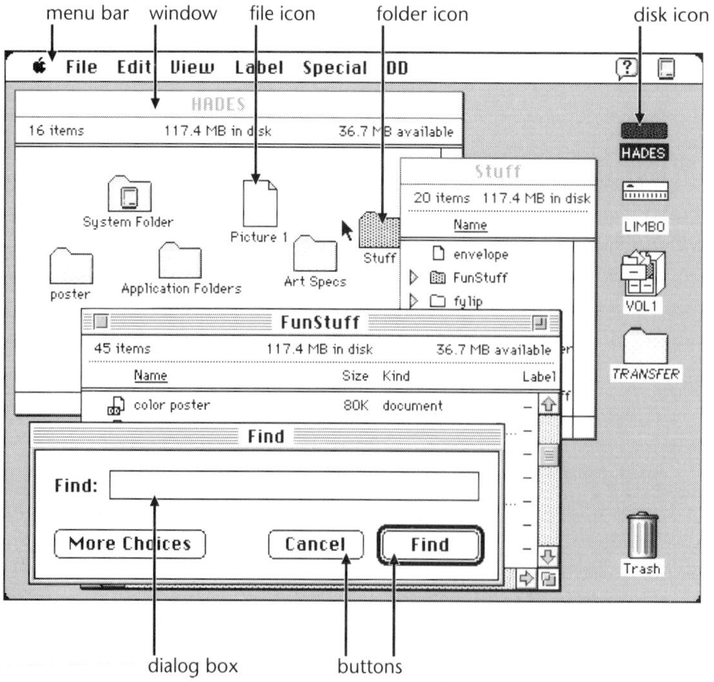

Figure 3.1
The Mac desktop

Macintosh Interface Standards

From the very beginning, Apple designed the Macintosh around a single software and hardware standard, meaning that Mac applications can share data transparently. This single specification also results in programs that behave the same way, making it easier to learn one application once you know another.

The rigidly controlled Mac specification has an even more important and far-reaching benefit: it gives developers access to a common set of system resources. Programs that handle graphics, for example, use the Mac *QuickDraw* utility (see below). This spares developers having to write their own basic graphics routines, but it also ensures a high degree of compatibility between applications.

One of the big reasons the Mac enjoys such a wide variety of sophisticated graphical applications is that developers can produce them quickly, without having to reinvent basic modules each time. Furthermore, the applications, freed of low-level constraints, can mature rapidly.

The **Finder** is a key part of the Mac's user interface, an application that shields the user from the inner workings of system software. It lets you drag a file to the trash can or to another folder instead of typing a command, as you would do in DOS, for example; the Finder handles all Mac file management utilities.

The Finder also lets you have more than one application open at once, so that you don't have to quit one application and start up another one.

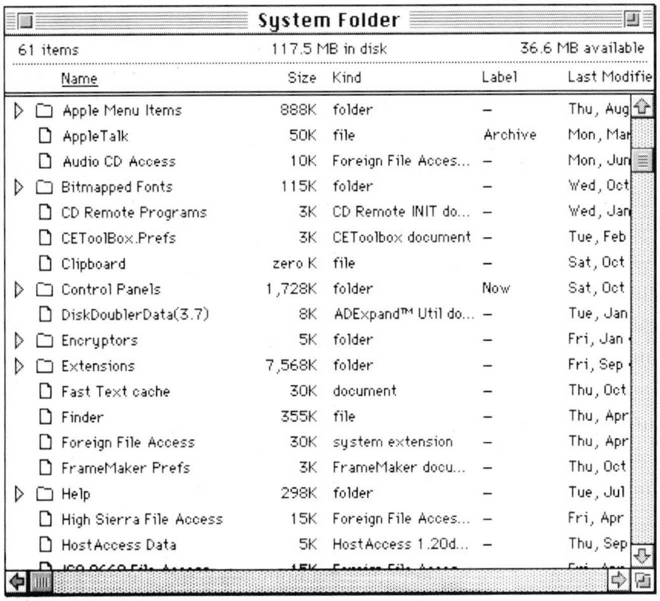

Figure 3.2 Contents of the Mac System folder

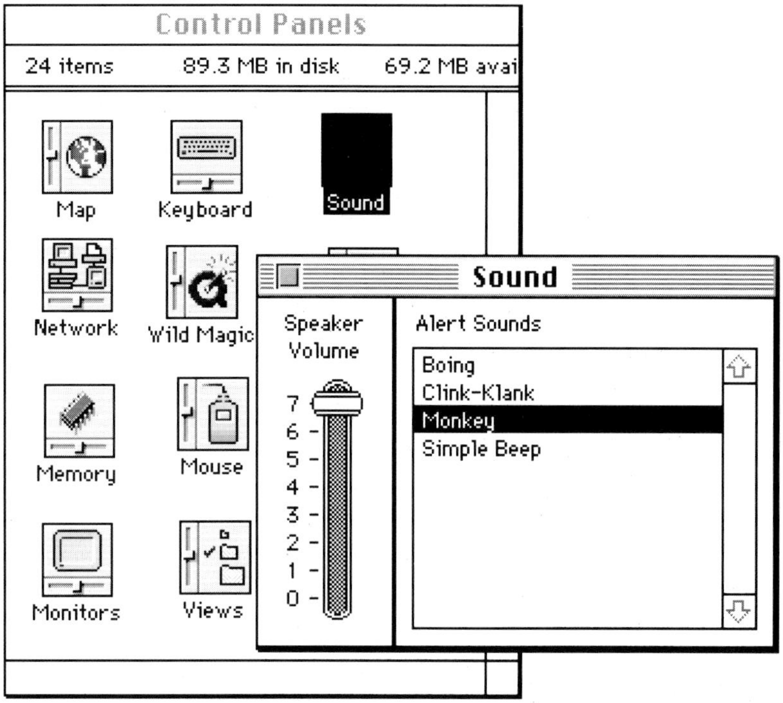

Figure 3.3 Main control panel and sound control panel windows

The **System file** contains software instructions that do not concern the end user at all, as well as *resource files*, such as screen fonts and sounds. When you open the System file, you'll see a list of these types of files. If you click on a font file, a window pops up with sample text in that typeface. Similarly, clicking on a sound file causes the Mac to emit the sound stored in that file.

Control panels (Figure 3.3) provide a means for customizing your Mac environment. The Mac comes with many control panels already installed, and others are added as CDEVs (control panel devices) when you install a new component.

Control panels let you customize your keyboard, mouse, memory, and many other aspects of your Mac operating environment. For example, the sound control panel lets you assign your own choice of sound to the alert tone the Mac uses to warn you of something. You can also adjust the volume of the Mac's speaker.

If you need quick access to files or applications you use frequently, you can drag their icons into the **Apple Menu Items** folder. As soon as you place the items into the folder, they are available directly from the apple symbol on the desktop. This saves you the trouble of hunting through file hierarchies and directories and windows to find often-used items.

Startup Items is a folder containing icons corresponding to applications that you want to launch automatically every time you start your Mac. For example, you might want the alarm clock desk accessory (*desk accessories* are small

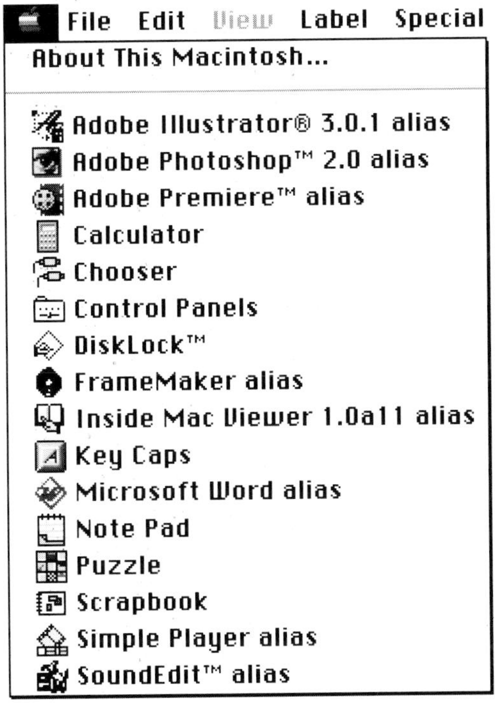

Figure 3.4 Apple Menu Items

applications) to be visible on your desktop at all times. To do this, you would simply drag its icon to the Startup Items folder.

When you customize an application to your own liking, your changes are stored in the **Preferences** folder. When applications launch, they check this folder for any customized elements. Normally, you won't have much to do with this folder, since changes are placed here automatically by the applications themselves.

The **Clipboard** is a sort of holding tank for text and graphics that you cut from an application file. You can go back to the Clipboard and get things you accidently deleted, or to move them to another file. The Clipboard is cleared each time you shut down the Mac.

Extensions

Extensions, also part of the System folder, bear special mention here because they are necessary for commonly used multimedia devices like videodiscs and CD-ROM drives, and because they are sometimes the source of conflicts and other difficulties.

Extensions are files that augment the basic functionality of the system software, and are typically loaded by the system at startup. Many extensions, such as the Chooser and control panels, are accessible from various areas of the desktop; others, like virus detection software, simply work invisibly. Extensions come in three basic types:

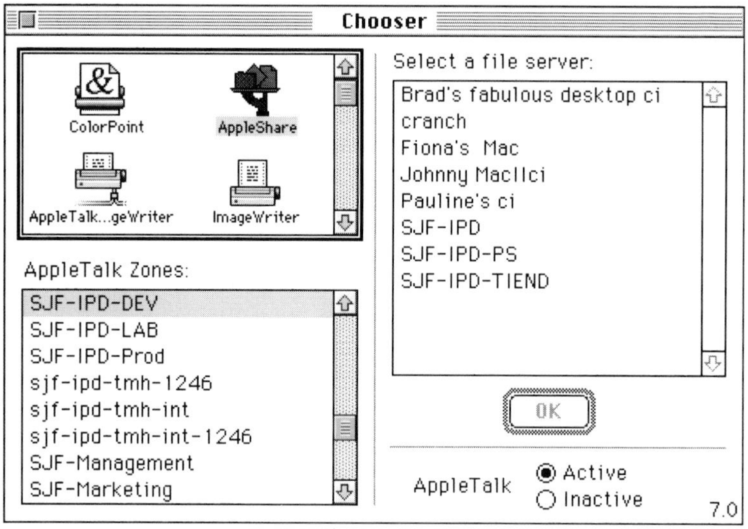

Figure 3.5
The Chooser

- *RDEVs* (AR-devs) are *drivers* that allow the Mac to work with any number of external devices, such as printers and fax modems. When you install a new laser printer, for example, it comes with a floppy containing the appropriate drivers and other software. When you install these files, the Finder knows to put them into the Extensions folder. The devices themselves are then selected through the *Chooser*, which displays an icon for each RDEV (Figure 3.5).
- The start-up file, or *INIT* (for "initialization resource"), is another common form of an extension. During system startup, INITs generally briefly display little icons at the bottom of the screen, indicating that they are present and active.
- The *CDEV*, or control panel device (discussed earlier), is a type of extension accessible through the Mac control panels. For example, you might install a new color monitor, and the accompanying software will automatically install itself in the Extensions folder, and will create a control panel just for the monitor. Here, you can fiddle with various parameters (See Figure 3.6).

Apple itself supplies QuickTime, an operating system extension of particular interest to multimediacs. See "QuickTime," later in this chapter for more information.

Extensions and CD-ROM Drives

TOOLS Macintosh CD Setup 120

CD-ROM drives come with the file access and driver software that allows you to retrieve information from the device; the Finder will generally automatically place these files in the Extensions folder. While installation is usually painless, it's a good idea to understand the basic components.

Since all Mac CD-ROM drives use SCSI (small computer systems interface) connectors, physical installation is simply a matter of cabling the drive to the Mac. Despite its convenience, however, SCSI is an ornery standard, so make sure to

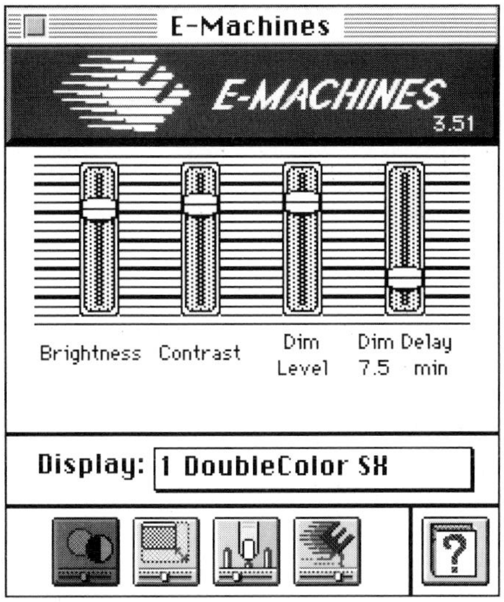

Figure 3.6 Monitor control panel

follow the manufacturer's guidelines when cabling and powering the drive on and off. In particular, *never* pull the cable out of the Mac when a SCSI drive is running—or you run the risk of damaging both the drive and your computer. See "Living with SCSI," later in the chapter.

Software installation is almost as easy; you just drag the drivers that come with your drive into the Extensions folder. These drivers will generally consist of several files, including High Sierra Access, ISO 9660 File Access, and Foreign File Access, which allow your drive to read CDs recorded in various formats.

CDs originally intended for the Mac are stored in Apple's native HFS (hierarchical file format). Other discs may be recorded in the High Sierra, or its successor, ISO 9660. Assuming that all of these files are present and are located in the Extensions folder where the Mac can find them, you really don't need to pay any attention to them—that is, if everything is working OK.

We installed CD Technology's popular Porta-Drive, and eventually got it running, though we had a few initial difficulties. Although the Porta-Drive INIT displayed onscreen as the Mac booted, the drive icon didn't appear on the desktop, and CDs in the drive wouldn't mount. We tried booting the Mac from a floppy containing a plain vanilla System folder, at which point the Porta-Drive mounted sucessfully and we could read CDs.

The problem we experienced resulted from a conflict between the Porta-Drive INIT and one of the others we had running. By booting from a floppy, we were able to quickly determine that it was an INIT conflict. Isolating which INIT was actually causing the problem was more challenging, as we had to remove them one at a time, rebooting in between, as described earlier.

Problems can also stem from a SCSI ID conflict. Every SCSI device is assigned an ID number. If you are trying to install a CD-ROM drive that has been assigned

Dealing with Rogue Extensions

Extensions, and particularly INITs, can frequently conflict with one another at start-up time, causing all sorts of strange problems, ranging from the disabling of one or more INITs to the total (temporary) paralysis of the Mac itself. For this reason, always keep a floppy with a System folder on it, so that you can start up from the floppy and then remove the offending extensions.You can also disable all extensions by holding down the Shift key at startup.

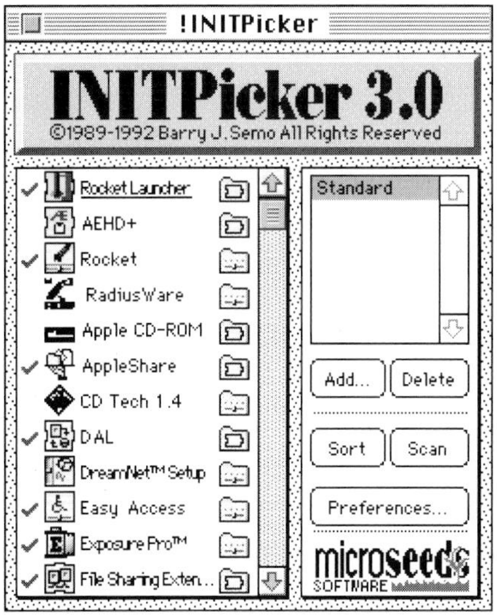

Figure 3.7 INITPicker helps you manage your start-up files.

Multimedia developers and users will often end up with a lot of extensions, which are necessary for the variety of devices and programs required by the medium. Any resulting conflicts are no reason for panic, but they can be annoying and time consuming to figure out.

If you are experiencing difficulties, the only sure way to get to the bottom of the problem is to remove all extensions and then add them all back to the Extensions folder one by one until the conflict reoccurs, at which point you'll be able to identify the offending extension. The problem with this brute force approach is that you'll have to restart each time you restore an extension.

Once you've identified the culprit, try renaming it—this will cause the Mac to load it in a different order at startup, which sometimes resolves conflicts. If that doesn't work, call the tech support department of the developer and describe the circumstances. Often, developers are aware of conflicts and can offer a solution or send a new disk that will resolve the problem.

If you're going to use a lot of INITs, you'll almost certainly run into conflicts of one sort or another. Several products (themselves INITs!) greatly reduce the hassle of INIT

box continued

conflicts. These little utilities let you turn INITs on and off individually without having to physically drag them out of the System folder (See Figure 3.7). You can also change the order in which INITs are loaded by the system, which can eliminate problems caused by INITs that don't like each other.

Baseline Publishing Inc. offers INITInfo Pro, a book and a HyperCard-based program that lists known INIT conflicts, and also includes a guide to isolating and solving conflicts. Help! by Teknosys will actually scan your system and prepare a diagnostic report that can lead you to the source of problems. Most INIT programs will also let you save sets of INIT configurations for use in varying circumstances.

Finally, as cool (and free!) as some shareware can be, it is rarely tested as rigorously as commercial software, and you have no recourse should problems arise. The best thing is to keep it simple: use only the extensions you really need, and clean house every once in awhile—extensions tend to stack up.

TOOLS
Extensions Manager 141

the same ID number as another SCSI device already installed and operating, such as a hard disk, there will be a conflict. In fact, if there is an address conflict with your main (or only) hard disk—the one you boot from—your computer might simply freeze up. In this case, you'll have to boot from a floppy and change the SCSI ID of your CD-ROM drive.

On external drives, you can usually reset the SCSI ID with a little thumb-wheel located somewhere on the unit. For an internal CD-ROM drive, you'll have to open the hatch on your Mac to get to the drive.

Occasionally, you'll run across a drive that doesn't have the necessary Mac driver software. If this happens, there are products such as Trantor Systems' CD-ROM Driver for Macintosh that includes drivers and file access software for dozens of different drives. Trantor's product also includes a desk accessory called Music Box that allows you to listen to audio CDs using your CD-ROM drive. (Apple CD-ROM drives come with a CD Remote INIT and Audio CD Access utility for playing audio CDs.)

Although the situation is changing, the majority of CD-ROM discs are intended for use with IBM and compatible computers running DOS. If you have the proper file access software (usually High Sierra or ISO 9660), you can mount the IBM CD on the Mac, locate the files you need, and translate them with a file conversion program such as Laplink (Traveling Software) or MacLink Plus (DataViz).

However, if you want to use the search engine that comes with a given DOS CD, you'll have to run some sort of DOS emulation software for the Mac. Insignia's SoftPC gives you a DOS prompt in a Mac window, and allows you to run DOS programs, including many CD-ROM search engines.

We use SoftPC on a Mac IIci and PowerBook with acceptable results. Even though DOS runs a little slow in software emulation, when used with a CD-ROM the speed of the CD itself is really the bottleneck, and access time doesn't seem appreciably slower than when running DOS native on a 386.

QuickDraw

From its earliest incarnation as a stubby little box, the Mac has long been a visually oriented computer. From its icons and scroll bars to its display of vibrant photorealistic images, the Mac is graphics-based to its very core.

The part of the system software responsible for the display of images on the Mac is called QuickDraw. QuickDraw is a set of graphics routines burned into the ROM chips of every Macintosh. QuickDraw is a very large piece of code, well over 100,000 lines, but it still manages to deliver images to the screen with great speed and reliability. This is due in part because the code is running directly from the chips, and because it is written in *assembly* language—very low level instructions that can be quickly understood by the computer.

QuickDraw functions are used by virtually all applications developers, which both preserves the Mac's legendary interface consistency and helps give rise to the diverse and rapidly developing base of graphics applications. Programs that do bypass QuickDraw, writing directly to the screen, do so at great risk, running the likelihood of incompatibility with the rest of the Mac world.

Originally, QuickDraw supported black-and-white images only, and indeed the Mac itself didn't get color until 1987, when Apple introduced the Mac II. With the new 8-bit QuickDraw, Mac II's could display 256 colors or shades of gray at one time. Eight bits can be turned on and off in 256 different combinations, defining the color limit of 8-bit QuickDraw.

Although this was a big improvement, there was increasing demand for *true color*, the ability to display photographic images, video, and realistically rendered "painted" images and animations. These very complex images far exceed the 256 colors that could be displayed by 8-bit QuickDraw, and in fact often contain *millions* of separate colors.

Meanwhile, the PC was becoming the preferred platform for high-end color applications, because of the wide range of input/output devices available. Not only that, but products like the TARGA video capture board were creating a low-cost color market based around the PC.

Apple struck back in 1989 with the release of 32-bit QuickDraw. Now Mac users could draw from a palette of more than 16 million colors. This unleashed a flood of applications and hardware add-ons, including 32-bit paint programs (see Chapter 5, "Imaging Tools,") and graphics accelerators (see Chapter 4, "Hardware Peripherals").

To display all of these colors, you need some additional hardware—a 24-bit display card (and a color monitor, of course). If you use a monitor bigger than the standard 13" display, you'll also need a graphics accelerator card. These cards have their own CPUs, which provide the necessary horsepower to move large true-color images around the screen in less than glacial time periods. See "Hardware," for more information.

A point of confusion is that the terms *24-bit* and *32-bit* are often used interchangeably. Actually, only 24 bits are needed to achieve the 16.7 million simultaneous colors that QuickDraw can display. The extra 8 bits, called the *alpha* channel, are used by applications developers to achieve a variety of effects, such as the effect created when two images intersect. Paint programs and image processing software like Photoshop use the alpha channel to create *masks* to protect part of an image from modification.

An important feature of 32-bit QuickDraw is its ability to directly drive the monitor's display circuitry. This eliminates the need to use color lookup tables, greatly speeding QuickDraw's performance. For those working in monochrome, 32-bit QuickDraw improves on the display of color images that are re-mapped for display on gray-scale monitors. Formerly, colors were mapped to a gray level based on their intensity, which often resulted in two completely different colors being assigned the same gray value. The new software does a better job of keeping colors distinct.

The new 32-bit QuickDraw, with its resulting availability of true-color products, large amounts of fairly inexpensive RAM, and the system-level standardization of the Mac, is the undisputed platform of choice for graphics applications of all types.

Adobe Type Manager and TrueType

Fonts are for desktop publishers, right? As a multimediac, your interest in type may be limited to adding flashy type effects that can be done in Photoshop, or creating titles for video. But fonts are such a key part of the Mac that type management is built right into the system software, and it helps to understand a few basics.

PostScript and Type 1, the page description language and font format from publishing software powerhouse Adobe, have long been the reigning type standards on the Mac (and indeed on all desktop computers). In 1989, Microsoft and Apple ganged up on Adobe by releasing new competing "standards," TrueImage and TrueType. The reason they did this has as much to do with market control as it does with the technical superiority claimed for TrueType over PostScript. Until challenged by the TrueType alliance, Adobe kept secret its type format specifications, securing its place as the standard source for font technology. This irked Apple and Microsoft, computing giants unused to depending on someone else's technology.

Under the Adobe method, there are two versions of every font: *bitmap* fonts, used to display type onscreen, and *outline* fonts, which are used by the printer. For each font, Adobe usually provides bitmaps in five or six sizes (typically, 10, 12, 14, 18, and 24 points). Bitmaps look fine as long as you don't want to use a size that isn't among the ones preselected for you. If you do, the Mac scales the closest available size. Since bitmaps are designed expressly for the sizes they come in, they do not scale well, resulting in ugly looking "jaggies."

QuickDraw GX

In 1992, Apple announced the latest incarnation of QuickDraw, QuickDraw GX. This newest version is a major enhancement that narrows the gap between the existing QuickDraw, which governs the display of images onscreen, and PostScript, which controls the printing of these images.

Ideally, the same software that displays images onscreen would be used to print them as well. This would theoretically yield an exact printed replica of a displayed image, a concept known as a *unified imaging model.*

In fact, Adobe, makers of PostScript, have had just that since 1988, when they released Display PostScript. NeXT computers, the first to use Display PostScript, have used it from the beginning. As a result, NeXT users enjoy a relatively close match between displayed and printed images—at least to the limits of the hardware. (Since most monitors contain 72–90 dots per inch, and typical printers print at 300 dpi, the correlation is never exact anyway.)

Apple has opted to enhance QuickDraw rather than implement Display PostScript. The reasons are that Apple feels the PostScript isn't the best choice for screen display—it's not as efficient as QuickDraw, and would be slow on lower end Macs; it will not scale as well as QuickDraw over a wide range of computers, from Apple's new handheld Personal Digital Assistants to top-end machines handling color prepress; and finally, Apple doesn't want to pay Adobe royalties on every computer it sells.

Major QuickDraw GX enhancements include a built-in set of graphics objects such as curves, rectangles, and polygons that are completely resolution independent—they do not depend on any particular screen or printer resolution, and may be scaled onscreen with no loss of quality. These objects can be operated on in numerous ways, including transformations (rotation, scaling, or skewing) and placement in different perspectives. Such sophisticated support for objects means that graphics and drawing capabilities can easily be incorporated into applications by developers. Significant color enhancements include color space conversion, color matching, and implementation of the alpha channel provided for by 32-bit QuickDraw but never used.

Finally, QuickDraw GX includes many advanced text handling features. It will support double-byte characters, allowing the Mac to handle ideographic languages such as Japanese. A QuickDraw facility called the *line manager* will provide typographic controls like tracking, kerning, and optical alignment. The line manager also allows text effects such as rotation, skewing, and stretching. All this means that developers can use these routines rather than writing their own, which will lead to smaller, cheaper, faster, and more powerful applications.

By contrast, TrueType uses outline fonts to create type for *both* screen and printer use. Outline fonts are generally superior to the bitmap method. Because they are based on mathematical descriptions, rather than bitmaps, they can instantly and accurately be scaled to any size with no loss of smoothness. (See Figure 3.8.)

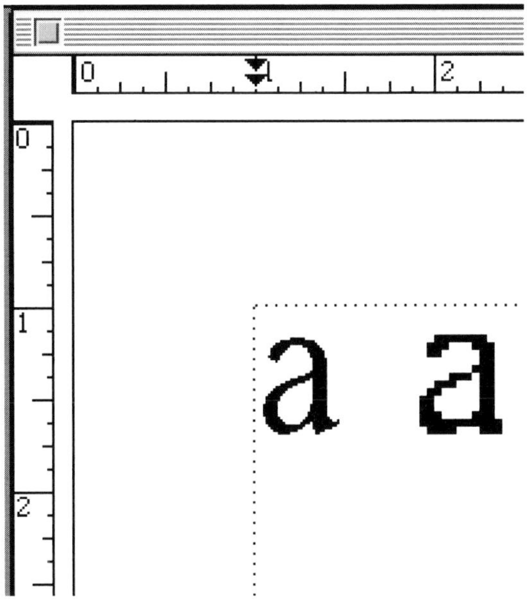

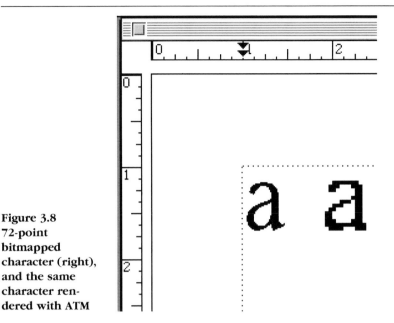

Figure 3.8
72-point bitmapped character (right), and the same character rendered with ATM

Adobe's answer was Adobe Type Manager (ATM), a CDEV that also uses outlines to create clean *screen* fonts in any size. While Adobe still ships both an outline and a bitmap version of all its fonts, with ATM you actually don't need the bitmaps. The trade-off is the old space-versus-speed question. Bitmaps kept in your System folder take up space, but are faster than outline type fonts, which must be created on demand. A good compromise is to keep bitmaps of the sizes you use a lot, and get rid of the rest, leaving ATM to cook up outline versions of other sizes for the odd times you may need them.

Adobe has also developed a new technology called SuperATM, which allows you to approximate a given typeface even if you don't have it installed on your system. Without SuperATM, when you open a document that uses a font you don't have, the Mac will substitute another font, which can throw off the entire format and layout of the document.

Both ATM and TrueType use a RAM cache to stash fonts so they can get them quickly when needed more than once. ATM allows you to set this cache size from the INIT's control panel (Figure 3.9). You can experiment with this cache size, depending on how many fonts you use at a given time and how much RAM you have to spare. (As a starting point, 192K seems to work well, but you can get by with far less if you use a lot of different fonts at one time.)

So, do you need to care about all this? Well, if you already have a number of PostScript fonts, then you probably don't need to bother with TrueType. The advantages of TrueType over PostScript are too slight if you already have an investment in type. If you don't, then you might consider using TrueType fonts

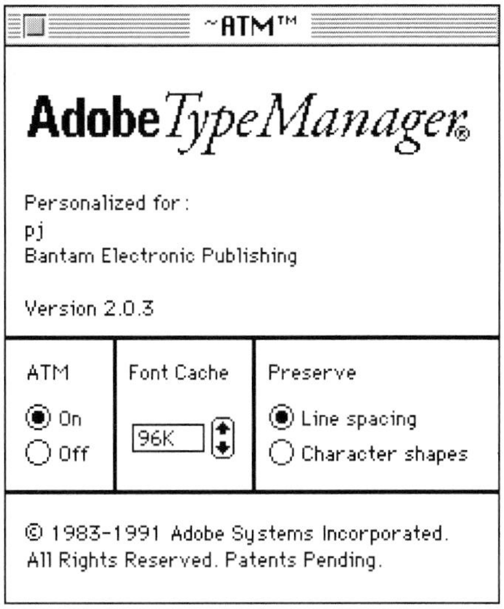

Figure 3.9 ATM control panel

for the simple reason that TrueType is built into the System; you won't have to buy and deal with another INIT (ATM) to get smooth type on-screen.

Also, Apple has built *optical font scaling* into QuickDraw GX, a technology which will potentially improve the look of TrueType even more.

But many of TrueType's initial advantages over PostScript and Type 1 have been reduced by the twin salvos of ATM and Multiple Masters (an Adobe technology that allows fonts to be incrementally modified for width, weight, style, and size), and indications are that Apple will incorporate ATM into future versions of System 7.

In the meantime, Microsoft and Apple, always uneasy partners at best (what with Apple suing Microsoft and all), seem to have retreated somewhat. Microsoft has pulled its TrueType programmers and put them in Windows development, and Apple has patched things up with Adobe.

The good news is that the emergence of TrueType has led to the incorporation of font technology at the system level, making it easier than it has ever been to work with type on the Mac.

Table 3.1 summarizes some of the pros and cons of both standards.

Managing Memory

A multimedia developer we interviewed said the first chapter of this book should contain nothing more than:

BUY RAM.

We agree that this is probably the single most important piece of advice when outfitting a computer for multimedia. Extra RAM allows you to have many programs open at one time, will stop annoying messages from the system about lack of memory, and will even prevent certain types of system crashes. Because of RAM's direct relationship with system software, we've elected to cover it here, rather than in the hardware section.

Table 3.1 PostScript vs. TrueType

PostScript	*TrueType*
User must buy third-party utility like ATM to get smooth screen fonts.	Fully integrated into Mac OS.
ATM seems to display screen type faster than TrueType.	Slower printing on PostScript printers, and no TrueImage laser printers yet.
Still uses two versions of type: screen fonts and outline fonts for the printer.	Uses a single outline font, making installation slightly easier.
Large existing library of Type 1 fonts	Type looks better at low resolutions.
Most service bureaus use Type 1 fonts.	Bundled with both System 7 and Windows, making it easier if you use both machines.

System 7 provides a range of options for memory management, most of which are selected from the Memory control panel (Figure 3.10). Of the four memory management options, 32-bit addressing is probably the most important because it makes very large amounts of RAM usable by the Mac for the first time (you'll still have to buy the extra RAM, though!)

RAM and 32-bit Addressing

The visual and time-based information generated by paint programs, image processing software, video and sound digitizers, and scanners makes for gigantic files that can be handled much more easily and quickly with lots of RAM.

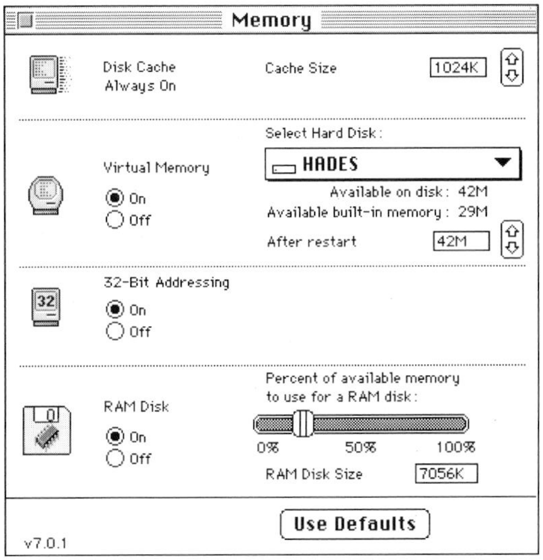

Figure 3.10 Memory control panel

System Limitations on RAM

For most Macs running System 7, adding extra RAM (also known as "high memory") is just a matter of buying it and plugging it in. Unfortunately, it's not as simple as that if you're using one of the earlier Mac II models or running System 6.

For starters, System 6 imposes a RAM limit of only 8Mb, despite the fact that the 68020 and 68030 processors in the SE/30 and Mac II series are technically capable of addressing up to 4Gb of physical (RAM) memory. (Compact Macs—the Classic, SE, and Plus—are limited to 4Mb under System 6.) While 8Mb is a lot better than the notoriously low 640K RAM limit of DOS, it's still very restrictive, particularly when it comes to multimedia.

32-bit Addressing

System 7 blew through the 8Mb barrier with *32-bit addressing*, a technique that allows Macs to use up to 128Mb of RAM. This is great and in itself is the reason why many decide to make the switch to System 7(see "Advantages of System 7" earlier in this chapter).

Unfortunately, critical system software burned into the ROMs of the Mac II, IIx, IIcx, and SE/30 are not "32-bit clean" and are thus constrained by the 8Mb RAM limit even when running System 7.

Luckily, there is relief available. Apple, perhaps embarrassed because they'd promised that System 7 would solve the RAM limit for all Macs, acquired an unlimited license for Mode32, a CDEV made by Connectix Corp. that patches the "dirty" ROMs in the Mac II, IIx, IIcx, and SE/30. With Mode32 in your Extensions folder, you can address the full 128Mb under System 7 with any of the Mac II series and the SE/30. Apple plans to include Mode32's functionality into a future release of their system software. For now, you can get download it from on-line services such as Compuserve, America On-line, and AppleLink.

Keep in mind that applications must also be 32-bit clean to take advantage of System 7's 32-bit addressing. Although most applications are 32-bit clean, some are not. If you need to use an application that is not 32-bit clean, you'll have to turn off 32-bit addressing, which reverts the Mac back to pre–System 7 24-bit addressing, with the 8Mb RAM limit.

In these situations, should you need to use more than 8Mb, you'll have to use a product like Connectix's Maxima, which extends the 24-bit addressing RAM limit from 8 to 14Mb.

Allocating RAM

The amount of RAM allocated by the Finder to each application program is called *application memory.* (Confusingly, total available RAM is also sometimes called application memory.) Each program automatically allocates the amount of RAM it thinks it needs, and you can select About This Macintosh from the Apple menu to review these allocations for all applications that are currently running (Figure 3.11).

The little bar graphs indicate how much of allocated RAM is actually in use at the moment, and the information is dynamic—you can leave this window up watch and System memory usage ebb and flow as you do different things (but only try this if you're really bored!). In the example shown in Figure 3.11, Photoshop isn't using much of its memory allocation because none of its files are open.

Speedometer 147

The whole idea of having plenty of RAM is so that you can improve performance by reducing hard disk access. You want to make sure you've enough memory set aside for each program so that the System can store the program code and the files you're working on in RAM.

As a rule of thumb, if the System goes to the hard disk in a given application for simple operations like clicking on icons or pulling down menus, you should probably increase the RAM allocation for that program. You can do that by selecting the application icon and typing the Get Info Command (-I),which brings up a dialog like the one in Figure 3.12. At the bottom of this dialog box, you increase or decrease the memory allocation. You can also get this box from within the application by selecting the program information item from the Apple menu. In this case, you'll have to quit and restart the application for the new allocation to take effect. The System controls its own RAM allocation, which is not configurable.

Be careful when decreasing the amount of RAM below the "suggested size." If you do that, you run the risk of an "unexpected quit"—a euphemism for a program crash—and in this regrettable case, you'll lose all data since your last save. Generally the System will warn you when it feels there isn't enough memory to launch an application, and sometimes it will simply refuse to launch a program altogether until you increase the RAM allocation.

Normally, if you reduce the amount of allocated RAM to less than 75% of the suggested size, you run the risk of an unexpected quit. If you're short of space, better to use virtual memory, or—you guessed it!—buy more RAM.

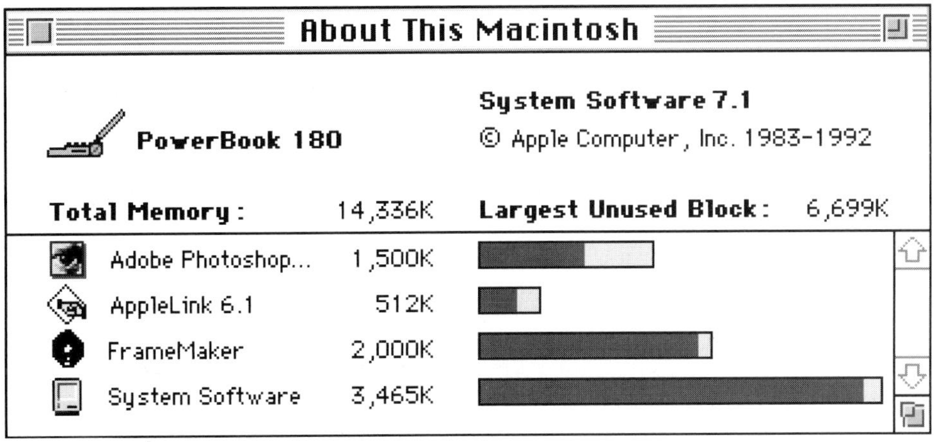

Figure 3.11 About This Macintosh

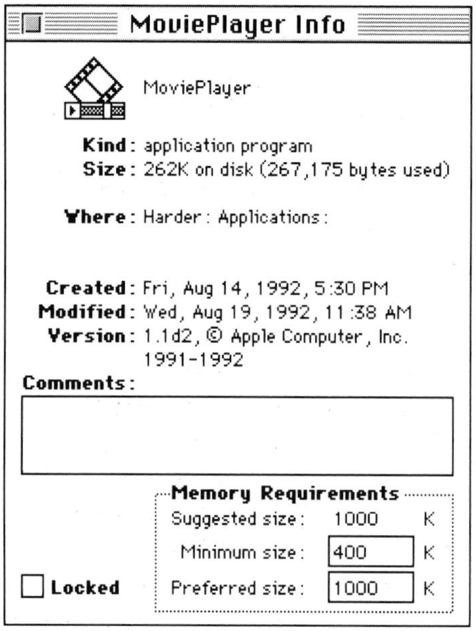

Figure 3.12 Get Info Dialog Box

How Much Is Enough?

Just how much RAM you should have depends a lot on what type of work you're doing. If you're involvement with multimedia is limited to playback of presentations, CD-ROMs, and the like, 8Mb should do fine. If you're developing heavy-duty applications that involve 3-D animation, video, or image processing, you'll want at least 16 to 24Mb. A Quadra 950 is capable of holding 256Mb of RAM

Using Virtual Memory

Virtual memory is a way to trick your Mac into thinking you have more RAM than you really do. You do this by allocating some of your hard disk as "virtual" RAM. If you're constrained by RAM limitations, as most of us are, virtual memory can be useful, what with the cost of RAM memory being about 10 times that of disk memory.

System 7 provides direct support for virtual memory through its Memory control panel. If you are using System 6, or an application that is not compatible with System 7 VM, there are inexpensive third-party products (such as Virtual from Connectix) that provide the same functionality.

Virtual memory works by allocating a special file on the hard drive called a *swap file*. As memory requirements exceed available RAM, the excess part of the file or application is tucked away in the swap file on the hard drive. When information in the swap file is needed, the system swaps it out from the disk. Since RAM is about 1000 times faster than typical hard disk access, virtual memory is slow, but it can also be the only way to open large files such as color images. In fact, paint programs such as ColorStudio and image processing software like Photoshop offered their own virtual memory schemes before Apple did it with System 7 VM.

Buying RAM

RAM prices have fallen dramatically over the last few years, making it possible to upgrade your Mac relatively inexpensively. Here are a few tips to keep in mind when buying upgrades:

1. There is a brisk business in mail order RAM sales, and you'll usually find the best prices here. You can generally get RAM for about $30 per megabyte. Check the ads in the back of Mac magazines.
2. Don't buy on price alone. Consider size and speed, quality, warranties, and the stability of the company you're buying from.
   - **Size**. RAM comes in the form of SIMMs—single in-line memory modules, small circuit boards that plug directly into banks on the Mac's logic board. SIMMs come in 256K, 512K, 1Mb, 2Mb, 4Mb, 8Mb, and 16Mb sizes. Of these, the most common today are the 1Mb, 4Mb, and 16Mb. Not all Macs will accept all sizes; check the capabilities for your machine before buying.
   - **Speed**. SIMMs come in different speed ratings, according to how fast information can be retrieved from them. The speed ratings are measured in billionths of a second, or nanoseconds (ns); the speeds are 150ns, 120ns, 100ns, 80ns, 70ns, and 60ns. The IIci, IIfx, and all Quadras need the fastest 80ns or better chips, while other modular Macs use 100ns or 120ns SIMMs. Compact Macs can get by with the 150ns chips. You can use faster than necessary SIMMs (e.g., 80ns in a Mac II), but this will cost you more and will not improve performance. The only reason for getting "overrated" SIMMs is if you plan to upgrade your machine in the near future, in which case you won't have to buy new RAM too.
   - **Quality**. Look for surface-mount RAM chips, which are more reliable, use less power, and generate less heat than those with older style through-the-hole mounting.
3. Some suppliers offer "lifetime" warranties, a good thing, but find out what is meant by "lifetime." The life of the SIMM, the life of the Mac you put them into, or what? Can you move the SIMMs to another Mac and still be under warranty? Also, what is the vendor's replacement policy? Some ship a new SIMM immediately, without waiting to receive the defective RAM back.
4. Buy from a reputable company, one that will be around for awhile. Saving a few bucks isn't worth it if the company disappears.
5. For a comprehensive and well-written guide to memory management, contact Connectix at 1-800-950-5880. They'll send you a free copy of *The Macintosh Memory Guide*. This excellent booklet has a wealth of information on all types of Mac memory. Its list of the memory capabilities of each Macintosh is especially useful. You can also get a HyperCard version of the book from on-line services. (To download from ZiffNet/Mac, a private on-line service on the Compuserve network, go to the central download library and download the file MEMORY.CPT.

System 7 VM has several limitations, and if you plan to use virtual memory, you might do better with Connectix's Virtual. First of all, while System 7's VM doesn't require contiguous disk space for the swap file, performance is much slower when the file is spread over the disk, or *fragmented.* (Over time, with much writing and deleting of information to your hard disk, it can become fragmented so that the system is forced write files over different parts of the disk.) If you use VM, it's a good idea to optimize (de-fragment) your hard disk with one of the many available hard disk utilities. Connectix's Virtual automatically optimizes its swap file. Virtual also require less hard drive space than VM, which requires 1Mb of disk space for every megabyte of RAM.

Virtual memory requires something called an MMU (memory management unit), which is built into the '030 and '040 processors used in most Mac II's and Quadras. The Mac II and the LC use the '020 processor, which does not have a MMU. You can buy one for about $150 for the Mac II, but the LC lacks an MMU slot.

Compact Macs don't work with VM but can use Virtual if they are accelerated with a '030 or '040 card, an expensive proposition.

Although System 7 allows you to assign as much as a gigabyte of disk space to virtual memory, in practice you should keep your VM allocation to no more than twice the size of RAM. This will prevent frequent hard disk access.

Virtual memory can definitely be a lifesaver when you're working with extremely large images, or when using a Mac with absolute RAM limits such as the LC. But if you're working a lot with color images, animation, or digital video, you'll be better off with a RAM upgrade.

RAM Caches and Disks

Aside from some very basic information stored on the Mac's ROM chips, the System must retrieve all information from the hard disk and place it in RAM, where it is immediately accessible. This includes everything from System information to programs and files. Often, the System as well as application programs will use and reuse certain chunks of code repeatedly. Once executed the first time, such code may be pushed out of RAM and must be again retrieved from the hard drive.

RAM Cache. In System 7, you can set aside, or *cache*, a portion of RAM for often-used data. Normally, the cache is 32K for every megabyte of total RAM you have installed, but you can change this number at the Memory control panel.

If you have a fair amount of RAM installed—say, 8Mb—you could increase the cache to as much as 2056K, but this probably isn't a good idea. Big caches don't noticeably improve performance, and any Ram that has been assigned to cache duty is unusable for other more important tasks. The default setting or even slightly less will be about right. In any event, performance enhancements yielded by RAM caches won't knock your socks off—you should only expect modest gains of about 5–15%. The only exception is if you are dealing with enormously large color files; in these cases, if you have the RAM, you might experiment with larger cache sizes.

Add-on cache cards can actually have a far greater impact, boosting performance to the 15–30% range.

RAM Disks

RAM disks are the opposite of virtual memory: instead of assigning part of the hard drive as "RAM," you configure part of RAM to work like a hard drive. This makes often-used files accessible much more quickly than they would be if stored on the hard drive. The only problem with RAM disks is that the information you copy to them is lost once the computer is turned off.

System 7 lets PowerBook and Quadra users create a RAM disk from the Memory Control Panel. You can also buy "RAM cards," which are stuffed with RAM meant to used as a disk. If you want to create a RAM disk but aren't using a Quadra, PowerBook, or System 7, such products as Maxima from Connectix and Roger Bates's RamDisk+ will give you this ability. Maxima will also copy the contents of the RAM disk to and from the hard drive when you power the Mac on or off—a nice convenience.

Stripping Down the System Folder

Since the System folder is loaded into RAM at start-up and remains there until you power down, it's a big target for optimization. The System eats up at least 1.5Mb of RAM, and Apple recommends a 2Mb minimum. The System folder can actually grow much larger, however, depending on what fonts you have installed (about 10–40K a piece), and what extensions you've added (typically 20–500K each).

For these reasons, you should do all you can to reduce the size of the System folder. There are third-party utilities that can help, such as Fifth Generation Systems' Suitcase II and MasterJuggler from ALSoft. These programs are font and DA management programs that perform a number of useful functions, such as extending the number of fonts and DAs that can be installed at a given time, displaying samples as well as names of fonts on menus, and so on.

Most important of all, however, is that these programs compress and store fonts on the hard disk rather than in the System folder, where they normally reside. If you work with a large number of fonts, you can dramatically reduce your RAM usage, and even if you don't, you ought to be able to cut out 500K or so.

QuickTime

With the release of QuickTime in 1991, Apple cemented its commitment to multimedia. QuickTime is the one piece of Mac system software that is probably of the most interest to multimediacs, so we're devoting a lot of space to it here.

Simply put, QuickTime is system-level software that lets users combine and synchronize animation, video, and sound and incorporate them into Mac applications. Because it is built into the system, it brings the multimedia experience to a wide audience, and moves digital video as close to the mainstream as it has ever been.

Just as you now freely cut and paste basic data types such as text and graphics, QuickTime allows the basic editing and manipulation of dynamic or *time-based* media.

QuickTime for the End User

As with most Apple system software, you don't have to know very much about QuickTime to begin using it immediately. Simply drop the QuickTime INIT in your System folder, and you'll be able to play back QuickTime movie clips. QuickTime works on any 68020 or better Mac (including PowerBooks with gray scale displays) running 6.0.7 or later system software with at least 2Mb of RAM.

QuickTime Extension 160

QuickTime is currently an extension to the Mac System software and is available at no charge from a variety of sources, including Mac user groups, and the AppleLink, CompuServe, and America On-line electronic bulletin boards. For developers, Apple supplies a QuickTime Developer's Kit—a CD containing all the QuickTime system software, plus a number of movie clips and utilities. End users can buy the QuickTime Starter Kit, a CD that includes various utilities, QuickTime movie samples, and QuickTime itself. Eventually, perhaps by the time you read this, QuickTime will be integrated directly into Mac System software releases.

QuickTime-aware applications, both general purpose, like spreadsheets and word processors, and more specialized applications, bundle QuickTime and a means for playing QuickTime movies. You can also buy the QuickTime Starter's Kit, which contains QuickTime itself, utilities for capturing, trimming, and compressing movies and still images, sample movies and clip art, and other goodies.

MoviePlayer 161

Popcorn 162

To play a QuickTime movie, you need nothing more than a suitable Mac, the QuickTime INIT, and a simple application for playback (Apple includes MoviePlayer with both QuickTime kits for this purpose). The only other thing you'll need is a QuickTime movie to play. You can get these from friends, bulletin boards, or QuickTime movie collections (see Chapter 10, "Outside Resources"), or you can make them yourself. To create your own movies, you'll need a little a little more than the basics—see "Making Movies." Once you've installed the QuickTime INIT and have a movie to play, you simply click on it to open it like any other file.

You also can launch MoviePlayer, which gives thumbnail views of movies on your disk, a timesaver if you have a lot of movies from which to choose. When you select "Open File" from a QuickTime-aware application, you'll also get this same helpful movie selection dialog box (Figure 3.13).

Once you select the movie you want to see, it's displayed in freeze frame, with the *Standard Play Bar Controller* at the bottom (Figure 3.14). To play the movie, simply click the play button on the Play Bar Controller. The slider will move to indicate time remaining as the movie plays. You can also click and drag the slider to move through the movie, though this generally produces choppy playback with unsynchronized sound. You also can use the step forward and step reverse buttons to display the movie one frame at a time.

Click the play button during playback and the movie will pause. When you click on the speaker symbol, another little slider appears so that you can adjust the volume. If there is no soundtrack on the movie you're playing, the speaker will be grayed out in the standard Macintosh manner.

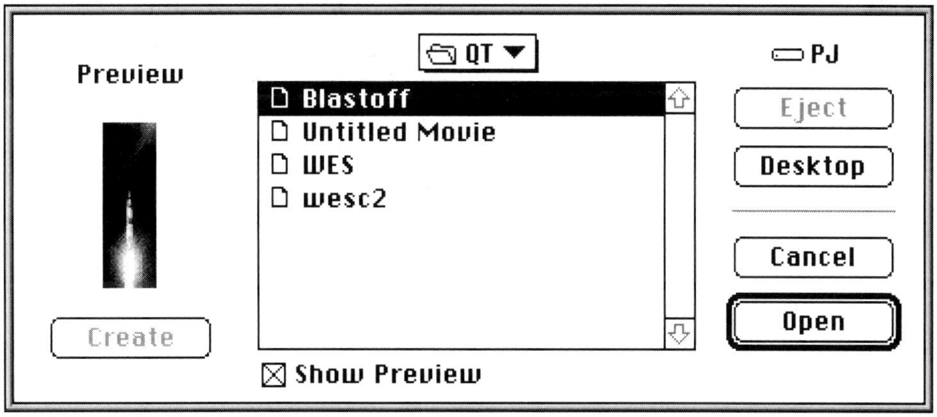

Figure 3.13
Movie selection dialog box

QuickTime's standard movie size is 320×240 pixels (about 3¾"×2½" on an Apple 13" monitor). You can enlarge a movie by click-dragging the standard Mac window handle in the lower right corner, but that degrades image quality rapidly, and sound synchronization may also be disrupted.

Just how fast movies will play back depends on the type of machine you're using. Apple claims that 320×240 movies play back at about 15 frames per second on a mid-range Mac like the LCII. In practice, you won't see that kind of performance except on Quadras, with their fast CPUs, hard drives, and bus architecture.

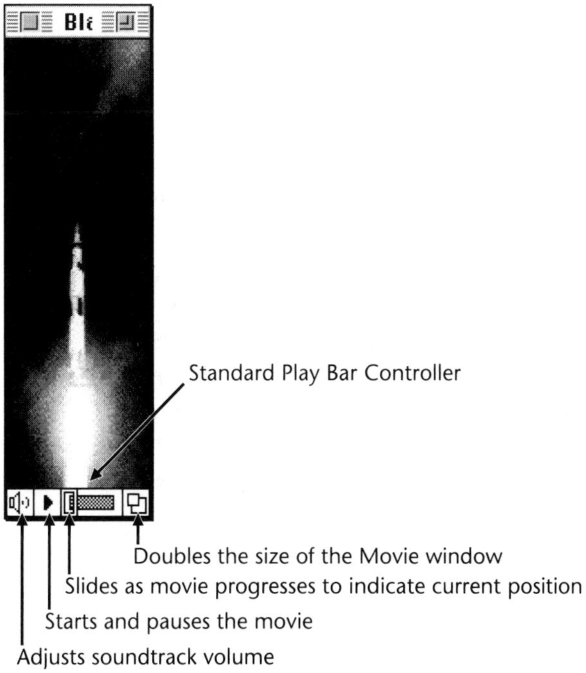

Figure 3.14
QuickTime movie

You should be able to play the smaller size movies at 15 frames per second on a mid-range machine. Add-in cards and third-party compressors make it possible to play back full-screen movies in real time (see Chapter 8, "Video Tools").

One of the interesting things about QuickTime is that it either fascinates immediately or completely disappoints. This seems to roughly correlate to the amount of computer experience the viewer has. Computer novices are disappointed by the so-so image quality and the jerky movements. Lay people naturally compare QuickTime to television, or even film, with which there really isn't any comparison at all. Both media have image quality many times higher than that of QuickTime's digital video.

By contrast, computer enthusiasts tend to go gaga over the tiny flickering images of QuickTime looking past the rudimentary feel of QuickTime to see the potential that lies ahead, once computers get a little faster and compression gets better. To the desktop computer user, so accustomed to dealing with visually arid text and simple graphics, QuickTime's moving images and sound synchronization seem revolutionary.

Playing with Magic

One of the most intriguing parts of QuickTime is a little utility developed by Apple France called Wild Magic (ah, those romantic French guys). Wild Magic is a control panel device that is bundled with the QuickTime kits, and is also available from user groups and electronic bulletin boards.

This CDEV allows you to cut and paste QuickTime movies into any application that supports the Mac Scrapbook and will import PICT files. Since PICT is the standard Mac graphics file format and the Scrapbook is a standard and well-used Mac utility, Wild Magic will bring QuickTime movies into applications that do not yet provide direct support for QuickTime.

TOOLS QuickTime Scrapbook 167

To use Wild Magic, simply drag the CDEV to your System folder. Then open a QuickTime movie, select it with the standard Mac Select All command (-A), and copy it to the Scrapbook (-C). This places the entire movie in the Scrapbook, where it can be retrieved and placed into an applications file. To do this, just open a file and type -V, and the movie will be placed (Figure 3.15).

The small icon in the lower-left corner, called a *badge*, is automatically placed here so that the viewer can distinguish the image from a normal PICT file. When you click on the badge, the Standard Play Bar Controller appears and the movie begins to play. The badge disappears during playback, and you can pause the movie using the pause button, or by clicking anywhere in the movie image itself. When you click anywhere outside the movie, the controller disappears and the badge reappears.

Wild Magic is in the public domain, meaning that you can use and distribute it free of charge. Type a letter to a friend, drop a QuickTime movie in it, put it on a

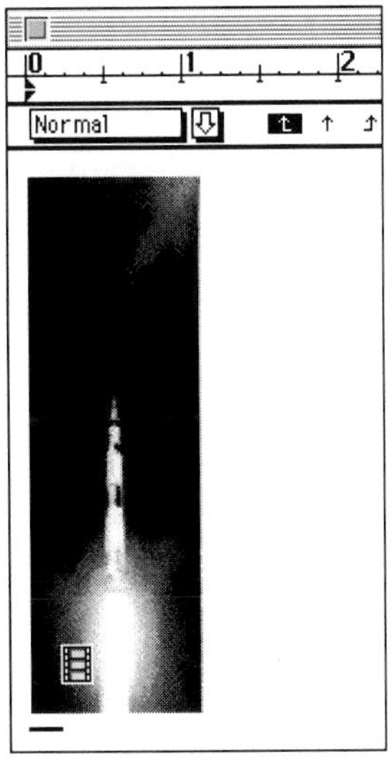

Figure 3.15
Movie imbedded in pre-QuickTime version of Microsoft Word

floppy along with the QuickTime INIT and Wild Magic, and you've got a portable digital movie that can be played back on any color-capable Mac in the world.

QuickTime Structure

If you want to do more than play back movies and place them in documents and files, it's helpful to know a little about QuickTime's components and architecture (Figure 3.16).

QuickTime consists of four basic component groups:

- System software
  - Movie Toolbox
  - Image Compression Manager
  - Component Manager
  - Media Handler
- Compressors
  - Photo compressor
  - Animation compressor
  - Video compressor
  - Graphics compressor
- File formats
  - Movies
  - PICT extensions

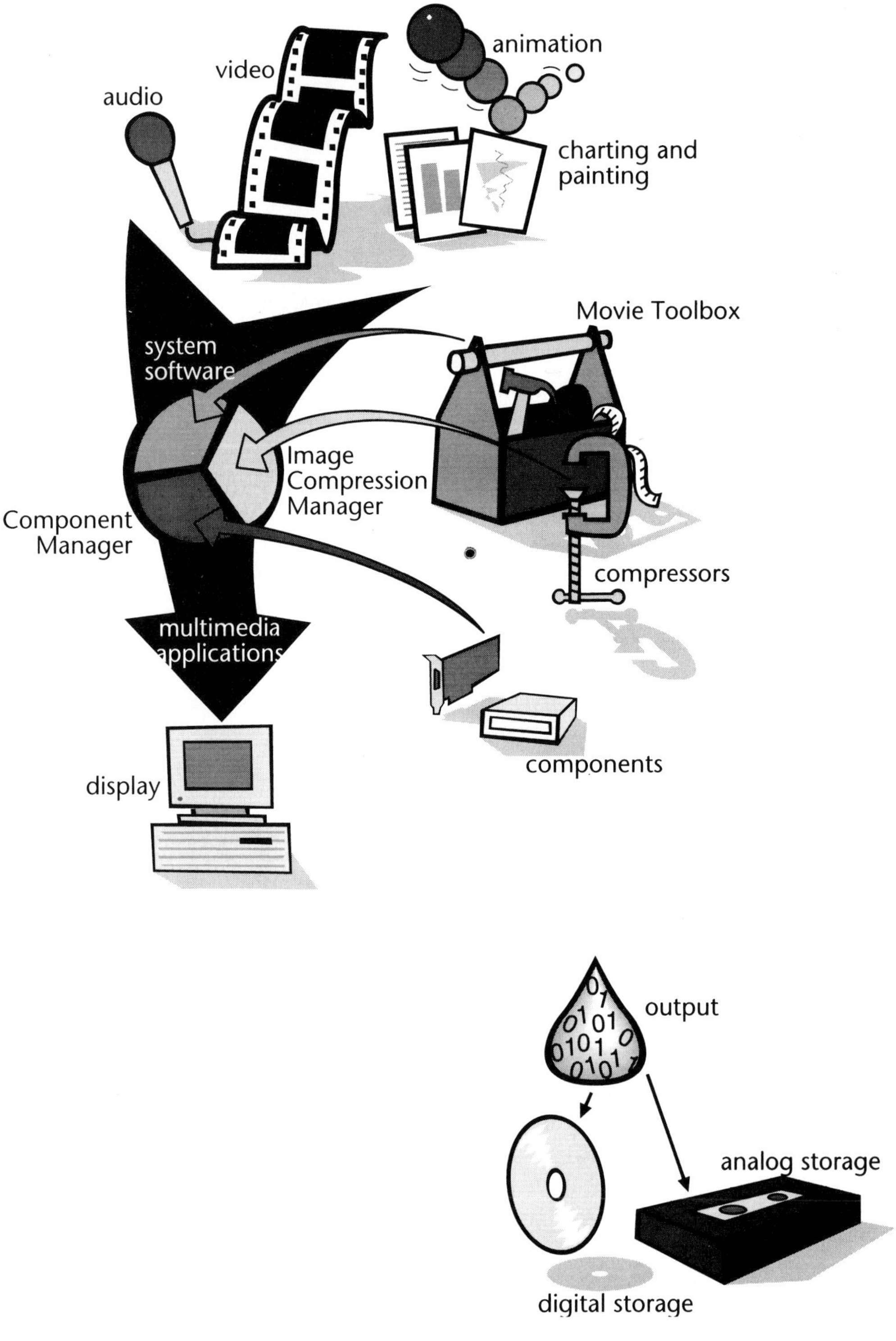

Figure 3.16
QuickTime
components

- Human interface

  Standard Movie Controller

  Extended Standard File dialog box with preview

  Guidelines for compression, capture, and more

Movie Toolbox

This is a set of system software services that allow third-party developers to incorporate support for QuickTime movies into their applications. Apple claims that the tools are so easy that developers have been able to incorporate basic functions such as playback and cut-and-paste in just a few days.

Image Compression Manager (ICM)

Since time-based data, like video, demands enormous storage capacity, QuickTime includes a variety of compression routines, all of which are software-based. These tools, called *codecs*, both compress video for storage on the computer and decompress for playback.

This sort of compression is called *symmetric*, because data is both compressed and decompressed by the user at the same rates using the same tools. (Asymmetric compression is done off-line, typically on mainframe computers—Asymmetric compression typically results in smaller files, with the trade-off being that it is not fully controllable by the user.)

The ICM controls the compression of QuickTime movies. When you want to compress and store a movie or other image (Apple supplies compressors for photos, graphics, and animation as well as video), from an application that uses the ICM, a menu provides access to the various compressors. When you select a compressed image for playback, the ICM selects the correct decompressor so that the image may be viewed.

The ICM accepts add-on compressors, so that QuickTime-aware applications will always have access to the latest in compression technology. When new compressors are added, the ICM menu is automatically updated.

Component Manager

The Component Manager manages external resources such as compressors and digitizers—which convert video and audio signals for use by the computer.

Before QuickTime, applications had to include individual drivers for each piece of video hardware, much as you need specific printer drivers to be able to print documents to various brands of printers. For example, to paste a video clip into WordPerfect, you'd need a special driver to bring the clip in from a particular video digitizing card; another driver would be needed for a different card.

With QuickTime, external hardware is transparent to applications. If you decide to make your own QuickTime movies and add a digitizer card, the application you use to control the digitizing of the video will rely on the Component Manager to communicate with the card. In this way, QuickTime frees software developers from writing a different driver for every digitizer board out there.

Media Handler

The Media Handler lets users and developers add different types of tracks to QuickTime movies. For example, after the initial release of QuickTime, Apple itself added support for a text track for titling and captioning.

Movies

Users integrate time-related data such as video and sound and store the results in a file format called the *Movie* (catchy, huh?). Each of the different components in a Movie is called a *track*, although the tracks do not themselves contain the data, but rather point to the data's location, type, order, playback speed, and so on. This arrangement keeps the Movie files small, since data can amount to several megabytes or more.

The Movie format standardizes organizing, storing, and recording time-based data. Each movie can have separate tracks recorded, each with its own timing, sequencing, control, and data description. QuickTime synchronizes the tracks and fetches the data. Initially Apple has defined two track types—video and sound. But the format is extensible, so that more track types can be added as they develop. By the time you read this, Apple may already have added support for MIDI and interactive controls tracks.

Each QuickTime movie includes three different "views"—a *poster*, which is an icon that represents the movie; a *preview*, which is a brief excerpt; and the full-length version itself.

Apple wants to make the Movie a cross-platform file format, and has published the specifications to make it easy for developers to include it in applications on various platforms (see Chapter 12, "Working Cross-Platform").

The Movie file format is fully supported by the standard Mac holding tanks, Clipboard and Scrapbook, so that you can cut and paste QuickTime movies as routinely as you cut and paste text and images. QuickTime will also recognize and convert various data types, such as PICS animation files and AIFF audio files.

With the release of QuickTime 1.6 in mid-1993, Apple added support for high quality audio with Sound Manager 3.0. Using a sound digitizer card, you can add CD-quality audio to your QuickTime movies.

PICT Extensions

Apple has extended PICT, its standard graphics file format. You can now compress PICT images, and preview them with thumbnail views. Any program that can view a PICT image now will be able to open a compressed PICT image as well, with no changes to the program.

Applications that support the new thumbnail PICT view will allow you to browse through a catalog of these small versions of PICT images. This will save a lot of time for those who work with large numbers of images.

Compressors

Apple is initially supplying four different compressor components: a photo compressor, a video compressor, an animation compressor, and a graphics compressor. These compressors are meant to be used with images collected from scanners, digitizers, paint programs, or any other sources that produce large, complex images.

TOOLS
TeachText 150

Along with an extension called Apple Photo Access, for example, QuickTime's built-in photo compressor will open pictures stored on Photo CDs. The photos are converted to PICTs and displayed in TeachText, where they can be copied into QuickTime movies.

All of Apple's compressors are software-based, which means they're cheap and readily available—definitely useful benefits. However, the structure of QuickTime is such that third-party compressors can be added easily and will be automatically managed and made available through the Component Manager. There are already both hardware and software compressors available from outside sources, most of which are faster than QuickTime's native tools.

Compression works by taking some of the information out of the image. If the removed information is redundant or not otherwise detectable by the human eye, the compression is known as *lossless.* But as the compression ratio gets higher, more information is removed and image quality degrades noticeably; this type of compression is called *lossy.*

For video, there are two additional types of compression. *Spatial* compression removes information from within a frame, and *temporal* compression takes away information between frames, a technique also called *frame differencing.*

There is a constant trade-off in compression, and you need to consider carefully the type of compression to use for a given image or movie. Higher compression rates will result in smaller files that take up less space on your hard disk, but the images may be of poor quality.

Say you have a short video clip that must fit on a floppy and is meant to be played back on a relatively low quality 8-bit display. Since the clip must be small enough to fit on a floppy, high compression can be used to make the file as compact as possible. Lower image quality resulting from high compression will not be a great problem because of the inherent limits of the displays that will be used to view the clip.

On the other hand, if you are making movies that will be played from a CD-ROM and viewed by many, you'll probably want the best quality images available, so you'd select low spatial compression, which will result in high quality images. You might also want to select high temporal compression, which will remove more information between frames, and will cause better playback of video from CD-ROM, which has low data transfer rates.

QuickTime provides a standard compression dialog box, shown in Figure 3.17. From this dialog box, you select the type of compressor (video, animation, graphics, or photo), as well as the quality ("Most" being low compression, and "Least" being high compression). For video, you also select the number of frames per second and "frame differencing," or temporal compression. Unless the "Frame Differencing" box is checked, both spatial and temporal compression are selected in tandem using the same slider.

Human Interface

Apple clearly cares about how users interact with computers. After all, they invented the Macintosh, certainly the most usable of computers. Apple has long provided exhaustive user interface guidelines for developers. This ensures that applications will be consistent and familiar, so that once you know one Mac program, its easy to pick up another one.

True to form, Apple has published human interface guidelines for developers who will be incorporating QuickTime into their applications. These guidelines include the basic design and functionality of the Standard Movie Controller, the Standard File dialog with Preview, and the Standard QuickTime Compression dialog, all shown above.

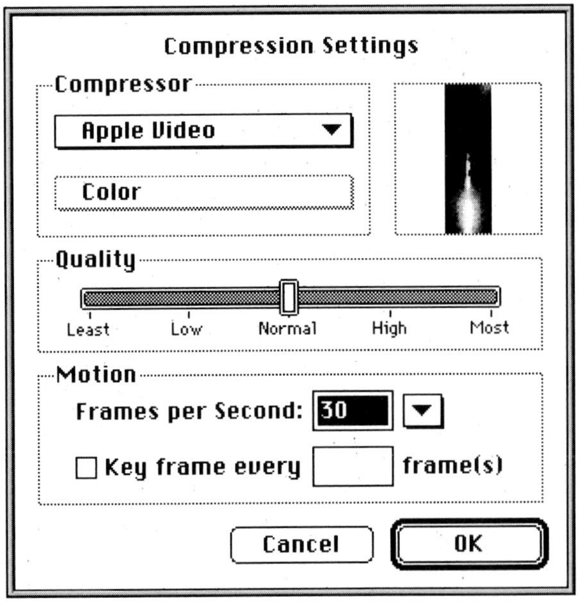

Figure 3.17 Compression dialog box

What's QuickTime Good For Anyway?

If you're the skeptical type, you may be wondering if there's really any use for tiny little low-quality movies. The following examples give an idea of the range applications that have already been found for QuickTime.

- QuickTime is at the heart of athletic shoe maker **Nike's** electronic merchandizing system. Nike store retailers can use an interactive system to select images and build 3-D models of store interiors, placing racks and product displays where they want them. Then they can "walk through" a simulated 3-D environment to see how the store would look. QuickTime is used to compress and playback the images.
- **Northwest Airlines'** Operations Analysis and Automation team uses QuickTime to make animated movies of weather patterns. The movies are put on a network file server, where schedulers worldwide can use them to help direct airline flight paths around storms and other disturbances.
- **Learningways Inc.**, a maker of educational software, is using QuickTime to put together a presentation for the National Science Foundation. The presentation is designed to help convince the agency to fund a new grade school mathematics program.
- **Ben & Jerry's**, makers of premium quality ice cream, have developed an interactive kiosk-based presentation featuring over 30 minutes of QuickTime video. The clips show the various steps in the ice cream making process. The idea originated as a way to entertain impatient tourists as they waited in line for a tour of Ben & Jerry's Vermont plant. The company plans to place kiosks in Ben & Jerry's franchises nationwide.
- **CK Media**, the multimedia branch of a San Francisco ad agency, developed a CD-ROM for Pixar's ShowPlace product. The CD contains the complete product—software and documentation, as well as an interactive walk-through of the product. QuickTime was used to animate several parts of the product demo.
- Using **Systat**, a statistical analysis and graphics package from Systat Inc., you can animate graphs and charts and store them as QuickTime movies. The animated graphs can make complex mathematical and statistical concepts and relationships easier to understand. Once created using Systat, the animated graphs can be incorporated into any QuickTime-aware application, just like any other QuickTime movie.
- KidPix Companion, from **Broderbund** software, is a children's paint program that makes very creative use of sound and motion. You can view QuickTime movies in KidPix's built-in "movie theater," Wacky TV.

TOOLS

QuickTime Tools 160–179
VideoShop Demo 242
Premiere 240

Making Movies

You may want to go beyond playing back QuickTime movies and venture into making your own. To do that you need surprisingly little: an inexpensive video digitizer, such as VideoSpigot from SuperMac, and an editing program like DiVA's VideoShop or Premiere from Adobe. You'll probably also want a sound digitizer such as MacroMedia's MacRecorder. You should be able to get the complete setup for under $1000.

Of course, you'll also need some source material, which can come from a camcorder, VCR, videodisc, or even a CD-ROM. For a guide to making QuickTime movies, see Chapter 8, "Video Tools," and Chapter 17, "Creating Video."

Macintosh Hardware

From its very earliest days, the Mac was destined to be a multimedia machine. Even before there was such a thing as multimedia, Macs were designed to handle graphics and sound as well as text.

As a result, nearly all the Macs Apple makes today are multimedia ready—even the low-cost LC has built-in color capability and sound digitizing. But the Macs that are truly suitable for multimedia development are the machines in the II, Quadra, Performa, Centris, and new Cyclone and Tempest series.

Apple still makes two machines in the old familiar Mac housing—the Classic and Classic II—but these lack expandability and color capability, making them all but unusable even as multimedia delivery machines. Although Apple doesn't make the SE/30 anymore, we have included it in the discussion below because it has an expansion slot and can drive an external color monitor.

Mac Models

In an effort to capture a larger market share of personal computer sales, Apple has released nearly 30 new Macintosh models over the past year or so. Keeping track of all the new machines and their capabilities is a formidable task—and still Apple keeps pumping out new boxes on almost a monthly basis. Still, most Macs fall into families defined by their architectures and targeted market. We'll take aim at a few of these moving targets here.

II, IIx, and IIcx

The Mac II was the first Mac that looked like a real computer—with a monitor separate from the CPU housing. No longer manufactured, and overshadowed by the more capable IIsi and IIci, there are still a number of Mac II's floating around. Outfitted with an 8-bit color monitor and 8Mb of RAM, this unit makes an adequate if unremarkable multimedia playback machine.

Several limitations make it a poor choice for a development machine. First, the Mac II's 68020 processor limits RAM to 8Mb, unless you buy a physical memory management unit (PMMU). Also, the floppy drive will read and write only 800K floppies, instead of the larger and more prevalent 1.44Mb disks. Finally, the processor and bus are just too slow to get decent performance with large multimedia images.

The Mac IIx is an improvement, as it uses the 1.44Mb floppy (or "SuperDrive") and its faster 68030 processor supports memory above the 8Mb limitation.

The IIcx was the first computer stuffed into the smaller Mac II housing, eliminating three of the six expansion (or "NuBus") slots, and upgrading the Mac IIx's 16MHz 68030 chip to 20MHz.

SE/30

The SE/30 (dropped by Apple in 1991 and replaced by the Classic and Classic II) put the power of the '030 in the original cramped Mac packaging. The SE/30 was also the first Mac to use a special expansion slot called "processor direct," or PDS. PDS cards (which will not work in NuBus slots, and vice versa), are faster because they communicate directly with the CPU.

It's possible to put a color card in an SE/30, so that you aren't limited by the tiny built-in black-and-white display. The SE/30 also supports the SuperDrive, and has both a math coprocessor and a 32-bit memory bus, which speeds calculations and memory access. If you can find a used one with a color monitor, the SE/30 would be an inexpensive multimedia machine, though you'd be better off with one of the more expandable machines in the II series.

LC and LC II

Apple released the LC in 1991, and by 1992 it was the company's best-selling computer.

With its low cost (a street price of less than $1500 for the base model), built-in 8-bit color monitor, and sound digitizer, it was ideal for the education market, long a special area of interest for Apple.

A big reason for the LC's popularity with educators is the availability of an Apple IIe card for the LC, enabling schools to continue to use their IIe software. This is important because of the extensive use of the IIe in schools.

The LC is certainly an excellent choice as a low-cost multimedia playback unit. As a development machine, it is hampered by its lack of expandability. It will accept only one expansion card, and only cards built to the LC spec—not cards built to the more ubiquitous NuBus standard. There is also no socket for a math coprocessor—a chip that can accelerate calculation-intensive tasks like animation rendering. Some LC expansion cards do include a math coprocessor, but there goes your one slot.... The LC is also limited to 10Mb of RAM, making it a poor choice for memory-intensive multimedia applications.

The newer LC II is an LC with an '030 instead of an '020 processor.

LC III

A 25 MHz '030 and a 32-bit bus, which allows the LC III to move data faster, makes the latest in the LC series twice as fast as the LC II. The new LC also improves on the II's memory capacity—you can pack it with up to 36Mb of RAM. The LC III supports 8-bit color on monitors of up to 16". Given that the III sells for about the same price as the II did in early 1993, it's quite a bargain. Envious LC II owners can buy an LC III logic board from Apple for under $500.

IIsi

The Mac IIsi is an inexpensive basic computer targeted at the business market. Like the IIci, it has built-in support for 8-bit color video. It's noticeably slower than a IIci, but faster than the IIcx it replaces. Its one expansion slot will accept either '30 direct or NuBus cards. Since there are a great number of cards built to the NuBus spec, this is an advantage of the IIsi over the LC, which will accept only LC expansion cards.

While attractively priced and reasonably capable, the machine isn't ideal for multimedia development because of its lack of expandability. Also, like the other current low-end Macs, the LC II and the Classic II, the IIsi is hampered by an inadequate power supply. Many cards, such as graphics accelerators and 24-bit color cards, exceed the 15-watt Apple limit. In fact, Apple's own 24-bit card draws 20 watts, leading the company to recommend against using 24-bit color in the IIsi.

IIci

The Mac IIci could well be the workhorse of multimedia. It's fast, expandable, and you can find used models for under $3000, complete with color monitor and medium-sized hard disk .

The ci fits into the smaller II housing, so it only has three NuBus slots, but it also has direct support for 8-bit color video on the motherboard, so all three are available for other uses. If you want more than 8-bit color, you'll have to install an adapter card, though.

The ci also has a faster PDS slot, into which you can install a "cache card," which will up overall system performance by as much as 75 percent. Apple ships the ci with the cache card included these days, but if you find a used ci without the card, you can buy the card for only $150 or so, well worth the expense.

As good as the venerable ci is, the new IIvx, which replaces it, is probably better. It costs about the same, and runs as fast as the ci with a cache card.

IIfx

Until the Quadras came along in late 1991, the fx was pretty much the computer of choice for high-end multimedia developers. And until the Quadra can get some of its compatibility problems squared away, the fx still looks pretty good.

It achieves near workstation level performance by using a 40MHz version of its mainstay CPU, the Motorola 68030. Performance is enhanced by a 40MHz math coprocessor, which speeds calculation-intensive tasks such as the rendering of 3-D images. Custom chips relieve the CPU of I/O responsibilities for the floppy drive, mouse, keyboard, and serial ports.

Other fx innovations include the use of static RAM, which acts as a buffer between the CPU and regular RAM, so that the normal Ram's relative slowness doesn't clog the CPU.

The fx is also popular with multimediacs because it comes in the original larger Mac II housing, and has six NuBus slots as well as a PDS slot. Unlike the IIci, though, it does not have a built-in color video adapter, so you'll have to use up one of the NuBus slots for a video card.

Apple discontinued the IIfx in 1992, shortly after it launched the Quadra, which is now the flagship Mac line.

Mac IIvx

Also in 1992 (a busy year for Apple), the new Mac IIvx appeared on the scene. (A similar model, the IIvi, is for sale only outside the United States.) With the introduction of the IIvx, Apple retired the IIci, long the choice of cost-conscious multimedia developers and users. The IIvx's three NuBus slots match the IIci's configuration in this respect, but the IIvx substitutes an accelerator slot for the ci's PDS slot. The IIvx uses a speedy 32MHz version of the old dependable ' 030 CPU. The machine also sports a math coprocessor and 32K of RAM cache, so you won't have to use precious standard RAM for buffering frequently used data.

The IIvx accepts a special Apple internal CD-ROM drive, which means, for one thing, that you won't have to mess with SCSI ports and termination. The drive itself, the AppleCD 300i, boasts a Sony dual-speed mechanism, which doubles the transfer rates of Apple's standard drives.

The IIvx has built-in 8-bit video, with 512K of VRAM (Video RAM), which will drive a 12" display at 16-bit color depth, or a 13" monitor at 8-bit color. You can add another 512K of VRAM to get 16-bit color on 13" displays.

As good as the IIvx is, is does have at least one curious lapse, especially considering that it's Apple's first "multimedia machine." Unlike previous Mac II's (including the ci it replaces), it cannot play back digitized stereo sound. When you open a stereo sound file, the vx simply discards the right channel sound. This is especially odd, since even the lowly LC at least mixes the two channels together, playing sounds monaurally.

Apple ships the IIvx with the new Macintosh Color Display, a 14" monitor that has excellent color fidelity, low distortion, and better brightness. Consumers will be able to upgrade the IIvx to the new Centris 650 (see below).

Performa 200, 405, 430, 450, 600, and 600 CD

With its launch of the Performa line in 1992, Apple continued the drive into multimedia that it had begun a year before with the introduction of QuickTime. As part of its new consumer marketing strategy, Apple even sought a distinct persona, boldly dubbing the machines "Performa" rather than "Macintosh," a name almost synonymous with Apple.

The Performas are true multimedia computers, boasting fast 32 MHz '030 processors, built-in color support, and in the case of the 600 CD, a built-in CD drive as well. The Performa 200 is simply a re-labeled Classic II renamed for the consumer marketplace, where, like the other Performas, they will be sold through retail outlets like Sears and Price Club. The 400 series Performas are based on the LCII and 2CIII machines.

The 600 is nearly identical to the IIvx, with a few critical differences. First, the IIvx has a math coprocessor, making it more suitable for tasks requiring a lot of calculations—such as rendering. Even more important, the IIvx has 32K of cache memory on the logic board, making it 25–33% faster than the 600. You pay an extra premium for these features, which Apple expects won't be as important in the IIvx's business market as in the more cost-conscious consumer niche that is the Performa's target.

All Performas ship with a new version of System 7, dubbed 7.0.1P. The OS variant includes features that should make Macs easier to use for first-timers. The biggest change is the Application Launcher, a window with oversized buttons that need to be clicked on only once to open an application. Apple says that its research shows that even double-clicking can be tricky for neophytes. Users also have a choice as to whether they want to use the standard System 7 Finder or an overlay called At Ease! that simplifies such chores as file management.

Quadras

If you have the dough and you're in multimedia development for the long haul, buy a Quadra. These machines, the 700 and 950, are the closest thing you can get to workstation performance in the Macintosh environment.

The Quadras have suffered from early compatibility problems—many programs simply won't run. By the time you read this, most of these problems should be sorted out, as applications vendors rewrite their programs to work with the Quadras' more complex 68040 CPU.

Quadras are the first Macs to use Motorola's speedy '040 processor, a chip that crams 1.2 million transistors *and* a math coprocessor on a ½" chunk of silicon. Quadras have built-in color support, and if you upgrade VRAM to the 2Mb max, you can drive a 13" or 16" color monitor at 24-bit resolution. If you want to use a larger color monitor, you'll have to buy an adaptor card, however.

The machines are bundled with a variety of software, further boosting their consumer appeal. Another innovation is incorporation of the system software in ROM chips, which greatly speeds access time and cuts down on both RAM and disk space.

Quadra 950

Once the fastest Mac of all, the 950 passed that mantle to the Quadra 800. With its built-in video support, the 950 can drive a 16" monitor at 16-bit color, or a 21" monitor at 8-bit. Other improvements on the Mac theme include a SCSI bus running at twice the rate of the standard SCSI interface, making data transfers from SCSI devices like CD-ROMs much faster. Data transfers between NuBus cards are also sped up considerably.

The 950 is built in a "tower" configuration, and is made to sit deskside. Networking capability (via Ethernet) is built in, eliminating the need to buy a separate networking card, if linking the 950 to other Macs is important to your application. The 950 has five NuBus slots, but you won't need to use up any of them for a network or color card.

Quadra 700 and 900

Both of Apple's first Quadras, the 700 and 900, were superseded by faster models within a year of their introduction. The 900 was replaced by the 950, and the

Wombat 25 replaced the 700. Better still, Apple reduced prices on the newer models, as part of its continuing price-reduction program, designed to answer long-standing criticism of the Mac's price-performance ratios in comparison with PCs. When the Quadra 700 came out, it cost $6999 for a 4/160 configuration; the Wombat 25 that replaces it sells for a whopping $2500 less in a similar configuration. For $8499 you can get an 8/230 Quadra 950, the same price as the slower 900 in a 4/160 configuration.

The Quadra 700 is packaged in the small II housing, and has only two NuBus slots. It also has a much smaller power supply, but this is OK, since power consumption comes mainly from expansion cards and you can use only two in the 700 anyway.

The 700 is also limited to only 20Mb of RAM using current 4Mb memory modules (as opposed to the 64Mb limit of the 950). However, once 16Mb modules become widely available, you should be able to stuff as much as 68Mb in the 700.

If you're short on cash, you might be able to pick up a used 700 or 900 for a good price; if you already have a 900, Apple offers a 950 upgrade.

Quadra 800

Apple's "mini-tower" is its fastest Mac yet. While priced less, and theoretically a notch lower in the Mac pecking order, the Quadra 800 actually matches (and in some cases exceeds) the 950 in computational power. You can also pack in more RAM (although the 950 does have a faster SCSI and card slots, so add-in cards should perform faster).

Centris 610 and 650

The Centris 650 fits in the same case as the IIvx, but is powered by a fast 68LC040. This chip is the '040 without the math coprocessor, which allows Apple to compete with 486-based PCs at a low price point. The machine has built-in Ethernet, three Nubus slots, and one PDS. Memory can be expanded to 136Mb using 4Mb SIMMs.

The Centris 610 is Apple's least expensive '040 box, which also uses the 68LC040 processor. The machine has only one NuBus slot, and it will accept only cards of 7" or less, which limits its expandability, as most cards are longer than 7". Both machines have built in video support.

Apple's New AV Macs and More

Just as we went to press, Apple introduced two machines that will give you a head start on producing multimedia: the Quadra 840AV and the Centris 660AV (the AV stands for audiovisual). These feature fast CPUs; a built-in DSP (digital signal processor) chips; video input and output (in multiple formats); video digitizing on the motherboard; Apple's Casper voice recognition technology; built-in phone/fax capability; and a bundled set of key third-party software programs. The high-end Quadra 840AV, carrying a retail price of just over $6,000 and sporting a 40MHz 68040 processor, can be purchased with 16Mb of RAM (expandable to 128Mb), a 1-Gbyte hard drive and an internal, duel-speed AppleCD 300i CD-ROM drive. The Centris 660AV comes with a 25MHz '040 and is expandable to 68Mb of RAM.

Software bundled with the AVs includes VideoFusion's Fusion Recorder, for capturing video to QuickTime format and recording sound at 16-bit resolution; Apple's Video Monitor, for displaying 16-bit, full-motion video at full-screen size; ExperVision's ExperFAX, for translating fax to digital text; and The Electronic Studio's ES.F2F videoconferencing program.

Beam Me Up, Scotty

While some criticized Apple for waiting until the end of 1992 to release a low-cost computer with a built-in CD-ROM drive, that machine was just the beginning. By all accounts, Apple is readying a slew of progressive machines that should be of particular interest to multimedia developers and users. Although Newton, Apple's pen-based personal digital assistant (PDA), has grabbed all the headlines of late, there are machines on the way that will be of greater interest to the multimediac.

A handheld multimedia device code named "SweetPea" will reportedly feature a CD-ROM drive and color monitor enabling the playback of a whole raft of multimedia titles. With commensurate advances in compression and storage technology, SweetPea could even be used as a QuickTime player, turning the diminutive gadget into a portable movie. SweetPea is also expected to implement wireless cellular file, fax, and e-mail transfer.

You've Got the POWER

As part of its alliance with IBM, Apple is developing a new generation of CPUs that promise to help boost multimedia computing into the mainstream. The Apple/IBM/Motorola joint venture will produce a series of RISC (reduced-instruction-set-computing) CPUs based on IBM's POWER chip set. RISC chips are able to process information much more quickly than conventional CISC (complex-instruction-set computing) CPUs. RISC processors are now widely used in the workstation industry, driving such machines as Sun's SPARC line and SGI's Iris Indigos.

The so-called PowerPCs are expected to appear beginning some time in 1994, and the three companies are taking the venture very seriously, spending over a billion dollars on the effort. Motorola will build the CPU, and Apple and IBM will use it for their respective machines.

The alliance plans four versions of the POWER CPU: the 601, 603, 604, and 620. The 601 will drive mid-priced desktop systems, while the low-power 603 will be used for low-end and notebook systems. The 604 will be used for more powerful desktop systems, while the 620 will appear in high-end systems in the $8000–$10,000 range.

Table 3.2 Macintosh Models

Macintosh	*Processor*	*Memory (base/ capacity)*[1]	*Expansion*	*Built-in Color Video Support*
SE/30	68030	1/8Mb	1 NuBus	no
LC	68020	2/10Mb	1 LC	yes; 8-bit
LC II	68030/16MHz	2/10Mb	1 LC	yes; 8-bit
LC III	68030/25MHz	4/36Mb	1 LC	yes; 16-bit[2]
II	68020/16 MHz	1/8Mb	6 NuBus	no
IIx	68030/16 MHz	1/32Mb	6 NuBus	no
IIcx	68030/20 MHz	1/32Mb	3 NuBus	no
IIsi	68030/20MHz	2/17Mb	1 NuBus or PDS	yes; 8-bit
IIci	68030/25MHz	1/32Mb	3 NuBus/1 cache	yes; 8-bit
IIvx	68030/32MHz	4/68Mb	3 NuBus/1 accelerator	yes; 16-bit
IIfx	68030/40MHz	4/32Mb	6 NuBus	yes; 8-bit
Performa 200	68030/16MHz	4/10Mb	none	no
Performa 405/430[3]	68030/16MHz	4/10Mb	1 LC	yes; 8-bit
Performa 450	68030/25MHz	4/36Mb	1 LC	yes; 16-bit
Performa 600	68030/32MHz	4/68Mb	3 NuBus/1 accelerator	yes; 16-bit
Performa 600 CD	68030/32MHz	5/68Mb	3 NuBus/1 accelerator	yes; 16-bit
Quadra 700	68040/25MHz	4/20Mb	2 Nubus, or 1 Nubus & 1 PDS	yes; 24-bit[2]
Quadra 900	68040/25MHz	4/64Mb	5 NuBus, or 4 Nubus & 1 PDS	yes; 24-bit[2]
Quadra 950	68040/33MHz	8/64Mb	5 NuBus, 1 PDS	yes; 24-bit[2]
Quadra 800	68040/33MHz	8/136Mb	3 NuBus, 1 PDS	yes; 16-bit[2]
Quadra 840AV	68040/40MHz	8/128Mb	3 NuBus, 1 PDS, 1 DAV	yes; 16-bit
Centris 610	68LC040/20MHz	8/68Mb	1 NuBus	yes; 16-bit[2]
Centris 650	68LC040/25MHz	4/136Mb	3 NuBus, 1 PDS	yes; 16-bit[2]
Centris 660AV	68040/25MHz	8/68Mb	1 PDS, 1 DAV (NuBus optional)	yes; 16-bit

[1] Using 1 Mb memory modules (or 4Mb where possible). Limits will be higher with availability of 4 Mb modules.
[2] With addition of extra VRAM.
[3] The Performa 405 and 430 are identical, except the latter has a larger hard drive.

Users will reportedly have their choice of three operating systems: the new Taligent object-oriented system, some version of good old system 7, and Apple will port the interface from its A/UX Unix variant to IBM's own AIX Unix system to create the PowerPC operating system, PowerOpen (ouch). This should improve on System 7 in a number of ways, by implementing features long enjoyed by Unix users, such as preemptive multitasking, multithreading, and protected memory. Preemptive multitasking assigns CPU time to applications in turn, making background processes run much more smoothly than they do now. Multithreading will allow you to perform system and application tasks at the same time, making it possible to, say, copy a file onto a floppy while you launch a new application. Protected memory will allow your other applications to keep running when an application you are using crashes and would otherwise take the entire system with it.

Apple will also introduce *agents*, which will sort, interpret, and process information for you in an intelligent manner. Agents are behind Newton's pen-based technology as well. Newton's agents will interpret your handwriting and drawings, making a keyboard unnecessary. But that's not all; you'll be able to write instructions like "fax to Joe," and agents will automatically launch the fax application, look up Joe's fax number, and fax the information to him.

Another agent is Casper (making its first appearance in the Cyclone and Tempest computers, as noted earlier in this chapter), a voice recognition technology that will allow you to give instructions to the computer by voice. Other agents will sort incoming faxes and e-mail and forward them to another location as necessary.

These intelligent services are enabled by the tremendous computational power of the new Power PC chips. As an extra bonus, the new technology will follow the curve of increasing performance for the same amount of money: all systems shouldn't cost any more than corresponding Macs available today.

All of these features will add up to very high performance computers that should be ideally suited to the demands of multimedia. Rotating 20MB TIFF files, for example, should happen in real time, something definitely worth the wait. In fact, you might want to wait a few years and open that really big TIFF file on a PowerPC, because if you start to open it right now, it might just appear about the same time the new machines do....

4

Hardware Peripherals

The basic components of multimedia—photographic images, graphics, animated sequences, video, and sound—are much more complex than text and carry huge amounts of information. Add to this the fact that most of these components are not static, but change over time, and you can see why multimedia places enormous demands on computer hardware.

Consider full-motion video, by far the most demanding of multimedia components. Video is shot at 30 frames per second, and when digitized for use on a computer, each frame consumes up to 1Mb of space. Thus, just to store a two-hour movie would require over 200Gb of disk space. Assuming such storage capacity is likely or even possible on the desktop—which it presently is not—a desktop computer capable of moving that much data from disk to screen has not yet been invented. Despite these limitations, there are still many uses for video on the computer, and ways to process it effectively.

A Trip to the Hardware Store

The processing of multimedia data by computer affects every element of basic system resources—CPU, RAM, I/O channels, storage devices, and display. Multimedia also requires at least a few additional components. If you are simply going to view multimedia presentations, electronic books, or interactive demonstrations, you can get by with a relatively modest system; a mid-range machine such as the Mac IIsi, a 13" color display, a CD-ROM drive, and at least 4Mb of RAM will do. If you plan to create presentations, or animation, or to work with video, you'll need to add a few components to your existing system. Most of the options are illustrated in Figure 4.1, which gives an idea of how the peripherals fit into the computer and relate to one another.

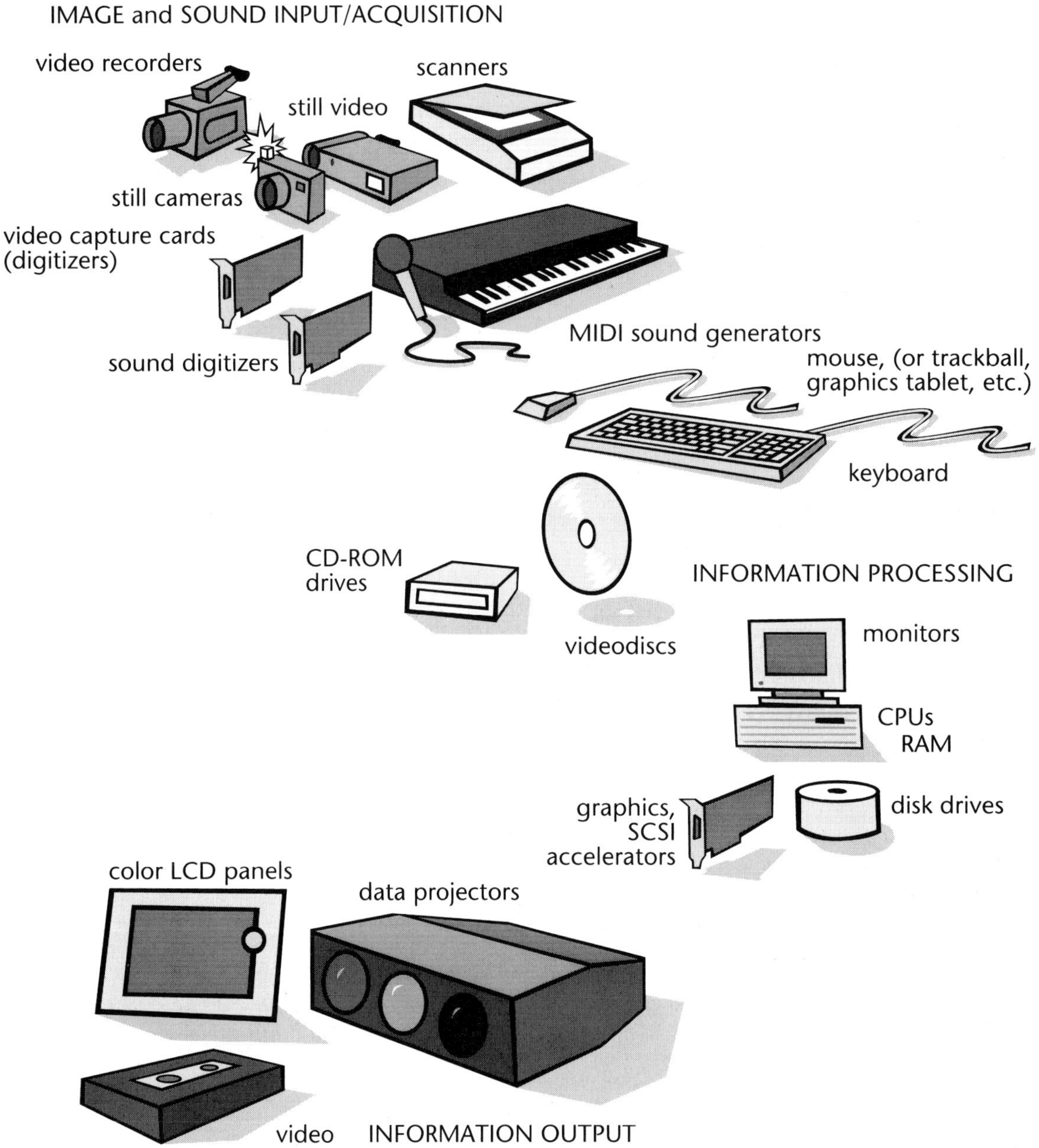
IMAGE and SOUND INPUT/ACQUISITION
video recorders
scanners
still video
still cameras
video capture cards
(digitizers)
sound digitizers
MIDI sound generators
mouse, (or trackball,
graphics tablet, etc.)
keyboard
CD-ROM
drives
INFORMATION PROCESSING
videodiscs
monitors
CPUs
RAM
graphics,
SCSI
accelerators
disk drives
color LCD panels
data projectors
video
INFORMATION OUTPUT

Figure 4.1
Multimedia hardware

Although this section is intended simply as an introduction to the different hardware components used in multimedia viewing and production, it is difficult to discuss them without commenting briefly on the various techniques and trade-offs involved in their use. For a full discussion of these aspects, however, see the various chapters devoted to multimedia creation.

For the sake of explanation, we've divided the hardware components into three categories—those that bring images and sound into the computer (discussed in the following section, "Image and Sound Input/Acquisition"), those that process, store, or display images on the computer ("Working with Images") and those that send images out, such as to tape or projection ("Image Output").

Image and Sound Input/Acquisition

The processing of real-world images and sound is one of the foundations of multimedia. Computers, originally able to handle text only, quickly progressed to the creation and manipulation of full-color graphics. Today, computers are processing all types of external images as well—photographs, noncomputer graphics, video, and sound.

The demand for computer access to these real-world images has led to many new and highly capable acquisition devices, including 24-bit color scanners, digital cameras, and video capture hardware. Despite their power and sophistication, these devices are beginning to be well within the reach of the desktop user, both in terms of price and usability.

Once images have been converted to digital form, there are a variety of programs that can enhance, transform, and incorporate them into multimedia creations of all sorts. The first step is to get the material onto the computer in the first place, a process that is becoming less daunting, yet still tests skill and patience.

For a discussion of video cameras, digital camera, and video capture cards see Chapter 8, "Video Tools." Sound capture and MIDI cards are covered in Chapter 6, "Sound Tools."

Keyboards and Mice

Used to be, not so long ago, that a computer's keyboard was enough of a challenge, and the mouse was just flat out baffling to a lot of people. When Hewlett-Packard conducted usability tests of its first mouse-equipped computers, some puzzled subjects aimed the mouse at the screen and punched its buttons as if it were a remote control; others rolled it around the computer screen. Of course, these days, most people have grown accustomed to mice as well as to the basic keyboard, and there are many interesting variations of both.

Keyboards

Keyboards haven't changed a whole lot since the first PCs came out in the early '80s, but they have been refined and standardized somewhat.

Nearly all keyboards for desktop machines now require about 2 ounces of force to actuate the keys, and key travel is between 0.14 and 0.18 inches. This is very important to touch typists, who are sensitive to the slightest variations in key characteristics. One reason why laptop and, especially, notebook computer keyboards are problematic for many users is that their relentless miniaturization means short key travel.

Another key consideration (har har) is the feel of the keyboard. There are two basic types: those that put up slight resistance before giving way with a click, and those that have linear travel—so-called "mushy" or "spongy" keyboards. The former is the classic noisy IBM keyboard, while the latter is the norm in the Mac world.

Keyboard Ergonomics

All of these things are part of the ergonomic design of the keyboard itself, and are more important than you may think—if a keyboard doesn't feel right to you, minor aches and pains can develop into cumulative trauma injuries like tendonitis or carpal tunnel syndrome. Major hardware manufacturers like IBM, Apple, Hewlett-Packard, Digital Equipment Corporation, AT&T, and Xerox have all been slapped with suits alleging hand and wrist injuries caused by keyboards. You can avoid these problems by trying out a keyboard before buying it and the computer it's attached to.

Keyboards vary slightly in the curvature of the keys and their degree of slope. But many aches and pains are not due to the keyboard itself, but to the position of the hands and wrists relative to it. The basic rule is to avoid flexing your wrists, which should remain relatively "unbroken" so that your hands stay on the same plane as your forearms. To facilitate this posture, you can get a wide variety of orthopedic aids such as wrist pads that lie in front of the keyboard, or supports that you wear like gloves. There are even little pads that you stick on your mouse to reduce clicking stress.

Keyboard Alternatives

Beyond these central considerations, a keyboard is pretty much a keyboard, but there are a few variations that may be of interest. In 1993, Apple itself introduced its Adjustable Keyboard, which splits in half so that you can adjust it to suit more natural hand alignment. The keypad also includes detachable palm rests. Apple makes no claims that the new keyboard reduces repetitive stress injuries (RSI), but it seems like a step in the right direction.

Infogrip of Baton Rouge makes an interesting alternative keyboard called the Bat. It is a "chordic" keyboard—so called because it has only seven keys, which you press in combination ("chords") to type characters. Unlike other ergonomic alternative keyboards, the Bat is used with only one hand, and operation in combination with a standard keyboard is not necessary.

Another unique device is the Twiddler, from Handykey Corp. of Mount Sinai,

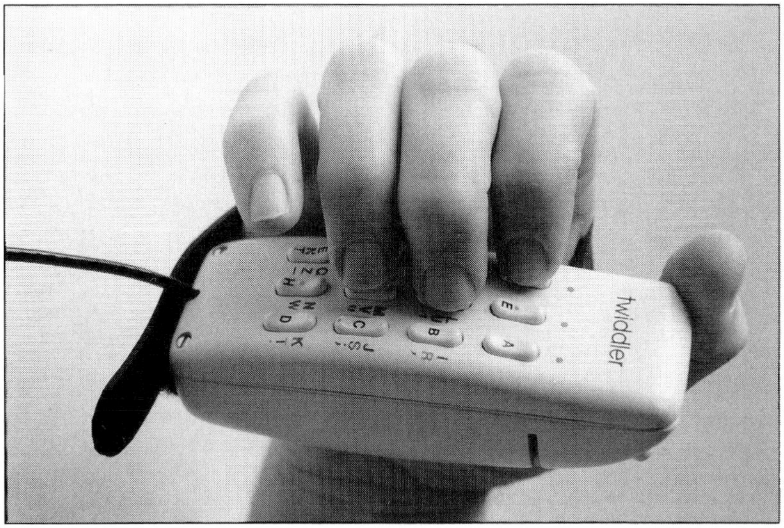

Figure 4.2
The Twiddler

New York (Figure 4.2). The Twiddler is about the size of a large mouse, whose functions it incorporates along with those of a keyboard. Using the Twiddler's 18 buttons, you can type any character that can be generated from a standard keyboard, as well as use it for normal mouse pointing and clicking. Once mastered, the Twiddler can be a convenient tool when giving computer-based presentations to a group.

Mice and Trackballs

There are dozens of alternatives to the familiar Apple mouse, many of which improve on its basic design. Mouse innovations include 300 dpi resolution (greater precision than the 200 dpi Apple mouse), ergonomic designs that fit the hand, and a choice of right- or left-handed models.

The familiar type of mouse has a little ball on the bottom, but many mice are optical. Optical mice work by bouncing light from a little LED off a reflective mouse pad. These mice are probably more durable due to fewer moving parts, but you must keep the reflective pad well dusted; otherwise, little dust motes can interfere with the light reflections and cause your cursor to behave erratically.

Trackballs—basically, upside down mice—are very popular, and of course have become almost indispensable on notebook computers. When Apple successfully incorporated a trackball into its first PowerBooks, there was a mad scramble as PC notebook manufacturers fell over themselves to belatedly incorporate trackballs into their own notebooks. Besides taking up less space, trackballs offer several advantages over traditional mice: they don't get tangled up, it's easier to move the cursor over the wide area of large monitors, and some people find them more accurate.

Some mice are programmable, letting you assign commonly used commands or keystrokes to their second and third keys. Others, such as Logitech's

MouseMan, even allow you to program keys with different sequences depending on what program you're in. When you switch between applications, the button assignments change. Now that's a smart mouse!

Still other mice follow the cordless craze, using infrared technology to transmit mouse commands and location to a tiny receiver plugged into the mouse port. Some of these gadgets may seem silly, but what the heck, they're selling: about half of all personal computer users opt for some sort of alternative input device.

Flying Mice and the Future

Speaking of alternative devices, you'll probably want to trade in your mouse or trackball when they start offering screens that sense what you're looking at—which you'll then select by blinking at it. These new selection devices, based on fighter plane heads-up displays, are still a few years away, but they're something to look forward to.

There are already voice recognition devices, such as Articulate Systems' Voice Navigator. These products are still a little rough around the edges, but may eventually prove to be better mousetraps.

A little more down-to-Earth, but still odd, are the flying or 3-D mice now being offered by such companies as Gyration, Mouse Systems, and Logitech. These mice are cordless gadgets that are meant to be used for mobility during demos and other presentations. The devices sense and track motion digitally, without relying on surface or position. While flying mice can be used as normal 2-D input, they are meant for the manipulation of 3-D objects; Gyration's unit, the Gyropoint (Figure 4.3), uses gyroscopes for motion sensing, and has six degrees of freedom—height, length, depth, roll, pitch, and yaw.

Graphics Tablets

Graphics tablets have been around for a while, but they've really taken off recently, propelled by revolutionary new painting tools. Computer art, once tainted by a telling computer-generated look and relegated to an artistic backwater, has been reenergized by new pressure-sensitive paint software, such as Fractal Design Painter and Time Arts'Oasis. These programs and others like them allow you to create textures and patterns by applying varying degrees of pressure—much as you'd create effects using traditional art tools. Effects include brushes, pencil, pastel, crayon, charcoal, oil paint, water color, and many more. You can also select the surface, such as canvas, different types of paper, even rock. And all of these surfaces can be given different textures, which interact with the paint effects to yield results that can be quite stunning—and very uncomputer-like. (See Chapter 5, "Imaging Tools.")

One of the enabling technologies of this computer art renaissance is the graphics tablet, once used mainly for CAD/CAM applications. Tablets are typically 12" square units that lie on a flat surface and resemble an oversized Etch-A-Sketch. You use a stylus to draw patterns and shapes on the tablet's flat surface, and you can also tap the stylus on the drawing surface to make

Figure 4.3
Gyropoint

selections, just as you would click a mouse's buttons, stylus is typically cordless and generally includes a button that can be programmed to behave like a second mouse button.

Pressure Sensitivity

Clearly, much of the appeal of tablets lies in their resemblance to the real world: drawing with a stylus is a more natural process than trying to create a complex or freeform image with a mouse. But the real secret of their success when used with one of the new painting programs is their sensitivity to pressure. When you press lightly on the tablet, you'll get a thin line; press harder, and the line comes out fat and bold. You can get styluses with different pressure sensitivities, depending on your preference (and grip).

Some tablets have an electrostatic field that clamps paper to the drawing surface for slip-free tracing. This is a quick alternative to scanning and can be used to digitize and embellish images in a single operation.

Programs that take advantage of pressure sensitivity include, in addition to those already mentioned, Photoshop, ColorStudio, Digital Darkroom, Easy Color Paint, SuperPaint, Studio/32, and UltraPaint. Leading tablets include the Wacom SD-421-E and the CalComp DrawingBoard II. The Wacom (Figure 4.4) is known for its sturdy construction and the excellent feel and response of its instruments, while the Calcomp tablet uses the Mac's serial port, which provides several times the throughput of an ADB connection.

Scanners

It may be easier to trace and digitize a simple graphic with a tablet and stylus, but for capturing the nuances of complex color images, there is nothing like a scanner. Factor in the plummeting prices of 600 dpi 24-bit color scanners, and you have an indispensable tool of the multimedia revolution.

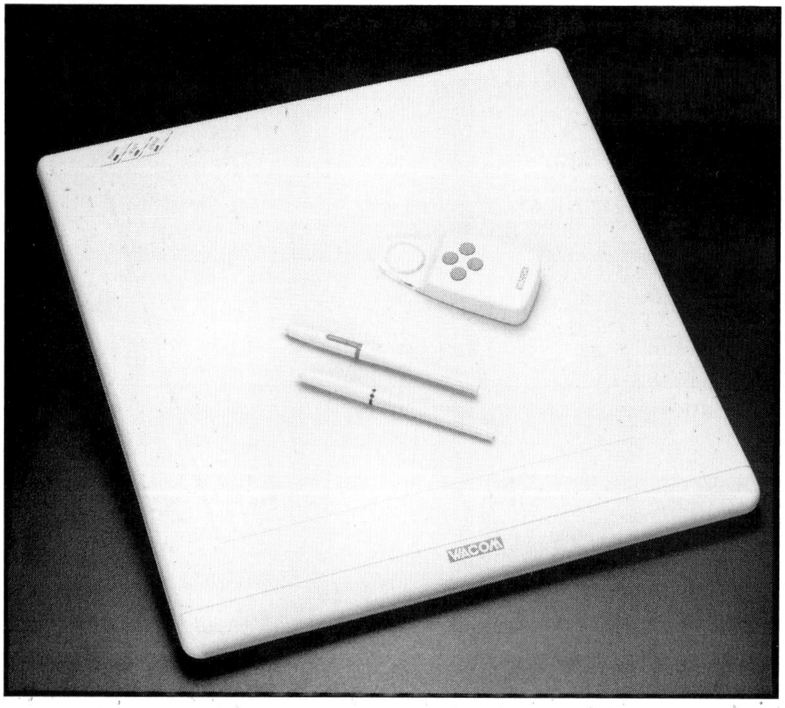

Figure 4.4 Wacom graphics tablet

When first introduced, scanners were mainly used in conjunction with optical character recognition (OCR) software to scan and recognize text. This had wide application in converting hard copy documents into digital form that could then be manipulated by computer.

The general excitement surrounding multimedia and the advent of digital processing powerhouses like Photoshop, ColorStudio, and Digital Darkroom has helped to drive the popularity of scanners and has pushed their application into areas far beyond simple text handling.

While there are a number of different types of scanners, the color flatbed scanner has the best combination of versatility, quality of results, and cost. There are also good gray-scale scanners available, but the falling prices of 24-bit color models make gray-scale scanners less attractive, as most color scanners will also handle gray-scale images quite nicely, and are priced only slightly higher.

In the following pages, we offer a rundown of the major scanning considerations: quality, speed, and control. We also include some tips for achieving good scans, and some advice for buying a scanner.

Image Quality

Image quality is certainly the ultimate concern in the scanning process. You can always busy yourself during slow scans, and fiddle with, correct, and otherwise process an image once scanned, but you simply cannot make up for poor image quality.

Resolution and Resolvability

Resolution is commonly measured in two different ways: *optical* and *interpolated.* The difference is important, although vendors don't always make the distinction.

Optical resolution is a measure of the scanner's ability to resolve images at the claimed resolution using only the optics of the scanner itself.

Although a scanner with a resolution of 300 dpi is theoretically able to resolve lines one three-hundredth of an inch wide and one three-hundredth of an inch apart, this ain't necessarily so. If a line happens to fall between two CCD-array elements, it will be incorrectly detected or not detected at all. (CCDs are the elements that measure and convert light intensity to digital format.)

Interpolation boosts the optical resolution through software that "interpolates," or adds, extra dots to smooth out jagged diagonal lines and curves. Different algorithms are used for interpolation: pixel averaging adds pixels with a value equal to the average of surrounding pixels, and pixel doubling simply duplicates nearby pixels. Some scanners use one or the other method, while others such as the HP ScanJet II use a combination of the two.

Since interpolation adds no new detail, it does not represent an increase in actual resolution, but it can improve an image. A scanner with an optical resolution of 300 dpi boosted to 600 dpi using interpolation should produce better scans than a 300 dpi scanner that does not use interpolation. On the other hand, a scanner with an optical resolution of 600 dpi should be better still.

Interpolation is not generally used to more than double optical resolution because as interpolated dots outnumber "real" ones, unwanted effects such as artifacts (stray pixels) can begin to appear. Also, while interpolation can be successfully used to smooth lines, it can undesirably thicken very thin lines. This effect has to do with a phenomenon known as *resolvability.* Resolution boosted beyond a machine's inherent optical resolution does not improve the scanner's ability to resolve detail, but can only fool the eye with the optical trickery of interpolation.

Noise Level

All scanners introduce a little something of themselves into each scan—in the form of electronic noise that manifests itself as image irregularities, color shifts, and blurriness. Some of the effects can be cleaned up in an image processing program, but they can be difficult to fix, since filtering tools treat the entire image, not just certain portions that may be affected by stray pixel noise. Filters themselves can even be hampered by noise; sharpening, for example, makes stray pixels even more distinct.

Color Fidelity

Poor color fidelity happens when the scanner incorrectly identifies colors and decides to substitute its own instead of the correct values. Unfortunately, this happens quite frequently, due to the inexpensive optics of desktop scanners, and the inherent inaccuracies of their lenses.

You can't eliminate unwanted color variations completely, but you can deal with them to some extent. While you can color-correct using image processing software, it's a lot easier to get it right the first time. The first remedy is to buy a good quality scanner that handles color sensing well; the trade press is an excellent source of information and benchmarks for scanners as well as other computer equipment.

You can also avoid color infidelity by using pre-scanning software to preview and correct images prior to scanning, and by using image editing software after the scan. Finally, there are programs that will help you calibrate your scanner, which will reduce color problems and other variations. This is particularly important as your scanner ages, since its optical and digital components will vary over time.

Calibration software is also useful if you use a number of different scanners in your work; the software will help you maintain consistent imagery across different scanners. Candela's Scan-Cal and Savitar's ScanMatch are examples of popular scanner calibration programs.

Registration and Shadow Detail

These are measures of a scanner's tendency to imperfectly merge the colors that make up a given image. The effect is particularly noticeable in black areas, which can exhibit little fringes or halos of color. In general, today's scanners are pretty good at accurate registration of images.

There is some evidence that one-pass scanners (see below) are less prone to registration errors than three-pass scanners, which must scan an image three times to collect all the colors in an image.

Shadow detail is a measure of a scanner's ability to distinguish between subtle gray values in dark areas of an image.

Scanning Speed

Speed is always a central consideration in working with computer equipment of all types; nobody likes sitting there watching those little watch hands go around and around. It can take from 2 to 15 minutes to scan and process an 8×10 color image.

You can dramatically reduce scan times (and image size) by scanning at lower resolutions or bit depths, when you don't need high resolutions or the range of colors provided by 24-bit scanning. Naturally, this results in a lower quality image, but the difference may not be critical in multimedia presentations, where images are usually viewed on a monitor.

One-Pass versus Three-Pass

Scanners digitize images by shining a light on the object being scanned, and then diverting the reflected light to a *charge-coupled device* (CCD), which in turn measures the intensity of the light and converts it to binary code. Most color scanners must scan the image three times: once for each primary color (red, green, and blue) reflected by the image. Some models scan color images in just one pass, by using three different colored lights that flash in sequence, or with three different CCDs, or with both.

You may encounter marketing hype claiming that one-pass is a superior technique because it reduces scanning time, but experience proves this is not always true. Some one-pass scanners are faster, while others using three-pass technology produce scans more quickly. It does seem that one-pass scanners are prone to fuzzier images caused by lighting errors in their flashing light technique.

These are probably minor points, however, created by sales and marketing departments to sell machines. There are other, more real, concerns when selecting a scanner (see "Buying a Scanner").

Scanning Software

All scanners include some sort of software that allows you to control aspects of the scan either before or after the image is scanned in. This software is sometimes proprietary, but increasingly, scanner vendors are bundling top image-editing software such as Adobe Photoshop, which has more sophisticated processing controls and filters. Sometimes these are "light editions" that don't include all the features of the full program.

The filters and adjustments that can improve scan quality are best made both before and after the scan is made to give you the best shot at the best image. You do what you can with pre-scanning adjustments, and then use powerful image editing software to make further adjustments.

Pre-Scanning Controls

Most scanners include simple controls for adjusting brightness and contrast. These can improve a scan, but should be used with care. When you brighten an image to bring out dark areas, you wash out light parts, thus enhancing one part of the image while eliminating essential information in other areas.

Better scanners offer *gamma control,* a correction technique that can improve a scan without compromising the overall image. For example, you can use gamma control to bring out detail in shadows without a corresponding lightening effect on brighter areas.

Image scaling allows you to reduce or enlarge size of the image being scanned.

A scanner's *threshold* is the point at which it reads a dot as either black or white. This is critical, because if set incorrectly, the threshold can cause some areas to drop out or plug up. Some scanners supply a preview mode so you can set the threshold and check the results without going through the time-consuming process of first scanning, then checking. For example, careful tweaking of threshold controls can be used to minimize the unwanted thickening of thin lines caused by interpolation.

Apple bundles Light Source's Ofoto scanning software with its Color OneScanner. Ofoto (which is written by Robert Cook, who also worked on Pixar's RenderMan)

TWAIN

A consortium of hardware and software suppliers has announced a new image acquisition standard called Twain. "Oh no," we hear you groan, "not another industry alliance!" Well, this one may actually produce something. Twain was developed by Aldus, Eastman Kodak, HP, Caere, and Logitech, and many other vendors have chimed in with their support as well.

The idea is that software vendors will have to write only one device driver that will work with all scanners that support the standard. Since Twain will take care of the details of how images are brought in to applications, programmers can concentrate on their own applications, rather than spending their time writing drivers.

For the end user, this should mean that many more applications will support the direct acquisition of scanned images right into the application itself, much the way Photoshop plug-ins work now. You should see an "Acquire Image" item popping up on menus of your favorite applications any time now. This will save you from having to exit your app, launch the scanner software, save the image to a file, reenter your application, and import the file.

is outstanding software that for the first time provides automatic pre-scanning adjustments to make great scans possible without a lot of tweaking. Light Source also sells Ofoto separately.

Note that you can make any of these pre-scan adjustments in an image processing program, but doing so before scanning can be faster and easier.

Post-Scanning Controls

Most scanners come with some sort of scanning software that allows you both to set certain parameters of the scan and to edit the images once scanned.

Scanners often come bundled with "plug-ins" to popular image processing programs such as Photoshop, Digital Darkroom, and ColorStudio (see Figure 4.5). This lets you scan from within the program—a nice convenience, since that's where the images usually end up for correction anyway. Sometimes, scanners are even bundled with full-fledged versions of these programs, or with "light editions" that do not have all the features of the shrink-wrapped products.

There are many filters you can use and adjustments you can make to an image. Two of the most common are *diffusion dither* and *sharpening.*

Dithering patterns reconfigure the dot patterns of a scan to improve image clarity. Diffusion is one of the most common and useful of these filters. Sharpening reduces blurriness, particularly in details. Generally, sharpening is done after the scan in an image processing program, but a few scanners include a sharpening filter in their software packages.

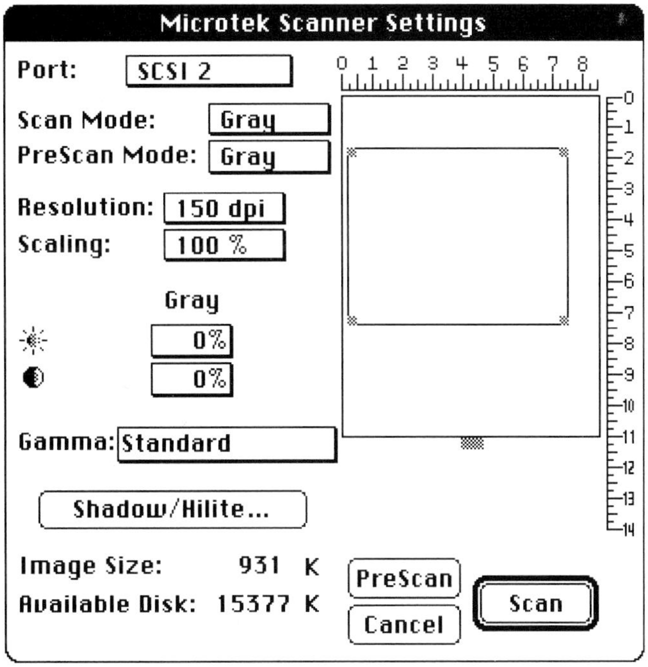

Figure 4.5 Scanner plug-in dialog box

Getting a Good Scan

Scanning is an acquired skill, and getting acceptable results can require much repetition and trial and error. While there is no substitute for experience, here are some tips that can help you get started:

- *Remember—Garbage in, garbage out (GIGO).* Start with the best possible images. You can correct a lot with image processing software, but you'll get the best results by starting with a clean image.
- Before scanning an image, concentrate on the darkest and lightest areas; if you get these right, chances are the rest of the image will follow suit.
- *Be prepared to tweak.* Although push-button scanning is now upon us, you may have to process scans to get the best results.
- Many factors contribute to *scan quality*. Flatbed scanners typically have a "sweet spot" in the middle, where scans will be sharpest. If your scans start out sharp in the middle and get gradually fuzzy, your images are probably too big for the bed.

If your image is fuzzy throughout, your scanner may not be calibrated correctly. Scan an image of thick black lines and see if they register correctly. If there are colored halos around the lines, your scanner needs to be calibrated to tighten up registration.

If white areas of scans are too dull or bright, or have color casts, the intensity of one of the light sources is out of whack; you can correct this condition with white balance calibration.

Handling Large Images

24-bit color scans produce some of the largest files ever encountered by the desktop computer. It is not uncommon for some images to reach 20, 30, or even 50Mb and more. Even an 8×10" color image scanned at 300 dpi will be well over 15Mb. This means you won't even be able to open such images without much more memory than the average Mac is born with.

As we mentioned earlier, 24-bit images aren't really worth the trouble for multimedia projects that will be shown on a standard 72-dpi monitor. However, if you plan to, or are already handling these large color files, you may find the following tips helpful:

- *Buy lots of memory!* The more memory you have, the easier it will be to manipulate large images. Remember that you'll need to have free RAM equal to twice the size of the typical images you work with, so that you can undo image edits if necessary.
- *Get a video accelerator.* Even if you do have a lot of RAM, screen redrawing on complex color images can be glacial. If you work with these images a lot, consider investing in a video accelerator, which will greatly speed up drawing operations. See the section "CPU, Video, and SCSI Accelerators."
- *Use software compression.* Software compression is not a new concept. Often large programs are compressed to reduce the number of disks in retail software packages. But existing compression algorithms were developed for text, and will generally provide only about 50% (2:1) reduction of the bitmaps that make up scans.

There are many utilities that use the *JPEG* compression standard, an algorithm developed specifically for image file reduction. These programs include QuickTime, PicturePress, Colorsqueeze, and ImpressIt.

Text compression algorithms use *lossless* compression, which does not remove any information as it squeezes files. Clearly, you don't want the computer deciding what words or sentences you don't really need. JPEG, on the other hand, uses *lossy* compression, which does cut out some, theoretically expendable, information. You can adjust how much data is removed; the more you eliminate, the smaller the file. Savings can be tremendous, even when the information removed does not result in any detectable image degradation. Using one of the JPEG utilities, you can reduce a 15Mb file to 1Mb or less.

- *Scan at high resolutions only when necessary.* Consider your delivery medium. Again, if your scans are part of a multimedia presentation that will be played back on 8-bit color monitors, there is no point in overscanning at 24-bit. Avoiding overscanning will considerably decrease the size of image files.

Buying a Scanner

We've covered most of the really critical issues of scanner performance, such as resolution and image quality, but how do you apply this information when buying a scanner? Probably the best way is to take an image to your local computer store and try scanning it in using a few different models. This will give you some feeling for the process, and also for what is possible with the current technology.

Another excellent source of information is the trade press. Magazines such as *MacWeek*, *MacUser*, and *MacWorld* publish excellent equipment reviews, and the monthlies usually do a yearly scanner roundup.

Here are a few tips to keep in mind when shopping for a scanner:

- Look for a scanner with a color preview feature, which can save time by letting you look at a representation of the scanned image before you actually make the scan. This allows you to make image tweaks and corrections and see the results before you scan.
- Some scanners will save images to disk, a real convenience when working with limited memory.
- Make sure that images are saved in common file formats that can be read by most applications.
- If you are scanning fine detail such as line art, invest in a scanner with a high optical resolution, such as 600 dpi. Remember, however, that high-resolution scanners will also readily detect unwanted detritus, such as dirt on the scanning surface and flaws in the object being scanned.
- Bundled software isn't always "free": it can add to the cost of a scanner. You may be able to save money by buying an image processing program separately.
- Scanners that connect to the SCSI port rather than the modem or serial ports will be faster.
- If scanner color and tonal accuracy are of the utmost importance in your work, and you have the time, you can scan the same image using a number of different scanners, and save the images to disk. Then open them in an image processing program such as Photoshop. Choose "Histogram" from the Image manu, and you'll get a graph of the distribution of pixel values for each color channel. By comparing histograms of the same image produced by different scanners, you can tell if a given scanner is capturing too much or too little of a color or tonal range.
- Avoid hand held scanners; they're hard to hold still and generally produce poor results in comparison with their deskbound cousins.

CD-ROM Drives

The CD-ROM is one of the driving forces of multimedia. The players are inexpensive; and the disks themselves are inexpensive to reproduce, and hold a whopping 650Mb apiece. Even so, the silvery disks have been a little slow to catch on. This may be because until recently, few hardware vendors have built them into their computers, and because standard CDs cannot be written to by the end user. However, driven by several recent market and technology developments, the CD medium is catching fire—buyers were expected to purchase over 5 million drives in 1993.

- Kodak's Photo CD has introduced the writable or *multisession* CD (see "CD 'Standards'" later in this chapter).
- New CD technology is leading to the release of faster drives with even greater storage limits (see "CD 'Standards'" below).
- In late 1992, Apple introduced the IIvx, IIvi, and Performa 600 CD (see "Macintosh Hardware" in Chapter 3) all of which come with a CD drive installed or as an available option. Apple has stated publicly that it intends to drive CD-ROM into the mainstream.
- Major software vendors such as Microsoft, Apple, Novell, and Macromedia are delivering their products and documentation on CDs instead of floppies.

Ironically, just as CDs are gaining momentum, manufacturers are confusing the market by introducing a number of competing formats that are fully or partly incompatible with one another. This has slowed the release of titles on a given

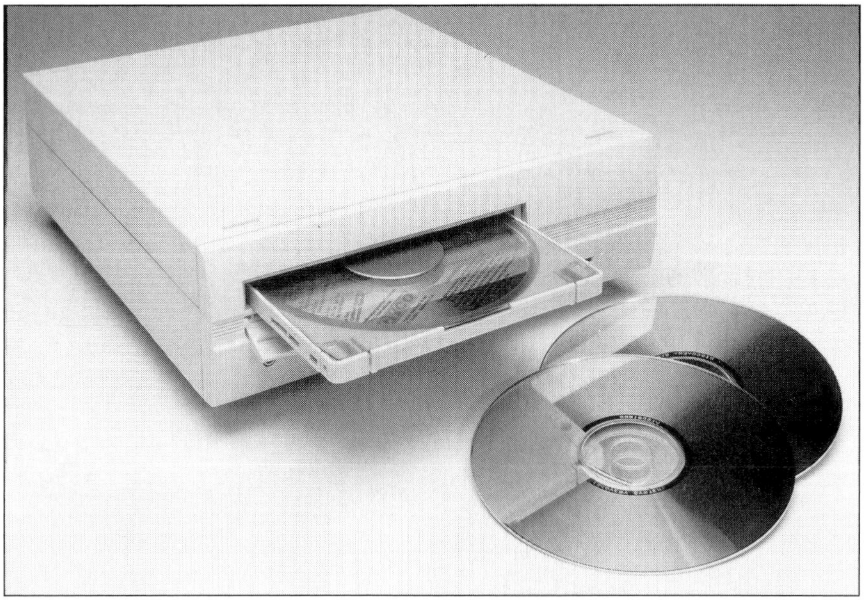

Figure 4.6
CD-ROM drive

format, as software developers wait to see which format will win, and buyers wait for titles. Unless otherwise noted, references to CDs in this section are given in the prevalent CD-ISO format (see "File Formats" later in this chapter).

CD-ROM drives hook up to your Mac's SCSI port and can be daisy-chained like any other SCSI device. As with all SCSI devices, don't connect or disconnect the drive while either it or your computer is on.

The Need for Speed

Standard CD drives perform adequately for electronic books that don't have too many graphics. CDs have proven an excellent storage and retrieval mechanism for text, enormous amounts of which can be searched quickly.

However, standard CD drives are obnoxiously slow for interactive presentations that depend on immediate response. When CDs began being used for multimedia presentations, the tremendous increase in the size and complexity of these images was offset by only a small increase in drive performance. The fastest drives can get at data in about 150ms, a far cry from a fast hard disk, which has an access time of about 10ms.

Even so, the most important consideration when buying a CD-ROM drive is speed, particularly when it's being used in an multimedia application. Speed is measured in two ways: *access time* and *transfer rate.* These parameters were originally defined in the '70s for audio CDs by Sony and Philips, in their Red Book standard. The standard was extended to CD-ROMs with the Yellow Book addendum in the '80s.

Access time, or seek time, as it's also known, measures how long it takes a drive to find a particular chunk of data. This is most important in CD-ROM–based text databases, in which the drive must hop around and find lots of bits of information. Access times of under 300 milliseconds (ms) are considered decent; under 200ms is excellent. It's generally agreed that QuickTime movie playback from CD requires an access time of 400ms or less.

Transfer rate is a measure of how fast a drive can read and transfer information to the CPU and display. For multimedia, in which rapid and smooth display of images is paramount, this measurement is more important than access time. A transfer rate of 150K per second is acceptable, but if you can find a drive with 300K transfer rates, that's even better.

Look for a drive with a data buffer—most have them these days—and the bigger the better. Buffers smooth the drive's delivery of data to the computer, eliminating gaps and pauses. For multimedia playback, we recommend a buffer of at least 64K (256K is better).

CD-ROMs and Audio CDs

Everyone wonders why they can't save a few hundred bucks and just hook up their $99 audio CD player to their computer and read CD-ROM discs. Well, you just can't, so stop wondering.

Seriously, even though the blank discs themselves are identical, the data types of audio and computer CDs are incompatible. CD-ROM players have special electronics that check and recheck data several times as it's being read. When you listen to an audio CD, you won't miss a skipped bit or two, but of course with computer data, every bit is critical.

Audio CD players do not have the beefed-up drive and head mechanisms that allow CD-ROM drives to survive repeated data access. And, naturally, most audio CD players lack SCSI interfaces.

On the other hand, many CD-ROM drives do incorporate the Red Book standard, meaning they will play audio CDs, so if you don't have either type of CD player yet, buy an audio-compatible CD-ROM drive. That way, the next time your computer won't boot, you can shove it out the window and still be able to play some nice Brahms to soothe your nerves. Apple itself offers the Power CD, a multiformat drive that will play CD-ROMs, audio CDs, and Photo CDs. It is, however, (being from Apple), a little on the pricey side, and finds data at the very slow rate of 550ms.

File Formats

The International Standards Organization (ISO) has established a standard CD-ROM file system format. ISO 9660 ensures that different computer systems will be able to recognize the files on any CD conforming to the standard. This standard, also known as CD-ISO, has been widely adopted, despite the flood of competing formats (see "CD 'Standards'" below).

TOOLS
Macintosh CD Setup 120

The Mac's native file system format, the Hierarchical File System (HFS) differs from the ISO standard. However, with both the ISO 9660 driver and Apple's Foreign File Access extension in your System folder, you should have no trouble reading most CDs intended for the Mac. These drivers are normally bundled with CD-ROM drives.

Note that there is a big difference between file *recognition* and file *compatibility*. Even though most CDs are now recorded using the ISO 9660 spec, if you are using a Mac, you'll be able to read and use only those files on the CD that are *Mac* files. For any other CDs, such as one intended for use under DOS, the ISO spec means only that you can mount the disc and transfer its files to your Mac. The files are still DOS files and you would still have to convert them using file translation software. And of course, any application software on the CD would be for DOS and not compatible with the Mac.

CD "Standards"

Until recently, there was basically one type of CD-ROM; but in their never-ending quest for cash, technology vendors have unleashed a flood of CD-ROM formats, despite the adverse effect on the market. While CD-ISO is still the safest bet if you haven't yet picked up a drive, you should at least be aware of the growing number of options.

Computing-Based Formats

CD-ROM/XA

CD-ROM extended architecture (XA) improves on the basic CD-ROM standard in two ways. First, it compresses data so that more will fit on a CD. Second, it *interleaves* audio, text, and graphics data for smoother and more efficient retrieval of integrated information.

A drawback is that XA requires an add-in card that contains the hardware necessary to encode and decode the interleaved data. This makes XA drives more expensive than their less capable cousins. XA drives will, however, read normal CD-ROM discs.

Kodak uses XA-compatible discs to store its Photo CD images. A confusing point is that you don't have to have a full XA drive to play Photo CDs, but only a drive that will recognize and mount Photo CDs. This is why you'll see drives that are advertised as "XA-ready." They don't have the additional hardware necessary to read XA discs, but they will read Photo CDs. If you get one of these drives, you can add the card later if you want to read XA discs other than Photo CDs.

Sony's MMCD

Sony, coinventor (with Phillips) of the CD format, has released its Multimedia CD player. The player includes a small LCD screen and keyboard, and will play both audio and XA disks. The portable device will also drive stereo speakers and an external color monitor. It will not, however, act as a standard CD peripheral for a computer, which limits its usefulness.

Multisession CD-ROM

CD-ROMs used to be read-only devices (indeed, it's in their name, ROM, for "read-only memory"). Even manufacturers, when creating a master CD, could only write to it once.

Now, all of that is changing. When Kodak was developing Photo CD, they realized that consumers would go to their photo-finishers and put a couple of rolls worth of exposures on a Photo CD, and still have a whole bunch of room left. So Kodak and a few drive manufacturers wrote the *Orange Book*, or multisession CD spec.

A multisession drive will read Photo CDs that have been written to more than once—a capability you'll need if you plan to put a lot of pictures on Photo CD. Multisession drives are also required for some interactive disc products. If you don't already have a drive, get one with at least single-session Photo CD compatibility; that way, you'll be able to tap into the large store of stock photos being released on Photo CDs.

Double Speed CD-ROM Drives

New drives from such manufacturers as Pioneer, Apple, NEC, Sony, and Toshiba double both the access speed and transfer rates of standard drives. Apple's 300i double-speed drive is available as an option in some machines, including the newer models in the Mac II line, as well as in the Quadra, Centris and Performa lines; the unit is also available for purchase separately.

Even though the double speed drives do find and move data faster than standard drives, you may not notice the difference, depending on the type of data you're working with. For example, QuickTime clips may run somewhat faster and more smoothly when played from a double speed drive, but in general, you won't notice much difference.

The reason is that most QuickTime movies are optimized for the current 150Kps standard transfer rate; until movies are tailored for the new 300Kps transfer rate of double speed drives, the faster drives will make little difference. Furthermore, most CD-ROM publishers produce QuickTime movies for general consumption—the lowest common denominator—so don't expect a lot of movies optimized for the higher transfer rates right away.

On the other hand, if you work with large graphics files (or any large files) stored on CD, such as PhotoCD images, a double speed drive can make quite a difference. That's because such files simply hold a lot of data—the faster you can blow it over the wire to your computer, the better.

Double speed drives also improve access time, which is definitely noticeable when you're looking for a specific bit of information. Those who regularly use CD-ROM-based encyclopedias, news compilations, and databases will enjoy marked improvements. Depending on the model, you can expect anything from incremental improvements to actual doubling of access time over standard drives.

If this is all good news to you, it gets better: CD-ROM drive transfer rates are expected to double every year or so for at least a few years: by 1994, 600Kps drives should be prevalent.

Consumer-Based Formats

3DO: Coming On Strong

Perhaps the most promising consumer multimedia system is one being put together by 3DO, a new consortium backed by entertainment conglomerates Time Warner Inc. and Matsushita Co. of Japan, and led by Electronic Arts founder Trip Hawkins.

3DO is not just building its own home multimedia technology (based on what it calls its "custom animation engine" chip), but, like Phillips, is intent on licensing it to other manufacturers in the hope that it will become the standard for home multimedia.

The 3DO system will feature an "Interactive Multiplayer," about the size and shape of a small VCR, that plugs into a TV set and plays Photo CD- and audio-compatible CD-ROMs. Matsushita says that it will market its version of 3DO as a Panasonic product, available by Christmas, 1993 for about $700.

The conglomerate will make sure that the system has plenty of home entertainment software available when it is released. MCA/Universal Studios and Warner Brothers, subsidiaries of Matsushita and Time Warner, respectively, will produce interactive movies in the 3DO format, while Electronic Arts will develop its own line of games and simulations for the technology. Third parties are getting into the act as well, including most of the leading entertainment-based multimedia development firms.

3DO predicts that future models will feature a connector to local cable television systems for use with interactive television services now being developed by cable companies.

Compact Disc-Interactive (CD-I)

CD-I represents nothing less than an attempt by one of the world's largest consumer electronics corporations to establish a worldwide consumer multimedia delivery standard. The company, Phillips, has spent the better part of a decade developing the new device, which it finally released in 1992.

Phillips has published the specifications for CD-I, enabling any company to introduce its own CD-I devices, which Phillips hopes will encourage the standardization of CD-I. The device itself is a CD player that will play CD-I discs, standard audio compact discs, CD-based game discs, computer-based CD-ROM/XA discs, and Photo CD discs. You hook up the player to your television set, which serves as the display.

If CD-I turns out to be a success, plans are to release modules that will allow playback of full-motion video. This could have many applications, ranging from hyper-realistic games to video-enhanced tutorials. CD-I's big claim to fame is that it brings interactivity to the static, brain-numbing world of television. CD-I titles, mostly video games and interactive learning programs, let you explore their contents at will.

"CD-I Ready discs" is Phillips' marketing term for discs that are principally meant to be played on an audio CD player, but which have some extra bits and pieces that are available when the discs are played on a CD-I unit.

Many are skeptical about CD-I's chances for survival. For one thing, its internal components are proprietary, and it's based on technology that's a bit older, and a step or two behind, 3DO (see below). CD-I players are also expensive, at least for now, and most of the titles available so far are less than overwhelming.

Still, CD-I is important because it brings the world of interactive multimedia to a wide audience. Ultimately, its viability will depend on the quality of titles and on Phillips' success in convincing consumers they need yet another appliance connected to their TV sets.

Tandy's Video Information System (VIS)

This is another interesting play for the couch potato crowd. As with CD-I and CDTV, users buy the VIS box and plug it into their TV sets, and then control the action with a wireless remote. VIS is actually controlled by Modular Windows, a derivative of Windows 3.1. Microsoft and Tandy claim that developers can easily port their MPC applications to VIS. This portability makes VIS an attractive platform for developers, and by the end of 1992, just one month after the release of VIS, there were over 100 titles on the market. VIS will play audio CDs but not standard CD-ISO discs.

Commodore Dynamic Total Vision (CDTV)

Commodore, maker of the Amiga personal computer, has its own consumer CD player called CDTV. In fact, the CDTV player is basically an Amiga 500 with a CD-ROM drive. Like Phillips, Commodore wants to reach consumers who are interested in entertainment rather than in experimenting with computer-based multimedia. Also like CD-I, the CDTV console looks like any other generic black box, and is controlled with a joystick-equipped remote.

Add a keyboard and a hard disk and you've got a full-fledged Amiga. CDTV also has MIDI ports for control of digital musical instruments. Unlike CD-I, which plays audio CDs with full 16-bit digital fidelity, CDTV reads its 8-bit audio from disc into RAM, which reduces memory and speed available for video playback.

Cutting Your Own CDs

A side effect of the Orange Book spec is that it caused prices for CD recorders to fall overnight, from $30,000 to as low as $4000. Inexpensive recorders are now being made by Sony and Phillips. Companies such as Meridian Data Systems, Kodak, and Dataware sell these drives under their own labels, sometimes bundling them with large hard disks from which to transfer data to the CD (see Figure 4.7).

Some of the drives contain big data buffers of several megabytes or more, which helps when writing data from a slow hard disk or other storage device. The hard disk you use must be relatively fast, sustaining data transfer rates of at least 150K

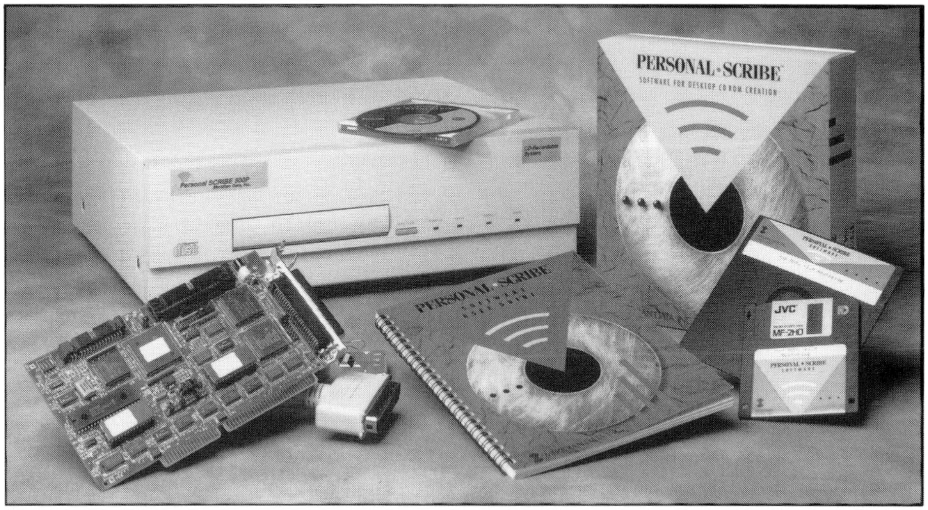

Figure 4.7 Meridian Data Systems' Personal Scribe CD-ROM recorder

per second to drive the recorder. The drives write data at 15–20Mb per minute, which means you can cut an entire 600Mb CD in about a half an hour or so.

If you're in the market for a recorder, look for one with "on-the-fly 150 recording." This feature allows you to transfer data directly to the recorder without first having to create a space-grabbing "disk image" in you hard disk.

The blank CDs themselves run between $30 and $80, though these prices should fall to the $10 range once the new technology catches on. The discs are coated with a photosensitive dye that is burned away in intricate patterns by the CD recorder's laser. These patterns carry the CDs data itself, and simulate the patterns of tiny pits used in commercial CDs.

When the disc is read, light from the reader's laser is reflected from the disc's surface. When the laser hits a pit, less light is reflected. These reflections are converted to the digital data that is readable by the computer.

Although you cannot change the data once it is written to the CD, thanks to the multisession technology, you can append data as many times as you want, up to the total capacity of the disc. When you are finished recording a CD and don't plan on appending any more data in future sessions, you "fixate" the disc. Though you can no longer append data at this point, fixated discs can be read by standard CD-ROM drives, while discs that have not yet been fixated can only be read by multisession drives. Regardless of the disc's state of completion, all are recorded in standard ISO 9660 format.

The new CD recorders make it easy to cut your own CDs, letting you do fast and inexpensive prototyping, but they simplify only the physical process of CD publishing. There are still many considerations in creating a successful CD-ROM product, including data conversion and filtering, database definitions, indexing, and other aspects of software design and development.

Besides the obvious implications for CD-ROM publishing, CD-ROM recorders pave the way for a new inexpensive storage medium, and are even beginning to rival both the storage capacity and speed of magneto-optical disc (see "Storage Systems," later in the chapter).

Videodiscs

Videodiscs, sometimes called laserdiscs, are an excellent source and playback medium for video. The resolution is much higher than videotape, (at least 400 lines, compared with 240 for VHS) and information access is generally faster too. In addition, laserdiscs offer a rock-solid source of still video frames, far better than tape, which often yields jittery and out-of-focus still frames.

Laserdiscs are frequently used as the playback medium in training and public kiosk applications, where interactivity and high quality are important. While laserdiscs are beginning to be eclipsed by digital video, until CDs get to the point of handling full-motion video, laserdiscs are the best bet if your application demands high quality video playback.

A number of vendors offer computer-controllable videodiscs, which, by the way, also play back regular videodiscs; once you see *Star Wars* on disc, you'll pitch your VCR. Many of these players also feature digital sound. Top manufacturers of videodisc drives include Sony, Panasonic, and Pioneer.

Players can have one or more of the following "control levels":

- Level I: You can control operation from the player or by remote control. This is the standard VCR-type control.
- Level II: Interactive branching software is imbedded in the disc and read by the player.
- Level III: The player can be computer-controlled.

If you're going to use laserdiscs in an interactive application, you'll want a player that offers Level III support. Level II support is important for industrial kiosk applications in which discs can be played back without a computer controlling them. When shopping for a drive, look for one with two channels of digital audio, for playing back high fidelity sound.

Like CDs, videodiscs are read-only media, but they are fairly inexpensive and quick to master. There are a number of service bureaus that will duplicate an interactive presentation onto videodisc in just a few days for under $500.

Working with Images

Once you've acquired images and sounds, the real work of multimedia begins. Using a media integration program like Director, you can combine your captured images and create dynamic presentations that have an impact far greater than simple text.

The equipment that supports this creation process—the display, acceleration, and storage facilities such as hard disks and RAM—affect the ease with which you can work with large and unwieldy image files.

Display Systems

TOOLS

DepthKey 140
ColorSwitch 153

Monitors are among the most important of computer components. After all, you spend a lot of time staring into them. Luckily, both advanced features and the range of choices have increased lately, while prices have dropped. Applications such as desktop publishing, color prepress, photo retouching, and animation have spurred a demand for bigger displays and 24-bit color.

This growing user demand and the competition among vendors for their business have turned monitors into hot commodities. This is great news for multimedia creators, who can make good use of more screen real estate and the realism of color.

The most important monitor attributes are size, resolution, and color depth—8- or 24-bit. (There are many excellent gray-scale monitors as well; we're assuming that color is more important for multimedia use.) A host of more specific qualities such as sharpness, contrast, convergence are covered in the Display Characteristics sidebar.

Size

Monitors fall into three size categories: small (12, 13, 14"), medium (15, 16"), and large (19, 20, 21"). Unless you already have a monitor, or are working on a shoestring, consider getting at least a 16" display. Today's graphical interfaces let you work between multiple windows, but much of this advantage is lost if there isn't room to see them. Also, with a smaller screen, you'll spend lots of time zooming in on images to see detail, and then getting impatient while the screen redraws. Finally, many people have reported problems with eyestrain and headaches from squinting at the tiny pictures displayed by the smaller screens.

The Mac IIci, IIsi, LC II, LC III, IIvx, and Centris line all have built in video so that you don't have to buy a separate video card when you plug in a 12, 13, or 14" monitor. (The Quadra 950 will handle 16" and 21" monitors as well.) Many of these new systems will also handle 16-bit video with the addition of inexpensive VRAM (see Mac comparison table in Chapter 3).

Until around 1992, the 13" monitor was pretty much the Mac standard, but now Apple has replaced it with a 14" model, and also offers a 16" monitor. This, along with the Quadra's built-in 24-bit color support, has pushed 16" monitors into the forefront. Prices have also dropped to well below $1000, and with 70% more pixels than a 13" monitor, all of this is good news for multimedia.

If you do use a larger monitor, you will have to use a video card; a large monitor has more pixels than a smaller one, so large screen redrawing is slower unless a video card with higher video transfer rates is added. Also, add-in video cards have more VRAM to support the extra information in 16- or 24-bit color for each of these extra pixels.

If you are going to use a smaller monitor for a Macintosh, shop around a bit—you'll save some money. Many people use the Apple 13" monitor, which is built around the well-regarded Sony Trinitron display. Instead, you can save a few hundred dollars and get a 14" multisync display made for the PC. Multisync monitors are so named because the PCs don't have a standard video frequency, so monitors must sense the video frequency coming from a given PC, and lock on or sync with it to display its signal. Because of high volume trade and intense competition in the PC markets, monitors are generally lower priced than in the Mac world. This is less true of larger monitors, which are more often found in the Mac market, where the graphics applications that demand them are more prevalent.

Resolution

Resolution is a bit of a puzzle, although it doesn't have to be. Basically, it refers to the number of pixels (*picture elements*—the little dots that make a display image) in a given display, and is usually expressed as dots per inch, or dpi. The lowest rung is 640×480 pixels, known as the VGA standard in the PC world (well, they have a few standards). This is the resolution found in small 13" and 14" displays.

Typical resolutions in larger monitors are 832×624 and 1024×768. These higher resolutions result in sharper pictures because a given image is drawn with more pixels than the same image on a lower resolution monitor.

Display Characteristics

The best way to choose among monitors is to go down to the monitor store and try them out for yourself. Bring a file of the type you'll be working with—video capture, scanned in photograph, 24-bit color graphic, or whatever. Once you have narrowed the field by choosing the size, resolution, and color support you want, you can consult the following list to familiarize yourself with some of the finer points.

If you walk in and ask for a monitor with low reflectivity and a high vertical scan rate, the salesperson may give you a blank stare, but at least *you'll* know what you're talking about. The trade press (particularly any of the monthlies beginning with "PC" or "Mac") do periodic exhaustive tests of monitors based on many of the criteria in this list.

Sharpness. A monitor that displays sharp images does not allow areas of detail to bleed together into fuzzy patches. Not surprisingly, sharpness is easier to maintain in higher resolution monitors (over 72 dpi), where pixels are packed closer together.

Brightness. Lots of people like to crank up the brightness on their monitors (we do this on our notebooks when traveling and end up with about 10 minutes of battery life). But brightness is related to sharpness and focus; the higher the brightness, the more intense are the beams blasting electrons at the screen to make a picture, and as the beams grow more intense, they focus less precisely.

Contrast. Contrast is the range between the darkest and lightest values that can be displayed. For nice crisp images you want this range to be as great as possible.

Convergence. This is a measure of how precisely the red, green, and blue electrons align to render different colors onscreen. *Misconvergence* is what happens when the electrons don't align so well—you'll see a little rainbow-colored halo around objects and type. In fact, looking at small type onscreen is a good way to see if a monitor's colors are converging properly. If you work with type a lot, misconvergence is particularly noticeable and will drive you batty very quickly. (A similar effect, *registration,* is described in the earlier section on "scanners.")

Curvature. The electron beams that sweep across the inside of the screen first pass through a device called a *shadow mask*, a grid of little holes that helps to align the beams. But when the beams get to screen edges, the angle causes electrons to leak through a few adjacent holes as well, which makes a fuzzy screen image. A curved monitor keeps the beams aimed at the correct holes even at screen edges. The technology for flat screens has made them more costly than curved screens, even with recent advances that have brought down their price; but many people find they look better and have less distortion.

Distortion. Monitors should show objects the way they were originally intended. Thus a circle should be displayed that way and not as an oval, and a square should be square and not some other sort of rhomboid.

Reflectivity (antiglare). Some manufacturers put an antiglare coating on their screen to keep light reflections from becoming a nuisance. The best way to prevent glare is to use the display in an area free of direct lighting.

box continued

Calibration. If you are creating images with colors that must be as accurate as possible, choose a monitor that includes *gamma correction* software. This is the same technique used in image processing and scanning programs. Gamma correction allows you to adjust a monitor's tracking to precisely match the colors in a scanned-in image or the color values of a printer or another monitor.

Refresh Rate (Vertical Scan). The refresh rate measures how fast the screen is redrawn from top to bottom. Make sure your monitor has a vertical refresh rate of 65 hertz or higher; otherwise, it may flicker.

Dot Pitch. This refers to the proximity of the screen pixels. In 12" to 14" monitors, a dot pitch of .28 or less is good. For larger monitors, look for a dot pitch of less than .31.

The Mac display system is based on 72 dpi. Monitors that have 72 pixels in an inch of screen space will display an image that it is the same size as it will be once printed. Thus, 72 dpi monitors are called WYSIWYG, for what-you-see-is-what-you-get.

People working with photographic images often prefer monitors with higher resolutions of 77, 82, 85, or 88 dpi. This is because the pixel grid—the space between pixels—is reduced in these monitors, making displayed images more tightly composed, smoother, and more like photographs. However, these monitors will display images that are smaller in size than when they are printed, which is an annoyance (see Figure 4.8).

Choosing a Monitor

As in choosing most hardware, selecting a monitor has a lot to do with what you spend most of your time doing. The two biggest questions are probably what size monitor to get and whether to get a 24-bit display card.

Desktop publishers prefer 16" or larger monitors so they can display multiple pages and windows at once. Certainly multimedia developers can also have a lot of windows open, so big screen displays can be very useful. As for 24-bit color; don't get it unless you really need it; if you're not sure, you probably don't need it.

Despite the advantages of large monitors and 24-bit color, a great many multimedia developers stick with the basic Apple 13" monitor and 8 bits of color. A big reason for this is that the vast majority of multimedia consumers have this setup themselves. It's important to test on machines that your target audience is using.

Here are a few things to consider when monitor shopping:

- The ability to display 24-bit images is a function of the display card, not the monitor, so you can always start out with an 8-bit display system and upgrade to a 24-bit card later, keeping the same monitor.

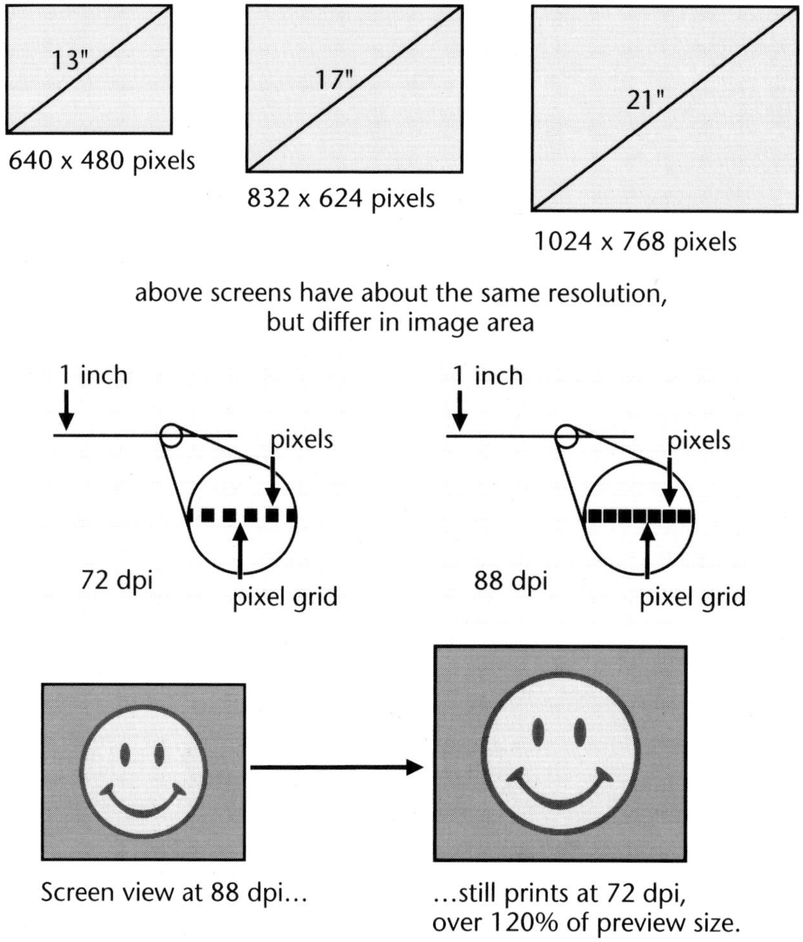

Figure 4.8 Resolution and image size

- Monitors that use BNC connectors at the display end of the cable generally produce sharper images onscreen. If your monitor comes with a cable with a DB15 connector but has the BNC connectors on the back of the monitor, consider upgrading the cable with BNC connectors.
- If screen glare bugs you, look for a monitor with an etched instead of polished glass screen. You can also get antiglare coatings. Be careful of the type of glare coating you opt for, however, as heavy coatings can reduce image clarity.
- Monitors, like a lot of other computer equipment, are heavily discounted, so shop around. You can save a lot by ordering through the mail, but repairs may be a problem if something goes wrong with the display while it's still under warranty.

The Bad ELF

The world has become much safer ever since we've realized what a dangerous place it is. Asbestos, saccharin, PCBs, other people's cigarette smoke, disappearing ozone layer—the list is growing.

Now there is concern over radiation emitted from monitors. (Actually, your mom knew this a long time ago—remember about not sitting too close to the TV?) although monitors give off a stunning variety of emissions, attention has centered on extremely low frequency radiation, or ELF. There is not yet definitive evidence that ELF emissions are in fact harmful, but several tests have raised doubts. A Finnish study published in late 1992 found that pregnant women using VDTs were three times more likely to suffer a miscarriage than those who were not exposed during pregnancy.

ELF emanates from all parts of the monitor, but tests show that the highest radiation is from the back and sides. This is a good thing, since not many people stare at the back of their displays for long periods of time (except when trying to figure out how to turn them on).

If you are concerned about ELF, try and find a monitor that meets the stringent "MPR" standards of the Swedish government. The International Radiation Protection Association (IRPA) has also adopted standards regarding ELF emissions.

Currently, several well-known monitor vendors offer displays they claim meet the Swedish standards. Apple, always more environmentally aware than the average company, has remanufactured some of its monitors, resulting in up to a 98% reduction in radiation. One of two optional 14" monitors Apple offers for the Performa 400 and 600, the Performa Display Plus, meets the Swedish specs, as do a number of other units from other manufacturers.

Apple, IBM, and Compaq have chipped in a total of $2.5 million to found the Center for VDT and Health Research at Johns Hopkins University.

CPU, Video, and SCSI Accelerators

Next time you're staring dumbly at your computer while it spends 18 hours rendering a 24-bit 3-D image, consider adding an accelerator card rather than throwing out your box altogether and buying a new one.

Image processing speed can be greatly enhanced when you add some sort of accelerator card. These come in several varieties:

- **CPU accelerators.** These cards speed up your machines' central processing unit, but also other functions such as I/O (input/output), keyboard, mouse, and hard drives.
- **Video accelerators.** Also know as graphics or QuickDraw accelerators, these cards accelerate the graphics routines that display images onscreen.
- **SCSI accelerators.** These cards speed up the transfer of data from disks and other SCSI devices.

TOOLS Speedometer 147

Since multimedia development and playback stress every element of system hardware, all of these accelerators can help. So, which should you look at first? The consensus seems to be that you'll realize the most immediate benefits from a CPU accelerator.

CPU accelerators are best installed when you're doing heavy-duty image processing, such as image enhancement and rendering. But you'll also realize overall system speed enhancements, whereas video and SCSI accelerators are targeted at specific tasks and applications. Also, on slower Macs in the II series, the CPU is typically the bottleneck, not QuickDraw or the SCSI interface.

Clearly, if you're constantly working with really big image or sound files and you already have a fast or accelerated Mac, you'll want to give serious attention to both SCSI and video acceleration.

CPU Acceleration

CPU accelerators take many forms. Some are chips that replace your old CPU chip. Replacing a chip is a delicate operation that requires dexterity and good static protection. Note that you should never replace or install any of your computer's electronics without being properly grounded. The static electricity that every human carries to some degree (depending on environmental and weather conditions) can fry delicate electronics in milliseconds. Many board manufacturers ship disposable wrist straps for installing their products; these divert any static to a ground source such as the third pin of a power outlet. You can also buy the wrist straps at computer and electronics supply stores. If you must fiddle with you computer's circuitry without a wrist strap, touch the power supply (the big metal box) before touching anything else; this will discharge to ground any static buildup.

Other accelerators are entire cards that plug into different slots, depending on the Mac. Accelerators for a IIci usually plug into that computer's cache slot, while cards for computers such as the LC and IIsi use the PDS slot. Other cards plug into NuBus slots. Sometimes acceleration involves revamping your entire computer—you send it to the manufacturer, who sends it back, sometimes in a new housing.

Radius makes a really innovative product called the Radius Rocket, which is an add-in card that has a fast CPU on board. This turns the Mac into a true "Multi-tasking" machine, allowing you to divide tasks between the two CPUs. Many multimediacs use Rockets to render animation or do batch image processing while they continue to use the Mac for other jobs.

Since most people will be accelerating Macs in the II series, we'll concentrate on the boards made for this purpose, which are straightforward in their installation, and surprising in their performance enhancement.

Types of Acceleration

Most accelerators work by using a faster CPU than the one that comes with your Mac. A Mac IIci, a typical acceleration candidate, uses a 25MHz 68030 processor. You can boost the performance of your IIci by adding an accelerator that has a

33-, 40-, or 50MHz '030. Even though these accelerators use the same Motorola 68030 chip, they boost the clock speed, which increases the speed with which the CPU does everything.

We'll take a look here at a few of the acceleration options for the Mac IIci and the IIfx, two of the most popular pre-Quadra (PQ) multimedia Macs, and excellent candidates for acceleration. If you don't have a ci or fx and still want to upgrade, don't worry. There are accelerators available for most Macs—even for 68000 machines like the Plus, although these are getting scarcer with the majority of Macs now being based on the '030 and '040 chips.

Accelerators using the '030 sometimes give you the choice of also getting an FPU (floating point unit, or math coprocessor, as they're also known). Before you opt for this extra chip, check to see if the software you use most often relies on a math coprocessor for calculations, if so, it's a wise investment.

Multimedia applications that typically rely on FPUs include rendering and image processing, but the apps themselves have to be specifically written to take advantage of the FPU. The '040 CPU has a built-in FPU, so you won't have to add one separately. But the integrated '040 FPU is different from its predecessors, meaning that apps have to be specifically written to use that FPU.

Accelerating a Mac IIci

A 50MHz '030 accelerator in a IIci will put the machine in about the same performance class as a Quadra 700. DayStar Digital, Sigma Designs, and Fusion Data all make leading '030 accelerators for the IIci. You can also buy Apple's Quadra 700 upgrade for the IIci. While more costly than the other accelerators, it gets you a lot more, such as built-in color and sound support.

The newest rage in acceleration are the '040 accelerators, which use the CPU found in the Quadra series. You can get '040 accelerators in two flavors: 25MHz (the CPU used in the Quadra 700 and 900) and 33MHz (used in the Quadra 950). Keep in mind that a 50MHz '030 -based accelerator will perform about the same as a 25MHz '040. You might find a good deal on the former as '040's take the spotlight.

Another thing to consider is that some applications still have problems with the '040 chip. Major differences in architecture between the '030 and the '040 have caught some applications vendors unaware, and many apps simply won't run on the '040.

Despite these problems, which are on the wane, '040 accelerators can definitely boost your Mac into the stratosphere. For example, a 25MHz '040 accelerator such as Fusion Data's TokaMac LC will lend IIfx performance to the relatively lowly LC. By the same token, 33MHz '040 boards from such vendors as Radius, Impulse, and Fusion Data Systems will turn a IIfx or IIci into a Quadra 950, although the Quadra 950 has an accelerated SCSI interface, built-in color support, and Ethernet, to name a few goodies that CPU accelerators don't incorporate.

RAM Acceleration

If you're dealing with mountains of graphic data, one of the main bottlenecks is getting the information out of your storage systems. RAM cards offer an interesting alternative, and are about five times faster than the fastest hard drives.

Basically, you just buy a NuBus card, such as DayStar Digital's RAM PowerCard, and cram it with as much memory as you can afford. The card holds up to 1.25Gb, so start counting those pennies. You can use the card with System 7's Virtual Memory, which further optimizes performance.

At current prices, populating a RAM card with sixteen 4Mb SIMMs will cost you about $1500 for the RAM, plus about $500 for the card. It's a bit pricey, but worth considering if you find yourself spending a lot of time waiting for large graphic images to arrive from your hard disk.

Accelerating a Mac IIfx

There are a number of interesting acceleration options for the IIfx, probably the most popular Mac for heavy-duty multimedia applications in the PQ era. Newer Technology makes fx/Overdrive, which can be tricky to install, but accelerates the fx by at least 25% (or your money back). The fx/Overdrive includes software that allows you to dial-up the clock speed of the upgraded '030 CPU in 40-, 45-, 50, and 55MHz increments.

Perspect Systems makes the Nexus fx, which the manufacturer installs for you. The upgrade includes cache RAM (see below), and a beefed-up 55MHz CPU.

Certainly, the most intriguing fx upgrade comes from Sixty Eight Thousand, Inc., in the form of the dash 30fx. You send them your fx, and you won't recognize it when you get it back. The manufacturer replaces most of the components and repackages it in a tower housing. You get an accelerated 50MHz CPU, a fast-SCSI-2 card (see "CPU, Video, SCSI Accelerators"), a 250-watt power supply, extra fans, and plenty of room for future upgrades—all this for $3995 plus your old fx.

Another fx acceleration option is the TokaMac II FX 33 from Fusion Data Systems. This board is based on the 33MHz '040, and does not require RAM of its own, but relies entirely on system RAM.

Upgrading RAM

To squeeze the most out of your accelerator, you may also have to upgrade the RAM in your machine. RAM comes in different speed ratings—150, 120, 100, 80, 70, and 60ns (for details, see "Buying RAM" in the previous chapter). A stock Mac IIci typically uses 100ns RAM. This may diminish the performance gains of an accelerator, which will generally require RAM speeds in the double-digit range.

Most accelerators employ a RAM cache, used to store often-requested data and instructions. RAM caches provide additional speed by reducing the number of times the accelerator must go to the system RAM for memory access. You will often need to come up with the RAM for this yourself. Depending on the card, you can sometimes just move some of your motherboard RAM onto the accelerator board to supply the cache.

Video Acceleration

Once you start dealing with 24-bit images and large screens, you start placing heavy demands on QuickDraw, the Mac's screen drawing utility. The system simply has many more pixels to update than it does with 1-bit images on 12" screens. The result is the agonizingly slow screen refreshing that graphic artists have been suffering for years, but that is being experienced by a whole new generation of multimedia developers and users.

QuickDraw is also impeded by the greater number of bits that have to travel across NuBus, which was just not designed to handle the heavier traffic. Video accelerators speed up screen drawing in at least three ways:

- By using ASICS (application specific integrated circuits) to handle frequently used QuickDraw commands.
- By using special *GWorld* and video RAM caches. GWorld is the set of QuickDraw graphics routines. GWorld RAM speeds graphics display by storing off-screen video data, which improves scrolling speed. Applications must be written to use GWorld RAM (and not all boards use it).
- By using NuBus only to transfer the QuickDraw commands themselves; the huge stream of data for screen display is sent directly from the accelerator board to the screen, bypassing the narrow NuBus (which can handle only about 4.4Mb per second).

Video accelerators are available for all bit depths and monitor sizes, though boards that handle 24-bit color and 20" or 21" screens are more costly. If you already have a 24-bit color card, you may not need a video accelerator: many color cards include video acceleration. Depending on your base machine and the type of work you're doing, you can expect screen drawing to speed up about fivefold with an accelerator.

If you're not sure if you need an accelerator, you might benefit from waiting to buy one a little longer, for a couple of reasons. First, Apple will release QuickDraw GX in 1993, and it's unclear whether the current generation of video accelerators will be compatible with this major upgrade. Second, Apple is readying QuickRing, its new bus architecture that will replace NuBus and accelerate bus transfers by 10 to 20 times. This may reduce the need for video acceleration, though, as noted, NuBus is only one of the reasons for video crawl.

SCSI Acceleration

Computers are complicated and modular, so even though you may have an accelerated CPU and a video accelerator to boot, you might still find yourself celebrating another birthday before that giant paint or image file opens up. That's

On the Horizon: SCSI-3

Even though the SCSI-2 spec was fully defined about three years ago, third-party vendors and off-the-shelf Macs are only just starting to incorporate the spec. The slowdown is the result of pending approvals by ANSI and ISO, the American and international standards bodies.

Meanwhile, work is already beginning on SCSI-3, a complex series of interrelated standards that promise to further refine and upgrade the basic SCSI spec. Innovations that will actually make it into SCSI-3 are still being reviewed, but multimedia will benefit from several of the likely candidates.

- Data moving at a sustained transfer rate of 100Mb/sec will make SCSI-3 more than twice as fast as current 68040 Quadras, and more that five times faster than other Macs.
- Switching from the parallel connections of current SCSI to a serial interface will allow higher actual throughput, since serial connections are less prone to electromagnetic interference.

The so-called Fibre-Channel Protocol is another possible SCSI-3 connection type, and one that promises transfer rates of 1 Gb/sec.

because the Mac's SCSI interface is transferring data from your hard disk at only about 1.5 to 2Mb per second (or about 3Mb/sec if you're lucky enough to own a Quadra).

Faster hard drives use a newer version of the SCSI standard, SCSI-2, that is capable of higher transfer rates. Since exiting Macs do not yet implement SCSI-2, you must add a SCSI-2 board to your NuBus or PDS slot if you want to realize these gains. These boards are available from such manufacturers as ATTO, MicroNet, PLI, and Storage Dimensions.

The SCSI-2 spec allows for both *Fast* and *Wide* options. The current SCSI-2 cards implement the Fast option, which boosts SCSI performance to the 5–10Mbs range. The SCSI-2 Wide option doubles the SCSI data path from 8 to 16 bits. Fast and Wide cards, now appearing on the scene, will theoretically be capable of slamming 20Mb/sec from your hard disk to the CPU. They are being offered by Daystar Digital, FWB, Loviel, and Storage Dimensions.

SCSI-2 cards can make a big difference when transferring large files from a fast hard disk, but make sure your SCSI device *is* fast—otherwise, an accelerator won't help.

Storage Systems

Of all computer resources, multimedia places perhaps the greatest demands on storage systems. Multimedia poses a triple threat to storage media: space, access time, and transfer rate. Some *single* 24-bit images won't even fit on the average hard disk, let alone in RAM. Then there is the problem of access time. Experts recommend, for example, a hard disk with an access time of at least 18ms for getting four-track sound files off the disk. And, of course, the storage device that will handle real-time transfer of full-motion video has yet to be invented.

The third problem is transfer rate. The fastest hard disks will transfer about 4–5Mb per second, but the SCSI interfaces in non-Quadra Macs will only support rates of 1.5 to 3Mb/sec. If you're constantly moving large files back and forth between your storage devices and RAM for display and manipulation, you'll definitely want to look at adding SCSI acceleration (discussed in the preceeding section).

Another issue is portability; transporting large multimedia files can be a challenge.

Removable hard disk cartridges offer a solution, but if you need to move big files around a lot, you'll have to use a portable drive in addition to your fixed storage systems. While removable disks perform fast enough to use them as primary storage for everyday work, their access and transfer rates can't cope with large multimedia files.

Luckily, there has been an explosion in storage technologies over the past few years, with many large capacity options from which to choose. While none of these technologies by themselves solve all of the multimedia demands of large capacity, fast access, high transfer rates, and portability, several in combination will do the job (see Figure 4.9).

Hard Disk Drives

Disk space usage has a way of staying about the same, regardless of your disk's capacity; so if you have a 40Mb disk, it's generally about as full as a 120Mb disk would be. That's just the way life is. But that shouldn't deter you from getting a mid-size or large disk, because you're going to need it. These days, mid-size disks are about 200Mb, a good size for multimedia work.

Disk speed is a consideration too. If you're using a relatively high-powered machine such as a Mac IIci, Quadra, or 486, you should spend a little more and get a disk with fast access time (in the neighborhood of 15–20ms) and a transfer rate of at least a few megabytes per second. The CPUs in these machines are fast enough so that disk speed would be a limiting factor.

Generally, very high capacity drives of 1Gb and over also offer the fastest access times and transfer rates. This conveniently gets you the key performance considerations along with capacity in one package. But you'll pay for it too, since fast, high-capacity drives cost several thousand dollars.

If you are in the market for a high capacity drive, make sure it is rated to handle time-based data like video or sound. While these components are in binary format like any other type of computer data, they are more susceptible to an effect called *thermal recalibration.* This is a process performed by the drive's controller to compensate for variations in the disk's substrate as it heats during use. While the recalibration process—a few hundred milliseconds every hour or so—is very rapid, I/O functions are temporarily suspended. That means that during the very long read/writes for video or sound, you may loose some data as the drive recalibrates.

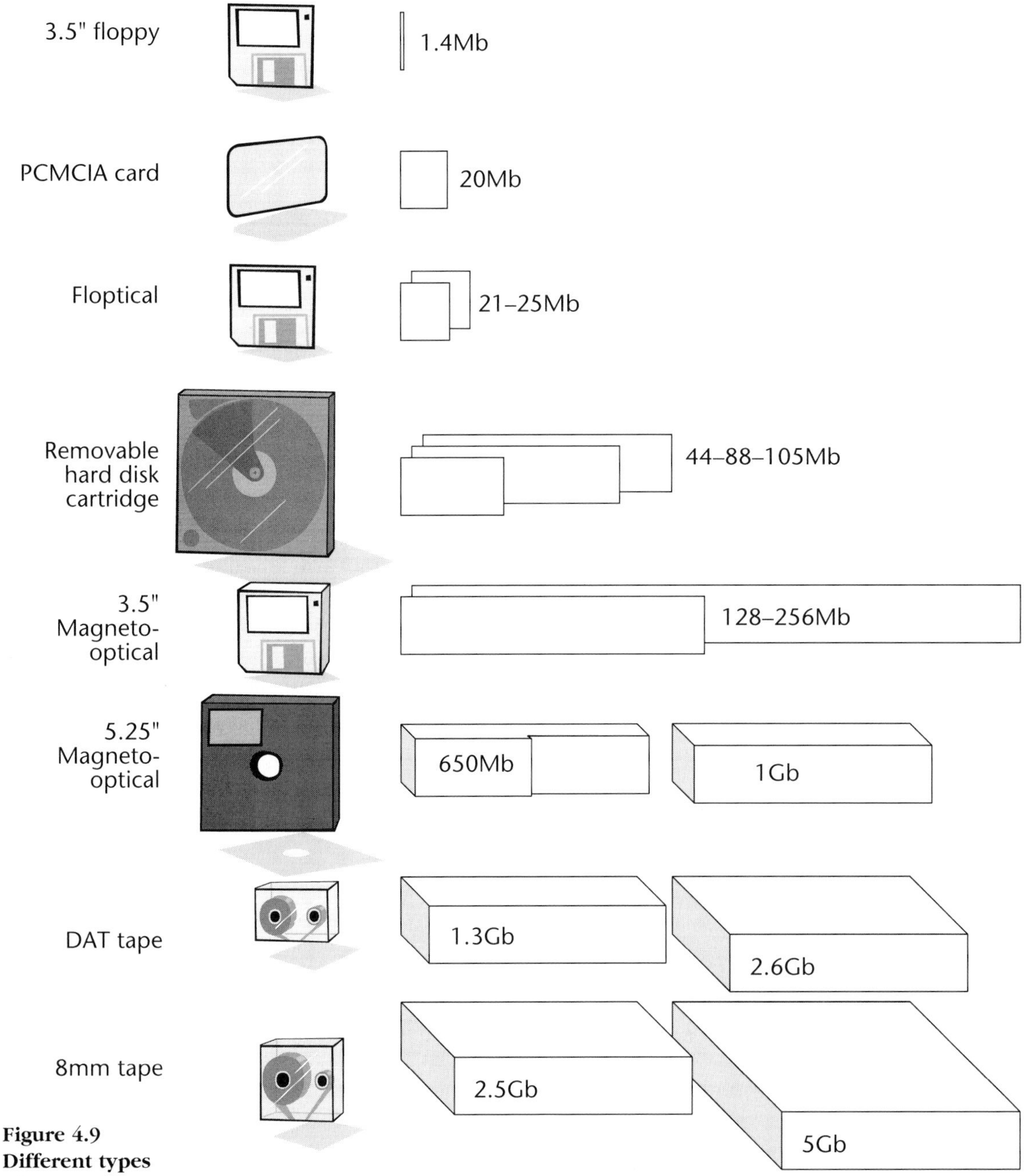

Figure 4.9 Different types of removable storage media

Before multimedia became widespread, no one noticed this effect, since most I/O operations for text or graphics are only a few seconds long. As large drives are more frequently used to store time-based data, the problem is likely to go away, because manufacturers can simply modify drive controllers so that they don't do recalibration during I/O.

RAID and Striping Technology

RAID (for Redundant Arrays of Inexpensive Disks) systems use groups of at least two disks in tandem to reduce access time and boost transfer rates. The disks can also mirror one another, so that if one drive fails, the other still has a copy of all your data. This fault tolerance could be very important if you can't afford to lose data should a disk burn out between saves.

Despite its name, RAID (also known as "striping") is not all that cheap, costing at least $5000, and easily ranging up to $50,000. Still, when combined with SCSI acceleration, RAID offers the best performance for those engaged in the most demanding of multimedia applications—digital video editing or digital audio recording on the desktop.

Removable Hard Disks and Flopticals

Many people supplement their hard disk storage with a removable cartridge drive, which can be a great convenience. These cartridges hold up to 90Mb apiece, and the drive mechanisms themselves are nearly as fast as hard disks. In general, as a multimedia creator, you should have the fastest disk you can find. Saving graphics images, a task that you will do (or are doing) constantly, is one of the most disk-intensive activities there is.

If you take files to a service bureau for processing and printing, removable drives are very handy. The most popular are those built around the SyQuest mechanism. The 44Mb version is pretty much a standard in service bureaus, so if you're looking for compatibility, get one of these. If you just want the flexibility of cartridge storage, and don't have to worry about interchanging the cartridges, consider one of the 88 or 90Mb drives.

If you're willing to pay a little more for flexibility and storage capacity, SyQuest has a new mechanism, the SQ5110C, which reads and writes both the 44 and 88Mb cartridges. Among the vendors using the new mechanism is PLI, which offers the Infinity 88/RW44. The only catch is that the unit was really designed for 88Mb disks, and writing to a 44Mb cartridge takes about three times as long. This is an interesting problem, since the 44Mb disks aren't big enough to hold the largest multimedia files, while the 88Mb cartridges generally do have the capacity. Perhaps the newer 88Mb cartridges will catch on sufficiently so that service bureaus will feel obliged to install them.

In 1993, SyQuest released a 105Mb removable disk drive that uses diminutive 3½" media, much smaller than the old disks, which are about 5" in diameter. The 105Mb mechanism has a seek time of under 10ms, less than half that of the 44- and 88Mb drives, and rivaling that of even fast fixed hard disks.

Another type of removable disk is the "floptical." Flopticals combine optical technology with the familiar 3½" floppy format. Floptical disks hold 21Mb or 25Mb, and floptical drives will also read standard 3½" floppies. The downside of flopticals is that they are only as fast as floppies, making them unsuitable as primary storage devices.

Optical Drives

For multimedia developers, whose storage requirements regularly run into the hundreds of megabytes, magneto-optical (MO) drives are an attractive alternative. They come in a 3½" size, which stores 128Mb or 256Mb, and a 5¼" size, which holds 650Mb or 1Gb. The smallest drives cost about $1200, and the largest are in the $2500–$4000 range.

The disks themselves go for about $50, and are erasable and rewritable. If you have invested in older and incompatible WORM (write-once read-many) technology, you can get a "multifunction" drive that will read both WORM and MO disks.

If the cost and storage capacity of magneto-optical drives better that of removable hard drives, their overall performance does not. Both transfer rates and access times fall between those of CD-ROM drives and hard disks. In 1993, rates for the 5¼" drives began to drop within shouting distance of removable hard disks.

Two recently released drives, Pinnacle's PMO-650 and Alphatronix's Inspire II F, boast access times in the 20ms range, making them comparable in speed to a standard hard drive. The Pinnacle achieves this performance in part by doubling disk rotation speed to 3600 rpm, and it auto-senses older disks and will read them at 1800 rpm.

Until these faster disks catch on, MOs do at least offer much better access times than tape, and are a good choice for a backup and archival system. They're also fast enough for playback of QuickTime movies.

Tape

Of all storage mechanisms, tape still offers the highest capacity, holding up to 5Gb of data. Tape also boasts the lowest cost per megabyte—from 1 to 15 cents per megabyte. By comparison, MO disks cost about 40 cents per megabyte, while fixed and removable hard disks are in the $2–$3/Mb range. Of course, tape is also the slowest of storage media, and is suitable only for long-term archiving and backup.

There several different types of computer tape:

- **DC2000.** Holds between 80 and 120Mb. Once the most popular format, DC2000 is now fading as the newer high capacity DC6000 is on the rise.
- **DC6000.** Incompatible with the older DC2000 format, DC6000 drives hold between 150Mb and 1Gb.
- **Teac.** Comes in 60Mb, 150Mb, and 600Mb sizes. The 150Mb is the most popular and is offered by many manufacturers. The 60Mb size is on the wane, while the 600Mb capacity is newer and is being adopted rapidly.

- **DAT.** Uses the 4mm DAT audiotape, and comes in 1.3Gb and 2.6Gb sizes.
- **8mm.** Uses 8mm videotape, and is generally slower and more costly than DAT. The most common size is 2.2Gb, but some drives more than double the capacity to over 5Gb.

Which is for you? If your disk drive holds less than 80Mb, don't bother with tape; get a removable hard drive for backups, or use floppies. For backing up medium-sized disks, a drive using the Teac 150Mb mechanism is probably the best choice. For backups of between 150Mb and 600Mb, consider a drive based on the DC6000 mechanism; for larger chores, DAT is the way to go. We recommend the slower and more expensive 8mm only if your backups are exceedingly large. DAT is also more popular than 8mm, making it a better choice when interchangeability is an issue.

Image Output

Once you've put together a multimedia work, there are number of ways you can present it. If the presentation is interactive and meant to be viewed by one person at a time, the computer itself will work fine.

If your presentation is to be viewed by an audience, and it is not interactive, one option is to print it to tape using a video out card; once on tape, the cassettes are easy to duplicate for wide distribution. Some more advanced 24-bit display and video capture cards include video-out capability.

If your presentation is interactive and also needs to be given to an audience, you'll need to use some sort of projection equipment hooked up to the computer.

Data Projectors

You can connect the computer to a *data projector*, which translates the computer signal into three light beams, red, blue, and green; these combine to form the proper colors and are projected onto a large screen. Data projectors are good for large audiences, because they can project an image of up to 8 feet across.

They do, however, have several drawbacks. First, they are quite expensive, costing up to $20,000. They are also large and bulky, making them unsuitable for road trips. Further, data projectors aren't compatible with all computer graphics cards. Finally, it takes some experience to get the three beams to converge properly.

Color LCD Panels

Fortunately, technology has again sped to the rescue, this time in the form of compact, full-color projection panels (see Figure 4.10). These panels, about the size of a notebook computer, are ideal for traveling presentations, and recent advances in color display technology have yielded surprising results in quality.

Like data projectors, LCD panels are driven directly from the computer. A panel is placed on an overhead projector, which projects its image onto a wall or screen. LCD panels are of two basic types: passive and active matrix. Passive matrix

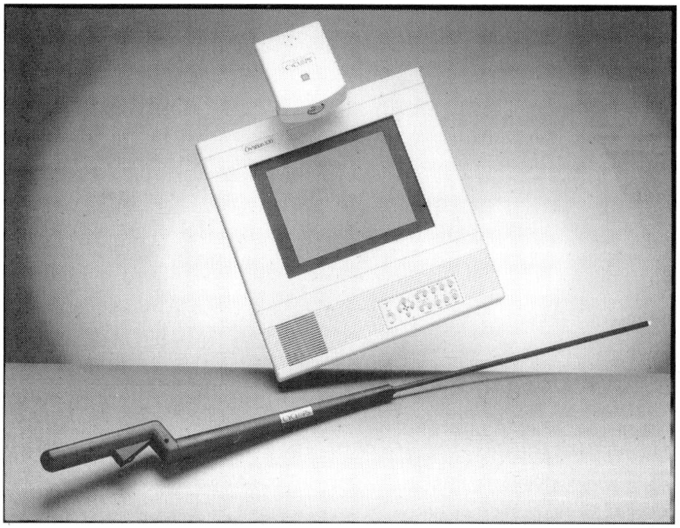

Figure 4.10
Projection panel

screens are most commonly found in today's notebook computers, although more expensive units feature the active matrix technology.

Passive matrix panels, while costing much less than the newer active matrix models, are unsuitable for multimedia presentations, because their scan rate is too low to cope with rapidly changing images. (The same thing happens when you're using a notebook with a passive matrix screen: you move the cursor, and are then unable to find it because the quick movement causes it to disappear temporarily.)

Active matrix screens solve this problem with a much higher refresh rate, and their color support is also much better, with newer models able to display full 24-bit color. Contrast and resolution are also excellent. If you plan to display full-motion video through a projection panel, you'll definitely need an active matrix panel, and one that has the appropriate video in ports.

These new display panels are also ideal for multimedia presentations because they support a number of input sources. Many can handle three or four simultaneous sources, either computer or video. This allows you to give presentations that might have bits and pieces on videotape, videodisc, and several different computers. You can toggle between the sources with a remote control without interrupting your presentation to reconnect or switch anything. The remote controls can even be programmed to issue computer commands so that you can give an interactive presentation with out stepping over to the computer.

The only disadvantage is the cost of these products, which is currently in the $4000–$8000 range. Active matrix screens are driven by an individual transistor for each pixel, which accounts for their high scan rate and high contrast. It also means that if a single transistor misfires, it could change the content of the data being displayed. For this reason, quality controls are stringent, keeping prices high. Once the manufacturing process is optimized, prices will come down, and this technology will undoubtedly become prevalent (at least until the next toys arrive from Japan).

Actually, the newest LCD technology may come from, of all places, the United States. The technique, called *active addressing*, features the performance of active matrix without the price. By mid-1993, look for products incorporating the new technology from such vendors as Motif, a joint venture of Motorola and LCD maker In Focus.

5

Imaging Tools

"One picture is worth a thousand words."

—Fred R. Barnard
(commonly misattributed as Chinese proverb)

In 1927, Barnard coined this phrase in the magazine *Printer's Ink*. What many people don't know about the popular saying is that he changed it from "One look is worth a thousand words," which he had written in the same magazine six years earlier. Barnard wouldn't take credit for the saying, as he hoped people would take it more seriously if he called it a Chinese proverb.

Today, the message carried by those same words has been altered again, especially as it relates to the computerized massaging and delivery of images. A picture may be worth a thousand words when printed on paper, but after it has been scanned, digitized, enhanced, or manipulated, it can be worth not just a thousand words, but a thousand, one hundred thousand, or even one million pixels.

While multimedia most often conjures up the idea of movement, its central element is actually the single, static image. This could be the opening screen of an interactive demo, the background graphics for a slide presentation, or a single frame of animation.

Images are now defined by both words and pixels. Within the past few years, it has become as easy to change and move pixels around using a desktop computer as it has been, for over a decade, to change and move words via word processing software.

With programs like Adobe Photoshop, Fractal Designs' ColorStudio, and Aldus Digital Darkroom, handling images to be used in multimedia presentations has become fast and, for the most part, friendly.

This chapter provides an overview of tools used to create images, especially as they relate to multimedia. Topics range from the use and importance of images, to Photo CD, to "color gamuts." While software for handling images has become much easier to use in recent years, it can still seem daunting to those who are

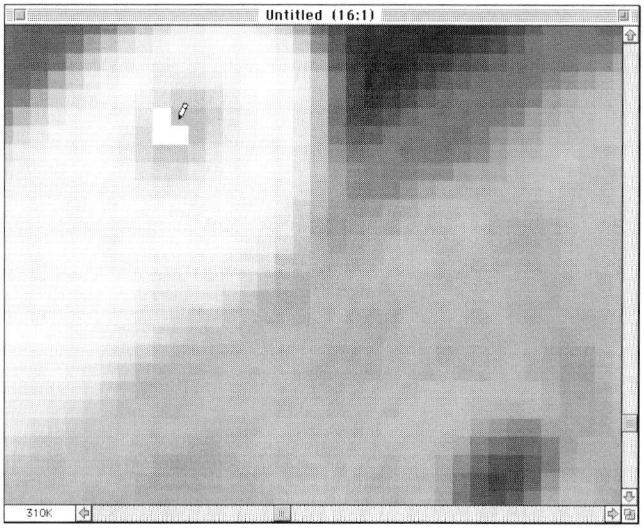

Figure 5.1
A computerized image is made up of thousands of pixels. Using image editing software, each one of the pixels in this screen shot can easily be altered, thus challenging the old bromide that "pictures never lie."

unfamiliar with its quirks. In fact, the learning curve can seem like the first hill of a roller coaster. We hope the following information helps with the ride.

The Importance of Images in Multimedia Presentations

There is no doubt that images are an important part of effective communications. Educators, for example, have long known that appealing to as many of the senses as possible enhances the message they're trying to get across. The same idea applies to creating a multimedia presentation. We have already learned to communicate solely with sound in the form of radio; images and words alone in the form of books; and moving images with sound in the form of television. Now it is possible to combine all of those media in communicating an idea. Multimedia promises the ability to deliver words, sound, and still and moving images with great fluidity, clarity, and influence.

Despite the kinetic quality of multimedia, the static images are at the core. The powerful impact of a still image or illustration can be formidable. Moving images and video simply do not have the content-laden history of still images. Who can forget some of the famous frozen moments in time of the last few decades? The raising of the American flag at Iwo Jima; a woman screaming over the body of an injured student during the Kent State uprising; Jack Ruby shooting Lee Harvey Oswald in the hallway of a Texas jail; Harry Truman triumphantly holding a newspaper's incorrect prediction over his head; these images are instantly recognizable and easily remembered. Images spark the viewer's mind and stimulate imagination.

Drawing versus Painting

To oversimplify somewhat, drawing tools are typically used when precision is necessary—in technical drawings, for example. Paint tools can help you create work that is more like paintings created with traditional tools. Paint programs also offer finer color control, down to the individual pixels.

There is another important difference between paint and draw tools. Objects created with paint tools are *bitmap* objects, so called because they are made up of a collection of dots (or pixels) that correspond directly to one or more "bits" of computer memory. As a practical matter, this means that you can't manipulate individual sections of a painted image without affecting the rest of it (except through the use of masking and channels; see the Image Processing section later in the chapter). To select part of a paint image, you use a tool such as "lasso" or "marquee." If you then drag the selected area to move it, there will be a gap left behind.

Bitmap graphics also do not resize well, because the individual dots that make up the image become too large, causing *pixelation*, or distortion. Since bitmap images are fixed at a particular resolution, their integrity is based on a device that matches that resolution. This is usually not a problem for images that are destined for display onscreen. Higher end paint programs support output at a variety of resolutions without compromise of image quality.

By contrast, graphics created with drawing tools consist of individual objects known as *object*-ori*ented* or *vector* images. To manipulate these objects, simply select them with a mouse click and have at it. When you create a background, and then draw an object on top of the background, the two elements are treated by the computer as separate entities. You can move the foreground object to a new location without affecting the background. These objects can be treated individually because the computer represents them as mathematical calculations. When objects are moved or otherwise manipulated, the computer recalculates the new position.

Some programs provide "autotrace" tools that allow you to trace a bitmap image to create an object-oriented image that can be manipulated. Others employ both a paint and draw layer so that you can use both types of tools on a given image. When in paint mode, paint tools won't affect drawn images, and vice versa.

In general, when type is part of an artwork, or when text and colored shapes are combined, a draw program is probably a better choice. For complex illustrations with gradations of color, or for photographic image retouching, a bitmap paint program is more suitable. However, it's key to remember that multimedia presentations are based on bitmapped screens displayed on a monitor. For that reason, paint is the essential environment for multimedia. Even object-oriented "draw" images are ultimately rasterized to bit maps for touch-up and final display on screen.

Getting Images into Your Computer

There are a number of ways to get images into your computer, most of which are covered in Chapter 4, "Hardware Peripherals." Briefly, such hardware accomplishes the task of taking ideas and images from the "analog" world and turning them into the bits and bytes your computer needs to handle them. Slide scanners, flatbed scanners, hand-held and drum scanners are the most commonly used pieces of specialized hardware, along with graphics tablets, video digitizers, and electronic cameras.

Images are also commercially available on a variety of CD-ROMs and on floppy disks as clip art, usually grouped by their subject. One of the most exciting developments in recent months has been Kodak's Photo CD system (discussed near the end of this chapter). This convenient method is finding its way into the portfolios of many image providers and purveyors. More information on external sources of images can be found in Chapter 10, "Outside Resources."

Graphics Files

Twirl a spoon in a bowl of alphabet soup and you just might come across some of the myriad letter combinations that identify the most common image file formats. PICT, EPS, TIFF, GIF, and RIFF are all common names for how graphics or image data can be stored and understood by the computer. Fortunately, multimedia producers only have to deal with a few common types of file formats.

First, you must understand the difference between file formats and the different types of graphics and images that applications can produce. File formats are simply names for the methods used to store a graphic or image. We'll get to them in a minute. The two different types of graphics one must deal with on a Macintosh are *bitmapped* and *object-oriented*. It is easy to distinguish between the two if you remember that bitmapped graphics or images are made of tiny little

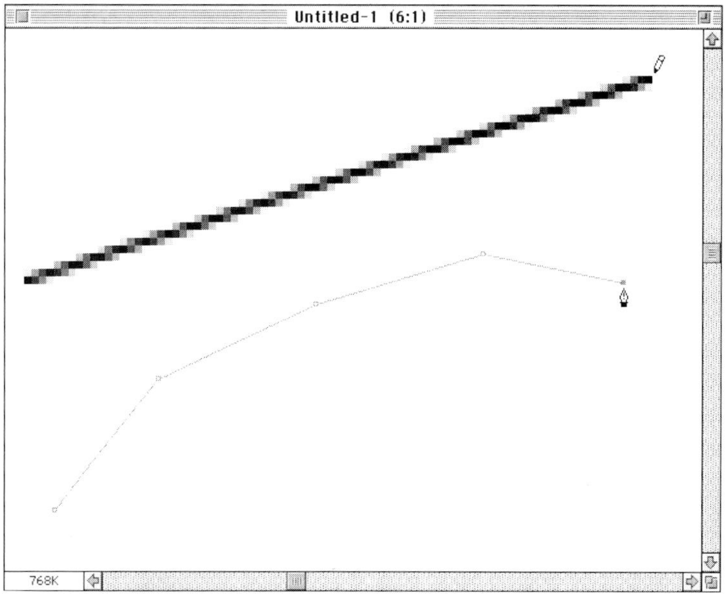

Figure 5.2 The difference between bit-mapped and object-oriented graphic types can be seen in this illustration. At the top is a bit-mapped line made up of individual pixels. Below, is an object-oriented line, determined in the computer by mathematical formulas and placed on the screen.

bits. Many millions of bits, or pixels, go into making up the image or graphic. It's just as if an artist had used so many little dabs of paint to make a picture that you couldn't tell the difference between it and a good photograph. This attribute is important if you are going to use a monitor or television screen as your output device, since monitors use rows of pixels to display images.

Object-oriented graphics are defined mathematically, rather than by how many bits or pixels they contain. In an object-oriented graphic or image, a simple line is not a row of bits or pixels to the computer, but an arithmetic description of where the line exists on the page (x and y coordinates) and its characteristics (how long, wide, color, etc.). This attribute is important when you are going to output a graphic or image to a printer. In fact, most printers made for the Macintosh are based on the fact that data sent to them for output will come in the form of lines of code and not millions of pixels.

Bittmapped graphics, while large compared with object-oriented files, are more suitable for handling images with subtle detail and extensive variations in shades, such as photographs. For more on the essential differences between bitmapped and object-oriented graphics, see Drawing versus Painting later in this chapter.

Graphic File Formats

Mac users have to put up with comparatively few graphics formats—TIFF, PICT, and EPS are the main ones. Most Mac programs can read and write at least one of these in addition to their native formats. The PC world, by contrast, supports a large number of proprietary and near-standard formats, but TIFF and EPS are the most widely used. The following list describes the most common graphics file formats on both platforms.

BMP

This is a common PC bitmap file format, brought on by Windows. BMP files are not compressed, so they are fast to open, but BIG! The file format can be edited on the PC by both Windows Paint and PC Paintbrush. Many file conversion utilities will convert BMP files for use by Mac programs.

CGM

The Computer Graphics Metafile format stores images that have the vector graphics advantages of compact size, scalability, and theoretically, better cross-platform compatibility. But while CGM files are quite common on the PC (and Unix), they are nearly unknown on the Macintosh.

Some conversion programs (such as MacLinkPlus) and paint/image processing software (like Canvas) will import some CGMs, but not all. If you need to get a lot of CGMs over to the Mac, lay your hands on a copy (by paying for it, of course!) of MetaPICT from GSC Associates. MetaPICT converts CGM files to PICTs very capably. One footnote: Once converted, the resulting PICTs cannot be edited, so do any necessary editing on the CGM file first.

CGM files are not as flexible a vector format as EPS. While you can edit CGMs, the format does not support gradient fills and bezier curves. This results in smaller files.

EPS

While EPS files are great for storing images and graphics to be output to a printer, they are not meant, necessarily, for output to a screen. Furthermore, EPS files are not popularly supported by most multimedia software.

EPS files include a low-resolution PICT component that allows the files to be displayed on systems without Display PostScript (which is most of them). This provides for quick and dirty display of the image onscreen without the overhead of PostScript interpretation. EPS files that do not contain the PICT component will display as the old familiar—and ever helpful—crossed-out rectangle.

Object-oriented EPS files (except those generated by Adobe Illustrator) generally cannot be ungrouped, refilled, or recolored. Although the EPS format can carry bitmaps, it is notoriously inefficient code when turned to this purpose; such EPS files are large and gobble up lots of disk space and other system resources.

GIF

TOOLS GIF converter 131

Graphic Interchange Format was created by the CompuServe network, and was specifically designed to minimize file transfer times when uploading or downloading images from the network. Since the format is designed for compact file size, images are stored with maximum compression (using the LZW algorithm), and the files can therefore take awhile to unpack. As CompuServe offers thousands of GIF files, it is a good source of clip art and scanned images (though all are limited to 8-bit color).

The format is more popular in the PC world than on the Mac, but it is read by good old Photoshop. There is also a shareware utility called GIF Converter that is included on the Power Tools CD.

MOVIE

TOOLS QuickTime 160

Apple's QuickTime movie format stores any dynamic data—video, animation, sound. The movie files contain only track and timing information; the actual data is stored elsewhere. The movie format also supports a *poster*, a still image representing the movie, and a *preview*, which is a short trailer taken from the movie itself. For a detailed overview of QuickTime, see Chapter 3, "Mac Software and Hardware."

PAINT

This is the Mac's original graphics file format, the native format of MacPaint. Almost archaic now, with its 1-bit black-and-white graphics, it is nonetheless firmly entrenched in the Mac world, and many programs (Canvas, PixelPaint, DeskPaint, Photoshop, and of course, MacPaint) still support it. If you need to do a simple bitmap, the format is quite serviceable, and very compact.

PCX

This is pretty much the standard PC bitmap file format. It dates back quite a ways into the murky swamp of the PC's past. Since it was originally intended as a drawing image format, its compression schemes are not optimized for bitmaps. The PCX format doesn't compress scanned or dithered images very well either.

Also, it was developed for the paltry 16 colors of VGA, and though newer versions do handle both 8- and 16-bit images, incompatibilities abound.

Most PCX files can be edited with Photoshop, and on the PC using Paintbrush, the program from which it originally sprang.

PICS

PICS files are simply collections of sequential PICT or PICT2 files used to generate animations. The format is used by Macromedia Director (and a few other programs, like SuperCard) to store animated files. Because of Director's popularity, some vendors' programs read PICS files directly. For example, Adobe Photoshop will import PICS frames for editing. It's also an output option for 3-D applications—Swivel 3D Professional, Strata Vision 3d, and Infini-D, for example—that can animate objects or viewpoints to produce sophisticated action, simulations, and structure walk-throughs. PICS files have a size limit of 15Mb.

TOOLS
PACo Producer Demo 218

Since PICS files can be monstrously big, compression is sometimes implemented. However, since there is no standard for PICS compression, a compressed PICS file may not be readable by programs other than the one that created and squashed it in the first place.

PICT

Another pillar of Mac graphics formats, PICT was designed for moving graphics between different programs on the Mac. While PICTs have a limited 8-color range, they are widely read by Mac programs, are the native format for the Mac's Clipboard, and drive the drawing functions of QuickDraw, the part of system software responsible for the construction and display of images on the Mac.

The PICT format allows comments about the image it carries, such as PostScript definitions of the image and curve-smoothing information. If the application reading the PICT file cannot handle this information, it is simply ignored.

TOOLS
PICTviewer 133
Capture 227

QuickTime extends the PICT format to allow storage of compressed still images and image previews. Any program that can now open a PICT file will also be able to read a new compressed PICT in the extended format.

PICT2

The PICT2 format is an extension of PICT that comes in two versions, one that handles 8-bit color images, and another that holds the 16.8 million colors of 24-bit images. Some programs are beginning to use PICT2 as their default PICT format; these applications include Studio/8, SuperPaint, and PixelPaint.

The PICT2 format (many applications now just call it PICT, since the original PICT format is almost extinct) is perfect for multimedia presentations because it supports bitmapped as well as object-oriented graphics and images and because most applications will import and export in the PICT2 format. The PICT2 format is the preferred format for producing multimedia presentations with software such as Adobe Premiere, Adobe Photoshop, VideoFusion, and Macromedia Director.

Using the 8-bit version of PICT2, you can save a custom 256-color palette with the image, ensuring accurate color information as the file is transferred and reopened by different applications. Beware of this feature, though—some applications don't save the palette along with the image, and you may get a rude surprise as another application performs color substitutions while opening the image. Also be careful when pasting parts of other PICTs into a PICT file with a custom palette—the pasted image's colors are not drawn from the custom palette, and you'll experience color shifts.

TIFF

Introduced by Aldus, and designed to accommodate the sophisticated images brought into the computer by scanners, TIFF (for Tagged Image File Format) is now pretty much the format of choice for color image files. It also stores black-and-white and gray-scale images.

Although close to a cross-platform format, TIFF is something of a joke as a standard, for vendors use it to their own ends, sometimes rendering TIFF files unreadable by programs supposedly designed to support it.

PC TIFF and Mac TIFF are different from each other. Both contain sequential representations of the pixels, but put them in a different order. Conversion utilities will handle this difference, and some Mac applications, like Photoshop, can save in PC TIFF format.

The different TIFF "dialects" are further complicated by the fact that there are actually three TIFF subtypes. Monochrome TIFFs store 1-bit black-and-white images; gray-scale TIFFs hold 256 grays, and color TIFFs can hold up to 16.8 million colors. TIFF files tend to be on the heavy side, so they are often encoded with compression schemes, but these differ and are not recognized by all programs. TIFF 4.0 uses the most widely recognized compression standard, and the newer TIFF 5.0 sports features such as variable compression formats.

Despite these variations, TIFF is still the most reliable format for exporting gray-scale and color images to other programs, ensuring that image tones and resolution are faithfully interpreted by the importing application. Unfortunately, some of the most popular multimedia software, such as Adobe Premiere, does not support TIFFs.

JPEG File Compression

This is not a file format, but a compression algorithm specified by the Joint Photographic Experts Group to compress 24-bit color images. By removing nonessential information, the technique can reduce files to 1/20 of their original size. At this compression ratio, images look virtually identical to their uncompressed counterparts. While JPEG can produce more highly compressed images, and therefore smaller files, image degradation becomes apparent at ratios above 20:1. (See Compression/Decompression later in the chapter.)

Dealing with Graphics Files

All in all, the whole business of graphics file formats is troublesome and not a little frustrating. To keep yourself from inflicting damage on your computer when your carefully adjusted multihued image turns green as you open it, it's best to stick to a few tested formats that you are most familiar with.

During the bleakest moments, an excellent resource is *The Graphic File Toolkit: Converting and Using Graphic Files* by Steve Rimmer (Addison-Wesley, 1992). The book also comes with a disk containing an award-winning program called Graphic Workshop that will read and convert virtually any bitmap format.

Software for Imaging

The tools used to manipulate and enhance images once they are transferred into your computer can be a bit intimidating, and just choosing among them can make your head spin. Fortunately, most packages are fairly intuitive, and with a little practice they can become powerful allies.

Imaging creation and processing programs are among the most powerful on the desktop. With their capability to handle images made up of millions of multicolored pixels that can then be filtered, sharpened, cropped, rotated, colored, airbrushed, painted, cloned, and erased, determining the differences between packages can be as difficult as making sense of the enhancement options.

Any multimedia production using desktop computer equipment will certainly involve more than one piece of software. In the creation and processing of images, producers will choose among software for painting, drawing, and handling scanned images. Each of the packages, although retaining some of the Mac's friendliness, also has its quirks. For example, all paint programs don't, unfortunately, incorporate brush tools in the exact same manner. It makes no sense to purchase four different paint packages solely to work with four different kinds of brush tools. Moreover, while some packages tout themselves as "all-in-one" godsends, you are much better off choosing software based upon what you will be producing most often.

Most people, excluding masochists, will standardize on a "suite" of software. A full-featured, well-supported set of products in each of the categories will pay off in the long run by reducing the number of programs one must learn and by saving a good bit of money! Magazines like *MacUser, MacWorld*, and *Macweek* often run detailed, side-by-side comparisons of the programs in each category. It would be wise to refer to such reviews before committing any funds. Input from friends and associates doing the same work is also valuable.

It is also prudent to be as sure as you can that the software you purchase will not become orphaned. This does not mean that you should disregard otherwise valuable software simply because it comes from a company you have never heard of. But while nothing is forever, you should be asking yourself some tough questions about the availability and cost of future upgrades; customer and technical support; competitiveness with similar software; and how "standard" the software seems to be among multimedia producers.

Following are descriptions of the software categories and brief examinations of some of the most popular software packages in the painting, drawing, and image processing categories with a bent toward their use in creating multimedia presentations.

Paint Programs

Paint programs are the closest you can come on a computer to dipping a brush into paint and spreading it on a canvas. Images created in a paint program consist of the manipulated pixels to create a bitmap - a pixel-by-pixel screen description. Many multimedia authoring packages include paint and drawing tools that can be used to create backgrounds and objects, special effects, even simple animation. If your needs are basic, these tools will save you the trouble of learning a specialized program. You also won't have to worry about importing images from a separate application.

However, due to the enormous variation and complexity of visual images, designers often opt for specialty programs to create them, and then import them for incorporation into a multimedia presentation. These programs have tools for creating and modifying images in ways that are beyond the means of most authoring programs. Paint programs are also among the most accessible of computer software. Anyone can sit down and immediately have fun dabbling and drawing.

Even professional artists have grown more interested as the tools have become more sophisticated. Some Products are now offering a range of painting techniques based on traditional methods, and the availability of graphics tablets has spawned a new category of paint programs that support pressure-sensitive effects (see Oasis and Painter entries later in this chapter).

Paint programs are used to create original images. Programs such as Adobe Photoshop and Fractal Designs ColorStudio, on the other hand, are commonly used to process preexisting images, even though they possess many of the same capabilities as paint programs. Most paint programs lack the specialized functions to adequately manipulate and enhance scanned images.

The tools used in painting programs affect each pixel they touch. Parameters such as color, brush type, wetness, opacity, and spray are almost infinitely variable by the advanced programs. Some even allow the user to define the type of painting surface to be used. Rice paper, canvas, charcoal paper, concrete, linen, and slate are just a few of the options. The ability to create masks that will protect parts of an image you don't want altered is another advanced option. Other things to consider when choosing a painting package include the maximum resolution and image size a program can handle, the intuitiveness of the interface and the tools, the number and variability of colors, and the ability to work with a number of file formats.

There are a great number of paint programs to choose from at many different prices. We've included extended descriptions of the three we believe to be the most useful and the best value for the money, as well as those that are the most popular among multimedia producers.

Basic Features

While paint programs differ in the particulars of their interfaces and tool sets, most offer similar groups of tools and resources.

Design Tools and Techniques

Tools provided by digital design programs range from simple drawing and painting functions to a variety of filters that can completely transform images.

A common set of drawing and paint tools has evolved as graphics programs have come into widespread use. Though these basic tools vary somewhat from product to product, they are for the most part fairly standardized and derive from MacPaint, one of two programs bundled with the first Macs back in 1984 (the other program was MacWrite).

For creating realistic paint effects, tools include paintbrushes, spraycans, and paint buckets. Most programs allow you to create custom brushes by editing the "brushprint" one pixel at a time. Paint programs also have blending tools so that you can smudge and swirl colors as on a canvas.

Palettes and Patterns

One of the main reasons for the success and proliferation of paint programs is the high degree of color control that they provide. Programs contain several standard color and pattern palettes from which you choose colors. Most also let you create and edit custom palettes that can be saved and reused. In some, you use an Apple-style color picker to select colors by clicking on the color wheel. Other programs supply matrices of colors from which to choose.

Paint programs also provide color mixers for more precise color synthesis. Mixers imitate real-world color mixing by allowing you to use tools to dab and blend colors just as you might with a paint spatula and palette in the studio.

The more useful programs let you "tear off" palettes and mixer windows so that you can place them onscreen for easy access. Stock patterns are also supplied, so that you can apply backgrounds and textures such as grids, checkerboards, and dot patterns. You can also create or use scanned-in images and designate these as custom patterns.

Fills and Gradients

Paint programs typically apply color to a wide area of the "canvas" by "pouring" the color from a "paint bucket." Such areas of color are known as fills, and they can be applied in different ways.

Gradient fills combine two colors in a smooth transition, automatically filling in the thousands of colors necessary to smoothly blend between the two colors. Most programs provide a set of fill effects—you can select fills that go from top to bottom, that fade from one color to another and then back to the first, and so on.

Radial fills let you simulate a light source for an object, and then fill the object with colors or grays that range from dark to light. Some programs allow you to store frequently used gradients for easy access.

You can even apply "color cycling" to achieve an animation effect. For example, you can create a flame effect by choosing different shades of red, yellow, and orange, which are then alternately displayed in sequence, giving the flickering effect of fire.

Filters and Masks

Many paint programs supply filters that can be applied to the whole painting or to selected areas. Basic filters, supplied with all programs, include ones that blur and sharpen. More specialized filters can transform paintings with transparency effects that give the illusion of depth and a three-dimensionality. Others make the painting appear as if viewed through distorted glass, or blended with numerous tiny brushstrokes, yielding an impressionistic effect.

A particularly useful effect, available in most paint programs, is the *antialiasing* filter. This filter smooths the jagged lines that sometimes occur in bitmap programs, especially as images are resized. Antialias control is also convenient for smoothing type that is imported into the paint program. Programs that do antialiasing automatically via a filter are much preferable to those that force you to do it pixel by pixel.

TOOLS
Kai's Power Tools 134

You can also buy plug-in products that offer a wide variety of filters to supplement those included in your favorite paint program. Kai's Power Tools is an imaginative and powerful collection of Photoshop plug-in filters, (which also works with many paint programs), providing tools such as gradient, fractal, and texture generators. Aldus makes a series of products called Gallery Effects that includes numerous filters, and Delta Tao Software's Monet creates impressionistic images from imported paint files.

Masking can be used to define the boundaries of different shapes, or to "protect" an image from being treated by a paint effect. Low-end products like Color MacCheese and DeskPaint let you mask only the entire painting. The mask consists of a separate transparent layer on which you can try out a paint effect. If you like it, you can merge it with the original layer. If not, you simply discard it, with no effect on the original layer. Products with professional features, such as Studio/32 and PixelPaint Professional, offer more masking control. Using these programs, you can mask not only specific areas, but also colors, even specific ranges of colors.

Although some paint programs include an impressive array of masks and filters, and support for plug-ins as well, the most sophisticated effects are found in image processing programs—see "Image Processing Software," later in this chapter.

Painter

Painter, from Fractal Designs, is arguably the most powerful and useful 24-bit paint program for multimedia currently available. The big strength of the program is its ability to simulate traditional artist's tools. Charcoal, watercolor, crayons, felt pens, chalk, and pencil are among the "natural" media which users can wield with almost infinite variability.

Painter has excellent support for Wacom, Kurta, and CalComp pressure-sensitive tablets across all of its tools as well as relating pressure to tool performance. In the latest version, Fractal Designs has added a number of new media options including diffused watercolors, marbling, distorted glass, and an airbrush which spatters.

Antialiasing is a part of nearly every tool, which makes for smooth effects, particularly for multimedia presentations destined for playback on a computer monitor. Painter has a very useful magic wand tool, much like the one in Photoshop, which makes it much easier to create *friskets* (masks) than by trying to select with a lasso-type tool. One of Painter's most intriguing options is the ability to "shine" different types of "lights" on an image created or imported into the program. In minutes, Painter creates a look similar to what a 3-D program would take hours to ray-trace.

Painter is also known for giving the user the ability to apply the styles of different artists to images. Seurat, van Gogh, and Cubist characteristics are available to users with the click of the mouse, surely to the chagrin of art teachers everywhere.

Multimedia producers will be especially interested in Painter's ability to restrict the usable colors in an image to those that can be displayed in NTSC or PAL formats. Painter does not come with any image-enhancing filters, but it supports Photoshop plug-ins and can save images in PICT, RIFF, TIFF, ColorStudio, and Photoshop formats, making it a great adjunct to the heavy-hitting image processing programs. Painter also supports virtual memory for work on large, detailed images. Painter is reasonably priced and should become a staple for multimedia producers.

Studio/32

Electronic Arts' Studio/32 is a robust 32-bit paint program with a well-rounded set of features. While Studio/32 is no match for Painter's "natural" tool feel, the program does possess some very advanced painting functions. Studio/32 supports pressure-sensitive tablets, but does not possess Painter's capability to link pressure sensitivity to a tool's characteristics. Transformation and selection features are excellent, and the program supports virtual memory for working with large, detailed images.

Multimedia producers will appreciate Studio/32's text tool, which offers an independent layer for working with PostScript text. The program also contains a masking ability to protect layers of work. Studio/32 imports and exports PICT, MacPaint, TIFF, and EPS files. While Studio/32 holds a place at the upper echelon of full-featured paint programs, so does its price in comparison to it's competitors.

Color It!

Color It!, shown in Figure 5.3, is a very inexpensive but full-featured 32-bit color paint program. With Color It!, users can edit images of any kind, from line art to direct color. The program uses a nice virtual memory scheme and supports up to 15 levels of undo and redo. Color It! supports antialiasing and can sharpen, blur, and retouch photographic images. A very handy feature is the program's

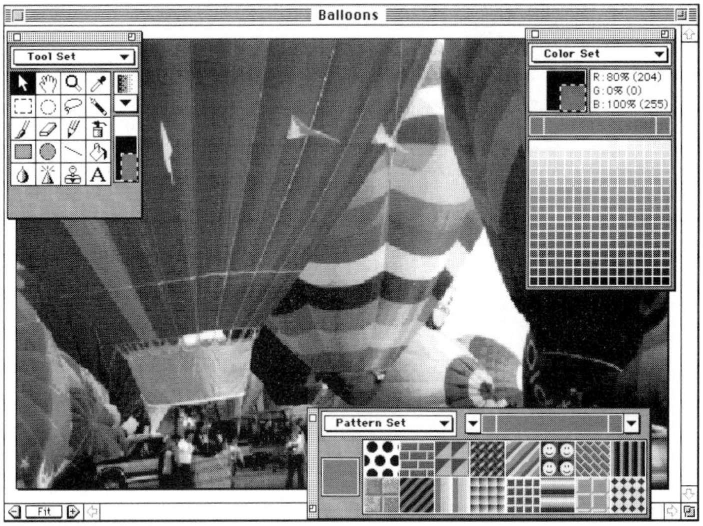

Figure 5.3 Color It! from TimeWorks is an inexpensive paint/image processing program that has many advanced features.

ability to open and save Photoshop files, and it also supports Photoshop filters and plug-ins. Color It! saves in several other file formats, including MacPaint, PICT, TIFF, and GIF. The program also has masking ability with variable levels of transparency, support for pressure-sensitive tablets, and an antialiased text tool.

Multimedia producers on a tight budget would do well to consider Color It! as a well-equipped painting program without all the advanced capability of Painter. Color It! also doubles as a very adequate image processing application, with enough features to handle all but the most demanding tasks.

SuperPaint

SuperPaint from Aldus (Figure 5.4) is a half-paint, half-draw program that doesn't accomplish either job as capably as stand-alone paint or draw applications. (see "Drawing versus Painting" below). But that's fine when you consider what you get for SuperPaint's price. SuperPaint is the best of the paint/draw programs when it comes to painting, although its tools are still weak when compared to a program like Painter. SuperPaint's strengths are its ease of use, its support for a variety of plug-ins, and its ability to save in a multitude of file formats including PICT, EPS, StartupScreen, MacPaint, and TIFF. SuperPaint will also import QuickTime frames from movies for manipulation.

On the down side, SuperPaint only supports one tool for pressure sensitivity and doesn't have any antialiasing capability, an important consideration for multimedia producers. Serious users should consider the purchase of a true paint and a true draw program for heavy work, but SuperPaint will suffice for those on a shoestring.

PixelPaint Professional

PixelPaint Professional, from Pixel Resources, has been handed down from company to company over the past two years. What was a great paint program now sits near the lower end of the market as other programs have caught up. Painter, Oasis, and

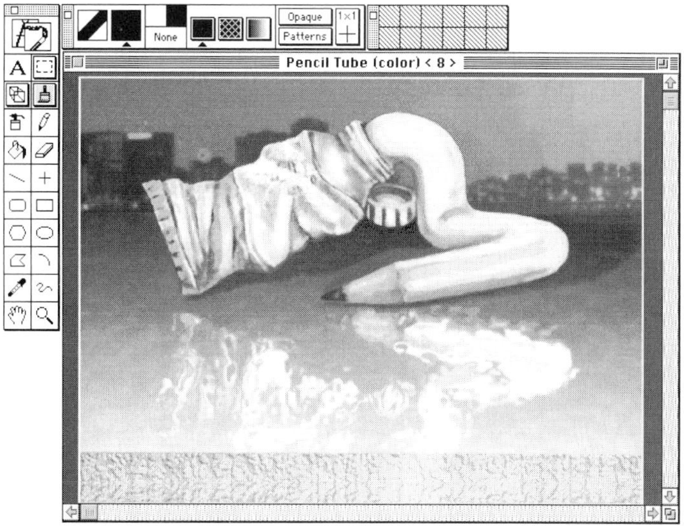

Figure 5.4 SuperPaint, from Aldus, is a combination paint/draw program that doesn't excel at either task.

Studio/32 possess equal or greater functionality, and the best of the bunch, Painter, is less than half PixelPaint's price. No serious multimedia producer would consider PixelPaint Pro without a long, hard look at its competitors.

Oasis

Oasis (Figure 5.5) was a ground-breaking program when it was introduced, but it has fallen by the wayside both in features and in its hefty price. Marketed by Time Arts, Inc., it would be well suited to the multimedia and video production environments, but its features need some updating.

While Oasis supports alpha channels, Photoshop plug-ins, and restriction to video-legal color palettes, it provides no magnification tool, and is frustratingly

Figure 5.5 Oasis specializes in tools to work on video images, but its features need updating.

sluggish to use for painting. The program has the capability to simulate traditional art media, including pencil, charcoal, oil, pastel, and watercolor, but it does so in a cumbersome, unintuitive way involving multiple tear-off menus and frustrating interfaces. It does support pressure-sensitive tablets and has an interesting Lightbox feature that enables users to "trace" over images as if they were translucently lit from beneath.

Drawing Packages

It is a bit easier to choose among drawing applications than among those in the painting realm. Unlike paint programs, where images can be imported directly into multimedia productions with relative ease, most draw packages are designed less for screen display than for output to a PostScript printer, although Canvas, FreeHand, Illustrator, and MacDraw Pro allow files to be saved as PICTs. You must be careful, however, when attempting to save files created with draw programs that contain specialized fills, gradients, or text effects. While most PostScript printers can easily handle such files when saved and output as EPSs, those same files saved as PICTs will be stripped of most of the extra-fancy stuff.

The most popular drawing programs are Aldus FreeHand and Adobe Illustrator. Deneba Software's Canvas is no has-been, however, since it combines many features of both paint and draw programs. Claris's MacDraw Pro, while not as sophisticated as the others, offers a well-rounded drawing environment. All of the drawing programs are great for producing original images in a more precise manner than that possible with painting tools, and not so good for manipulating photos or scanned items. Because they offer features not easily incorporated into painting programs, no multimedia producer should be without one of these powerful, full-featured drawing packages.

Canvas

Deneba Software's Canvas (Figure 5.6) is a hybrid paint/draw program with a definite emphasis on drawing. Its ability to be expanded and updated via plug-in tools has solidified its position as a "Swiss-Army knife" among image creation/manipulation programs. Canvas has a complete set of drawing tools and an adequate set of painting tools. It can also import and export a stunning variety of file formats, which makes it a natural for massaging files for multimedia. Canvas can be a daunting program for novices to start out with, but its versatility and flexibility pay big rewards in the end.

FreeHand

FreeHand, from Aldus, provides a generally friendly, if sluggish, drawing environment but lags behind both Canvas and Illustrator when features are compared. FreeHand does have many useful features for multimedia producers, though: support for pressure-sensitive tablets, the ability to export files in the PICT or PICT2 formats, up to 99 undos, bitmapped fill patterns, onscreen display of text effects, and TIFF-import and color balance capabilities (Figure 5.7).

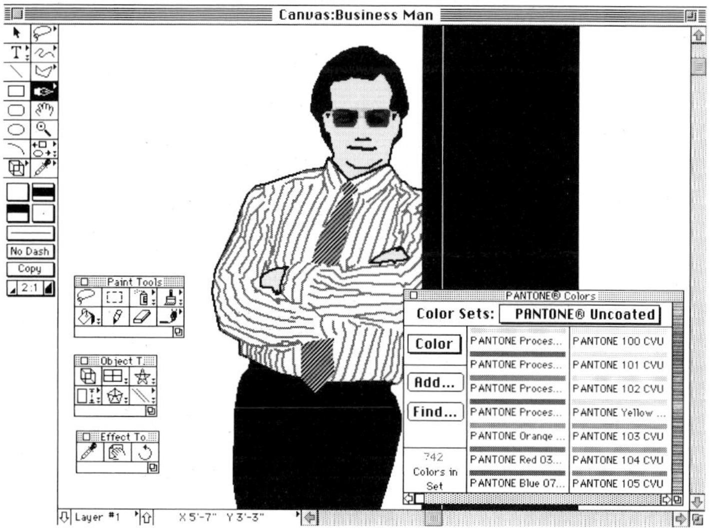

Figure 5.6
Canvas is a powerful paint/ draw program with a dense interface but much versatility.

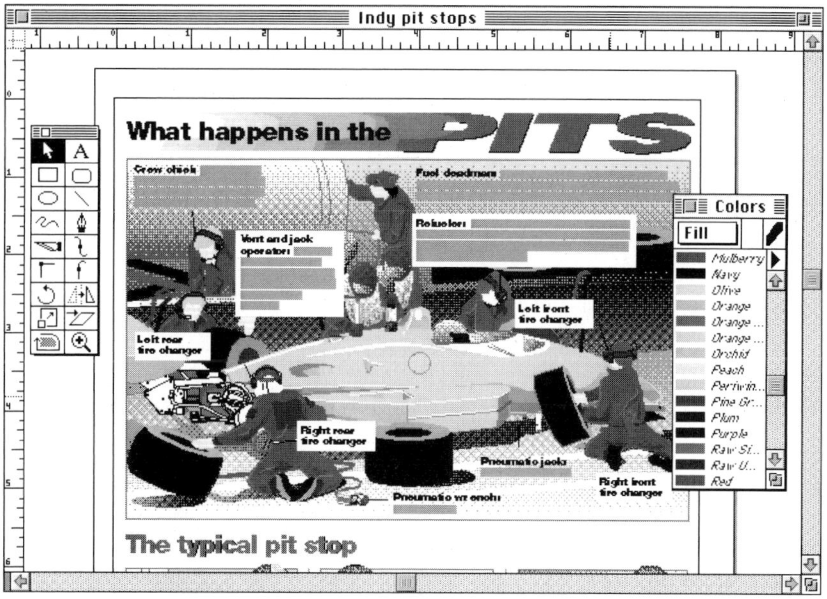

Figure 5.7
FreeHand's 99 undos and the ability to export its files as PICTs make it a good environment for drawing, but its text tools need work.

Illustrator

TOOLS
Adobe Illustrator Demo
223

Adobe Illustrator is a powerful design tool that includes superb text handling capabilities and handy automatic graphing (Figure 5.8). Some people prefer Illustrator's elegant interface to FreeHand's one-tool-for-each-job approach, but FreeHand still seems to be the more popular of the two. Multimedia producers will want to consider Illustrator's ability to save in an EPS file format that is fully compatible with Photoshop and Premiere, but EPS files are definitely not the norm

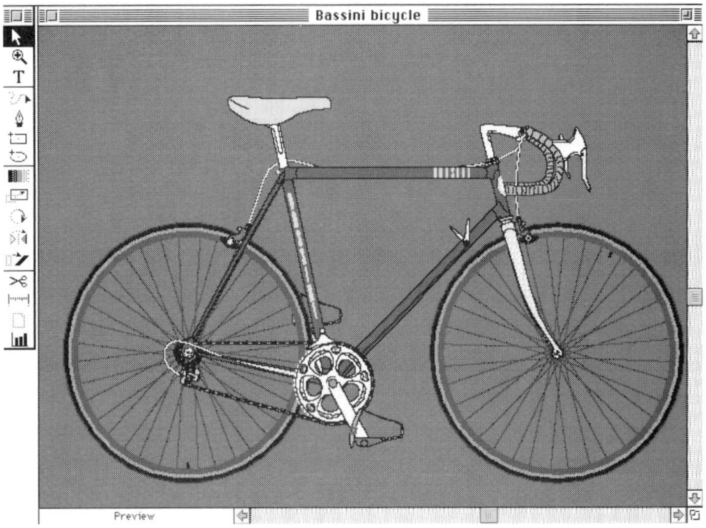

Figure 5.8 Illustrator is an excellent drawing program with good text handling features and seamless file compatibility with Photoshop.

for onscreen productions. One other advantage of using Illustrator is that clipping paths created in Photoshop can be imported and exported between the two programs easily.

MacDraw Pro

Claris's MacDraw Pro is a solid draw program for both new users and those with a bit more experience (Figure 5.9). As a professional drawing tool, however, it doesn't compare with Canvas, FreeHand, or Illustrator. It is System 7–savvy and supports QuickTime. Multimedia producers on a shoestring will appreciate its

Figure 5.9 MacDraw Pro is a good program for novices, but more advanced users will want to consider FreeHand, Illustrator, or Canvas.

support for a variety of file formats, but you can get Canvas and all of its advanced features for about the same price.

Image Processing Software

Despite the great number of capable design programs and the beautiful art that can be created using them, multimedia imagery more often comes from the real world.

Photographs, video captures, art, and 3-D objects can all be scanned in and used as the basis for multimedia design elements. In fact, it is quite common for designers to scan *rocks* to achieve the granite look so popular these days. For more information on scanners and the scanning process, see Chapter 4 "Hardware Peripherals."

Scanners provide quick and relatively easy access to a huge array of imagery, and the quality of scanned images is very high. Image processing software provides the opportunity to meld scanned imagery with paint and type effects, thus creating unified images that can be imported into multimedia presentations.

Basic Features

Images can be manipulated in almost any way imaginable through a variety of tools. Image processing programs are very similar to paint programs in that they work on data at the pixel level. In fact, many of the tools in image processing programs are identical to those in paint software. Image processing software, however, usually includes special functions to retouch and enhance scanned images and provide high-resolution printed output.

Tools

Color image processing programs like Photoshop and ColorStudio include refinements of basic design and selection tools found in paint programs. For example, the *magic wand* lets you select all connected pixels of common or similar hues. A *feathered* selection includes pixels outside the selection boundaries, which it fades to give a misty effect.

Like the lasso, Photoshop's *pen* is a tool that allows selection of irregular areas of an image. But the pen allows more precise selection, outlining areas by drawing *bezier curves.* The area of selection can then be modified after the fact by clicking and dragging the curves' control points.

Color Control

Image processing software can be used in lieu of stand-alone paint programs, but it is more useful for its array of filters that allow you to manipulate and totally change the appearance of images, and for its unsurpassed color retouching capabilities. It allows you to separate an image into its various color components, or *channels.* You can work with each channel separately, adjusting color, contrast, and brightness. Exact control over color is further extended through *remapping,* in which you modify colors by adjusting a *colormap curve*—a graphic representation of an individual color.

Some programs, such as Photoshop and ColorStudio, even have color separation capabilities, and offer multiple adjustments for color values and levels. The ability of these programs to do real-time CMYK color editing is a real advantage for those using desktop color separators. Before these features were available, if you wanted to retouch or manipulate images and produce files for four-color printing, you'd have to work in the computer's native RGB mode and then convert to CMYK.

Retouching and Filtering

Retouching tools include "water drop" and "finger," which can smooth specific areas by spreading pixels around. The individual attributes of retouching tools can be precisely specified. For example, you can set paintbrush shading preferences so that shading alternates between light and dark over a specified period of time. You can also set width, rate of paint flow, and so forth.

Filtering is one of the most delightful of the features of these amazing programs. Using special effects filters, you can blur and diffuse images, sharpen, posterize, outline contours, and trace edges. Wave and ripple filters produce interesting effects, and you can even turn an object into a sphere, complete with light reflections, refractions and transparency. Edge detection filters, which outline an image so that just its edges remain, are used to create embossed effects.

Industry leading programs like Photoshop offer more than a dozen such filters, and you can buy third-party plug-ins that supply supplementary filters. Paint programs usually include some filtering effects, but none approach the diversity and capabilities of image processing software.

There are a variety of image processing programs available. A brief discussion of some of the most popular follows. You should remember that no one program is likely to fill all of your needs. For example, many people rely on Photoshop for heavy-duty image handling and manipulation, and on a more intuitive painting package such as Painter for creating images from scratch or for applying artistic effects. Make sure the software you choose can handle the appropriate file formats and that its files can be easily ported to any multimedia creation or authoring software you might use.

ColorStudio

Fractal Design's ColorStudio (Figure 5.10) has long been a second cousin to Adobe's powerhouse, Photoshop. While ColorStudio is not the industry-standard image processing program that Photoshop is, its features are comparable, and it even offers a few surprises. ColorStudio is a very dense program and is definitely not for the faint of heart. While providing all the image manipulation and enhancement features of a good image processing program, it also has a decent suite of drawing tools. ColorStudio has the ability to convert text into editable paths and to access special characters not available from the keyboard.

ColorStudio's filters are numerous and powerful, some more powerful than Photoshop's. The program does support Photoshop filters and can import

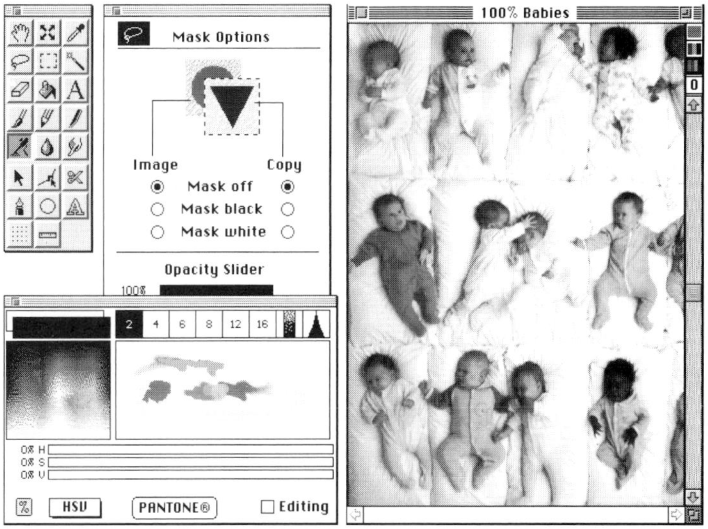

Figure 5.10 ColorStudio's features are almost equal to those of Photoshop, but it lacks any clear superiority to the ubiquitous Adobe product.

Photoshop files. Users with limited disk space may want to consider wheter they can give up over 5Mb of disk space and wade through the three manuals it takes to cover all the features.

ColorStudio is a close second to Photoshop in both functionality and ease of use. Multimedia producers will find it very useful, but need to ask themselves if they can afford to swim against the Photoshop tide.

Photoshop

Adobe Photoshop (Figure 5.11) is nothing less than an industry standard for image processing and handling. Its presence is so widespread that not using it might be considered heresy. Serious multimedia producers simply must have this program.

Photoshop's initial claim to fame was its sophisticated color editing and color separation capabilities, which it brought to the desktop for the first time. For the multimedia producer, its photo editing and filtering features are probably of more interest.

TOOLS
Adobe Photoshop 222

Photoshop groups filters to speed identification and selection. There are some interesting ones in addition to the familiar blur and sharpen filters. The Wind filter streaks images as if they were rushing by a camera lens. The Tiles filter splits an image into a mosaic pattern, while Crystallize gives a stained-glass effect. The emphasis is always on control. For instance, the Wind filter has three separate streaking directions, and Tile can be set according to the number of tiles as well as their offsets.

Those working with video will find good use for PhotoShop's video filters, which remove even or odd scan lines from video images and interpolate pixels to create a smooth image. A filter that restricts image colors to those that will reproduce most accurately on videotape or television is also excellent. New dodge and burn tools are fantastic, as is a new color correction method based on choosing an image that looks best to the user and not on arbitrary individual color channel changes.

Figure 5.11 Photoshop is a "must-have" for serious multimedia producers, and its features, except text handling, are generally beyond compare.

Photoshop also lets you import EPS (Encapsulated PostScript) files and treat them as vector images. This is important because PostScript is an industry standard and many graphics are stored in the EPS format. Photoshop's support for vector images is not as extensive as ColorStudio's, however.

Photoshop is renowned for its user interface, which is approachable and deceptively simple. In fact, it wins the ultimate accolade in this respect: for all but the most advanced work, you might think you don't need the manual. However, the manual is clearly written, contains color graphics, and includes tips on how to get the most out of the tools and filters. Also, it covers shortcuts that are nearly impossible to find by coincidence, but are extremely useful once they are used.

New on the Scene

TOOLS
DeBabelizer Demo 228

PROJECTS
PageMaker Demo 040

Two image editing newcomers are of particular value to multimedia developers. The first is DeBabelizer from Equilibrium Technologies. DeBabelizer, which has been described as an "image operating system," simplifies many repetitive image processing tasks. The program translates from and to over 40 graphics file formats, and lets you automate, or "batch" tedious manipulation and editing operations. DeBabelizer, only released in 1993, has already won the hearts and minds of professionals across the range of multimedia, from animators to interactive programmers.

"I can't say enough good things about it," says Matthew Fass, a multimedia producer for Ikonic in San Francisco. "An extremely useful batch processor." Among its many functions, DeBabelizer uses a "Super Palette," which automatically creates the best palette for a series of images, reducing the "dithering" that degrades image quality. For a description of this process see the PageMaker Demo project on the Power Tools CD.

Another new image editing program is Advanced Imaging S.A.'s Live Picture. The high-end program (which sells for thousands of dollars) lets you perform

Under Pressure

Graphics tablets, devices that use a natural-feeling "pen" instead of the more conventional Macintosh mouse as a pointing device, have recently achieved great popularity. Their appeal lies in the superior precision and control users have over the movement of their on-screen cursor and tools. While drawing or painting with a mouse has been likened to creating with a bar of soap, graphics tablets, such as those from Wacom, Kurta, and CalComp, use lightweight, smooth-handling "pens" that are a natural extension of the hand. With the support of a multitude of programs, graphics tablets have become "must-have" devices for any serious user of drawing or painting programs.

Pressure sensitivity is a feature of an increasing number of tablets that has taken the painting and drawing realm by storm. Pens designed to react with great precision to downward pressure on the tablet have enhanced the usefulness and creativity of software that supports them. Technically, the workings of pressure-sensitive graphics tablets are fairly complicated, but fortunately, their application is simple and straightforward. With the right software and a little practice, users become unaware of how they are using a pen and can transfer more energy and concentration to their work.

Pressure-sensitive pens incorporate tiny switches in their tips that act like a mouse button when clicked or double-clicked against the tablet. Pressed against the tablet with varying force, the pens act like a pencil does on paper. Press lightly and a light line is drawn, press hard and the line becomes thicker.

Painting software, especially, has made great use of the capabilities of pressure-sensitive tablets. Painter, by Fractal Designs, includes extensive support for pressure sensitivity. Using tools like felt pens, charcoal, and, of course, paintbrushes, users can create stunningly un-computer-like paintings. Brushstrokes can start out as a delicate whisper and end with dense gusto. Felt pens can be made to increase in color application as pressure is applied. Precise control over selections becomes second nature. The ability to trace hand-drawn art, maps, or photographs with a tablet and a pen is worth the price of the hardware alone if you do that kind of work often and find using a mouse unbearable.

While all pressure-sensitive tablets will increase a user's capabilities, it is important to consider features. Wacom tablets are known for quality construction, speed, and superior feel. CalComp tablets offer good value for the money and are lightweight. Many Kurta tablets include on-tablet selection of often-used commands. Consider tablets that use non-battery-powered cordless pens. Tablets that connect through the serial port of a Mac are generally faster than their ADB-attached counterparts. Some also allow the use of a puck, a sort of mouse without a tail, for more precision.

Among the packages that include support for pressure-sensitive tablets are Photoshop, FreeHand, Illustrator, ColorStudio, Painter, Sketcher, SuperPaint, and Canvas.

complex operations on gigantic images in seconds. The secret of Live Picture's high powered performance lies in a technology called Functional Interpolating Transformation System, or FITS.

FITS lets you manipulate large files (of up to 1 gigabyte), performing rotations, scaling and zooming in near real time. While Live Picture itself may be out of reach of the average desktop experimenter, look for the FITS technology to pop up in mainstream programs costing less than $1000.

Images on Screen

Now that we've covered the software needed to create, enhance, and manipulate images for multimedia productions, what do you need to worry about next? Why, getting them to look good when displayed, of course. There is a big difference between preparing images for printing and preparing them for viewing on a computer monitor or television screen. Most of the problems have to do with color and how it is represented by different media and the hardware associated with those media. The technical details could fill an entire book this size, so we will cover only the very basic concepts here.

As a multimedia producer, you will generally be producing work for presentation on a computer screen or monitor of some sort. This means that you have much less to worry about than someone producing a piece that is to be printed. Images presented on a screen do not need to be created at the high resolutions (from 300 to over 2000 dots per inch) of output to a printer. Most monitors have resolutions of from 72 to 90 dpi depending on the size of the tube and the display card used. Lower resolution images mean smaller file sizes. A full-color image at 72 dpi will take up a little less than 1Mb of hard disk space. While 1Mb files can quickly turn into monsters if you have enough of them, they're much easier to work with than the multimegabyte files routinely used for output to paper.

TOOLS Klutzz 132

Color is one of the main factors involved in showing images on a screen. Without going into the intricacies of bit-depths, color look-up tables, and color models, there are some basic things multimedia producers need to consider when displaying images on screen. First, how many colors can your computer display on the screen at one time?

TOOLS DepthKey 140
ColorSwitch 152

Macintosh computers equipped with 8-bit monitor cards or on-board video (up to 256 colors per screen pixel) are satisfactory for working with most images; however, to work in "full color" or to see images onscreen with photographic quality, you will need a 24-bit monitor card. These cards can display up to 16.7 million colors per screen pixel. (See Figure 5.12 for a comparison of 8-bit and 24-bit color.) What most people tend to forget when throwing around such numbers related to monitors and the colors they display is that humans can only discern about 380,000 colors. If your hardware will allow it, you should work in 16-bit mode, which allows the display of over 65,000 colors. This is usually more than adequate for viewing images onscreen, and it allows your computer to work faster because it doesn't have to crunch as much color data.

Figure 5.12 The difference between images viewed in 8-bit and 24-bit color can be seen in this illustration . However, be aware that 24-bit color has large processing and storage requirements that could bog-down your project.

The second issue related to color and images involves what are known as color *gamuts*. For multimedia producers whose final output will be to videotape or some sort of regular television screen and not a computer display, the issue of color gamuts is very important. Basically, a color gamut is a fancy name for the array of colors that can be displayed or printed to a specific output device.

There are colors that can be displayed on a computer monitor, but not on a regular television screen. Moreover, there are colors that can be displayed by a television screen or computer monitor but cannot be printed on paper, and vice versa. For example, certain printing presses have no problem printing metallic gold onto a sheet of paper, but reproducing that same metallic gold on a computer monitor or television screen is impossible. Thus, a printing press has a certain color gamut, or colors it can reproduce, and computer monitors and television screens have their own respective color gamuts.

Since most multimedia products will be viewed on a monitor or screen of some sort, the trick is to keep all the colors you use for your images within the capabilities of those devices. When you are dealing with output to standard television screens (those which adhere to some sort of color broadcast standard, like the North American Television Standards Committee standard), however, the trick becomes, well, tricky.

Fortunately, some software has the ability to restrict the colors you are using for an image to those considered "safe" for display on a television screen. Adobe Photoshop, for example, has a filter called "NTSC-legal colors" which, when applied to an image, adjusts the colors in that image to those within a TV's capabilities (Figure 5.13). Adobe Premiere, Fractal Design's Painter, and Color It! are some of the programs that possess the ability to adjust images for "NTSC-legal" colors.

Figure 5.13 Photoshop's NTSC-legal colors filter comes in handy when converting colors in images for viewing on a regular television screen.

Photo CD

One of the most promising innovations to affect multimedia producers who work frequently with still images is Kodak's Photo CD system (Figure 5.14). If you haven't seen the commercials, a description of how the system works and the hardware you require can be found in Chapter 4, "Hardware Peripherals." What the Photo CD system promises for those who handle lots of images is great convenience and time saving.

Film can be sent to Kodak for processing and returned to you in the form of developed negatives or slides, along with prints and a special type of CD-ROM called a Photo CD. A Photo CD can hold up to 100 images. These can be put on the CD at different times. For example, you can bring 25 slides to be put on a Photo CD one week, 50 more the next, and 25 more a month later. This capability, called "multisession capability" is new to the CD-ROM field, and hardware and software producers have been scrambling to add this feature to their products.

Photo CD images are scanned onto the disc at five different resolutions: 3072×2048, 1536×1024, 768×512, 384×256, and 192×128 pixels. The largest size is meant to be used for printing, the 1536×1024 size matches the HDTV format, and the 768×512 size is for display on a monitor. The smallest size is used for thumbnails (Figure 5.14). Compression factors in all but the two smallest sizes, and Kodak claims that the proprietary compression algorithms applied to the larger sizes results in no perceivable loss in image quality.

Kodak has recently introduced a number of new Photo CD formats aimed at professionals. These include the Pro Photo CD Master disc, which stores images from 35mm and larger film formats; the Kodak Photo CD Portfolio disc, which boasts larger picture capacity for distribution of interactive multimedia elements; the Photo CD Catalog disc, for easy distribution of digital catalogs containing up to 6,000 images; and the Photo CD Medical disc, for storing medical diagnostic images.

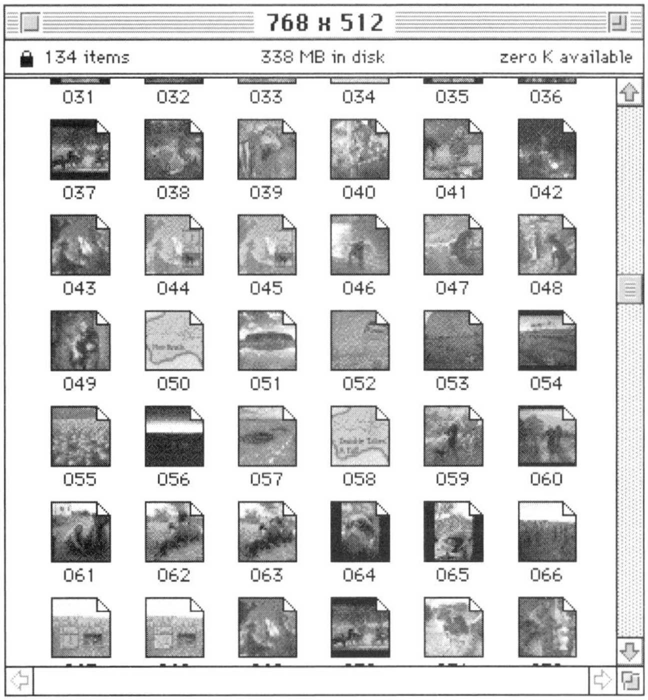

Figure 5.14 Kodak's Photo CD system presents users with the proper software and hardware to show a screen full of image thumbnails all scanned at varying resolutions.

Kodak sells a package for about $40, called Photo CD Access, which can open, display, and crop the images contained on Photo CDs. Photo CD Access also allows users to export Photo CD images in TIFF, EPS, and PICT formats. Kodak also markets a product called PhotoEdge, which provides all the same tools as Access, and also allows some limited image editing capability, such as sharpening a picture or adjusting color and contrast.

And there's more: Kodak Shoebox Image Manager Software allows you to create a database to manage thousands of images, QuickTime movies, and audio files; and Kodak Browser is a licensable, scaled-down version of Shoebox that can be used to navigate Photo CD catalog discs. (See Chapter 10, "Outside Resources," for more information on image data bases.

Kodak also sells hardware "authoring" systems for creating your own Photo CD images. These would be economical only if you plan to regularly digitize large image catalogs; otherwise, taking your film to the local commercial Photo CD processor is the best way to go.

Adobe Photoshop has the ability to handle Photo CD images if the required Apple CD-ROM drivers are in place. Adobe also has a plug-in for direct access to Photo CDs, and Apple's QuickTime also supports the format. Kodak is pushing the Photo CD technology very hard, so it is safe to say that almost all software that deals with images will support Photo CDs in the future.

Kodak also has plans to license the Photo CD technology to other vendors and to introduce new kinds of Photo CDs. The company has announced upcoming support for larger film sizes through the use of a new scanner that will be able to handle larger film. Photo CD formats that hold catalogs of images and that allow the addition of sound to the images for complete slide shows are also in the works.

The great convenience of the Photo CD system is that multimedia producers can save enormous amounts of time by having Kodak do all the scanning of their slides and negatives and put them on a Photo CD. The images are scanned in at standard resolutions varried to suit anything from onscreen presentation to high-end printed output. If you had 100 slides to scan for your multimedia production, just think of how much time it would take to prepare, scan, and enhance each one. We're not trying to hype the Kodak system too much, but the time savings that can be realized, especially for those who work alone, are staggering.

Compression/ Decompression

When working with images, the issue of size becomes increasingly important—not the size of the image as displayed, but the size as stored on your hard disk. A color image at screen resolution takes up approximately 1Mb of disk space. While not a huge number by itself, imagine multiplying that by hundreds for a multimedia production that makes use of a lot of stills. Enter image compression and decompression. A look at compression and decompression and how it relates to video, animations, and QuickTime movies can be found in their respective chapters.

TOOLS
Picture DecomPress 130

Compression is a widely employed technique to reduce the size of large image files without appreciably changing the way a viewer sees the images. Once compressed, an image must be decompressed before it can be used. Compression and decompression take time because the processes are processor-intensive. The more a file is compressed, the more computer power it takes.

Compression and decompression can be accomplished by software alone or through the use of a combination of software and hardware. Compression software analyzes an image and finds ways to store the same amount of information using fewer bytes. Compression hardware usually consists of a ROM chip with built-in compression routines for faster operation, or a coprocessor chip that shares the computing load with the computer's main processor.

Differing levels of compression are usually offered through the software. *Non-lossy* or *lossless* compression means that no information is lost or thrown out as a result of the compression process. Images look unchanged after compression, but the file size is not reduced as much as with *lossy* compression schemes. Lossy compression discards more information as it compresses, thereby reducing file sizes dramatically. However, images might not look as good as they did before they were compressed. *Pixilation*, or the appearance of blocks of color in areas of solid tones, is a usual result of drastic lossy compression methods.

The most common method for compressing images is called *JPEG compression.* "JPEG" stands for the Joint Photographic Experts Group, which came up with a standard way of reducing image file sizes that discards information the human eye could never discern. JPEG compression methods are used by image processing software such as Photoshop and ColorStudio and by multimedia software like Premiere and VideoFusion.

Compression and decompression of images is a complicated process made easier by standard methods like JPEG and powerful new hardware to free the computer's main processor from extra work. Multimedia producers who expect to use many large images should consider exploring further the available options. Compression and decompression are here to stay for a while, at least until we can buy computers with unlimited speed, power, disk space, and bandwidth.

For more information on compression as it relates to video and animation, see Chapter 3, "Mac Software and Hardware," and Chapter 8, "Video Tools."

Using Images with Multimedia Software

Software for producing multimedia is in many ways like a glorified meat grinder. You throw video images captured from cameras and VCRs—animations, audio recordings, backgrounds, and still images or graphics—at the software, and, with a bit of work, you can produce a fantastic presentation. Obviously, there is a lot more to it than "a bit of work." For information on using images within multimedia applications see the appropriate "Tools" and "Creating" chapters throughout the rest of the book.

6

Sound Tools

There's no doubt that multimedia presentations have a greater impact when sound is integrated into the production. You only need to view a videotape for a minute or two with the volume turned off to realize the importance of the marriage of sound to visual imagery. In nonlinear interactive environments, sound can aid in navigation in the same way that graphic backgrounds, button groupings, or color schemes orient users to their current location in the program.

The value of a memorable musical "logo" or sound effect is easier to grasp when you realize that those whose livelihood is creating such sonic materials often command up to $10,000 a second, and sometimes licensing fees as well as residuals. Consider the associative properties of the Delta Airlines sound logo or the sound effect you hear when you use your calling card on an AT&T phone line.

And consider this example of aural power: Back in the 1950s and '60s, we baby-boomers would often be playing outside on Sunday evenings. Suddenly, from various windows, we'd hear the strains of "When You Wish Upon a Star" and we'd all rush inside to watch *Walt Disney Presents* on television. In the 1970s, when so many of us became excruciatingly health conscious, MacDonalds suddenly changed its musical logo to "You Deserve a Break Today," using a melody remarkably similar to the Disney tune. Were they hoping that all of us health-food fanatics would march off for a Big Mac in a trance reminiscent of H.G. Wells's *Time Machine?* We'll probably never know, but there's little doubt that the jingle served as a powerful subliminal enticement for millions.

When it comes to desktop-based multimedia, the creation of decent music to fit a particular visual sequence is no small task. It can't be automated in the manner of, say, animation. You can hold down the Shift key to draw a straight line in many graphics programs, but you can't hold down any key to compose a beautiful melody.

It's common to divide multimedia into five data types: video, animation, still graphics, text, and sound. However, these really fall into two larger data groups: Video and audio, and the latter can be subdivided into music, sound effects, ambiance, and narration. Apple reaffirmed these two super classes of data when it released QuickTime with two tracks: one for movies and one for sound. The movie track can hold all four types of visual data and the sound track can contain all four types of audio data.

Types of sound can be broken down even further. Speech can occur either as dialog or voice-over. Similarly, to borrow a few terms from the film industry, music can be either *source music* or *underscore*. Sometimes called score or, erroneously, background music, underscore is devoted to reinforcing, commenting on, or otherwise enhancing the dramatic content of the film. In all cases, underscore is music that would not be present if the scene were occurring in reality—the characters in the scene would not be able to hear it. On the other hand, source music is music that would be present if the scene were played out in reality—it might be coming from a radio, record player, night club band, or Muzak; in other words, source music is music that the characters in the scene would be hearing in their current situation. A further distinction is between visual source music, where we, the audience, can see the source of the sound, and nonvisual source music (sometimes called off-screen music), where we can't see the source but we can believe it is there (for example, a car radio heard in an interior shot of the back seat of a car).

There are rough correlations between music and video, sound effects and animation, still graphics and ambiance, and text and narration. The interrelation of the four sound elements is just as important as the interrelation of the four visual elements. And, like the various visual components, the music, sound effects, ambiance, and narration can be assembled separately—and are sometimes assembled by different specialists. Sound can be added to a project before, during, or after the visuals. Finally, your sound or musical data can be delivered in three different flavors: MIDI (Musical Instrument Digital Interface), 8-bit digital audio, or 16-bit digital audio. Some projects combine all three formats.

This chapter will examine some of the tools you can use to create and manipulate sound in multimedia.

Sampling and Sound Capture

The most popular form of sound used in multimedia is called *sampled* sound or digital audio. Another format, called MIDI (Musical Instrument Digital Interface), is a much more efficient and desirable way to deliver sound in a multimedia presentation, but current computers are not equipped to easily accommodate MIDI data for multimedia purposes. The difference between sampled sound and MIDI is very similar to the difference between bitmapped fonts and outline fonts, such as those offered by PostScript or TrueType: Bitmapped fonts contain the actual visual data to create font characters, whereas outline fonts contain instructions that control an output device.

The Speed of Sound

Digital audio relies on a phenomenon similar to persistence of vision in a film, video, or QuickTime movie. To achieve the illusion of visual motion, many consecutive still images are displayed as quickly as required. Although motion in the real world exists within a continuous, or *analog*, sequence, only 24 frames per second are necessary to fool our eyes into believing that we are seeing a representation of reality. Sound also is fundamentally continuous. Sound sampling captures still "snapshots" (called samples or frames) of a sound. To recreate the illusion of the original sound, these samples are played back very rapidly.

While the eye may be tricked by 24 frames per second (30 frames per second is the standard for American video), sound requires between 5000 and 48,000 samples per second to achieve comparable results. This wide range of playback rates affects aural realism in the same way that the frame rate of a film, video, or QuickTime movie affects visual realism.

As a reference point, consider that the rate used on an audio compact disc is 44,100 samples per second, or 44.1 *kilohertz* (kHz). Because at least two samples are required to represent any one frequency (according to a mathematician named Nyquist), digital audio on a compact disc can faithfully reproduce sounds up to 22.05 kHz, which correlates to the upper end of the spectrum for human hearing. Although the highest note of a piano is 4.186 kHz, well below the 22.05 kHz supported by CD-quality digital audio, many higher frequencies (called *overtones* or *harmonics)* are present in any given waveform. These overtones are what color a sound's timbre and provide the information that allows us to distinguish between a note being played on a piano and that same pitch being played on a flute or violin.

Digital Sound Sampling

Sample resolution plays an equal part in the faithful reproduction of sound through digital means (see Figure 6.1). Sample resolution refers to the number of bits used to represent the individual samples that are being output at 44.1, 22.05, or 11 kHz. Sample resolution exerts a similar effect upon the ear as the number of bits used to represent a pixel exerts upon the eye.

Two sample resolutions are common: 8-bit and 16-bit. The former restricts the range of sample values to 256, while the latter allows for 65,536 steps between values. The distinction is not as analogous to the difference between 8-bit color and 16-bit color as you might suspect; 8-bit sound sounds like an AM radio, whereas 16-bit sound is used on compact discs. Because each bit used to represent a sound sample adds 6 dB (decibels) to the signal-to-noise ratio of a sound, 8-bit sampling has a 48 dB signal-to-noise ratio, while 16-bit sampling approaches 96 dB. Current generation Macintosh hardware supports built-in 8-bit audio, although 16-bit Macintoshes are under development at the time of this writing.

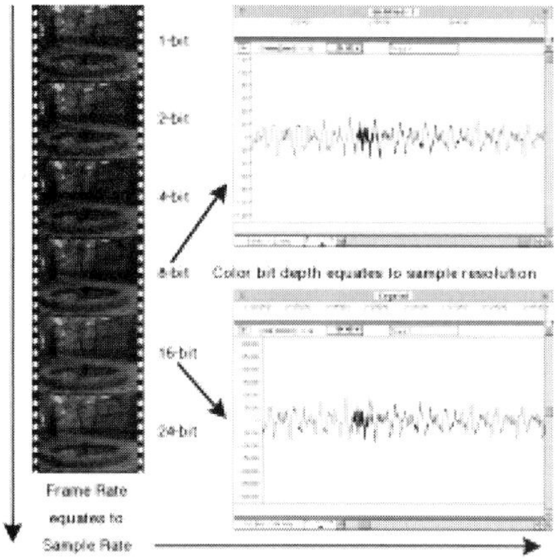

Figure 6.1
The factors influencing realism in digital audio are identical to those in film, video, and QuickTime. Audio sampling rate corresponds to frame rate, and sample resolution corresponds to color depth.

Recording Media

There are various ways you can record and store sounds before bringing them into your multimedia Mac environment. These include conventional analog recording tape, digital audio tape (DAT) and hard disk storage.

Analog Tape

Popular analog tape widths are ⅛ inch, ¼ inch, ½ inch, 1 inch, and 2 inch—each divided into 1, 2, 3, 4, 8, 16, or 24 horizontal tracks.

With analog tape, the larger the track width, the better the recording. However, noise reduction systems are available (and sometimes built in) to enhance the performance of ⅛ inch and ¼ inch systems (as well as ½ inch recorders) which divide the tape into 8 or more tracks. Transport speed is another factoring influencing fidelity because faster tape travel provides more horizontal space to encode additional audio data. Standard cassettes use 1⅞ inches per second (ips) or 3¾ ips for prosumer decks. Open reel recorders employ 7½, 15, and 30 ips transport speeds. Recorders that integrate a mixer into their box—the so-called "porta-studio" or "mini-studio" (usually cassette-based)—are an ideal solution for someone on a budget.

Digital Audio Tape (DAT)

Common digital audio tape widths are 4mm, 8mm, or ½ inch divided into 2, 4, or 8 tracks. Current disk-based systems range from 2 to 16 tracks. Speed of tape travel has no impact upon fidelity as practically all systems employ 16-bit samples at the industry standard rate of 44.1 kHz (although many decks offer options for 32 kHz and 48 kHz sample rates). By far the most popular format is 4mm DAT (digital audio tape), largely due to ever-dropping prices. Even systems offering more than 2 tracks and SMPTE-standard synchronization have dropped to the consumer price level. Newer formats such as DCC (Digital Compact Cassette) and MD (Mini-Disc), introduced by Phillips/Tandy and Sony respectively, promise even more affordable digital recording, albeit with some loss of fidelity.

Table 6.1 Storage Requirements for Digital Audio at Popular Sampling Rates TST Includes Audio Compressed with MACE (Macintosh Audio Compression and Expansion)

Sampling rate*	***Sample resolution***	***Channels***	***Number of bytes required for one minute of sound***
44.1 kHz	16-bit	Stereo	**10,584,000**
44.1 kHz	16-bit	Mono	**5,292,000**
22.254 kHz	8-bit	Stereo	**2,670,545**
22.254 kHz	8-bit	Mono	**1,335,273**
22.254 kHz with MACE 3:1	8-bit	Stereo	**890,182**
22.254 kHz with MACE 6:1	8-bit	Stereo	**445,091**
22.254 kHz with MACE 3:1	8-bit	Mono	**445,091**
22.254 kHz with MACE 6:1	8-bit	Mono	**222,545**
22.05 kHz	16-bit	Stereo	**5,292,000**
22.05 kHz	16-bit	Mono	**2,646,000**
22.05 kHz	8-bit	Stereo	**2,646,000**
22.05 kHz	8-bit	Mono	**1,323,000**
11.127 kHz	8-bit	Stereo	**1,335,273**
11.127 kHz	8-bit	Mono	**667,636**
11.127 kHz with MACE 3:1	8-bit	Mono	**222,545**
11.127 kHz with MACE 6:1	8-bit	Mono	**111,273**
11.025 kHz	16-bit	Stereo	**2,646,000**
11.025 kHz	16-bit	Mono	**1,323,000**
11.025 kHz	8-bit	Stereo	**1,323,000**
11.025 kHz	8-bit	Mono	**661,500**
7.418 kHz	8-bit	Stereo	**890,182**
7.418 kHz	8-bit	Mono	**445,091**
5.563 kHz	8-bit	Stereo	**667,636**
5.563 kHz	8-bit	Mono	**333,818**

*The sampling rates 22.05 kHz and 11.025 kHz are optimal for Sound Manager 3.0 (available with QuickTime 1.6), while 22.254, 11.127, 7.418, and 5.563 kHz are best for Sound Manager 2.0.

Hard Disk Recording

Hard disk-based systems can be stand-alone, expansion card-based, or involve hardware built into a computer (for example, 8-bit, 22kHz sampling features built into every Macintosh). With the exception of the latter, the recording specifications are predominantly 16-bit, 44.1 kHz.

There are many reasons to choose hard disk recording over analog tape. Having random access to any point in your soundfile allows you to use, reuse, and reorder sound material to your heart's content. That individual tracks are not physically time-aligned to one another, as they are on tape, offers similar benefits. Furthermore, tracks can be mixed in the digital domain *ad infinitum* without the signal degradation that occurs when you attempt to process in the world of analog tape.

Another advantage is that much of your editing is non-destructive, meaning that the original source material on your hard disk remains unchanged. EQs, fades, and other effects are applied on the fly during playback and even reusing and reordering of material is accomplished in real time.

About the only strike that hard disk recording systems have against them is the vast storage requirements (see Table 6.1). To store an hour of analog or digital tape will cost you less than $25, but that same hour of audio stored on a hard disk will require 600 MB of free disk space, and the hard disk itself will need to have an access time of greater than 28ms. If you are used to storing QuickTime and other memory-hungry visual material, you may not find the sound storage requirements to be a stumbling block.

The Sound Manager

Apple's Sound Manager utility takes care of recording, playback, and saving sound on the Macintosh at 8-bit or 16-bit resolutions (current hardware limits playback to 8-bit), at rates of up to 64 kHz (current hardware places a 22.254 kHz ceiling on the rate). Apple has promised that 1993 will see the release of Sound Manager 3.0, representing a major overhaul of this package of routines, resources, and drivers. Sound Manager 2.0 requires System 6.0 or greater (6.07 or greater for 8-bit sound input), whereas Sound Manager 3.0 may require System 7 or greater. Certain features of either version of the Sound Manager are only available if you are running System 7—in particular, direct-from-disk playback and multichannel sound. Further, your Macintosh model will dictate whether you hear the left, right, or both channels of a stereo sound when using its internal sound capabilities (see Table 6.2).

All Macintoshes since the IIsi have shipped with a sound input port optimized for their bundled microphone. You can still record sound using earlier Macintoshes, provided you have a third-party digitizer and your System folder contains the drivers that support it. Popular third-party 8-bit digitizers include Macromedia's MacRecorder, Premier Technology's MacMike, Articulate Systems' Voice Impact, Voice Impact Pro, and Voice Navigator, while CD-quality options come from

Table 6.2 Channel Capabilities of Various Macintosh Models (All Macintoshes support 8-bit, 22 kHz sound)

Model	*Internal speaker*	*External audio port*
Plus	left (channel)	left (channel)
SE	left	left
SE/30	mono mix of left and right	stereo
II	left	stereo
IIx	left	stereo
IIcx	left	stereo
IIci	left	stereo
IIfx	left	stereo
IIsi	mono mix of left and right	stereo
IIvx	mono mix of left and right	stereo
Classic I	left	left
Classic II	left	left
LC I	left	left
LC II	left	left
LC III	mono mix of left and right	stereo
Performa 400	left	left
Performa 600	left	left
Quadra series	mono mix of left and right	stereo
Centris series	mono mix of left and right	stereo
Powerbook 100	left	left
Powerbooks (others)	mono mix of left and right	stereo

Digidesign, Spectral Innovations (MacDSP), and MediaVision. Apple includes the drivers for many of these products on the QuickTime Developers' CD-ROM and also provides a driver for SID+, a build-it-yourself 8-bit digitizer, the schematics for which are available from most on-line services.

MACE, short for Macintosh Audio Compression and Expansion, is an audio compression scheme that reduces soundfile size to ⅓ or ⅙, depending upon whether you choose 3:1 or 6:1 compression. Note that 6:1 compression is not suitable for music; and once you have compressed a sound using any compression scheme, including those offered by some third parties, you will not be able to edit that sound with any current sample-editing software.

MACE will decompress sound while it is being played back (however, not on the Mac Plus, SE, or Portable), and provides sample rate conversion options for all Macintoshes on the Mac II and beyond.

Version 2.0 Problems

Sound Manager 2.0 has some bothersome characteristics, including one in particular (discussed in the next paragraph) that crops up when you use more than a single sound channel. Unfortunately, with the possibility of unlimited soundtracks in QuickTime, and the fact that many multimedia productions employ sound effects or narration in conjunction with musical tracks, multiple sound channels are the norm rather than the exception. Because we will be in a period of transition to Sound Manager 3.0 throughout 1993 and possibly into 1994, the lowest common denominator, platformwise, may still be Sound Manager 2.0—take steps accordingly.

Sound Manager 2.0's multichannel problem occurs because to output multiple channels, the software simply adds the sample values and divides by the number of channels for the purpose of scaling output volume to avoid clipping (a nasty phenomenon that occurs when your sample values exceed the maximum value of your sample resolution—i.e., your volume meters are in the red). The result is that the volume of two tracks is sealed to 50% of normal, four tracks to 25% of normal, and so on. This won't be a problem if you have continuous sound on all tracks. Unfortunately, music, narration, and sound effects are likely to drop in and out, and every time this occurs there will be an immediate and drastic reduction or increase of volume.

To get around Sound Manager 2.0's undesirable multichannel sound implementation, you can keep unused tracks playing silence at all times. The downside is that certain authoring programs will reserve space in your file even for these predominantly empty tracks and increase the storage requirements significantly. Premixing your multiple tracks down to a single track using dedicated sound editors such as SoundEdit Pro, Audioshop, or Alchemy is the best solution if you are forced to accommodate Sound Manager 2.0. (See the section on sound editors below.)

Version 3.0: The Way to Go

Apple's Sound Manager 3.0 has solved the multichannel problem and adds a great number of new and useful features. Among the new features are device independence—with the appropriate drivers, 16-bit tracks will automatically be routed to NuBus cards that can handle them. Forthcoming Macintoshes eventually will support built-in 16-bit audio, and Sound Manager 3.0 will be ready for them when they are released. Until then, Sound Manager 3.0 performs automatic 16-bit-to-8-bit file conversions. While Sound Manager 2.0 performed such processor-intensive (read: reduced frame rate for QuickTime) conversions by throwing away every other sample and dropping the low byte of every 16-bit word, Sound Manager 3.0 offers better methods for sample conversion.

Another feature of Sound Manager 3.0 is support of plug-in audio CODECs (compressor/decompressors). Such sound compression/decompression schemes automatically will be available to the Sound Manager and Sound Manager-compatible software. This digital signal processing pipeline also will provide for plug-in software-based digital EQs, filters, reverbs, and many DSP functions that usually require external hardware. The drop-in modular approach allows third parties to develop components (sometimes called "sifters") to enhance Macintosh-based sound. Sound Manager 3.0 will include a number of these components, including a sample rate converter, a mixer, and CODECs for MACE and ADPCM (a popular DOS/MPC 4:1 compression format).

Finally, Sound Manager 3.0 plays back 2 to 3 times faster than its predecessor which allows for increasing QuickTime frame rates by 1 to 3 frames-per-second. Apple guarantees full compatibility with Sound Manager 2.0, even though the standard sampling rates have change slightly (22.05 and 11.025 kHz in Sound Manager 3.0, as opposed to 22.254 and 11.127 kHz in the previous version).

Sound Manager 3.0 and QuickTime

TOOLS QuickTime Extension 160

QuickTime relies heavily on the Sound Manager. QuickTime 1.5 and earlier used Sound Manager 2.0. To use Sound Manager 3.0 with QuickTime, you will need QuickTime version 1.6 or beyond. Theoretically, QuickTime's dependence upon the Sound Manager means it can store an unlimited number of audio tracks in any combination of stereo, mono, 8-bit, or 16-bit, and at any sampling rate up to 64 kHz. QuickTime 1.5 and earlier mix all tracks down to one monophonic 8-bit track on output.

Sound does add processing overhead to QuickTime movie playback, and this can increase the CPU load by 25% to 50%, lowering your effective data rate (frames per second) accordingly. With this in mind, don't expect to reliably play more than four channels on a Mac Plus or Classic, four to eight on an LC, or 12 to 24 on a Quadra. If your sound is compressed with MACE (or ADPCM with Sound Manager 3.0), the processor time associated with on-the-fly decompression will have a negative impact on the speed of your visual elements.

Sound Digitizers

If your Macintosh does not support sound input through built-in hardware (look for a microphone jack on the back panel), there are still many options for sound digitization open to you. Third-party external digitizers and NuBus cards offer compatible or better-quality sampling for any Macintosh. Some popular examples for multimedia production follow.

MacRecorder

Macromedia's MacRecorder package includes a self-powered 8-bit monophonic digitizer box that connects to either of your serial ports. You need two MacRecorders for stereo sampling, and you can also use two MacRecorders to achieve stereo recording on Macintoshes that provide monophonic sound input. The full package includes SoundEdit Pro software (see below).

Voice Impact Pro

Articulate Systems Voice Impact Pro is an 8-bit digitizer similar to MacRecorder, with one important distinction: MACE compression is built into Voice Impact Pro (the non "Pro" version has no on-board compression). Having MACE built into the hardware allows you to use the compression scheme on pre-System 6.07 Macintoshes and also frees up CPU time required to apply the compression algorithm.

The full package includes SoundWave software, although you can use Voice Impact Pro soundfiles with any sample editor.

16-bit NuBus Cards

The built-in sound input and the external digitizers just mentioned currently limit you to 8-bit sampling at 22 kHz. For 16-bit, 44.1 kHz (CD-quality) recording, you will have to add a NuBus card to your computer. Available options are Digidesign's Sound Tools, Audiomedia, and Pro Tools packages; Mark of the Unicorn's Digital WaveBoard; and MediaVision's Pro Audio Spectrum 16. For direct-to-hard-disk recording, you should have an unfragmented, preferably high-capacity, hard drive with a seek time of 28 ms or less. Drive mechanisms that perform thermal recalibration too frequently are not suitable for hard disk recording or playback.

Audiomedia and Audiomedia II

Digidesign's original Audiomedia card and its current Audiomedia II card are excellent solutions for multimedia production requiring CD-quality audio. At $1295, the only thing less expensive is MediaVision's Pro Audio Spectrum 16 board, which limits you to stereo soundfiles. Most QuickTime capture boards will work in conjunction with an Audiomedia card if they detect one on the NuBus. The RasterOps MediaTime board includes the Audiomedia hardware.

Video Cards That Capture Audio

QuickTime video capture cards usually provide some mechanism for recording sound either during the recording of video or after the fact. Note that you will achieve better frame rates if you record video and audio separately. If you choose to add sound later, most multimedia authoring software can accommodate you (see Chapter 9, "Authoring Tools," for more details). Just recording your sound as a sound-only QuickTime movie is usually sufficient to make it available to other software. Use Audioshop, Director, or PROmotion for this. Any QuickTime editing program will let you combine the sound with a QuickTime video; or you can choose to use SoundToMovie, the HyperCard QuickTime stack, or Audioshop.

Spigot and Sound Pro, and DigitalFilm

SuperMac's VideoSpigot and Sound Pro accomplish 8-bit sound recording at sampling rates up to 22 kHz by bundling a Macromedia MacRecorder (see above) with the package. If you require higher fidelity, SuperMac's DigitalFilm card offers 44.1 kHz at a nonstandard 10-bit resolution. Remember that the extra two bits will theoretically only increase your signal-to-noise ratio by 12 dB (bringing it up to 60 dB).

VideoVision

Radius's VideoVision card is particularly versatile for sound capture. It is the only card currently offering treble and bass controls in addition to volume adjustment on input. VideoVision's external connector box offers options to mix non-Macintosh-based audio with QuickTime output to bypass current generation 8-bit, 22 kHz limitations. Further, VideoVision will "take over" any Audiomedia card it finds on the NuBus to provide CD-quality recording.

MediaTime

As we have mentioned, RasterOps' MediaTime has Digidesign's Audiomedia hardware built right onto the card. This allows MediaTime to offer stereo sampling at either 8-bit or 16-bit resolution and at rates up to 44.1 kHz. Note that most current generation multimedia authoring software will not play back 16-bit, 44.1 kHz sound at full resolution.

Sound Editing Software

Sound editing software is crucial to multimedia production, if only for mixing soundfiles and adding fades. However, sampling editors offer as many important bells and whistles as many image-processing programs. Cut, copy, and paste procedures let you reorder and reuse music and sound material to create endless new arrangements from an existing file. Like their image manipulating counterparts, most sound editors support the full range of soundfile formats that your authoring software will require. For example, SoundEdit Pro supports SoundEdit, Sound Designer II, AIFF, Instrument, 'snd' resource, and System 7 soundfile formats.

The standard representation of a soundfile is a waveform timeline made up of dots or lines, the height of which indicates amplitude at any point in time. Such displays are usually zoomable, so you can edit with the precision of a single sample—that's 1/44, 100th of a second in the case of CD-quality sound.

Where sample editors really shine is in the area of digital signal processing and special effects. Menu options typically offer amplification, various types of fades, equalization, sound reversal, pitch bending, echo, flanging, and reverberation. Time compression and expansion is a useful (but not standard) option that lets you lengthen or shorten a soundfile or region thereof without changing its pitch. Conversely, pitch shifting lets you change the key of your soundfile without effecting its duration.

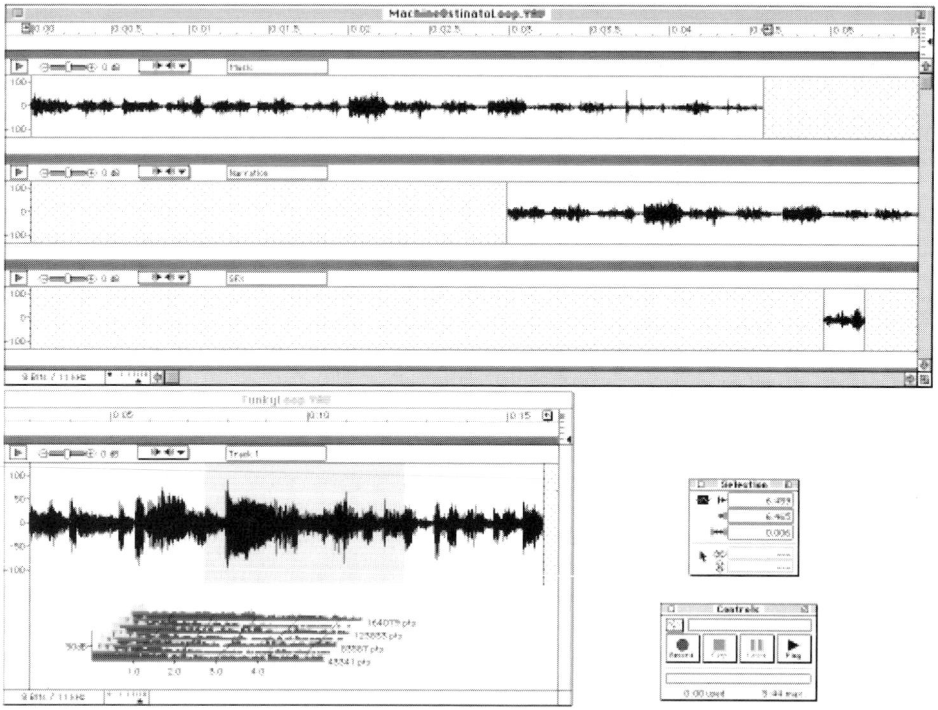

Figure 6.2 Macromedia's SoundEdit Pro is the foremost sound editor for multimedia. The software supports multiple tracks of direct-to-and from-disk digital audio in many file formats, and provides for extensive editing and effects.

SoundEdit Pro

SoundEdit Pro 201

Farallon's SoundEdit and its current incarnation as Macromedia's SoundEdit Pro are the most popular 8-bit sample editors. The software may be purchased as a bundle with Macromedia's MacRecorder 8-bit, 22 kHz digitizer (see above), although it will function perfectly well with sound digitized using any device, including the built-in options of newer Macintoshes.

SoundEdit Pro is a necessity if you need to record 8-bit sound directly to hard disk—that is, for soundfiles that will not fit in your available RAM. The software supports 8-bit stereo sampling at 22 kHz, 11 kHz, 7.3 kHz, and 5.5 kHz. In addition to 6:1 and 3:1 compression, SoundEdit offers proprietary 4:1 and 8:1 compression options.

Although you can edit 16-bit soundfiles sampled at 44.1 and 48 kHz, SoundEdit Pro does not provide any option for playing these CD-quality sounds at a fidelity higher than the native Macintosh's 8-bit, 22 kHz.

Of all the 8-bit sound editors, SoundEdit Pro (see Figure 6.2) offers the most processing options. These include mix, amplify, reverse, bend, echo, reverb, graphic envelope editing, 5-band graphic EQ, flanging, rudimentary FM synthesis, emphasize (to boost upper harmonics), noise gating, pitch shifting, and time compression/expansion.

SoundWave

SoundWave (see Figure 6.3) is an editor that ships with a variety of multimedia tools; notably, Articulate System's Voice Impact Pro. Compared to those of

SoundEdit Pro, its editing options are somewhat limited, and recordings must fit into RAM rather than be stored directly to disk. Although the same sampling rates are supported, if you are using the Sound Manager (which you probably will be), you are limited to 22 kHz recording with options to employ MACE compression. However, to get around this, the program offers sample rate conversion (for noncompressed sounds). The only file format unrecognized by SoundWave yet found in SoundEdit is 16-bit AIFF (SoundWave does support 8-bit AIFF).

Audioshop

Opcode's Audioshop (see Figure 6.4) offers playlist editing, a valuable feature that is missing from all but the very high-end sound editors such as Digidesign's Sound Designer II. With Audioshop, you can arrange a list of 8-bit soundfiles in any order and intermix these with CD audio tracks, assuming that you have a CD-ROM drive that is capable of playing audio CDs. The program offers 8-bit recording at the four standard Macintosh rates. Editing, limited to 8-bit soundfiles, includes cut, copy, paste, scale amplitude, pitch bending, echo, vibrato, flanging, sound reversal, and looping. Although playback can be direct-from-disk, both recording and editing are limited to soundfiles that can fit in your available RAM. Once recorded or opened into Audioshop, a soundfile may be saved as an AIFF, SoundEdit, System 7, HyperCard, Director 'snd resource, or a QuickTime movie. A bonus is that sounds may be saved to existing movies.

Alchemy

Passport recently discontinued Alchemy even though it was the most popular program for sample editing on the Macintosh. The reason for dropping the

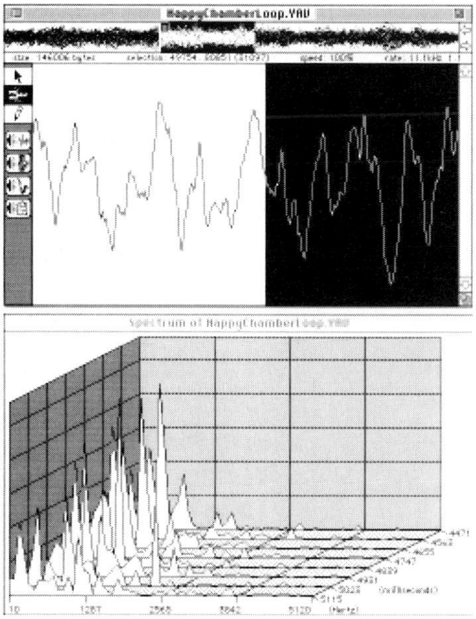

Figure 6.3 SoundWave is a functional 8-bit soundfile editor that offers a subset of the features found in SoundEdit Pro.

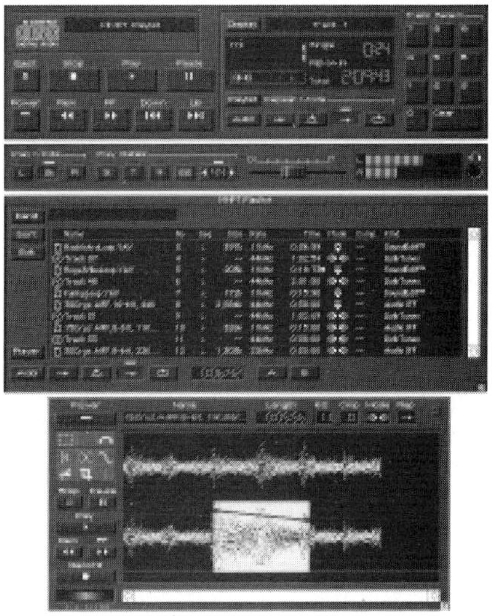

Figure 6.4 Opcode's AudioShop lets you intermix CD-based audio with disk-based 8-bit and 16-bit soundfiles in playlists. Basic editing of non-CD audio is supported.

product was excessive piracy (the program was not copy-protected). At the time of this writing, Alchemy is up for sale; and by the time you read this, another vendor may well be distributing the software.

One reason for Alchemy's popularity is that it supports 8-bit and 16-bit sounds without distinction. The program will play back (but not record) sound through any Digidesign NuBus audio card if one is available; otherwise, playback is through the Macintosh speaker or external audio port.

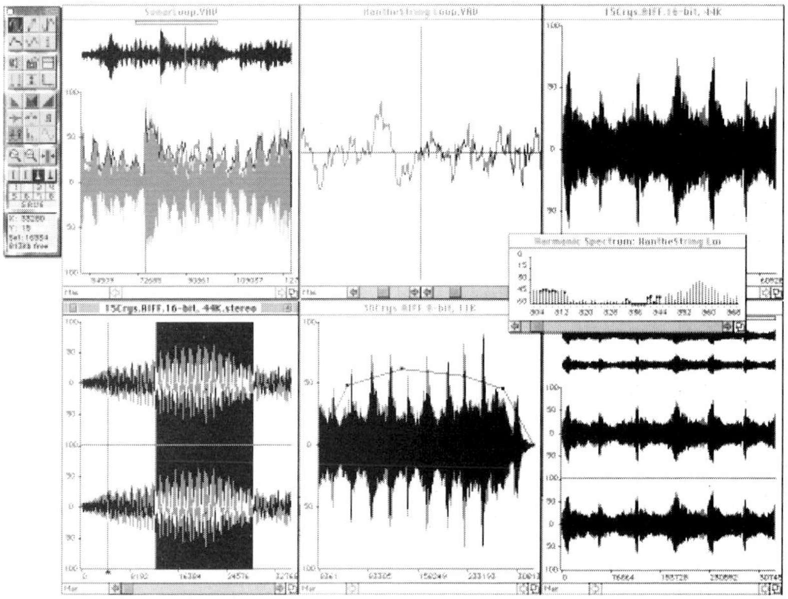

Figure 6.5 Passport's Alchemy is a very powerful 16-bit sample editor. Besides supporting most common audio formats and converting between them, the software is compatible with most popular hardware sampling devices.

Alchemy is a professional tool, and the $695 price is reasonable for the RAM-based editing options the software provides: cut, copy, paste, replicate, reverse, invert, gain adjustment, crossfade, mixing of two files, looping, resampling, sample-rate conversion, pitch shifting, time compression/expansion, parametric EQ, graphic editing of amplitude and frequency envelopes, and editable FFT (Fast Fourier Transform) frequency plots. Recognized file formats include Sound Designer I and II, 8- and 16-bit AIFF, SoundEdit, SoundLab (an ancient 8-bit editor's format), 'snd ' resource, and Dyaxis (see Figure 6.5).

AudioStack

Voyager's AudioStack (see Figure 6.6) offers a unique approach to adding sound to a multimedia project. You can use any off-the-shelf audio CD as sound material, provided that playback is by way of a CD-ROM drive. Considering the restrictions of musical copyright laws, this might not seem to be a viable alternative to Macintosh-based sound. However, there are numerous applications of this software in the field of music education, and there are also hundreds, if not thousands, of CD-based production music libraries that could be applied to other types of projects.

AudioStack is a HyperCard-based authoring tool that relies on the fact that there are over 300,000 unique addresses on an audio CD when that CD is being played

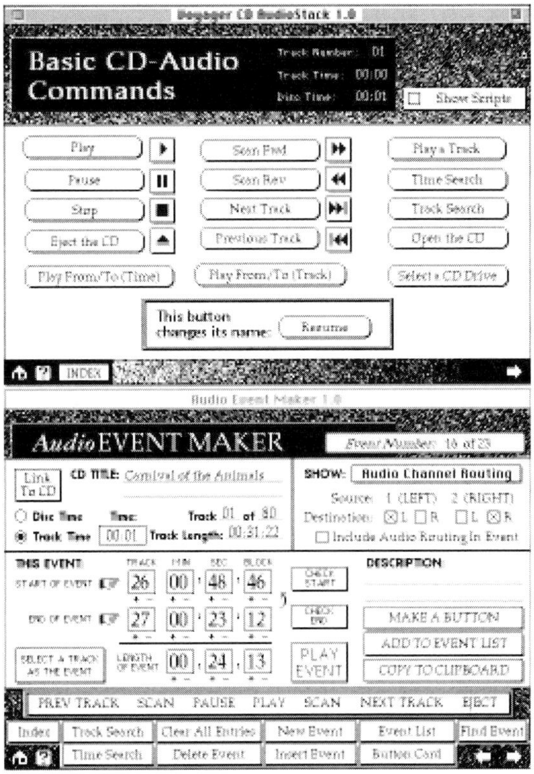

Figure 6.6 Voyager's AudioStack automates the process of creating interactive buttons to control off-the-shelf audio CDs being played back on a CD-ROM drive.

on a CD-ROM drive. Near random-access is possible. However, when constructing projects, you must keep in mind that during CD audio playback, your Macintosh can't retrieve any data from its hard drive. That means that any interactivity, animation, or video that you want to take place during playback must be resident in RAM prior to commencing audio playback. This is not as restrictive as it might sound, because whenever audio playback stops momentarily, your project can retrieve the next chunk of visual data from disk.

This versatile stack and XCMD set automatically creates buttons and HyperCard scripts to play from any point to any other point on a CD. Furthermore, you can create sequences of audio clips, not unlike the playlists discussed above. You are not limited to controlling a single CD-ROM drive.

Sound Synthesis

Early sound synthesis was accomplished through analog methods that have now given way to digital approaches. Interestingly, the components of digital synthesis are roughly the same as those of the analog ancestors.

A general model of digital sound synthesis starts with a sound source that produces a waveform at a user-specified pitch, often user-specifiable as a square, triangle, sawtooth, or other shape. An oscillator (OSC), digitally controlled oscillator (DCO), or digital waveform oscillator (DWO) generates this raw sound data.

Next in the synthesis signal chain is a filter used to remove, reduce, or emphasize specified frequencies or frequency bands. Filters that remove the upper frequencies are called low pass filters (LPFs), while those that remove the lower frequencies are referred to as high pass filters (HPFs). Band pass filters (BPFs) remove all but a specified frequency range or band, and notch filters do just the opposite—that is, they remove a specified frequency range. Sometimes, filters that can be placed under digital control are referred to as variable digital filters (VDFs). Variations on this theme are seen in time variant filters (TVFs).

Before the sound can be output it must be amplified, so the final link of the synthesizer signal chain is an amplifier. Amplifiers that can be controlled digitally are often called variable digital amplifiers (VDAs) or, in some manufacturers' devices, time variant amplifiers (TVAs).

Along the way, other waveform processors may be applied to a sound. Low frequency oscillators (LFOs) produce waveforms that are below the threshold of human hearing. When a sine wave LFO is applied to the VDA, it produces *amplitude tremolo* or a continual fluctuation of loudness. On the other hand, when applied to an oscillator, an LFO can produce the continual pitch variance known as *vibrato.*

Envelope generators (EGs) are used to impose a simple or complex variation of intensity over time. When applied at the amplifier stage, EGs can specify how fast a sound rises to its peak volume and how slowly it decays, among other things. Special effects can be achieved by applying an EG at the filter stage of the signal chain.

Synthesis has reached a stage of development where nearly all of the components in the signal chain—OSC, VDF, VDA, EG, and LFO—can easily be controlled by software or by way of the front panel buttons on a device.

Within the framework of the synthesis signal chain, a great number of approaches to synthesis have been developed, adapted, or appropriated by various synthesizer manufacturers to endow their instruments with a unique signature sound. These are (in approximate order of appearance on the scene): subtractive synthesis, additive synthesis, frequency modulation synthesis (FM—sometimes known as algorithmic synthesis), phase distortion synthesis (PDS), resynthesized pulse code modulation (RS-PCM) synthesis, Karplus-Strong synthesis (also known as plucked string synthesis), linear/arithmetic synthesis (L/A), advanced integrated synthesis (AI), advanced vector synthesis (AV), and variable architecture synthesis technology (VAST).

In subtractive synthesis, a complex waveform, generated by one or two oscillators and often mixed with white or pink noise, is filtered by a VCF, with EGs and LFOs thrown in along the way. Additive synthesis takes the opposite approach. Sine waves or other waveforms are simply added together, often with each waveform responding to a separate EG to vary its pitch over time.

Frequency modulation or FM synthesis was created by John Chowning and eventually licensed to Yamaha, where it gave birth to Yamaha's legendary DX7 synthesizer. FM synthesis uses the same principles as FM radio, applied to waveforms in the range of human hearing. The process starts with at least two frequencies, one of which is used to control (or modulate) the other. The result is a very complex waveform that is usually extremely interesting to listen to. The problem is that it is difficult to predict what will result from combining any two or more waveforms. Fortunately, an army of sound designers has created tens of thousands of stock sounds that are either built into FM instruments' ROMs or loadable in their RAM.

Phase distortion synthesis, popularized by Casio, is similar to FM synthesis, except that a waveform is applied to an out-of-phase copy of itself. If you can picture a sine wave, you can imagine how two copies of the same wave could be shifted so that they do not reach their peaks at the same time. This is referred to as being *out of phase* and forms the basis of PD synthesis.

Resynthesized pulse code modulation (RS-PCM), popularized by Roland, is similar to additive synthesis. The difference revolves around the fact that the choice of the component sine waves is mandated by an analysis of an FFT (Fast Fourier Transform) of a sampled sound rather than through random or procedural processes.

Karplus-Strong synthesis was developed by Kevin Karplus and Alan Strong. Karplus-Strong synthesis models the sound of plucked strings by starting with a sound source that resembles a plucked string and then filtering it to produce the effect of the subsequent vibrations of that string. Strings of any length and circumference can be modeled using this technique, including those which could never exist in the real world.

Synthesizers and Samplers

Electronic devices that generate sound through this wide variety of synthesis techniques are the instruments of the late 20th century. Most available devices are marketed in two formats, one with a keyboard (not necessarily the 88 notes found on a traditional piano) and one (referred to as a sound module or rack-mountable module) without a keyboard meant to be controlled by a separate keyboard or by software. The sound-generating innards of the keyboard and module versions of a device should be identical.

Electronic instruments have evolved to the point where most devices nowadays are capable of sounding a maximum of 16, 24, or 32 different notes simultaneously. This characteristic is referred to as 16-, 24-, or 32-voice polyphony. If a 24-voice polyphonic synthesizer is currently sounding 24 notes together and is requested to play a 25th note, one of the other 24 will immediately drop out to free up the software mechanism required to generate the newly arrived note.

Most devices also can play back a maximum of either 8 or 16 different types, or *timbres,* of sounds at once. This feature is referred to as 8- or 16-channel multitimbrality. This is not to be confused with the number of different timbres that an instrument contains in its ROMs or loadable RAM. Here you will typically have 192 sounds available at all times, even if only 16 may sound simultaneously.

Many people refer to all electronic sound-generating devices as synthesizers, but, technically, synthesizers form only one class of such devices. Synthesizers produce sounds from electronically generated waveforms and, thus, rarely produce a sound that might occur in nature. Samplers, on the other hand, simply play back sounds that have been digitally recorded and stored in ROM chips or loaded into RAM. A further distinction exists between samplers that can make their own digital recordings to play back and sample-players that rely exclusively on sounds stored in their ROMs or loaded into their RAM.

Many more recent approaches to electronic sound generation combine synthesis and sampling techniques into a hybrid process. The first widespread use of such a hybrid sound-generating technique was popularized by Roland in the Linear/Arithmetic (L/A) synthesis. Sampled attacks of real instruments, traditionally the most difficult portion of a sound to synthesize and often the most interesting, are pasted onto the front of synthesized tones. Korg followed with their advanced integrated synthesis (AI), employing a similar approach to L/A and, shortly thereafter, advanced vector synthesis (AV), which relies upon the interaction of sequences of stored waveforms.

Finally, Kurzweil introduce variable architecture synthesis (VAST) in 1991. VAST utilizes custom chips that can be software-configured to replicate any of these synthesis techniques in combination. The chips are flexible enough to be configured for as yet unimagined forms of synthesis.

Macintosh-Based Synthesis

If by now you believe that there doesn't seem to be anything that a computer couldn't accomplish in software, you're correct. Although there are not many tools available to accomplish software synthesis on the Macintosh, one in particular, Digidesign's TurboSynth, is extremely powerful.

TurboSynth offers a modular approach to software synthesis (see Figure 6.7). All the traditional components and many other far-out ones are represented as icons that you interconnect by using the mouse to drag virtual input and output cables between them. It's relatively easy to model additive, subtractive, amplitude modulation, and carrier/modulator-type synthesis techniques. Additionally, you can use and edit sampled soundfiles in place of waveforms or wavetables at any stage of the signal chain.

The software offers icons for oscillators, filters, amplifiers, spectral inverters, digital delays, time "stretchers," time compressors, pitch shifters, frequency envelope editors, amplitude envelope editors, resonators, mixers, wave reshapers, and AM/FM modulators. All icons can be double-clicked to reveal control panels under their "hoods." Going in the other direction, you can "collapse" any configuration of modules to a soundfile equivalent to the state of the sound up to that point in the signal chain.

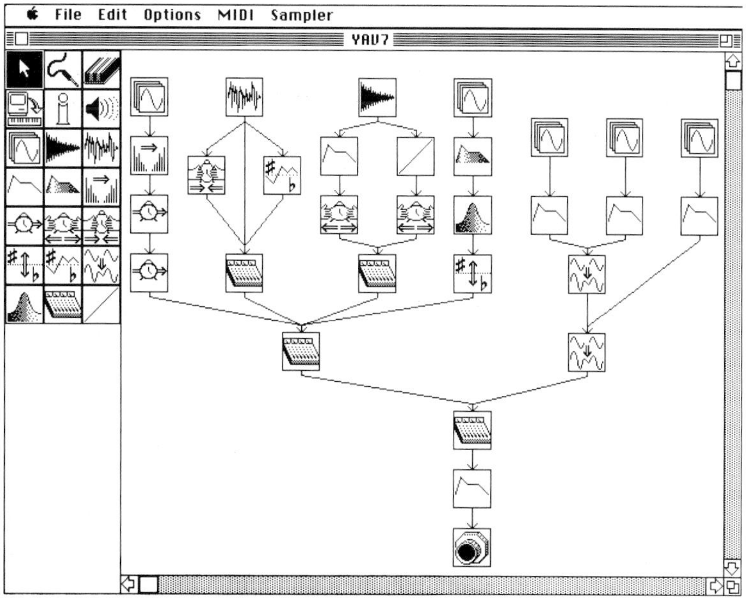

Figure 6.7 Digidesign's TurboSynth offers an icon-based approach to software synthesis.

With a Digidesign audio NuBus card installed, you can preview any sounds in 16-bit resolution; otherwise, sounds are output to the Macintosh speaker or external audio port.

At the time of this writing, Apple is close to the release of a software-based synthesizer that will work in conjunction with QuickTime's new music track. The music track contains a representation of MIDI data (see below) and, until Apple's software-based synthesizer is released, will therefore require an external MIDI device connected to a serial port or a synthesizer on a NuBus card such as Digidesign's MacProteus (a card version of E-mu Systems's Proteus 1 sample-player).

With the new music architecture, QuickTime's music track will use a General MIDI synthesizer existing entirely in the RAM of the Macintosh, and send its output to the Macintosh speaker or sound output port. In this case, additional CPU load can be expected. Playing four-voice polyphony on a Mac Plus will consume an additional 35% of the CPU; six-voice polyphony on an LC will require an overhead of 25%; and 16 voices on a Quadra will eat up 45% of your CPU bandwidth. Sophisticated note allocation algorithms, operating under the principle of "graceful degradation," will assure the best possible approximation of, for example, a 16-voice file played back on a machine that can only support eight voices.

MIDI

Developed in 1982, MIDI is an international specification used by musical instruments that contain microprocessors to communicate with similar devices of different manufacturers. The format of MIDI data was codified by representatives from synthesizer manufacturers in a document called the MIDI Specification, published in August of 1983.

Several multimedia authoring and video editing tools let you take advantage of the economy and flexibility of the MIDI format. Notable among these are Passport Producer, Macromedia Director, and Adobe Premiere. When Apple releases the Music Track in an upcoming update to QuickTime, the whole MIDI-multimedia connection will be solidified. It doesn't take very long to realize the significance of the fact that MIDI files that are used to produce sound tracks are minuscule in comparison to the digital audio files (even 8-bit) that their data would produce. When you use MIDI instead of digital audio for an interactive multimedia project, you can alter many sound characteristics during playback. Furthermore, you can change the tempo or key of the music; mute, solo, or fade individual tracks; loop beat-delineated regions; or completely reorchestrate and remix the music—all from a single version of the file.

MIDI data requires serial cables with 5-pin DIN connectors, at 31.25 kBaud. Most MIDI messages are assigned to one of 16 independent channels. In a multi-timbral MIDI device, you can assign a different sound to each MIDI channel.

A MIDI interface is required to convert MIDI data into a format that your computer

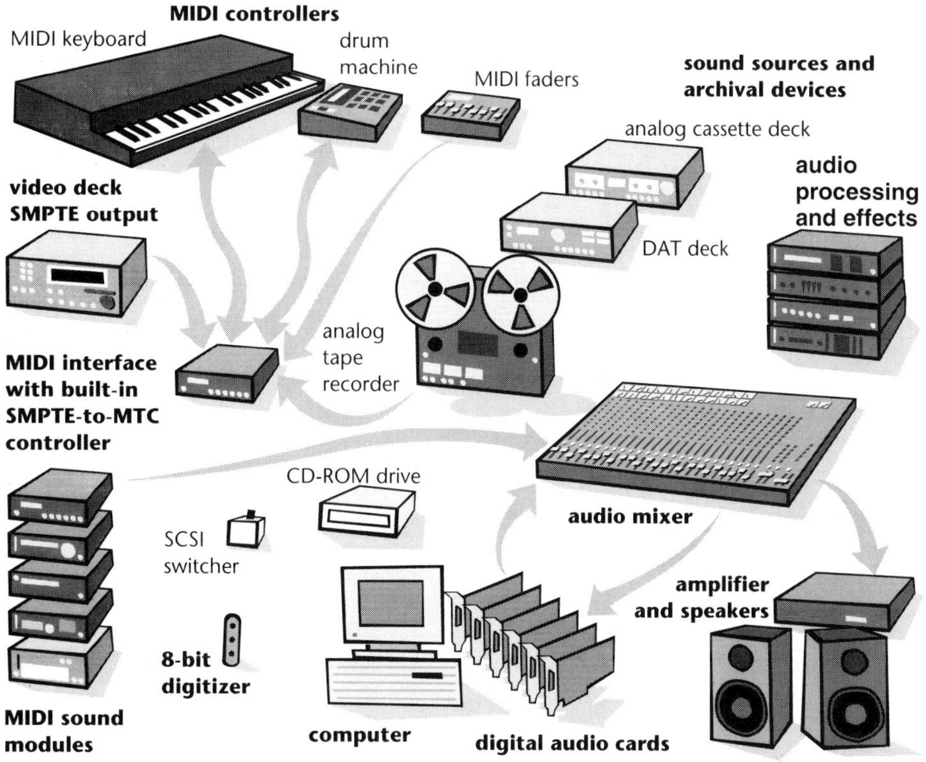

Figure 6.8 This configuration lets you take full advantage of MIDI and digital audio in both 8-bit and 16-bit formats. There are many variations on this theme and some components could be omitted, depending upon the level and type of production you are engaged in.

can understand, and vice versa. MIDI interfaces come in three types: those that support a single set of 16 MIDI channels, those that support two sets of 16 MIDI channels (sometimes referred to as dual interfaces), and those that support more than 32 channels (sometimes called multiport, multicable, or cableized interfaces). See Figure 6.8 for an example of a typical MIDI setup.

The MIDI specification has had several addenda. In July of 1988 Standard MIDI Files (SMFs) were made official and have now become analogous to ASCII text files in word processing. A file saved in one program as an SMF can usually be opened, played, and edited with another program. Additionally, SMFs are compatible across all computer platforms. Since their introduction, SMFs have formed the basis for a growing "clip MIDI data" market (don't forget that copyright issues apply to SMFs as well as to actual recordings of music).

In 1991, the MIDI specification was updated to include a General MIDI mode to facilitate a plug-and-play approach for multimedia. General MIDI mode defines a standardized list of sounds that are always assigned to the same patch numbers. When a device is in General MIDI mode, for example, patch 1 is always an acoustic grand piano, patch 41 is a solo violin, and so on up to 128. Prior to that, there was no guarantee that a MIDI sequence recorded on one device would sound anything like it was supposed to when played back through another

Table 6.3 General MIDI Sound Set (MIDI Program Numbers 1 - 128 on all channels except 10)

1	Acoustic Grand Piano	29	Electric Guitar (muted)	57	Trumpet
2	Bright Acoustic Piano	30	Overdriven Guitar	58	Trombone
3	Electric Grand Piano	31	Distortion Guitar	59	Tuba
4	Honky-tonk Piano	32	Guitar Harmonics	60	Muted Trumpet
5	Electric Piano 1	33	Acoustic Bass	61	French Horn
6	Electric Piano 2	34	Electric Bass (finger)	62	Brass Section
7	Harpsichord	35	Electric Bass (pick)	63	SynthBrass 1
8	Clavi	36	Fretless Bass	64	SynthBrass 2
9	Celesta	37	Slap Bass 1	65	Soprano Sax
10	Glockenspiel	38	Slap Bass 2	66	Alto Sax
11	Music Box	39	Synth Bass 1	67	Tenor Sax
12	Vibraphone	40	Synth Bass 2	68	Baritone Sax
13	Marimba	41	Violin	69	Oboe
14	Xylophone	42	Viola	70	English Horn
15	Tubular Bells	43	Cello	71	Bassoon
16	Dulcimer	44	Contrabass	72	Clarinet
17	Drawbar Organ	45	Tremolo Strings	73	Piccolo
18	Percussive Organ	46	Pizzicato Strings	74	Flute
19	Rock Organ	47	Orchestral Harp	75	Recorder
20	Church Organ	48	Timpani	76	Pan Flute
21	Reed Organ	49	String Ensemble 1	77	Blown Bottle
22	Accordion	50	String Ensemble 2	78	Shakuhachi
23	Harmonica	51	SynthStrings 1	79	Whistle
24	Tango Accordion	52	SynthStrings 2	80	Ocarina
25	Acoustic Guitar (nylon)	53	Choir Aahs	81	Lead 1 (square)
26	Acoustic Guitar (steel)	54	Voice Oohs	82	Lead 2 (sawtooth)
27	Electric Guitar (jazz)	55	Synth Voice	83	Lead 3 (calliope)
28	Electric Guitar (clean)	56	Orchestra Hit	84	Lead 4 (chiff)

Table 6.3 *continued*

85 Lead 5 (charang)	100 FX 4 (atmosphere)	115 Steel Drums
86 Lead 6 (voice)	101 FX 5 (brightness)	116 Woodblock
87 Lead 7 (fifths)	102 FX 6 (goblins)	117 Taiko Drum
88 Lead 8 (bass + lead)	103 FX 7 (echoes)	118 Melodic Tom
89 Pad 1 (new age)	104 FX 8 (sci-fi)	119 Synth Drum
90 Pad 2 (warm)	105 Sitar	120 Reverse Cymbal
91 Pad 3 (polysynth)	106 Banjo	121 Guitar Fret Noise
92 Pad 4 (choir)	107 Shamisen	122 Breath Noise
93 Pad 5 (bowed)	108 Koto	123 Seashore
94 Pad 6 (metallic)	109 Kalimba	124 Bird Tweet
95 Pad 7 (halo)	110 Bag Pipe	125 Telephone Ring
96 Pad 8 (sweep)	111 Fiddle	126 Helicopter
97 FX 1 (rain)	112 Shanai	127 Applause
98 FX 2 (soundtrack)	113 Tinkle Bell	128 Gunshot
99 FX 3 (crystal)	114 Agogo	

device. Now, there are many General MIDI synthesizers and synthesizer modules. Roland's Sound Brush, about the size of a Stephen King paperback, is a good example of such a device.

General MIDI mode also includes a standardized mapping of percussion sounds to note numbers (see Table 6.4). Prior to this, playing a percussion part on a different percussion machine than the one for which it was created always resulted in cacophony—on one device, the G above middle C might be a snare drum; on another, it might be an crash cymbal.

General MIDI may be a major proponent in the CD+MIDI Specification (designed to provide a MIDI data track on audio CDs), and Apple is jumping on the General MIDI bandwagon with great enthusiasm.

Apple's MIDI Manager

Apple created the MIDI Manager tool set (system software including an INIT, a driver, and a program called PatchBay) to handle communication between MIDI software and the serial ports. MIDI Manager makes it possible to route the output of one MIDI application into one or more other MIDI Manager-compatible programs while all communicate with the serial ports. The software also offers

Table 6.4 General MIDI Percussion Map (Channel 10)

Key	*Percussion sound*	*Key*	*Percussion sound*	*Key*	*Percussion sound*
35	Acoustic Bass Drum	51	Ride Cymbal 1	67	High Agogo
36	Bass Drum 1	52	Chinese Cymbal	68	Low Agogo
37	Side Stick	53	Ride Bell	69	Cabasa
38	Acoustic Snare	54	Tambourine	70	Maracas
39	Hand Clap	55	Splash Cymbal	71	Short Whistle
40	Electric Snare	56	Cowbell	72	Long Whistle
41	Low Floor Tom	57	Crash Cymbal 2	73	Short Guiro
42	Closed Hi-Hat	58	Vibraslap	74	Long Guiro
43	High Floor Tom	59	Ride Cymbal 2	75	Claves
44	Pedal Hi-Hat	60	Hi Bongo	76	Hi Wood Block
45	Low Tom	61	Low Bongo	77	Low Wood Block
46	Open Hi-Hat	62	Mute Hi Conga	78	Mute Cuica
47	Low-Mid Tom	63	Open Hi Conga	79	Open Cuica
48	Hi-Mid Tome	64	Low Conga	80	Mute Triangle
49	Crash Cymbal 1	65	High Timbale	81	Open Triangle
50	High Tom	66	Low Timbale		

extensive support for the Macintosh, including a full implementation of internal and external synchronization.

With MIDI Manager you deal with virtual MIDI ports—representing both hardware serial ports and inputs and outputs provided by MIDI Manager-compatible applications. Connecting "in" ports to "out" ports is as simple as using the mouse to drag a virtual patch cable between ports (see Figure 6.9).

MIDI Sequencers

A sequence of musical events played or intended to be played on a sound-generating device, such as a synthesizer or sampler, is called a MIDI sequence. MIDI sequencer software allows you to record, edit, and play back such sequences (see Figure 6.10). The data stored in a MIDI sequence is similar to piano-roll data in that actual sound (waveform) data is not recorded, only the instructions that are required to trigger specific sounds on an external or internal hardware synthesizer or, in the case of Apple's new music architecture, a software-based synthesizer.

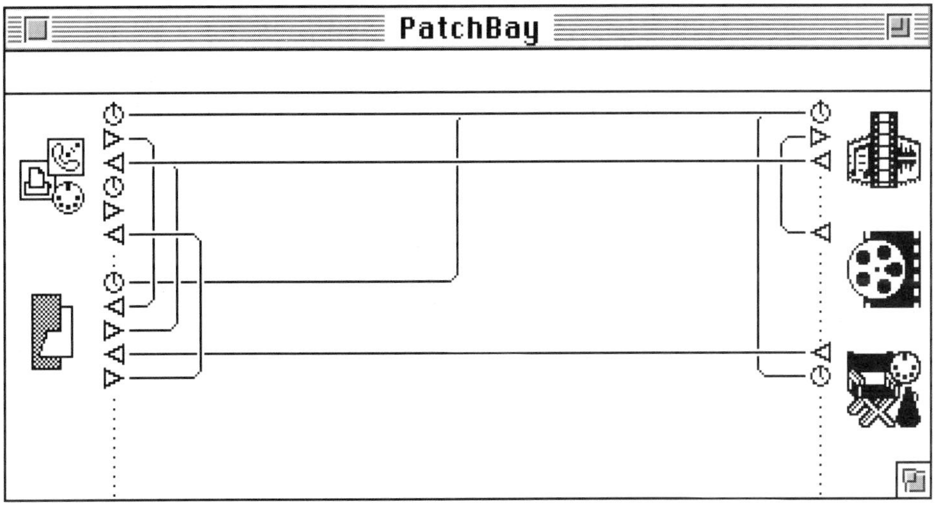

Figure 6.9 Four applications have been interconnected using virtual data cables in Apple's MIDI Manager PatchBay. This configuration provides for SMPTE (converted to MTC) synchronization arriving at the modem port to act as a master to Passport Producer. Producer can, in turn, function as a sync master to Macromedia Director and OSC's MIDI sequencer Metro. SPP synchronization triggers may be sent from Adobe Premiere to Producer and also from Director to Metro. MIDI data arriving at the modem port is sent to Metro, while MIDI output from both Metro and Producer is routed to the modem port. Metro can send additional MIDI output to the printer port.

Acoustic music concepts relating to sound waves—pitch, volume, timbre, rhythm, and articulation—correlate to control codes describing performance actions with MIDI data. Pitch equates to a note number, volume to velocity of keystroke, timbre to "patch change," and articulation to controller number and setting. Because of this, each time a MIDI sequence is played, the result is a repeat performance of the original or edited performance.

MIDI data is quite different from the data stored on analog tape or in digital soundfiles. Taped music is frozen and can only be edited with great difficulty. On the other hand, MIDI data can be examined and edited at the individual note level. Mistakes can be corrected with little effort. Transposition and tempo modifications are simple edit options. The rhythmic correction that MIDI permits, known as quantization, has no correspondence for files consisting of actual sound data, whether analog or digital.

There are currently ten MIDI sequencers shipping for the Macintosh. Based upon options such as synchronization features, number of tracks, Standard MIDI File (SMF) compatibility, and event editing, it is possible to divide the available software into entry-level programs—Ballade, EZ Vision, One Step, and Trax—and professional-level sequencers—Metro (originally released as Beyond), Cubase, Notator Logic, Performer, Pro 5, and Vision. There even are several shareware sequencers, including MIDI Companion and MiniTrax. At the time of this writing, Multitude, a new sequencer from Canadian-based Oktal Software, is due for imminent release.

Some of the entry-level sequencers are merely "junior" versions of professional sequencers offered by the same company. Opcode's EZ Vision has many of the same options as the company's Vision. Passport's Trax is simply Passport's Pro 5 professional-level sequencer with a restricted feature set.

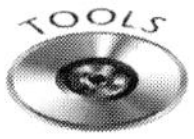

MasterTracks Pro 5 200

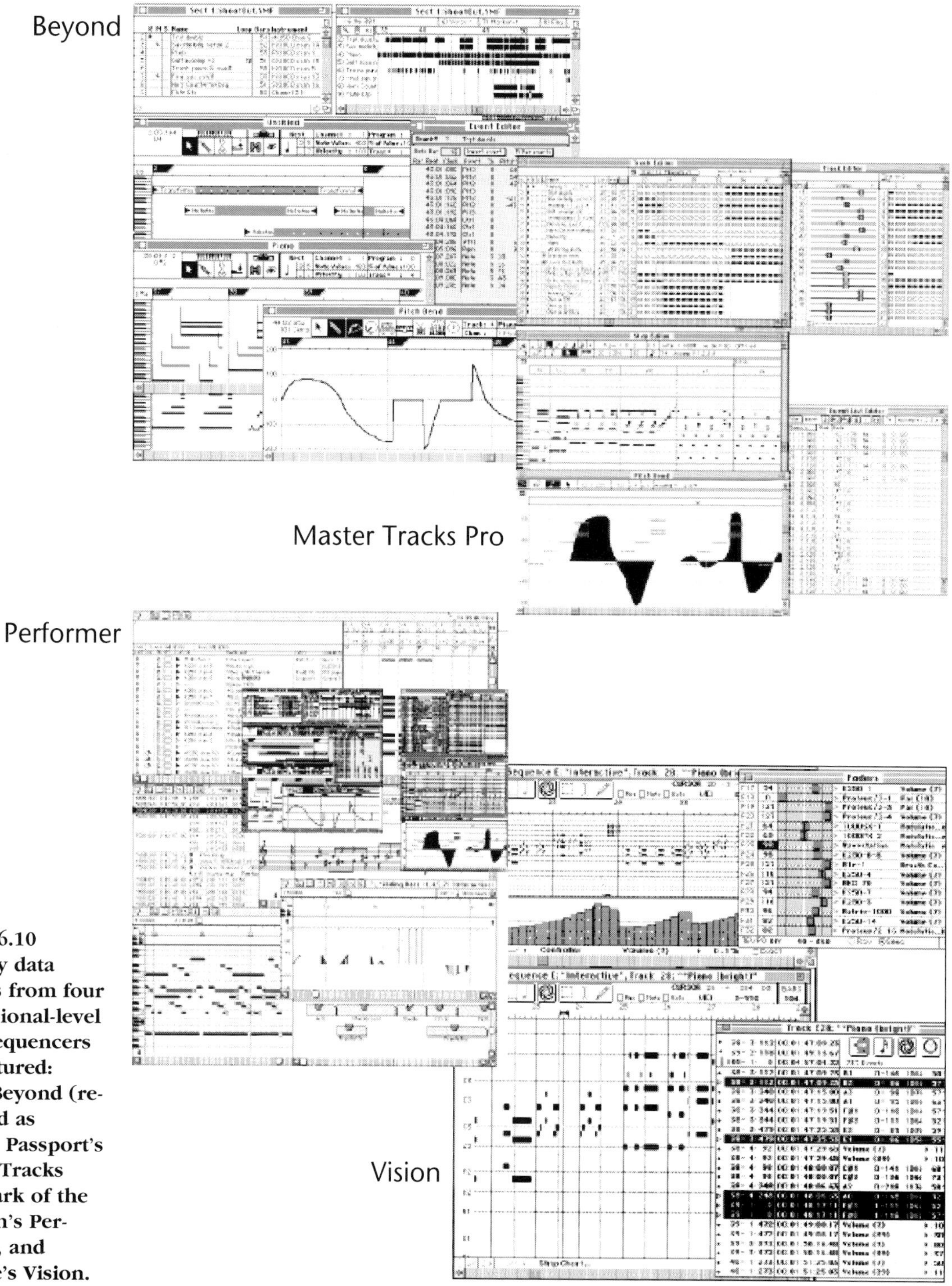

Figure 6.10 Primary data screens from four professional-level MIDI sequencers are pictured: OSC's Beyond (re-released as Metro), Passport's Master Tracks Pro, Mark of the Unicorn's Performer, and Opcode's Vision.

There are versions of Cubase, Performer, and Vision that support multiple 16-bit, 44.1 kHz digital audio tracks (Cubase Audio, Digital Performer, and StudioVision). Additionally, OSC's Metro integrates with OSC's Deck 2.0 software to provide CD-quality digital audio features. Finally, there is a version of Trax called Audio Trax that provides for 8-bit, 22 kHz digital audio tracks.

Music Generation

Automatic music generation software is an often neglected category of MIDI software that will, out of necessity, gain more and more importance in the creation of multimedia. Such tools let you generate credible music without having to worry about copyright infringement. Each of the current Macintosh products for automatic composition focuses on a different musical style or styles.

Cybernetic Composer is a shareware program developed by algorithmic composition pioneer Charles Ames (with Michael Domino) for the Kurzweil Foundation Automated Composition Project (see Figure 6.11). The program will generate as many pieces as you need in four styles—ragtime, standard jazz, rock, or Latin jazz—at the push of an OK button. You are free to choose between styles, forms, key, and instrumentation, or you can let the software make all the choices for you randomly. You can play its compositions by way of MIDI or through the Macintosh speaker or audio port. Batch processing is available so that you can set the software in motion, go to the beach, and come back to hundreds of MIDI files meeting your requirements.

Butch Mahoney markets two programs: Evolution #9 (for 12-tone serial music reminiscent of Arnold Schoenberg) and Music Box (for pandiatonic or "white-note" music). Evolution #9 generates, plays, and saves to SMF format. The program requires that you make a few decisions regarding the order of pitches in the original row (you don't need to use all 12 if you don't want to), rhythmic

Figure 6.11 The Kurzweil Foundations shareware Cybernetic Composer generated this license-free ragtime at the push of a single button.

motifs, dynamics, length, tempo, note density, and number of parts (up to eight). MusicBox generates 1940s-style pandiatonic music with options limited to specifying tempo, length, note density, and scale type (major, minor, harmonic minor, or melodic minor).

Power Tools Theme 012

EarLevel Engineering's HyperMIDI (described below) includes two sample stacks for automatic composition accompany the software. The Algorithms stack by Jeff Roan lets you create a musical score from general descriptions in the form of "Long Notes, Short Notes, Hi Note, Low Note, Play Chord, Stop Chord." Redmon's Fractal Music Generator gives you more control over pitch and rhythmic material, but generates musical forms from fractal geometry.

MusicLines by Bengt-Arne Molin requires you to use a pencil tool to draw melodic contours. Within the drawing window, the vertical axis represents pitch and the horizontal axis represents time. MusicLines maps your graphic representations onto an editable rhythmic data file to generate original music.

Besides these six programs, none of which require musical training, there are a number of interactive composition tools that you might consider if you have some musical background. In this area, Dr. T's Music Software markets Jam Factory, M, UpBeat, MusicMouse, OvalTune, and Interactor. Most of these import SMFs, so you might, for example, process clip music to produce generated works that are probabilistic variations on your original data.

Adding MIDI Options through XCMDs

The marriage of MIDI and multimedia was consummated in 1988 with the release of Nigel Redmon's HyperMIDI 1.0 set of XCMDs and XFCNs. Already extremely powerful in its initial shareware release, HyperMIDI went on to become version 2.0, a commercial product, in 1991.

Two similar MIDI utilities were introduced in 1991: Passport Designs released its HyperMusic software (with XCMDs and XFCNs written by Nigel Redmon), and Opcode Systems released its MIDIplay set of externals.

You can install any of these XCMDs and XFCNs into any XCMD-compatible application, using a resource editor such as Resorcerer or ResEdit—for example, a Director document or Director itself. Then, the XCMD inputs and outputs appear in PatchBay as if they were a separate application, even though they are resident in the program in which they have been installed.

HyperMusic

Passport's HyperMusic is the easiest of the three options for MIDI in a program such as Director. The HyperMusic stack comes with a JukeBox and Mixer card and 10 sample MIDI files.

HyperMusic consists of three XCMDs: hmus_Open, hmus_Close, and hmus_Play. The stack also includes the XFCNs, hmus_Slider, hmus_MIDIfile, and hmus_Utilities. There are no additional licensing fees required to use and distribute HyperMusic externals (noncommercially) in your own stacks and multimedia documents, although you must acknowledge Passport's copyright.

HyperMusic will play back any Standard MIDI File (SMF), and Passport markets hundreds of SMFs in its Music Data series. These include many elegantly programmed sequences of just about any kind of music: pop/rock, country, R&B, Beatles, oldies, jazz, standards, and classical. These are preconfigured for Roland's MT-32 and CM series synthesizers, but can easily be adapted for any electronic MIDI sound generator.

HyperMIDI lets you control the MIDI volume (called "Controller 7" in MIDI parlance) of the current sequence on a track-by-track basis in real time. You also can set the master volume of the sequence, change the patch assignments for each channel, and mute or solo individual tracks. Because there are three popular sound numbering schemes, HyperMusic provides a welcome courtesy feature for patch (sound) change: You can specify the numbering system as 1 to 128, 0 to 127, or A11 to B88 on a local and global basis.

MIDIplay

Opcode's MIDIplay offers considerably more options than HyperMusic (but not as many as HyperMIDI—see below). MIDIplay is made possible by Andy Wolpert's MIDI XCMD driver. You can play SMFs and edit certain aspects of their playback—volume, muting, looping, transposition, and program change. MIDIplay comes with two preconfigured synthesizer setups, one for E-mu's Proteus and the other for Roland's MT-32 and CM series of instruments.

MIDIplay lets you set global track effects for any sequence. This editing does not change the file's MIDI data, but can be applied on output whenever you play a particular SMF. You can edit the volume (Controller 7) settings, mute tracks, change MIDI channel assignments, set an initial program change message, and set a transposition. All of these options are available on an individual-track basis.

MIDIplay makes it easy to designate a specific segment of the file to play back. If you don't like the introduction of the file, you can skip it. You can choose a start and end point, specified in bars (measures). Here, you also can set a looping segment (and specify how many times to loop), and you can adjust tempo by percentage or by specifying the overall song duration, whereupon the program calculates tempo.

When you use MIDIplay with HyperCard, the Track Editor's Export Options let you automatically create a button in another stack that will play the current MIDI file (including your edits), or a card that will play the file when you open the card. MIDIplay writes all the necessary scripts for you automatically. There is also an option to have this automatically generated script transferred to the Clipboard, so you can paste it into your Director document or other document created by a similar XCMD-compatible authoring tool.

HyperMIDI

EarLevel Engineering's HyperMIDI (developed by Nigel Redmon) provides for MIDI input, an option missing from MIDIplay and HyperMusic. This lets you control an entire Director presentation by way of external MIDI events. For example, a sprite might undergo a transformation every time a C-major-ninth chord is played, the palette might change when you play in a different key, or specific melodic passages, cause the animation to jump to a specified frame. This sort of external control needn't issue from a MIDI keyboard. There are many external MIDI boxes consisting entirely of sliders and buttons dedicated to sending MIDI commands (e.g., JL Cooper's FaderMaster).

HyperMIDI offers a host of other MIDI functions besides MIDI input and output. In fact, this set of XCMDs and XFCNs is so powerful that you can create just about any kind of MIDI application you want, often as powerful or more powerful than commercial programs dedicated to the same purpose. Fortunately, HyperMIDI makes it relatively simple.

To make things even easier, HyperMIDI treats all data as text strings rather than as explicit data types such as integer, real, or character. Furthermore, you can use decimal numbers in HyperMIDI scripts, so you don't need to know about the binary or hexadecimal system.

HyperMIDI lets you create up to six input and output ports in MIDI Manager and also supports MIDI Manager's Timing port (for synchronization), allowing data to be time-stamped as it passes into HyperMIDI. You can choose from three time-stamp bases: milliseconds, beats, or MIDI Time Code (in 24, 25, 30 drop, and 30 nondrop formats).

HyperMIDI also imports and exports Standard MIDI Files and provides a number of useful user interface elements that make dealing with MIDI data a pleasure.

Once you start using MIDI in conjunction with your favorite multimedia authoring tool, you'll discover a whole new world of musical possibilities. Your files will be much smaller and your soundtracks will sound much better than 8-bit soundfiles that are constantly getting out of sync.

Passport Producer

Passport's Producer is the ultimate media integration tool, allowing you to combine 8-bit and 16-bit soundfiles (AIFF format up to 44.1 kHz), CD-ROM-based audio, and Standard MIDI Files with QuickTime movies, PICS animations, PICT graphics, and text (see Figure 6.12).

Each media element or "cue" is displayed as an icon containing information about its contents. Master volume sliders and elastic duration borders let you get everything in sync quickly. You can drop cues into vertical tracks at SMPTE addresses (a time code standard for synchronization employed by the Society of Motion Picture and Television Engineers).

TOOLS Passport Producer 216

Passport will lock to incoming SMPTE data that has been converted to MIDI time code. In fact, at the time of this writing, there is no other way to achieve SMPTE synchronization among the various media types (particularly QuickTime and CD-ROM-based audio) without Producer. Further, Producer can function as the synchronization master to external slaved devices.

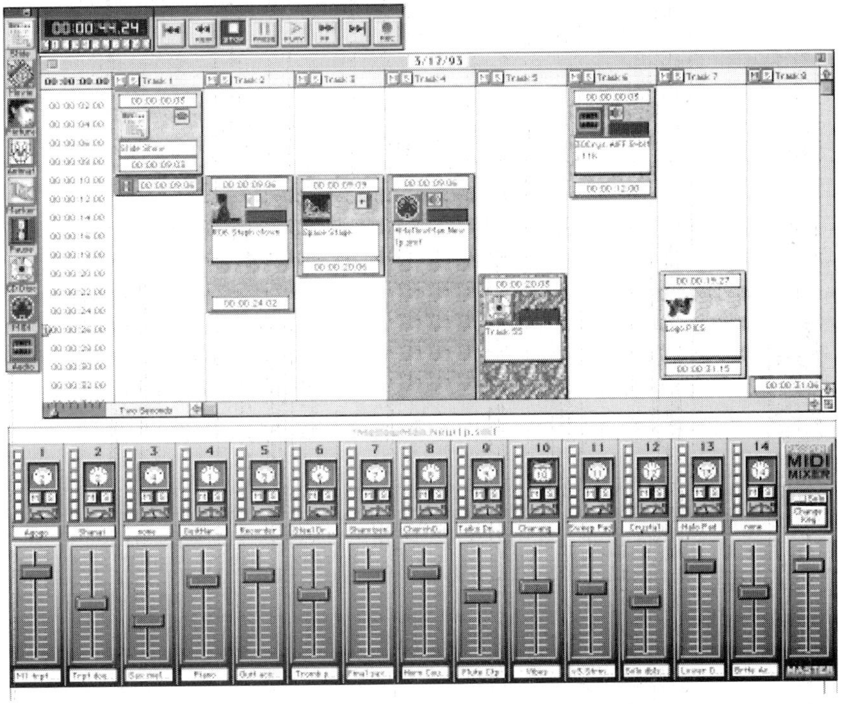

Figure 6.12 Passport's Producer integrates all types of media commonly found in multimedia. The icons at the left represent the various media types, and the cue-list controls the location and playback of media placed upon each track. You can edit most of the data types using built-in editors, such as the MIDI file editor displayed, or by creating links between various data types or individual cues to third-party editors.

Most supported media types can be recorded directly into Producer. Conversely, you can simply import files. Once a file is imported or recorded, double-clicking a cue opens Producer's built-in editor for that media type or, if you have designated an alternate editor (such as your favorite MIDI sequencer or QuickTime editor), that program will launch with the clicked-on cue data loaded.

Producer is ideal for multimedia presentations. Your presentation can loop, pause for durations you specify, or wait until the next mouse click, keystroke event, or MIDI event to trigger the following portion of your presentation.

Sound Databases: Fetch and Mariah

Once you have accumulated a wealth of digital audio data in various formats, there are several utilities that can help you keep track of your soundfiles. Two good examples are Aldus Fetch and Symmetry's Mariah. Besides supporting the gamut of graphic file types, both utilities let you maintain a database of soundfiles in a number of popular formats. One main difference is that Fetch stores references to the location of soundfiles on disk while Mariah stores a copy of the actual sound data and even lets you copy sound resources embedded within files. This makes Mariah files much larger than those of Fetch but also lets Mariah offer you the option to record new soundfiles directly into your database. While Fetch

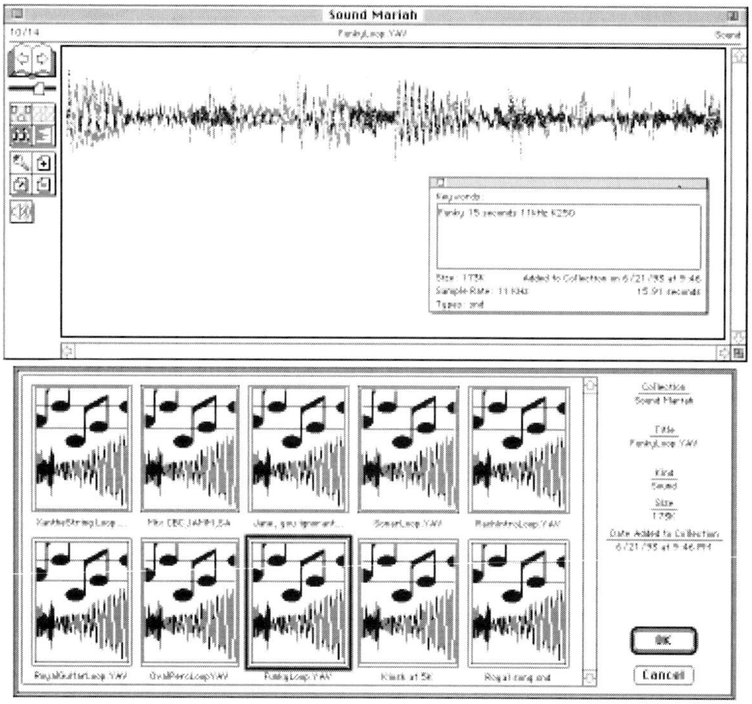

Figure 6.13 Mariah vs. Fetch. Mariah (top) and Fetch let you catalog your sounds in a searchable database. While Fetch supports a far greater number of soundfile formats, Mariah offers built-in recording and rudimentary editing features. On the other hand, Mariah files contain the actual sound data so they tend to be quite large whereas Fetch files only contain pointers to the location of the soundfiles on your hard disk.

TOOLS
Fetch 230

lets you add new soundfile formats to its list of supported file types, Mariah's compatibilities are built into the program.

Fetch displays the icons of your soundfiles and Mariah displays the actual waveform and lets you copy and paste regions to new pages of your database. With Fetch, if you want to edit a sound, you have to jump into a dedicated sound editor. As in Passport Producer you can assign an editor to open automatically.

Both Fetch and Mariah let you associate key words, phrases, and comments with a file and execute Boolean searches to narrow your selection. Detailed information about each member or the database is available as are a variety of options to sort your soundfile list.

For more information on media databases, see Chapter 10, "Outside Resources."

Speaker Systems

Amplifiers and loudspeakers (monitors) fall at the end of the recording chain (see Figure 6.14). All audio signals originating from your recording system or mixer must be amplified before you can hear them, and you must take care that your amplifier's output level (measured in watts) does not exceed that of your loudspeakers.

Most professional studios have at least three sets of monitors. If you are on a budget you might want to enlist your home stereo system for this purpose—or even a set of headphones. It is important to have a set of speakers that approximate the lowest common denominator that you may reasonably expect for playback of your project. In a Macintosh-based system this issue is an easy one because all Macintoshes have a cheap built-in speaker that you can assume to be the worst playback scenario. Because the playback characteristics of loudspeakers at either end of the spectrum are so different, it is a good idea to continually check your mixes on your best speakers as well as those you are using to simulate the worst-case scenario.

Multimedia producers, presenters, and consumers have a wealth of self-powered speakers to choose from. Such desktop sound systems include self-contained amplifiers optimized for use with audio originating from your computer, sound card, CD-ROM drive or all three. Most powered speakers designed for the desktop market contain magnetic shielding to prevent the powerful magnets in the speakers from distorting your screen. Newer desktop sound systems sometimes include built-in CD-ROM drives, mixers, effects such as reverberation, circuits that simulate stereo from a mono sound source, MIDI interfaces, and even full-blown MIDI synthesizers. Such integrated systems can save you considerable money on additional peripherals and are also easier to transport.

Some pairs of powered speakers consist of two units, each with its own amplifier or with an amplifier in one that drives both speakers. Such configurations let you to place the left and right channel speakers at any location you desire. Other models that incorporate both the right and left channel speakers into a single box have the advantage of portability, easy configuration, less cable clutter, and optimal sound disbursement and stereo separation characteristics fixed by the manufacturer.

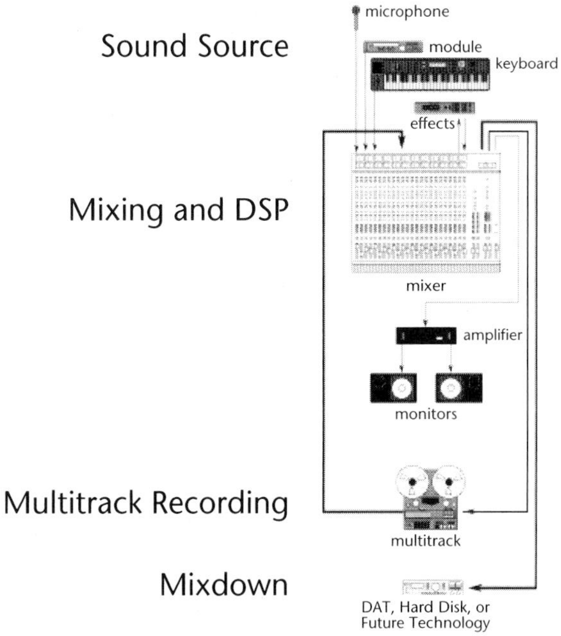

Figure 6.14 The Recording Signal Chain. The axiom: "a chain is only as strong as its weakest link" applies to the recording signal chain as well. Note that the mixer, DSP effects, amplifier, and speakers usually do double duty in the recording process.

Figure 6.15 Roland Self-Powered Speakers for Multimedia/ Model MA-12C. For multimedia development and presentation many companies now offer desktop sound systems with self-contained amplifiers (sometimes called powered speakers) optimized for use with audio originating from your computer, sound card, CD-ROM drive, or all three.

The speakers themselves may consist of one full-range speaker cone designed to handle the entire frequency spectrum or two or three cones for different frequency ranges: woofers designed to handle low frequency sounds, tweeters optimized for high frequency reproduction, and possibly a mid-range speaker to handle the frequencies in between. In some cases, internal circuitry may automatically boost certain frequency ranges that result in a more pleasing effect on the listener. You may or may not wish this type of meddling with your living room stereo system sound reproduction capabilities; however, this type of attention to detail in a system designed specifically for desktop multimedia can be a definite bonus.

Ready to Roll

TOOLS

Clip Media Sound/Music
900-993

In this chapter we've covered the basic types of hardware and software you'll need to produce sound on your Mac. You'll find a large number of valuable sound resources on the Power Tools CD, including save-disabled demos of Passport Designs MasterTracks Pro 5 and Macromedia's SoundEdit Pro 2.0, as well as extensive libraries of license-free sound clips that you're free to use immediately. For detailed information on using all these tools to produce professional-quality audio for your multimedia projects, refer to Chapter 13, "Producing Sound."

7

Animation Tools

Animation is one of the most compelling elements of multimedia, and good animation can make the difference between a ho-hum presentation and one that stuns and delights its audience. No other multimedia category approaches animation in range and depth.

The past few years have witnessed a confusing proliferation of animated presentation programs, media integration software, 3-D typography programs, 3-D drawing packages, 3-D animation software, network rendering programs, and animation utilities. Adding to the market confusion is a cloying 3-D jargon filled with arcane terms that are often used interchangeably. To name a few, there are lofting, loafing, and skinning (all referring to the same basic cross-sectional modeling technique); NURBs, splines, and Beziers (various methods for drawing smooth curves); procedural, reflection, and bump maps (assorted ways to project and render surfaces onto 3-D objects); and motion control, morphing, and keyframes (different animation techniques).

In this chapter, we'll try to slice through this snarl of competing products, overlapping categories, and pervasive jargon. For easy reference, we've broken product reviews into the following groups:

- **Presentation Software.** Programs that allow you to incorporate simple 2-D animation into multimedia presentations.
- **3-D Type and Illustration Programs.** These products let you take 2-D images from a drawing program and create uncomplicated 3-D images.
- **3-D Modeling, Animation, and Rendering.** This category includes programs that specialize in one or more phases of the 3-D process.

Finally, we've thrown in two sidebars, one on various animation utility programs, and another on products that speed the 3-D rendering process.

2-D and Not 3-D

Let's face it, 3-D animation gets all the attention. With its simulated dimensionality, subtle reflection and lighting effects, and sophisticated animation, 3-D is one of multimedia's darlings. On the other hand, it's not for everyone or every application: Creating 3-D is enormously time consuming and places great demand on hardware resources. Many times, 2-D animation is just as effective, and it's far easier to master.

Presentation Software

Back around 1988, presentation packages, such as Aldus' Persuasion and Microsoft's PowerPoint, began hitting the scene. These programs are used to create computer-based slide shows to enliven boardroom snooze-fests. Common program features include basic slide outlining; templates for slide backgrounds, type, and graphic elements; graphics and sound libraries; and conversion of spreadsheets to graphic charts.

When combined with a data projector—a compact portable screen that displays a computer's output onto a common overhead projector—these programs are indispensable for on-the-road presentations (see Chapter 4, "Hardware Peripherals").

More recently, presentation software has become even more powerful, as traditional programs have started to incorporate more advanced features, blurring the lines between media integration programs, such as Director, and newer multimedia presentation packages, such as Action and Cinemation.

Using new versions of PowerPoint, Persuasion, CA-Cricket Presents, and Symantec's More, you can create basic 2-D animations for your slide shows; design simulated 3-D graphs; and create interactive links that branch to new slides, depending on user input. Although these programs are impressive in both features and usability, they do not yet approach the sophistication and multimedia support of the new breed of programs that are the focus of the following section.

Multimedia Presentation Programs

Support for 2-D animation and QuickTime digital video is what sets *multimedia* presentation software apart from traditional presentation packages. In fact, experimenting with one of the multimedia presentation programs can be an excellent introduction to multimedia.

"Presentation" is something of a misnomer, by the way, as programs, such as Action, Cinemation, and PROmotion (see below), can actually be looked at as "lite" versions of powerful media integration packages, such as Director. For the purposes of this chapter, we'll concentrate solely on the animation features of these programs. For detailed information on media integration (authoring) tools, see Chapter 9.

Basic Animation Techniques

Using one of the programs reviewed below, you'll be able to create realistic *path-based* animations, and even exercise rudimentary *motion control.* Path-based animation lets you create movement by dragging an object from one point to another; the program then animates the object along this path. Many 2-D and 3-D animation packages use a more sophisticated version of this technique that allows you to specify "keyframes," with the program filling in the "in-between frames."

Most animation packages us a *timeline*—a pop-up window that lets you position objects at any point in time. A few packages, such as Cinemation and Animation Stand, mimic traditional *cel-based* animation techniques instead of using path or keyframe animation. With this technique, you create one frame or *cel* at a time. These cels are then overlaid to create a finished animation. Cel animation is sometimes referred to as *onionskinning*, after the transparent paper Hollywood animators used to sketch cels.

Motion control, also called *motion scripting,* is a catch-all term referring to the refinement of movement, in which you specify such attributes as acceleration. More advanced motion control, such as camera movement, spline-based motion paths, and motion filters, is the province of 3-D animation programs. Discussed later in this chapter and in Chapter 15, "Creating Animation."

Common Features

For starters, you shouldn't expect a multimedia presentation package to have all of the features of traditional presentation software. If you're going to be creating slide shows and working mostly with text and charts, you're better off with such old-guard mainstays as Aldus Persuasion and Microsoft PowerPoint, both of which offer complete text and charting facilities. These programs also offer features such as slide sorters and presentation outliners.

In general, you'll trade these traditional slide-based graphics and text creation tools for such multimedia features as device control, interactivity, and animation. Specifically, these are some common features of multimedia presentation software:

- **Graphics support.** You can expect at least basic draw and paint tools, such as pens and brushes, line styles, and fill patterns. Some programs, such as Cinemation, even include image processing tools like lassos, and eyedroppers. While many users prefer to turn to more specialized paint and image programs, it's handy to have these features in one program. Most programs import PICT or animated PICS files; some also accept EPS and TIFF files.

- **Templates.** Most programs have an assortment of prefab templates that include backgrounds, actors, and movements that you can customize for your own purposes. These are very helpful for the beginner: Assembling a presentation from templates is a good way to learn a program without the frustrations of starting from scratch.
- **Transitional effects.** All programs provide a slew of special effects, such as wipes, dissolves, and fades, that are useful for transitions between scenes. A more advanced version of these effects is the *automated build*—the gradual overlaying of elements in a scene.
- **Interactivity.** The ability to explore seemingly random areas of an on screen presentation is one of the cornerstones of multimedia. With many packages, you can incorporate interactivity by designating an object as a "button." When the button is subsequently selected with the mouse, the program plays a sound file, or branches to another slide.

Macromedia's Action

Action is a program that divides a presentation into "scenes" that have static backgrounds against which objects can be arranged and animated. These objects can be text, graphics, animations, or even QuickTime movies. The action is orchestrated using the Timeline Window, which helps you sequence objects and their movements.

The timeline concept was pioneered by Macromedia, which first introduced it as the "Score" in Director. It is now used in one form or another in nearly all leading 3-D animation programs. If you plan to move on to the more rarefied world of 3-D, you can get used to the concept with the timeline, which is probably the most complicated part of Action.

You create animation with the Path menu by specifying points along a path (keyframes) and the overall duration of the motion. Action then fills in the intermediate frames, creating smooth motion.

Action provides good control over individual objects: Click on an object, and you can adjust parameters such as the object's duration in a scene. If object creation and control leaves you cold, you can use one of Action's predefined templates, complete with text, graphics, and animation. Using templates as a starting point, you can replace template objects with your own, and adjust the existing animation. We recommend this technique to beginners, who may be put off by the timeline and its moderate learning curve. By adjusting a template's animation parameters and then viewing the results, you can learn a lot.

After you've imported or created your various objects and choreographed them with the timeline, you can add transitional and multimedia effects, such as sound or a QuickTime clip. Action has a particularly well-stocked arsenal of transitional and motion effects. Objects can be designated as interactive triggers that, when clicked, will pause or resume action, play a sound or movie file, or go to another scene.

In general, Action is geared more towards media integration than animation, and does not offer the more sophisticated techniques of a program like Cinemation.

Vividus' Cinemation

Cinemation (Figure 7.1) offers excellent animation tools. You can create motion by setting a beginning and ending frame for an object; Cinemation will fill in the intervening frames in a process called "tweening." If you prefer, you can click a Record button and simply drag the object at the speed and in the direction you want it to go.

Cinemation also lets you animate using a cel-based technique in which you edit a sequence frame by frame, giving you the most precise control (and, quite possibly, a headache!). This feature lets you display grayed-out images, or "ghosts," of previous frames that you use as guides to trace objects for subsequent frames.

The movie-within-a-movie is another fairly advanced feature that lets you achieve effects like a planet spinning as it simultaneously revolves around a sun. You can also stretch or compress animated sequences simply by increasing or decreasing the number of frames.

Cinemation includes basic image creation facilities, such as paint and object tools, and comes with a large assortment of templates, backgrounds, and clip animation.

Motion Works' PROmotion

Like other 2-D animation programs, PROmotion lets you create paths that describe the motion of objects. After creating paths in PROmotion, you can edit them by smoothing and by adding or deleting points. Like Cinemation, PROmotion includes an onionskin feature that displays grayed-out versions of previous

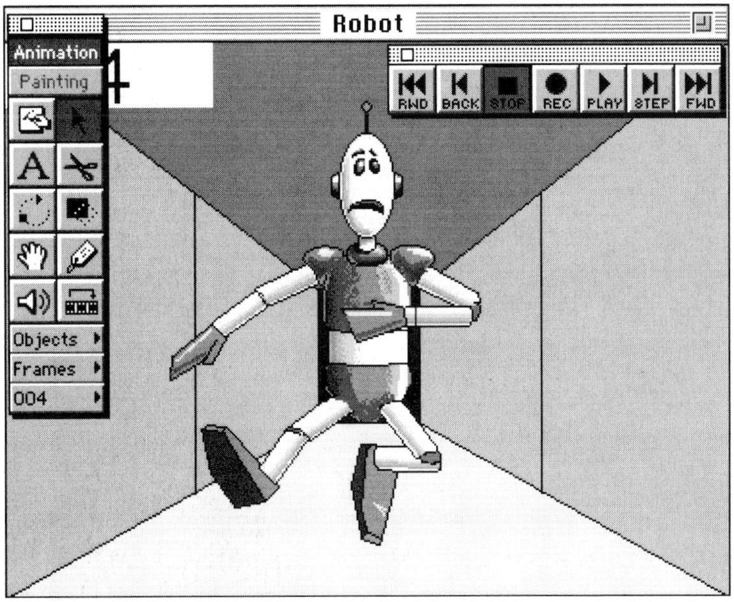

Figure 7.1 Using Cinemation, you can put together simple but effective animations.

frames as a guide to creating new frames. PROmotion uses a timeline feature to control sequencing, much like Action's TmeLine window.

PROmotion 213

An other standout feature of PROmotion is its excellent control over interactivity, including it's ability to control a variety of external devices such as laserdisc players. PROmotion also supports Apple Events—messages between different programs. For complex presentations, this feature can be used by one program to trigger an animated sequence from PROmotion.

PROmotion will save animations to videotape by writing them one frame at a time. To do this, you'll need an animation controller and frame-accurate videotape deck. Included with the program is the PrimeTime CD that's packed with actors (various objects), props (still graphics), and sounds that you can use as the basis for your animations.

Macromedia Director

Macromedia Director is the premiere media integration, or authoring tool. It's used by multimedia developers to integrate and playback multimedia productions of all types (see Chapter 9, "Authoring Tools"). Because Director is relatively complex and expensive, you wouldn't want to use it for animation alone, but if you're assembling a presentation using the program, you'll find its built-in animation tools very handy.

Director 210

Director's Studio module has a set of paint tools for creating bitmap objects, as well as a basic set of drawing tools. Other features include 32-bit color support and blend tools, and an antialiasing feature for smoothing jagged edges.

Animation in Director is similar to animation in other 2-D programs; you assemble and sequence objects using a timeline, which MacroMedia calls the Score, and then specify beginning and ending frames. Director interpolates the intermediate frames. There are tools for accelerating and slowing down objects, and you can animate a variety of imported objects, not just ones you create in the Studio.

CoSA's After Effects

Released in 1993, CoSA's After Effects has quickly moved into the forefront of multimedia programs. While it has many animation features, After Effects is based on QuickTime, so we've elected to cover it in Chapter 8, "Video Tools."

Its animation features include alpha channel compositing, allowing you to create a wide range of transparency and masking effects; a sub-pixel editing feature that offers fine control over image detail; an "object-oriented" approach that lets you easily combine objects that move independently of one another, yet are still treated as single unit (such as the moving wheels on a speeding train).

3-D Type and Illustration Programs

It's easier than ever to experiment with 3-D graphics, thanks to a new category of programs that has sprung up in the past year or so. Two of the programs, Typestry from Pixar and Strata's Strata Type 3-d, allow you to turn type into fully rendered

3-D objects. Using these products you can create 3-D type for publications or presentations, even animating type for that movie-of-the-week look.

Adobe's Dimensions and Ray Dream's addDepth are designed to take PostScript art from programs, such as Illustrator and FreeHand, and give it a 3-D look. The programs are excellent and inexpensive bridges to higher powered 3-D software, and are much simpler to master.

Pixar's Typestry

Typestry will take any PostScript or TrueType font, "extrude" it into three dimensions, and then rotate or scale it. You then add one of several bevel styles to give the type a rounded, chiseled, or beveled look. Once you've established the basic appearance of the type, you select from a library of textures (Pixar calls them "Looks"), such as shiny metal, wood, and plastic. Pixar bundles over 30 Looks and sells plug-ins of additional textures. Pixar's Looks are well known in the 3-D industry for their outstanding quality, which results in very slick effects. In addition to Looks, you can apply special effects, such as "perforations," which pierce type with different shapes.

Typestry offers precise control over lighting, and you can have up to 18 different light sources. Each light can have one of six different "gels" that cast shadows, or simulate window panes or venetian blinds. You also can specify the color and spot diameter of lights.

When animating objects using simple path-based techniques, you even can apply a motion-blur filter that results in some eye-catching effects. Typestry will save these animations as a QuickTime movie—a neat and useful feature.

After you've selected textures and lighting for your type, it's time to "render"—that is, for the computer to calculate and apply all of the effects you've specified. Typestry offers three levels of rendering quality. The first level results in a draft appearance that is suitable for making sure you're on the right track before you commit to a higher-quality render.

A word to the wise: Start with small test objects to get the look you're after before rendering a full-size image. Full-screen images can easily take an hour or two to render on a IIvx or IIci machine. Of course, rendering time is dependent on the number and complexity of effects you've applied, as well as on the sort of Mac you're using, and will take much longer for an animated sequence than for a single frame.

Strata's Strata Type 3d

Strata Type 3d gives you more control over the basic look of your type objects than does Typestry. You can choose from 17 bevels, or create your own using smooth Bezier curves. Extrusion depth is controlled with a simple slider. The program also supports "kerning," the adjustment of space between two letters.

With Strata Type 3d, you can render type using textures of your own design. You can "map" scanned or painted imagery onto type for a custom look, an effect that is possible in Typestry only when you purchase a separate module.

Strata Type 3d's lighting effects are similar to Typestry's, and include multiple sources, gels, and preset washes. It's rendering quality isn't up to the professional results possible with Typestry, but then you have to have a very fast Mac to make Typestry's rendering times tolerable on complex jobs.

Adobe Dimensions

While they are similar in many respects, Adobe Dimensions (and addDepth, below) differ from Typestry and Strata Type 3d in at least one fundamental way. The latter two programs convert outline type, which are vector graphics, to a bitmap format. By contrast, both Dimensions and AddDepth work on type in its native vector format.

Neither method is necessarily superior, but there are important trade-offs with each approach. Generally, you can achieve a higher-quality, more painterly look with bitmap images, but they're bigger and do not scale as well as vector graphics. Also, once a vector image is converted to a bitmap, it's made up of fixed pixels, and you can make only a minimum of useful adjustments to the image.

By contrast, vector graphics can be resized, broken down to its component parts, and have different stroke and fill patterns applied—all with no loss to image quality. (For a complete discussion of the two formats, see Chapter 5, "Imaging Tools.")

After you turn an Illustrator image into a 3-D image using either Dimensions or addDepth, you can bring it back into Illustrator and manipulate it as you would any other Illustrator file. In fact, Dimensions is basically designed for users of Illustrator who want to fiddle with 3-D effects, but don't want to subject themselves to the intricacies of a full-featured 3-D program. This fact is plain when you open a Dimensions window: There are no tools for text creation, and only simple drawing tools.

Figure 7.2
3-D illustration programs are particularly useful for adapting 2-D art for applications such as package design.

As in the type programs, you can extrude objects to give them depth. Dimensions has a nice "trackball" feature that lets you rotate objects with great facility. Surfaces effects are limited to PostScript blends and fills. You can, however, map an Illustrator or FreeHand file onto an object, which can be very useful for such tasks as package design.

Dimensions includes very basic animation features, and while you can't save the result as a QuickTime movie, you can use Apple's Movie Player (or another utility) to convert to QuickTime.

Ray Dream's addDepth

Ray Dream's product (see Figure 7.3) is very similar to Dimensions, offering the same basic approach to simple 3-D effects. The main difference is that, while Dimensions is being marketed as an Illustrator add-on, AddDepth is a stand-alone product. Unlike Dimensions, addDepth lets you generate type and print directly from the program.

Figure 7.3
Ray Dream's 3-D illustration program pushes 2-D art into shape.

Animation Utility Programs

Along with the plethora of full-featured animation programs, there is a whole category of utility programs that are fun to fiddle with—and some are actually useful:

TOOLS
Morph 229

Morph. Metamorphosis, popularized in movies, music videos, and TV ads, seems to have captured people's imaginations. While the feature is offered in several 3-D programs, Gryphon Software's Morph lets you try this high-end effect on two-dimensional artwork.

Using the program is simple—you designate key points on two PICT images to be morphed, then map the points to one another. You can save the resulting morphing sequence as a PICS animation, QuickTime movie, or single PICT file of an intermediate image in the morphing sequence.

JAG II and Smoothie. Image processing software has long offered antialiasing features that smooth the jagged edges of bitmap files, but these two utilities do the job particularly well. Smoothie accepts only object-oriented files from drawing programs. JAG II will import bitmaps as well; however, Smoothie does the better job on object-oriented art.

Both programs will accept either single or multiple images automatically in batch mode, so you can treat animation frames unattended. For animators working under tight resource constraints, JAG II is particularly useful. You can turn off the anti-aliasing feature in your 3-D rendering program to save time, then run the frames through JAG II to smooth them out.

TOOLS
PACo Producer 218

PACo Producer. PACo, short for PICS Animation Compressor, compiles and compresses PICS files, QuickTime movies, and PICT files into a proprietary format that can be played back on the lowliest Mac Plus with only 1Mb RAM. Compare this with QuickTime, which needs a minimum of 4Mb RAM and a 68020-class machine. PACo files can be played back on other platforms as well, including Windows, and Sun SPARCStations.

3-D Modeling, Animating, and Rendering Software

There are at least 20 products that fit into the 3-D software category. Some of these specialize in one of the phases of 3-D, such as modeling, while others do it all. First, some definitions:

- **Modeling.** This is where 3-D creation begins. Typically, you start with simple objects such as squares and circles, then push or *extrude* them into 3-D objects. By manipulating these simple forms, you "model" the objects that ultimately will make up your 3-D world. More advanced modelers supply sophisticated tools that let you make precise refinements. For example, *vertex editing* lets you manipulate single points on an object.

When modeling, you generally work with outlines or *wireframes* of objects. If you were to work with fully rendered objects, operations would slow to a crawl. Most modelers supply quick shaded views, to give you a rough idea of what models look like with surfaces. Some programs, such as Infini-D, Swivel 3D, and MacroModel, are fast enough so that you can work in quick shaded view instead of wireframe mode.

- **Animating.** Once your models are complete, you animate them using a variety of techniques. Most 3-D programs use the *keyframe* method, in which you position your models at key points, and the program creates the remaining frames. Motion control techniques allow you to vary the acceleration of animation, simulate the effects of centripetal force, and refine the continuity of motion. To improve performance, animators generally work in wireframe or quick shaded mode while working out moves. During this phase, you'll also position lights and cameras.
- **Rendering.** Finally, you'll select surfaces and textures for your animation, determine color and type of light, and specify effects such as shadows and masks. You'll probably want to do several test renderings on small parts of your work before rendering an entire scene or sequence of frames. When you're ready to go, the program and your CPU take over and perform the intensive set of calculations necessary to render realistic colors, textures, light, and shadow. This process can take from several minutes to days or even weeks, depending on the complexity of your art and the number of frames that must be rendered.

For a complete description of the 3-D process, see Chapter 15, "Creating Amination."

Modelers

While some of the following programs also will do animation and rendering, they specialize in the modeling phase of the 3-D process. A trend, however, is to combine all 3-D processes into a single product. Specular has done this successfully with Infini-D, and MacroMedia plans to create a 3-D powerhouse by combining its advanced modeler, MacroModel, with its high-end renderer/animator, Three-D.

All modelers provide basic shapes, called *primitives*, for constructing 3-D objects using *lathing* or *cross-sectional* modeling techniques. These are simple techniques that will help you create simple 3-D objects quickly and with little effort. Basic modelers, such as Swivel 3D and Super 3D, create *polygon-based* models, in which even curved shapes are made up of small segmented lines.

More advanced modelers, such as Form Z, MacroModel and Presenter Professional, let you make more complex shapes with techniques such as *sweeping* and *drilling*. Using these packages, you also can create smoother *spline-based* curves as well as polygonal models.

Higher-end modelers give you more control over model refinement as well, with such features as *vertex editing*, which lets you manipulate single points, or *vertices*, along a model's surface. *Boolean operations* are another advanced technique in which you sculpt models by applying intersecting shapes. For examples and more information about all of these modeling techniques, see Chapter 15, "Creating Animation."

Selecting a Modeler

Before you invest in a modeling program, make sure you really need one. You might be better off with a general purpose 3-D package, such as Designer or Infini-D, that includes a modeler.

However, if you need to create intricate or unusual surface geometry and can make good use of advanced features, such as spline-based tools, vertex editing, and Boolean operators, then you'll probably want to look at a high-end modeler, such as MacroModel or Form Z. The modelers in all-purpose programs generally lack advanced modeling capabilities like these. VIDI's Presenter is an exception to this rule, combining powerful high-end modeling and rendering features.

Finally, as there is no standard file format for models, if you go with a stand-alone modeler, make sure you can export the models to the renderer you're going to use. While all modelers have their own proprietary file formats, DXF is a common interchange format, and many modelers export to Pixar's RIB format.

Macromedia's Swivel 3-D Professional

Swivel 3-D 220

Swivel Sample Models 820–829

Swivel is the granddaddy of Mac modelers, beginning its life in the mid-'80s as the modeler for virtual reality pioneer VPL's simulated worlds. Even though it has been surpassed by better modelers, such as Macromedia's own MacroModel, Swivel is still used by professionals for a number of reasons.

First, its straightforward interface appeals to many users, allowing both novices and professionals alike to quickly build workable models. Its cross-sectional modeling metaphor (sometimes called "skinning" or "lofting") makes it easy to build many of the objects that are difficult in other modelers. (For example, it's much easier to create a bar of soap via cross section than with the lathing tools found in other modelers).

Second, Swivel has a complex system of hierarchical links and locks necessary to build complex models, such as human figures, that have many joints and points of rotation. (For more on hierarchical models, see "Locks and Linking.") Finally, Swivel has an excellent quick shading mode that allows you to work with smooth-shaded models rather than wireframes.

Despite these advantages, Swivel has some drawbacks and suffers in comparison to many new generation modelers, notably MacroModel. For one thing, Swivel lacks a spline tool, which means that the only way to get really smooth curves is to use many polygons—a painstaking process that also results in slow rendering. Swivel models also tend to contain a lot of internal geometry, which makes complex models unwieldy.

While Swivel is primarily a modeler, it has basic rendering and animation capabilities suitable for modest needs. Swivel does export to Pixar's RIB format, so you can take advantage of RenderMan's state-of-the-art rendering features. However, Swivel's compatibility is not total, and you may find that certain elements, such as shadows, do not carry over well. Macromedia bundles Swivel with RenderMan in a package called SwivelMan.

Marketed by Macromedia under license from VPL, Swivel's future may be somewhat in doubt, as it lingers in the shadow of MacroModel. In fact, the program hasn't been updated for sometime. However, with its long history and strong base of influential power users, it's likely to be around for at least a little while.

Autodessy's Form Z

Form Z is unique in that it provides the *solid* modeling techniques used by design engineers and architects with the *surface* modeling tools normally found in 3-D animation products.

Some forms are more easily produced with solids than with surfaces. For example, windows can be cut from walls, and shapes can be refined by sculpting them with other shapes (see Figure 7.4.) In addition, a complex shape created with solids is a single shape, and not made up of many forms the way a complex surface model may be. As a result, it is more compact and will render faster.

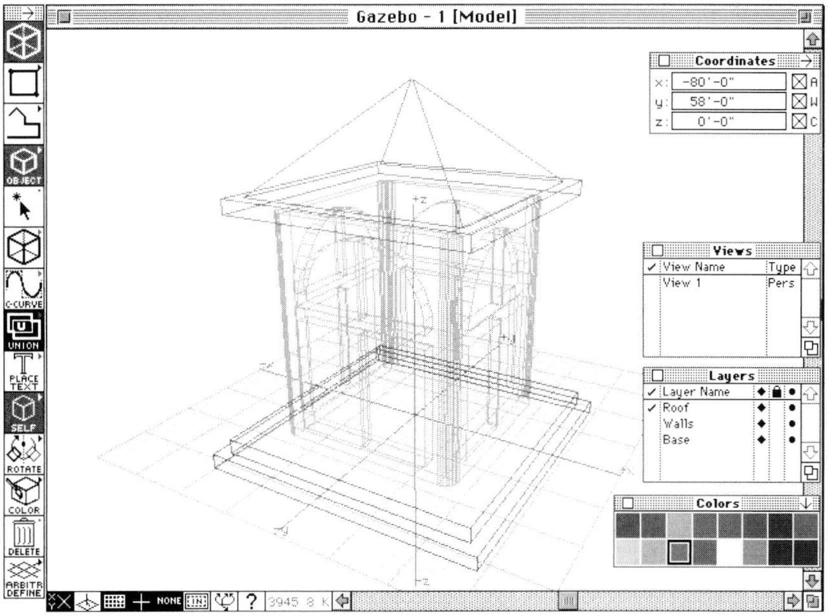

Figure 7.4
Form Z's solid modeling technique of cutting windows from walls and refining and sculpting shapes.

Among Form Z's solid modeling features, you'll find a variety of powerful tools, including Difference, for carving one solid with another; Add, for combining two solids; and Intersection, for creating the space formed where two solids intersect. These tools, collectively known as *Boolean operations*, are rarely found in other programs.

Form Z's surface modeling tools are equally as strong and rival those of most advanced surface-only modelers, such as MacroModel. You can create smooth curves with splines, Beziers, and NURBS (an advanced form of splines), among other tools. Such tools give you an unusual degree of control over smooth surfaces.

Surface models can be edited by manipulating the *mesh* that makes up a wireframe model, this process is similar to the *vertex editing* offered by other programs, in which you manipulate single points on a mesh. Form Z's mesh-editing feature is considered superior, because it's easier to edit a grid of points instead of the individual points themselves.

In another innovation, Form Z lets you build solids using surfaces, which you combine using the Stitch tool. This technique allows you to produce very complex shapes that would be difficult or impossible to create any other way. Once the Stitch tool has been used on a group of surfaces, the object is a solid that can be further refined using any of the Boolean operators.

Like all modelers, Form Z's rendering capabilities are rudimentary and lack advanced features, such as texture mapping. You can export Form Z models as DXF files that are accepted by many renderers.

Form Z is one of the best solid modelers on the market, and if you need both solid and surface modeling in a single package, you won't find a better tool.

Alias Sketch!

Alias Research Inc. makes advanced workstation-based 3-D packages targeted at industrial design applications. With Sketch!, Alias is aiming to appeal to Mac 3-D designers by incorporating some advanced features and wrapping them in an approachable interface.

Like other advanced modelers, Sketch! lets you create smooth curves using spline curves. Sketch! uses a spline variant called NURB. This is powerful, but may take some getting used to. Luckily, you also can import the more familiar Bezier curves from Illustrator and FreeHand.

Sketch!'s object editing features are also powerful, letting you alter *isoparms*—isolated details of a larger object. You also can pinpoint and edit object elements using a Finder-like library catalog.

Unlike most modelers, Sketch! offers a fairly complete set of rendering tools, including surface mapping and lighting options, and will export models in Pixar's RIB format if you prefer to render using that program. Finally, Sketch! has a unique and noteworthy feature that lets you match a 3-D model's perspective to that of a 2-D image, such as a photograph.

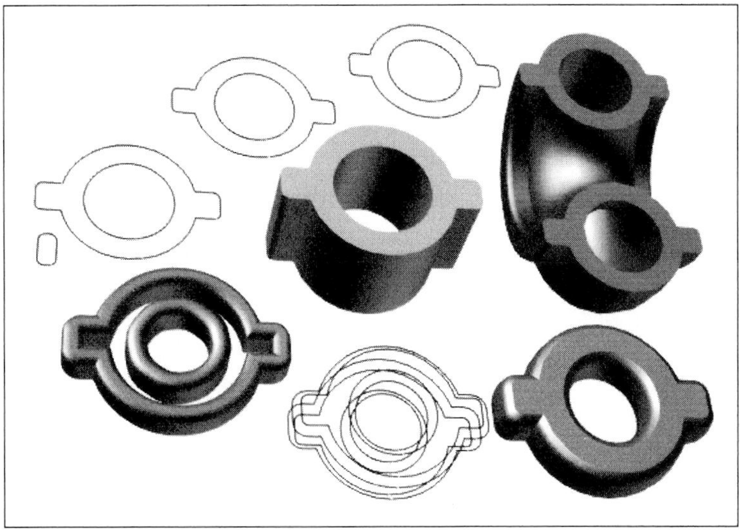

Figure 7.5 MacroModel's sophisticated tools make it possible to produce a variety of shapes and forms.

Macromedia's MacroModel

MacroModel 221

MacroModel is the new kid on the block, and it has moved in and made itself at home very quickly. Macromedia designed the program from the ground up, with the goal of producing a high-performance modeler with an approachable interface.

As in Swivel, MacroModel objects can be manipulated in a surprisingly fast and fluid smooth shaded mode that gives a good representation of the model's form. Using a virtual "trackball," you can interactively rotate a model to make on-the-spot adjustments. These two features give MacroModel its admirable real-time feel that makes modeling seem more natural and less mathematical.

Like Sketch!, MacroModel's organic feel is abetted by a drawing metaphor that will be familiar to users of Adobe Illustrator and other drawing packages. The emphasis is on intuitive creation, rather than on the visual and spatial skills demanded by other modelers. Accordingly, MacroModel is a spline-based modeler that creates smooth and easy forms.

The program supplies a full set of conventional object creation tools, including extrude, lathe, cross section, and sweep (for definitions, see Modeling Tools). Far from run-of-the-mill, however, are MacroModel's "Deformation" tools, which allow you to create complex models on-the-fly, by twisting, bending, and tapering them (see Figure 7.5). This real-time feature is particularly powerful and illustrates the progressive nature of the program.

For refining models, the program neatly categorizes editing into three modes that offer increasingly detailed object views:

- **Compound Geometry** lets you adjust the gross dimensions of your models—height, width, and so on.

- **Surface Geometry** lets you edit an object's surfaces using spline-based control points. In another of MacroModel's friendly innovations, the control points are accessible even in smooth shaded mode.
- **Mesh Geometry** reveals a model's smallest details, allowing you to reshape and make micro-fine adjustments at the mesh level (a technique commonly known as "vertex editing").

In MacroModel, as in addDepth and Dimensions, you can import object-oriented art, such as Illustrator files. However, in the case of MacroModel, imported vector art is converted to bitmap form, complete with associated geometry that you can adjust as if you had created it within MacroModel.

Macromedia also has incorporated a group of capabilities suitable to the more formal demands of computer-aided design. You can "nudge" object position, scale, and angle from the keyboard, and objects can be manipulated with numeric precision. People working with hierarchical models will be pleased to see that MacroModel equals Swivel's excellent support for links and joints. Another timesaving touch is an auto-copy tool that allows you to mirror structures such as aircraft wings.

Snapping tools are equally impressive. By default, snapping occurs in the 2-D working plane, but you also can accurately align 3-D surfaces. This last feature is particularly important, because it helps you avoid small surface defects that may be visible only after time-consuming rendering.

MacroModel includes basic rendering tools, but serious designers will want to import models into a full-featured rendering/animation program. MacroModel supports a fair range of export options, including DXF, RIB, and Swivel.

MacroModel is aimed at the high end—with a price to match—and probably is the best modeling-only program on the market today. Its sleek interface and intuitive tools will appeal to multimedia developers creating free-form shapes, and its CAD features will make engineers and industrial designers feel right at home, too.

Integrated Programs

3-D programs in this category combine modeling and rendering, rendering and animation, and sometimes all three phases of the 3-D process. It's difficult to group these programs according to features, price, or performance, because these criteria are not as interrelated as they are in other software categories. Strong 3-D market competition, an unusually large field of products, and rapidly evolving technology have combined to create a somewhat confused market segment. Despite this, it's possible to make a few generalizations.

Creating Surfaces

All renderers let you wrap models in basic matte, shiny, and transparent surfaces. For heightened realism and detail, you can create surface textures through different *mapping* techniques:

- **Texture maps.** Using this process, you place a 2-D image onto a 3-D object. Programs offer different mapping modes, depending on the shape of the object.
- **Reflection maps.** Also called environment mapping, this is a specialized form of texture mapping in which you simulate reflections by projecting an image of an object's surroundings onto that object. The technique cuts down on rendering time, since the program does not need to calculate reflections.
- **Bump maps**. These surfaces simulate various surface irregularities, giving the illusion of rough, uneven surfaces.
- **Procedural maps.** Computer-generated images that can yield effects ranging from realistic to surreal.

Nearly all renderers have these surface-mapping features: The differences are in the amount of control they give you over their application, and how fast they render the results. For example, Infini-D has a wide range of rendering effects, with average-quality rendering. StrataVision also has an excellent array of effects, but renders rather slowly. At the high end, ElectricImage is known for its wide range of effects, high quality, and very fast rendering, but this is unusual; most programs do only one or two of these things well.

Shading and Rendering

Aside from the flat shading draft mode, renders usually offer *Gouraud* and *Phong* shading. Gouraud is relatively quick to render and looks OK for sharp-edged objects. Phong yields smooth surfaces, but takes longer to render.

Photo-realistic rendering is most commonly achieved with "ray tracing," which gives excellent results but in glacial rendering times. Pixar's proprietary RenderMan techniques also offer excellent results.

Lighting options include four different types of effects: ambient, spot, distant, and radial. Not all programs offer all lighting options, but higher-end programs, such as Presenter and Three-D, do. In the mid-range, Infini-D and Strata offer excellent lighting options.

Controlling Motion

On the animation side, most programs offer keyframe animation, which gives a fair degree of *motion control.*

Selecting a Package

Beyond the range of basic to high-end features, programs differentiate themselves by including an assortment of specialized features that may or may not be of interest to you. For example, Infini-D will let you create animated surfaces by projecting a QuickTime movie onto an object; StrataVision boasts a texture map library whose permutations could take months to explore; several programs, including Presenter, Three-D, and ElectricImage, let you create very smooth transitions by "morphing"—changing one object into another over time; and with Topas and RenderMan, you can create atmospheric effects like fog and "depth cueing"—which blurs background objects to make them appear distant.

One last feature that is genuinely of use to almost everybody is the so-called *alpha channel*, which will be familiar to Photoshop users. An alpha channel can be used to isolate an image from its surroundings. This image then can easily be overlaid or *composited* into another scene without rerendering. Alpha channels have many other advantages as well (see Chapter 5, "Imaging Tools," for more information). Unfortunately, alpha channel support is generally limited to more advanced programs, such as Three-D, Topas, and Presenter. However, in the mid-range, Designer, Infini-D, and RenderMan support the feature.

With their mixed bag of features and unpredictable trade-offs, choosing a 3-D package can be tough. But we can offer a few general suggestions—hey, that's our job. If you don't need precision control over textures and movement, you'll be happy with a mid-range program, such as Infini-D, StrataVision, or Designer (for still images). Using any of these programs or others listed below, you'll be able to create convincing, realistic, and dynamic imagery with reasonable balance between time and quality.

On the other hand, professionals working in broadcast environments, realistic simulations, or photo-realistic applications definitely will want a higher-powered program, such as ElectricImage, Presenter, or Sculpt 4D. You actually may wind up with several programs, since no one application does it all with excellent results.

Ray Dream's Designer

Designer is aimed at the vast cadre of Mac graphic designers who want to incorporate 3-D into their work, but who are turned off by arcane and expensive 3-D software. The program creates beautifully rendered still images that are ideal for the print medium, and certainly suitable for multimedia scenes and backgrounds.

The program is divided into two modules—LightForge for modeling, and Scenebuilder for assembling, lighting, and rendering. Ray Dream uses Apple Events to pass information between the modules but, even so, hopping between them gets a little old.

Designer's modeler is more than adequate, and includes a lofting feature (for creating shapes whose cross sections vary along their length), spline curve tools, and even vertex editing. A virtual trackball makes it easy to rotate objects for viewing from alternate perspectives. These tools make it possible to create all but the most convoluted and intricate shapes.

When you've modeled a cross section and then given it an elevation, Designer automatically renders a full-color shaded view—a nice feature. Ray Dream offers a full set of textures and lighting options for creating surfaces, and supports an alpha channel, which greatly aids in image compositing and rendering.

Figure 7.6 Rendering still images in Ray Dream's ray tracing mode yields beautiful photo-realistic art.

Designer's ray tracing rendering mode is one of the best, and produces near photo-realistic images (Figure 7.6). As a result, rendering is comparatively slow but can be sped up with DreamNet, Ray Dream's network rendering option.

All in all, Designer is a good beginning-to-intermediate package, similar in philosophy to 3-D drawing packages (and such programs as Sketch!) but more powerful and full-featured.

Strata Inc.'s StrataVision

Like Designer, StrataVision is capable of rendering very high quality photo realistic imagery. It's modeler is satisfactory, but lacks the flexibility and creation tools of other mid-range packages, such as Infini-D. StrataVision does have one interesting modeling technique called *flexing*, which allows you to create skinned objects that can be animated to flex like a snake or tail.

StrataVision's real strength lies in its texture mapping and rendering capabilities. Its surface libraries are vast, and you can create endless variations on your own. Alpha channel support also is good, allowing you to use alphas for lighting effects and image layering.

TOOLS
StrataVision 226
StrataShapes 802
StrataTextures 812

Animation support is OK, but not great. The animation component is keyframe based, and you can adjust frame rate with a timeline. More advanced motion control features are lacking, but you can animate textures so that they dissolve (morph) into one another, a useful feature.

StrataVision, like Designer, can render beautifully, with rendering speed being the main trade-off. Strata Inc. does offer RenderPro, a network renderer that greatly reduces rendering time if you have access to a number of machines over a network. Strata offers a proprietary version of the *radiosity* rendering technique,

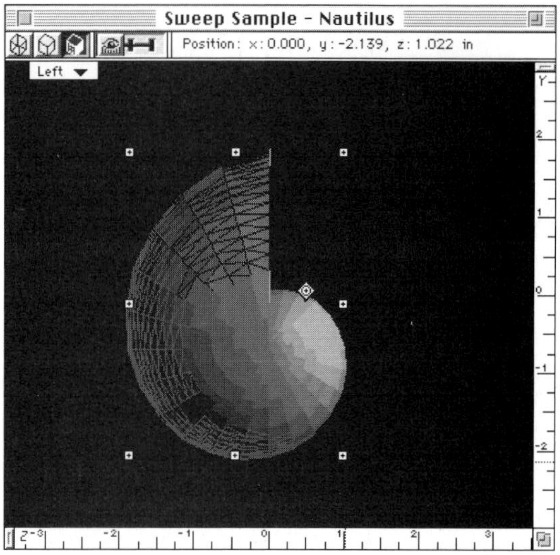

Figure 7.7 Among its many features, StrataVision boasts a strong modeler.

an advanced algorithm that can account for nuances, such as the effects of reflected light. The technique can yield spectacular results, but rendering time is prohibitive on all but the fastest machines.

Pixar's RenderMan/ ShowPlace

RenderMan is a standard renderer that works on all major desktop platforms. This universality and RenderMan's outstanding quality have made it the rendering engine of choice for many professionals.

However, RenderMan lacks a graphical interface, forcing you to set rendering options and parameters using a difficult text-based interface. Actually, the fact that RenderMan's textures are "procedural"—defined by text files—is the very reason why the program is so powerful. You can edit these files to create unlimited textural variations. In fact, third-party vendors, such as The Valis Group, offer dozens of textures (called "looks") that plug into RenderMan.

As its name indicates, RenderMan neither models nor animates, but focuses squarely on rendering. Pixar has softened RenderMan's formidable interior by offering an interface module called ShowPlace. ShowPlace accepts objects imported from modeling programs in the RIB format, and also includes some basic "ClipObjects." You can position and scale these objects, then light them and select rendering options. The program's lighting control is excellent, providing a selection of options, such as ambient, distant, and spot.

Rendering is RenderMan's claim to fame, and it does it quite well, with the usual speed/quality trade-offs.

Specular's Infini-D

Using Infini-D is sort of like going to your favorite sushi bar: You can choose from a glittering array of exotic yet accessible treats. Well, maybe you don't like sushi, but you might just cotton to Infini-D (see Figure 7.8).

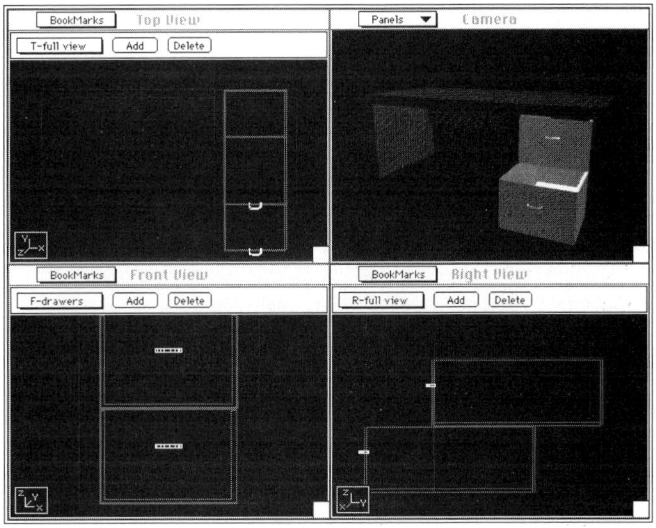

Figure 7.8 Infini-D's interface appeals to many 3-D artists.

Infini-D has a complete set of modeling tools, and provides simultaneous views from four perspectives as you work. The program lacks a spline tool or vertex editing capabilities, so creating free-form shapes and curves can be tricky.

An excellent set of textures, including an unusually complete group of procedural textures, are highlights of Infini-D. All textures can be fully manipulated and adjusted according to several attributes. The animated-surfaces feature is nice, allowing you to project QuickTime movies onto objects. You also can morph objects and textures using a simple interface that produces very pleasing results.

Infini-D is one of the few modelers that takes advantage of Apple's Publish and Subscribe facility. You can use it to import 2-D art from a drawing program, which Infini-D will convert to a 3-D image. When the original 2-D art file changes, Infini-D updates the 3-D derivative as well.

Infini-D's alpha channel support is particularly excellent, allowing you to seamlessly composite such images as a tumbling 3-D logo against a sky backdrop. Rendering modes include Ray Tracing and Phong shading, which will render shadows for heightened realism.

Infini-D's animation facilities are well-developed and offer many advanced features. Animation is controlled with a well-designed timeline window, through which you can easily adjust frame rate, smooth the velocity of motion, and animate objects, cameras, and lights.

Traditionally, animators have spent much of their time trying to achieve smooth motion. In response, Infini-D's Animation Assistant gives you further control over motion through "procedural" animation techniques. For example, you can smooth motion by aligning to camera path, aligning direction to motion, or automatically banking a camera. You can thus program motion fairly haphazardly, then clean it up with the Animation Assistant.

Infini-D is an integrated package that's an excellent choice for the intermediate-to-advanced user, and its effective interface makes it ideal for beginners, too.

Topas

Topas, like Infini-D, is an integrated package that offers complete control over the 3-D process. A high-end package that has been in use by 3-D professionals for some time, Topas has many advanced features.

Its modeler features high-end tools such as spline curves, Boolean operations, bending, twisting, and beveling. A complete set of surface options and libraries, lighting types, and rendering effects highlight Topas's rendering capabilities. Topas's rendering speed is better than average.

Animation features are also strong—it supports both keyframe-and path-based methods—but many motion control options must be specified with text commands, rather than through a more intuitive interface.

Macromedia's Three-D

With Three-D, Macromedia has clearly focused on the animation phase of 3-D. The program has no modeler, leaving this in the capable hands of its cousins, MacroModel and Swivel 3D.

Three-D uses the time-based approach to animation, which gives you fine command over every detail of movement for multiple independent objects (Figure 7.9). This may sound complicated, but Three-D's timeline animation control window, the Score, simplifies operations (although, it does take a little getting used to).

You can point an object at a camera, light, or another object, which makes it easy to create smooth and precise movement. For example, you can attach a

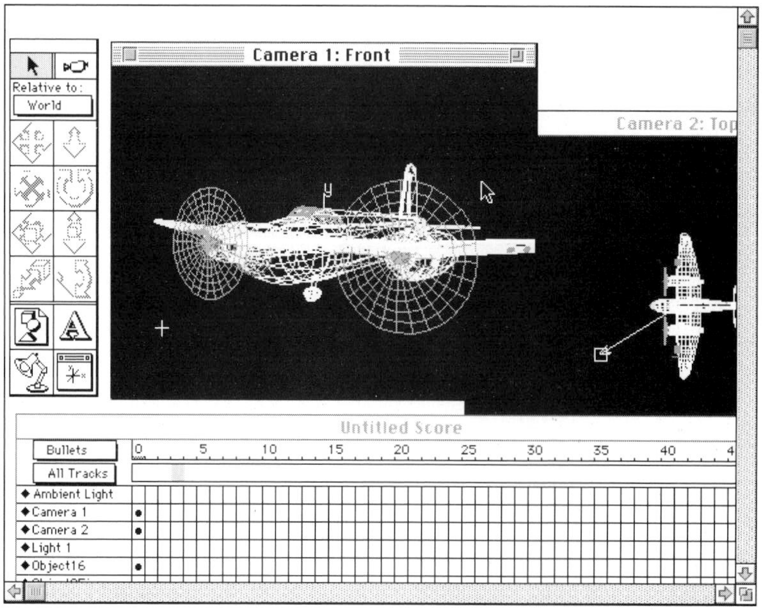

Figure 7.9 Three-D gives you excellent command over the placement, movement, sequence, and timing of animation.

Speeding Up Rendering

One of the frustrations for amateur animators as well as professionals is the time it takes to render their work. Current desktop Macs simply are not powerful enough to perform the immense number of calculations necessary to render complex 3-D animation in a reasonable amount of time.

Effects such as lighting, color, antialiasing, procedural mapping, transparency, alpha channels, and motion itself are as time consuming to calculate as the results are beautiful to look at. In response, vendors have come up with a number of solutions—all of which will cost you more money, but may be worth it to you:

Network Renderers. Specular (Infini-D/Backburner), Strata (StrataVision 3d/RenderPro), and Ray Dream (Designer/DreamNet) all have network rendering software that works with their particular 3-D packages. The idea is that you can commandeer otherwise idle machines on a network, and split your rendering job among those computers.

The speed advantage is equal to the number of machines working on the job, minus the 10–15% overhead necessary to split the job, send the chunks back and forth, and reassemble the rendered frames on the originating machine. The performance improvement can diminish somewhat as more machines are roped in, increasing network traffic.

If you have access to a network and already use one of the 3-D products that has a companion network renderer, you'll definitely want to consider this option. The packages are relatively inexpensive, and the performance gains are significant.

Coprocessor Boards. Manufacturers such as Yarc and StarTech make hardware cards with special processors that take over rendering tasks from the Mac's CPU. Using these cards, you can cut rendering times by as much as a factor of 10.

While these cards most commonly accept Pixar's RIB file format, they are beginning to support other file formats, including those of Presenter and Sculpt 4D. Although they are much more expensive than network rendering software, rendering cards have the advantage of local installation, and they don't require a network to operate.

Workstations. Using Pixar's NetRenderMan, you can send RIB files to a Unix workstation for rendering. You'll also need an Ethernet networking card in your Mac for connection to the workstation. If you have access to a Unix workstation, such as a Sun, NeXT, or SGI, this is an attractive option that can give you performance rivaling a whole network of Macs.

camera to an object for cinematic "fly-bys." Similarly, lights can "look at" objects, which makes it much easier to align components.

To further refine animation, you can view graphs of motion and tweak them simply by adjusting the motion curve, which is spline-based for easy editing and smooth motion.

Three-D offers a decent set of surface and rendering options, certainly adequate for most uses, but not up to its professional animation tools. Many 3-D pros use Three-D for its animation control, and export frames in RIB format for rendering with RenderMan.

VIDI's Presenter

This is a professional high-end tool that integrates modeling, animation, and rendering. Presenter's modeling tools are among the best on the market and include all advanced techniques, such as spline curves, mesh editing (which VIDI terms "digital clay"), and bending/twisting/tapering.

Presenter has a full range of texture-mapping options, including computed procedural surfaces. Lighting options also are good, with a variety of instrument types, colors, and intensities. Both ray tracing and Phong shading are supported, and Presenter has strong links to RenderMan. Animation is via the standard keyframe method.

Sculpt 4D

Sculpt 4D is another integrated high-end 3-D package that includes a particularly powerful modeler. The interface is known for its complexity, however. Rendering and animation facilities are good, but probably not up to the strength of the modeler. Some professionals use Sculpt for modeling and ElectricImage for animation and rendering, a formidable combination.

ElectricImage

ElectricImage is the ultimate professional 3-D tool, noted for its particularly strong broadcast and film animation features (see Figure 7.10). EI has no

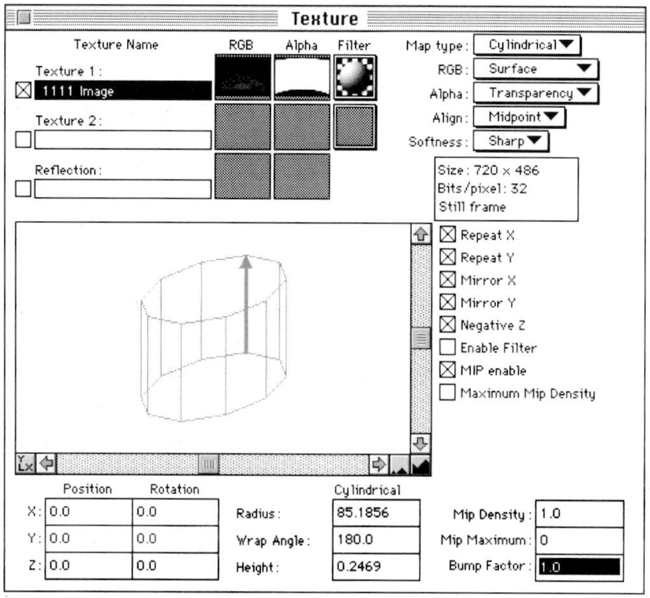

Figure 7.10 ElectricImage's Transparency Mapping interface lets you specify an object's opacity.

modeler, but it does have the best file import facilities of any animation package on the market.

The program has many features that have made it the darling of the Hollywood animation set. You can write animation to 8mm tape for further work at a postproduction house, or save to a digital broadcast video format. This last option renders each field of interlaced video independently, so the output is well integrated—very important for broadcast work.

You also can work with action-safe indicators, ensuring that your work won't be cropped when transferred to video. A *rotoscoping* feature (allowing you to combine live action and animation) and Mr. Font (for creating titling) further endears EI to the lotusland crowd.

EI's animation features are equally sophisticated. Not only can you animate objects, but also textures, transparencies, reflectivity, lights, and more. Velocity graphing allows you to adjust spline-based representations of motion, and you can even transfer predefined motions from one object to another.

EI also is known for its absolutely blazing rendering speeds, which it achieves through proprietary machine-level coding. The sheer speed of the program lets you view wireframes at 30 frames per second real-time. Not surprisingly, rendering quality is the best in the business—essential for the quality demands of the broadcast medium.

8

Video Tools

Desktop video is the latest digital revolution of the 1990s. Although it has been around in one form or another since the late 1980s, desktop video has now been made practical for most people by the convergence of Apple's QuickTime—the standard system architecture for handling moving images—and outstanding video capture and editing products from third parties. It represents one of the crowning achievements of desktop computing. The new accessibility and economy of desktop video tools means you now can make real-time video sequences an integral part of your multimedia presentations.

In this chapter, we'll introduce you to digital QuickTime-based video on the Macintosh, and we'll provide a description of features and capabilities of the hardware and software tools for QuickTime applications. We'll also give you the information you need to make informed buying decisions, based on your particular needs. Don't be intimidated by the jargon or by the wealth of choices for special effects described in the software sections; many features can be implemented with point-and-click simplicity. Frequently, you just copy and paste your audio and video into place, choose a filter, and make your movie. As you become more accomplished in this task, you will have new appreciation for the information you're about to read.

Desktop Video's Evolution

Desktop video has evolved from two family trees: one descending from television, the other from microcomputers and graphics software. These have been combined to form tools that address traditional video production tasks with convenience and economy.

Broadcast Roots

The first television shows preceded the invention of videotape and were by necessity broadcast live, for want of an effective way to store and edit them. When videotape first arrived on the scene in 1956, the only editing tool was a pair of scissors. The tape was spliced or taped together like film, which proved to be quite inadequate. Editing videotape—an analog, non-digital medium—has matured into a familiar process of electronically transferring the analog video signal from the source tape, or raw footage, to a master edited tape, which can then be sent out for duplication. This process of non-digital editing continues to this day, although increasingly, digital effects are used, and computers assist in the editing process.

Several significant drawbacks are inherent in the traditional process of analog videotape editing. One is the need to lay down each sequence in a linear fashion, making changes difficult after the fact. In order to effectively replace a segment from earlier in the editing session, the new segment has to be exactly the same length as the original. Furthermore, every time video is transferred to another tape the quality of the signal deteriorates, a phenomenon known as generation loss. If the raw footage is edited onto a master tape, the new master is a second generation tape. When duplicates are created from the master tape for distribution, they are third generation. If special effects are needed, the final tape may be fourth generation or more, and the deterioration in quality can be pronounced.

Now you can have your cake and eat it, too. These shortcomings are not present in digital video, where scenes can be edited in any order, and each copy or duplicate is identical in every respect to the original (although some generational loss can still occur as a result of compressing and decompressing digital footage—more about that later). At the same time, digital video features all of the high-end special effects that have evolved in all those years along the analog route. And, of course, the comparatively low cost and incredible convenience of digital video have been major factors in sparking the new revolution.

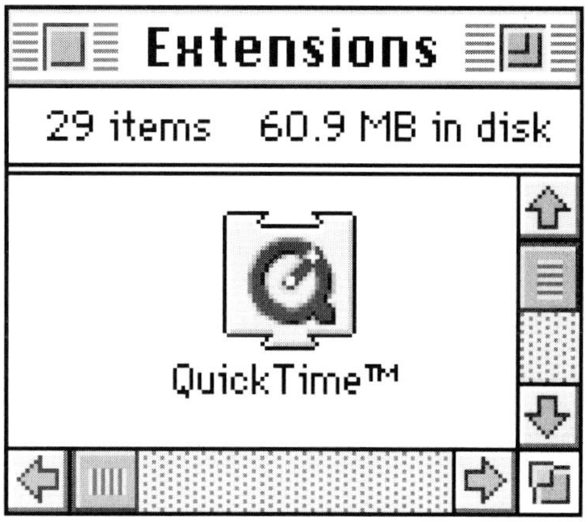

Figure 8.1 QuickTime in the Extension folder

Digital Roots

Desktop video's digital heritage also is plainly visible in today's new tools. QuickTime tools incorporate cut-and-paste simplicity, and have evolved from Apple's experience with the Macintosh Desktop metaphor of file folders, double-clicks, menus, and, of course, the ever-present trash can. Video editing software is a descendent of the photographic quality graphics technology found in Photoshop, photorealistic 3-D products such as Ray Dream Designer and StrataVision 3D, the motion and interactivity features of Macromedia Director, and the sound capabilities of Sound Edit Pro. Combining these attributes with the traditions and aesthetics of the broadcast world has resulted in a tool set that brings desktop convenience to professional producers, while providing professional power to the Mac-based multimedia producer.

QuickTime

The first tool in the multimedia workshop for anyone who is serious about digital video on the Macintosh is QuickTime, the system extension and file format that makes multimedia manageable, reliable, and standardized. QuickTime is installed as an Extension in the System folder (Figure 8.1).

TOOLS
QuickTime 160

QuickTime has become an instant success due to the integration of three important components that define a format for digital video, and provide the capacity and flexibility to withstand a period of rapidly changing technology. These components are the user interface, video compression, and hardware independence. The latter allows QuickTime files to run not only on a Macintosh, but also on PC compatibles under QuickTime for Windows, on Silicon Graphic Stations, and on many different types of QuickTime-compatible graphic cards. Let us take a closer look at each of these three components.

User Interface

The most obvious feature of QuickTime's interface is the controller below each QuickTime movie. This allows you to play the movie in forward and reverse, step through it one frame at a time, play it rapidly or slowly, increase or decrease its audio volume, move to a new location in the sequence, or cut and paste frames from one movie to another. To control the speed at which the movie plays, you can hold down the Control key while pressing the step forward or step backward arrow on the controller; this displays a new control bar for regulating the speed. You can press down the Shift key and move the scroll bar to select the portion of the movie you wish to copy and paste (Figure 8.2).

This standard user interface is the hallmark of the Macintosh philosophy. While different third-party software may implement the QuickTime interface with minor variations, the basic controller should remain intact for most applications.

Video Compression

Digital video requires huge files—as big as 30Mb for each *second* of playing time. QuickTime utilizes new software compression technologies to shrink the size of QuickTime movie files and increase their playback frame rate. It does this in a

Figure 8.2 A portion of the controller bar turns black in MoviePlayer to indicate the selection made for copying and pasting.

manner that permits new compression technologies, called codecs (compressor/decompressors), to be used with QuickTime as soon as they are available with existing software applications. This software-independent approach to compression will permit QuickTime to avoid obsolescence and adjust to new technologies, such as fractal compression, as they become available.

The more common compressors use *symmetric* compression, so named because they take the same amount of time to compress and decompress a file. They can compress video sequences, save them (to a hard disk), and play them back (from a hard disk or CD-ROM) on-the-fly, in real time. *Asymmetric* compression usually takes much more time to compress (an hour or more for one minute of video), but creates a more highly compressed file packed with more data, which can then be decompressed relatively quickly. An example of an asymmetrical compressor is Apple's Compact Video, which may take as much as an hour or more to compress a minute of video, best done unattended overnight or during a good football game. While they take longer, asymmetrical compressors usually can create a smaller file and provide better playback from a slow drive such as a CD-ROM.

Lossless versus Lossy Compression

Even though QuickTime operates in the digital domain, this doesn't mean that all data is perfectly preserved. It depends on what type of compression is applied to the images. *Lossless* compression keeps all the information from the original image. If you were to compress a picture with lossless compression, then decompress it and compare the data to the original on a pixel by pixel basis, there would be no difference. All of the current products which compress space on your hard disk use this form of compression. You wouldn't want to find even one character changed or dropped from your word processing document! The QuickTime JPEG codec when used in the highest quality setting results in lossless compression.

When dealing with images, however, there is quite a bit of data that can be removed without our noticing much of a difference. This is called *lossy* compression. The codecs will carefully analyze the image data, and toss out information that may not be missed. If you were to do a pixel by pixel comparison again, thousands of pixels may have been changed. But if you view the original and compressed images side by side, you may hardly notice a difference. It depends on the effectiveness of the codec, as well as the quality setting you choose. The lower the quality, the better the compression (the resulting image will take up less space on your hard disk), but the more obvious the differences will be in the comparison.

One more important point about lossy compression. Every time you recompress an image using lossy compression, additional degradation will occur. When making a QuickTime movie, you are better off working from the highest quality image you can afford to store on your disk (higher quality means more disk space is required), then wait until the very end of the editing process before you apply compression.

Spatial versus Temporal Compression

There are two other ways to classify compression. *Spatial* compression looks at an individual image or frame and finds data that can be removed. For example, if the video was shot in front of a solid yellow background, then the codec may reduce much of the similarly colored area to a few bytes of information.

Temporal compression (also called *frame differencing)* deals with the similarities and differences in consecutive frames of a QuickTime movie. If the camera was mounted on a tripod and pointed at an actor sitting in front of a fixed background, then the only thing that will change from frame to frame is the actor's movement. Rather than saving the entire frame of data, temporal compression throws out the entire background in subsequent frames, and only include the portion of the actor that moved. This can save an enormous amount of storage. In Chapter 17, "Creating Video," we'll provide some tips to take advantage of QuickTime's compression while shooting your movie

The Apple video compressor is a good choice for saving to a hard disk, because temporal and spatial compression are accompanied by symmetrical compression. While Compact Video is a very efficient way to compress video, postpone using it until your project is completely finished so that the slow compression speed does not interfere with your creative efforts.

Hardware Independence

QuickTime is adaptable to different kinds of hardware, allowing you to create and play movies using many different kinds of hardware and software combinations. It is designed to synchronize audio and video on any QuickTime-capable Mac, regardless of the machine's peculiarities in managing and processing data, and provides a basic architecture that can be expanded and enhanced as ever more powerful platforms and tools come to market. QuickTime respects the natural evolution of computer technology, so that it can adapt to changing environments without becoming useless.

Older third-party software offering audio, graphics, or animation capability on the Macintosh now boast updated export commands converting the final product to the QuickTime format. In addition, an avalanche of new special-effects packages, software designed for digital editing, and other QuickTime-specific applications, as well as new hardware, has brought QuickTime tools to a high level of maturity in an incredibly short period of time.

QuickTime Reference Movies

One of QuickTime's features that makes it so flexible is its ability to create *reference movies*. Reference movies have no video or sound data of their own. Instead, they have pointers to the original, or source, movies. This makes editing QuickTime movies fast and efficient because instead of copying huge amounts of data from the source movies to your edited movie, only a relatively few bytes of index information are needed (including the name of the original file, where it resides on your disk, and exactly where the scene is located in the source movie). When the new reference movie is played, the indices are used to find the frames in the original host movies. Everything you see is actually from the original movies, and not contained within the edited reference movie.

Reference movies allow you to make an unlimited number of new movies without ever altering the originals, or having to allot disk space for the large files that new QuickTime movies would otherwise require. You can also afford to experiment with many versions of an edit without using up precious disk space. And if a friend already has all the source movies you are using, you can send her a new reference movie on a floppy disk since they are so small.

On the other hand, there are a few major drawbacks to using reference movies. They are completely dependent on the original host movies in order to play. If you delete any one of the host movies, your reference movie won't be able to play! If you rename or move a host movie, you will also have problems. QuickTime will notice it can't find a source movie, and ask if you want it to search for it. If it fails to locate it on your mounted hard drives of CD-ROMs, it will ask you to show it where it is, or to give up. So, to save yourself this trouble, don't move or rename the original host movies.

Another problem with reference movies is disk access time between scenes. If you have a fast hard drive, you may not notice any problems. But when the host movies are located on a CD-ROM, the delay caused by the drive searching for the next scene in a different host movie may interrupt the flow of the movie.

To solve these problems, simply convert a reference movie to a self-contained, or *flattened*, movie. This is a standard QuickTime movie that contains a complete copy of all the video and audio data from the source movies. Most QuickTime applications have the ability to create flattened movies. It's usually an option of the Save or Save As dialog box. Make sure you flatten a movie *after* you are satisfied no more changes will be made, *before* passing it on to someone who doesn't have all the referenced host movies, or *before* you've removed your host movies.

Other Digital Video Standards

Alternative digital video standards continue to coexist with QuickTime. One of the earlier attempts to create compressed digital video on a computer was RCA's DVI (Digital Video Technology), which was sold to Intel. DVI was not intended to give hardware and software independence like QuickTime, but relied instead on specific hardware and compression technologies that Intel was committed to putting on a single computer chip. The earlier versions took up three slots in an IBM PC. However, the compression on which DVI relied for good results had to be done on a mainframe computer, which was neither a practical nor an affordable solution. QuickTime, on the other hand, was designed to be independent of any particular hardware or software, allowing new hardware and compression techniques to be used with existing QuickTime-savvy products.

Intel has responded by releasing Indeo, a compression algorithm that can be built into hardware such as DVI, or can work as a software-only solution, for near-real-time compression on the desktop. Indeo is made available by Intel under both QuickTime and Video for Windows, the PC solution from Microsoft. Thus, the horse race for standards continues. Nevertheless, Apple Computer's licensing of QuickTime to Silicon Graphics for use on its workstations, and marketing of QuickTime for Windows, ensures that Macintosh users also can distribute their movies on other platforms (see Chapter 12, "Working Cross Platform.")

QuickTime Is Here to Stay

In creating QuickTime, Apple had its eye on the future: QuickTime is designed to evolve as new technology becomes available. QuickTime's open architecture ensures that the product will continue to evolve, abetted by any number of movie and audio tracks, special purpose tracks, compression algorithms, interactive scripting, control of devices such as videodisc players and VCRs, and synchronization standards. For more information on QuickTime, see Chapter 3, "Mac Software and Hardware."

Uses of Digital Video

QuickTime movies can complement other computer-generated media in desktop presentations; the QuickTime movies themselves also may be created from text, PICT and PICS files, other image files, scanned photographs, audio files, and other types of media. Live video may be brought into the computer with a SuperMac, RasterOps, Mass Micro, Radius, Truevision, or other digitizing cards. At the same time, the range of filters, transitions, and other special effects that can be used in a digital video production on the Macintosh is nothing less than spectacular. For more details on all of these options, see the hardware sections that follow.

In addition to being used in presentations on a computer monitor, QuickTime can be printed to tape—if your hardware supports the output of video (also discussed later in this chapter). The resulting quality is lower than that of regular video, and should be judged on its own merits, based on how it looks to you and the intended audience. Using hardware like the Radius VideoVision card, resolution can approach that of S-VHS. (See the sidebar on video tape formats later in the chapter.)

Interactive multimedia using digital video allows a single Macintosh to handle applications that range from simple control of the flow of QuickTime movies to interactive tutorials, interactive training, and advanced applications. If the highest-quality video is required, a videodisc player, such as the Pioneer LDV-4400 or the Sony LVR-5000 or LVS-5000, can be added to the presentation under the control of the Macintosh.

Real-World Multimedia Video

QuickTime is a wonderful technology. Still, most multimedia producers don't expect professional-quality video in their presentations. QuickTime architecture is capable of handling full-screen images at 30 frames per second—broadcast quality. However, that level of performance requires a large investment in storage, compression, and raw processing power—at a cost that may bust the budgets of most desktop producers. Thus, before launching your dream project, take a few minutes to ponder not only what is possible but also what is practical.

If your goals are like those of most multimedia productions on the Macintosh, you may choose to incorporate motion video at, say, 15 frames per second in a quarter-screen window—still highly effective. Video capture cards such as the SuperMac VideoSpigot permit you to do some remarkable things on almost any color Macintosh. Programs that previously displayed only static images can be converted to utilize real-motion video in just a few minutes. For interactive multimedia or CD-ROM projects, the low-cost VideoSpigot card is all you need to do interesting work (see the hardware sections later in the chapter). Software for editing QuickTime movies provides the means to knit together raw footage—with impressive results.

If you want more, keep in mind that the capabilities of software such as Premiere and VideoFusion are limited only by what the hardware can do. In theory, some of the software packages can support high-definition television and other resolutions up to 4000×4000 pixels, and video frame buffers like the Truevision NuVista+ board are capable of making state-of-the-art QuickTime movies. Before you try such high resolution for a feature-length production, however, you may need to wait for the hardware to catch up with the capacity of the software.

Equipment for Shooting Your Own Video

There are two primary ways to acquire video for your multimedia project: You can buy prepackaged video clips from a variety of vendors (see Chapter 10, "Outside Resources"), or you can elect to shoot your own video. The latter really is hard to avoid for most multimedia presentations. In all likelihood, your particular project is going to require at least some original video. Fortunately, it's fairly easy and inexpensive to "roll your own," requiring only a consumer-quality camcorder or video camera, and perhaps a video casette recorder (VCR) for playback and review of the pre-digital footage.

Choosing a Video Camera and Video Deck

Choosing the appropriate video camera or deck depends on the quality you require and the budget that is available.

Video equipment is usually categorized as consumer, prosumer, industrial, broadustrial, and broadcast-quality, which pertain more to the skills of the user than the characteristics of the equipment itself. The first three categories require little technical expertise to use, whereas you really have to understand video technology to get the most out of broadustrial and broadcast equipment. Still, when it comes to digital video presented on a Macintosh, there are diminishing returns per investment on the high-end equipment.

- *Consumer* equipment encompasses all the standard camcorders and VCRs we've become familiar with over the past several years. These are low-end production tools that are inexpensive, exceedingly easy to use, and suitable for average-quality QuickTime video. Consumer cameras start at about $500 and range in price up to $2000. VCRs start at only a few hundred dollars.
- *Prosumer* tools also are relatively low-end and inexpensive, but are more feature-laden than the consumer models. They feature such bells and whistles as on-board character generators, special transitions, and image stablizers. The Cannon A-1 Series of Hi-8 cameras is a good example of prosumer equipment; they feature auto-everything. Cameras and decks in this category generally cost up to $3000.
- *Industrial* equipment tends to be basic and rugged. It is not necessarily chock-full of features, but can stand up to repeated use in a labor-intensive, multiple-user environment. The Hi-8 tape format increasingly is used in the industrial equipment, replacing the venerable ¾-inch U-matic standard, the Sony DXC series. Industrial-quality equipment generally is priced in the $5000–$7000 range.
- *Broadustrial* equipment boasts more features, and can be plugged into larger professional systems. It incorporates features necessary for stabilizing and monitoring signals for cable and broadcast applications, such as time-based correctors, vector scopes, and waveform generators that monitor and manipulate the integrity of the signal. A typical broadustrial video system, such as Sony's BetaCam, costs upwards of $25,000.
- *Broadcast,* of course, refers to the top-quality, highly controllable, technically demanding equipment used in professional video production.

Prosumer equipment is a good choice for desktop video, but consumer cameras and VCRs may be adequate to create QuickTime movies in many instances. If the videotape needs to be edited using traditional analog methods, generational loss will occur, and a higher-quality raw tape will be needed to make up the difference. On the other hand, a consumer camera may be sufficient for acceptable results if the raw footage is digitized directly into the computer from the original tape, and not from duplicates. The quality of the video equipment should be in proportion to the quality of the final delivery system, whether that is a multimedia system or videotape.

Before making a final decision, consider what other future uses of the videotape are likely. An important advantage of shooting high-quality video to begin with is that everything you do with it will benefit, and in addition, the original footage will be available for reuse for future projects, which might not be possible if the quality of the video is not on par with the new application.

Bringing Video into the Mac

Minimum Equipment

All you need to bring video into a Macintosh is a QuickTime digitizing card (also called a *video capture board*) such as the SuperMac VideoSpigot or RasterOps 24MxTV, movie recorder software, and a VCR, video camera, or camcorder. Digitizing cards plug into a slot within your Mac, and feature one or more video and audio input connectors. VideoSpigot includes only one RCA video port, and no audio input. In order to import audio with the video, you need to run the audio lead to the audio input of your Macintosh (if it has one—it will if it came with a microphone), or through an audio digitizer such as the MacRecorder. Other cards, such as VideoVision, Digital Film, and MediaTime, have inputs for S-Video, audio, and other connectors. In order to print to video, the card must have an appropriate video output connector.

Recording Software

Most digitizing cards come with recording software that provides controls for their particular features. The VideoSpigot card includes ScreenPlay for recording, while RasterOps boards include MediaGrabber software. In addition to their primary editing features, third-party QuickTime editing software packages, such as Premiere and VideoShop, support the ability to record.

If you want to use one vendor's recording software with another's card, you must install a *VDIG* (video digitizer) extension, supplied by the board's manufacturer, in your System folder. This is a standard device interface that allows editing software to effectively communicate with your hardware digitizer. If you do not have the proper VDIG, contact the board manufacturer, or download a VDIG from an on-line information service such as CompuServe or America Online. Even if you purchased your digitizing card prior to the release of QuickTime, you probably can obtain a VDIG or equivalent software from the manufacturer. The QuickImage 24 board from Mass Microsystems, and the RasterOps offerings, including the Colorboard 364 and 24STV boards, feature

VDIGs for popular software packages. You also can get a VDIG for the Truevision NuVista+ board, even though its function is primarily that of a high-end video frame buffer. Truevision also offers the QuickTime-specific Bravado 32.

Basic recording software also can be obtained through other channels. Apple Computer includes the MovieRecorder in the QuickTime Starter Kit. Several different kinds of recorders also are available in Apple's QuickTime for Developers CD-ROM, which anyone can purchase through the APDA (Apple Developer's Association). Capabilities include the ability to digitize from Hypercard Stacks, to control frame-by-frame digitizing from Pioneer LDV-4400-compatible videodisc players to record from frame-accurate VCRs.

ScreenPlay: Recording Tool for the VideoSpigot

ScreenPlay (Figure 8.3) tries to grab as many frames per second as the speed of the computer permits. In order to maximize the frame rate, it gives you the option to record directly to RAM, faster than directing captured frames to the hard drive. It also allows you to limit the frame rate through the Preferences menu. After recording, files can be compressed using different schemes in order to save hard disk space.

Other ScreenPlay features include the ability to record only a small window within the movie, or to record motion video up to 320×240. ScreenPlay also will record still images at full frame size (640×480).

MediaGrabber: Recording Tool for RasterOps Boards

The features available with MediaGrabber (Figure 8.4) are dependent on which RasterOps board you have. The software has more sophisticated control of image quality than does ScreenPlay, which lets you control the quality only for compression purposes. MediaGrabber's Image Color Editor permits control of brightness and contrast, setting the white and black levels, and individual control of the red, green, and blue channels. While both boards permit recording sound and video together, some of the RasterOps boards have direct support for input

Figure 8.3 ScreenPlay recorder software for the VideoSpigot

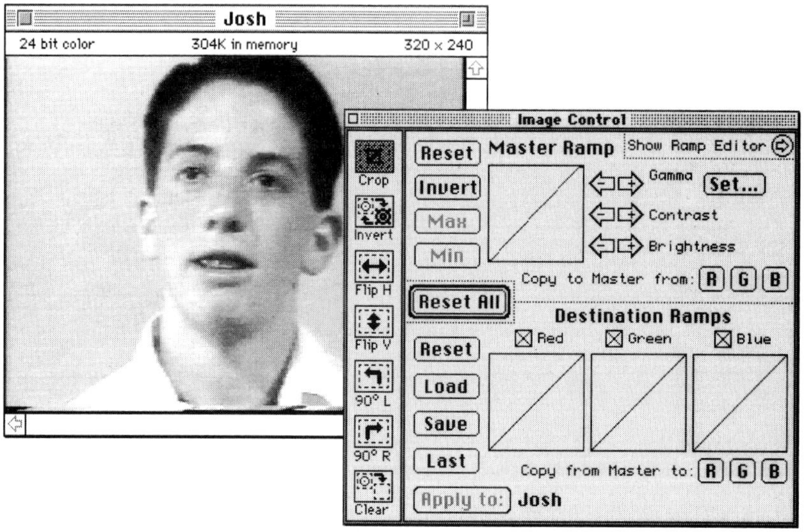

Figure 8.4 MediaGrabber Image Control Utility for RasterOps boards.

of audio, and the software provides more controls over the quality of the sound. MediaGrabber permits recording to hard disk or to RAM, and allows you to set frame rates and key frames.

Choosing a Hardware Digitizing Card

Video capture cards vary widely in their capabilities. Low-end cards are inexpensive (less than $500), but are suitable for capturing still images only. More expensive boards, ranging in price from $1500 to $5000, can capture full-motion video.

In many instances, an inexpensive digitizing board, such as the VideoSpigot or one of the lower-priced RasterOps models, is all you will ever need to create professional-quality QuickTime movies for such applications as desktop presentations and CD-ROM. Many new high-end QuickTime boards, such as the Digital Film card from SuperMac, feature the capability of storing 30 frames per second on the hard disk at full-screen resolution on a 13" monitor of 640×480. However, those require a lot of processing power—you'll need at least a Quadra 800 for this kind of work.

When moving to a more capable board, give careful consideration to the actual cost of using it. If the board can capture 30 frames per second at full-screen resolution, ask yourself how fast a hard disk will be needed to keep up with this board, how long it will take to compress the movie, and how much disk space you will need to store it. If the answers are unacceptable, then use a lower-end board, create wonderful media quickly and affordably, and pocket the difference.

In view of the rapid changes in technology, give consideration to obsolescence before making a major investment in QuickTime cards. Manufacturers protect their customers against this in various ways—or sometimes, not at all. While neither video nor QuickTime is in danger of becoming a fossil, compression algorithms are in flux. Some boards, such as the DVI-based eyeQ board from New

Consumer Videotape Formats

Broadcast-quality ¾ inch videotape remains the standard format for professional videographers, Most of the industrial editing studios have been using ¾ inch decks for years, and their availability is an argument in their favor. However, the equipment required to shoot and edit ¾ inch tape is much more expensive and cumbersome than that used for the more readily available "consumer" videotape formats on the market today, and the latter are quite suitable for use in multimedia. These consumer formats are increasingly compatible with each other in the sense that you can edit them together or digitize them for use in making QuickTime movies.

VHS and VHS-C. The most common consumer format is, of course, VHS half-inch tape, used in virtually all VCRs in the home. This format is adequate for making QuickTime movies from original footage, but quickly loses quality if duplicated, due to generational loss. A sister format is VHS-C which is simply a small VHS cassette for use with miniature camcorders.

8 MM. An increasingly popular consumer format is 8 mm videotape. Its small size allows 8mm camcorders to be very compact, which is not only convenient for the person holding the camera, but often results in shots that would have been impossible to obtain with a larger, more bulky camera, due to the intimidating effect the latter may have on the persons being videotaped. Furthermore, 8mm picture quality is generally regarded to be higher than that of VHS.

Hi8. Hi8 is perhaps the best consumer format, coming close to the broadcast quality of ¾ inch tape. Hi8 carries separate signals for chroma and luminescence to give a higher resolution approaching that of high-end video systems. Many persons in the video industry complain that Hi8 tape starts to flake or becomes unstable when a single tape is used repeatedly for editing. For that reason, Hi8 often is transferred to ¾ inch editing sessions. However, the stability of Hi8 continues to improve, as does the availability of editing equipment designed for this format.

S-VHS. Another popular high-quality consumer format is S-VHS, which is half-inch in size but, like Hi8, carries separate signals for chroma and luminescence.

Video, are programmable, permitting them to serve new functions by means of software updates from the manufacturer.

Other boards rely on the flexibility of QuickTime to permit new compressors to be used. Some companies have good upgrade policies and allow a trade-in value for older boards, or for boards from other companies. RasterOps has created a modular system where hardware compressors can be added as daughter boards to existing digitizers. The MoviePak daughter board provides real-time JPEG compression for the RasterOps 24STV, 24MxTV, 24XLTV, or MediaTime board without requiring an extra slot in the computer.

Despite some hassles associated with any new technology, capture boards are a very convenient way to bring video clips into your Mac, and the only way if the clips you want are not commercially available as part of a video clip CD-ROM, videodisc, or QuickTime movie. (For information on CD-based video collections, see Chapter 10, "Outside Resources." There are a number of video clips included on the CD-ROM packaged with this book.)

Capture boards offer a wide variety of features, but they all do basically the same thing: capture video frames, digitize them, and then save the digitized images to disk in PICS or QuickTime movie formats. Some high-end cards also double as display cards for large-screen monitors.

The capture process itself is essentially the same, regardless of the type of card you use. The card's software displays the video in a window on-screen, and you can set controls such as hue, saturation, and brightness. When you're ready to capture, a mouse click does it. (See Chapter 17, "Creating Video.")

NTSC Support

NTSC is the dominant broadcast standard in the United States and Japan, but it is not widely used elsewhere in the world. PAL is the standard for most of Europe, and SECAM is used in France, Eastern Europe, and the former Soviet Union.

If your source material is in PAL or SECAM, you'll need to make sure you have a card that will accept and digitize these input signals. Virtually all capture cards support NTSC and PAL, and many support SECAM natively or as an option.

Most cards also will accept several different types of NTSC video signals:

Composite. This is the most common video signal. Since it mixes together the chrominance and luminance parts of the signal into one channel, it's also inferior to the other two types.

S-video. This is the two-channel signal (for color and luminescense) put out by the two types of higher-end consumer cameras, S-VHS and Hi-8 (see the Videotape Standards sidebar).

RGB. This is the norm in the professional video industry. It's a three-channel signal—one for each color—plus a sync channel.

Advanced Features

Manufacturers are cramming more and more features into video cards. The trend is to pack into a single card 24-bit color display, image compression, video effects, and video out. Until recently, each of these functions would have required a separate card.

In fact, several vendors offer cards that combine seemingly unrelated functions. ColorLink cards from E-Machines Inc. drive large-screen monitors and include Ethernet connectivity.

The most common dual function cards combine 68030 acceleration with large-screen display capability. These cards, available from Systech, Nutmeg Systems, and Mobius Technologies Inc., are targeted at the Mac Plus and SE machines—Macs that have slower performance and small screens.

Some of the features found in more advanced cards include:

24-bit display. Cards that combine 24-bit display with video capture give a much closer approximation of the final captured images. If you don't need 24-bit color, then you don't have to bother with this feature.

Video display. Due to the huge amount of data it sends to the screen, digital video greatly taxes the Mac's built-in display technology. Some cards include on-board display hardware that accelerates image display. Again, if you've already got a video accelerator (see Chapter 4, "Hardware Peripherals"), you're set. If not, give cards that offer this feature close attention if you're going to be spending a lot of time working with digital video.

Compression. As we've seen, video takes up a lot of disk space. Some cards address this problem by deploying on-board compression chips that can write video to disk in a compressed format. When you want to view an image or sequence, the board decompresses the images for display. Hardware codecs are superior to software compression because they perform the task much more quickly.

Video out. Some capture cards also come with video out—the ability to write, or encode, a computer's output to tape.

Live video preview. Some high-end cards feature a full-motion, full-color preview window. This is a great convenience because it makes it easier to capture just the frame you want.

Video effects. A few of the more expensive boards allow you to overlay computer graphics on video, and add titling and other on-board effects.

Automatic sequence capture. Another advanced feature that lets you precisely grab an entire sequence of frames.

A card with some of the integrated features you need is a real convenience, because getting multiple cards to work together can be a headache.

Video Editing Software

The real fun and creativity of creating QuickTime movies comes in the editing stage, when you can put on your director's hat and turn raw footage into a finished production, complete with professionally inspired sequences and special effects. This truly is the good stuff, made possible by sophisticated, QuickTime-based video editing software. Today's video editing software is a postproduction house in a box, combining desktop convenience and simplicity with capabilities previously available only in million-dollar postproduction studios.

In this section, we'll take a look at the four leading editors for digital video: Adobe Premiere, DiVA's VideoShop, Video Fusion Ltd.'s Video Fusion, and CoSA After Effects. Before we delve into the applications themselves, however, we want to provide you with the basic video editing features and the interface metaphors these packages use to combine power and efficiency. Once you understand these, you'll be better equipped to select the package that most directly addresses your situation and needs.

Metaphors for Desktop Video Editing

Because digital video on the desktop is so new, no one could predict for certain what approach to software would best facilitate its use. The Macintosh desktop utilizes file folders and a trash can to create a metaphor about a business person's desk. Videotapes, however, are stored on shelves, and not in file folders, and are erased rather than trashed.

Furthermore, the people who need to understand and use this software come from different backgrounds. Persons who come to desktop digital video from the video industry are used to previews, in-points, out-points, perform edit, titling, and the like. Those who come by way of the film industry are used to relying on another set of tools, while others have experience with Macintosh graphics programs and have totally different expectations. The end result is that digital video software is a rich amalgamation of metaphors and jargon from many different disciplines. The approaches range from software modeled on traditional video editing to that which uses new metaphors designed to take advantage of the unique nature of this new medium.

In selecting a software package, your own background and experience may be an important factor in helping to make the right choice. You should know what approach is taken by each software package, and whether that approach will facilitate your ability to work effectively with the features of the software. The following are some of the common metaphors used by digital video software.

Macintosh Desktop Metaphor

Apple Computer encourages all software to subscribe to the basic interface of the Macintosh desktop, using cut and paste, file folders, and so on. This makes each new Macintosh program easier to use, since you already are familiar with the desktop. With a few notable exceptions, such as DiVA's VideoShop, most digital video software *does* conform to the most important features of the desktop. VideoShop, with roots at the M.I.T Media Research Lab, has been designed from the ground up to create a new working environment most appropriate for digital video.

Video Editing Metaphor

The more support a software package has for traditional analog video editing through the control of videotape recorders, videodisc players, and other external devices, the more likely it will subscribe to the video editing metaphor. A good example of this is Adobe's Premiere, which currently is limited to editing two video tracks in a manner similar to professional video editing studios, with a third super track for superimposing. This type of software frequently assumes that, as with videotape, only one format or image size, will be used as material in the creation of a particular production.

Digital Photography Metaphor

Morph 229

If you already have experience with programs like Photoshop, designed for digital photography, you will appreciate software that has filters, RGB channels, alpha-channels, and the like. Software that relies heavily on the digital photography metaphor includes VideoFusion and Premiere. If you think of video as a series of still frames, be aware that the same techniques used in digital photography apply to digital movies. However, the techniques used in digital photography may be augmented for digital movies to permit change over time. For instance, a filter from Adobe's Premiere QuickTime editing software may gradually alter the movie frames over time, beginning with no noticeable effect and gradually increasing the amount of the effect.

3-D Rendering Metaphor

StrataVision 226

A common vocabulary is used among 3-D programs such as Infini-D and StrataVision. For instance, renderings can be done to various degrees of detail, from wireframe to shading to high resolution for final rendering. Objects are created in three-dimensional space and can be manipulated and rotated separately. An example of a digital video software package that is modeled on such 3-D programs is CoSA's After Effects, which allows movies of different dimensions to be combined in a window by treating them as separate objects.

Metaphors for New Paradigms

Some say that the metaphor for digital video software should be designed from scratch to best exploit the capabilities of this new medium. Others insist that you should start with what people are already familiar with, so that they do not have to reinvent the wheel in order to use it. VideoShop by DiVA is an example of the first philosophy; it creates an environment optimized for digital video. Even the Macintosh desktop is revised to capitalize on what works best for that medium.

VideoShop's approach departs from common conventions on the Macintosh for opening files, file folders, and other Macintosh Desktop conventions. However, the advantage of VideoShop is that it creates a seamless environment in which to work, including access and search of files, making movies, and rendering interactive presentations using the movies you make.

Software Features

Digital video editors include organizing tools for your QuickTime movies or other media files; windows for multiple views of your project, such as storyboards and timelines; movie recording capabilities; and most important of all, the filters, transitions, special effects, titles, rotoscoping, and alpha-and other channel capabilities that turn these software packages into power tools.

Organizing Your Media Files

Most digital video programs have devised ways to help organize the movies or other media files for a particular project; some also tackle the bigger picture of organizing all of your QuickTime or media files on your hard disk for ready access during an editing session.

Databases

TOOLS

Aldus Fetch 230
Kudo Image Browser 224
EasyPlay 166

The purpose of a database is to give you access to media stored on your hard disk or elsewhere that has been categorized for your convenience, to help in retrieving the right movie for a current project. There are many independent visual databases, such as Fetch by Aldus. A built-in database, however, generally provides better integration within a software editing package for effective access to files as needed. DiVA's VideoShop comes with a Visual Catalog, which functions as a database of files that are compatible with with VideoShop. (For reviews of image databases, see Chapter 10, "Outside Resources.")

Folders

TOOLS

Folder Icon Maker 142

Since the Macintosh desktop includes a system of folders in which you can put your media (or more folders), you have a ready-made system to organize your media files. However, some programs allow customization of this process. DiVA's VideoShop, for example, alters the Macintosh desktop to allow special views of only those folders and files that can be used with QuickTime (See Figure 8.5). Media can then be moved from a folder directly into the Storyboard view of the application.

Projects

Most digital video editing packages import files into a project window that holds all of the files for a particular project, whether you actually use them or not. In addition, Premiere offers a library, which consists of files that can be reused in other projects.

Recording Video

In addition to the recording software that came with your QuickTime video digitizing card, video editing software also frequently provides for the convenience of recording video from within the editing session. The advantage of recording within an editing package is the convenience of bringing video into the computer when needed in the project. In some instances, the ability to record

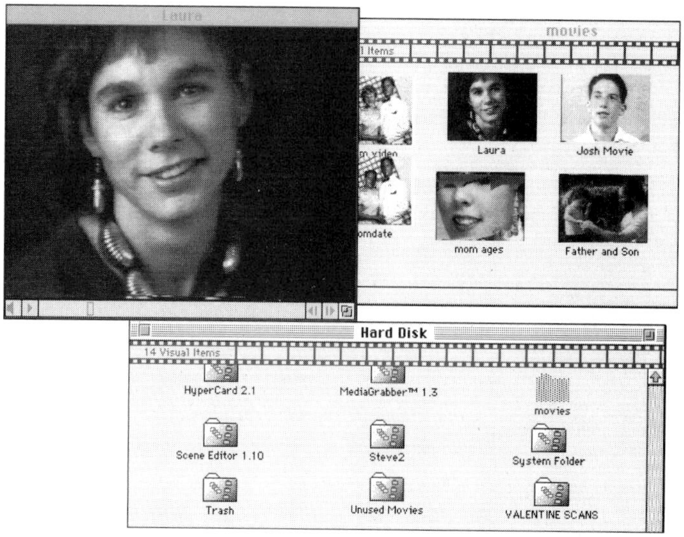

Figure 8.5 The VideoShop environment converts the Macintosh desktop folders and creates Micons to illustrate QuickTime movie files.

during an editing session extends the capability of the editing package to off-line editing and other specialized purposes.

Multiple Views of Your Project

A significant advantage of digital video over tradition videotape editing is that you can look at the video information anyway you want to, or at least, anyway the designers of your editing software anticipated would be useful. The following are some of the more common views, or windows, in which to view digital video information now being supported by software packages. Most software packages support views of your project through a timeline, a preview, and a movie player. Other views of a digital video project may include an object-oriented view and a motion picture script view.

Timeline View

A timeline is the most important view in the software program, because it permits synchronizing audio to video, and allows editing on a frame-by-frame basis. Most software editors support this view, which shows you the entire movie frame by frame, second by second, or by whatever particular time reference you choose that is supported by the software. Frequently, this is the view in which you will add transitions and special effects, and in general create the important nuances that make your movie what it is.

Movie Player View

TOOLS
MoviePlayer 161
Popcorn 162
TheaterMaker 165

Several different species of movie players may come to your attention, depending on which software packages you are working with. The most common permits you to play any part of an existing movie that is part of your project. VideoFusion software has the unusual feature of permitting you to play in its entirety the current edited version on which you are working. In order to achieve this laudable goal of real-time playing, this software creates the transitions and special effects as soon as you apply them, rather than waiting until you are ready to make the whole movie. The movie players also permit you to mark in-points and out-points for segments, and to cut and paste portions of your movie.

Preview View

In traditional videotape editing, a preview allows you to see a segment you are about to edit, including any transitions or special effects, before you actually finalize or perform the edit and record it to videotape. A preview in software digital editing is somewhat more flexible. In traditional editing, you are creating one edit at a time. However, in digital editing, you can create the entire movie before you start transferring any of the individual edits. As a result, a preview in digital editing gives you much more flexibility to choose any portion of the project that you want to preview. Depending on the particular software and preferences you have designated, a preview may be in a smaller window, and at a lower resolution of video or audio, than the final movie. The point of the preview is to let you see what is going to happen, without having to wait for delays caused by a slow compression algorithm or other necessary steps in making the entire movie.

Storyboard View

A digital software storyboard serves to fulfill all of the functionality of a traditional storyboard, and a great deal more. (See Chapter 2, "Project Planning and Design.") Storyboards were originally devised as a means of communicating between the production people and the client. A secondary use is in helping the designer to visualize the project. Digital storyboarding can not only help in the design process, but directly contribute to building the final video product as well. Storyboard views use a single still image to represent an entire segment of a movie. You can design the movie simply by reordering the video segments in the storyboard. Because the storyboard collapses each segment, regardless of its length, to a single image, this view is ideal for obtaining a broad overview of what the project will look like. Examples of software that provide this view are VideoShop, CoSA After Effects, and VideoFusion (see Figure 8.6).

Object-Oriented View

An object-oriented view may be featured in editors that permit the combination of movies, PICT files, and other media that may be of different sizes and shapes. Premiere, for example, does not support such a view because it requires all files to be in the same size format. CoSA After Effects, in contrast, provides very complex layering of movies, text, images, and other visual information of different shapes and sizes. Until the movie is finalized, each visual element of the movie remains a separate object that can be manipulated, made closer or farther, larger or smaller, or fused together with another object, or on which special effects can be separately imposed.

Motion Picture Script View

Many productions are preceded by a motion picture type of script consisting of a written description of every scene, including the dialog and other information necessary for creating the movie. Taking advantage of the ease with which QuickTime movies can be incorporated into word processing documents, some software editors support a view of the movie based on a motion picture script format. As more of the movie is actually finished, the resulting QuickTime movie can be

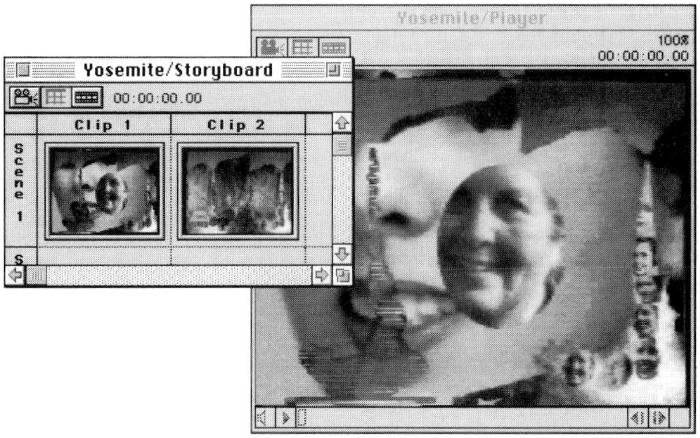

Figure 8.6 Storyboard view and the Player window from VideoFusion

inserted into the appropriate location in the written script, and viewed simply by clicking on it. An example of a software package supporting this view is VideoFusion.

Editing Capabilities

The editing capabilities of digital video software on the Macintosh are extraordinary. Within a year after the release of QuickTime, almost anything was possible. We see exciting new features every day. Following is a list of categories that should help you to understand what the capabilities are and when to use them.

Titles

Adobe and TrueType fonts so common on the Mac are designed with parameters that can be altered for use in desktop publishing. Digital video can do even more with these fonts. Editing software, such as Premiere, permits all of these parameters to be manipulated in real time as the letters go flying, spinning, and growing across the screen. New versions of QuickTime will support a separate titles channel that could permit you to change the fonts and their parameters even after the movie is made, as well as to do word searches.

Video and Sound Channels

In theory, QuickTime supports an almost unlimited number of video and audio channels. In practice, access to them may be limited by the capabilities of your software. In some instances, you may prefer to combine the channels in the final movie to optimize the playback speed. Multiple sound channels can be used not only for stereo, but also to manipulate the volume or other aspects of the audio relative to other audio channels. Some programs rely more heavily than others on channels to create filters, transitions, and special effects.

PICT Files and Other Media Formats

TOOLS
Capture 227
CameraMan 241

In addition to combining existing QuickTime movies and titles, some editing software permits you to add PICT files and other Macintosh media formats to your movies. Since many Macintosh programs that use other formats now can convert them to QuickTime, you may not need to utilize this capability very often for animations. However, you certainly will find it convenient to scan images on a scanner and import them into your QuickTime editor.

Filters

TOOLS
Kai's Power Tools 134
DeBabelizer 228

Whatever the original meaning of the word "filter," the important thing to remember is that filters operate on a single movie to make dramatic changes in the image or sound. Filters may operate on the entire movie or any portion of it. They may operate on only one color channel (red, green, or blue), or on all channels at one time. While photographic filters change the color, digital video filters can turn the movie upside down, reverse its color, cause it to spin in three dimensions, or anything else.

Unlike Photoshop filters, which operate on a single still image, digital video filters can change the nature of the image over time. The filter might slowly increase the contrast of the movie, make it darker, bluer, cause the image to rotate and turn, or create any number of other effects.

One very promising aspect of the use of filters is the move toward standards. Adobe publishes the standards for Photoshop filters so that third parties can provide their own. Many of these can be used with any application that is compatible with Photoshop filters, including Premiere and other digital video software. The day may be near when every program can use every other program's filters, so that you will be able to customize your software for whatever filters you choose to buy.

Transitions

Transitions differ from filters in that they require two different video segments; they perform their magic on the transition from one video segment to the other. Like filters, there is very little limit to what transitions can do, and they are beginning to be standardized.

Combinations

Combinations allow you to combine two different movies in myriad ways. The following are examples of combinations.

Chroma key. A term that comes from traditional video techniques, chroma key is used extensively on television. For example, it permits the weatherperson to point to details in a weather map that actually is not there. The weatherperson actually points to a blue screen, and chroma key is used to replace the blue screen with another image coming from a different source.

In digital video, chroma key permits you to designate a color (or range of colors) in a movie as transparent, so that you can see through it to a second movie, giving the weather map effect. Chroma key works best with high-quality RGB video that has been taken with chroma key in mind, using a brilliant color to be designated as the transparent color.

Arithmetic. This technique mathematically combines the pixels of one movie with those of another, which can result in impressive special effects.

Logical. These special effects rely on the logical manipulation of bytes that hold the pixel information. They are extremely fast and effective, and can cause images to look like color or black-and-white negatives, make colors disappear altogether, create ghost colors, and many other effects.

Composite. These include morphs and alpha-channels.

Morphs are very attractive special effects that cause a shape in one movie to change slowly into the shape of something very different in another movie. Morphs have been overused in television, and one can tire of them unless they are used for making an effective statement. Thus, think before you morph.

The only difference between a 24-bit movie and a 32-bit movie is that the latter includes a fourth data channel, called the alpha-channel, which allows special effects in digital images. Movies that are stored in 24-bit RGB mode use 8 bits for red, 8 bits for green, and 8 bits for blue, with the remaining 8 bits reserved for such special effects as masks, mattes, overlays, and other manipulations. For example, the alpha-channel might contain a black-and-white oval shape, permitting the combining of two movies, with one movie inside the oval shape and the other movie in the background. (For more information on alpha-channels, see Chapter 15, "Creating Animation," and Chapter 5, "Imaging Tools."

There are several different types of alpha-channels, and they frequently are supported by 3-D software, digital photography software, and other programs that can export QuickTime movies. Although QuickTime does not ordinarily display information in an alpha-channel, it will nevertheless carry the information to a software program that can display it. Photoshop and Premiere both have support for alpha-channels.

Rotoscoping

The process of hand painting on one frame of a digital video movie at a time is called rotoscoping. A convenient way to perform this procedure is to export one or more frames from a movie into Photoshop or other appropriate digital photography software, where the image can be easily hand colored. Premiere supports a special file format, called a film strip, for exporting QuickTime movies to and from Photoshop.

Extensible Architecture

The trend in software development is for one company to encourage other companies to support add-ons to its software package, so that users can extend its capabilities by picking and choosing new features to add. Perhaps having learned the hard way with Adobe fonts, which Adobe did not publish as open standards until Microsoft and Apple challenged the existing font standards with TrueType, Adobe has taken the lead with Premiere in providing the necessary specifications to permit other software add-ons to be made compatible with it, as well as providing standards that other software packages can adhere to in order to utilize Premiere-compatible add-ons.

As in Photoshop, Premiere filters are standardized, and any company can design filters for Premiere. In addition, products such as VideoShop and VideoFusion are compatible with Photoshop or Premiere plug-in filters. Adobe also has published standards for other types of plug-ins for Premiere, including transitions or special effects, video filters, audio filters, device control, exporting EDL's (Edit Decision Lists), and other standards.

Printing to Tape

The Macintosh desktop uses general terms for cutting, pasting, printing, and so on, which can be redefined to meet the needs of new file formats. The term "printing to tape" actually refers to using an output device to send a digital video file to be recorded on a VCR. In order to print to videotape, RasterOps provides another add-on, the VideoExpander, which encodes the Macintosh signal so that it can be recorded to videotape. Radius offers VideoVision, which is a medium-priced one-board solution with inputs and outputs for stereo audio, composite video, and S-Video. It utilizes a propriety convolution technique obtained from Apple Computer that stabilizes the Macintosh signal when it is converted to video.

VideoVision can deliver a very high-quality North American NTSC, 4.43 NTSC, or PAL composite video signal for writing to video tape or driving a standard television monitor. By itself, VideoVision does not have the power to deliver full-screen, full-motion QuickTime movies, though Radius plans to introduce a daughter board that will provide this capability.

Not all QuickTime hardware is designed to print to tape, and if the hardware does not support printing to tape, neither will the software. Hardware cards that support printing to tape must have one or more outputs where a VCR or other device can be hooked up. If your hardware card does support output, then look for software that allows you to print to videotape. If you do not have the necessary hardware, you still can videotape your movies by pointing your video camera at the Macintosh monitor and videotaping that image. You will not be satisfied with the results, however, unless you do something to eliminate the flicker that is invisible until the tape is made. Flicker can be reduced by using appropriate software accessories, such as Apple's Video Synch.

Device Control

In addition to controlling VCRs to print to tape, software packages also can control VCRs, videodisc players, and other devices in order to bring video into the computer, or for other purposes.

Software Packages

Now that we've looked at the features and capabilities common to most video editing packages, let's focus on the particular characteristics of the leading applications.

Adobe Premiere

Adobe Premiere 240

Premiere is the leading software package for QuickTime digital video, due in part to Adobe's marketing clout and presence on the Macintosh with such other milestone graphics packages as Photoshop and Adobe fonts. Many thousands of packages of Premiere were bundled with the VideoSpigot card and distributed for free. Premiere benefits from Adobe's experience with Photoshop and utilizes the same or similar filters. In addition, the new text editor in Premiere gives the user control over many of the parameters of Adobe fonts. Premiere also includes a powerful editing system for combining two QuickTime movies; as well as the Super Channel for superimposing titles, movies and special effects; and support's professional applications requiring SMPTE timecode for off-line editing, extensibility, add-ons, and more (see Figure 8.7).

Features in Premiere permit the intuitive creation and alteration of QuickTime movies. Users can control complex parameters simply by moving a line up and down to create paths in the Title window, audio in the Timeline window, and animation paths in the Motion window.

The Construction window, providing a timeline view of the current project, is at the heart of Premiere. Two primary movie channels are separated by a special-

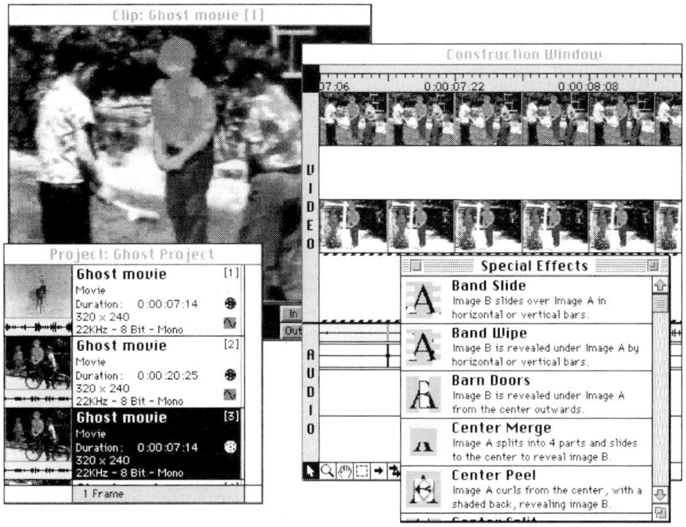

Figure 8.7 Premiere 2.0 with the Movie window, Project window, Construction window, and Special Effects Tansition window

effects channel for the placement of transitions. Audio channels also are supported. A third movie channel, known as the *Super track*, permits whole movies to be displayed over the other two movies in a variety of ways. Using the simplicity of manipulating lines, the transparency function allows the movie in the Super track to be seen as a split screen or a mask, to serve as an alpha-channel, to be used for superimposing titles, and so on. The Construction window permits video and audio to be stretched or shrunk to fit, and facilitates proper placement of video sequences.

Premiere, like all software packages, also has its weaknesses. Premiere is sometimes slow to redraw the movie frames within the Construction window, but has some workarounds. One is the ability to create miniature movies during the editing process, and return to full-size movies at the time of final compilation. There are extra steps involved in making miniatures, however. Premiere works best with finished video segments that are ready to be edited together with titles, transitions, and limited kinds of motion. With the plethora of filters and special effects available, virtually anything can be accomplished, but Premiere does not directly support the simultaneous combination of different movies and images of many different sizes. A great deal of manipulation of filters and special effects may be necessary to create a smaller movie within a movie.

In addition to the Construction window, several other views are available. A Project window holds all the movies and other media chosen for the project (however, the scissors tool in the Construction window, which permits cutting a movie into many smaller pieces, can quickly clutter it). A Library window stores media libraries for future projects.

The Clip window allows you to view clips, as well as change the in-points and out-points of specific segments. The current movie can be viewed, with varying degrees of accuracy, using the Preview window, in which you can designate the portion of the movie to be previewed, and the size and resolution of the preview. A Sequence window permits rapid creation of simple cuts by combining all of the movies placed in it.

As it continues to be enhanced by Adobe, Premiere will undoubtedly flourish as one of the most significant QuickTime digital editing packages.

VideoShop

If you are looking for a software package that creates a complete environment in which to work, from video editing to interactive multimedia, DiVA's VideoShop offers the complete answer. It features a world of internal consistency built around a proprietary data format called a *Micon*. The purpose of a Micon, the parameters of which you can control, is to provide a motion preview of the movie anywhere on the hard disk or elsewhere within VideoShop. Even when porting to HyperCard for interactive presentations, VideoShop takes its Micons along for the ride. A few clicks of the mouse are enough to create a simple interactive presentation. While this approach may not fit everyone's needs, those who are comfortable with the VideoShop environment will have a very productive tool they can stay with. VideoShop even provides its own Visual Catalog database in which to store your media.

TOOLS
VideoShop 242

Micons have their own peculiarities that take some getting use to. For instance, a generic Micon is available for any movie on the hard disk, but each movie must be selected individually to create a custom Micon to represent it. Do not even think of creating a custom Micon for a movie on a CD-ROM, because the Micon data must be attached to the movie itself, which is not feasible on media that is read-only. Once Micons are created, your hard disk and VideoShop data turn into a visual feast of accessible information.

Like Premiere, VideoShop features a timeline view, but in this case the number of video channels is virtually unlimited, providing some of the capabilities of CoSA's After Effects in permitting the combination of different QuickTime movies without regard to shape or size (see below). In addition to the filters and transitional effects that come with the software package, it supports Photoshop Plug-Ins.

VideoShop is a general editing package with all of the features necessary to create first-class QuickTime movies.

CoSA After Effects

Billed as a complementary tool for mainstream editors, such as Adobe Premiere and DIVA's VideoShop, CoSA After Effects is designed for combining movies of different dimensions, as well as PICT files and other media of different sizes, into a single new movie. Under the object-oriented paradigm CoSA has borrowed from 3-D editing software, each movie or other media becomes an object in the Composition window.

The power of this tool is that at any point in the Composition window, which will become the new movie, you are free to move individual objects around relative to each other, to blend them together in many different subtle ways, or to apply special effects to each object individually. Permitting an unlimited number of objects to be layered together, and providing extensive support for the alpha-channel and other effects, this software package is more like a media creation tool than a video editor.

As with 3-D editing software, you can render a movie at different levels of quality to facilitate rapid development. There's a wireframe mode for viewing the relative positions of objects. In the draft mode, the movie is visible at a medium level of quality, and not all effects are calculated. In the best mode, all pixels are displayed, full antialiasing is provided, and plug-in effects are fully calculated. Whereas most other editing software relies on QuickTime to determine quality levels during the editing process, the 3-D model of rendering provides CoSA After Effects with greater flexibility in giving the user an appropriate level of quality for the task at hand, thus speeding up the editing process.

After Effects supports a number of different views, or windows, providing surprising differences from other editing packages (see Figure 8.8). While it features a Project window, it distinguishes between the whole project and a composition, which is the use of the media in a particular project. As a result, many different compositions can be present at one time. As they are created, they show up in the Project window and become raw ingredients for a larger project.

Borrowing again from 3-D software, CoSA Special Effects utilizes its own brand of keyframes to demarcate the length of special effects or transitions. The time view allows you to quickly travel from one keyframe to another, providing a convenient way to design and navigate a movie in various stage of production.

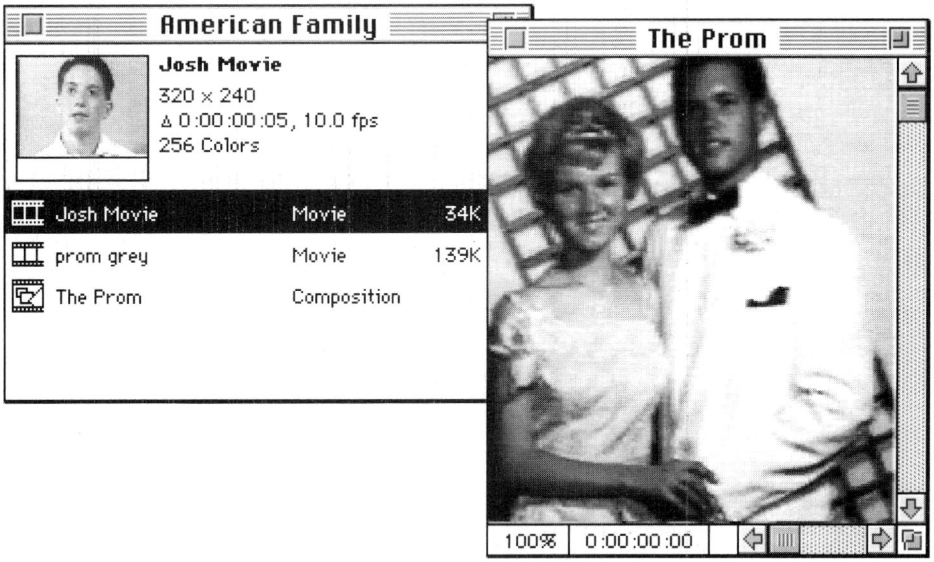

Figure 8.8 Project window and Composition window in CoSA After Effects

VideoFusion

VideoFusion, marketed by Video Fusion Ltd., includes special-effects capabilities beyond those of the other packages, and offers an excellent assortment of views for evaluating a movie. Because VideoFusion compiles special effects as they are created (in Premiere, you compile all at once), it lends itself to experimentation. The results of each preview can be saved to the hard disk and then added to the Storyboard view. Since everything is compiled as it is created, the Movie Player can play the entire movie even while it is being constructed. When you are assembling the final movie, having to wait to process transitions and special effects each time they are created can be burdensome. However, if you are especially interested in the particular effects, this process is ideal.

In VideoFusion, the Storyboard view is the most important, although the Movie Player and Timeline views are conveniently accessible at any time. In fact, a consistent interface allows any view to be switched easily to any other view. The Storyboard view allows the composition to be designed merely by changing the order of the movies or other media. Clicking on any file permits a filter to be used on it. Clicking on any two files permits a transition or a combination to take place by choosing the appropriate special effect and then creating and previewing it. The Timeline is used primarily for synchronizing audio to the video, and for adjusting individual frames within a movie.

VideoFusion enhances rapid experimentation by allowing you to choose and preview various options interactively. For example, logical combinations can be tried by clicking on the choices of "And," "Or," and "Xor." Arithmetic combinations can be sampled by clicking on Add, Subtract, Multiple, Differences, or Superimpose. Replacements can be tried with regard to the red, green, and blue channels, through hue, saturation, and brightness, and so on.

The more advanced features include use of mattes and traveling mattes, morphing one movie to another, rotoscoping, and the like.

VideoVision Studio

Just as *Multimedia Power Tools* went to press, Radius had released VideoVision Studio, the first QuickTime editing and production system to support full-screen, full-motion video at 60fps. Priced at just over $4000, VideoVision Studio comes with a NuBus card that allows 24-bit graphics on 13-inch displays and 8-bit graphics for monitors up to 21 inches; Adobe Premiere; and VideoFusion (see above). It also features a connector panel with a variety of input and output ports for external audio and video devices.

Other Editors and Movie Players

In addition to these sophisticated software editors, you also can find less powerful utilities suitable for simple editing. For instance, Apple supplies MoviePlayer, which allows movies to be edited by using cut, copy, and paste. VideoFusion offers a low-end editor called QuickFLIX. There are also numerous other QuickTime editors coming to market monthly.

Tools for Controlling VCRs and Other Video Equipment

You also can find tools that control VCRs and videodisc players for the purpose of editing video, or to assist in the creation of digital video. The type of hardware/software combination determines how accurately you can control the VCR or other equipment, which is dictated by your needs. The capability of your VCR and the task at hand determine whether you need sophisticated hardware to control your equipment, or whether software control is sufficient (see Chapter 17, "Creating Video").

Tool Features for VCR Control

Not a great deal of accuracy is required for bringing video into the computer, since QuickTime editors allow you to trim the video after creating it. The video can be edited in the computer and the final result can be output to tape without precise control of the VCR. However, multiple prints to the same tape require more precision.

Logging

The process of viewing and describing the scenes in a videotape is referred to as logging. The entire videotape can be logged, or you can select only those scenes that may be used in a production. The computer can assist in the logging process, providing the frame numbers for the beginning and the end of each scene. QuickTime-based logging software can provide a QuickTime preview of the in-point and out-point of each scene.

Off-Line Editing

More precision is required to do off-line editing than is necessary for logging only. Once the in-points and out-points are established, they can be assembled in order to create what is called an edit list. The edit list can be taken to a high-end video

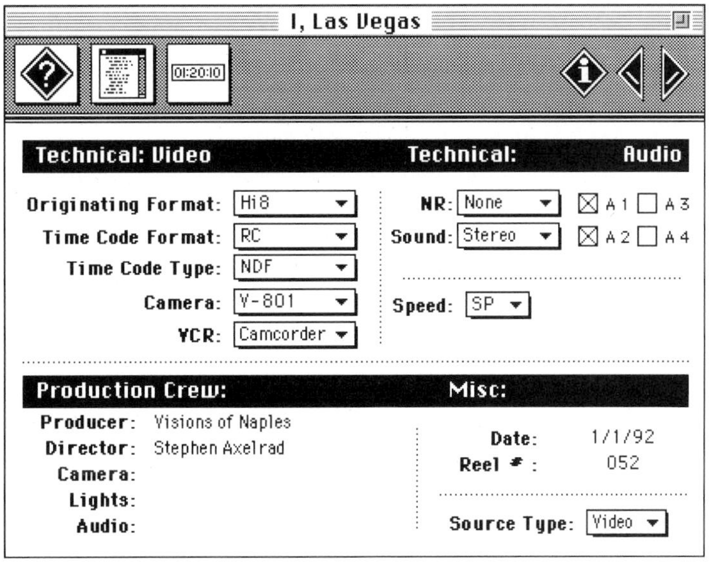

Figure 8.9 A screen from CueTrack HyperCard stack from VideoToolkit permits rapid logging and database management of videotape.

facility, where the final video can be edited using very expensive equipment in a very short period of time, because all of the decisions have already been made.

Using software such as Premiere, the entire production can be created as a QuickTime movie, including the transitions; the software can then export an edit list sufficient to reproduce the movie in its entirety in a high-end video facility. In order to obtain sufficient accuracy to do this properly, the QuickTime movie should include time code at 30 frames per second. This is possible using only some of the more advanced QuickTime digitizing hardware.

On-Line Editing

The process of using the computer to edit videotape without bringing the video into the computer is called on-line editing. The computer acts as a controller to synchronize the videotape player and transfer the video to the videotape recorder. This requires almost no computer memory, since none of the video has to enter the computer. A controller system that is precise enough to begin and end on the designated video frame is said to be frame-accurate. More likely, on-line editing will be accurate within a few frames. The use of time code is necessary for frame-accurate editing.

VCR Control Software and Hardware

While some software tools for VCR control rely on the Macintosh itself for hardware, more expensive solutions utilize additional hardware for more precise control. The VideoToolkit, which comes with interfacing cables, is an example of an excellent software package that is a complete, inexpensive solution not requiring additional hardware. The primary focus of this software is logging, control for digital video, and off-line editing, although it can also be used for on-line editing.

The FutureVideo EditLink 3300 Series desktop controller is an example of a hardware/software solution (Figure 8.10). The primary focus of this package is on-line edits, although it can also be used for logging, control for digital video, and off-line editing. While the FutureVideo EditLink 3300 Series can simulaneously control three VCRs for logging or bringing video into the computer, its primary purpose is for on-line editing while also controlling external special-effects generators, such as the Video Toaster. Two different videotapes can be combined with transitions created by a special-effects generator and recorded onto a third VCR. This process is called A/B roll, and the ability to trigger the special-effects generator is called a GPI. The FutureVideo EditLink 3300 controller comes with editing software compatible with all current Macs.

Videodisc Control

Videodisc players can be utilized to bring video into the computer, or for interactive presentations utilizing the computer for the limited purpose of controlling the player. The Voyager VideoStack provides a HyperCard solution for controlling videodisc players and creating interactive presentations. Most industrial players with computer interface ports, including Sony and Pioneer videodisc players, are supported. Many of the consumer players also are supported by the Voyager VideoStack by means

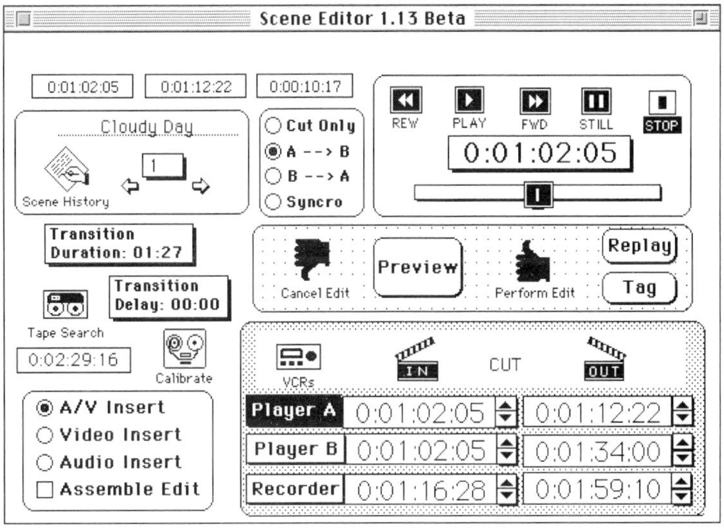

Figure 8.10 FutureVideo's EditLink 3300 Series controller with Scene Editor software for the Macintosh

of an additional hardware interface that can be purchased from Voyager. The interface provides infrared communication through emulation of the commands of the player's own hand controller.

Two of the most popular videodisc players are the Pioneer LDV-4200 and its successor, the LDV-4400. Players that use commands compatible with these players, including the high-end Pioneer LDV6000, can be controlled by the Pioneer MovieMaker, which is distributed on the QuickTime Developer's CD-ROM from Apple. This utility can control the videodisc player one frame at a time to permit bringing all frames into the computer, even with hardware not designed to capture all 30 frames in real time.

MovieShop for CD-ROM

QuickTime movies destined for CD-ROM will benefit from treatment by MovieShop, a utility from Apple Computer and available on the Apple QuickTime Developer's CD-ROM. A QuickTime movie looks like a snake that has swallowed a few mice, in that the data has lumps in it which are too large to transfer at the proper speed on a CD-ROM player.

MovieShop compresses a movie's data so that it can be played back within a specified data rate. If there is too much information per second, then the movie will appear jerky, or the sound will begin to skip. If a movie is intended to play back from a CD-ROM, you'll want the data rate to be no higher than 90–100K per second. (The newer double speed drives can deliver twice this data rate, but you should use the lower rates for backwards compatibility). To reduce the data rate, you can select which of MovieShop's compression techniques should be applied. These include lowering the frame rate, reducing the quality of the sound, shrinking the image size, lowering the image quality by increasing compression, dropping similar adjacent frames, and many others.

Currently, the Apple Compact Video codec is the most effective in reducing data rates and supports smooth playback of QuickTime with a surprisingly large window size. This codec can be selected from within MovieShop. In Chapter 17, "Creating Video," we suggest the MovieShop settings you should use for optimal results from this codec.

The Future of Digital Video Tools

While the quality of existing tools for digital video already is very impressive, the medium is still in its youth and has many years of exciting growth ahead of it. There are many new and evolving features in third-party software. Apple Computer itself has made a significant commitment to digital video and can be expected to contribute to its evolution. One possibility would be an operating system that permits all of the best tools from each third-party supplier to be combined. Thus, you would be able to use filters from one company, a timeline from another, and transitions from a third company to virtually design your own software environment.

QuickTime also has an exciting and extensible future. Because its inventors knew that digital video was a rapidly changing format, they created QuickTime with the flexibility to grow and change, and you can be sure that it will. Andy Soderburg, an important member of the team that developed QuickTime, suggested at a 1992 conference in Los Angeles that the following areas were likely candidates for improvements:

1. **Device Control.** Additional video tracks in QuickTime could be used to synchronize videotape, videodisc, external audio equipment, etc. to events within a QuickTime movie production.
2. **Midi.** Support for synchronizing Midi instruments to QuickTime so that electronic music could be orchestrated directly from the instruments themselves.
3. **Interactive Scripts.** Navigable movies could permit you to explore an object or place by moving all the way around it, above it, or below it.
4. **Media Servers.** Since reference movies can function separately from the digital video original movies from which they are composed, a central media server makes a lot of sense, assuming that QuickTime can access it fast enough to run the movie from somewhere else on a computer network. This permits the original videos to be used by many persons on the network, who can incorporate the videos into new productions without duplicating files and taking up disk space. Future versions of QuickTime could have direct support for this capability.
5. **Video Conferencing.** As more people communicate in real time with video, QuickTime may incorporate support for video conferencing within its specifications.

6. **Filters, Transitions, and Special Effects.** Since most digital video on the Macintosh is now based on QuickTime, Apple Computer is in a good position to help standardize the specifications for standard features in different software packages, to increase interchangeability of features like filters, transitions, and special effects from one software package to the next.
7. **Professional Video Support.** As QuickTime and the Macintosh computer increase in speed and memory capacity, the demand for professional video support for QuickTime also will increase, and Apple has indicated an interest in this market by providing support for SMPTE time code. More professional support is likely in the future.
8. **New Compression Algorithms.** Compression is something that will continue to be enhanced in QuickTime. Indeo, which will give QuickTime DVI compatibility, has already been announced. Eventually, fractal and other compression may arrive.

Desktop tools for creating broadcast-quality video are still somewhat expensive and technologically demanding. Nevertheless, relatively low-cost multimedia-quality video tools and applications are now accessible to nearly everyone. In addition to low-cost hardware such as the VideoSpigot, the software lets you create state-of-the-art special effects. CD-ROM offers storage capabilities for large projects, and provides an inexpensive means for distribution. By the end of the decade, the transition to digital video may be complete, and analog video may become a thing of the past. In the meantime, digital and analog video can be used together by borrowing from the best of both worlds. Chapter 17, "CreatingVideo," looks further into these topics.

9

Authoring Tools

Dramatic video, beautiful sound, and delightful animation won't give you multimedia—not unless they're combined together in a cohesive, interactive whole. That's where *authoring* tools come in: They're the software programs you'll use to take all those building blocks—as beautiful as they may be individually—and orchestrate them in a way that creates a powerful, synergistic, final product that is far greater than the sum of its parts. With authoring tools, you become a multimedia director, with total creative control over the storyline, the set, and the actors that make up your project.

Most authoring tools allow you to create and modify backgrounds and visual effects for your project's interface. Many allow you to control external devices, such as videotape decks and laserdisc players. However, the most important features are those they offer for creating links between graphics, text, and audiovisual elements. These features work through buttons, scripts, hardware device drivers, and other means of creating interactivity between the user and the project.

In this chapter, we'll take a look at all the major authoring software applications, including Macromedia's Director and AuthorWare Professional, Discovery Systems International's Course Builder, and those old (yet highly effective) standbys, Apple Computer's HyperCard and Aldus's SuperCard. We'll also touch on less sophisticated, more economical applications that provide decent authoring power, including Passport Producer, Vividus Cinemation, and Motion Works PROmotion.

Authoring Software Features

When evaluating authoring software, you should carefully consider issues such as interface, capabilities, and features. Does the software have all the necessary tools for creating links between your interface and your data? Can you customize the software and write custom scripts to perform special functions that might be considered outside of the norm? Most importantly, is the interface sensible and organized for the task you have set for yourself?

You should also look for programs that support current graphics, animation, and video standards. QuickTime support is crucial if you're planning on using small video segments off hard drives or CD-ROMs. Also, emerging compression/decompression technology means that many of the authoring programs will soon be supporting full-screen video directly off your hard drive.

There are so many features and capabilities to keep track of, yet you can conveniently place them into a few major categories.

Master Windows

Most authoring packages feature some type of master window, where you can get a bird's-eye view of your project, including all of its elements and their relationships. Sometimes this screen takes the form of a flowchart, as with Authorware Professional or Course Builder; other times it may resemble a spreadsheet, as with the Director's Score found in Macromedia Director.

Objects and Scripts

Most authoring packages allow you to create the sequence of your presentation, and link its elements together, simply by selecting and connecting screen icons that represent the various pieces of the presentation. This *object-oriented* type of interface is very intuitive and allows almost anyone to successfully choreograph a presentation from the get-go. Some packages give you even more power and precision in this area by including a *scripting language*. However, a scripting language takes some time to learn, and can be daunting in some situations.

The Object-Oriented Approach

Working with objects is the easiest way to create a multimedia ensemble. For example, to allow you to create a button that leads to an animation on-screen, most programs will offer some sort of "make button" command. Once you've made the button, you'll have the option to associate a visual graphic with it and place a name on it, such as "Play Animation." You can then *define the button's properties*—tell the button where to look for your animation on the hard drive, and give the instruction to play the animation once the button is clicked—via some type of "button info" dialogue.

As you can see, this is a fairly straightforward procedure. You simply create an object and then give it instructions about what it should do when activated. The same button that plays an animation could have just as easily been programmed to play a segment of video from a laserdisc, show a PICT file on the screen, or even navigate to another screen that contains more buttons.

Of course, a professional multimedia project usually will involve much more complexity than that represented with simple "go directly from here to there" relationships. It often will also involve the concept of "branching," which means setting up the paths and options for how your data is accessed. We'll get into branching and other considerations for constructing an interactive project in Chapter 19, "Interface and Interactivity."

Scripting

Many major authoring programs, including Director, HyperCard, and SuperCard, include a scripting language that can give you great precision in determining how your multimedia elements will interrelate, and how well your project will interface with external programs, routines, and devices. Although multimedia scripting is generally a lot easier to master than traditional programming languages (you don't need to have a degree in computer science), it does have a steeper learning curve than that for pointing and clicking on objects. However, once learned, scripting will allow you to add that extra polish to your project.

File Formats

An attractive interface is one of the most essential ingredients for a successful multimedia project, so most authoring packages come with tools and features that allow you to import various graphics and sounds. Perhaps most important is the capability to import the most popular graphics and motion-graphics formats, since you certainly will be using graphic elements created in other packages. Most authoring packages will accept PICT, PICS, and QuickTime formats, as well as a number of others. Color support also is an important consideration for professional-level multimedia.

On the sound side, most packages support AIFF, SoundEdit, MIDI, and Sound Designer II formats. For more information on these formats and their use, see Chapter 6, "Sound Tools," and Chapter 13, "Producing Sound."

Graphics and Animation Tools

Authoring packages also provide varying capabilities for manipulating graphics. Many come with built-in drawing and painting tools. Some boast sophisticated animation tools for movement, timing, and transitions. Most have controls for transitional effects and wipes from one window to another. Some applications, such as HyperCard and Passport Producer, are weak in these areas. However, there often are ways around a program's shortcomings, usually requiring more work in "outside" graphics and animation applications before the sequence is brought into the authoring environment.

Connecting to External Devices

Many multimedia presentations rely on external devices, such as CD-ROMs, laserdiscs, or VCRs. How and to what degree your authoring program controls these devices can greatly affect the scope and impact of your project. Most authoring packages do this through add-on routines called *external commands* (XCMDs), which follow a standard originally established with HyperCard. AuthorWare Professional not only supports XCMDs, but also boasts built-in control for laserdiscs.

Playback

"How will people be using my project? Will it be a kiosk in a hotel lobby? Will it be mass distributed on a CD-ROM, or on a laserdisc?" As we suggested in Chapter 2, "The Multemedia Production Process," you must ask yourself these questions early on, as they will have a huge impact on what authoring tools you'll need to put your project together. Most authoring packages support run-time playback, which means that users can view the final project whether or not they have the application in which it was created. This is a critical consideration if you will be distributing your project via CD-ROM. Macromedia Director even features a Windows Player for running Mac-created multimedia projects in the Windows environment on IBM PC compatibles (see Chapter 12, "Working Cross-Platform," for more details).

Software Packages

Now that we've looked at the features and capabilities common to most authoring packages, let's focus on the particular characteristics of the leading products.

AuthorWare Professional

TOOLS
AuthorWare Professional
214

Macromedia's AuthorWare Professional is one of the leaders for interactive authoring. Perhaps its greatest strength is that it is entirely based on using icons for creating interactive links, so there is no scripting necessary. AuthorWare's icons and their associated dialog boxes act as tools for building a project and creating links between elements, so the learning curve is relatively shallow. AuthorWare Professional also has built-in support for multiple file formats, as well as for 24-bit graphics, laser disc control, and HyperCard XCMDs. AuthorWare Professional has good animation tools as well, allowing you to easily add movement to your project. Animations are created through the use of dialog boxes, which greatly simplifies the process so that you can concentrate more on the task of building an interactive presentation.

AuthorWare's primary interface is centered around a flow-line map, which is a visual representation of your project (see Figure 9.1). This enables you to get a quick overview of the structure and branching paths of your project.

AuthorWare's graphics facilities include a draw-type graphics environment, complete with patterns, fills, and transparency layering options (see Figure 9.2). It also has a variety of transitions as well as many built-in erase options, which include a number of options for helping get rid of graphic elements that are no longer needed on the screen. Also, object-oriented draw graphics, such as those created with MacDraw or Deneba's Canvas, can be imported in such a fashion that you can access and modify their component lines and shapes. The potential for attaching more information, such as animation data, to imported draw graphics provides the opportunity for an entire new level of interactivity. AuthorWare Professional supports the importation of 24-bit PICT files, unlike most authoring tools, which only support 8-bit graphics.

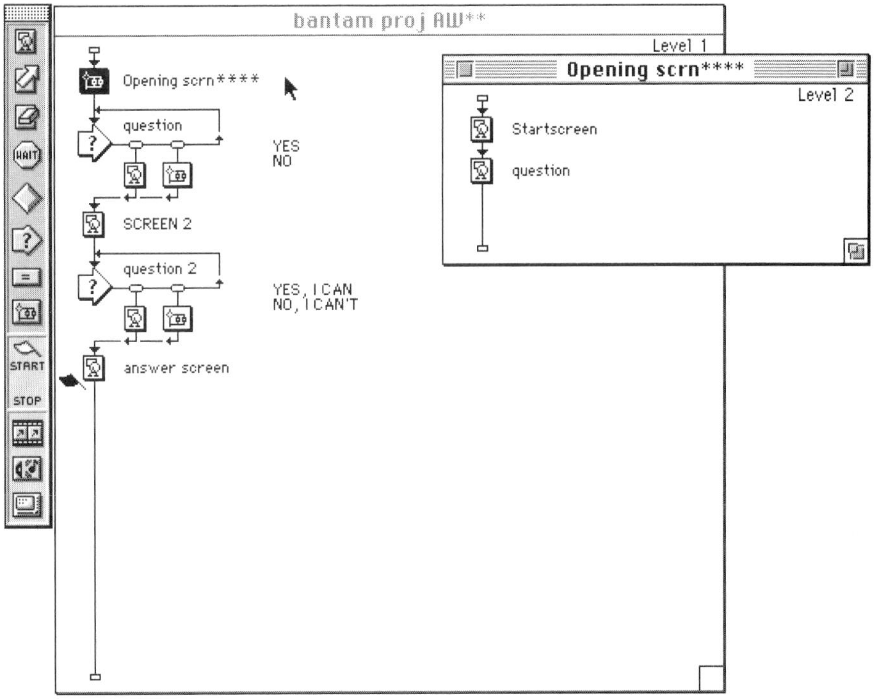

Figure 9.1 **AuthorWare's Flow-line window is the main window for plotting the flow of your project. Icons are dragged into the Flow-line window, where they can then be linked together to create interactivity between elements.**

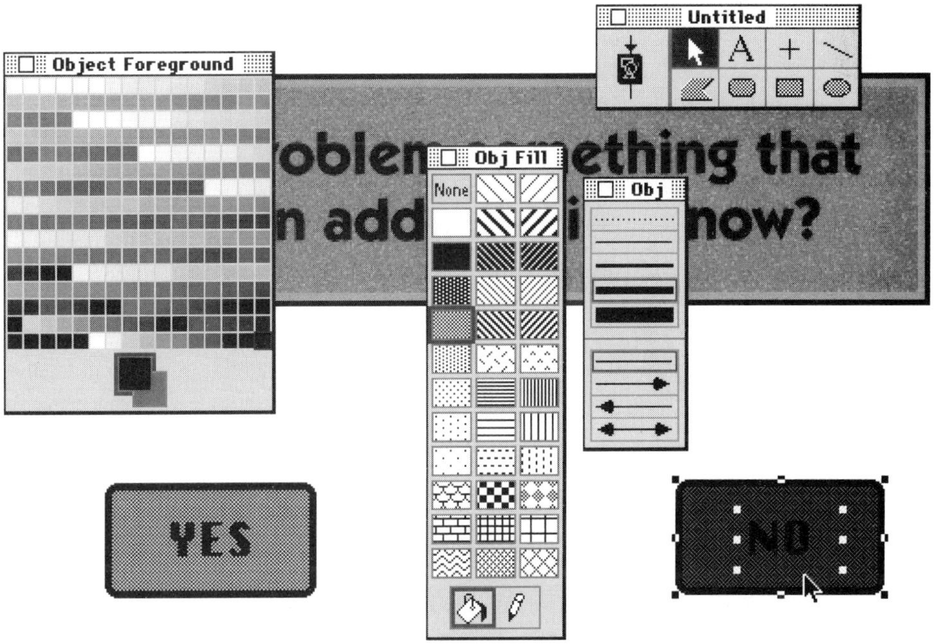

Figure 9.2 **AuthorWare Professional has fairly extensive graphics capabilites, with palettes for creating graphics and text, as well as modes for layering and transparency.**

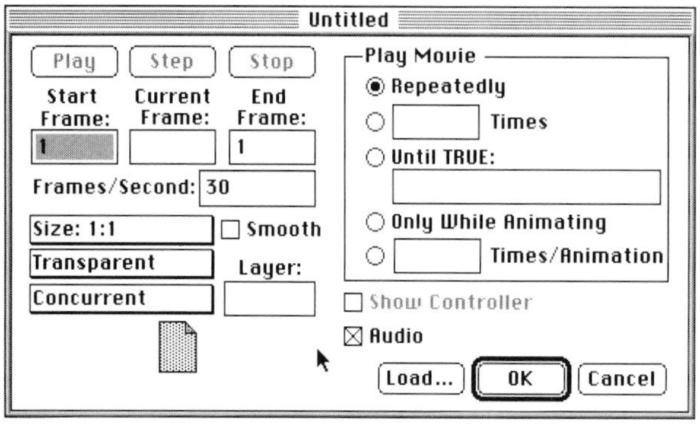

Figure 9.3 AuthorWare Professional offers a Digital Video dialog for controlling the playback of QuickTime movies and DVI files.

AuthorWare Professional provides all the necessary animation support a multimedia producer could want. There are built-in, path-based animation functions, as well as direct support for Director "movie" files. So, if you can't create the animation you want in AuthorWare Professional, it's easy to import it from Director. AuthorWare Professional also can import sounds, QuickTime movies, and Digital Video Interactive (DVI) files, which are compressed digital video files that will play back as full-screen video at 30 frames per second—right on your computer display, assuming you've installed a DVI compression board (see Figure 9.3).

Another of AuthorWare Professional's strengths is its ability to track test results. It has established itself as the leader for authoring interactive learning applications, partially because of the result-tracking capabilities, which makes it ideal for training applications. AuthorWare Professional has a large collection of built-in system functions and variables for keeping track of users' responses, as well as their response times, so it's fairly easy to measure the efficiency and performance of students being tested. Although AuthorWare Professional does not support scripting, it has extensive text-handling capabilities for updating projects. Generally, the icons on the tool palettes will be more than adequate for authoring tasks.

For distribution, there is a run-time version that will launch your project but won't allow anyone to make changes to it. AuthorWare Professional also is available as a Windows package, and it has the same user interface on both platforms, which makes cross-platform development relatively painless (see

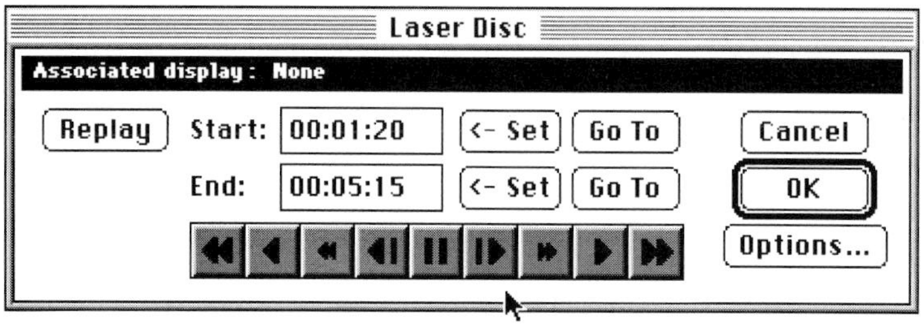

Figure 9.4 AuthorWare Professional offers direct control of external analog video devices, such as a laserdisc recorder.

Chapter 12, "Working Cross-Platform"). If you need to create a project that can be modified on both the Mac and the PC, AuthorWare Professional certainly is worthy of consideration.

AuthorWare Professional allows you to create Media Manager libraries of source files for multimedia projects that can be interactively shared. You can have a number of projects access the same library, or inversely, you can have one project access a number of libraries, as may be found in a cataloging and archiving system. You also can have machines on a network share access to libraries. For large projects and networks, this approach can maximize resources, especially if you're using large amounts of animation and digitized video.

How It Works

AuthorWare Professional projects are created by dragging icons into a flow line map that allows you to quickly see the visual flow of your project and also provides its structure and foundation. There are eleven icons in total, and these provide the means to create any part of an interactive project, whether it's adding a QuickTime movie, a button, or a path that branches off to other areas (see Figure 9.5). At any point in the design process, you can double-click on an icon to set its parameters, thus telling it how to interact with the other elements in your flow map. You also can try a dry run at any time to see your progress as you build your project. Integration of laserdiscs, QuickTime movies, animations, sounds, and other multimedia elements is quite simple, since there are dedicated dialog boxes for each of these types of data.

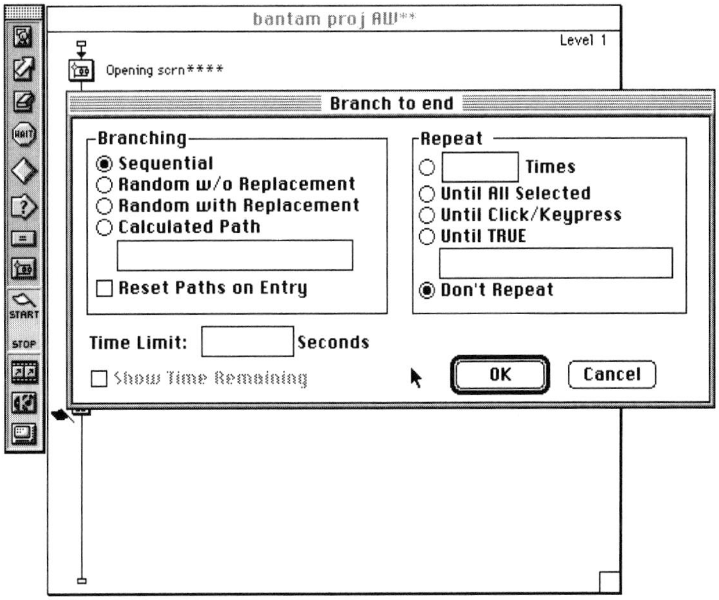

Figure 9.5 AuthorWare's Decision icon allows you to determine what types of branching you would like to assign to an element.

Summary

AuthorWare Professional, the most expensive of all the authoring tools available ($8000), also seems to have the broadest range of capabilities. Its support for QuickTime, laserdiscs, and DVI digital video files make it unsurpassed in the ability to incorporate video in a project. As for animation, while it provides a basic path-based approach, it also directly supports Macromedia Director files. And it supports 24-bit graphics and stereo sound. This should be just about everything on a multimedia producer's checklist. Its Media Manager, which allows libraries of source files to be accessed by a number of different projects or machines, is a key element for managing system resources, especially with large multimedia projects.

AuthorWare Professional is designed and billed as a tool for interactive learning. It has extensive tools for building projects that test and keep track of results. This, plus the fact that it is a well-developed product existing on both the Mac and PC platforms, ultimately justify the steep price tag. And even though the developers state that it is specifically designed for creating interactive learning applications, it has the potential to accomplish much more than this for those willing to take a creative approach to authoring.

Macromedia Director

Macromedia Director is extremely popular for creating graphics-oriented multimedia projects in all budget ranges. Director's strengths include the ability to create animations and to control such external devices as laserdiscs, and its custom scripting environment. For projects based on animation, sound, and interactivity, such as an interactive game, almost all of the work can be done within Director.

TOOLS Director 210

Director has two primary working areas for creating projects. There is a basic, introductory area for creating interactive presentations, called the Overview mode, and then there is the nitty-gritty animation and serious multimedia authoring area, called the Studio mode. The Overview mode forces you to sacrifice many of the specifics you might require for an interactive project, but it is very good for the quick and easy creation of a linear presentation (see Figure 9.6). Elements can be layered, complete with transitions between different sections of a presentation, and you can even build in pauses, where the computer waits until you're ready to continue, at which point you simply click the mouse to move on. The Studio mode is where most users will spend their time, as it is the environment for creating sophisticated animations as well as for building complex interactivity into a project.

Director has its own scripting language, called Lingo, for creating interactive links between the various elements and peripherals in a project. Lingo provides a robust selection of tools for linking elements together, with pull-down menus that are chock-full of commands, functions, operators, constants, and more. As with most multimedia programming languages, Lingo is an object-oriented language, so it's quite easy to attach a script or command to a graphic or animation

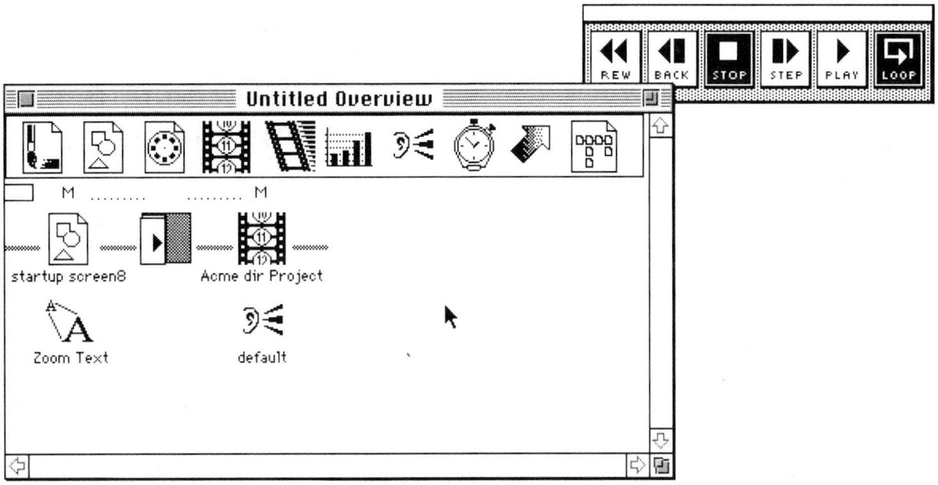

Figure 9.6 Directors' Overview mode allows you to quickly compose a presentation simply by dragging icons into place along a timeline. Elements such as graphics, text, sound, and animations can be layered and organized in a linear fashion, complete with transitions from one section to another.

element. The statements created in Lingo are similar to those used in hypertext-based applications. By constructing simple statements and referencing other functions, it's relatively easy to create fairly complex projects. This is not to say that it is easy to learn. Director can be more difficult than other authoring environments, especially if you need to learn how to create animations as well as interactivity.

Macromedia also offers a Windows player for projects created in Director. This means that you can create a project on the Mac and play it back on a DOS machine running Windows. This type of cross-platform capability often can be the deciding factor for companies with a heavy investment in DOS-based systems (see Chapter 12, "Working Cross-Platform").

How It Works

Since serious interactive projects will demand that you work in the Studio mode, we'll direct our working comments to this area of the program. Director's Studio mode uses theatrical metaphors to create an understandable environment for building the visual parts of a project. Graphic and animation elements are considered Cast members, the screen is considered a Stage, and choreography of your animation elements is controlled via a Score. This conceptual model works well, as it allows you to orient yourself quickly to the various audio/visual tasks involved with animation and multimedia producing. Once you are oriented to Director's approach, the layout is quite logical (see Figure 9.7).

The Score is the central area for organizing and controlling your data. Besides having virtually unlimited layers available for graphics, it features channels for tempo, audio, transitions, and scripting. The Score is basically a spreadsheet with a series of cells laid out in a grid. Graphics and animation elements are layered from top to bottom, with the bottom layer being the elements that are in the fore-

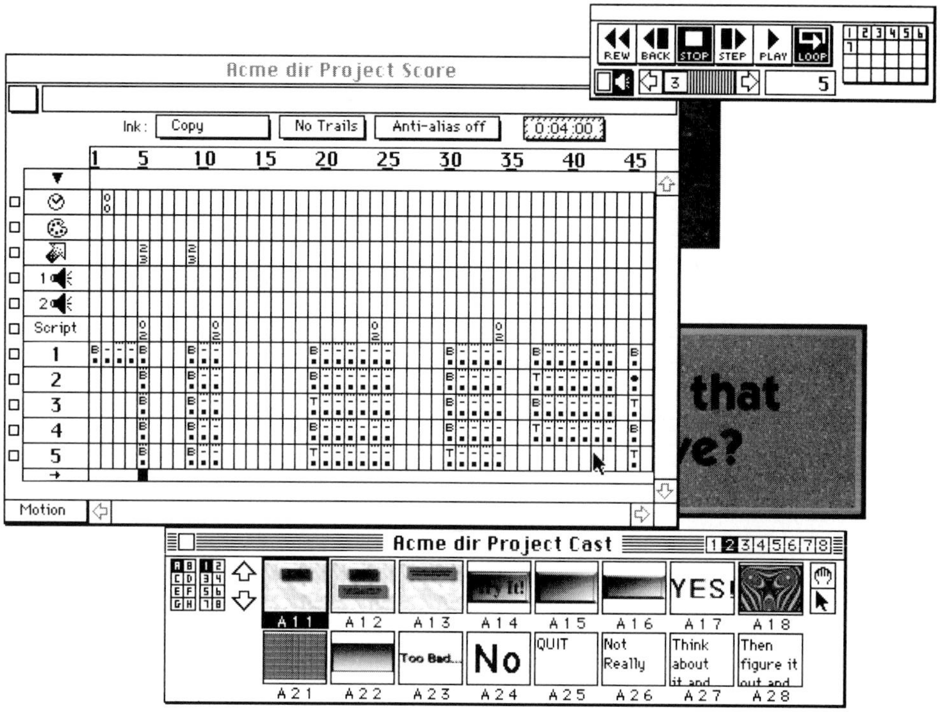

Figure 9.7
This image shows the key elements of Director's Studio mode; the Score, Cast, and Playback windows. The Score is a command sheet where you organize the layers, structure, movement, and interactivity in your project. The Cast is where you keep the graphics, animation, and text elements of your project. The Playback window is used to play a project, much like you would play it on an audio or video player.

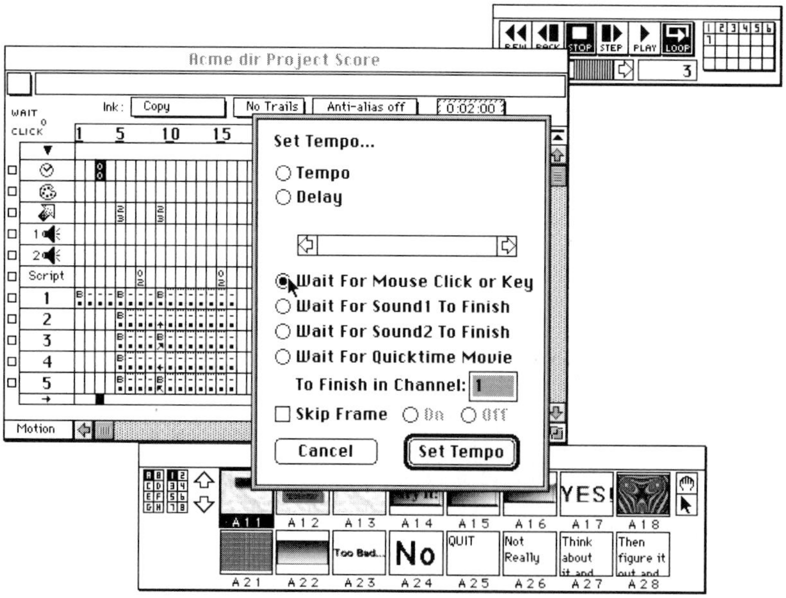

Figure 9.8
Tempo settings can be applied at any given point in a project, with controls for predetermined wait periods or instructions to proceed upon the completion of a sound or movie. You also can instruct the project to wait for the user to click the mouse or hit a key before proceeding.

front visually. The left-to-right organization of cells represents a linear timeline. The top six channels in the score are dedicated to tempo settings (including "wait for mouse click" commands), color palette transitions, graphic transitions (such as wipes and dissolves), audio, and Lingo scripts (see Figure 9.8).

Other notable windows include those for Cast and Paint. The Cast window is where Director stores all of the project's visual elements. This includes all graphics, animations, and text overlays, as well as animated loops and QuickTime movies. The Paint window is actually Director's built-in paint program. Although not as slick as some of the dedicated paint programs on the market, it offers a fairly full-featured set of tools for creating and modifying graphic elements (see Figure 9.9). Arrow buttons in the Paint window allow you to toggle through your entire cast of graphic elements, providing easy access for making changes. Among items available in the Paint window are user-definable gradients, patterns, and textures, painting and drawing tools, and rotation and distortion tools for modifying graphics.

Summary

All in all, Director is a very capable program. It has a reasonable price (about $1000), and has become something of a standard for multimedia authoring. While it's not the most sophisticated paint, animation, or authoring tool, it does a great job of combining all three in a powerful environment. Users should be forewarned that both the animation and scripting parts of Director have fairly steep learning curves, but the program comes with plenty of samples and tutorials from which the dedicated multimedia artist can learn. Furthermore, through XCMDs

TOOLS

Director Training 211

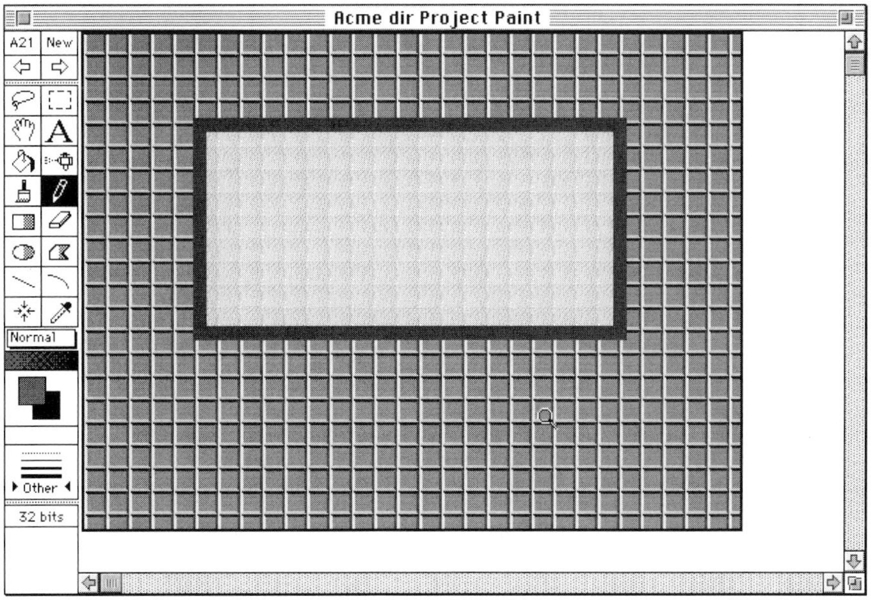

Figure 9.9 Director contains a fairly complete paint environment, with a variety of brushes, drawing tools, gradients, patterns, text tools, and more.

and Lingo scripting, Director can be configured to control external devices, adding another level of power for those needing serious video or audio integration in their projects.

Course Builder

Course Builder, from Discovery Systems International, is a program designed primarily for testing and education, although it certainly can be used for a wide range of applications. It is unable to support 32-bit graphics, and is not particularly strong on animation, but it does have built-in control for laserdiscs, as well as support for Macintalk, Apple's current voice synthesis technology (see Figure 9.10). It seems clear that Course Builder will be building on future voice synthesis technology, so keep an eye on it as Apple's Casper technology develops.

Course Builder is another object-oriented program that, like AuthorWare Professional, uses icons and dialog boxes as tools for building projects. Course Builder also supports HyperCard XCMDs for external device control, and extensions to other custom programs. Course Builder can import 8-bit graphics and their associated custom palettes, so it is possible to have color of reasonable quality in your projects. It also has fairly in-depth animation control, with motion path editing capabilities for fine tuning an animation.

The graphics creation tools in Course Builder are quite complete, with a draw and paint mode for creating 8-bit graphics (see Figure 9.11). You can use custom imported palettes as the source colors for any graphics you create, or you can default to the Apple 8-bit system palette.

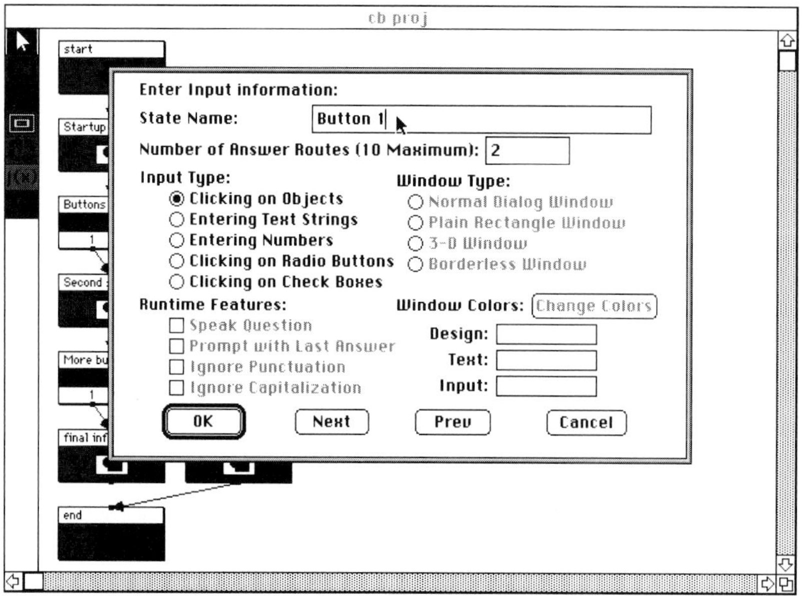

Figure 9.10 Course Builder's Design and Text input dialog allows you to define properties of the element you are working with. Programmable elements include everything from the type of input used, such as a mouse click or text, to the use of Course Builder to compose a voice synthesize response with Macintalk.

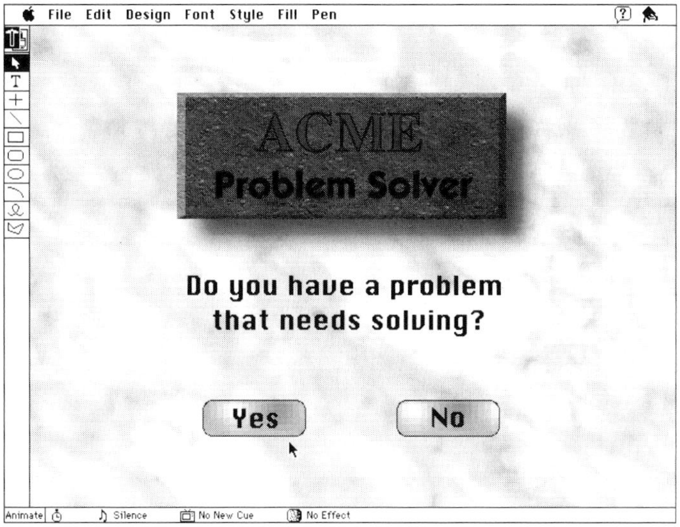

Figure 9.11 Course Builder's Graphics State window allows you to create paint or draw graphics and animations, as well as import PICT files for foreground or background elements.

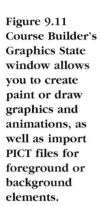

The product's branching and interactivity capabilities are very strong. It offers a number of methods for creating links for everything from a button to an animated sprite. The branching tools are also quite strong, allowing you to create branches quickly and easily.

Course Builder's major strengths lie in its capabilities for responding to user input. Projects can be structured to request a variety of mouse, typing, or touch-screen responses (see Figure 9.12). It also has extensive capabilities for dealing with testing scenarios. There are options for users to hit radio buttons, click check boxes for multiple choice entries, enter text or numbers for answers, and more. There are even options for allowing users a certain number of attempts at answering a question before forcing them to move on. And there are built-in mechanisms for creating a log of students' answers, even noting how much time

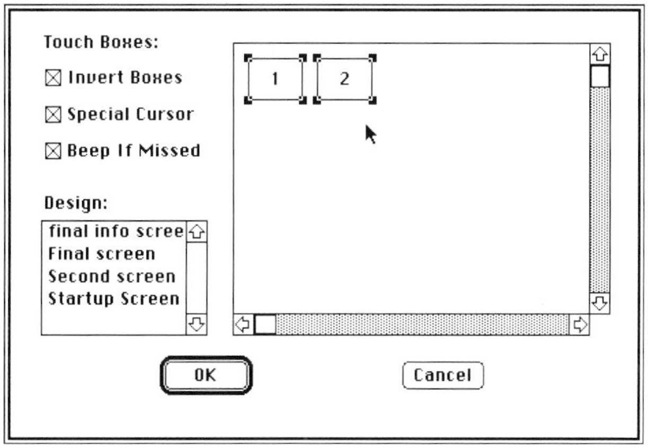

Figure 9.12 The Mouse Input State view allows you to define the size and location of up to ten Touch Box regions on a screen. The output of each box can be routed to other screens when clicked.

it took for a student to get the right answer. The tools for building this type of interactivity are accessible through dialog boxes, making it easy to compose sophisticated test-response monitoring into just about any project. Needless to say, these features could also be put to excellent use in projects for museum kiosks, trade show exhibits, games, and other situations where questions and user responses are central.

Course Builder features extensions for running projects over a network, allowing teachers to easily monitor the results of an entire classroom of machines. You can create bridges between different projects, enabling you to link large amounts of material together. Finished projects can be turned into stand-alone applications, without the need for a run-time version of the program.

How It Works

Course Builder is icon-based. Its main screen allows you to construct a map of your project, which clearly shows the links between the various elements (see Figure 9.13). Like a roadmap, the path of your project can take you through various "states" via a variety of routes. This roadmap metaphor seems to work fairly well.

Projects are built by dragging icons into order on the Course Map. By clicking and dragging on the in-and-out points of an icon, you can easily link the various elements of your project together visually. Double-clicking on an icon will give you access to its parameters for creating specific linking data and other options.

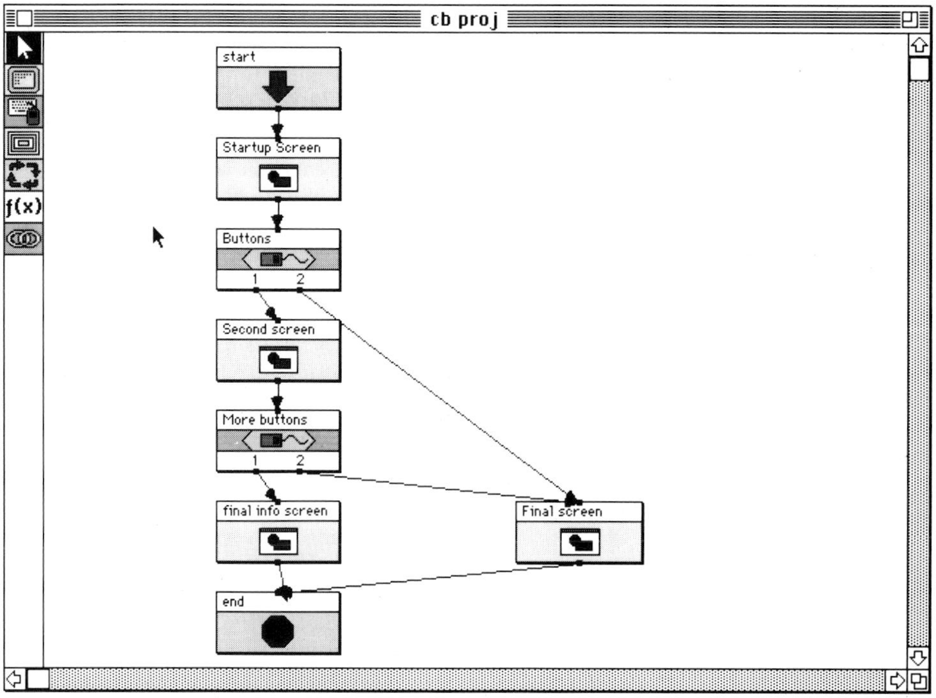

Figure 9.13 Course Builder's main screen allows you to construct a map of your project. The lines connecting the boxes show the relationships of the various elements.

Summary

Course Builder ($1495) is a very complete environment for authoring. Like Authorware Professional, it is geared toward interactive learning. It has good color graphics and animation capabilities, support for such video devices as laserdiscs, and extensive tools for user interactivity. All this, combined with the ability to record test results, make it a good candidate for creating multimedia teaching and testing applications, as well as public question-and-response exhibits.

Passport Producer

TOOLS Passport Producer 216

Passport Producer is a time-based media integration and assembly tool designed for creating synchronized presentations. For video and audio devotees, Producer offers an environment for combining graphics, animations, MIDI, and digital audio files. It uses Society of Motion Picture and Television Engineers (SMPTE)-standard time code as the means for synchronizing elements, which can be a great boon to dedicated audio or video professionals who are already working with SMPTE. It provides a very consistent playback result regardless of the CPU speed of the computer.

How It Works

Passport Producer uses a graphical timeline called a "Cue Sheet." The Cue Sheet is a bit different from timelines in other multimedia authoring tools in that it displays the time scale along its vertical axis and uses tracks along its horizontal axis to provide for simultaneous tracking of data elements. You also can switch this orientation around if you wish. The timeline can be scaled to show the data in different resolutions. It also can show time in different formats, including hours: minutes: seconds: hundredths of seconds, as well as SMPTE standard time code.

The Cue Sheet allows you to integrate different media elements called "cues." Each occupies a single track, matched to a location in time. Cues are created by clicking on a icon in a Cue palette and dragging it into the Cue Sheet. Producer then opens up a dialog which allows you to select a disk file which contains the data you wish to attach to that cue.

Once created, cues are displayed showing a visual reference to the type of data it represents, an image thumb of the cue's image if available, the name of the file that the cue's contents originate from, and the starting and ending time within the Cue Sheet for the cue and a number of controls. The controls allow you to set the volume for a cue's audio, the speed at which animation or QuickTime cues are played, and the portion of a cue's content which is used.

You can quickly align multiple cues with each other and resize them in a number of ways by dragging the mouse or typing settings into dialogs. You also can print the Cue Sheet for use in a paper edit, group review, or as a storyboarding aid. Producer will let you open multiple Cue Sheets to make it easy to cut, copy, and paste cues between different presentations.

You can create audio cues using 8- or 16-bit AIFF, Sound Designer, MIDI type O or type 1 files, or CD audio tracks (see Chapter 6, "Sound Tools"). Also, Producer will allow you to directly input digital audio cues through a microphone or audio digitizer, and input MIDI cues through MIDI devices such as a keyboard or sequencer. Image and animation cues can be media elements from any presentation software that saves files in TEXT, PICT, and PICS formats. In addition, you can apply transitions to still images as they appear on-screen. Producer also supports use of QuickTime movies as cues, and the conversion of PICT, PICS and AIFF files into QuickTime movie format before assignment as cues. Cues can be edited using built-in media editors at any time, or you can link individual cue types to third-party applications if desired.

Producer also supports two special cue types: marker and pause. You use marker cues to identify specific sections of the Cue Sheet through user-entered notations, navigate quickly to different locations of the Cue Sheet, and act as guides for exact alignment of other cues. You use pause cues to pause a presentation at the time specified by its location in the Cue Sheet. Pauses can be for a specified number of seconds, until the mouse is clicked or a key is pressed or until an event is received through the MIDI interface.

Producer presentations are displayed on-screen using a user-defined "stage." This can be a single-color background or an image imported from any graphics program. Producer's stage can be as big as any single monitor's display or it can span several displays at once—making it useful for creating multimedia video walls. Visual cues can be located anywhere on the stage, and can be stretched and resized to fit specific areas.

You control your Producer presentations using a VCR-like control panel. In addition, a separate time counter provides you with exact control over the current selection within the Cue Sheet.

You also can use Producer for multitrack recording and soundtrack production, and for combining MIDI music with live instruments and vocals. It works with most popular MIDI sequencing and audio editing software to form a complete audio postproduction system.

Summary

Passport Producer ($395) is a very important tool for anyone creating linear presentations where the synchronization of the data is of primary importance. Producer's slaving to Society of Motion Picture and Television Engineers (SMPTE) time code also makes it an ideal tool for musicians and other MIDI users who are looking for a method to create multimedia productions. If you are in need of interactivity beyond pausing, or MIDI control systems, you will want to use a different multimedia authoring tool.

Vividus' Cinemation 1.0

Vividus' Cinemation is an animation and presentation tool which uses a frame-oriented timeline approach. Cinemation can be used to create animations and to add motion to slides created in such applications as Microsoft PowerPoint and Aldus Persuasion. Cinemation animation sequences can integrate text, still images, animations, digital audio, QuickTime movies, and other Cinemation files. You also can directly capture and edit digital audio to add to your production.

Cinemation includes a 24-bit color paint program for creating and editing images. A special Ghosting feature displays any series of frames through a transparent easel, so you can paint in-between frames or align objects using other frame images as a reference.

Cinemation comes with over 12Mb of clip animation, art, sounds, and music created by professional artists and composers to help you get started building your productions. Collections of clips include business, creatures, transportation, marquees, and buttons. Sounds include music loops, intros, finales, and button sounds.

For HyperCard users, Cinemation includes a MovieWindow XCMD that plays Cinemation productions from within HyperCard. The MovieWindow XCMD also can be used to obtain detailed control over user interaction, branching, and object positions via HyperTalk.

How It Works

Cinemation displays each frame of animation in a series or "filmstrip". Individual frames have no direct correlation to actual time—instead, there is a global setting that can be used to specify the number of frames per second that Cinemation should try to play the animation.

Frames can have a transition or sound attached to them, which are used when the frame is displayed. Transitions include wipes, dissolves, reveals, cuts, and more. Sounds that start playing at a specific frame continue until the sound ends, another sound is played, or a command to stop the sound is encountered.

In addition, frames and visual objects can have links attached to them, which provide a number of controls over the flow of a presentation. First, you can apply a pause to a frame. Pauses include waiting for a specified number of seconds until the mouse is clicked, until an object in the frame is clicked, until the currently playing sound or QuickTime movie is finished playing, or until Cinemation has finished loading all of the remaining frames to accelerate their playback.

Second, links can direct playback to other frames in the presentation. This includes branching playback to the next or previous frame in the filmstrip, to a specified frame, to another file, to the last frame displayed, or halting altogether.

You can manage the flow of a presentation through another Cinemation tool called the Organizer, which allows you to manipulate named groups of frames all at once. It displays this groups in an outline format. Groups can be quickly rearranged or even temporarily disabled during playback. You also can work with the sequence of more than one presentation through this interface.

If you are using traditional slide-based presentation tools, you add animated effects to the slides you have created through use of Cinemation's AutoMotion feature, which automatically animates presentations created in PowerPoint or Persuasion. For example, you can add animations or sound to Persuasion

Scrapbook files by importing them and converting each slide into an individual Cinemation frame. You can then add custom effects or apply one of Cinemation's AutoMotion templates to lines of text and graphic objects on the slide.

Alternatively, you also can use AutoMotion in conjunction with templates that are provided with Cinemation to create your own animated slides. Design templates include backgrounds and border designs which can be customized simply by typing in text.

Animations can be easily created within Cinemation through either real-time recording of an object being moved around the screen or through a feature called Fill In Motion, which automatically fills in the motion of an object between two frames. Cinemation also provides filling in motion for cropping, scaling, and rotating an object.

Once you have built your presentation, you can distribute it with the included CinePlayer run-time engine on a royalty-free basis. This enables someone who doesn't have Cinemation to use your productions. You also can export presentations created in Cinemation into QuickTime format, so that they can be imported or pasted into other applications.

Summary

Cinemation ($495) is a unique animation and presentation tool useful for business presenters, trainers, and educators. Cinemation simplifies many of the tasks involved in creating animated multimedia productions. If you don't need exact control of synchronization and timing of your animations, Cinemation may be a good tool for you to use.

Motion Works' PROmotion

Motion Works' PROmotion is a color animation creation and editing tool which can be used with other applications to create an interactive multimedia production. You can use PROmotion to create color animations that integrate path-based animations and background images with digital audio tracks.

Like Cinemation, PROmotion uses a frame-based timeline approach to sequencing of data. You can import data from several other data formats, including PICT, PICS, digital audio, and QuickTime. PROmotion also will allow you to directly record and edit digital audio using a microphone or sound digitizer. Imported sounds can be edited in their waveform, and such special effects as volume fading, amplifying, echo, and reversing can be applied. PROmotion comes with a full-featured 24-bit paint tool which supports advanced animation editing techniques such as cel-based editing and onion-skinning (see Chapter 15, "Creating Animation").

TOOLS
PROmotion 213

Animation features include cel tweening, cel sequencing, antialiasing, and automatic scaling. Multicel animations are called "actors" and can be treated as objects when sequencing them in the timeline. You create your production simply by sequencing actors and backgrounds on the screen. The motion of actors can be controlled through paths. PROmotion provides sophisticated path editing tools to enable complex animation motions. Backgrounds can have a wide range of transitions applied to them as well.

How It Works

You control animations—as well as playback of your presentation, use of actors and background, and access to other tools—using a VCR-like panel called the Media Controller. You also can use the timeline and Media Controller to sequence animations with multiple audio tracks and MIDI.

You can add interactivity to a PROmotion production in a number of ways. PROmotion allows you to establish conditions, called "cues," which can trigger interactive events. You can attach cues to a frame or range of frames. Cues can cause a pause for a specified amount of time, until the mouse is clicked anywhere or on a specific object, a key is pressed, or the currently playing sound is finished. Cues can also control branching of the presentation to another frame or animation, force a halt to playback, change the playback frame rate, play a QuickTime movie, or send a message to HyperCard, Userland Frontier, or other AppleEvent-aware applications. PROmotion includes support for over 200 AppleEvents, so it can be controlled by another application to provide multimedia playback.

PrimeTime 530

Included with PROmotion is the PrimeTime, a CD-ROM-based collection of multimedia clips that includes over 100 Mb of animated actors, background props, and sound clips for use with Motion Work's PROmotion and ADDmotion II animation processors, as well as animation and presentation programs from other vendors. You can use the animated characters, backgrounds, sounds, buttons, and QuickTime movies as they are, or use other applications such as PROmotion to edit content to better suit your own needs.

Once you've created a production using PROmotion, you can distribute it in several different ways. PROmotion lets you save a file into a special run-time format which can be played back later without the need for PROmotion itself. Run-time formats are royalty-free.

You also can export your animation to QuickTime format. This allows you to use your animations in other programs, such as word processors, presentation tools, and video editing applications. Another export option makes it possible for you to create custom After Dark screen savers. Animations also can be saved in PICS format.

Finally, you can record your animations to videotape using PROmotion's Print-to-Video feature. PROmotion supports Control-S, Control-L, and Sony VISCA device control protocols. Suuport for VISCA allows you to connect your video devices to your Macintosh using a SONY V-Box interface.

Summary

PROmotion ($349) allows you to quickly create presentations, videos, training, and educational applications and then distribute them royalty-free. Its complete support for HyperCard and AppleEvents makes it an ideal tool to use to create applications through the combination of PROmotion and HyperCard or other AppleEvent-aware applications.

HyperCard

Apple XCMD's 110

Apple Computer's HyperCard is quite possibly the most widely used program for authoring, mainly for these three reasons: It's fairly simple; it's based on HyperTalk, a highly accessible programming language; and it has been shipped free with every Macintosh since its original launch. (Now you have to buy the developer's version of HyperCard, although the run-time version of the program that comes with every Mac makes for a huge, ready-made, installed base of HyperCard players.) HyperCard allows for easy creation of buttons that can be attached to a variety of user-definable routines. What's more, it was the application for which XCMD device controllers were originally designed.

HyperCard initially was designed to run on monochrome Macs, so it is capable of dealing only with black-and-white graphics (although color support is rumored to be on tap for a future release). Color and/or gray-scale graphics must be imported through special windows, and cannot be used as background or "card" elements—you can't overlay any elements on top of them. However, you can now run QuickTime movies within HyperCard, thanks to a QuickTime Tools stack distributed as part of the Development Kit.

HyperCard uses the metaphor of creating stacks of filecards, so each project is considered to be a "stack," and is composed of a series of interrelated "cards." The card metaphor works quite well, allowing you to place backgound graphics on the background layer of the card, and then overlay any buttons, moving graphics, windows, or other elements that your project requires (see Figure 9.14).

All HyperCard-created "applications" are actually just HyperCard stacks that require the core HyperCard "engine" in order to work. HyperCard users are

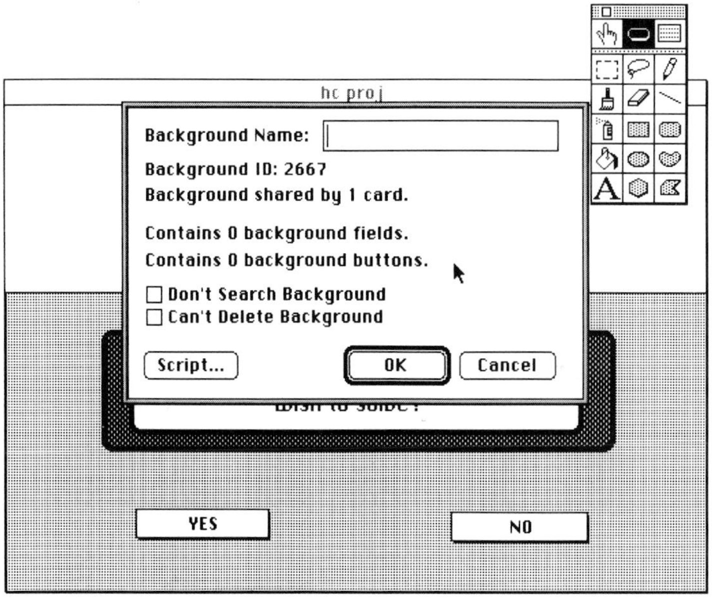

Figure 9.14 Hypercard's Background Info dialog contains information about the current background as well as access to any script that might be attached to it.

accustomed to considering a stack as an actual program. For instance, if you create a database of names and addresses based on a HyperCard stack, you will use it much as you would a dedicated database—only, you need HyperCard to launch it. HyperCard also comes with a "Home" card, which can be customized with buttons to launch your favorite stacks. In fact, there is a command-key equivalent that will bring up your Home card no matter where you are in a HyperCard application; hence, you are always close to the "main menu" of any stack.

Interactivity in HyperCard is user-defined, meaning that you can control the level of interaction that users will have with your project. There are five user levels to HyperCard, ranging from browsing to scripting. This means that you can create a project at the scripting level, complete with all the necessary buttons to navigate through it, and then you can lock the project into browsing mode, which allows users to click on any of your buttons without being able to modify your project or any of the scripts contained in it. This is a key element to HyperCard, and one of the things that allows a single application to be an appropriate tool for programmers and beginning users alike.

HyperCard also has an auto-save function, which makes it rather unlike most Mac applications: It constantly saves your work as you go. This is all the more reason for different user levels, as beginners may want to limit their ability to alter a stack so that they don't destroy it in the process of getting comfortable with HyperCard. There is a "Save a copy" function, so you can always make a copy of a stack and then proceed to mess it up and rip it apart without having to suffer the consequences.

There are thousands of public-domain and third-party HyperCard stacks available, with applications ranging from databases and clip art collections to video output controllers for animators. The public-domain products are free (available through bulletin boards and user groups); third-party stacks may cost as much as a few hundred dollars, but can be well worth it if their purposes suit your needs. There are compiling add-ons, which allow you to compile your scripts into XCMDs that will dramatically improve performance. Heizer Software and Teknosys both offer compilers for HyperCard. Dartmouth College and Language Systems both offer collections of useful XCMDs for those who would rather not spend the time developing their own. More dedicated products, like HyperSound from Farallon and the Video Toolkit from Abbate Video, will be of great assistance to those who need advanced control over sound and video.

These are just a few of the products available as extensions to HyperCard. Depending on the focus of your project, there are bound to be public-domain and third-party add-ons that can make your task much easier, so look around if you think HyperCard might be the core building-block of your production.

How It Works

Projects are built in HyperCard by creating a new stack. Screens are built in layers, from the back to the front. First is the backgound, where you can create graphic elements, text fields, and buttons that will remain consistent throughout a project.

Cards are the next level, and are for placing elements that will change from screen to screen. Types of elements that can be superimposed over a card include graphics, fields, and buttons. Graphics are black-and-white, and can be animated. HyperCard has a graphics tool palette that easily allows you to change from button or field creation mode to browsing mode, so it's easy to create a button and then test it without going through any extra steps (see Figure 9.15).

The tool palette also features a number of paint functions. The paint tools are based on the original MacPaint program and are limited, yet easy to use. There also are palettes for creating and choosing fill patterns for your graphic elements.

The main substance of a HyperCard project is created through the dialog boxes associated with backgrounds, cards, fields, and buttons. Each of these elements can have an associated script, where you create the links between the various elements in your project. You can easily create a new button and then double-click it to get at its properties and characterstics via the Card Info dialog box. From here you can go directly to its script and start building links into your project.

Summary

HyperCard ($199) is most definitely script-dependent. Although you don't have to be a serious programmer to use HyperCard, the more serious your project gets, the more you'll have to know about programming. Also, HyperCard is not the choice for heavily graphics-oriented projects, as it lacks the ability to deal directly with color graphics, but instead must import color through special windows that are not interactive. However, cataloging and cross-referencing functions can be created, and when tied to XCMDs and laserdiscs, it can be the basis for very powerful video archiving and retrieval. For advanced multimedia, you'll have to make extensive use of XCMDs.

SuperCard

SuperCard, now up for sale by Aldus Corporation, was originally designed to be a better version of HyperCard, adding full-screen color and a few other features that HyperCard did not have. In fact, SuperCard is based on the HyperTalk script

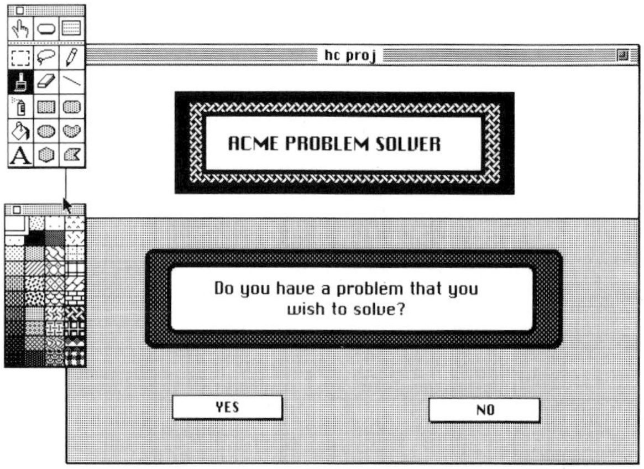

FIgure 9.15 HyperCard's graphics tool palette contains tools for accessing buttons and fields, as well as the tools necessary for creating graphics and text elements.

language and uses the same HyperCard metaphor of stacks, cards, and buttons, although it is not a HyperCard-based product. SuperCard consists of two main applications: SuperCard and SuperEdit. Projects are created in SuperEdit and played back via SuperCard. Once you've completed the final version of your project, you can turn it into a stand-alone application that doesn't require either application to run. HyperCard stacks can be converted to SuperCard in order to take advantage of its enhanced capabilities.

SuperCard does indeed offer HyperCard users an easier-to-use and more powerful environment for interactive programming. Standard commands and properties that need to be typed into HyperCard scripts are built into pop-up menus in SuperCard. Imported color graphics can be used as both background and foreground layers. Although SuperCard only supports 8-bit graphics, you also can import 8-bit custom palettes or custom look-up tables for special colors that may be associated with your graphics.

Animations can be created from within SuperCard, and although the program may not have the most sophisticated animation tools, they certainly can enhance an otherwise static screen. SuperCard also can display cards from more than one window at a time, which can serve to increase the depth and complexity of your project.

SuperCard has two graphics creation modes, paint and draw, which are based on the original MacPaint and MacDraw programs. The combination of paint and draw modes are actually a mini-version of Aldus' SuperPaint; when combined with SuperCard's selection of 8-bit color palettes, they provide a wide range of graphics capabilities.

SuperCard also supports Apple Events, which means you can send data from SuperCard to other applications—for example, exporting numerical fields into a Microsoft Excel worksheet.

How It Works

Projects in SuperCard are structured through a series of hierarchical windows (see Figure 9.16). A project window contains background windows, which, in turn, contain card windows. The project window also can contain custom menu information, as well as system resources, such as custom 8-bit color palettes and sounds. At the background and card levels, you can easily add buttons, fields, and graphics. There are custom palettes for drawing, painting, button creation, and field creation.

These tool palettes are great enhancements to the kind of basic offering that HyperCard gives you. The graphics palettes offer a complete selection of paint and draw tools, with the addition of 8-bit color. The field palette allows you to create a variety of different text fields for displaying or calling up text on a card. The button palette gives you a variety of button tools for creating buttons with different graphic characteristics: invisible, radio button, checkbox, and so on.

The authoring process is quite efficient in SuperCard. Most elements, such as fields and buttons, can be quickly created by clicking and dragging with tools

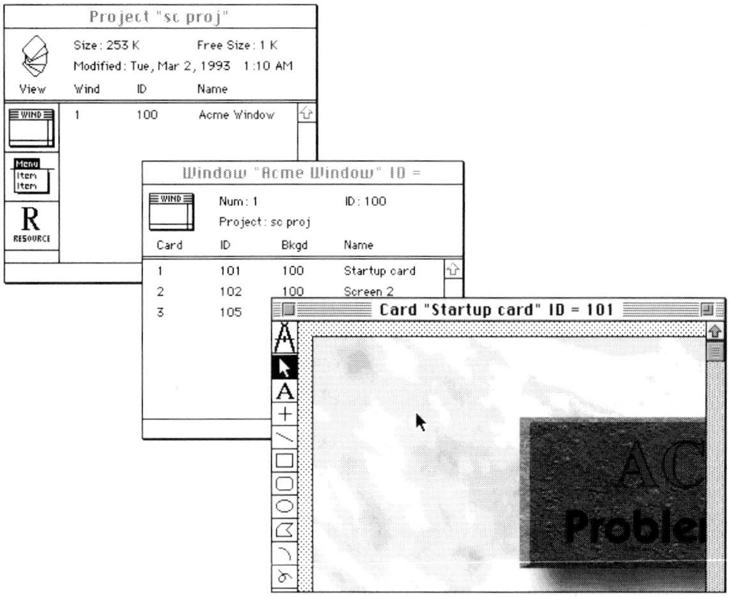

Figure 9.16 SuperCard works via a series of hierarchical windows. The Project Overview contains a list of windows, resources, and menus; the Windows Overview contains a list of cards; and each card contains its particular graphics, text, or button elements.

from the associated tool palette. Elements also can be easily modified by double-clicking on them to access info dialogs. The further addition of pop-up menus shortens the amount of time required for scripting, especially when compared to the authoring process defined by HyperCard.

Summary

SuperCard ($299) is a great extension to HyperCard, especially for those who wish to convert existing HyperCard projects into color. Stacks can easily be converted into SuperCard format, and then turned into stand-alone applications. Fancier buttons and sliders also are available as objects in SuperCard, so control of multimedia peripherals can be enhanced as well. The graphics, fields, and button palettes, combined with the pop-up menus for creating scripts, all serve to greatly speed the authoring process. And, with the addition of windows listing all your backgrounds and cards, double-clicking your way through the structure of a project is extremely easy.

The Apple Media Kit

Finally, The Apple Media Kit, announced just as this book was going to press, provides entry-level users with a vehicle for creating Mac or cross-platform multimedia presentations without having to do any scripting. Priced at less than $3000, the full package includes an object-oriented authoring program called The Apple Media Tool (available separately for less than $1500), and the VideoFusion QuickTime editor. It supports Kalieda's ScriptX cross-platform authoring environment (see Chapter 12, "Working Cross Platform.")

The Apple Media Tool works with QuickTime movies, PICT graphics, snd and AIFF soundfiles, and fonts in either Adobe Type 1 or TrueType formats. It is relatively simple to use, relying on icons that are positioned on screen to establish relationships between media elements.

Putting It All Together

All of the programs discussed here are good authoring tools, depending on your budget and the type of project you're doing. Of course, if you use the wrong tool for the job, you're bound to have some insurmountable problems, so make sure that your system has all the hardware and software components you need, and make sure that they're compatible with one another.

Also, don't neglect the importance of giving yourself ample time to become adept at interactive authoring. Despite the friendly interface of the Mac and the helpful tools that these programs offer, an ambitious interactive project will demand a lot of hard work and a thorough knowledge of the tools you're using. Hopefully, you'll be able to maximize your success while minimizing the frustrations by checking out the project case studies on the Power Tools CD-ROM, and by reviewing Chapter 19, "Interface and Interactivity."

Also, keep in mind that planning is often the key ingredient in the successful development of any project, and that's certainly the case with interactive multimedia. There are many ways to approach a given project, so make sure that you think it all the way through before leaping into action. Once you've considered your options, picked your objective, and settled on a set of tools to use, building interactive projects can be a very rewarding and enjoyable process.

10

Outside Resources

A fundamental promise of multimedia lies in its power to enable almost anyone to fashion dynamic and complex creations right on the desktop. Still, as any multimedia developer will tell you, content development is one of the great challenges of the field, and is especially difficult for the neophyte.

Clip art libraries have long been a convenient source of imagery when time is short or inspiration fails, but the rise of multimedia has spurred a demand for content far beyond static artwork. In this chapter, we'll list some of the sources for art, photos, animation, sound, and video. (The Power Tools CD contains many ready-to-use samples from leading collections.) We'll also look at the resources provided by service bureaus, including some of the new multimedia bureaus that are springing up.

All content collections include images and sounds that are legally licensed by the manufacturer, or are in the public domain. Your own use of these materials, however, is restricted under U.S. copyright law designed to protect the intellectual property of the original copyright holders. Consult the last section of this chapter, "Content and Intellectual Rights," for a discussion of these issues.

Sources for Art

Clip art has been around since the early days of the Mac. Business users have long used stock images to dress up presentations, and small companies use them to design quick and inexpensive brochures and marketing collateral. Even professional designers rely on them when backed into a corner by looming deadlines.

Vector versus Bitmap

There are lots of clip art libraries around, and they generally contain images in either vector or bitmap format. Vector images are composed of instructions that tell the computer how to draw lines, arcs, fills, and so on. Vector files are scalable

Figure 10.1 Letraset markets Fontek, a collection of high-end vector illustrations in a font format.

without loss of image resolution, and will reproduce at the limits of the output device. You also can break down a vector image into its component parts, modifying elements, or discarding ones you don't need.

Vector clip art is most often stored in the EPS format, which is widely readable by applications programs. Some clip art libraries are designed for use with specific drawing programs, and are available only in formats readable by those programs.

Not all EPS images are editable; some can only be placed and viewed or printed. Only graphics stored in the "editable EPS" format (also called the "AI" format, after the EPS files created by Adobe Illustrator), can be fully modified. Typical changes include recoloring, adding gradient fills, or changing existing ones.

Vector art is composed of a series of objects that are grouped to form the image. Getting at a specific object—to color it, for example—can be frustrating if the original designer didn't make that object a separate entity. Likewise, if objects are not made up of logical groupings, it can be easy to leave part of an image behind when you move it.

Images that use colors and gradient fills also can be problematic if the application you're using doesn't support them. In fact, to ensure universal compatibility, clip art images often simulate gradients with closely spaced bands, which look inferior to true gradients and can be hard to color. But you can always use a paint or image processing program to substitute real gradients.

Figure 10.2 Typical Bitmap clip art image by Form and Function

Vector graphics files, since they do not contain the images themselves, are also much more compact that bitmap image files. As convenient as they are, though, many vector images look cartoonish, and do not approach the pixel-for-pixel accuracy of bitmaps, which are ideal for highly detailed photographs, animation, and other types of complex art. Figure 10.2 shows a representative bitmap image.

Bitmaps are composed of the actual pixels that make up the image. When you scale up a bitmap, the "jaggie" effect, or *pixelation,* will become noticeable; scale down and the image may become muddy and indistinct.

Image processing programs have made it possible to edit bitmaps by supplying tools, such as magic wands, to isolate elements so that you can, for example, recolor them.

Most clip art collections offer images in both vector and bitmap formats. In the Mac world, this generally means the EPS format for vector art, and TIFFs for bitmaps. For a complete guide to graphics formats and their uses, see Chapter 5, "Imaging Tools."

Distribution

CDs are a perfect storage medium for large clip art collections, and are, of course, much easier to work with than a distribution of 30–50 floppy disks. Happily, many vendors are now producing their collections on CD as well as floppy.

All of the collections listed below are available on Mac-compatible floppies or CD-ROMs, but there also are a lot of clip art collections for the PC. Many of the images in these collections are stored in the EPS or TIFF formats, which are readable by Mac programs. See Chapter 12, "Working Cross-Platform," for information on how to read PC disks and CDs on your Mac.

Many collections include software to help you find the images you're looking for, usually by displaying catalogs of "thumbnails"—tiny versions of the images themselves. Those that do not, generally provide thumbnails in the documentation. There are several good databases that specialize in image management; if you often work with many images, these products are well worth looking into. See the sidebar on "Image Management."

Clip Art Libraries

Backgrounds for Multimedia
⌘601-605

The following is a small sampling of some of the best of the great number of clip art libraries that are available for the Mac user:

- **ArtBeats.** Several comprehensive collections, including *Dimensions 1–3*, which contain background images, patterns, and designs; *Natural Images 1* and *2*, for art depicting the natural world—wildlife, plants, and the weather; and *Backgrounds for Multimedia*, which can be used as backdrops for presentations. You can get all collections on a single CD or on a multitude of floppies. Images are in EPS, PICT2, TIFF, and GIF.
- **Artright Software: Artright Image Portfolios.** Excellent and well-executed collections in a number of volumes. The entire library is a complex and varied collection including images of people, transportation, technology, world flags, borders, and signs and symbols. Most images are in EPS or CGM, and the collections are available on both floppy and CD. Artright, like a number of other suppliers, also offers a clip art subscription service.
- **DS Design: KidBAG.** A collection of illustrations made by children. The package has black-and-white and color EPS and TIFF images, which were scanned from original designs created with magic marker, paint, and crayon.
- **Dubl-Click Software Inc.: WetSet.** Dubl-Click's WetSet is a CD containing all 10 volumes of its WetPaint clip art libraries. WetSet is huge, containing over 7000 images, and with this number of graphics, it's a good thing that Dubl-Click includes viewing and search utilities. Categories range from tropical images and animals to caricatures, decorations, and ornaments.
- **Dynamic Graphics: Designer's Club.** Long a supplier of traditional clip art, Dynamic Graphics now offers a clip art subscription service. Each month, subscribers get more than 50 black-and-white EPS graphics. Quality is very high, and the subscription comes with a monthly newsletter offering tips and techniques. You also can buy a year's worth of libraries on CD.
- **FM Waves: Graphic News Network.** This is also a subscription service, specializing in political graphics. Each month, you get EPS and TIFF graphics depicting current events and people in the news, such as Pee-wee Herman. FM Waves also produce a CD collection offering more typical images, such as icons, borders, and decorations.
- **Image Club Graphics Inc.: ArtRoom.** This is a large collection of more than 9000 black-and-white EPS images. The CD includes a version of Aldus' Fetch cataloging software that helps in locating images on the disc.
- **Innovation Advertising & Design: AdArt Series.** Several volumes specializing in logos, trademarks, and international symbols. The EPS images are very well executed and useful for corporate presentations, map making, and package design.

- **[metal] Studio Inc.** This company has a number of collections that group images by format, such as EPS silhouette or black-and-white TIFF.
- **Metro ImageBase.** Various collections with artistic images drawn from the archives of Metro Creative Graphics, which has been supplying traditional clip art since 1910. The graphics are mainly TIFF bitmaps, but collections include EPS images as well. Collections run the gamut from everyday images to specialty categories such as health care and religion. Image quality is superb.
- **New Visions Technology Inc.: Presentation Task Force.** A gigantic collection and one of the best values around, Presentation Task Force offers over 3000 CGM images. Collection specialities include cartoons, business themes, and people. Most images, however, are in the CGM format, which is not well supported on the Mac, and is not as editable as the EPS format.
- **Quanta Press Inc.: Fresh Arte.** A CD with over 1500 black-and-white PICT images. Categories include people, animals, food, and travel.
- **Sandhill Arts Publishing Co.: Funny Business.** Includes EPS cartoons about business, travel, and technology. Subscribers get a disc each month with 15 new cartoons.
- **Seattle Support Group: Medley.** A selection of over 300 PICT images in three different resolutions. Categories include nature and wildlife, people, and sports.
- **T/Maker: ClickArt.** A venerable and complete collection of EPS and bitmap images. The image quality is very high, but the economically constructed EPS images can be difficult to edit. The images are made up of relatively few lines, arcs, and other objects; it can be tricky to recolor just one part of an image, since it may be connected to another part that you don't want affected. Still, all in all, this is an impressive collection.
- **Teach Yourself by Computer Software Inc.: EduClip Series.** This series includes EPS and PICT files meant for use in the classroom. Individual volumes center around such categories as school subjects, letters and numbers, and sports and holidays.
- **TechPool Corp.: Atmosphere Systems.** These collections of EPS backgrounds, in several volumes, are targeted at the print and desktop publishing industries. Images include patterns and geometric designs and come in both gray-scale and color versions. The collections feature a utility that converts the images to their formats, such as TIFF and PICT.
- **3G Graphics Inc.: Images With Impact!** These volumes, which include EPS images of symbols, people, and business themes, are designed for easy editing. The objects in the graphics are arranged in modular groups that can

easily be rearranged, ungrouped, and recolored or otherwise edited. The CD version of the collection also includes over 450 colorized images.

- **Wayzata Technology Inc.: EPS Pro.** Several CD collections of EPS art, each containing over 600 images ranging from maps and flags to symbols and borders.

Textures, Backgrounds, and Filters

Multimedia undertakings, such as presentations, interactive demos, and QuickTime movies, have created a demand for "secondary" art, such as textures and backgrounds. Texture libraries also are useful for mapping surfaces onto 3-D objects (see "Creating Surfaces"). Figure 10.3 shows a textured background image.

The power of image processing programs to alter images with specialized filters also has encouraged vendors to market supplemental filter collections. A partial listing of texture, background, and filter libraries follows:

- **Aldus: Gallery Effects.** Aldus's San Diego-based consumer division (formerly, Silicon Beach Software) has produced this popular filter collection for some time. You can supplement your image processing program's basic filters with such effects as chrome, mosaic, and film grain. Gallery Effects plug-in filters work with many popular image processing, video editing, and paint programs, including PhotoStyler, Painter, Photoshop, and Premiere. You also can use Gallery Effects as a stand-alone application or Desk Accessory. Aldus also makes **Classic Art**, another effects collection sporting such filters as Bas Relief and Glowing Edges.
- **Aldus**: **Texture Art.** These textures, over 125 of them, were created by Pixar, and are being packaged and sold by Aldus. Categories include Marble, Metal, and Brick, and all can be mapped onto 2-D or 3-D surfaces. You can view

Figure 10.3 Textured image by Wraptures

low-res thumbnails of all 125 images on the CD, but you'll have to buy an unlock code from Aldus for each image you want to use.

Marble and Granite ⌘621-623

- **ArtBeats: Marble & Granite.** This CD collection of stone textures includes hi-res TIFF images, lower-quality PICT files suitable for presentations and QuickTime movies, and a set of gray-scale marble and granite images, too.
- **Cameo Interactive Ltd.: Material Worlds.** A series from Japan offering background textures in both 8- and 24-bit formats. Textures include stone, glass, metal, wood, paper, and fabric.

Wraptures ⌘731-739

- **Form and Function: Wraptures.** The various Wraptures collections contain PICT textures and backgrounds, such as cloud formations, water reflections, and architectural elements. Some are even PICS animations that you can import into your presentation, movie, or demo. The discs also include QuickTime video clips. Each image comes in several resolutions and bit depths, and may be repeated ("tiled") seamlessly to cover larger surfaces. The Wraptures discs feature a nice Hypercard-based browser that shows what a given texture will look like when mapped onto a 3-D surface. The browser also has a copy facility that transfers texture files from the CD to your hard disk. Figure 10.4 shows the browser for the Wraptures Two disc.
- **Letraset: Phototone Background Image Resource.** Another set of photographic textures, including wood, metal, paper, and stained glass. You can peruse an image selection catalog, and scan in or copy low-res versions of the images. When you find ones you want to use, Letraset will send you a slide or color transparency for an extra fee.

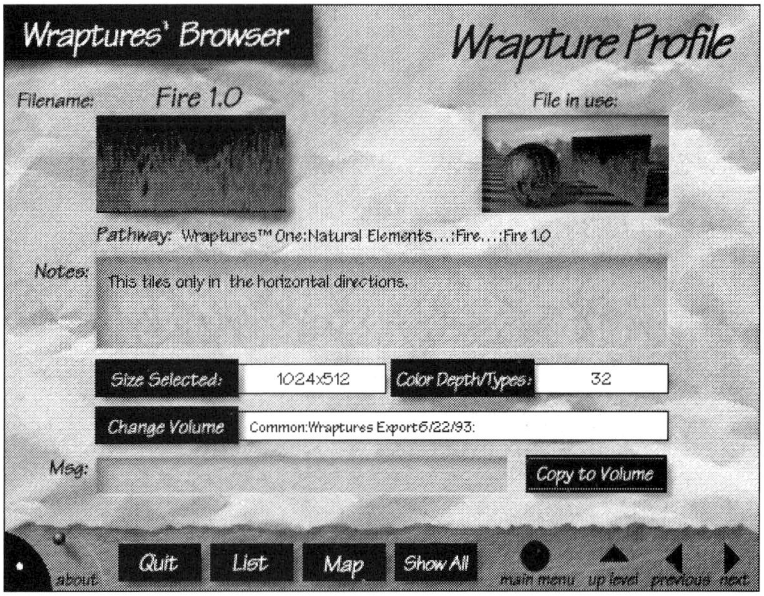

Figure 10.4
A Wraptures
texture browser

- **Wayzata Technology Inc.: Gallery of Dreams.** A selection of surreal 24-bit TIFF images for use as backgrounds and textures.

Sources for Photography

The big news in digital photography is Kodak's PhotoCD, which lets you put your own pictures on a CD, where they can be edited on the Mac and incorporated into multimedia creations (you also can view PhotoCD photos on your TV screen; see Chapter 15).

The CD also is an ideal distribution format for stock photography. For years, print designers have used stock-photo agencies to locate images for their publications. Traditionally, you'd look through catalogs to locate the image you want, then contact the agency for a color print or transparency. Prices range from perhaps $100 to many thousands of dollars, depending on the photo's importance to the overall piece, how widely it will be distributed, and the reproduction size of the photo. Typical CD photo catalogs have from 100 to 5000 images, depending on resolution and color depth.

Today, many stock agencies are releasing their catalogs on CD, as well as making them available through various on-line services. Although the selection process is much the same, and you still have to send away for the real thing, digital photo catalogs offer several advantages. For one thing, digital photos can be incorporated directly into your electronic layout or multimedia presentation. Often, these images are 72dpi FPO (for position only) or "comp" photos that you can use for rough layouts, client approval, and so on. Since 72dpi is the most common screen resolution anyway, the catalog versions of photos are often just fine for presentations that will be displayed by computer.

There are, however, use restrictions. You're merely licensed to use images in very specific ways. They're still owned by the agency or original photographer. Most suppliers limit their catalog photos to use in in-house applications, such as company newsletters or the preliminary layouts described above. A few agencies extend the allowable use of their catalog images to noncommercial business presentations, advertisements, and broadcast. No agency allows you to resell photos or distribute them to others.

Definitions of such terms as "noncommercial" are somewhat murky; be sure you understand what constitutes legal use before you incorporate a digital photo. If you're not sure, we recommend you contact the appropriate stock agency, who will be glad to clarify use restrictions on a specific photo. For further information, see the section "Content and Intellectual Rights" at the end of this chapter.

If you prefer to download digital photos, there are several agencies that offer this service (see "Digital Photo Collections" later in this chapter). After you've logged in, sort through photo catalogs in the same way you would using a CD catalog. When you've found the image you're after, you download a compressed version, which cuts down connect time. Compressed 72dpi digital photos are typically, about 50K and take around 5–10 minutes to download at 9600 baud. Once on your computer, the images decompress to about 500K.

Hardware Requirements

Some collections offer higher-quality 266 or 300 dpi images, as well as the more common 72dpi resolution. While these images themselves may be suitable for more demanding print applications, most collections don't include a great many, since they can easily run to 20Mb or more.

24-bit high-resolution color photos make big files. Really big. If you're going to edit digital photos, you'll need free hard disk space and plenty of RAM (we recommend at least 16Mb). If you're going to work with digital photos a lot, you also might consider both CPU and video accelerators. For a rundown of these and other peripherals, see Chapter 4, "Hardware Peripherals".

Like other clip media collections, digital photo catalogs usually bundle some sort of image management software that helps you sort through and locate photos.

Digital Photo Collections

- **Aris Entertainment: Media Clips Series.** A set of CDs organized by such categories as business, wildlife, and various backgrounds. Images are stored as 8- and 24-bit PICT and TIFF files, and most are at 72dpi. Some Aris discs also have QuickTime Movies; see "Sources for Video" later in this chapter.
- **CD Folios.** A set of CDs that divide images into such categories as business, wildlife and the outdoors, and various backgrounds. Images are stored as 8- and 24-bit PICT files, including some high-resolution compressed photos scanned at 2000dpi.
- **CD-ROM Galleries Series.** These CDs specialize in nature and architectural images, most of which are stored as 8- and 24-bit PICT files. Resolutions include 300 and 1200dpi, as well as the standard 72dpi.
- **Comstock, Inc.: Desktop Photography Series.** Comstock has a gigantic database of over 3 million photos, some of which are available in digital form on a set of CDs. The digital photos are stored as 24-bit TIFF files, and may be used for noncommercial in-house applications, as well as for comps. Comstock also runs an on-line photo service, with over 12,000 images as of this writing.
- **Digital Gallery Ltd.** This company has several volumes of digital photos, specializing in landscapes and cityscapes.
- **Digital Zone Inc. Series.** These discs specialize in very high quality photos of nature, business, and geography. The 24-bit images are compatible with Kodak's PhotoCD format, and are each stored in four resolutions.
- **Discimagery Professional Photography Collections.** A series of CDs with photos in several black-and-white and color versions. You browse through the high-quality images with the help of a printed catalog.

Folio I ⌘651-656

- **D'pix: Folio 1 Print Pro.** These images are designed for use in printing applications, and include many high-quality 24-bit images stored as 266dpi TIFF files.

International Graphics Library ⌘741-742

- **Gazelle Technologies Inc.** Gazelle offers a series of CD-based photos, all of which are marketed through its San Diego-based subsidiary, Educorp. Collections include Aquatic Art, Swimsuits, and People. All images are stored in 24-bit color TIFFs, 8-bit gray-scale TIFFs, and 8-bit color PICTs. HyperCard is included for browsing thumbnails or image listings.

Digital Photographics ⌘641-642

- **Husom & Rose Photographics.** A CD series that includes Digital Photographics and Nature Photographics. The former is an eclectic collection of people, backgrounds, textures, and landscapes. Not surprisingly, Nature Photographs has scenes of wildlife and the outdoors. All images include hi-res 24-bit TIFF and PICT versions, and the package includes utilities for image browsing.
- **The Image Bank.** This well-established provider of stock photography now puts out its catalog in PhotoCD format. The images are in a low-resolution format suitable for viewing. When you locate the images you want, you can send for transparencies, or download a hi-res electronic version.
- **Kodak's Picture Exchange.** This is a worldwide on-line image service. Instead of browsing a CD for photos, you use search utilities to sort through images on-line. Then, you can call a number to order or download the "real" image. Images are in Kodak's PhotoCD format.
- **Metatec Corp.: Best of Photography Series.** These images are drawn from the company's Nautilus electronic magazine (see "Magazines" later in this chapter) and are stored as 24-bit TIFFs and 8-bit PICTs.
- **Mirror Technologies Inc. Stock CD Series.** Each Mirror CD has over 5000 TIFF images that are drawn from several stock houses, including AllStock Inc., FPG International Corp., and The Stock Market Inc. The CDs are searchable using both thumbnails and keywords, and when you double-click on a photo, you'll get copyright and ordering information. For those who do not have a CD drive, Mirror bundles a set of CDs with one of its drives and 3M's CD-Stock image management software. Images may be used as comps only.

The Multimedia Library ⌘671-684

- **Multimedia Library Inc.** Collections in this series focus on great world art. Volumes include the Art of Ancient Egypt, and Arms and Armor, both photos of art and artifacts from the collections of New York's Metropolitan Museum of Art. All images come in three versions: 24-bit color TIFFs, 8-bit gray-scale TIFFs, and 8-bit color PICTs.

PhotoDisc ⌘691-699

- **PhotoDisc Collections.** Each of the CDs in the PhotoDisc collection includes several hundred 24-bit color TIFF files. Each volume centers around a theme, such as Business and Industry, Lifestyles and People, and Nature, Wildlife and the Environment. The collections are bundled with LightBox,

Figure 10.5
Multimedia
Library photo

Figure 10.6
Digital Photo
from PhotoDisc

image management software that helps you to organize, browse, and import the images into applications. Photos can't be used in for-sale enterprises, but may be used in ads, presentations, and in-house newsletters.

- **PressLink.** This is an on-line service run by the Knight-Ridder news agency. Images are targeted at newspapers, but are available to anyone willing to pay either a monthly or per-image download fee. Photos are stored in resolutions and line screens commonly used by newspapers, but the images are often large, allowing them to be downsized, which increases resolution.
- **TechScan MaxImages A2.** Like PhotoCD, TechScan's CD offers different versions of each phot o—8- and 24-bit color, and gray-scale. This reduces the number of images that will fit on a CD, but provides more options for their use. The 60 TIFF images are geared toward the graphics market, with photos of backgrounds, borders, and textures.
- **Tsunami Press: The Right Images.** 8- and 24-bit PICT images, mostly centering on space travel and other astronomical themes.
- **21st Century Media Photodiscs.** This is a CD series, with each disc containing photos selected according to a common theme. Themes include business and industry, sports and travel, and nature. Each disc contains over 350 32-bit color TIFF photos measuring about 4" ×6" each. The images come from Seattle's West Stock/Photolink Inc. stock house, and can be used without restriction (but not for resale). Each CD includes image retrieval software that helps you quickly locate images by thumbnails, keywords, or full-screen previews.

TOOLS
SpaceTime and Art
⌘711-712

- **Wayzata Technology Inc.: Photo Pro.** A series of CD-based digital photos that center on such categories as people in action and nature.
- **Westlight Collections.** Westlight is a large stock photo house with access to over 2 million images. Images are available in every conceivable category, from textures and backgrounds to primary images and color separations for printing. Westlight has started to convert some of its vast image holdings to digital format on CD.

Sources for Animation

Animation libraries include everything from 3-D backgrounds and clip 3-D models, which you can render according to your own needs and tastes, to basic 2-D and more complex 3-D animations.

- **East•West Communications: ProGraphix.** These CD collections, available in several volumes, feature 8- and 24-bit TIFF and PICT 3-D background images, as well as animations in the PICS and MacroMedia Director formats.

- **Mac Illusion Industries Creative Services: IllusionArt.** These floppy-based collections contain animated clips and static clip art for use with Macromedia's Director application. Animations, including opening and closing doors, can be used as is by beginners in Director's Overview mode, or can be modified in Director's studio.

TOOLS
Swivel 3D Pro:
Sample Models
⌘821-829

- **Macromedia: SwivelArt.** These volumes feature sets of 3-D models that you can render and incorporate into your multimedia productions. Objects include office and computer equipment, anatomical models, cars, planes, ships, and map collections. Figure 10.7 shows a Swivel model of an airplane. The collections include a version of Macromedia's Swivel 3-D modeler for making adjustments to the models. Most models are high quality and well-detailed (the more advanced models were licensed from 3-D modeling specialists Viewpoint Animation Engineering). Keep in mind that working in 3-D, like working with large TIFFs, requires a fast machine and lots of RAM. (For more information, see Chapter 15.)

TOOLS
Media in Motion
Animation Clips
⌘501-505

- **Media in Motion.** San Francisco-based Media in Motion has several floppy-based 2-D animated clip collections targeted at the business presenter. Clips include an unfolding notebook computer, a TV with flickering screen, and a camera taking a picture. All animations are designed to be customized; for example, you can superimpose your own images on the notebook screen, TV, and the developing picture taken with the camera. Images are in the Director, PICS, or QuickTime formats, and are available as black-and-white line art and 8-bit color, and with associated sounds.

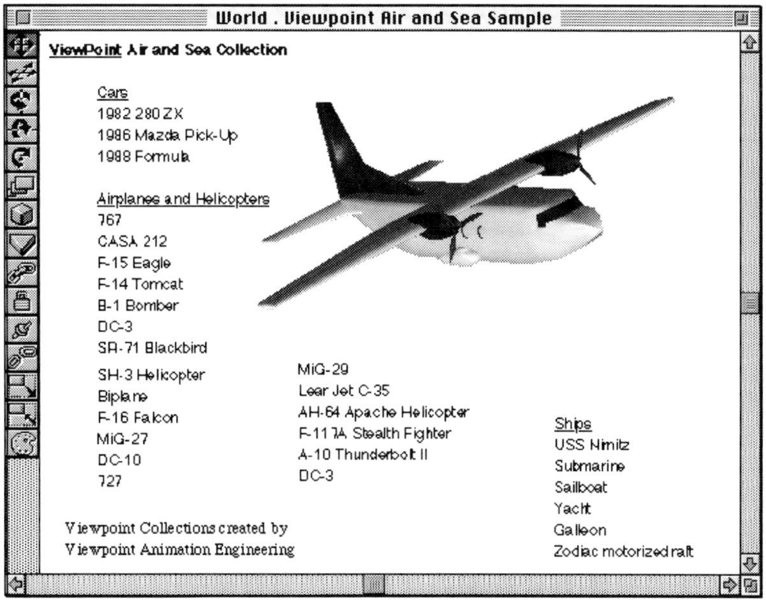

Figure 10.7
A SwivelArt image

- **MicroPlacement Inc.: AniMedia.** Another floppy-based collection of simple clips, such as flying titles, and animated characters. Clips are JPEG-compressed 8-bit color images, and are stored as PICTs, PICS, and Scrapbook.
- **Vanguard Media: The World of U.S. Manga Corp.** This collection has over 1000 24-bit color still images, as well as more than 100 QuickTime movies featuring Japanese animations, including comic book and science fiction characters.
- **NEC Clip Art 3-D.** This is a huge collection of over 2500 images on a CD. Image quality varies, but is perfectly adequate for computer-based presentations. The scope of images is vast, from everyday objects to vehicles, people, maps, and landmarks. There is also utility software for altering and rendering the models.
- **MacRenderMan and ShowPlace Plug-ins.** A number of companies make texture libraries for Pixar's MacRenderMan 3-D rendering program, and models for use in Pixar's ShowPlace 3-D modeler. **The Valis Group's VG Looks** and **VG Shaders** are surface libraries for MacRenderMan, and include, in several volumes, such textures as brick and stone masonry, shingles, polished metal, blistered paint, and translucent plastic. The textures also can be used with any renderer that supports the Pixar RIB format (see Chapter 7).

  Special effect shaders are available from **Videographics Corp.**, with various effects that will transform cones to mountains, and rectangles to skyscrapers. **Acuris** makes several volumes of **ClipModels** for use with ShowPlace, including furniture, natural elements, and people. **Acme Animation Group Ltd.** also has several libraries of its **ClipProps**, including outdoor furniture, glassware, and models of various Mac computers.
- **Specular International: Replicas.** The makers of the Infini-D animation package (see Chapter 7) offer these collections of fully rendered 3-D objects in such categories as office furniture, interiors, and flying logos. Figure 10.8 shows an animation of a helicoptor landing. You can use the objects as is, or rerender them to suit your taste. Textures used to render the models also can be reused for your own Infini-D models. Some objects are animated. The animations make use of hierarchical links and predefined constraints (see Chapter 15), meaning that such objects as drawers will slide in and out and will stop before they fall out. Specular bundles a neat Replicas interactive demo with Infini-D, so you can try before you buy.

Sources for Video

Professional videographers have been working on the desktop for at least a short while, but the appearance of QuickTime has ushered in an era of digital video for even the uninitiated. But as you build your presentations, demos, and other

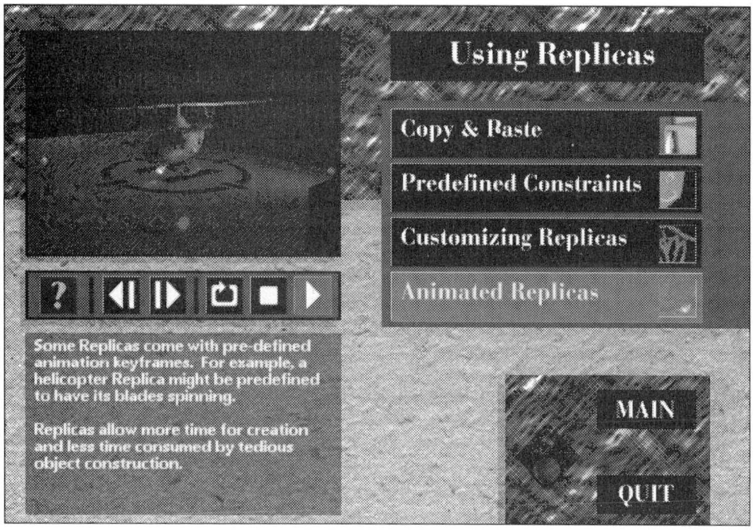

Figure 10.8 You can browse Infini-D's Replicas 3-D clip art demo, then order the clips that you want.

multimedia creations, you may quickly tire of shooting and digitizing your own video. And, of course, pirating copyrighted material off the TV or tape is not an option.

Luckily, clip media collections have begun to crop up, and most contain clips that are cleared for at least noncommercial use. (For a complete discussion of copyrights and the legal use of content, see "Content and Intellectual Rights" in this chapter.)

- **Alpha Technologies Group: ClipTime Series.** These CD collections each contain 250 16-bit color clips, most of which also play back at 15fps, and are selected through a HyperCard directory. Volumes include American Media, which focuses on U.S. presidents, American landscapes, and national parks, and which also has songs and sound effects in the AIFF format. Hollywood Classics has digital clips from old favorites such as *It's a Wonderful Life*.
- **Apple Computer: QuickTime Starter Kit.** Apple's introductory QuickTime CD, which contains QuickTime itself, some useful utilities, and over 400Mb of QuickTime clips. The library is indexed so that you can quickly browse its contents, which include animation and static images, as well as movie clips. The bundled utilities allow you to play back the movies, as well as to compress them, convert existing content to movies, and digitize source material (you'll still need a hardware card to digitize—see Chapter 4).
- **Aris Entertainment: World View.** The focus is on the Earth and other planets in this CD collection of 25 QuickTime clips, more than a hundred 8- and 24-bit PICT still images, and music clips.
- **Audio Visual Group: The Multiple Media Tour.** As its title hints, this CD sampler has a little bit of everything: PICT background images, textures, photos, sounds, animations, and QuickTime movies.

- **Beachware: MultiWare.** This collection is a sampler that has QuickTime movies, background art, textures, and sound and music clips.
- **Bliss Interactive Technologies: Resource Library.** These collections of over 500 24-bit images and over 60 Quicktime clips have the advantage of material that is completely in the public domain. Topics range from nature and the environment to people, space, and the weather.

TOOLS BMUG ⌘581-585

- **BMUG: TV-ROM.** BMUG (Berkeley Macintosh User's Group), one of the largest and best established user groups in the country, has produced TV-ROM, a CD containing 500Mb of QuickTime movies, sounds, and PICT images. The 16-bit color clips are organized with a HyperCard directory and play at the standard QuickTime 15 frames per second. BMUG includes its own movie player, called Popcorn.
- **Compact Designs: PROclaim!** Another CD-ROM clip media directory devoted mainly to QuickTime clips. There are over 250 clips on a variety of topics, as well as digitized sounds in QuickTime format, and some still images, too. Generally, the sounds and images are not up to the quality of the movies.
- **Figment: FigTime.** A quarterly CD-ROM "magazine" that contains QuickTime clips, viewers, and instructions on how to make movies, including special effects and techniques.
- **Macromedia: ClipTime.** This is an assorted mix of movies, music, animation, and special effects. The clips are stored in the Director, PICS, and QuickTime formats. The disc is probably a better source of art and music than of video clips, of which there are relatively few.
- **Media-Pedia Video Clips Inc.** This company, video clips on VHS, S-VHS, Hi8, ¾ SP, and Betacam SP tape. The clips, which include nature, technology, and people, are designed to be digitized into QuickTime movies.
- **The San Francisco Canyon Company: Canyon Action!** 50 QuickTime clips featuring music videos, movie clips, and computer animations. The clips are playable on the Mac, as well as on the PC, using Apple's Movie Player for Windows, which is supplied.
- **WPA Film Library.** This company has a huge film collection totaling over 10,000 hours of material. Footage includes films, TV shows, documentaries, and travelogues. Rights to use the material are negotiated on a case-by-case basis. CD samplers and a catalog are available from the company, which is based in Alsip, Illinois.

Sources for Sound and Music

The use of music is of special concern because most of it is copyrighted, and most of us aren't composers. You can always go down to the beach and videotape waves crashing on the rocks, and then digitize the video, but it's a little harder to write and play background music. Sounds and special effects are a little easier, since you can record these yourself or lift them from a collection of copyright-free material.

Clip Audio

BMUG ⌘981

- **B & B Soundworks: Sound Effects.** 100 sounds on floppy in 'snd' resource format.
- **Berkeley Mac Users Group: BMUG Sound Library.** Public-domain sounds on floppy disks and CD-ROM. No licensing fees or restrictions.
- **Desktop Music Company: Desktop Music.** CD with 200 musical selections in 'snd' resource format.
- **Digidesign: Clip Tunes.** 300 megabytes of music on CD in many styles, and sound effects, all sampled at 44.1kHz in 16 bits. Developed jointly with Prosonus, these files are stored in Sound Designer 2 format for use with Digidesign's digital audio cards.
- **Educorp: The Sound Machine.** 450 sound effects and classical music clips on CD. Educorp's **Sound/FX** CD adds 225 additional sound effects.
- **Hologlyph, Inc.: Sound/FX CD Series.** Six volumes of sound effects on floppy disks.
- **Killer Tracks Multimedia Music Library: Killer Tracks.** Three CD-ROMs, each containing more than 30 pieces of music.
- **The Multimedia Library: Royalty Free Series.** CDs containing 200 music clips 15 seconds to 3 minutes in length. The four MIDI file discs contain 4000 classical music themes, 23 Mozart string quartets, and Beethoven symphonies 5 and 6.

The Multimedia Library SOUND Series ⌘961-967

- **The Music Bank: Stingers.** A series of CD-based music and sound effects libraries, whose clips range in length from a few seconds to a few minutes. Sounds are stored in 44.1kHz (CD-quality) and 22kHz versions in the Mac AIFF file format.
- **Olduvai Corporation: Sound Clips.** Three volumes containing sound effects.
- **Optical Media International: Desktop Sounds.** 400 sound effects and music fragments in 'snd' format.

DeskTop Sounds ⌘971-975

- **OSC: A Poke in the Ear With a Sharp Stick.** These collections, spanning several volumes, include more than 1800 musical sounds, special effects, and industrial noises; in AIFF format.
- **PassPort Designs: QuickTunes.** This is a CD collection of over 80 MIDI sound clips.
- **Presto Studios: Hi Rez Audio.** Presto offers several volumes of digital music. Styles run the gamut from classical to R&B. The CDs contain 42 tunes

Hi Rez Audio ⌘921-929

Media Management

Programs that examine disks for a variety of image, graphics, sound, and movie files and bring them all together in the form of a visual catalog are becoming a necessity. As multimedia creation becomes more and more popular, folders chock-full of the different files needed in a typical multimedia production can quickly become unwieldy. Cataloging software takes over the task of organizing multimedia files and presents them in an organized form that can be varied according to the needs of individual users.

Features

Although these programs vary in their specific features, most offer the following services:

- **Thumbnails.** Instead of the familiar Finder lists or icons representing files, images are represented by small pictures, saving you the trouble of opening files to see what's inside.

PICTpocktet ⌘225

- **Search and Retrieval Mechanisms.** You can generally attach associated information to images, such as subject, date, and caption. Then, when looking for a specific image, you can search based on these keywords. Some programs, which are really multimedia-capable databases, have sophisticated query languages, such as *Boolean operators*, providing a way of limiting searches to very specific criteria.

Photoshop ⌘222
ACTviewer ⌘133

- **Image Editing.** Most programs give you the ability to perform simple manipulations, such as cropping, scaling, and rotating images. As in image processing programs, such as Photoshop, you also can open images without the application that originally created them. Image managers typically will open files stored in a whole slew of formats, including PICT, EPS, TIFF, Photoshop, Photo CD, AIFF sounds, and QuickTime Movies.

Programs

Image management has grown with the popularity of multimedia, and now there are a number of programs that have found their niche in the cataloging, retrieval, and manipulation of images (and sounds). Following is a sampling of currently available software and features:

Aldus Fetch ⌘230

- **Aldus: Fetch.** Released only late in 1992, Fetch has quickly become a very popular program. You can search for images based on patterns that you can store as menu items—a nice feature. Thumbnails can be stored in 1-, 8-, or 32-bit versions for faithful representations of the original images. You can create custom catalogs of images, and Fetch will analyze folders containing the original image files and update catalogs with only those files that have changed since the last update.
- **DeltaPoint: FreezeFrame.** FreezeFrame catalogs images, and also converts them to over 50 Mac, Windows, OS/2, and Sun graphics formats. The program includes over 500 color EPS images, and in addition to the graphics formats, supports QuickTime, animation, and sound files.

Kudo Image Browser ⌘224

- **Imspace Systems Corp.: Kudo Image Browser.** Support for many file formats is a particular strength of Kudo Image Browser, which will handle QuickTime, PhotoCD, and a number of graphics formats, as well as many PC formats, such as PCX and

box continued

GIF. Images can be located and cataloged on a variety of volumes, including hard disks, CD-ROM drives, and network storage devices.

- **Kodak: ShoeBox.** The cataloging of Photo CD images is the focus of Kodak's image manager. Keyword searching and large thumbnail views are supported.
- **Loop Software: PictureBook+.** PictureBook+ organizes images into collections called books, which you then can search based on file attributes and keywords. The program features an unusually complete set of editing tools, including text manipulation, as well as cropping and resizing of images.
- **Multi-Ad Services: Multi-Ad Search.** This program has many features designed to help manage files over networks and multiple volumes. You can find images that were once in a particular folder but have since migrated to other locations. Multi-Ad Search supports a full set of thumbnail representations and search capabilities.
- **Nikon Electronic Imaging: ImageAccess.** This program supports the usual thumbnail and information retrieval features, and will automatically assign file name, date, location, image size, and so on.
- **Symmetry Software: Mariah.** Using Mariah, you can catalog not only image files, but also animations and sounds. You can search for images and sounds by such attributes as file type, as well as by keyword. Unlike other programs, Mariah catalogs copies of images and sounds themselves, rather than just pointers to the original files. This requires you to store the same file twice, which wastes disk space.

and 23 sound effects, all in three sampling rates—44.1, 22, and 11 kHz—in Red Book, AIFF, SoundEdit, and SoundEdit Pro formats. No licensing fees, unless used for broadcast or phonorecords.

- **Prosonus: MusicBytes.** 28 tunes played by some of the foremost session musicians of Hollywood. Most tracks have four additional versions, 60, 30, 15, and 5 seconds in length. All files are available as Red Book (CD-quality) audio, 22 K AIFF, 11 K AIFF, and Standard MIDI Files. Additionally, over 100 sound effects are included in Red Book, 11 K AIFF and 22 K AIFF formats.
- **Tactic Software: Sound Clips.** These floppy-based collections contain mainly special effects, such as police sirens, airplanes taking off, and toilets flushing. Have a ball.
- **Wayzata Technology: Sound Library 2000.** More than 2000 sound effects on CD. The company also distributes **Porcupine Productions' Music Madness** in various volumes. The collections comprise sound effects, spoken phrases, and music clips in various styles. The CD includes QuickTime and a utility that allows you to combine sound clips. Sounds are stored as AIFFs, as well as in System 7 and HyperCard sound formats.

Clip MIDI

- **Golden MIDI Music: Golden MIDI Sequences.** Standard MIDI Files on floppy disks.
- **Dr. T's Music Software: MIDI Clips.** Standard MIDI Files on floppy disks.
- **Romeo Music International: MIDI Editions.** "Over seven million notes" of classical music. These are $19.95 per composer. Collections, CD-ROMs available.
- **The Parker Adams Group: MIDI Jukebox.** Preconfigured for Roland's U-20, U-220, D-10, D-110, D-5, MT-32, CM-32-L, CM-64, Sound Canvas, Sound Brush, MC series (sequencers), Alesis Data Disk, and the E-mu Proteus 1 and 2. Each song includes custom sounds. On floppy disks.
- **Mac Media: MIDI Minus One.** Standard MIDI Files on floppy disks.
- **Opcode Systems: MIDI Play.** 46 Standard MIDI Files that come with the company's MIDI Play HyperCard MIDI XCMD stack.
- **Passport Designs (Music Data Division): MIDI Records.** Nearly 500 Standard MIDI Files in all styles, on floppy disks or CD+M discs. Preconfigured for Roland's CM series of synthesizers and the Sound Canvas. $10 to $20 per song.
- **Trycho Tunes: Trycho Tunes.** Over 1000 Standard MIDI Files on floppy disks. Preconfigured for Alesis MMT8; Ensoniq EPS; Kawai Q80; Korg T series; Roland W30, MV30, MC50, MC300, and MC500; and Yamaha QX3, QX5FD, and V50. They offer custom sequencing at $100 per song—otherwise, $11 to $16 per song.

Multimedia Books and Magazines

Electronic publishing is one of the hottest areas in the computer industry, and multimedia is having a serious impact on this emerging phenomenon. Voyager has been turning out its annotated books for some time now, and even mainstream such publications as *MacWeek* and *Newsweek* are experimenting with the new medium.

A big reason for the explosion of offerings is the continuing consumer acceptance of the CD-ROM, which is an ideal (if a little slow) multimedia distribution medium. Here's a sampler of some of the best and most interesting multimedia books and magazines for the Mac:

Magazines

- **Nautilus.** Subscribers to this engaging magazine get a new CD every month. But "magazine" really fails to describe these discs, which are crammed with articles, clip art, photography, games, freeware, and shareware. Some of the images (there is an excellent monthly gallery of digital photos) are cleared for reuse by subscribers. Contact Nautilus at (800) 637-3472.

- **Macworld Interactive.** Sumeria, a spin-off of IDG, publishers of *Macworld*, releases a multimedia CD version of the magazine every few months. (See Chapter 1 for more on MacWorld Interactive.)
- **Newsweek Interactive.** In early 1993, *Newsweek* dove right into the fray and became the first general-interest magazine to publish a CD version. The quarterly publication, produced by Software Toolworks, includes audio interviews and selected *Newsweek* articles, as well as those from sister publication *The Wall Street Journal*. You must have a CD-ROM/XA drive to read NI disks (see Chapter 4 for more information).
- **Verbum Interactive.** *Verbum* was on the scene early, publishing a CD version of its computer art magazine in 1991. The two-disc magazine features a huge array of multimedia art, projects, how-to's, and samplers. The scope of *VI* is truly awesome: We've been using it for well over a year and are still unearthing new discoveries. A potential drawback: *VI* requires Finder 6.0.7 and will not work with System 7. Figure 10.9 shows *VI's* main content screen

Books

- **Voyager's Expanded Books.** Voyager targets its HyperCard-based electronic books at PowerBook users. Editions feature carefully chosen typefaces, illustrations, and many computerized features, such as page marking, user annotations, and text searching. Titles are shipped on floppy disks, and include Michael Crichton's *Jurassic Park* and *The Complete Hitch Hiker's Guide to the Galaxy* by Douglas Adams.

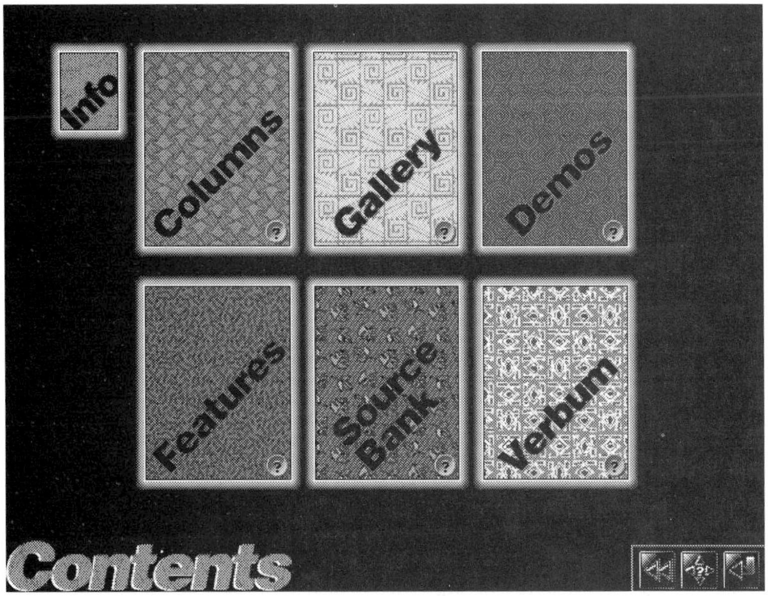

Figure 10.9 The main content screen from Verbum Interactive

Service Bureaus

Desktop publishing was the killer phenomenon of the '80s, a true revolution that clinched the Mac's success as a serious machine. The fact that you could lay out, typeset, and print reasonably professional documents—right on the deskto p—was essential, but only part of the story.

Vendors of high-end typesetting and printing equipment scrambled to make their equipment compatible with the Mac's new DTP tools, getting a big boost from Adobe's PostScript. You could fiddle around with inexpensive software and equipment on the desktop, and then send files to a service bureau, which would typeset or print them on high-resolution equipment. Thus, you had a powerful mix of creative control on the desktop, and state-of-the-art output without investing in high-end equipment.

Long a mainstay of desktop publishers, service bureaus have evolved considerably. Right from the beginning, you could send your work via modem, but early on, this was fraught with problems ranging from font substitutions to indecipherable communications software. These problems have eased considerably, and in fact, communications have become quite sophisticated:

- Many service bureaus now let you transmit your files through custom bulletin boards that automate much of the transfer process. Many interfaces duplicate the Mac desktop look, allowing you to send files simply by dragging your file to the service bureau folder. There even are icons that help you specify fonts, linked files, and file compression.
- These bulletin boards also will manage multiple modems at the service bureau, so that they can receive several jobs at one time. The software will then automatically queue, image, and invoice each job.
- Some bureaus let you write file specifications and special instructions off-line, so that you save phone time. Others provide chat lines so that you can communicate directly with the service bureau "sysop" at the same time as your file is being transmitted.
- You even can have the service bureau disconnect and call you back to provide an extra level of security. These service bureaus have your phone number on file, so if someone claiming to be you phones up, they will be denied access.
- Sites that are constant users of outside services can install digital phone service to send files at 56,000 baud, or 5–6 times the speed of a 9600 baud modem.

Content and Intellectual Rights

Content is, perhaps, the greatest of multimedia's many challenges. Multimedia tools—authoring packages, 3-D modelers, sound editing software, and so on—somewhat arcane and complex now, will get easier to use; but creating professional, artful content will remain a hurdle. As a result, many will turn to the clip media collections, such as those described in this chapter, to brighten and supplement their own work.

There's no question that these content libraries also will encourage the further development and acceptance of multimedia in the mainstream. However, uncertainty over the application of current U.S. copyright law has hampered the development of clip media collections.

Copyright law was designed to protect the rights of those who create and publish original works. In fact, according to the Copyright Act of 1976, works do not even have to be published to fall under the protection of the law; their very existence is enough to guarantee protection.

The problem is that the digital age—in which vast stores and many types of information are being converted to digital formats—has created a crisis in the interpretation of copyright law. Apple's famous five-year (so far) lawsuit against Microsoft alleging copyright infringement is a prime example of the complexities and confusions surrounding use of intellectual works in electronic form.

All of this has made such copyright holders as museums reluctant to grant the use of their materials in electronic form—at any price. They, like everyone else, don't yet understand the implications of electronic use, and fear that existing law may be inadequate to defend them against unfair use.

Intellectual works, like any information converted to digital format, are simply too easy to copy, distribute, and profit from. The Office of Technology Assessment, an arm of Congress, has recommended changes in the law, which may eventually provide better protection for intellectual works in the electronic medium.

The music industry is a potential source of inspiration for positive change in copyright protection. In the 1920s, with the advent of radio, many recording artists worried about their rights in the face of global exposure over the airwaves. BMI (Broadcast Music Inc.) and ASCAP (American Society of Composers, Authors and Publishers) were formed to safeguard the rights of their members.

Some organizations, such as the American Society of Magazine Photographers, are considering starting copyright collectives that would act as agents for artists wishing to sell electronic rights.

Multimedia, of course, incorporates intellectual property from the entire spectrum of human ideas, including the major categories of art, text, photography, and music; the potential and temptation for illegal use is high. Photographers, in particular, are wary of exploitation. For years, they have depended on sales to stock houses to supplement their income. The potential for unbridled abuse of digital photos threatens to upset this successful licensing system.

Protecting Others

Central to U.S. copyright law is the concept of *fair use.* With the exception of certain research and review purposes (noncommercial use), copyrighted material may be used only with the permission of the copyright holder. When you buy and use a clip media collection, you are implicitly agreeing to a license for its use. Licenses vary widely; read them so that you know what restrictions apply. The clips on Apple's QuickTime Starter kit, for example, are restricted to noncommercial use.

Following is a list of the basic types of intellectual property usage:

- **Noncommercial Use.** You can copy, manipulate, and edit the work to your heart's content, as long as it stays in your own possession or within the confines of your organization. You definitely cannot resell the work or incorporate it into another work for sale. This is the category most clip media collections fall into.
- **Commercial Use (One Time).** You can incorporate the work as part of larger product and sell it (or broadcast or publish it), but you cannot use it again without paying an additional fee. The fee you pay depends on how you are going to use the material, how many people will see or use it, and so on.
- **Commercial Use (Multiple)**. You can use and resell the work more than once. Usually, there is a time limit, so that you have to renew the license when the period expires, but sometimes the license is in perpetuity.
- **Public Domain.** It belongs to no one; you can do anything you want with it.

The only way to make sure you are using content fairly and legally is to read the license agreement that comes with the clip media collection. If you're still not sure, call the vendor.

Remember that copyrighted materials are protected even if you modify them. If you take a copyrighted photograph, and crop it, run it through an image processing filter, recolor it, or whatever, the result is a *derivative work*. Derivative works are subject to the same use restrictions as the original copyrighted work from which they are derived.

The underlying principle of the whole issue is fairness: If it's not yours, don't steal it.

Protecting Yourself

As a multimedia developer, you're creating content that is a protectable resource. If you are concerned about your rights, include a copyright notice with your work. It's just a simple sentence that states your name, the year the work was created, and add the copyright symbol (©) or the word "copyright."

You also should register the copyright with the Copyright Office in Washington, DC. There's a $20 filing fee, and you must send a copy of the work along with your application. Note that you don't have to include a copyright notice or to register works—they're protected anyway; but registered copyrights whose works also include a notice are considered pretty much bulletproof in court.

To further protect yourself against piracy, you can imbed a tiny identifying mark in your work. This could be a logo, or your company name, which would, if necessary, prove your ownership of pirated material.

Part Two

CREATING MULTIMEDIA ON THE MACINTOSH

11

Project Planning and Design

Advanced planning is essential to any multimedia project, from a short presentation to an interactive CD-ROM. Planning ensures that your project has a cohesive message and that every element used in the production helps convey this message. The work you do in this critical planning stage also ensures that the product you envision is produced within the allotted time frame and budget constraints. It also allows you to focus on marketing and logistics issues, such as audience definition and product positioning. This blend of foresight and paperwork allows the actual production to be a free-flowing, creative process.

Chapter 2 contained an overview of the production process, covering everything from the initial idea to the final product. This chapter focuses on the detailed aspects of preproduction and project design. Specifically, it explains many of the types of decisions that must be made during preproduction.

The basic steps of preproduction involve defining your purpose, determining external factors that will affect your production, and then deciding on the specific needs of your project. During the design phase, you transform these ideas into prototypes that your team can use to create the elements of a cohesive project.

Exploring Content

Generally, when you think about starting a project, you have a vague notion, a simple idea, or a nebulous project description from a client. This is a great starting point—you just have to flesh out the details. The easiest way to do this is to look at the full range of multimedia products already out there. Explore their "content" in terms of subject matter, components, and interface.

Look at all types of projects, even if they are nothing like what you want to do. This exercise will both stimulate your creativity and help you become familiar with the marketplace. With the changing nature of the computer industry, the latest features can be exciting, but last year's technological innovation might appear dated.

As you examine multimedia offerings, note your reactions—are they fun, and interesting, or confusing, dull, and boring? What did you find particularly effective in the presentation of the information? Which multimedia elements were used? How were they implemented?

Note the things you did not care for in presentations. Did some seem too flashy? Did you want to turn off the sound after two minutes? Was the interface like a maze? Were the fonts too small? Was there too much or too little text?

Evaluate the equipment necessary to run various types of multimedia projects. Look specifically at projects that appear to have been produced on a budget and scale similar to yours. By examining the decisions reached by others, you can see what is practical. Often the magazines have articles about the pros and cons of different equipment setups, and we extensively cover tools and platforms in this book. At trade shows, you might discuss this with knowledgeable people at the booths.

Keeping Abreast of Technology

For most multimedia professionals, keeping informed of industry innovations is an ongoing task. Publications specializing in multimedia, such as *New Media* Magazine or the *Digital Media* and *Inside Report on New Media* newsletters, cover what is happening in the field. There are magazines focusing on every facet of multimedia: *Verbum* covers multimedia design and content development; *Videography* provides the latest in video production coverage; *MacWeek, MacWorld,* and *MacUser* all yield insights into Apple Computer hardware and software, and other goings-on.

You also should actually try out some multimedia products—pick up a few that look interesting and explore them thoroughly. Trade shows such as MacWorld Expo, Comdex, or any of a multitude of smaller regional conferences have exhibits that give you a chance to test out numerous programs in a short time. These shows may have conference sessions given by multimedia professionals, which can provide additional insights and ideas.

In browsing around the multimedia world, spend time learning about technologies that intrigue you. Most productions use a blend of older and newer technologies. If you see a 3-D animation that you can't stop looking at, maybe it is worth getting familiar with the tools and techniques used to produce it. An exciting animation may be just the thing to attract someone to a kiosk or wake up the audience in the middle of a long presentation.

Be aware of which authoring systems are commonly used for specific types of multimedia. (see Chapter 9, "Authoring Tools"). Many presentations are created using HyperCard, which is a quick way to assemble a project, especially if you don't mind a bit of programming.

TOOLS

Journeyman Project Demo
⌘243

Figure 11.1
"The Journeyman Project" by Presto Studios uses extensive 3-D graphics and special effects for its high-tech adventure. It has a version that runs on 5Mb machines, and another that requires 16Mb. Both require a CD-ROM player.

Figure 11.2
In contrast, Amanda Stories, published by Voyager, uses line drawings and gentle sounds to get users involved emotionally. They are available in black-and-white floppy files to run in HyperCard, or in a color CD-ROM version.

Macromedia Director and HyperCard are the most popular authoring systems for large projects. Director is used most often for projects utilizing color, detailed 2D animation, and high-quality sound. Other types of productions can be put together more quickly in HyperCard with excellent results. Multimedia systems that require complex data searches and work mainly with stills or videodisc images can be built very effectively using HyperCard.

TOOLS Director ⌘210

Examine as many systems as you can, including those featured in projects and demos on the Power Tools CD. Learn from what has worked for others, then use this knowledge to make the most of your production time. Looking at the work of others takes time and may cost some money, but it also helps you to focus on ways to implement multimedia elements you want for your project, and decide what you need for production and distribution.

Thinking About Focus and Design

There must be a reason for your multimedia project to exist. The idea might be your own vision and inspiration for a creative project, or come via someone with a concept and funding. Regardless of the source, the idea must have merit. For a multimedia project to be a success, it has to provide an end user with information, entertainment, or the impetus to purchase something. If it does not, there is no reason for your audience to spend time with your hard work.

These decisions are just as important when you are working alone as when you are working with a large team. With a project of your own, you have the final say over concept, budget, and implementation. For commercial ventures, the final word over each aspect of the production comes from the clients. Even if they have done most of the preproduction, you must review their decisions to make sure that you fully understand the intent of the requests.

For example, suppose you have been requested to create an exhibit on the Civil War, and are given a script with text and photographs. This is not sufficient information for you to work from, because it does not fully explain the intent of the exhibit. It may be designed to show the extent of the war and the role of the first photojournalists. In this case, you would not take creative liberty with the photographs, but would display them in their entirety (Figure 11.3a). On the other hand, if the client is interested in the effect of the war on individuals, you may choose to crop images and position them so that the facial expressions are obvious to the viewer (Figure 11.3b).

Define the Message

Your initial project idea will probably be simple and may be vague. Think of how the product might be written up in a short catalog listing. Think about all the movie listings in TV Guide. No matter how involved the plot, any movie is described in 25 words or less. Try to come up with a concise and concrete statement of your concept. Once you have a main idea, try to think of what you

Figure 11.3a and b "Lt. James B. Washington, a Confederate prisoner, with Capt. George A. Custer of the 5th Cavalry, U.S.A." by Civil War photographer James F. Gibson. The image on the left shows the original photograph. The image on the right shows how a cropped close-up focuses on the facial expressions.

want your audience to take away from the multimedia experience. Should the presentation inform, evoke emotion, or entertain? Be general with your goals as well; list categories rather than specifics.

The main idea and goals of each of the sample projects on the Power Tools CD can be summarized in a single sentence. For example,

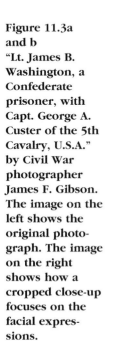

PROJECTS

Hip Hop Hits ⌘011

Rock and Roll Star ⌘013

Lawnmower Man Logo ⌘022

Title: "Hip Hop Hits"

Idea: Provide users with information about how digital audio editing is used to construct Top 40 hits.

Goal: Inform

Title: "So You Want to Be a Rock and Roll Star?"

Idea: Let amateur musicians experience the excitement of playing with a rock and roll band and make learning music fun.

Goals: Inform, entertain

Title: "Lawnmower Man Logo"

Idea: Produce an animated corporate logo that fits the image of a fictional company used in the movie "The Lawnmower Man."

Goal: Entertain

Title: "The Madness of Roland"

Madness of Roland ⌘032

Idea: Create an extremely rich media environment to tell the story of contradiction and dichotomy from multiple points of view.

Goals: Evoke emotion, Entertain

Who Is the Audience?

Once you have an idea of what you want to do, you should focus on the viewer. If your project is to design an animation to be shown on MTV, you can easily picture your audience, and probably have some idea of what will or will not appeal to them. Since MTV attracts a young audience, references to famous musicians from the past such as Frank Sinatra, Bobby Darin, and even the Beatles (!) could go by unrecognized and add nothing to a presentation.

Another thing you know about MTV viewers is that they enjoy watching images that change as rapidly as once or even several times per second. This may affect your design decisions. You can imitate this fast-paced style, or try to create a purposeful contrast by using a slower pace. Choosing a direction to take should be a conscious decision based on what you know about the audience.

Sometimes a project idea defines a target market from the outset—the idea was created to fill a specific need. The audience for "Hip Hop Hits" from the Power Tools CD is a select group of individuals interested in digital audio editing. "So You Want to Be a Rock and Roll Star" has a broader audience. Think about who would be interested in playing along with a rock and roll band. This is a very general idea, and so producer Steve Rappaport still had to make some important decisions about his target audience. Did he want to intrigue closet musicians and shower singers, or attract users that simply liked to listen to some tunes and learn about how the musicians made it to the top? He had to decide what types of music would appeal to his audience, and the songs he ultimately chose were those that appeal to people who listened to rock and roll in the early 1960s (see Figure 11.4).

Any idea can be presented in hundreds of way. By looking at your audience and your goals, you can narrow the scope down to fit your objectives.

Style

The presentation and interface style of a multimedia project can attract or repel users with surprising force. Even if the content is exceptional, the style must appeal to the user. Symphony lovers adore seeing black notes on a white page while high-quality orchestral music is played. As long as the imagery is clean and classic, it can be very appealing to this audience. The MTV generation, by contrast, seems to favor chaotic, fast-paced graphics.

After deciding if color is important to your audience, you should decide on the type of palette that might appeal to viewers. If you are designing a system to

Figure 11.4 "So You Want to Be a Rock and Roll Star"

inform patients about how to live with a serious illness, you are better off using relaxing colors like blue or green rather than alarming reds and yellows or ominous black.

At this point, you don't need to make hard decisions about style; just think about the users and what will reach them. Stylistic decisions based on what your audience would enjoy will further define your project.

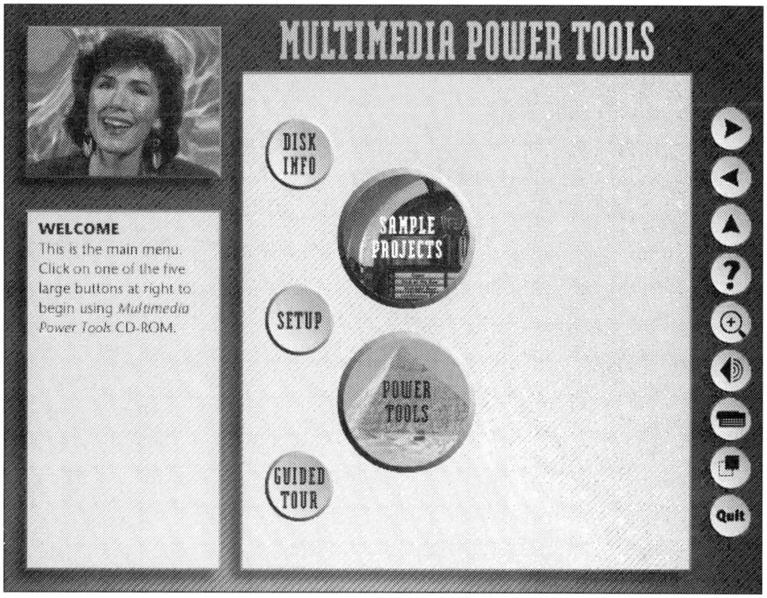

Figure 11.5 The main interface of the Multimedia Power Tools CD. Color and style are essential parts of any presentation.

Other Factors

Outside influences affect how any multimedia project is received, regardless of the age or interests of the audience. Before actually designing your project, you should identify where it will be used, how often, and the type of equipment on which it will operate.

Location

Where will the project be used? This is a weighty decision that will have repercussions on the total design and style of your project. If the program is to be used in a library, it should not contain loud audio. If it will be used primarily in a busy shopping area or trade show, expect the users to spend no more than a few minutes looking at the program. The interface must be intuitive, as well as colorful and flashy to attract attention.

Educational products might be used at home or at school, where the user will have time to explore without distraction. Here the subject matter can have more depth. The pace can be slower, and the style less flashy than for programs designed to attract attention. The interface should be geared toward the age and attention span of the user. Think about the special needs and distractions around home and school locations.

Number of Uses

How many times will a user view your product? Animation, the element of surprise, and a sense of humor are all valuable qualities in any presentation. A multimedia production created for a single showing to each audience should use these elements differently than a program that will be used on a regular basis. In the latter case, some special effects and techniques can easily change from exciting to annoying. Imagine a multimedia catalog for identifying and ordering auto parts. If the catalog had a picture of each type of auto part so that a quick visual identification was possible, as well as a search engine and lots of cross-referencing, the end user would be thrilled. Now imagine the same project, but this time with QuickTime movies in place of each still picture. The same user would be infuriated, if he or she had to repeatedly view a 3-D animation of black exhaust spewing from a loud, faulty muffler while attempting to identify parts for customers.

Target Equipment

A final consideration is the type of computer equipment that your audience will be using to view your product. The sophistication, speed, and abilities of these target computers will have great bearing on your design.

Try to determine the type of machine your users are most likely to have. Apple Computer produces a range of business and consumer Macintoshes (see Chapter 3, "Mac Software and Hardware"). If your product is to be used by small businesses or people at home, remember that they might not be able to run animation that will look good only on a Quadra. You may need to take the high-end animation and convert it to a QuickTime format that is not as aesthetically perfect, but at least puts forth the idea in an accessible way.

Appropriate Use of Technology

Hardly a week goes by without some announcement of a new multimedia technology. Industry professionals and members of the techno-elite love this constant and rapid pace of change. As a producer, however, you need to think seriously about when and where to use these dazzling new effects. Before using them, you must decide if the technodazzle really adds something tangible to your product.

A well-designed multimedia project focuses on its message and its audience. The producer must keep each development area working toward presenting the message in the most effective way. It is all too easy to get sidetracked by these fun, new bells and whistles that may cause your project to go over budget and not get done on time —or even worse, only to play on expensive equipment that cuts out 90% of your potential market.

In 1992, morphing—making one image magically transform into another by a sequential blending of the pictures—was all the rage (see Figure 11.6). Various programs ranging from low-cost Morph for the Macintosh to high-end versions used in postproduction houses became available. Suddenly, there was morphing in movies, television advertisements, and various forms of multimedia.

Figure 11.6 This was done using Gryphon Software Corp.'s Morph.

TOOLS Morph ⌘ 229

Morphing is fun to watch, but does it have a place in your multimedia project? Sometimes a special effect of this sort is essential to your message. In the movie *Star Trek VI,* an alien changed form before our eyes and turned into Captain Kirk—that was impressive. The alien did have unusual powers, and the viewers got to see this alien being rearrange its own face. The technology furthered the development and believability of the story.

Similarly, you may have seen the television commercial in which a leaping tiger transforms into an automobile, infusing the image of a car with the power and agility of a tiger.

In both of these cases, the morphing technology serves its purpose: It carries and drives home an appropriate message, while entertaining the viewer. On the other hand, if the morph causes the viewer to think, "Wow, I wonder how they did that," but has no real bearing on your message, it is nothing more than a distraction.

Sometimes there's no clear-cut indication as to whether technology will really add to your project. In this case, the decision to morph or not to morph has to be made based on other factors. Can you afford it? Fancy technologies take time and money. You have to learn how to use the program that creates the effect, and then implement it. Will the effect bring a user's playback machine to its knees?

Don't squander time and money on technodazzle when they would be better spent on the actual content of your product. On the other hand, if you have a place where the new technologies will enhance your message and you have the time and money to get the job done, by all means use them.

Health Care Kiosk ⌘042

For presentations, you must consider what equipment is available at the end site, and what you will need to bring or rent. For kiosks, think about what is appropriate and within the budget constraints.

You also may need to develop a project for playback on non-Macintosh equipment. For an overview of the considerations required for this scenario, see Chapter 12, "Working Cross-Platform."

Planning the Process

During the planning phase, you will develop your idea into a detailed overview of the project. The overview begins with a complete definition of the content to be presented, then includes information about interactivity, graphics, and use of sound. Each of these elements must be viewed in terms of the message, the audience, and the budget. At the completion of the planning phase, your overview should contain all the information necessary for designing the actual script, visual images, and sounds required for production. The Multimedia Power Tools CD contains a number of graphics and sound libraries for your use.

Content

Content is the essential element of any multimedia production. Content may be text, or may be mainly sounds or visual images, but it has to tell a story and relate information in a meaningful way.

Your central message needs to be expanded into an outline of the main points that will be covered. This generally assumes the form of text written on a word processor, outlining, or flowchart program. The outline needs to be detailed, covering all the topics, subtopics, and tangential information that will be included with the project. Even the most interactive project must have an internal structure that makes sense.

The outline format compels you to make decisions about the relative importance of each item you wish to include in your project. This will become important as you design the menus and any interactive elements.

Interactivity

A diagram or flowchart gives you a visual image of how the parts of your program relate to each other, and reveals the nature of the navigation issues the user will face. Major diagram elements often become main menu items that, in turn, branch to the subtopics (see Figure 11.7).

Although it's not the only way to design interactivity, the flowchart is a powerful tool, allowing you to plan the type of interface most effective for your project by consolidating a navigation plan, audience needs, and project content.

You don't need to decide on the details of the interactivity, but you should determine the nature of it. Recall your observations of other systems as you consider how interactivity fits into your own project. If you will be using a touch screen, the buttons have to be big enough for a finger to manipulate. Does your

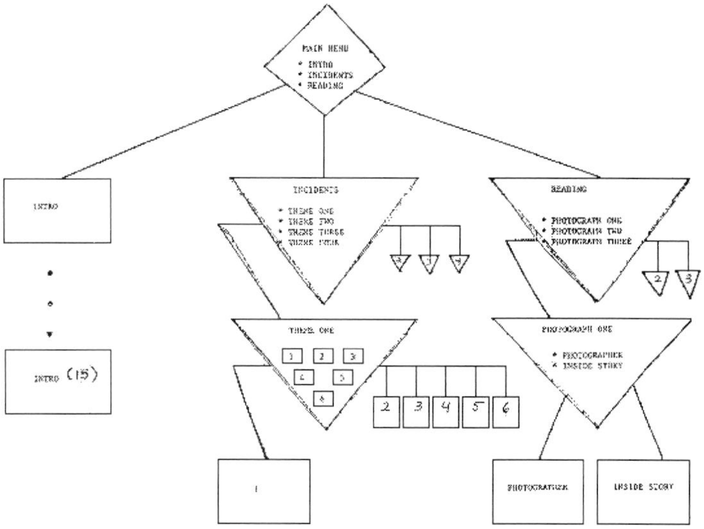

Figure 11.7 This flowchart of the user interface created for the exhibit "Incidents of the War: The Mathew Brady Photographs of the Civil War, 1861-1865" in the Library of Congress American Memory prototype.

topic lend itself to text menu items that work like the table of contents of a book? Would a set of index icons down one side of the screen be appropriate? Will your audience members all speak the same language? If not, an icon approach to menus may be essential.

Graphics

Look at your flowchart and try to locate where visual images are essential to your message. Multimedia is a highly graphic medium, so a graphic element is generally present on-screen at all times. Sometimes the graphic image is the primary focus; other times, the image simply illustrates a concept or enhances an interface item.

Expand the flowchart to include the types of graphics you need for your message and your audience. You don't need to specify particular images, but try to mark where still images would be useful, where video might be better, or where animation might enhance the user's perception of information.

Think of the types of graphics that are available on your topic. Actual movie footage of Revolutionary War battles is hard to come by, but movies of the Voyager spacecraft passing through the rings of Saturn can illustrate the immensity of space travel. Would a CD on baseball be the same without QuickTime movies of great home runs? Is there an existing videodisc with high-quality images that could be licensed as part of your product?

Animated graphics can be two- or three-dimensional. They can be simple or complex rendered images. Consider your budget, capabilities, and message to determine what level of animation is appropriate for your project. Do you want full animation or a few carefully selected animations that can add excitement to your topic?

During this phase of preproduction, try to get a good mental image of the visual style your project needs. Should it have simple screens, lots of pictures, or a highly stylized look created by a graphic artist? Think in generalities rather than specifics. Which graphic elements are essential, which are attractive and might be nice, and which are beyond the needs of the project?

Sound

Sound is too often forgotten or considered as a last minute add-on. Yet, audio can add enhance your message as much as any other multimedia element. Much of the power of Ken Burns's seminal PBS documentary on the Civil War stems from the expert use of sound effects, narration, and music.

Chapters 6 and 13 focus on the types of sound tools available and the means to produce the audio for your production. Read through these chapters before making your decisions about sound, especially if you haven't previously paid much attention to sound as a multimedia element.

Sound can be as simple as an audio click when a button is pressed, or a beep to indicate a response of some kind. Some sounds are cute and fun, especially in multimedia targeted toward children.

The audio may be narration of a passage read by the original author. Many people dislike reading text from a screen, but will listen to the information when delivered by an interesting voice.

Musical tracks can be produced which add to the style and heighten the emotion evoked by the multimedia experience. Musical scores go particularly well with animations and video, and add enormously to presentations, kiosks, and trade show productions.

Decisions about sound should be made early enough to ensure that the audio is available for the programmer when the various elements are combined to make the final project. Even recording a few beeps with a MacRecorder takes some time to do right. The sound needs to be produced and properly recorded. The computer needs enough memory to digitize and store variations until the decision is made for the ideal sounds. If you will be licensing music, someone must listen to a large quantity of stock sounds to locate the snips you want for your project; then you must obtain a written license to use the sounds.

Determine the types of sounds that are necessary—and those that would be ideal—during preproduction, so that you can work sound into the budget.

Budget

No developer likes to think about budgets. They can really cramp your creativity and set limits on what you want to do. Despite this, budgets somehow continue to exist. The reality is that without planning for time and money, most projects would never get done. Like outlining, budgeting forces you to make difficult decisions about time and resources, while you are looking at the entire project as a single entity. It requires you to set priorities, milestones, and constraints. Once this is done, you are freed from worrying about these things, as long as you respect the schedules you have set.

When you start a project, you must determine how to make use of the money that has been allocated for the budget by balancing your financial and time resources against your needs during development. Some projects are small, requiring only a few hours from one person. The bigger projects require additional people, equipment, and time. Large projects with huge budgets will have top professionals creating the various multimedia elements. Regardless of the size of the project, time and money must be managed carefully in order to ensure that the resources last until it is completed.

When putting together a schedule, allot time to solve special problems and to work around software and hardware difficulties. Curtis Wong, who has produced numerous products for Voyager, advises, "Whatever time you budget, it will invariably take twice as long as you think. Especially if you are working with new technology. Plan for this, and deadlines will match realities."

Building the Production Team

Once you have a firm idea of the needs of the project and what you can afford, you must decide how to get the work done. Can you do it all yourself? If not, is there a team available to work with? Can you license pieces from other sources? Do you know how to create the various elements you will need? Do you need to hire outside contractors? How these questions are answered depends on your environment and your project.

In-House Talent

If you are working in a corporate environment, you may have access to talented people to help in your project's development. There may be programmers, graphic artists, writers, and other experts who can be brought in to help with parts of your production.

You may be in a position to hire people to work on a permanent multimedia team. In this case, a core team usually consists of a project manager, a programmer, an artist, a writer, and, depending on the project's sophistication, specialists in video and sound. For small jobs, some individuals may perform more than one function, while on large projects, several people may be working in each area.

Each member of the team requires equipment and software. Most multimedia is produced on machines more powerful than those required to run it.

Black-and-white programs can be produced on an 8Mb machine. If you are working with color, especially 256 colors or more, you may need 20Mb of RAM or more. An image processing program like Adobe Photoshop requires a minimum of 2Mb of memory, although Adobe recommends 4–8Mb. Macromedia Director does say that it requires a minimum of 2Mb of RAM, but in reality needs about 8Mb.

During the production phase, several applications often are open at once, for image processing, word processing, or sound processing. If you don't have enough memory, expect unsightly bombs that will threaten the integrity of your data, as well as frustrate your creativity. Recovery from these bombs takes time and causes general paranoia. Weighed against these concerns, 20Mb of memory seems worthwhile for any serious production (especially as chip prices plummet).

Think about the speed of computers you have available compared to the work that has to be done. If there are many graphics to be processed or extensive programming code to be compiled, a faster machine will save time in the long run. Chapters 3 and 4 have information about hardware considerations. Read these chapters with your project specifications in mind. If you cannot afford the equipment, you might reconsider some elements of the production that can be done with available components.

Contractors

One way to get specialists for specific areas of your production is to hire independent contractors. Experienced contractors may be expensive, but they will do the job as you ask for it and get it to you on time. Contractors have their own equipment and software, which you would otherwise have to supply for employees. Professionals are available for any type of work, from producing the entire project to designing layout, programming, sound production, animations, or whatever your needs may be. Chapter 10, "Outside Resources," has additional information on working with contractors.

Licensing Considerations

Instead of hiring people to do work for you, you can license materials from companies that specialize in photographic images, sound, or any other element you might need. The costs are usually lower than they are for having the work done specifically for you, but make sure that you have a good license agreement in order to reproduce the work. Sometimes, you can get permission to use the work in your product without any fee. Make sure to get the permission in writing for your own protection.

The licensing of copyrighted materials for multimedia productions can be complicated. A license for an image or sound may include print rights, movie rights, video rights, audio rights, or magneto-optical rights. You must make sure that you have the license to use the image or sound on the media that you use for final distribution. The safest license is one that includes unlimited multimedia use.

Every part of a sound, movie, or image may be under copyright. The image of a person may need licensing, even if the photograph is now in the public domain. Fictional characters may be trademarked and require licensing. Choreography, background music, or even the entire production may need individual releases. Even tiny clips of music or images can be traced by the copyright holder, who may contact you for back royalties if you do not obtain written permission to use them beforehand.

You may wish to enlist the aid of a competent intellectual property attorney to ensure that you have a properly written release or license agreement for any sound, movie, or image used in your multimedia production. Many multimedia producers prefer to avoid these complications by creating as many of the elements as possible for a production. For more information, see Chapter 10, "Outside Resources."

Selecting End-User Equipment

The last step in the preproduction phase is to make a decision regarding the final form of your project. This decision must be made during preproduction to ensure that money is budgeted for manufacture of a CD-ROM or videodisc, or for projection equipment if your final product will be displayed at a kiosk, corporate demonstration center, or convention hall.

Projectors

When you present your multimedia project, it is important that the audience can see it. There are a variety of projection devices available, the most popular being LCD (liquid crystal display) and CRT (cathode ray tube) projectors.

LCD panels are relatively inexpensive and are portable, weighing between 4 and 6 pounds. Most of these units sit on the bed of an overhead transparency projector, so make sure one is available. LCD panels come in color or black-and-white. Color panels produce images from a spectrum of about 24,000 colors. The weak points of LCD panels are that the pixel quality is not as sharp, and many are slow to refresh the screen. LCD panels are much less expensive than most multimedia projection equipment, ranging from $4000 to $9000. For $8000–9000 you can purchase LCD projection systems that do not require the overhead transparency projector.

The three-gun CRT projectors are good for convention meeting rooms or corporate presentation rooms, where they can be set up and then left in place. They have a high scan rate—that is, the projected image keeps up with the screen image from the computer. CRT projectors produce clear, sharp video that is essential for data projection and fast animations. These units cost between $11,000 and $35,000.

The highest-quality projection is produced with the LCLV systems, which cost anywhere between $50,000 and $500,000. These are great for large projections, such as stadiums and rock concerts. Because of their weight and price, they are usually rented.

Another type of video projection that is gaining in popularity is the video wall. It is often seen at trade shows, but is popping up in hotels, museums, and retail locations. A video wall is composed of monitors, called cubes, set side by side and stacked vertically. Larger walls might include any combination of cubes up to about 12 by 12 (144 in all). Each individual monitor, or cube, is about 40 inches diagonally and 4 feet deep, about twice as deep as a regular computer monitor. A computer generally controls the image on the video wall, which can display one large image spread over all the cubes, or a variety of images at once. The advantages of this system are that the wall can be used in a bright room, does not require projection space, and can display a variety of eye-catching effects.

CD-ROM

Many multimedia projects are best distributed on a CD-ROM. CD-ROMs have numerous advantages for multimedia. They hold large quantities of information. They are relatively indestructible, impervious to viruses and other contamination, and relatively inexpensive. And CD-ROM readers—the devices used to play back CDs—are catching on very quickly.

If you choose to run a CD-ROM from an authoring system, you need to be able to access the CD-ROM from the system. Voyager's Voyager AudioStack 1.2 provides detailed information about how to use CD-ROM with HyperCard. It demonstrates the use of external commands (XCMDs) that may be licensed from Apple Computer in order to allow sound plaback. Macromedia Director has XCMDs that control external devices, and movies that show how to write the LINGO code to operate the CD-ROM.

For detailed information on the CD-ROM standard, and on CD players and recorders, see Chapter 4, "Hardware Peripherals."

If you decide to put your project on a CD-ROM, you can make the decision about what quality sound you want for your production. Using CD audio will limit your users; some CD players don't have audio output, or may not have the required external speakers hooked up. If you decide to have CD-quality audio available, producers often provide access to the audio through the computer speakers for users who do not have the more sophisticated equipment.

Videodisc

Videodiscs specialize in storing video images and associated sounds. These are used most often for collections of still images, or for movies. You would not put your main program on the videodisc. Some large multimedia systems use CD-ROMs and videodisc. Advantages are high quality images, and quick random access to the images.

Picture quality and easy access to individual frames make videodiscs essential for certain multimedia projects. Videodiscs are particular, effective for kiosks and exhibits used in museums, libraries, and other institutions. Corporate presentation centers generally have this sort of equipment.

If a videodisc will be a part of your multimedia production, you must include a videodisc driver with your program. The Voyager VideoStack 2.2 has excellent

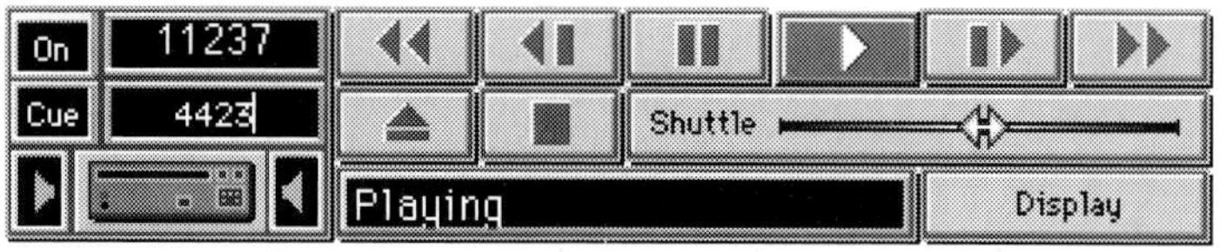

Figure 11.8 "Color CD Sound Panel" comes with Macromedia Director 3.1. It uses the AppleCD XObj to control audio on a CD player from within Director.

Figure 11.9 Color Videodisc Panel using XCMDs to control videodisc player from Macromedia Director 3.1

drivers that can be licensed for about $500. This interactive product provides extensive information about accessing and retrieving data from videodiscs using these external commands from HyperCard.

Macromedia Director includes XCMDs, which control Sony and Pioneer videodisc players. A movie has sample scripts that show how to use these controllers from your Director movie.

The Design Process

The preproduction process provides a focus and helps you determine what should and should not be a part of your multimedia production. It is a highly logical operation that clears the way to allow full creativity during the design process.

From preproduction, you have a detailed outline for the content, of your project, along with an overview of the needs for interactivity. You also have a good idea of the types of graphics and sounds you need for your production.

In the design phase, you get specific about each topic you outlined during preproduction. During this time, you may flesh out the outline, or write a detailed script covering all the text and narration used in your project. (Which road you take depends upon the nature of your project.) You also will select the exact illustrations you need and decide on your specific audio requirements.

Creating a Detailed Outline or Script

The core element of the multimedia production is usually a detailed outline or specific script. This contains all the text used in the production and specifies the images needed. It mentions when important sound is required, and focuses on the message and how it can be best presented to the audience. This is where the content is polished and delivery style determined.

The script or outline can then be used to determine actual budgets for time, and is the guide for the programmer who will integrate all the multimedia elements.

Greg Roach wrote the "Madness of Roland" as a serial that appeared in HyperBole, an interactive multimedia magazine. This story served as the basis for the production script. The story of Roland is told using the media that best convey the story, imagery, or emotions at each moment. Sometimes there is multicolored text on the screen; other times, QuickTime movies or dramatic audio conversations. Regardless of the media used, the script maintained the message and structure throughout the production.

Prototypes

Once you have created a detailed outline or script, you may wish to create a prototype to try out your ideas, layout, and interface to see if they work. The prototype may be a few screens with graphics, text, and sound, or a mock-up of what the actual scenes will look like. This can be done in any outlining program, in HyperCard, or even in the authoring system you have chosen. The prototype lets you make final decisions on style, fonts, color palettes, screen design, and the look and feel of the interactive elements.

The prototype lets you try out your ideas in the many dimensions of the interactive program. Use your imagination to try out various possibilities. Make decisions based on feedback from as many people as is practical. Comments and suggestions on interface, layout, and content are important at this point, particularly because it is easy to make changes when you're still at the prototype stage. Once production begins, these same changes can cause delays, wasted work, and added expense.

With the script written, and the look and feel of the project prototyped, the interface needs to be fully defined. Interactivity is one of the hardest areas to visualize. A flowchart is the most effective way to visualize how a user can progress from one screen of the program to another. This is a multidimensional process, which can be viewed in a number of ways. Many producers use simple sketches with a pencil and paper. This method is fast and does not require art skills; rough boxes, stick figures, and arrows are sufficient.

Some producers build a small, sketchy prototype in a program such as HyperCard. This works well for very small teams, but is not as readily understandable as a paper flowchart. Complex projects involving many people can be prototyped using powerful organizational tools like Microsoft PowerPoint, Aldus Persuasion, Symantec More, or Claris MacProject Pro. Programs like these have features that allow you to view static ideas and outlines in a variety of ways.

Chapter 19, "Interface and Interactivity," covers the full spectrum of considerations for creating an effective interface. Once the interface is fully designed, the script may need to be updated to reflect the new environment. A prototype of the interface should then be tested on a wide range of individuals, some familiar with the project, others with no prior involvement in the design process.

Storyboarding

From the tested prototype comes the final design stage. Generally, this takes the form of a storyboard, which is a sketch of where each element will appear sequentially in the project. It allows you to move screens to more logical locations and to see the elements of your production on a sort of visual timeline. You can see if there is sufficient visual variety and if there is enough continuity to prevent the user from getting lost.

Storyboards can use the same range of tools used for interface design, from a clean sheet of paper (or the back of a used envelope) to a complex planning and presentation package. For a simple project, a few quick sketches are sufficient. For large, involved projects, detailed storyboards must be created. Again, presentation programs can be very helpful in this process. Some of these programs allow you to view thumbnails of the images that you can shuffle around until the flow of the presentation is just the way you want it. Major projects can be dealt with easily when the pieces are planned individually.

Rarely is a multimedia project storyboarded from start to finish before production begins. More often, a scene or animation is sketched out just prior to its production. The prototyping and planning done to this point has defined the elements of the project. Storyboarding can save immense amounts of time—and money—when you are renting time at a postproduction house that can cost hundreds of dollars each hour. Although most multimedia is created in less expensive environments, time is always at a premium.

Make your decisions about how and when to storyboard based on your time and budget constraints. Also, think about the people you have working on the project. It makes sense to take advantage of the creativity of artists and programmers when you have time, but make sure that the innovations fit with the decisions you have made during preproduction.

Focus Groups

At each stage in the design process, you should bring in others to give you feedback on the interface and every other element of your project. This can be done formally, as with a focus group, or informally, just showing the project to others in the office. When you near major decision points, such as the interface design, you should try to get feedback from people who are likely to be using the program.

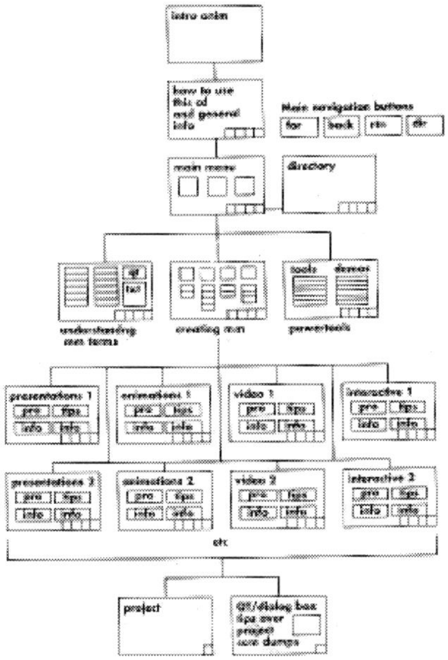

Figure 11.10 Early storyboard used for a portion of the Multimedia Power Tools CD.

Figure 11.11a This is a handwritten outline of the user interface created for an exhibit in the Library of Congress American Memory prototype.

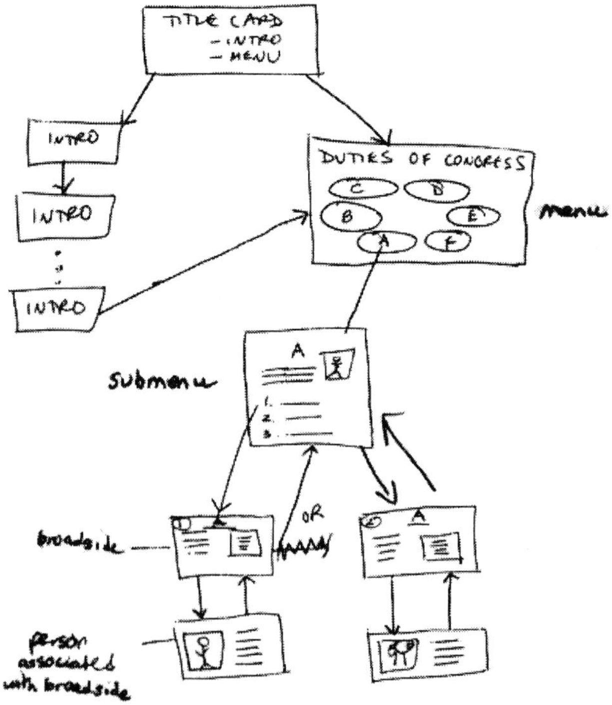

Figure 11.11b This example from the Library of Congress American Memory prototype shows a simple flowchart for the "To Form a More Perfect Union:" exhibit about the Continental Congress and the Constitutional Convention.

Flowcharting and Outlining at the Library of Congress

The American Memory project at the Library of Congress shows how the vast information held by the library can be made available electronically throughout the country. Collections of material are electronically catalogued. Some collections are introduced by an exhibit, very like a museum exhibit. The project uses both CD-ROM and videodisc technology.

Figures 11.11a and 11.11b show how the interface for an exhibit for the American Memory project was mapped out. The work was done using pencil and paper flowchart, starting with an outline. From that outline, Joanne Freeman, the author, drew a flowchart showing interactivity of the project.

Starting with the title, the user can take either of two paths: the introduction or the main information menu. The introduction is sequential and can be viewed from start to finish. If the user chooses to go to the main menu, a submenu shows the available topics. From the submenu, the user can choose to see a Congressional broadside—a document posted in pubs and public places, and information explaining why it was important. Hyperlinks connect the user to in-depth information about people or events mentioned in the text.

The plan for the program structure was reviewed and discussed to determine if this interface would work. After testing the interface on several individuals, the team decided not to allow users to roam freely throughout the miscellaneous information. It would be too easy to lose track of the relationship between the Congressional broadside and the associated individuals and events. As you can see in Figure 11.10b, the arrow connecting the related information has been deleted. This flow chart shows the flow through one menu item down to the end of one path.

This method of flowcharting was very clear and easy to work with; it was simple and to the point. Everyone involved in the project, from the project supervisor to the programmer, was able to quickly see the scope of the exhibit, how it worked, and how it was to be assembled.

The actual script was written. The text for each card in the HyperCard stack was displayed on a single page. Each page contained all text, including titles, menu items, and captions. Every other page was a photocopy of the still graphic image that was to be used to illustrate that page. The photocopy ensured that the programmer would know exactly what the image in the caption looked like.

```
Page1
                 To Form a More Perfect Union:
               The Work of the Continental Congress
               and the Constitutional Convention

                    An  Interactive  Exhibition

                         *  Introduction

        * The Work of the Continental Congress and the
                   Constitutional  Convention
```

box continued

Page2
[menu]

The Work of the Continental Congress
and the Constitutional Convention

Organizing a War

Fanning the Flames of Patriotism

Incorporating the Western Territories

Relating With Native Americans

Identifying Defects in the Confederation

Creating a Constitution

Page 8
[submenu]

Organizing a War

The huge task of organizing thirteen separate governments and militia into a united, effective fighting force was a main concern of the Continental Congress. The hastily assembled Continental Army had no precedent; Congress had to create rules for organization and conduct, and invent an effective system of raising money to fund the war.

Congress makes rules for plundering enemy ships

Congress provides for prisoners of war

Congress reorganizes the army

Image & Caption:
Das erste BHrger Blut, zu GrHndung der Americanishen Freyheit, vergossen bey Lexington am 19ten April 1775. [The Battle of Lexington].
Daniel Nikolaus Chodowiecki (1726-1801).
Engraving, 1784.
(Reproduction number: LC-USZ62-26669).

Page 9
[Congressional Broadside #49]

Congress reorganizes the army

Throughout the Revolutionary War, the Continental Army suffered problems of low recruitment, supply shortages, and sinking morale. In January 1778, at **General George Washington s** urging, Congress sent a committee to military headquarters at Valley Forge, to confer with Washington on necessary improvements. Although the committee made proposals for reorganizing supply procedures and revising recruitment regulations, Congress s response was slow and piecemeal; other issues, such as the **controversy surrounding a prisoner exchange,** kept Congress distracted. Congress did not approve the displayed plan for rearrangement of the army until May 1778, and it was November before implementation was completed.

box continued

```
Page11
[related  information]
                      #49 - image and sidebar (#2)

              General George Washington (1732-1799)

                During his lifetime, George Washington was admired, respected,
              and praised to a degree unmatched by any other figure in Ameri-
              can history. With America s victory in the Revolutionary War,
              many gave General George Washington most of the credit for the
              birth of the American nation.
                Before the Continental Congress named him Commander-in-Chief
              of the Continental Army in 1775, Washington was already recog-
              nized as a statesman and soldier. As early as 1755, at the age
              of twenty-three, he was in command of all Virginian troops dur-
              ing the French and Indian War. Born to a landed family in the
              Virginia countryside, Washington was skilled in surveying land,
              managing a plantation, entertaining the gentry, and playing
              politics. Although he had a fierce temper, through sheer
              strength of character he kept it under control. This same
              strength of character enabled Washington to endure nine years of
              commanding a novice army during a war with one of the world s
              great powers   the British empire.

              Image & Caption:
              General Washington (1732-1799).
              Painted by John Trumbull (1756-1843).
              Engraved by Valentine Green (1739-1813).
              Mezzotint, 1781.
              (Reproduction number: LC-USZ62-45197.)
```

Getting Ready for Production

The final step of preproduction involves getting ready for production. Specific assignments need to be made for the appropriate groups, and a detailed time schedule written. The detailed script and storyboard simplify the assignment process tremendously. Everything needed for your multimedia production has been defined and is ready to become a reality.

Scheduling and Budget

Before production begins, you should make a realistic timetable. Try to set definite goals, such as "Approve the final artwork for the main menu screen" or "Get written license for main theme for introduction." The goals should be worded so that their achievement is not debatable. The artwork got final approval or it did not. Either you have a license in your hand or you do not. A nebulously stated goal such as "Work on artwork for menu screens" does not provide a solid landmark; the deadline can come and go, but as long as someone worked on the artwork, one could argue that the goal was met.

With a detailed schedule, you can determine if your project is behind schedule and if so, how far. Track the actual timing for projects so that you can make more realistic projections for other creative efforts. Remember Murphy's law: "Everything takes longer than you think."

Finally, keep a list of ideas that the team comes up with that might enhance the project. These ideas may be capable of adding depth to the project, but if you approve all of them, it will never get finished. When the project is near completion, try to use as many of the good ideas as timing and budget allow.

Summary

Preproduction can be tedious, but it's critical to any multimedia project. Planning your project before starting it ensures that you can deliver a cohesive product to your audience. It allows you to make realistic decisions about which elements must be in your product and which may enhance it. Realistic budgeting and schedules are the best way to get a project finished and into its final form sometime near its deadline.

12

Working Cross-Platform

"If you go to the bathroom during the fourth quarter, you'll be sorry."

1984 Super Bowl Sunday; Apple's advertisement in the San Francisco Chronicle.

Not many who saw the legendary 1984 Super Bowl commercial would soon forget it. The ad begans with a line of blue-suited figures marching off a cliff while singing a tuneless ditty. (It didn't take much imagination to realize that these unfortunate souls must be IBM customers—or victims). Meanwhile, a female athlete pursued by storm troopers bursts into a room full of downtrodden people, who stare dumbly at the giant, flickering image of "big brother."

The woman abruptly spins around and hurls a sledge hammer through the screen, and as a fresh wind blows through the auditorium, a legend appears: "On January 24th, Apple Computer will introduce Macintosh, and you'll understand why 1984 won't be like 1984."

From the beginning, it was war.

In 1981, when $40 billion behemoth IBM entered the personal computer market with its PC, Apple was a $600 million upstart that owned 80% of the desktop computer market.

With his trademark blend of arrogance and idealism, Steve Jobs welcomed IBM into battle with a national ad whose headline read, "Welcome IBM. Seriously." It went on to say, in part, "Welcome to the most exciting and important marketplace since the computer revolution began 35 years ago. And congratulations on your first computer."

Apple and Jobs clearly relished the David and Goliath struggle that lay ahead, and no doubt assumed that their size and agility, as well as their head start, would give Apple the critical competitive advantage.

But Apple's opponent was no stranger to either adversity or market dominance. When IBM itself was on the rise in the 1950s, it too was puny in comparison with General Electric and RCA, the giants it challenged. But by the mid-'50s, by building a reputation for technology leadership and sensitivity to the customer,

IBM had 75% of the computer market. And in the personal computer war with Apple nearly three decades later, the story was much the same. A year after joining the fray, IBM had captured nearly 20% of the market, and by 1983 it was recognized as the leader, displacing Apple, which had enjoyed such a commanding lead just a short time before.

By the early '90s,the competitive landscape had shifted again, and both Apple and IBM had all but ceded control of the personal computer market that they themselves had spawned. By making the PC market open to encourage the PC's acceptance, IBM had lost market share to such clone manufacturers as Compaq, AST, and Dell.

Apple, too, had continued to lose share to both IBM and the cloners (although its Macintoshes are, of course, now fully expandable, with hundreds of peripherals available to supplement the performance of a stock Mac).

The two pioneers of personal computer technology collectively held barely one quarter of the market they had created. By mid-1992, even the Mac's edge as a graphical environment was being challenged, when for the first time, market research reports indicated that GUI buyers at corporate sites were acquiring more Windows than Macintoshes.

Given these cold facts, perhaps the IBM/Apple alliance should have come as less of a shock. Yet when the two companies announced their partnership in 1991, it rocked the industry.

In this chapter, we'll examine the fledgling set of cross-platform multimedia standards, including the fruits of the IBM/Apple relationships, followed by some practical information on cross-platform development. Since the Mac and the PC/Windows are the dominant multimedia environments, we'll cover the main issues involved in developing on the Mac for delivery on the PC.

We'll also take a look at some of the applications that offer the best cross-platform compatibility. And finally, we'll present an overview of the major multimedia computers, including MPCs and Unix workstations.

Multimedia Standards

The computer industry is plagued by a lack of true standards for file formats, data of all types, devices, and software architecture. This sad situation has many ramifications: It's tricky or impossible to move data between programs and platforms; product development costs are high; technological innovations are hampered; and the user frustration factor is in the stratosphere.

Of the approximately 5 million Macs installed at corporate sites in 1992, 65–75 percent were connected to multiplatform networks. Yet, interoperability remains elusive. As vendors struggle to differentiate themselves and their products, they build walls by creating proprietary systems that communicate imperfectly and only with great difficulty.

Bolt-on filters often are used by vendors to convert data from one format to another; but this process requires extra steps to transfer and open files across platforms and between applications, and usually results in only partial conversion. To be truly transparent, applications must incorporate interoperability into their core code.

Part of the problem lies in the appearance of the graphical user interface (GUI) following the Mac's rise to prominence in the 1980s. Now, GUIs are everywhere: Windows for PCs, Motif for Unix, and Presentation Manager for OS/2. In the days of the ugly but effective command-line interface, an application written in a high-level language such as C or Pascal more or less guaranteed its portability.

But despite GUI similarities in look and feel, beneath their clever and colorful desktops lurks code that is largely incompatible across systems. Every GUI has a complex and unique set of functions that governs the display of menus, windows, and icons, and specifies keyboard and mouse interaction. All this means that while GUIs make it much easier for users to interact with computers, they make it a lot harder for programmers to develop interoperable applications.

However, the explosion of multimedia, with its new file formats for video, sound, and graphics, has reemphasized the need for interoperability, and there has been a flurry of action in the renewed rush to establish standards.

Even Microsoft CEO Bill Gates, in a *MacWeek* interview, has predicted that there will be content standards, at least: "The key elements, the audio and video that you put your money into, will be shared. . . . we can hide [differences in the platforms] for a content producer, and make those things look the same." Gates says that vendors will retain their edge by competing on the basis of applications; "otherwise, the differences [in platforms] cease to have separate value added."

Below, we'll outline a few of the most promising standards efforts, focusing on their impact on multimedia.

Kaleida's Script X and Bento

Kaleida, one of two Apple/IBM joint ventures, soon will introduce Script X, a universal multimedia scripting language for developing cross-platform applications. Once written, these apps can use run-time engines for playback in Windows, Unix, OS/2, and System 7. The applications also will play on Kaleida's Consumer Operating System (COS), which will run on hand held multimedia players like Sweetpea, as well as on PDAs made by Sony and Toshiba.

TOOLS QuickTime ⌘160

According to Kaleida, QuickTime will be incorporated into the Script X environment, and QuickTime movies will play on Script X-compliant machines, including PDAs.

Kaleida also will support Apple's Bento standard for vendor and system-independent multimedia products. Bento (a Japanese word meaning "boxed lunch") allows compound documents containing different types of data to be read by multiple applications. For example, a word processing document with graphics could be opened by an illustration program, which would operate on only the portion of the file it understands—the graphics. Companies who have joined the Kaleida Association (for a $1 million membership fee) will be allowed to develop applications that incorporate the Bento specification.

While all of this new technology sounds promising, Kaleida has a tough row to hoe, for Apple and IBM have been pursuing their own unique multimedia strategies for some time now.

Apple has encouraged (and provided, notably in QuickTime) the tools necessary to "roll your own" multimedia presentations and creations, including The Apple Media Kit (see Chapter 9, "Authoring Tools). IBM has spent its time developing industrial-strength multimedia training applications, and such point-of-sale products as information kiosks. The two companies also plan to continue to develop their own competitive edges, labeling their joint ventures "precompetitive cooperation."

Odd times, indeed; one can hardly imagine two stranger bedfellows. And at some level, both IBM and Apple must agree—certainly, the two companies' hapless employees do. Spencer the Katt, the popular *PC Week* gossip columnist, reports that Apple people are especially wary, comparing the situation to the Star Trek movie in which Captain Kirk helps save his archenemies, the Klingons. As Apple employees suspiciously eye their alien counterparts from IBM, they're thinking (Spock) "We have to save them, Captain. they're dying." (Kirk) "They're animals, Spock. Let them die."

IBM people apparently feel the same, as they reportedly are continuing the development of their own Script X alternative—just in case.

Interactive Multimedia Association's CPC

The IMA is a nonprofit organization that was formed in 1991 by a group of engineers and managers who wanted to develop, through their Cross-Platform Compatibility (CPC) group, a set of international multimedia standards that could eventually be adopted by such influential bodies as the International Standards Organization (ISO). The IMA is actively supported by a number of key computer vendors, including Hewlett-Packard, DEC, Intel, and Compaq.

The IMA wants, like everyone else, to develop a standard file format, and specifications for multimedia components such as digital video. The IMA has pursued a software-only video decompression standard. Software-only solutions have a better chance for cross-platform compatibility, as they are not tied to proprietary hardware.

Through its Digital Audio working group, the organization is also addressing standards for audio, an important multimedia component. The group is developing a set of digital-coding, data-format-exchange standards that will allow up- and down-sampling between low-quality 8-bit audio and 44.1-kHz, 16-bit CD-quality sound. Member company Intel is trying to get the IMA to adopt its Audio Video Kernel (AVK), which Intel claims will allow multimedia files to be played back on any platform using an Intel processor.

The IMA is leveraging the experience and technology of its powerful member organizations to develop recommended standards and practices for all multimedia components. The organization also is cooperating with the Object Management Group (OMG), an HP/SunSoft joint effort that is developing interoperability standards that will allow multimedia applications to move between workstations and desktop machines.

Symantec's Bedrock and Apple's MacApp

For some time, application developer Symantec has been using cross-platform development tools in-house to develop both Windows and Mac versions of its programs. Symantec calls this technology "Bedrock," which is an application framework that provides a common set of programming building blocks, or objects. This approach incorporates the object-oriented technology that is now sweeping the computer industry.

Bedrock will allow software developers to develop and maintain a single version of source code that will run on a variety of platforms. Initial platforms supported are the Mac and Windows, with future versions to support the OS/2, Unix, and Windows NT environments.

Apple's own development environment, MacApp, will be modified to incorporate Bedrock. The hybrid technology, which will be available by mid-1993, is expected to speed the development of applications that will run on both Windows and the Mac, and could further bolster the Mac's position as a major cross-platform multimedia development system.

Developing on the Mac for Delivery Under Windows

The jostlings and posturings of major corporations and standards organizations aside, the realities of today's cross-platform tools are such that if you want to develop cross-platform multimedia productions, you have your work cut out for you.

Since the most popular multimedia platforms are the Mac and PC/Windows, we'll focus on some of the cross-platform considerations for those two environments. The Mac being the platform of choice for most multimedia developers, we'll concentrate mainly on the issues in developing multimedia on the Mac for delivery under Windows.

Know Your Target

A central problem in cross-platform development is the wildly variable range of PCs and their peripherals. Designer/developer Jim Collins of Smoke and Mirrors, in San Francisco, points out that you can generally predict multimedia performance on the Mac. A presentation may play at a certain speed on an LC II, a little faster on a IIvx, and faster still on a Centris or Quadra.

By contrast, the PC world is populated by a jangling array of monitors, drivers, cards, and other peripherals. It's simply not possible to estimate how a given multimedia production will behave on the tremendous range of PC hardware, even with the unifying influence of Windows. Says Collins, "The vagaries of PC hardware are just a killer."

To combat these uncertainties, experienced multimedia developers agree that a key to creating successful cross-platform apps is to lock down your target PC, if at all possible. If the playback machine is a particular type of PC—say, as part of a kiosk—you're in luck, because then you can obtain a PC just like the target machine, test your work, and be sure that your multimedia will always perform consistently.

Unfortunately, more often than not, multimedia presentations are bound for a variety of PCs. In these cases, you still can dampen, if not eliminate, performance problems by specifying a few key parameters: processor type and speed, RAM and hard disk capacity, and color capability. If your multimedia production is a product or custom app, make sure that your product packaging states these requirements, or that clients are aware of them.

If the target machine is known, Collins insists that clients provide him with one so that he can test projects before delivering them. If the work will be played back on an unknown range of PCs, he informs his clients of minimum hardware requirements, and then tests on his own similarly configured machine. Even then, he makes sure clients know that performance may not be consistent across the range of PCs out there.

Beyond the complexities of interoperability and performance, there are issues of design and of look and feel that are just as daunting. For many, it's enough just to get an application or project to perform acceptably. But for others, the inherent differences in look and feel of the Mac and Windows lead them to develop custom interfaces.

Dave Arnowitz, vice president of software development for Arnowitz Productions Inc. in Mill Valley, California, says that "the biggest problem in cross-platform development is that, if you want a product to have a consistency of look and feel, you can't rely on the native appearances of either environment." Accordingly, Arnowitz Productions builds large-scale interactive productions that are designed around custom interfaces.

Is It Worth It?

With all the intricacies of cross-platform development, you may wonder if it's worth the trouble, and you're not alone. Collins, for one, has all but thrown in the towel. After three years of developing on the Mac for delivery under Windows, it's still "a huge pain, and probably not worth the time and money" in lost revenue from other, missed opportunities. Collins is considering not accepting any more cross-platform projects, to concentrate solely on Mac-based development and delivery.

But not everyone agrees; Britt Peddie, technical director for San Francisco-based Ikonic, while admitting that confronting cross-platform development hurdles can be grim, actually prefers the PC to the Mac, claiming that the PC's installed base, modest pricing, and improving apps make it an appealing development target. "And, anyway, I prefer some PC applications over Mac software," says Peddie, citing both Animation Studio and Micrografx's highly regarded Picture Publisher image-processing program.

Peddie certainly has a point about the cost of the PC. Consider Compaq's new ProLinea CDS—a multimedia PC with a 486 ×25MHz processor, built-in CD-ROM drive, 16-bit sound card, and external speakers, all for under $1700 list.

And the PC has become a more appealing machine with the advent of Windows, which has undeniably brought a unifying force to the machine. After all, speaking of configuration permutations, under DOS you need a different video driver for each *application*; at least under Windows, one driver per device is the norm.

For all the pitfalls of cross-platform development, it's certainly possible to build high-quality applications for presentation on the PC. Consider a screen shot of an interface (note, of course, that the original is in living color) created by Ikonic for PC-compatible manufacturer TriGem, shown in Figure 12.1.

The icons were actually shifting video images that were produced in the days prior to the release of QuickTime, so the motion video effect had to be achieved using Director's *puppet sprites*, "real gnarly little things," says Ikonic president Robert May. For a full account of the development of the TriGem interface, a rather harrowing and baroque process, see the June 1991 issue of *New Media Age* (now simply called *New Media*).

Figure 12.1 Ikonic's TriGem Interface

Choose Your Poison

There are two basic ways to play back on the PC multimedia that you develop on the Mac. The first is to create different components on the Mac—sound, graphics, animation, video; then transfer the files to the PC (see *"File Transfer"* below) and assemble them using a PC-based authoring tool such as Visual Basic or Toolbook. The other way is to develop a complete multimedia production on the Mac using a "multi-platform" application—one that is also supported on the PC.

With the current state of Mac/PC interoperability, and in particular the dearth of cross-platform multimedia tools, both methods involve compromise. Developing and then transferring elements one by one is time consuming, and then you've got to invest in and learn a PC authoring program.

Using the second method, you'll be able to tweak the multimedia elements with the authoring package directly on the PC, a distinct advantage. However, if you develop a complete production on the Mac using Director, for example, you'll have to spring for the $995 Windows Player, which compiles Director files for playback on the PC. More importantly, if something doesn't work or look right (expect this, at least to some extent), you can't modify elements on the PC. You'll have to go back to the Mac, make adjustments, recompile, transfer to the PC, and only then find out if things have improved.

If your multimedia production involves device control—external commands that fetch images and other data from peripherals such as CD-ROMs and laserdiscs—you'll pretty much have to put everything together on the PC, because these "compiled code resources," such as HyperCard XCMDs, must be replaced by equivalent Dynamic Link Libraries (DLLs) under Windows.

Using products like Macromedia's Director and Windows Player, you can develop multimedia productions on the Mac and play them back on the PC under Windows. The built-in transfer utilities take care of converting everything in the presentation—graphics, animation, sound, and text. But even when the conversion is handled for you in one big lump, that doesn't mean you won't run into problems.

If you do a lot of cross-platform development (you have our sympathy, first of all), you'll probably use both methods, as appropriate to individual projects.

Let's take a look now at the basics of cross-platform computing—file formats, file transfer and conversion, and screen capture. We'll also cover cross-platform conversion of multimedia components: colors, graphics, text, animation, video, and sound.

File Translation and Graphic File Formats

File transfer and translation are at the heart of cross-platform multimedia development. The following information and advice should help you through the thicket of formats and conventions.

File Naming

As a Mac user, you're used to naming your files descriptively, using up to 31 characters, including any combination of upper- and lowercase letters and punctuation (except colons). File naming under DOS (and Unix, too) is much more restrictive. In DOS, a file name can be up to only eight characters long, followed by a period and a three-character extension, which tells the OS what kind of file it is. DOS makes no distinction between upper- and lowercase letters.

In the Mac OS, application and system files are each linked to a companion file, called the resource fork, which is not visible in the Finder. The resource fork file yields to the Finder certain information about the file, such as its type, icon, and so on. When you transfer a file from the Mac to the PC, you'll see the file split into two files on the PC side, with the resource fork named identically, save for a percent (%) symbol at the beginning of the name. If the file is going to stay on the PC, you can discard the resource fork, whose information is conveyed to DOS by the three-character extension.

If you're going to do a lot of file transfers, you should consider using file names that both the Mac and DOS will understand. Use names of no longer than eight characters, and include a three-character extension—the Mac will just treat it as part of the file name, but the PC will recognize the extension and process the file correctly.

If you're going to be cutting a CD for your multimedia presentations, files, or product, file names must conform to ISO-9660, an international standard that defines a filesystem for CD-ROMs. If you have data on the CD that is compatible with applications running on multiple platforms, you'll also want the file names to be readable by different operating systems. The following file naming conventions will ensure this compatibility.

The ISO-9660 Level One specification outlines file naming conventions similar to DOS rules. File names are limited to eight single-case characters, a period, and a three-character extension. File names cannot contain symbols or special characters (no hyphens, tildes, equals, or pluses), only single-case letters, numbers, and underscores. Directory names cannot have the three-digit extension, just eight single-case characters.

Level Two ISO-9660 allows longer file names, up to 32 characters. But many of the other restrictions still apply. Level Two discs are not usable on some systems, notably MS-DOS. For further information, see Chapter 4, "Hardware Peripherals."

File Transfer

While direct content and application compatibility between the Mac and PC still lags, simple file transfer is now pretty routine. Apple itself has finally delivered on the promise of direct DOS file mounting it made when releasing the SuperDrive (which handles 1.44Mb floppies), back in 1988.

By Floppy. For $79, you can get Apple's Macintosh PC Exchange software, which allows you to read, write, and format DOS 720Kb and 1.44Mb disks on a

Mac. Contents of DOS disks appear on the Mac desktop as standard Mac files, and you can open, save, rename, move, copy, or delete them as you would any Mac file. You even can configure PC files to launch the appropriate application when you click on them.

An older utility, called Apple File Exchange, is included in the Mac's System software (in System 7), but you have to launch it separately—it doesn't offer the direct-from-the-desktop mounting of PC Exchange.

PC Exchange has a few drawbacks of its own: It works only under System 7, requires at least 3Mb of RAM and a SuperDrive (the standard drive on all post-Mac II machines), does not support DOS-formatted removable hard-disk or optical drives, and doesn't support Apple's own PC Drive 5.25.

Dayna Communications' DOS Mounter, and AccessPC from Insignia Solutions, which actually also wrote some of PC Exchange's code, appear to be a better deal. These two products do not have any of the limitations of PC Exchange (except that both also require a SuperDrive), and are priced similarly to PC Exchange.

By Serial Line. Directly connecting a Mac and PC by cable can be a cheap and fast way to transfer files. You can get the right cable from most computer suppliers for about $10 (PC 9-pin or 25-pin COM1 or COM2 port on one end, and the Mac's Mini DIN-8 on the other). Several products bundle these cables with file transfer software, and some, like MacLinkPlus and LapLink also will convert files to different formats before sending them.

On the Mac, you can run Zterm, a shareware transfer utility available from BBSs. Combine this with the cable, and you've got the cheapest transfer solution. Other commercial products include Argosy's RunPC, Microphone II from Software Ventures, and White Knight Telecommunications Software from Freesoft Co.

By Modem. You can use file transfer software in conjunction with a modem instead of a serial line if you need to connect to a remote machine. You also can join a network or BBS, and download or upload files with a modem.

By Network. All Macs have built-in networking capability via AppleTalk software. Buy an inexpensive connector for each Mac, connect them with ordinary phone wire, and poof—instant LocalTalk network, complete with printer and file sharing.

You can add AppleTalk capability to any PC by adding a card such as Daystar's LT200 Connection, PhoneNET Card PC from Farallon, or Sitka's TOPS FlashCard; all are in the $20 0–300 range.

If you're moving lots of big files around all the time, you should buy Ethernet cards for your Macs and PCs. AppleTalk's data transfer rate of 17.2Kb per second is OK for occasional transfers of small files, but Ethernet moves data at about 10Mb/second, making it ideal for pushing around giant multimedia files. You can get Ethernet cards for $40 0–500 apiece.

For connecting major networks of Macs and PCs, you'll need a "gateway." These higher-end products can be on the expensive side. A few are: GatorShare from

Cayman Systems, which connects Unix and Apple networks; MacLAN Connect from Miramar Systems, which connects PC and Mac networks; and NetModem/E from Shiva Corp., which allows Macs to connect to Novell NetWare networks.

Farallon's Timbuktu is an interesting software product that lets you view Windows files from a Mac and vice versa. You can move files from machine to machine across a network, and even give Windows users access to Mac shared printers, folders, and servers.

File Conversion

File interchange is the bane of the computer user. Getting one program to read a file created with another program can be frustrating and time consuming, and sometimes impossible. Often you end up stripping a text file of its formatting characteristics, importing it into the other program, and reformatting it.

Unfortunately, you can't do this with an image file, whose whole identity is wrapped up in its file format, without which it is a meaningless collection of bits. There are some graphics standards, and some of them are even adhered to by applications vendors (which used to be the meaning of "standard").

Many applications vendors pull self-serving stunts like reading files in a number of formats but writing out files only in their own proprietary format, thus encouraging (forcing) use of their program alone. Luckily, even mercenary software companies are recognizing the importance of interchange standards, and most graphics programs read and write to at least a few basic formats.

Integration programs (like Director) and image processing programs (like Photoshop) actually accept a wide variety of file formats. In fact, Photoshop supports so many formats that it is often used simply to convert an image from one format to another.

Using Director's Art Grabber II desk accessory, you can import files in a range of formats, making it a sort of media melting pot. For a more detailed summary of Director's capabilities, see Chapter 9, "Authoring Tools."

Once you have a connection established to the PC (or other computer), the next step is to invest in a good file translation package.

One of the most comprehensive is DataViz's MacLinkPlus, which offers over 400 conversion combinations, spanning word processing, database, spreadsheet, and graphics formats. MacLinkPlus will even auto-detect the type of data in a file (or at least hazard a reasonable guess). We once were piddling around trying to convert a text file of unknown origin, recklessly hit a button or two in MacLinkPlus's interface, and before we knew what was going on, the utility had converted the file to Microsoft Word.

If most of your work will be in graphics file translation, you may want to go with a program that specializes in this task. Inset Systems Hijaak supports and converts more than 60 graphics file formats, and SnapPro from Windows Painter Ltd. is another capable graphics converter that also includes image editing tools. Both programs run under Windows.

FGM Inc. has PICTure this, which lets Mac users convert graphics files from the PC, Unix, and Amiga environments into PICT files.

Graphics File Formats

Mac users have to put up with comparatively few graphics formats—TIFF, PICT, and EPS are the main ones. Most Mac programs can read and write at least one of these in addition to their native formats. The PC world, by contrast, supports a large number of proprietary and near-standard formats, but TIFF and EPS are the most widely used.

All in all, the whole business of graphics file formats is troublesome and not a little frustrating. To keep yourself from inflicting damage on your computer if your carefully adjusted multihued image turns green when you open it on the PC, it's best to stick to a few tested formats that you are most familiar with.

TOOLS
DeBabelizer ⌘ 228

Many now use a handy tool called DeBabelizer, a sort of Swiss Army knife of graphics utilities that can open most Mac and PC graphics files. See Chapter 5, "Imaging Tools."

During the bleakest moments, an excellent resource is The Graphic *File Toolkit: Converting and Using Graphic Files* by Steve Rimmer (Addison-Wesley, 1992—sorry Random House!). The book also comes with a disk containing an award-winning program called Graphic Workshop that will read and convert virtually any bitmap format. For a comprehensive list and description of graphics file formats, see Chapter 5, "Imaging Tools."

Screen Capture

Many developers will use the Mac to create presentations for playback on the PC. Often, they'll need to capture PC screenshots, bring them to the Mac, animate them if necessary to simulate a running PC application, incorporate them into the presentation, then send the whole thing back to the PC for playback.

Believe it or not, it's easier to simulate a PC program's functionality in this way than to have the presentation call the PC program in real time during playback. One of the essential cross-platform tools is a good PC screen capture utility.

Windows, like the Mac, offers a built-in screen capture capability. While limited, it does the trick and works well for most simple screen grabs. To capture a screen and save it to the Windows Clipboard, just hit the Print Screen key. To grab the active window only, type Alt-Print Screen. This utility saves the screen captures to the Windows Clipboard in bitmap format (BMP).

While functional enough, the Windows Print Screen utility has some drawbacks. For one, you cannot save grabs to a file or print them at the time of capture. And if you have a number of captures to do in sequence, you'll have to move captured images from the Clipboard one by one; otherwise they'll be overwritten by subsequent captures.

You can bring the screen grabs into Windows' Paintbrush utility, which can crop and otherwise process each image. Unfortunately, Paintbrush has an aesthetic sense of its own, and has been known to chop off portions of screen captures without consulting with you first. If these limitations put you off, there are a variety of utilities that might fit the bill. Some popular PC shareware screen grabbers are CAPBUF, GRABBER, and TXT2PCX. All are available from CompuServe and other bulletin boards. Commercial screen capture utilities include Capture, Collage, Hotshot Graphics, and Hijaak.

Capture ⌘ 227

In addition to simple screen capture into different file formats, many of these programs include tools for cropping and cleaning up stray pixels, or artifacts, which commonly accompany screen captures.

You'll also have to use a graphics file translator to convert the screen capture to something Mac programs can use. PICTure This and Imagery are two Mac programs that will convert a wide variety of graphics formats (including BMP) to more universal graphics formats like TIFF and PICT. PICTure This is available from FGM Inc, and Imagery is freeware available from bulletin boards.

For a quick way to get PC screen shots over to the Mac, many developers save the grabs in PCX. The native file format of PC Paintbrush, a popular PC paint program, PCX has become a de facto standard on the PC (see). Once saved in PCX, you can bring the screen captures into Photoshop, one of the very few Mac applications (perhaps the only one) that will read PCX. You can then use Photoshop to convert the graphics to PICT or some other native Mac file format.

Other Elements of Multimedia

Aside from graphics files, the other components of multimedia present their own challenges when you move them from one platform to another. Here, we'll look at some of the ins and outs of fonts, colors and palettes, video, and sound.

Fonts

Fonts are trouble, probably one of the biggest problems you'll run into in this line of work. Many believed that TrueType held the promise of font standardization. After all, the new type technology was incorporated into both System 7 and Windows. But TrueType for the Mac and TrueType for Windows actually use different methods for character encoding and font specifications.

Windows includes two TrueType fonts—Arial and Times New Roman—that are translated to Helvetica and Times when moved to the Mac. These substitutions are not exact matches, so line breaks and careful copy fitting will be for naught.

Truly interchangeable fonts, such as Adobe's Multiple Master product, are on the way, but they may take a while to get here. Adobe's new technology uses a single Multiple Master typeface, such as Myriad, to simulate specified typefaces—even if the actual typefaces themselves are not installed in the system. Myriad cooks up substitutions on-the-fly, while preserving both the appearance and metrics of the original work. This technology is a true gift to the world, and may forever banish the frustrations of imperfect font substitutions.

Until that great day, many developers work around the font problem by converting type to bitmaps, which they antialias (smooth) to improve appearance. A lot of designers do type effects such as fills and gradients, which require that fonts be turned into bitmaps anyway.

Of course, this won't help you if your presentation includes a lot of text. In this case, use basic fonts that are available in default configurations on both platforms, to minimize subtle inconsistencies that will throw off formatting. And even if you use fonts with direct equivalents, save a little room to account for subtle variations that may cause text to expand or contract when converted. In any case, be prepared to tweak text if you don't convert it to bitmap form.

Colors and Palettes

This is another very tricky area, due to the generally poor color handling of Windows and the relative paucity of colors handled by VGA, the predominant PC video standard. VGA handles 16 colors, and is the minimum configuration supported by the PC multimedia standard MPC.

Since most color Macs are equipped with at least 256-color 8-bit cards, this can cause problems when your 8- or 24-bit images are transferred to the PC. For example, when you convert a Director multimedia production for playback on the PC with Windows Player, it automatically *remaps 8- or 24-bit images to the 16* colors available for VGA displays.

This can produce strange results, because remapping simply substitutes one color for another based on their relative positions in their respective palettes. The substituted colors, because they are selected purely on their position, may bear no resemblance at all to the original colors.

To avoid these nasty consequences, many developers capture the standard VGA palette on the PC and use it as the basis for image creation, thereby ensuring that colors will transfer properly. To get this palette, you can open the "Colors" control panel under Windows, and do a screen capture of the palette that pops up. Save this as a TIFF file, transfer it to the Mac, and import it into apps that support custom palettes, such as Director. Using this technique, you can create images that use colors that are drawn only from the VGA palette.

Photoshop ⌘222

For an image that has already been created, you can use an image editing program like Photoshop to convert the image's colors to the standard VGA 16. In Photoshop, import the captured palette and name it something like "VGA palette." Open your image, and select Color Table in the Mode menu. Then select Edit Table, and you'll see the current palette. Click the Load button and select "VGA palette." Click "OK" and the image will be converted to the 16 colors of VGA.

This works fine if you have just a few images to convert, but can take a lot of time if you have many images, such as the multiple frames of an animation. In these instances, you can set up a macro to automatically fetch each image, apply the new palette, open the next image, and so on. Then you can go out and have dinner; make sure you have coffee and dessert, and maybe catch a movie on the way home, too, because the conversion process can take a long time! But this process is necessary only if you can't be sure your multimedia won't be played back on a plain old VGA display.

Happily, many PCs outfitted for multimedia now have Super VGA, which can display 256 colors, making it roughly equivalent to the Mac's 8-bit color. In fact, if you know that your multimedia will be played back on a Super VGA monitor, you probably won't have to worry about remapping the colors of your images. The 256 colors of the Mac standard 8-bit palette map reasonably closely—though not exactly—to the 256 colors of Super VGA.

Video

Just as the Mac has QuickTime, Windows users now can enjoy digital video with Microsoft's Video for Windows (Figure 12.2). VFW uses Microsoft's Audio Video Interleaved (AVI) movie file format, analogous to QuickTime's MooV movie format. VFW incorporates Intel's Indeo digital video compression and playback technology, but it also works with other compression schemes being offered by third parties.

There are ways to move VFW and QuickTime movies back and forth between platforms. Apple offers the QuickTime for Windows Starter Kit, with which you can play back on Windows QuickTime movies that you created on the Mac. Apple plans to release a full-blown QuickTime implementation for Windows, probably as part of QuickTime 2.0, which should be available by the end of 1993. This version will allow you to actually create QuickTime movies under Windows.

New Video has a version of the Indeo codec for QuickTime. With this utility, you can create an Indeo movie and save it in either the VFW or QuickTime

Figure 12.2 Microsoft's Video for Windows

formats. VFW also includes a QuickTime movie converter, which translates QuickTime movies with mixed results.

Media Vision, best known for its PC audio hardware, has come out with a QuickTime and AVI-compatible cross-platform video format called MotiVE. The technology plays back identical video files on the PC, Mac, Sun SPARCstation, and SGI Iris Indigo. While Media Vision doesn't market the product directly, it is expected to pop up in a number of multimedia authoring packages.

Another alternative is the Digital Video Interactive (DVI) format developed by IBM and Intel. DVI is not just a digital video format, but an ambitious project that specifies file formats, compression, and software interface specifications. While a proprietary format, DVI nonetheless preceded AVI on the PC, and seems to be gaining a foothold there.

Currently, DVI/QuickTime compatibility is limited, but you can get New Video's EyeQ board, which handles both formats. Using the board you can capture video, save it as a QuickTime movie for playback on the Mac, and save the same video in DVI for playback on the PC. An interesting option is a product called PACo Producer, made by CoSA (aren't these trendy upper- and lowercase names beginning to drive you nuts?). While mostly designed to compress and distribute animations, PACo can also pack QuickTime files, which can then be played back on the PC, on Sun SPARCstations, and from within PC applications. For more on PACo, see "CoSA's PACo" below.

If cross-platform digital video leaves your head spinning, you can bypass it and pull video from an external source like a CD or videodisc for playback. But even then, there is no escape from the problem of compatibility, because you'll have to alter the external commands that fetch the images from these devices, since the commands rely on platform-specific code.

Sound Files

From the very beginning, all Macintoshes have had at least primitive sound capabilities built right into the system. All but a few of the earliest Macs have a version of the Apple Sound Chip, which can play four voices of synthesized sounds for basic effects. Hardware-based digital-analog converters (DACs) yield reasonable sound quality when audio is played back through the Mac's built-in speaker.

All newer Macs, from the IIsi on up, can play back stereo sound through speakers plugged into rear outputs. And most also can record sounds when a mike is plugged into input jacks. All this means that viewers (and listeners) won't have to invest in a sound card to hear the sounds and music in your multimedia extravaganzas—that is, if they're played back on just about any old Mac.

It is, alas, a different story on the PC. Except for primitive system "bings" and "bongs," which can play back through the PC's internal speaker, no add-in sound board means no sound. So if your target PC doesn't have an audio card, the sounds in any multimedia presentations developed on the Mac won't be heard.

There is a workaround that may help. Windows version 3.1 brought better sound capability to the PC, at least on the software side; a sound card still is necessary for sound processing, indeed even for simple recording and playback. But Microsoft and other vendors have made available a driver that allows sounds stored in the Windows .WAV format to be played back through the PC's internal speaker. (MIDI files stored in the .MID file format still require a separate sound card for playback).

Because the digital-analog conversion necessary for playback is performed in software by the driver, the sound quality is inferior to what you get when playing back files through the dedicated DACs of a sound card, or even the on-board Mac DACs. But it works; well, sort of. It works on most Windows PCs and most Windows programs.

Anyway, Microsoft inexplicably left the PC Speaker driver out of the standard Windows 3.1 distribution, but you can get it free from the Microsoft Windows BBS (206 637-9009), or from a number of other BBSs, including Compuserve. You also can order it from Microsoft End User Sales (800 426-9400) for about $20. Similar drivers also are included in some Windows programs, including GRasp, a DOS-based authoring tool.

We expect that the driver eventually will make its way into the standard Windows distribution, giving most Windows machines simple sound playback capability. Even so, if your multimedia production includes complex sound and music and it is targeted at a PC, you'd better make sure that target machine includes a sound card.

Fortunately, with the advent of the multimedia personal computers (MPCs), sound cards are becoming more prevalent. But of course, as is always the case regarding PC "standards," you can't count on a standard level of sound support in the PC world.

Microsoft offers some sound tools for Windows multimedia developers in the Multimedia Development Kit (MDK). To convert audio files from the Mac's AIFF format to Windows' WAV file format, you can use the MDK's Convert tool. The converter will translate 11.025 kHz and 22.05 kHz sound files, but conversion of CD-quality 44.1 kHz samples is not supported.

Once converted, you can edit these sound files—setting volume, fades, and mixing channels—with the MDK's WaveEdit tool, or with a commercial sound editing package such as Turtle Beach's Wav for Windows.

Multi-platform Applications

Cross-platform applications that allow you to create a presentation on the Mac and play it back on the PC (and vice versa) have begun to spring up. These programs include total authoring environments such as Director and AuthorWare, which allow you to create integrated presentations incorporating sound, graphics, and even video. Other programs such as MediaVision's MotIVE and CoSA's PACo focus on cross-platform components like video and animation.

These programs can save you a lot of time and effort, and many developers who do a lot of cross-platform work will become expert in one or more of the tools. However, even if you rely on an authoring environment like Director, don't expect to develop your presentation once, sit back while it converts, and have it run perfectly; chances are, you'll still have to do a lot of tweaking of fonts, colors, and sound-file formats.

And of course, you'll have to do this by going back to the Mac, because most cross-platform multimedia tools have their complete authoring environment on only one of the platforms, with just a "runtime" version on the other.

Even programs that are completely duplicated in both environments—so-called "sibling applications"—have idiosyncracies that may drive you nuts. Fonts, fill and ink effects, placed art, and macros are particularly notorious for not making the crossing even between sibling applications.

One thing that will help ease the burden of transition, is to try the conversion many times during the course of development. Don't wait until you've finished a presentation before trying to convert files and checking them out on the target platform. Converting your work several times a day will help minimize the reworking process.

Macromedia's Director

Director is probably the most often-used authoring tool on the Mac, so it's no surprise that many cross-platform multimedia projects are developed on Director for the Mac, then converted for playback on the PC.

To do this, you'll need to buy the $995 Windows Player add-on. Windows Player converts Director files and creates "projectors" that run under Windows. These projectors are run time players only, so if any adjustments are necessary, it's back to the Mac. On the Windows side, playback machines need to have at least a 286 chip, VGA display, hard disk, and 2Mb RAM (4Mb recommended).

Director ⌘ 210

If you want to avoid spending money for Windows Player, there is another alternative. Microsoft has included Movie Converter in its MDK. This utility converts Director files to an MMM file format that can be played back stand-alone under Windows using Movie Player, or imported into applications such as Asymmetrix's Toolbook for playback. This method is free, but there are some limitations (not all ink effects, cast members, and palette effects are supported). Also, as the Windows utilities are system-level resources, you may have to do quite a bit of tinkering to get everything to work.

The MDK documentation has a pretty complete description of the entire process, and this documentation also is available in book form from Microsoft Press, in Microsoft Windows Multimedia Authoring and Tools Guide.

The Apple Media Kit

The Apple Media Kit provides entry-level users with a vehicle for creating Mac or cross-platform multimedia presentations without having to do any scripting. Priced at less than $3,000, the full package includes an object-oriented authoring program called The Apple Media Tool (available separately for less than $1,500), and the VideoFusion QuickTime editor. For details, see Chapter 9, "Authoring Tools."

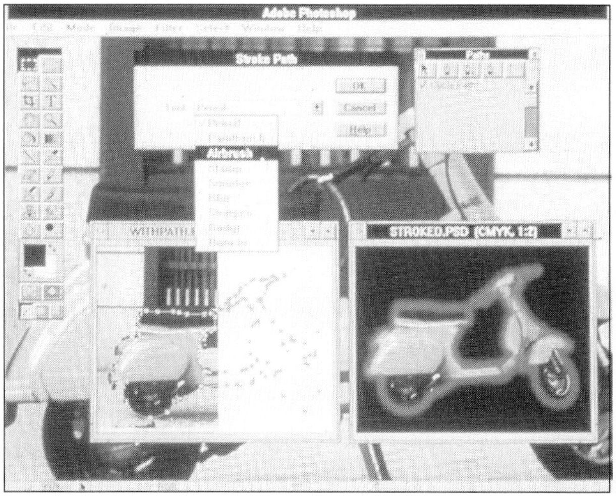

Figure 12.3 Adobe's Photoshop for Windows

CoSA's PACo

PACo ⌘218

Designed primarily to compress animation and sound files for playback on the Mac, PACo also has several add-on utilities that allow you to play back animation files, sound files, and QuickTime movies under Windows and the Sun SPARCStation. The Windows Player costs $199 and requires a Super VGA's 256 colors to play back animations and movies. You also can buy XPlayPACo for $199, which lets you play back PACo animations and movies from within HyperCard, SuperCard, and AuthorWare on the PC.

Other Cross-Platform Applications

AuthorWare ⌘214

In the past year, several important sibling applications have made their appearance. Adobe now offers a Windows version of Photoshop (Figure 12.3), and Aldus' PhotoStyler also has a Windows implementation. MacroMedia's Action, a popular multimedia presentation program, now has both Mac and Windows versions. For 3-D animators, Macromedia has also released a Windows version of its high-end modeler, MacroModel.

A few other programs offer cross-platform compatibility, but are not, strictly speaking, multimedia applications. AuthorWare Professional is a high-end authoring tool frequently used for building interactive training applications. It's expensive ($7995 for each platform), but it converts files very well, retaining most elements, with the exception of some fonts and external commands (see Chapter 9, "Authoring Tools," for more details).

Spinaker's Plus, modeled after HyperCard, also has good cross-platform compatibility. If your presentations are limited to basic multimedia effects such as simple animation, graphics, and sound, Plus is a good buy at $495 per platform. Plus supports 256 colors in its Mac version, but only 16 colors in the Windows implementation. Another way to get your Mac HyperCard stacks over to the PC is to use Convert It! from Heizer Software. This $199 package converts HyperCard stacks to a form usable by Asymmetrix Toolbook, a popular PC authoring tool.

13

Producing Sound

Sound should be an integral part of your multimedia project. It may be central to the project's focus, or it can be used to simply add polish to the presentation, fill disc access periods, or enhance navigation. This chapter introduces you to basic principles of sound and the recording process, followed by a discussion of special recording considerations for narration and electronic sound sources. It also examines the various file formats and considerations for importing and storing sounds, synchronization during the dubbing process, and its use with three popular multimedia production tools: Director, Premiere, and QuickTime. The chapter closes with a number of tips and tricks for digital audio, MIDI, and multimedia sound in general.

Audio Overview

Just from browsing through this book, you're probably starting to get a good grip on the science and technology behind multimedia's visual elements, whether they be still images, animation, or video. Now it's time to dive into sound. If you are going to produce sound for multimedia, you'll benefit by understanding some of the finer points of sound's quantifiable characteristics: frequency, amplitude, envelope, phase, and harmonic content. Some of this may seem technical at first, but will serve you well when you're using the incredibly precise controls afforded by digital sound tools.

Frequency

Sound consists of waves just as color and light do. One difference is that sound waves or sound-pressure waves are transmitted (propagated) through the air through periodic compression and rarefaction of air molecules by a vibrating body such as the string of a musical instrument, a loudspeaker, or your vocal chords. Further, compared to the blindingly fast pace of light waves, (186,300 miles per second), sound waves travel at the snail's pace of between 1088 and 1130 feet per second, depending upon temperature and altitude.

The term *frequency* refers to the pitch of a sound by relating it to the number of wave cycles (called periods) that occur in a second (see Figure 13.1). The number of cycles per second in this context is measured in *Hertz.* When a string is vibrating at 262 cycles per second (262Hz) we call that pitch "middle C." All multiples of this frequency are also referred to as "C"; we perceive them to be higher or lower variants of the same pitch. Therefore, 131Hz is the C below middle C (referred as being an octave below middle C), 524Hz is an octave above middle C, 1048Hz is the pitch two octaves above middle C. Most children have a hearing range of 20Hz to 20,000 Hz. Adults gradually lose the higher end of the spectrum down to 15,000Hz (15 kHz).

In the previous example, notice that the progression of frequencies is exponential. That is, the interval between 131Hz and 262Hz (an octave) covers 131Hz, but the distance between the C above middle C and the C two octaves above middle C covers 524Hz, although we perceive these distances to be equivalent (see Figure 13.2). Another unit of measurement, the cent, divides an octave into 1200 equal parts regardless of the difference in frequencies between the two pitches making up the octave.

Amplitude

The second important characteristic of sound is its *amplitude* (see Figure 13.3). This refers to the perceived loudness. You have experience adjusting this

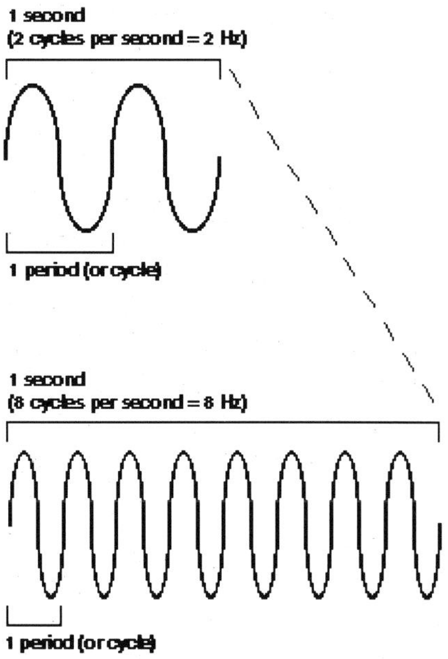

Figure 13.1 Sound Frequency. The number of cycles of a waveform determines the frequency of a sound expressed in Hertz. A single period consists of one complete positive (compression) and negative (rarefaction) cycle of the waveform.

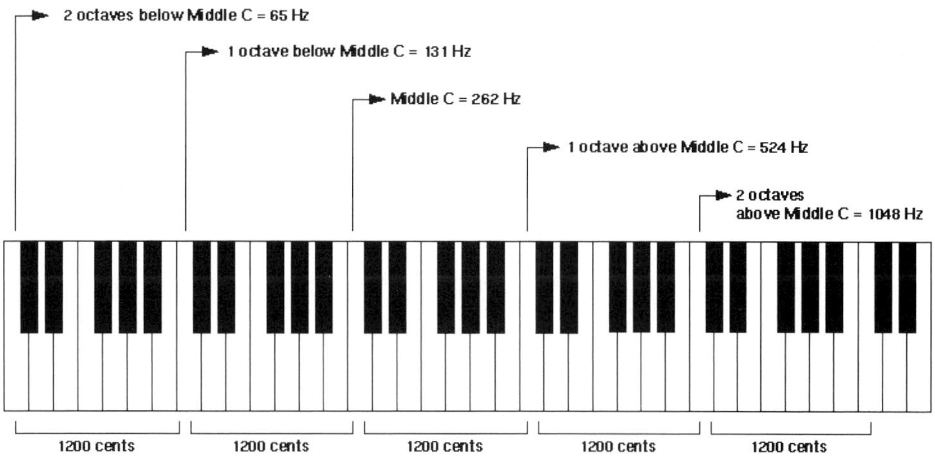

Figure 13.2 Octave Equivalence. Doubling the frequency of a sound, that is, increasing the number of cycles per second by a factor of two, raises the perceived pitch by one octave. There are 1200 Cents per octave.

characteristic using a knob on your stereo system. Amplitude is really much more complex than your stereo volume control makes it seem. The term designates the amount of pressure exerted by a single instance of a sound wave when compared to normal atmospheric pressure. Such pressure indicates a displacement of air molecules within a range of .00001 to .001 of an inch and is measured in units called *decibels* (dB). As a point of reference, the threshold of human hearing is assigned 0 dB. Audience noise is generally around 40 dB, while a jet engine exceeds 150 dB. Most conversation falls between 30 and 60 dB. A classical music performance rarely sustains levels greater than 95 dB, while rock music concerts can reach 115 and 120 dB for the people sitting in the front row. One hundred twenty dB is considered the threshold of pain.

Because the decibel scale is logarithmic, the amplitude of a 20 dB sound is 10 times that of a 10 dB sound and the amplitude of a 30 dB sound is 100 times that of a 10 dB sound. However, perceptually we experience every 10 dB increase in sound

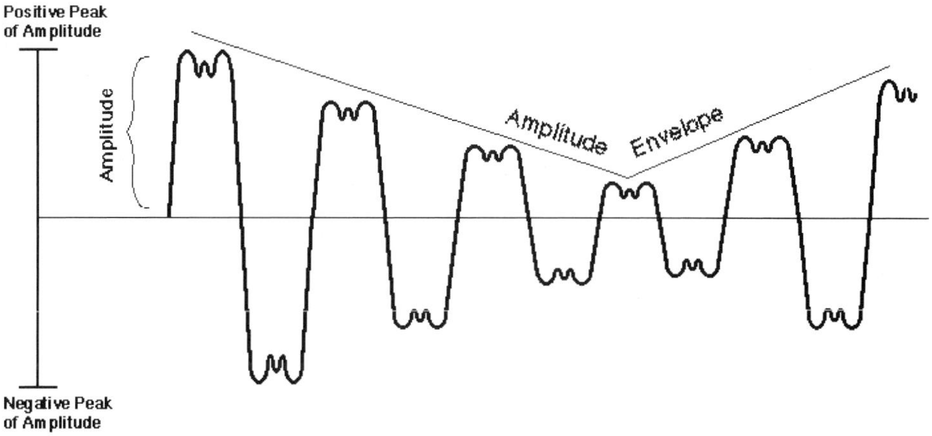

Figure 13.3 Sound Amplitude. Amplitude refers to the perceived loudness of a soundwave typically measured in decibels. The visual shape described by changes in volume is called the amplitude envelope. Notice that frequency is independent of amplitude.

amplitude as a doubling of volume. Incidentally, doubling the number of sound sources—for example, using two trumpets instead of one—only increases volume by 3 dB. Furthermore, as you move away from a sound source, the perceived volume drops 6 dB every time you double your distance from the source.

Envelope

More often than not, a sound's amplitude changes over time. About the first third of a second is referred to as the sound's attack. At this point there is an initial rise in volume, often to the maximum level of the sound in question. Following this there is sometimes a slight drop or decay in the sound's volume and then perhaps a lengthy sustained volume level followed by a rapid or not so rapid dying away of the sound. The four segments of this simplified model—attack, decay, sustain, and release (or ADSR)—represent the *envelope* of the sound. Note that complex sounds undergo many other changes of amplitude as the volume levels of their component frequencies transform over time. The attack segment is one of the primary characteristics of a sound that provides audible "clues" to aid us in distinguishing, for example, a trumpet from a flute. (Another important signature to a sound is its harmonic content, discussed below.)

Phase

Phase is an important sound phenomenon that happens when two identical sound waves are received by a listener or microphone at slightly different times (see Figure 13.4). Obvious causes of this are listening to two loudspeakers while being closer to one than the other. Another normal occurrence of phase takes place when a sound wave bounces off a reflective surface and arrives at your ear or microphone slightly later than the nonreflected sound wave. Phase is measured in degrees from 0 to 360. Remember that each cycle (or period) of a sound wave has a compression and rarefaction stage. In its simplest form, this can be represented as a *sine wave*. The beginning of the cycle is 0 degrees; the peak of the compression side (the positive side) is 90 degrees; 180 degrees is the point at which the sound crosses the zero point between compression and rarefaction; 270 degrees is the peak of the rarefaction stage; and finally, 360 degrees is the point at which the rarefaction stage returns to equilibrium at the end of the cycle. When a reflected copy of a sound wave begins just as the compression stage of the original sound is peaking, the sound waves are said to be *90 degrees out of phase*. When sound waves are 180 degrees out of phase they cancel each other out and silence is perceived. Many interesting special effects rely upon shifting the phase of a sound with respect to a copy of itself.

Harmonies

Sound waves are usually much more complex than simple sine waves. In reality, most sound waves can be demonstrated to be the product of many, many sine waves occurring simultaneously (the principle behind additive synthesis). When sound waves such as sine waves are combined, other frequencies are present in the resulting sound. These are called *partials*, *overtones*, or *harmonics* of that

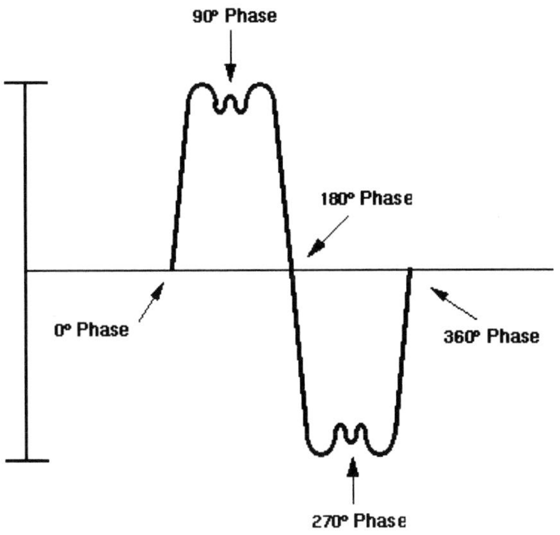
90° Phase
180° Phase
0° Phase
360° Phase
270° Phase

Figure 13.4 Soundwave Phase. Phase comes into play when a reflected or otherwise duplicated version of the same soundwave arrives at your ear slightly later than the original waveform. If the two sounds arrive 180 degrees out apart, the waveforms "cancel each other out and silence ensues.

sound (see Figure 13.5). The component sound wave with the lowest frequency is referred to as the *fundamental* frequency because this is the wave that determines the perceived pitch of the sound. The relative amplitudes of the upper partials making up a complex sound wave taken together determine the "timbre" of a sound and provide our ears with information that lets us distinguish one instrument from another when all other characteristics (frequency, amplitude, phase, etc.) are identical.

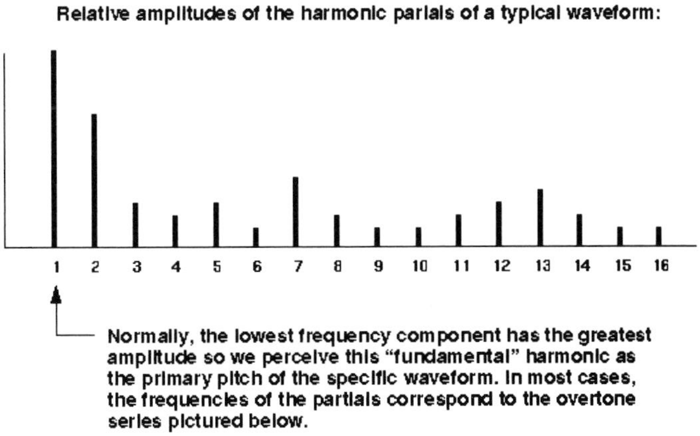
Relative amplitudes of the harmonic parials of a typical waveform:
1 2 3 4 5 6 7 8 9 10 11 12 13 14 15 16
Normally, the lowest frequency component has the greatest amplitude so we perceive this "fundamental" harmonic as the primary pitch of the specific waveform. In most cases, the frequencies of the partials correspond to the overtone series pictured below.

The overtone, or harmonic, series:
1 2 3 4 5 6 7 8 9 10 11 12 13 14 15 16

Figure 13.5 Harmonic Content. With the exception of pure sine waves or similar wave shapes, all sounds contain additional frequency components of lower amplitude. This phenomena is referred to as harmonic content and helps determine the timbre of a sound. The loudest—normally the lowest—frequency partial making up a sound determines the perceived pitch.

Recording Sound

During the sound recording process we often speak of the "sound recording chain." The links in this chain include microphones, mixers, signal processors, analog or digital recording systems, amplifiers, and speakers. Like any chain, it is only as strong as its weakest link. Using $20 microphones with a $2000 tape recorder is not going to sound any better than using $2000 microphones with a $20 tape recorder. However, using $2000 microphones with a $2000 tape recorder will make a difference. Unfortunately, multimedia producers typically have little or no control over the final link in the chain: the speakers used to play back the sound elements accompanying their endeavors. Because of this fact, it is important to provide audio of the highest quality possible.

Using Microphones

Microphones record sound by converting sound waves into electrical impulses as they strike a stationary transducer such as a thin sheet of conductive metal called a *diaphragm.* Although their outward appearance may be similar or identical, microphones exhibit different degrees of directionality. *Omnidirectional* microphones respond equally to sound arriving from any direction. *Bidirectional* microphones pick up sound in a "figure eight" pattern, with a dead spot in the center of the eight. There are three main types of *unidirectional* microphones available, all relying on a variation of a heart shaped (cardioid) pattern of sensitivity. *Cardioid, supercardioid,* and *hypercardioid* microphones provide progressively more focused response fields.

A microphone may be directly routed to your recording system; however, a mixer is essential when recording multiple sound sources. Mixers let you control the proportions of a large variety of sound sources by moving knobs or faders while monitoring the incoming and outgoing signal through VU meters or LED bars, most of which provide some indication, such as a red area, of when the signal is too "hot" and thus prone to distortion. Some mixers offer *equalization* (EQ), the capability of boosting or cutting various frequency bands (like the treble and bass controls on your home stereo); access to signal processing (effects such as reverberation, chorusing, flanging, compression, expansion, and limiting); and options to pan a signal in various degrees to the left or right channel of the stereo output to which the incoming audio is being mixed.

Special Recording Considerations

The nature of your source material—music, sound effects, or narration—may mandate a particular approach to the recording process. When recording live material, microphone placement becomes an issue. When recording from electronic sources, signal processing (often to simulate microphone placement) is a factor.

Miking Strategies

With a live sound source you must consider the type and proximity of the microphones as well as their directional placement. *Close miking* places the microphone less than a meter from the sound source. *Distant miking* employs microphones further than a meter from the sound source. When you are recording with distant miking, it may be advantageous to use an "accent" microphone placed in or near the close miking field to highlight one particular instrument or sound source. Likewise, when using predominantly close miking, it may be advantageous to add an "ambient" microphone at a distance where the room ambiance or reflected sound is stronger than the primary source.

Spaced Miking

Four popular techniques to stereo miking are spaced miking, X-Y miking, M-S (mid-side), and binaural miking. The *spaced miking* approach relies on the 3:1 principle which dictates that the distance between the two microphones should be at least three times the distance between the microphone and the source. For example, if the microphones are 10 feet from the sound source, they should be at least 30 feet apart. The rationale revolves around considerations of phase distortion. Obviously, this method is best suited for closer miking situations.

X-Y Miking

The *X-Y miking* approach employs two identical microphones (usually directional or cardioid) in the center of the stereo field, with their diaphragms as close together as possible at right angles to one another with the tip of the right angle pointed toward the sound source. Larger angles may be used to widen the perceived width of the stereo image.

M-S Miking

M-S miking (mid-side method) uses a "mid" cardioid microphone aimed directly at the sound source and a microphone with a "side" figure-eight response pattern directed 90 degrees from the mid microphone. M-S miking requires an additional hardware matrix system to assemble the stereo image from the two signals.

Binaural Miking

Finally, *binaural miking* is optimized for headphone playback. Two omnidirectional microphones are mounted in the ears of a dummy head (alternatively, you can place them about 6 inches apart with a baffle between). This miking method should not be used for material intended to be played back through loudspeakers.

Recording Spoken Words

You should take special care in recording narration or any spoken material included in your multimedia project. Try to record vocal material with a directional (cardioid) microphone placed 1 inch to 2 feet from the speaker, after experimenting to determine the optimum distance. Positioning a cardioid microphone too close to the speaker can increase the low frequency content, which may or may not be the effect you want.

Certain consonants can cause undesirable pops and noise during vocal recording. The letters "p," "t," and "k" are notorious in this respect. "Pop filters"

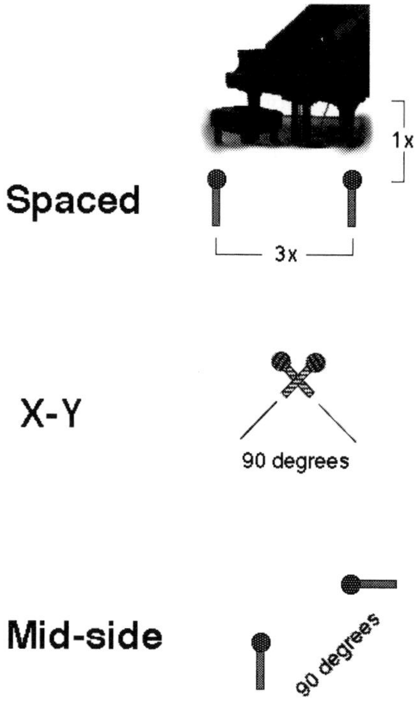

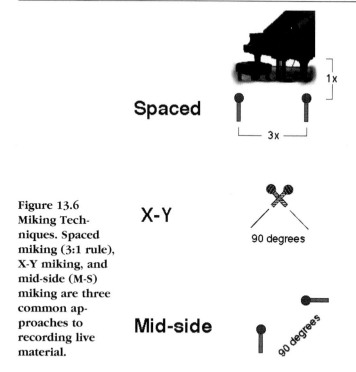

Figure 13.6 Miking Techniques. Spaced miking (3:1 rule), X-Y miking, and mid-side (M-S) miking are three common approaches to recording live material.

or foam wind screens affixed to the microphone can reduce these annoyances, albeit with the possibility of reducing high frequency response as well. The sibilants "s" and "sh" can introduce unwanted hiss into a recording. A special signal processor called a de-esser is one solution to this problem. Another solution for both popping and hissing is to angle the microphone so that the voice is passing across the response field rather than directly into the diaphragm.

Ambient Noise

When recording speech, keep aware of ambient noise. If some segments are recorded with ambiance while others are not, the effect is irritating. It's a good idea to record a few minutes of pure room ambiance as a precaution—if necessary you can mix this in with the voice to achieve an even effect.

Uneven recording levels can produce an effect on listeners similiar to unnatural handling of ambient noise. Apart from coaching your speaker in vocalization techniques, you can get around recording level disparities by using a signal processor called a compressor/limiter. Such devices, when used in their compressor mode, even out the dynamic levels to fall within a specifiable range. Sounds that are too soft have their volume levels boosted, while those that are too loud get softened. You will probably experience better results if you apply compression during the initial recording, although there is no reason not to do so during mixdown.

Direct Instrumental Recording

Electronic instruments such as synthesizers, samplers, sound modules, and electric guitars may be recorded "direct" without the use of a microphone. The primary concern is matching the device output levels with the mixer input levels. Many sound modules and signal processors are switchable from balanced or unbalanced +4 dB (1.23 volts) to unbalanced -10 dB (3.16 volts), but for those that are not, you may need to invest in a piece of hardware known as a direct box or direct insert box (DI box) to make the conversion.

The Mixing Process

When multitrack recording systems of any kind enter the picture, some method to mix the various tracks down to a single stereo or monophonic signal is required. When the source material is multitrack tape, the mixdown medium might be DAT, hard disk, or even analog tape (see Chapter 6, "Sound Tools"). During the mixdown stage, additional EQ, signal processing, and other effects can be introduced into the signal. For multimedia production, all sound will eventually have to be in a disc-based digital audio format, so keep this in mind when considering mixdown methods.

Ping-ponging

Often it is possible to mix a collection of tracks in any system down to two free stereo tracks on the same system, rendering the need for a separate mixdown system superfluous. This technique, called track bouncing or "ping-ponging," needn't be limited to the mixdown stage—it can also be used at intermediate points in the production process to reclaim tracks for new material. One important advantage that digital systems have over analog in this area is that whenever an analog track is copied to another analog track, about 10 dB of signal degradation is introduced into the audio. (This is called "generation loss" because each subsequent copy is referred to as a new generation of the original material. By the third generation the corruption will become audible for an average listener.) Analog track bouncing is subject to this progressive degeneration, whereas digital track bouncing results in no signal loss or additional noise.

Creating Special Effects

Signal processing, often called *effects*, refers to the ability to route from a mixer or synthesizer, via a jack labeled "effects send" or "aux send," a controllable amount of the incoming signal to an external device for modification. The transformed signal is then sent back to the mixer, via a jack labeled "effects return" or "aux return." A knob on the mixer usually provides control over the proportion of the original signal that is mixed in with the returning processed signal. Typical signal-processing effects include *reverberation* to simulate multiple reflections of a sound wave from one surface to another; *digital delay* to create echo effects that repeat a replica of the sound at varying intervals; *chorusing*, where an original signal is combined with delayed copies and the delay time is varied randomly or periodically to simulate multiple sound sources; *phase shifting* to produce a variety of special effects that depend upon the amount of phase between two copies of a waveform; *flanging*, by combining a signal with minute fluctuating pitch with an otherwise identical, nonfluctuating signal; *pitch-shifting* to alter the pitch of a sound without changing its duration; *compression* to decrease the width of the dynamic range of a signal (the distance between the softest and loudest levels); *expansion*, the opposite of compression; *limiting*, reduce the peak volume; *gating*, to pass through only those signals that are above a specified strength; and *spatialization*, to create 3-D effects or otherwise place a sound at a designated location.

Importing and Storing Sounds for Multimedia

SoundEdit Pro ⌘ 201

All audio for multimedia must be in a digital format. If you have recorded all your source material using a 16-bit hard disk recording system such as Digidesign's SoundTools, ProTools, or Audiomedia, Mark of the Unicorn's Digital Waveboard, or MediaVision's PAS16 (Pro Audio Spectrum 16—the 16 stands for 16-bit), or 8-bit systems such as Articulate Systems' Voice Impact or Voice Impact Pro, Macromedia's MacRecorder (bundled with SoundEdit Pro), or the built-in hardware of the Macintosh, you are well ahead of the game. If your source material is on analog tape, you have another recording stage to go through. If the material is on digital tape and you have a sound card supporting digital I/O such as those from Digidesign, you will probably be able to transfer the digital audio data without reentering the analog domain.

Play AIFF ⌘ 100

Snd Converter Pro ⌘ 101

Snd Player ⌘ 103

Snd Catalog ⌘ 104

The question arises as to what format to use for storing audio data in on your hard disk. You will recall from Chapter 6 "Sound Tools" that a wide variety of soundfile formats are available. Common formats include 8- and 16-bit AIFF and AIFC (compressed form of AIFF), 'snd ' resource, System 7 sound (type sfil—note the lowercase), SoundEdit (type FSSD), and SoundEdit Pro (type 'jB1 '), and Sound Designer (I and II, type SFIL—note the uppercase). Of these, AIFF is the most universal, followed closely by 'snd ' and System 7 sound. The latter have the advantage of being playable by double-clicking in the Finder, a good way to preview or audition sounds.

Dubbing and Synchronization

Synchronizing audio to visuals is not as simple as making sure that both elements start playing back simultaneously. Inevitably, they will drift apart. The film industry has taught us that even a two-frame difference between a visual event and its corresponding audio event in a video running at 30 fps will be perceived by the audience as being out of sync. With popular QuickTime frame rates hovering around 15 fps, this means that you cannot risk being more than a single frame off at critical synchronization points (often referred to as hit points, dead hits, or simply "hits").

When two or more elements—for example, a QuickTime movie and incoming audio data—are synchronized, the software or device controlling one element provides the master clock reference to which the other "slave" components are related. There are three common methods of synchronization: pulse- or clock-oriented, relative addressing, and absolute addressing (sometimes referred to as time code). Multimedia software generally supports the latter two approaches if any .

Relative addressing requires that synchronized programs keep track of the current location as an offset in standardized units relative to the beginning of the music or visuals. The most common form of relative synchronization originated in the world of MIDI and is called Song Position Pointer (SPP). During SPP synchronization all synchronized software tracks the number of sixteenth notes from the beginning of the video, animation, or music. This allows you to issue commands such as "advance to the 1597th sixteenth note." Software with this feature does not require you to count sixteenth notes; rather, conversions are built into the interface.

SMPTE Time Code

Absolute addressing is a more accurate method for synchronization in which every event has unique address. As we discussed in the video chapters, the film and video industry uses a protocol known as SMPTE time code (SMPTE stands for the Society of Motion Picture and Television Engineers). SMPTE time code provides an absolute address in hours, minutes, seconds, and frames for video. It is also used for audio data and to relate audio data to video data.

SMPTE time code addresses are called time code words. While in computer lingo a "word" is two bytes (16 bits), SMPTE time code words are 80 bits in length. You can think of this as 10 bytes; however, it is more accurate to consider these 80 bits as sixteen 4-bit "nibbles" followed by a 16-bit sync word. Each nibble can designate a number from 0 to 9. The SMPTE address "02:34:21:08," for example, means 2 hours, 34 minutes, 21 seconds, and 8 frames.

The fact that there are a number of different frame rates to which SMPTE time code is applied can be problematic in some situations. In the United States, video is standardized at 30 fps, although since the introduction of color, tape actually travels at 29.97 fps (more precisely, 29.97002617 fps). European videotape travels at 25 fps, and standard 35 mm film uses 24 fps.

Drop Frame Time Code

Because SMPTE assigns 30 addresses to a space in which only 29.97 frames pass, a system called "drop frame" time code emerged to correct for the extra 108 frame numbers per hour that result (if a 108-frame discrepancy per hour doesn't seem significant, remember that only two frames are necessary to perceive elements as being out of sync). Drop frame time code works like this: every time the "minutes" value of the time code address increments by 1, the first two frames

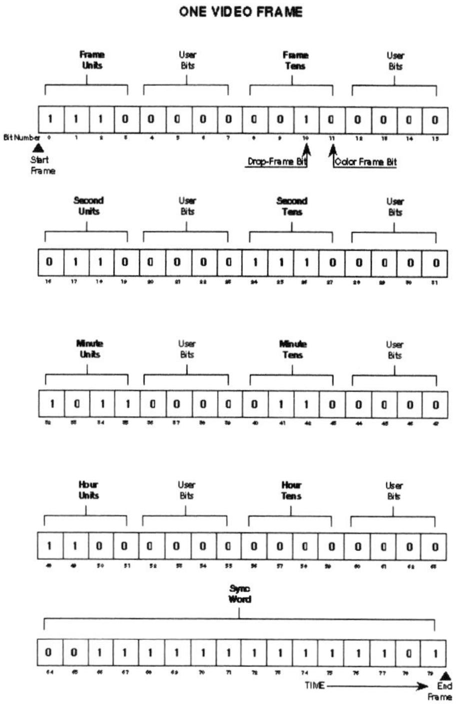

Figure 13.7
A SMPTE Word. Each SMPTE address requires 80 bits of data to express the digits representing a unique location expressed in hours, minutes, seconds, and frames.

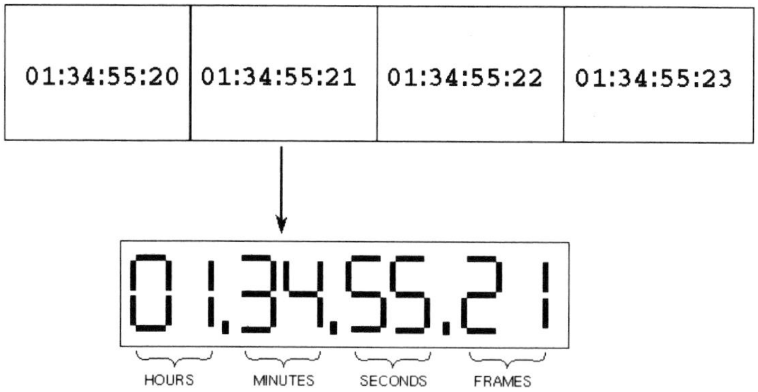

Figure 13.8
SMPTE Frame Rates. A table of the six most common SMPTE frame rates appear below a typical SMPTE display.

24 fps	Film
25 fps	European (PAL) video
30 fps non-drop	American black and white video (also used for audio applications)
30 fps drop-frame	American color video (will not agree with wall clock)
29.97 fps non-drop	American color video (NTSC — will not agree with wall clock)
29.97 fps drop-frame	American color video (NTSC and broadcast)

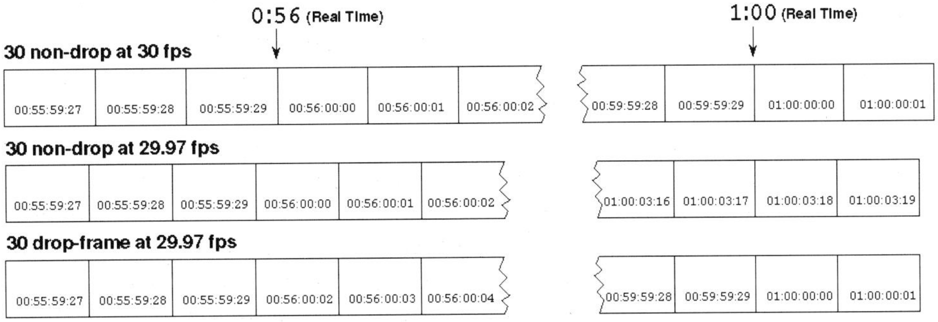

Figure 13.9 Drop Frame. Drop-frame SMPTE drops the first two frame numbers (not actual frames) after each minute passes (except at minutes 00, 10, 20, 30, 40, and 50) to ensure that video tape traveling at 29.97 fps agrees with the actual elapsed time,

of the next minute are dropped. In other words, the frame after 02:34:21:29 is 02:34:21:02, and not, as you might expect, 02:34:21:00. Dropping two frames every minute results in a loss of 120 frames every hour, so to reclaim 12 dropped frames, the two frames are not dropped at minutes 00, 10, 20, 30, 40, and 50, resulting in a total of 108 dropped frames per hour and thus guaranteeing that the frame count and the clock on the wall will always be in agreement. Note that the dropping of frames in drop frame time code only skips address numbers; no actual frames are omitted.

SMPTE time code is not directly compatible with MIDI, so when external MIDI devices or background MIDI software processes are in the synchronization loop, SMPTE time code gets converted to MIDI time code (MTC), a related protocol that was standardized in early 1987. The conversion is transparent to the user because all MTC compatible software expresses addresses in standard SMPTE formats.

At the time of this writing, all software offering SMPTE-to-MIDI synchronization relies upon Apple's MIDI Manager for timing support. MIDI Manager (discussed in Chapter 6, "Sound Tools") performs all the required conversions between the various MTC synchronization formats from 30 fps non-drop, 30 fps drop frame, 25 fps, and 24 fps to the format required by the software being synchronized.

(For more perspectives on synching sound and video, see Chapter 17, "Creating Video.")

Using Sounds With Applications

The sound capabilities of multimedia software are as varied as the interfaces to access these audio features. Compared to graphics software, where certain standardized interface conventions are observed, sound manipulation in multimedia is a regular turkey shoot. Examining three software options in detail—Macromedia Director, Adobe Premiere, and Apple's QuickTime—will clarify this state of affairs. For the most robust implementation of digital audio, MIDI, and synchronization in multimedia to date, check out the discussion of Passport Producer in Chapter 6 "Sound Tools."

TOOLS
Passport Producer ⌘216

Sound in Director

Stretching back to earlier incarnations as VideoWorks, Macromedia Director has a long history of audio support. One result of this extensive background is support of practically any soundfile format currently in use. Furthermore, the program provides access to CD audio, digital audio NuBus cards, and speech synthesis.

TOOLS Director ⌘210

Smaller sounds can be stored as a member of Director's "cast". Likewise, sound stored as sound only QuickTime movies can be designated as cast members. The disadvantage to this approach is that your file size increases accordingly, so it's usually a better approach to place longer sounds in Director's external "Sounds" file so they are loaded when required.

The enhancement to Director's Lingo scripting language that allows you to jump to a specified frame in a QuickTime movie essentially provides you with random access to soundfiles stored as sound-only movies.

Sound Syntax for Lingo

A more sophisticated use of Lingo for sound that often goes unnoticed allows you to open up an additional six channels of the Sound Manager and designate them for playback of different soundfiles. Such soundfiles must be accessed by way of the Sound play File and puppetSound commands. (The former requires only one line of scripting and bypasses PuppetSound, making it a simple solution for novice Lingo users.) For sounds controlled by Lingo you have the added advantage of executing controlled fades (both in and out) on an individual channel basis for durations specified in ticks (1/60ths of a second). Finally, Lingo offers you the full range of 256 volume levels for your puppetSounds.

puppetSound (Command) Causes the Sound channel to act as a puppet so that it can be controlled by Lingo (under script control). It is not necessary to place anything in the Sound channels of the score. In fact, puppetSounds override sounds that may simultaneously exist in the score's Sound channel. They continue to play even if you load another movie. At the time of this writing, the puppetSound command does not work with the second sound channel (i.e., the lower of the Score's sound channels).

puppetSound *castmemberName* Starts playing a sound stored in the Cast. Note: To use AIFF soundfiles as castmembers, you need System 6.0.7 or later.

puppetSound *menuItemNumber*, *subMenuItemNumber* Starts playing a sound stored in an external Director Sounds file. Specify the menu item number (if it is a letter, use A=10, B=11, C=12, D=13, E=14, F=15) and the submenu item number.

puppetSound 0 Turns off continuous sound and returns control of sound to the score's Sound channel.

puppetSound *midiOption* (see below under "MIDI in Director")

soundEnabled

set the soundEnabled = *expression* (Property) Turns sound on or off. Example:set the soundEnabled = not (the soundEnabled) Toggles the sound on or off depending on the previous state.

put the soundEnabled into *variableName* Returns TRUE if sound is enabled.

sound fadeIn (requires System 6.0.7 or later)

sound fadeIn *whichChannel [1 to 8]* Fades in sound on the specified channel for a period of frames, unless ticks (see next) are specified. If ticks are not specified, the default setting is 15*(60/(Tempo setting of first frame of fade in)).

sound fadeIn *whichChannel, ticks* Fades in sound on the specified channel for the specified number of ticks (1/60ths of second).

sound fadeOut (requires System 6.0.7 or later)

sound fadeOut *whichChannel [1 to 8]* Fades out sound on the specified channel for a period of frames, unless ticks (see next) are specified. If ticks are not specified, the default setting is 15*(60/(Tempo setting of first frame of fade out)).

sound fadeOut *whichChannel, ticks* Fades out sound on the specified channel for the specified number of ticks (1/60ths of second).

sound playFile (requires System 6.0.7 or later)

sound playFile *whichChannel [1 to 8], whichFile [name of file in quotes]* Starts playback on the channel indicated by *whichChannel* of an external AIFF sound stored in *whichFile.*

sound stop (requires System 6.0.7 or later)

sound stop *whichChannel [1 to 8]* Stops sound playback on the specified channel.

soundBusy (requires System 6.0.7 or later)

soundBusy(*whichChannel*) (Function) Returns TRUE (1) if the specified channel is currently playing a sound or FALSE (0) if it isn't. If you use soundBusy() to determine the status of a puppetSound, you must place an updateStage command between the puppetSound command and the soundBusy() function. Example: if soundBusy(1) then sound stop 1

the soundLevel

set the soundLevel to 7 (Property). Sets the level of sound playing through the Macintosh speaker or external audio jack. 0 = no sound, 7 = maximum volume.

put the soundLevel into *variableName* Puts the current sound level setting (0 to 7) into the specified variable.

the volume of sound (requires System 6.0.7 or later)

set the volume of sound *whichChannel[1 to 8] to level [0 to 255]* Sets the volume of the sound on the specified channel (Channels 1 and 2 are the Score sound channels) to a level between 0 and 255.

put the volume of sound *whichChannel[1 to 8]* into *variableName* Puts the volume of the sound on the specified channel (Channels 1 and 2 are the Score sound channels) into the specified variable.

the multiSound

put the multiSound into *variableName* (Function) Returns TRUE (1) if the current System software is capable of multi-channel sound playback or FALSE (0) if it isn't.

noSound

playAccel *whichFile,* noSound Used in conjunction with the PlayAccel command to play back an accelerated movie without any sound that may be associated with it.

MIDI in Director

Director's rudimentary MIDI implementation supports the standard SPP synchronization messages: Start, Stop, Continue, Beat (MIDI Clocks) , Song Select, Song Position Pointer. These commands let you trigger songs, and start, stop, and continue playback at any measure in external MIDI sequencers (for example, a Roland Sound Brush), or MIDI sequencer software running in the background, or both at once. Chapter 6, "Sound Tools," provides information for enhancing Director's and other multimedia software's MIDI capabilities through the addition of external resources known as XCMDs.

The following Lingo messages provide relative synchronization of MIDI sequences with Director:

puppetSound midiStart Sends a MIDI Start message to the attached MIDI Manager port. Sets the SPP to zero and starts playback at the beginning of the sequence.

puppetSound midiStop Sends a MIDI Stop message to the attached MIDI Manager port. Halts playback without resetting the SPP. All SPP counters retain the current value.

puppetSound midiContinue Sends a MIDI Continue message to the attached MIDI Manager port. Resumes playback at the current SPP location, often equivalent to the location stored when the last Stop message was issued. SPP counters resume their count from the current location.

puppetSound midiBeat, *[4 to 280]* Sets the tempo of the sequence being controlled by midiStart, midiStop, and midiContinue. Serves as the "pulse" or metronome: 24 PPQN (pulses per quarter note).

puppetSound midiSong, *[0 to 127]* Sends a MIDI Song Select message to the attached MIDI Manager port. Instructs sequencers (both hardware and software) that provide for multiple "songs" which song to cue up to be played at the next issuance of a Start message. (Message can only be sent when sequences are not playing.)

puppetSound midisongPointer, *beat[1 to 4], measure[1 to 1023]* Sends a MIDI Song Position Pointer (SPP) message to the attached MIDI Manager port. Sends a location (or address) of a beat measured in 16th notes (a 16th note is equal to six MIDI Clocks) from the beginning of the sequence. The software in your Macintosh or in a hardware sequencer keeps track of this number whenever you start playback of a sequence while using this method of synchronization. The maximum sequence length supported by SPP is 45 minutes.

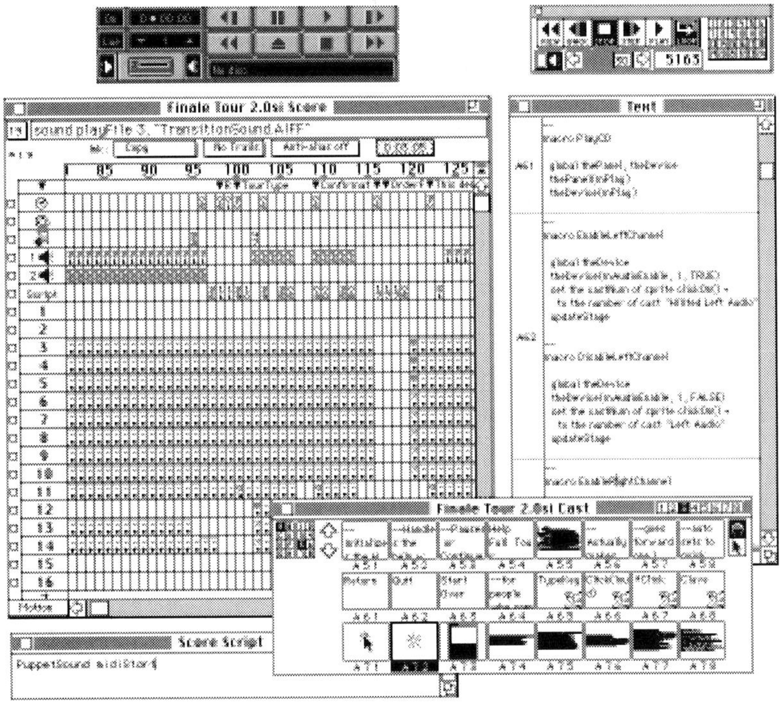

Figure 13.10 Sound in Director. Macromedia Director offers a flexible sound environment supporting many soundfile formats (both stored as "cast members" and external to the document) as well as CD audio, digital audio NuBus cars, speech synthesis, and MIDI.

Sound in Premiere

TOOLS

Premiere ⌘ 240

Adobe Premiere 2.0 supports up to three 8- or 16-bit, mono or stereo audio tracks at sampling rates of 5, 11, 22, or 44.1 kHz. Compatible file formats include AIFF, 'snd ' resources, 'sfil' format soundfiles, and SoundEdit files (but not SoundEdit Pro files), and any sound data you may have imported into Premiere may be exported as 8-bit or 16-bit mono or stereo AIFF files. Sound tracks are displayed as an amplitude waveform or, optionally, a simple line (to reduce the time required to create a waveform display). For stereo soundfiles only one channel is visible in the display. One annoyance inherent in Premiere's sound handling is that because all tracks are considered to be the same length, adding, for example, a single sound effect on a track will have the same impact on file size as if the track contained continual audio data.

Linking Audio and Video Data

As is often the case in professional sound editing programs, cut, copy, and paste are nondestructive operations that simply move pointers to the specified locations in your audio data. The razor tool lets you make logical splits in soundfiles that have no impact upon the actual file but permit you to deal with soundfile regions as if they were separate entities. Premiere provides frame-accurate designation of in-and-out points to any soundfile. If you need to work independently on the sound track of a movie that contains visual material, perhaps to move it to another location or another set of visuals, you must first unlink it from its associated visual data (drag on the track with the Shift and Option keys pressed to accomplish this).

Only at the point when you choose "Make a Movie" from the menu does the audio data actually get copied into the new movie file, reflecting the cuts, copies, and order you defined in the construction window. At this stage, you will have the option to set the audio interleave factor (or chunk size—see below,"Sound in QuickTime") of the sound as a half, one, or two seconds, or one or five minutes. If you want your sound to be loaded into RAM prior to the start of movie playback, specify a chunk size that is longer than the total duration of the movie—of course, if your movie exceeds five minutes, you're stuck with an interleaved format.

Other Controls

Premiere's interface to the control of sound track volume is much easier than Director's. An Audio Fade control runs under the waveform display of each audio event. You can add handles (breakpoints) to this line with a simple mouse click and drag these to any position to create fades and complex amplitude scaling factors. Dragging the handle at the far left scales the volume for the entire audio event, and Shift-dragging between two break-points lets you manipulate the contour they define without affecting surrounding amplitude contours.

Premiere offers access to a multitude of video and graphics filters for special effects. There are also several audio filters accessible on the sound tracks assigned in just in the same way you assign them to the visual tracks (option-clicking). Included among these are "Backwards" to reverse a soundfile's playback (useful for special effects); "Boost" to execute an algorithm similar to expansion options found in compressor/limiters which increase the volume of soft sounds without altering louder sounds; "Echo" to add digital delay in .01 or .02 increments within a range of .01 to 2 seconds; and "Fill Right" and "Fill Left," which serve to pan the sound element completely to the right or left channels. Note that any of these effects may be used in combination and all are nondestructive—they are applied on the fly during playback—until you choose "Make a Movie" from the menu.

Although this procedure is not accessible from the filters menu, Premiere also lets you set the rate at which soundfiles are played back (using the Speed option under the Clip menu). The range is from 1 to 1000 percent. This simply increases or decreases the speed at which samples are output. Because this is not a sophisticated time compression/expansion algorithm such as you might find in Alchemy or Sound Designer (see Chapter 6, "Sound Tools"), changing the speed in this manner also changes the pitch of the sound (or the key of the music).

MIDI in Premiere

Premiere's built-in MIDI support is even more limited than Director's. Premiere includes only the basic Start, Stop, and Tempo options for MIDI synchronization, whereas Director adds Continue, Song Select, and Song Pointer messages to offer the complete set of SPP synchronization messages.

SMPTE time code stamping is an option in Premiere, although this is useless for MIDI purposes because there is no mechanism to convert the time code to MTC. Premiere's rudimentary SMPTE implementation is designed to be used

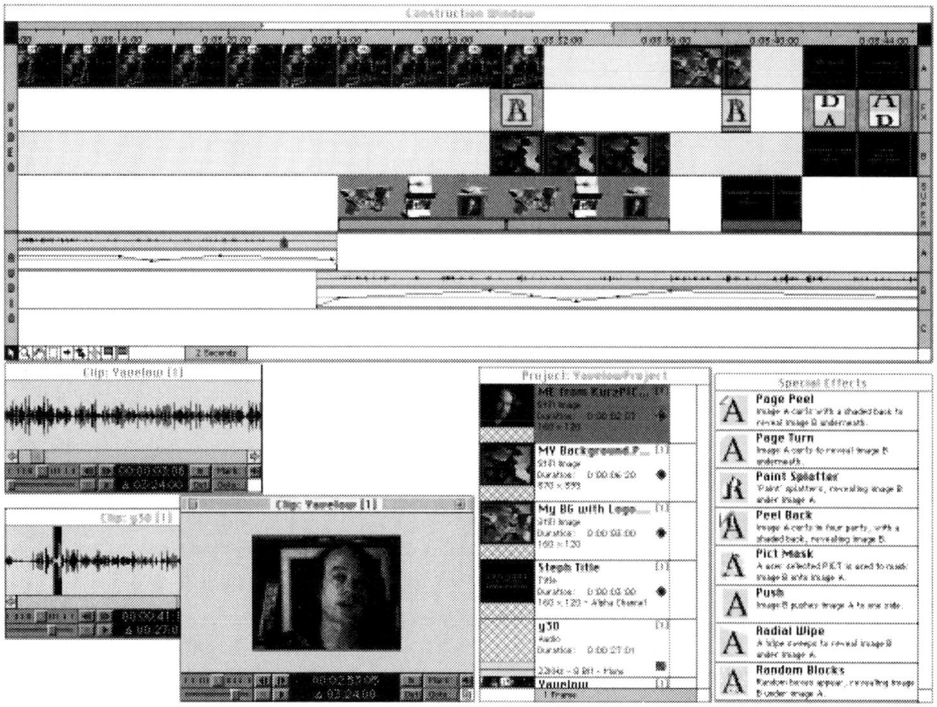

Figure 13.11 Sound in Premiere. Adobe's Premiere offers a functional yet limited set of editing features in a QuickTime editor. You can apply "elastic" amplitude envelopes to up to three sound tracks. Several sound "filters" (actually signal processing algorithms) may be applied to any segment of a sound track.

when you export Edit Decision Lists (EDLs) to CMX 3400 and 3600, Grass Valley, and Sony BVE video editing systems.

Sound in QuickTime

QuickTime's handling of sound tracks is interesting—the video will drop frames rather than glitch the sound track. As you learned in Chapter 6, "Sound Tools", sampling rate and resolution play a major role in determining the amount of storage required for Macintosh-based audio and therefore have a major impact on the file size of any QuickTime movie.

QuickTime ⌘160

QuickTime 1.5 supports AIFF, AIFF-C, sfil, and 'snd ' resources (QuickTime 1.6 adds ADPCM to this list of compatible file formats). Although the popular FSSD format created by SoundEdit, SoundCap, and SoundWave is conspicuously missing, QuickTime-compatible software such as Premiere can access SoundEdit files and convert them to QuickTime compatible formats.

QuickTime sound tracks support 8-bit and 16-bit sounds at sampling rates of up to 65,535 samples per second, although until Sound Manager 3.0 appears (see Chapter 6, "Sound Tools"), sound playback is strictly 8-bit, 22.254kHz (actually 22254.5454 samples per second). You may have an unlimited number of sound tracks, although with QuickTime 1.5 all your audio is mixed to 8-bit mono during playback.

At the present time, when QuickTime encounters a 16-bit 44.1kHz (CD-quality) sound in a movie, it automatically converts the data to 8-bit 22.25kHz. Because this occurs on the fly during playback, additional CPU time is required and your movie's effective frame rate is reduced accordingly. To effect the conversion of 16-bit, 44.1kHz sound, the Sound Manager discards the low byte of each sample, and every other sample as well.

Although QuickTime will play back MACE-compressed sounds (QuickTime 1.6 adds support of ADPCM compression through Sound Manager 3.0), it does not currently offer sound compression as an option during movie or sound capture. Using the more desirable uncompressed sound track can result in your audio data occupying a very large portion of your movie file—in some cases, the greater portion of the file. When QuickTime must decompress sound as well as video, there is an additional CPU load of approximately 20%.

Sound also has an impact on the data rate required for compressed video decompression. Because 8-bit 22kHz stereo requires pumping 44K/second through your system, you can expect a 44K/second increase in the overall movie data rate. Likewise, 8-bit 22 kHz mono and 8-bit 11kHz stereo sound both increase the data rate by 22K/second. QuickTime 1.5 exhibits an anomaly with 8-bit 11kHz mono sound which raises the data rate by 22K rather than 11K per second as you would expect.

Storing Audio Tracks in QuickTime

QuickTime offers two ways to store audio tracks in movie files. The first is having all the audio in one large chunk at the beginning of the movie (called "RAM-based" because all the sound is loaded into RAM before movie playback commences, freeing more of your CPU processing power to deal with the video to achieve better frame rates). The alternative is called "interleaved sound" and requires that the sound data stream off your disk continually along with the video data (see Figure 13.12). While the second approach is better for longer movies, where the entire sound track cannot fit into available RAM, this method does lower the maximum frame rate your video can attain due to the increased processing power required to continually fetch and schedule sound data from the disk.

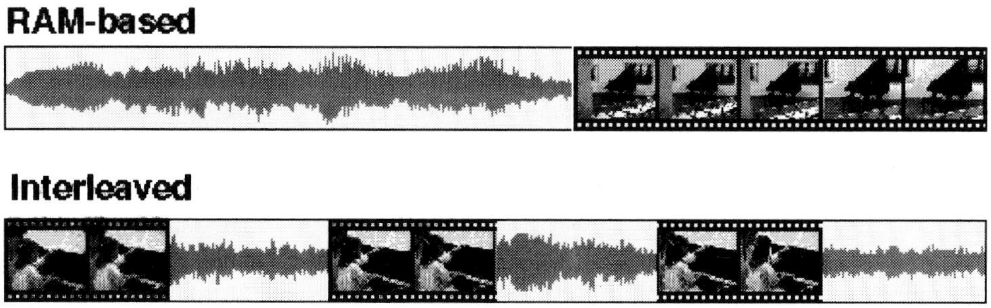

Figure 13.12 Interleaved Sound vs. RAM-Based Sound in QuickTime.

You can specify how often and in what size chunks QuickTime grabs interleaved sound data by setting the interleave factor (chunk size) with programs such as MovieShop and SoundToMovie, both found on the QuickTime Developers CD-ROM. SoundToMovie offers many other sound manipulation options that make your QuickTime activities easier. The program lets you create sound-only movies, add sound to existing movies, edit the chunk size, and convert 'snd ' resources to AIFF files. SoundToMovie also displays additional useful information about your soundfile such as the number of channels, number of samples, sample size, sample rate, compression settings, and current chunk size.

Copyright Issues and Challenges

The proliferation of sound in multimedia has created a rat's nest of problems and issues in the field of copyright and licensing. Simply stated, if you use someone else's music in a multimedia project without obtaining permission (in the form of a license), you are guilty of copyright infringement and liable for very large fines regarding which you will discover you have no legal recourse. The myth that you can use four bars or seven seconds of someone's music is simply that—a myth. You can be prosecuted for stealing much less.

The good news is that unless you are trying to license music for commercial use, meaning broadcast, resale, or theatrical display, licensing fees are relatively small—often much less than $200.

To avoid breaking the law, you can use anything composed before 1915, as it is in the public domain. Alternatively, you can use clip music, or algorithmically generated music (see Chapter 6, "Sound Tools," regarding both these options); or, better yet, hire a composer to write original music for your production.

It will serve you well to understand the Copyright code with respect to musical works. The relevant section is called Title 17 of the U.S. Code of the Copyright Act of 1976. Section 101 contains legal definitions of terms you need to understand throughout the rest of the code. For example, the term "phonorecord" refers to any medium upon which sounds may be stored, not just phonograph records. See Appendix C.

Context of Usage

Most publishers and copyright owners do want to have some say regarding the context of the usage and the possible attachment of secondary meaning to a song by, for example, changing the lyrics.

Steven Winogradsky, director of music business affairs for Hanna Barbera Productions (the folks who brought us "Yaba-Daba-Doo"), has had some interesting experiences along these lines with the Flintstones theme song. He recently denied a request to use the tune in a comedy show where the lyrics would be changed to "Flintsteins, meet the Flintsteins, the modern Jewish family." He also discovered an East coast "safe sex" campaign where the lyrics had been changed to "Condoms, use a condom . . ." and forced the infringers to pull it out of the campaign because "the *Flintstones* is basically a kids' show."

Winogradsky continues, "It all falls back on the rights of the copyright holder under the copyright law. Unauthorized use of copyrighted material is an infringement that is punishable by substantial fines. And along with that, each separate copy of a computer program that includes unauthorized copyrighted material is considered to be a separate infringement. So if the court decides that the infringement is worth $1000 and there are 500 copies of the program, the developer finds himself owing $500,000. Furthermore, if it is considered willful infringement, that carries fines up to $100,000 per infringement, especially if you have been notified. Shareware vendors are pretty bad about that, and when I find them I send them a strongly worded registered letter making demands on behalf of the copyright for monetary compensation. If they continue to distribute, they can no longer claim that it was unwillful because they were put on notice."

General Tips

Obtaining Music for Multimedia

As we stated in Chapter 6, "Sound Tools," the desire to compose music is not a reliable indication of talent. With graphics software, anyone with a mouse can draw a straight line while holding a control key down. But composers require a lifetime of training; we are a long way from software that could, for example, write a happy melody if you held the Shift key down and a sad melody with the Control key down. The best way to obtain music to accompany your multimedia presentation is to hire a composer to create something original and tailor-made to the rest of your content. Nothing can replace a trained human being who can respond to such suggestions as "this section should be mysterious and build in anticipation" or "I need the musical climax to synchronize precisely with the appearance of the corporate logo."

Let the Visual Element Dictate the Music

Music and sound effects can reinforce the rhythm, emotion, and historical setting of your visuals. Alternatively, your sound track can be used to add subtext, to comment, or to contradict what the audience is viewing. You can play upon expectations and associations by using a particular musical style, but don't reveal the punch line unintentionally. In most cases, the rule "less is more" applies to multimedia—the music needn't run from beginning to end, particularly if it would distract the viewer. Music under narration or dialog should be handled with extreme care. Silence can have a profound dramatic impact, especially when following a particularly audio-saturated section. Your favorite song will almost never be suitable.

Learn from the Film Industry

When you consider music for your multimedia production or QuickTime movie, it is a good idea to look at the way music is integrated into a theatrical film production. There are two primary types of music: underscore and source.

Underscore, sometimes called *score* or, erroneously, background music, is devoted to reinforcing, commenting on, or otherwise enhancing the dramatic content of the film. In all cases, underscore is music that would not be present if the scene were occurring in reality—the characters in the scene would not be able to hear it. On the other hand, *source* music is music that would be present if the scene were played out in reality—coming from a radio, record player, night club band, or Muzak—in other words, source music is music that the characters in the scene would be hearing in their current situation. A further distinction is made between visual source music, where we, the audience, can see the source of the sound, and *nonvisual* source music (sometimes called off-screen music), where we can't see the source but we can believe it is there (for example, if it is coming from a car radio in an interior shot of the back seat of a car). If you need a lesson in adding sound to visuals, go to a movie twice to allow you to effectively analyze the choice and placement of music without being distracted by the plot.

Exercise Care in Synchronizing Music to Visuals

If you are creating multimedia for distribution, you may have little control over the type of Macintosh that your work will be played on. Long soundfiles and MIDI sequences can get out of sync with the visual material if your masterpiece is played on slower or faster Macintoshes than the model you used to create the work. There is a simple solution for this. Test your project on every model of Macintosh that supports it and use a stopwatch. Most multimedia authoring environments provide a function to identify the "MachineType" and you can use this information in IF-THEN scripts to subtly change the playback tempo of the graphic element (if you are using digital audio soundfiles) or the music itself (if you are using MIDI playback).

Be Aware of the Synchronization Threshold

Take a tip from the film industry on synchronization (or verify it yourself with a poorly dubbed Japanese film): The human ear will notice a synchronization error as small as two frames at 24 frames per second. That equates to $\frac{1}{12}$ of a second, or 1 frame if your QuickTime movie is running at 12 fps. Keep this rule in mind when you need to create a "dead hit" where the visual and audio must be in precise synchronization—such as a gunshot.

Don't Ignore the Importance of Sound Placement in the Stereo Field

A sound track has a limited bandwidth. At maximum saturation, the dialog, sound effects, and music cannot add up to more than 100%. Using pan controls on your mixer or sound editing software to place different sounds at different locations in the stereo image can enhance the effect of your audio significantly. Narration is usually placed dead center. Look at an orchestral seating diagram or consider the normal spatial disposition of musicians performing in smaller ensembles to determine how far to the right or left to pan them.

Randomness Adds Interest

If you have ever wondered what you would use the "Random" function for in your multimedia authoring environment, you can put it to good use with sound. Interactive multimedia already provides random access to data, so why not select the sound (MIDI or digital audio) randomly for different segments? It makes the experience much more interesting for your users. A recent example of this technique is the Verbum Interactive CD-ROM, which randomly selects between soundtracks composed by Geno Andrews and Christopher Yavelow.

Play Through File Loading

No matter whether you are using MIDI or digital audio, if your multimedia work requires multiple files with pauses for loading, play music through the loading of files. For authoring environments that do not support playback during file loading, there are XCMDs available that offer this feature.

Avoiding Copyright Infringement (Plan A)

Fortunately, copyright law does make a distinction between public and private exhibition. Where it might cost $10,000 (or much more) to license a song for commercial use, say, in a motion picture, the price of a one-shot use of the same song in a QuickTime presentation at a board of directors' meeting would be negligible—often just the cost of the paperwork and well under $200. Sometimes you can get away with quoting popular songs, if they happen to be based upon folk songs. For example, "Love Me Tender" is really the public domain folk song "Aura Lee," although most people will think of Elvis Presley when they hear an arrangement of it in your multimedia presentation.

Avoiding Copyright Infringement (Plan B)

Commission a composer to write some original music. Everyone knows a composer or has a friend who does, and many of these composers are underemployed. Most would welcome the opportunity to write some music that would suit your presentation perfectly, often producing a better effect than pre-existing music that you try to fit to visual material for which it wasn't intended.

Avoiding Copyright Infringement (Plan C)

Another way to avoid copyright infringement is by using pre-licensed clip music, although you may have the same problems of trying to fit a round peg in a square hole. Clip music is currently being marketed in three forms: as MIDI data on floppy disks using the Standard MIDI File format (a generic format analogous to "ASCII text" in word processing)—licensing fees may be required in some situations (particularly broadcast); as digital audio data on floppy disks or CD-ROMs that you can play back with the Macintosh's internal sound capabilities (8-bit) or with various NuBus boards (16-bit)—licensing fees are usually not required; and as digital audio data on standard CDs (sometimes called "needle-drop" libraries)—these require relatively inexpensive licensing fees. (See Chapter 10, "Outside Resources," for more details.)

Use an External Sound System

The internal speaker of current Macintoshes cannot accurately play back sounds sampled at rates exceeding 11kHz. However, the rear-panel audio jack does support the Macintosh's highest resolution (22kHz). You can use portable powered speakers to greatly enhance your presentation.

Digitize the Video and Audio Separately

This is required in frame-by-frame grabs, and if you try to record audio simultaneously with video during real-time capture, you will reduce the frame rate of your video.

Increase the QuickTime Chunking Factor

Without intervention, QuickTime loads one second of your sound track into RAM before initiating movie playback. Programs like ComboWalker let you specify how many half-second chunks of sound to load into RAM before playback commences. It will often be in your interest to set a higher chunking factor than QuickTime's default, which is designed for the lowest common denominator with respect to Macintosh models.

Digital Audio Tips

Don't Record Digital Audio Too Hot

Carefully monitor audio recording levels. "Hot" levels (where the meters go into the red momentarily) are acceptable with analog tape. Digital recording meters only enter the red when the sound exceeds the maximum sample value; because there is no cushion above that number, the sample is "clipped," resulting in annoying clicks, pops, or otherwise noisy distorted audio. Use a compressor/limiter if necessary to set even recording levels.

Storage and Playback Requirements Have an Impact on Sampling Rates

Mono 8-bit digital audio sampled at 22kHz, such as that you record with MacRecorder, requires 1.3Mb per minute of sound. To save disk space, always use a playback rate of 11kHz. If your audio will be played back in mono, there is no reason to waste disk space and CPU bandwidth by using stereo soundfiles. Only use 22kHz in the final project if you are certain that your project will be played using an external sound system. If your project is destined for a CD-ROM, you should stick with 11kHz unless you have an intentionally low data rate (or frame rate below 8 fps in the case of a QuickTime movie). You can get by with a sampling rate of 7kHz if your audio consists entirely of speech. Remember, the lower your sampling rate, the more time the CPU will have to deal with the other elements of your production.

Record High, Downsample Later

Always record sound at the highest sampling rate of your digitizing hardware and then downsample the sound to 11kHz later. This is because many digitizers drop every other sample when sampling at 22kHz to achieve an 11kHz sampling rate, resulting in sound that is inferior to that achieved by recording at a higher rate

Figure 13.3 Clipping. Unlike analog recording, digital recording offers no "cushion" over the maximum sample value expressible by sample resolution (the bit-depth of each sample).

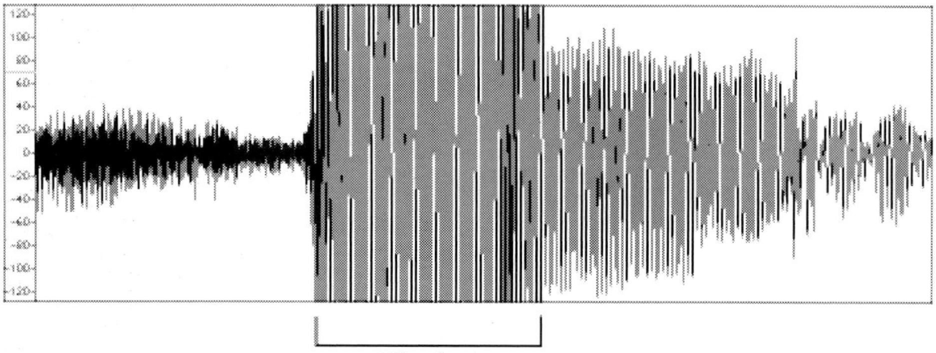

and using the "downsample" or "sample rate conversion" options of a sound editor. Downsampling and sample rate conversion options use filtering algorithms that don't necessarily result in dropping every other sample. With SoundEdit or SoundEdit Pro you will have the best results if you sample at 22kHz and paste the file into an empty 11kHz document. Always use the most exact sample rates your software permits: capture your audio at 22.254kHz and downsample it to 11.127kHz (for QuickTime 1.6 use 11.05kHz) rather than capturing at 11.127kHz or 11.05kHz.

Be Wary of Soundfile Compression

Before using MACE or any other compression scheme to compress your 8-bit soundfiles, make sure that your multimedia authoring environment lets you use compressed sound. Keep in mind that once you have compressed a sound, you won't be able to edit it with most sound editing software, so keep an uncompressed backup copy. If you must compress, don't go beyond a 3:1 compression ratio for music; 6:1 compression may be used for speech if you can tolerate the reduction in quality. The freeware Farallon Sound Expansion INIT allows any Sound Manager-compatible applications to play sounds compressed with Farallon's proprietary 4:1 and 8:1 schemes in System 6.0.7. Third-party drivers placed in your 6.0.7 System folder allow you to use Farallon's MacRecorder, Articulate Systems' Voice Impact Pro (formerly VoiceLink), or even a homemade digitizer in place of the microphone included with newer Macintoshes. Note that 4:1 and 8:1 Sound Manager playback is built into the MacRecorder Driver—don't install it and the Farallon Sound Expansion INIT on the same Macintosh.

Control an Audio CD Player

When you put an audio CD into a CD-ROM drive, every block of data has a unique address (over 300,000 separate addresses). The Macintosh can jump to any place on the disc almost instantaneously. There is no load time such as is associated with reading other forms of CD-ROM data; audio playback commences as soon as the data is located. Authoring tools such as Voyager's CD AudioStack automatically create buttons and XCMD scripts to play back audio sequences you designate by "scrolling" through an off-the-shelf audio CD. You can even control multiple CD-ROM drives, each with a different audio CD playing at your command. Macromedia Director also offers control of CD-based audio through its own XCMD.

MIDI Tips

Use MIDI as Soon as the Sound Manager Supports It

Another important advantage of using MIDI instead of digital audio is that you can alter many sound characteristics on the fly during playback. You can speed up or slow down a piece of music, transpose it to another key, mute or solo specified tracks, fade individual tracks in and out, loop beat-delineated regions, or completely reorchestrate and remix the music—all without having a separate version of the file. Furthermore, you can direct any or all of these operations to take place in response to user interaction.

When MIDI comes to Sound Manager and, therefore, QuickTime, the abundance of Standard MIDI Files that are floating around on telecommunications bulletin boards should create a renaissance in QuickTime music. Keep in mind the necessity to ascertain licensing requirements for copyrighted music, even in SMF format.

When You Use MIDI, Use General MIDI

If you are going to use MIDI sequences in your multimedia presentations, it makes sense to set them up so that they are compatible with the "General MIDI mode message" protocol that was added to the MIDI Specification in 1991. General MIDI was created specifically to address multimedia issues. Among other things, General MIDI consists of a standardized list of patches that are all assigned to the same numbers, a universal patch location scheme if you will. This means that when a device is in General MIDI mode, for example, patch 1 is always an acoustic grand piano, patch 25 is a nylon-stringed guitar, patch 41 is a solo violin, and so on. All 128 possible patch numbers have explicit assignments covering just about any instrument of the orchestra, as well as many standard electronic instruments, synthesizer timbres, and sound effects. General MIDI also defines drum sound to note number mappings. General MIDI lets you "plug and play" with the assurance that the sounds will be correct, regardless of the hardware you use for playback.

Use MIDI XCMDs to Increase Your MIDI Possibilities

Ear Level Engineering's HyperMIDI XCMD set can add a complete MIDI implementation to multimedia authoring environments that support externals such as XCMDs. There are also several HyperCard stacks available that play back Standard MIDI Files (a couple are Opcode Systems' MIDIplay and Passport Designs' HyperMusic). These stacks can automatically create buttons or scripts that play MIDI files in any XCMD-compatible multimedia authoring environment. You can even assemble lists of files that play back sequentially. There are thousands of files available in Standard MIDI File format.

Initialize MIDI Tracks

As the first event of each MIDI track, insert messages to reset controllers, set pitchbend to 0, set MIDI volume (controller 7) to 127 or the appropriate value, and include program changes (preferably in General MIDI format) to ensure that if these values have been altered during the course of the playback of another sequence, you will be starting from a clean slate. Another reason these parameters may have the wrong values is because an earlier version of your sequence was interrupted during playback.

Use MIDI Effects in Place of Digital Signal Processing

You can edit MIDI data to simulate almost every effect that you might otherwise use an expensive digital signal processor to accomplish. The following effects are easily achievable by copying, delaying, merging, scaling, and transposing MIDI data: echo, chorus, flange, compression/expansion, limiting, pan, and spatialization.

Had Enough?

You may not have realized how much there is to know about sound—especially in the digital environment of multimedia. Fortunately, once you understand the basic technology, you'll find that the process of adding sound to your multimedia project is more like creative play than tedious drudgery. In any case, the rewards of using sound's emotional power is well worth the mental and technological investment. It can be the polish of your presentation.

14

Sound Projects

Computer-based music generation and editing are among the most intriguing and least explored areas of multimedia. In this chapter, and in the step-by-step explanations on the Power Tools CD, you'll find fascinating discussions of the effect of digital music on popular culture, the use of rock songs to teach music theory, and how "intelligent instruments" allow beginners to create coherent and original compositions.

Hip Hop Hits

Hip Hop Hits ⌘011

Musical styles have always influenced popular culture. In the 1960s, music helped fuel the revolution—in fashion, politics, lifestyles, art, and even industrial design. Today, computers are increasingly influencing music. Many of today's hot new musical styles, like Hip Hop, Industrial, Rave, and Acid-House, are technology-driven, born out of new capabilities stemming from the marriage of computers and digital audio. Through the development of these new musical styles, computers are exerting a powerful influence on the popular style and culture of the '90s.

All these new styles share one characteristic—the prominent use of small bits of digitized audio called *samples*. Samples are small music clips, often only three or four seconds long, taken from old tunes that are dated but familiar. They are digitally recorded with a computer or sampling keyboard and usually played back as repeating loops (see Figure 14.1).

Many of today's musicians are really sound engineers. They take tiny chunks of old favorites, digitally chew them up, mix in a hot, new dance beat, and spit out a groove that's completely fresh. By its very nature, sampling allows musicians to pay homage to old styles like Funk, House, and Soul, while inventing

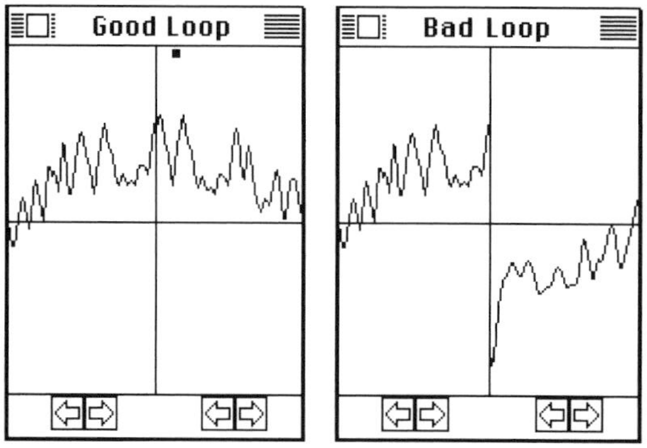

Figure 14.1 Editing sound loops to make sure they play seamlessly

something entirely new. That's why new songs on the radio sometimes subconsciously sound familiar.

What do Hip Hop, Industrial, and Acid-House have to offer multimedia creators? Through their use of sample loops, they show new ways to create long pieces of sound with small chunks of audio data.

Imagine the implications of this modular approach for multimedia! Not only are the problems created by space limitations drastically reduced, but audio starts and stops are smooth in an interactive environment. By using small, repeating loops, audio can be better molded around individual screens and buttons, eliminating graceless user-initiated stops and extended silences while projects move to the next screen.

Hip Hop Hits is really two projects in one. Mike Salomon designed the original project as a CD-quality audio track for the song *"Straight to the Point"* by the Hip Hop band, Dark Side Productions (DSP). Knowing that DSP would be playing additional elements live (lyrics, keyboards, and nonlooping samples), Mike wanted to keep the tracks simple.

Figure 14.2 The final digital tape of *"Straight to the Point"*

First trained as a recording engineer, Mike worked in studios and did live shows for two years, and later began doing Mac installations for studios working with MIDI and digital audio. In 1990, he went to work for Horizon Resources in San Diego, which integrates digital audio systems for recording studios and composers.

Dark Side Productions disbanded shortly after Mike completed the job, so he was happy to reincarnate the recording for the Power Tools CD.

Special Considerations

The project's biggest challenge, says Mike, was getting good sound out of the 8-bit internal Mac system. To optimize the sound quality, Mike did three things. First, he started a high-quality 16-bit 44.1kHz file, which was equal to the fidelity of an audio music CD.

Since the source was clean and high-quality, he had only to remove information to make an 8-bit file; this is much easier than trying to clean up lower-quality sound, which also will almost inevitably produce inferior results.

Next, Mike performed a process called *normalization*, to optimize the fidelity and dynamic range of the original music for playback on the Mac's relatively low-quality built-in sound. The process works by assigning the maximum number of bits to the loudest passages, thus getting the most natural sound possible from 8-bit payback.

Finally, Mike cleaned up the sound by editing the music's waveforms to remove the audible clicks that the Mac's speakers would normally emit at the beginning and end of each track.

Tips and Techniques

For those wanting to experiment with digital sound on the Mac, Mike recommends the new Audiomedia II card from Digidesign. While not as sophisticated as the Sound Tools system he used for the project, it allows you to play back, edit, and mix CD-quality sound, and can be had for less than $1000. Mike also points out that the budget conscious can pick up a used Audiomedia I card for around $300.

Mike recommends keeping an eye out for the new version of Sound Manager, rumored to be released by Apple by mid-1993. The system software extension could do for audio what QuickTime did for digital video, by providing standard audio drivers that will work with various applications and sound cards. Sound Manager also will automatically adjust digital music playback for individual Macs, much the way QuickTime will giddily drop video frames to keep in sync when playing back movies on slower Macs.

Finally, Mike warns those planning multimedia projects not to underestimate the importance of sound, and not to forget to budget for sound production. In an area that is often overlooked, attention to good audio production can help boost a multimedia project to professional levels.

Tools and Equipment

Mike used a Mac IIci and Digidesign's Sound Tools system, which consists of the Sound Accelerator Card, Sound Designer II editing software, and an outboard digitizing box.

Step by Step

To learn more about how Mike actually created the project, see the Power Tools CD. You'll experience firsthand how he digitized the original music, isolated each instrument, created the sound loops, mixed tracks, created the PlayList regions, and finally, recorded it all onto digital audio (DAT) tape.

Power Tools Theme

PROJECTS
Power Tools Theme ⌘012

"About one minute long and industrial." That was the extent of the guidelines Christopher Yavelow got before composing the theme for the Power Tools CD. But these brief and vague directions were enough for Chris, who has an award-winning and distinguished background in music and computers, is professor of composition at Claremont Graduate School, and wrote *The Macworld Music and Sound Bible.*

Special Considerations

To compose the music, Chris used M, interactive music software from Intelligent Music, Inc. "I normally use interactive music software only for live performance," says Chris, "but considering that the Power Tools CD is devoted to interactive multimedia, I decided to use an intelligent instrument to create the music."

M allowed Chris to accomplish several things. First, "M responds to performance gestures, by generating much more musical information than would be generated by the same gesture were it applied to a traditional instrument."

Even though the entire theme was composed of only four simple elements—one 17-note and one 13-note melody, a five-chord progression, and a 13-note rhythmic pattern—M generated "an astounding amount of material," says Chris.

Chris further points out that composing with M forces you to think about musical parameters that you would not generally even consider when using other computer-based tools (see Figure 14.3). These parameters include note density, relative volume ranges, probabilities, and event order, "the sort of things you would only think about were you composing for traditional instruments."

Chris says that composing with tools like M allows you to deal with the many levels of music composition from "greater levels of abstraction." "Rather than think of the actual notes that make up a pattern," he explains, "you think of the pattern itself."

This concept appeals to both trained and amateur musicians. "Professionals can deal with the processes that transform musical ideas," Chris says, "while neophytes can ignore the details, and get results by pushing larger conceptual blocks around, rather than tiny notes where any little mistake stands out like a sore thumb."

Tips and Techniques

Chris's primary advice is that novices should not be scared away by interactive music tools, sequencers, or MIDI. "I really believe that people with zero musical training can use these tools and have fun doing it. There are a lot of people out there attempting to do multimedia and needing music for it."

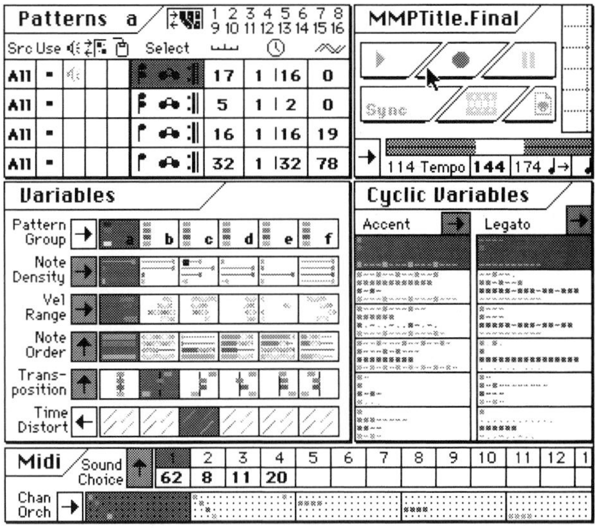

Figure 14.3
M allows you to control many different musical parameters.

Likewise, professional musicians should not be put off by computer-based tools, says Chris. "Desktop tools can reflect compositional philosophy just as successfully as traditional tools can," he asserts.

Another benefit of compositional tools is that you can create music with no license restrictions, since anything you compose belongs to you. This is a significant benefit, as content rights can absorb considerable time, effort, and economic resources (as in the *So You Want to Be Rock and Roll Star* project; see below).

Tools and Equipment

Aside from M, Chris used a variety of computer-based music tools, including Opcode's EZ Vision MIDI sequencer, Coda's Finale, Apple's MIDI Manager, Mark of the Unicorn's Performer, Kurzweil's 250 sampler and the Kurzweil 1000PX, SX, and E-mu's Proteus 2 sound modules, Panasonic's 3700 DAT deck, MediaVision's Pro Audio Spectrum 16, and Passport's Alchemy (see Figure 14.4).

Step by Step

In his tutorial on the Power Tools CD, Chris begins with an overview of the philosophy and strengths of interactive music software and intelligent instruments. He then provides a detailed overview of the many parameters of the M system, and the means he used to edit and record the final theme.

So You Want to Be a Rock and Roll Star

Rock and Roll Star ⌘013

In the mid-'80s, Steve Rappaport was an independent producer for Electronic Arts, the high-flying computer and video game developer founded by Trip Hawkins (now CEO of 3DO).

"Trip told us about this new technology, CD-I, that was going to marry a bunch of technologies that were already on the shelf," Steve notes, "Audio CDs, CD-

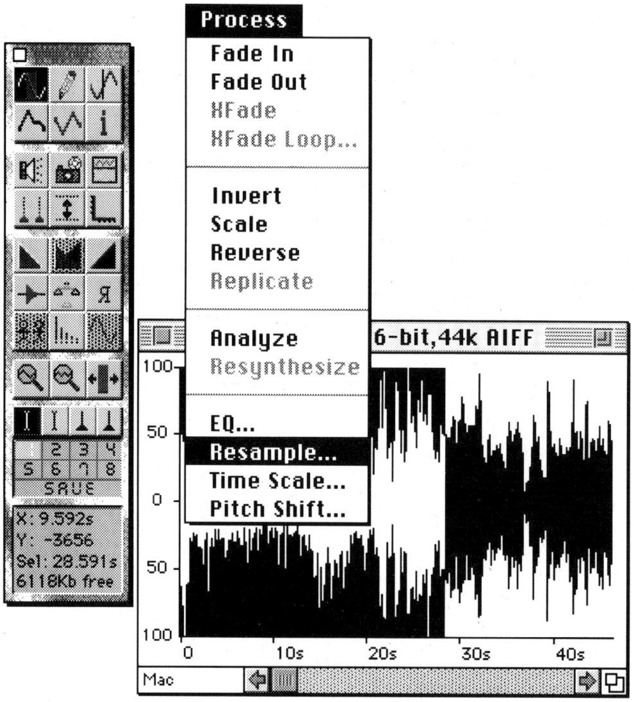

Figure 14.4 Chris used Passport's Alchemy to downsample his final sound file to an 8-bit file that would play back on the full range of internal Mac sound systems.

ROM, color technology, graphics—basically, all the parts that were integrated into CD-I and what we now know as interactive multimedia were already invented by the mid-'80s, but they hadn't been put together in a coherent piece of hardware. The software tools, like Director, didn't exist yet either, so that one could actually create interactive multimedia."

Hawkins urged his creative staff to think about uses for the new technology, because, Steve points out, "you can have all the hardware and software and tools you want, but if you can't create a compelling product, all of that doesn't mean anything."

With Hawkins's challenge ringing in his ears, Steve began to form the germ of an idea. A musician for over 30 years, he had always wanted to share his knowledge in a fun and educational way. An interactive CD might be the perfect medium, but Steve had to bide his time a little longer until desktop software tools made such a project economically feasible. In 1990, when MacroMind (now Macromedia) released Director 2.0, Steve saw his chance, and enlisted a partner, Greg McGee, to handle the technical aspects of the project.

TOOLS Director ⌘210

So You Want to Be a Rock and Roll Star uses classic rock songs to teach music and guitar. All six songs— *"Twist and Shout," "Stand by Me," "Runaway," "Crazy," "In the Midnight Hour," and "Sittin' on the Dock of the Bay"*—are illustrated with animations (Figure 14.5), and are recorded in 16-bit CD-quality sound.

You can simply enjoy the music and animation, or you can learn about music theory, chord structure, and the history of each song. Music theory is a pretty arcane subject to most people; but *So You Want to Be a Rock and Roll Star* teaches it in a context that is a bit more fun. Professional music teachers use the songs to teach piano and guitar, and you can even isolate various tracks to hear only the instruments you're concentrating on.

Special Considerations

A producer and musician by training, Steve has a refreshing angle on multimedia because he focuses on the content and human aspects of the genre, rather than the technical issues that seem to captivate and divert so many.

In fact, the most demanding aspect of the project didn't involve technology at all. "The single most difficult part of the project was licensing the music," says Steve. In the course of over three years, Interactive Records has obtained the rights to more than 400 songs. In many ways, Steve and his company have blazed the trail for producers of multimedia who seek to incorporate original musical works. "Now, everyone in Hollywood and Nashville, and New York has, at minimum, heard of interactive multimedia," he notes.

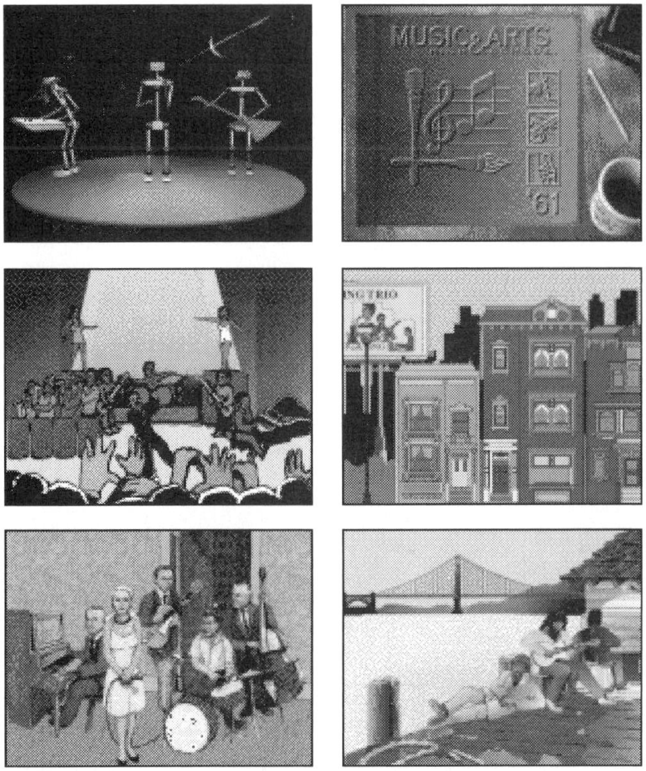

Figure 14.5 Each of *So You Want to Be a Rock and Roll Star's* six rock songs is illustrated with original animated art.

Steve also values and emphasizes personal relationships in his work. During the early phases of the project, he and Greg built a prototype and Steve took it on the road." I not only showed people what multimedia was, but I also demonstrated how it could be a source of completely unexpected revenue," Steve explains.

Steve was able to show music publishers that an early involvement in multimedia licensing would position them as the demand for electronic rights heats up in the '90s. "I would spend hours with these folks, and they came to see that they could trust me," he says. "One of the things you never hear about in discussions of obtaining content is the importance of personal relationships."

Another key aspect of the project was choosing the songs, which are at the core of the project. "We wanted to create a product that was transgenerational, so we chose songs that, although they were written and recorded in the '60s, had re-releases in the '80s, he notes. *"Sittin' on the Dock of the Bay"* was a top-10 hit for Michael Bolton in 1988. *"Runaway"* was not only a hit for Bonnie Raitt in 1977, but was the theme of TV's *Police Story. "In the Midnight Hour"* was a hit for The Commitments in 1990."

Tips and Techniques

Steve was careful to emphasize the originality and individuality of the songs, by choosing unique art to accompany and enhance the music. The rise of music videos and MTV during the '80s also was not lost on him, and he saw that each music video had its own style and sensibility. He auditioned over 40 artists before settling on the six who created animations for the songs.

Although Steve's original market inspiration for the project was CD-I, he quickly realized that the Mac and CD-ROM were better bet, for both development and distribution. "One of the beauties of the Macintosh is that, to some significant extent, the interface builds itself."

Although *Rock and Roll Star* is much more than simply a sound project (we could have easily included it in the interactive category instead), it *is* primarily about sound, and Interactive Records understandably focussed on the music.

One key concern was how to fit all of the sound on a CD. At 650Mb capacity, *it* would seem to have plenty of room, until one considers that audio CD-quality sound takes about 10Mb per minute. At that rate, the *Rock and Roll Star* CD would hold only about an hour of music and sound (with no room at all for text, graphics, and interactivity!).

Interactive Records solved the problem by recording the music at 15-bit CD-quality (also called Red Book Audio), and narrative voices, at a lower-quality 8-bit sound. With that ratio, the disc was able to hold a full three hours of sound and music.

Steve points out that developers have to be constantly aware of emerging multimedia products—not just to keep up with new technology, but also because new products can have an impact on maintenance of their own programs. *Rock and Roll Star* worked flawlessly in the early months of its release, and then Interactive Records began to get bug reports. They realized that all the customers

Figure 14.6 To create the project, Interactive Records used computer-based tools as well as traditional recording studio equipment.

who were reporting problems were using the new AppleCD 300i, which is a dual-speed CD-ROM drive.

It turned out that there was a conflict between this drive's software driver and Macromedia's Director Projector, which plays back the *Rock and Roll Star* CD. Code changes to both Apple's driver and Director turned out to be necessary, but meanwhile, it was Interactive's problem.

"It's not enough that your program is flawless today, it has to be flawless on new products that come out that are going to have new code," Steve notes. "So in a sense, you're never through with a product. And that's one reason why code has to be meticulously documented. So many people do not comment their code, and they may not realize that, two years from now, they're going to have to go through that code to find and fix problems."

Tools and Equipment

TOOLS

MasterTracks Pro ⌘ 200
SoundEdit Pro ⌘ 201

Interactive Records used a Mac IIci and IIcx, Farallon's MacRecorder and SoundEdit to digitize and edit sound, a Sennheiser 421 microphone for the vocal recordings, and all the tools you'd find in a traditional recording studio (Figure 14.6). Photoshop was used for image processing, HyperCard for prototyping, Director for building the interface, and Passport's MasterTracks Pro for sequencing.

Step by Step

Rock and Roll Star's entire production process is documented in great detail on the Power Tools CD, and is accompanied throughout by Steve's articulate narration. You'll learn, among other things, the importance of good script writing and editing, how Interactive Records chose its teachers and narrators, the impact of desktop sound tools, the sound recording and editing process, how the songs' arrangements had to be understood and analyzed, and how track recording and sequencing works.

15

3-D Modeling, Animation, and Rendering

" Jeethus Cristh, that' s a funny voithe! Where'd you get that voithe?"

—Studio executive, after screening premiere appearance of Daffy Duck, unaware that he himself was the inspiration for the character' s voice.

At a lunch meeting in the 1950s among Loony Tunes animators Friz Freleng and Chuck Jones, and studio owners Jack and Harry Warner, Harry told the bemused cartoonists that he had no idea where their cartoon division was, commenting, " The only thing I know is that we make Mickey Mouse." Of course, as any grade schooler will tell you, the famous rodent is a product of Disney Studios, not Warner Bros.

Another time, legendary Warner Bros. director Chuck Jones and a colleague were quietly working when their producer appeared in the doorway and blurted out: "I don't want any gags about bullfights. Bullfights aren't funny!" Jones's colleague turned to him and said, " I never knew there was anything funny about bullfighting until now. But Eddie' s judgment is impeccable. He' s never been right yet." Sure enough, *Bully for Bugs* became one of the best and best-loved Bugs Bunny cartoons.

The annals of early film animation are full of colorful stories, and in many ways, the state of today's desktop computer animation is similar to that of the pioneering days of cartoons. Both have wide popular appeal, each was revolutionized by new technology, and both are painstaking to produce.

Although 3-D animation tools are getting easier to use, they still require considerable time to master, which is one reason why 2-D animated presentation tools like Magic, Cinemation, and PROmotion have cropped up.

Beyond the technical skills that are needed to excel at 3-D animation, there is the looming question of aesthetic talent. Many overlook the fact that technical mastery is not the most important skill necessary for good animation. A feel for composition and design, and innate creativity are critical.

Jim Collins of Smoke and Mirrors in San Francisco, who designs 3-D animation and interactive presentations, laments the emphasis on technical detail that dominates the creation of computer-based images. He feels that as computer animation matures and the tools get easier to use, artists will begin to gravitate to the new medium, sparking a creative renaissance in computer animation.

Harry Marks, a broadcast graphics pioneer, has similar views. Marks believes that much control has been lost by broadcast graphics designers, who are now dependent on operators conversant with the complex and expensive equipment necessary to create broadcast-quality graphics. As desktop tools become more powerful and accessible, Marks predicts, artists and designers won' t have to be as reliant on technicians: " I think the most important thing about the computer is that, as the machine is being accepted more by designers, the control is coming back."

Don't let all this scare you away. Three-dimensional animation can be enormously rewarding, and with some patience and dedication, you can turn out stunning imagery. The point is that desktop animation (and all multimedia applications) are sort of in the Model T phase, with tools that can be difficult to learn, albeit much less complex than the specialized equipment they replace.

There is no substitute for an artistic sensibility—the tools eventually will get easier to master, but unless you have some knowledge of aesthetics, you may find 3-D animation daunting. This doesn' t mean you have to be Picass o—much about form, balance, composition, and design can be learned over time, or at least enough to help you produce reasonable-looking animation. So if 3-D animation turns you on and you don' t know the first thing about design, take a class or a seminar; you might surprise yourself.

In this chapter, we' ll cover the basics of animation, beginning with how to plan out an animation and continuing through basic structural definitions through modeling. Then we' ll discuss the rudiments of movement and animation, and go on to basics of rendering surfaces, textures, color, and light. Finally, there is a brief discussion of ways to distribute your final product.

Planning

For all but the simplest of 3-D images and animations, planning is essential—the 3-D process is too involved to leave anything to chance. You' ll need to plan such elements as shots, camera angles, and scene composition. Even if you're just animating a logo, it helps to visualize where the text will come from, and just what effects will be used: rotation, zooming, morphing, or some other manipulation. For more complex projects, such as animated presentations or very involved CD or videodisc-based games, planning is absolutely critical.

Animators have many horror stories about learning this the hard way. For example, animator Joe Sparks, creator of the popular CD-ROM games *Spaceship Warlock* and *Total Distortion*, tells of spending hours designing and modeling beautiful vases and other amenities for a room in *Total Distortion*. When it came time to set camera angles and motion, he realized that his carefully designed details would be completely off camera.

Video Quilt ⌘020

Some animators keep notebooks in which they record lists of frames, changes to be made after test renderings, client likes and dislikes, sketches of objects and scenes, and anything else they may have to consult later. Lynda Weinman, a Los Angeles animator who worked on the display graphics used for the cyborg's readouts in the film *Robocop*, made the entry in her notebook shown in Figure 15.1.

Although it pays to be as organized as possible, individual animators stress different parts of the process. Jim Collins, of Smoke and Mirrors in San Francisco, finds elaborate planning unnecessary and even limiting. He says those with background in computers tend to plan and organize more, while those with an artistic background value inspiration and happenstance over planning.

He cites as an example the project he did for Pixar's ShowPlace/MacRenderMan product demo, a clever and creative piece of work. At one point, there were a number of objects whirling around, including a teacup and pot. As he watched them pass each other, the thought came to Collins that it would be fun if the teapot poured tea into the cup as they flew by each other. "Everybody loved it, but it occurred to me on-the-fly. I certainly didn't plan the shot or storyboard it," says Collins.

By contrast, Drew Pictures's Drew Huffman, another San Francisco animator, makes very intricate models and spends a lot of time on that phase of animation. He also emphasizes the planning stages, and declares these considerations are too often overlooked, especially by novices who often want to just plunge ahead. Huffman's modeling on his new interactive 3-D game, *The Iron Helix*, is evidence that he follows his own advice: The models are beautifully detailed and rendered, and the story line is logical and well thought out.

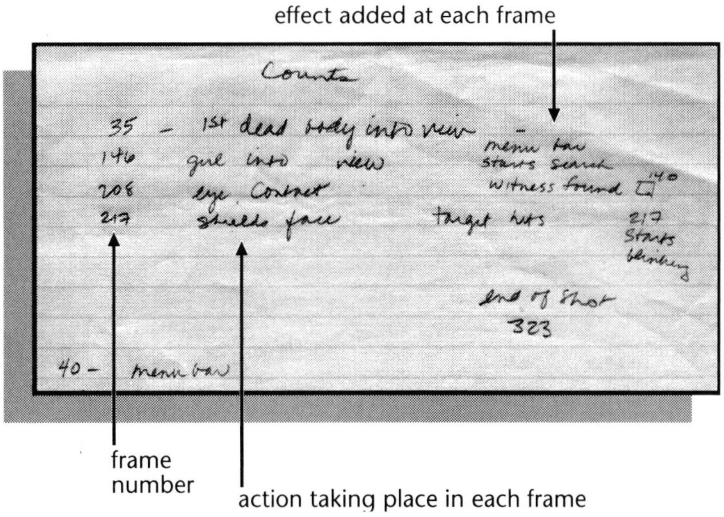

Figure 15.1 Excerpt from Lynda Weinman's *Robocop* Notebook

So, clearly, there's more than one way to skin a cat (or put surfaces on a spaceship), and you will evolve your own style as you gain experience; in the meantime, it's a good idea to understand the early phases of the animation process.

Storyboarding

The primary means for planning an animation is the *storyboard.* Now widely used by the broadcast and film industries to plan and visualize scenes, the storyboard was actually pioneered by early animators. In fact, Walt Disney himself kept as a souvenir part of the storyboard for *Steamboat Willie*, the cartoon that introduced Mickey Mouse to the world. (It was also the first cartoon to feature a synchronized sound track. The first film of any kind with sound, *The Jazz Singer*, had only been released the year before, in 1927.)

Syd Mead, a well known artist and industrial designer who has also worked extensively in film and multimedia, considers storyboards to be "an extremely important part of the planning process."

A production designer for such films as *Aliens, 2010,* and *Tron,* Syd also designed the V'GER entity for the first *Star Trek* movie, which trekkies will remember as the visual and dramatic climax of the film.

For the science fiction classic *Blade Runner*, Syd designed the street scenes as well as the vehicles. The storyboard for some of the film's sequences included Syd's original art, which he later annotated:

Storyboards are also key parts of the animation process for today's full-length animated movies such as *Beauty and the Beast*, which contains over 10,000,000 frames. Many people work on such complex animations, and the storyboard is a way to study the project in detail before committing the vast resources necessary to create the work itself.

Though your own animations probably won't approach the epic scale of a sci-fi epic or Disney movie, the storyboards are still your opportunity to visualize before you start work. The storyboard itself doesn't have to be anything too

FIELD NO.03: LOWER CENTER

VEHICLES FOR BLADERUNNER WERE DESIGNED TO BE CHARACTERS IN THE STORY. IN THIS CLOSE-UP, THE TAXI BECOMES AN ANGULAR, UTILITARIAN ADDITION TO THE CLUTTERED STREET SCENE; AN UN-GRACIOUS, BRUTALLY FUNCTIONAL UTILITY FOR PUBLIC USE.

Figure 15.2 Excerpt from Syd Mead's *Blade Runner* storyboard

involved. Basically, it's just sketches of key scenes with a place to write accompanying notes and script outlines.

The storyboard can save you many hours of wasted effort later. You' ll also find that when you sketch out scenes and look at them in relation to one another, other ideas will suggest themselves. Holes in the story and action also will become apparent through the storyboard. If you are working on a large project involving many people, storyboards also are a way to stay in sync with one another.

The "script" that goes along with the storyboard doesn' t have to be actual dialog or narration—your animation may not have any. The accompanying text can simply be information on content, ideas for color and texture, cues for music, notes on the "feel" and visual dynamics of the scene, or instructions for camera placement and quality and location of lighting.

Many animators also study comic books, a readily available source of storyboard art. Comics regularly use odd angles and forced perspective, and are generally very effective at suggesting motion and action.

You can buy preprinted storyboard blanks from art or video production suppliers, but you can just as easily create your own with a word processor.

In the end, it's less expensive to sketch something than to animate it.

Designing for the Medium

Another important part of the planning process is to scope out fully the target delivery method and platform for your animation. Is it to be played back on another computer? If so, what kind, and what sort of display will be used, and how much RAM is necessary? Your own equipment must be evaluated as well, to make sure it is up to the demands of the project. If the animation will be played back on a kiosk or from a laserdisc, or written to videotape, there are still other considerations.

One of the most important factors is the time you have to devote to the project. If you need to produce a 30-second broadcast-quality piece, you'd better have a lot of time on your hands (or some help), not to mention the extra equipment you' ll need, (such as a frame-accurate videotape recorder and video output hardware).

All of these issues are best contemplated before you actually start any work. This will spare you unpleasant surprises later, which could derail a lot of hard work.

Computer-Based Delivery

If you' re designing for playback on a computer, find out what the lowest common denominator is. You should know the target machine' s CPU, color capabilities, screen size, and both RAM and hard disk capacities. If the animation will be played from a CD or videodisc, the target audience obviously must have the appropriate playback device as well.

The target machine may be very different from your own development computer. If, say, you have a Quadra 700 and the target is an LC, then try to lay your hands on an LC for frequent testing of different pieces of the project as it evolves. You may well find that transitions and effects that work fine on your Quadra will crawl on the LC.

Lower-end machines like the II and LC II have limitations when it comes to multimedia. While they theoretically can hold more, they often are equipped with only 1 to 8Mb of RAM, small hard disks, and slower ' 020 and ' 030 CPUs.

Remember that, despite the fanfare surrounding 24-bit color, this capability is still relatively scarce among the masses. Working in 24-bit also will drastically slow development time, especially rendering. The resulting image files are also larger, thus requiring more disk and RAM space.

However, if you have a 24-bit card and the extra time and resources, it does make sense to create 24-bit images and then convert them to 8-bit for final output. This results in better image quality than if you were to work in 8-bit from the beginning.

If your work will be stored and delivered via CD, you also should do some tests to simulate performance, so that you can experience the delays that will be encountered by viewers as they wait for images to transfer from the device. The faster CD players will do an adequate job of transferring from the disc, but your audience may not have the latest equipment.

The faster data access of the videodisc makes it desirable as a delivery medium, but other factors are less favorable. For one thing, few people have videodiscs, which will limit the market for your work. On the upside, they *are* gaining in popularity, they are being used by many schools and corporations, and they are getting pretty cheap to master and produce.

Other performance trade-offs can be made during the production phase rather than in the initial planning stage, but you should be aware of them early on, too. These include rendering only what will be seen by the "camera" (the viewer' s point of view), using 2-D elements where possible, using antialiasing only when necessary, and selecting lower-quality shading when acceptable. All of these trade-offs of quality versus performance are discussed later in this chapter.

Kiosks and Videotape

When designing an animation that will be played back on a kiosk, you may be able to bank on a more robust delivery platform. Industrial-strength kiosks often use higher performance computers and maybe even videodiscs. But this is not always the case, so, again, make sure you try out the delivery platform ahead of time and, if possible, have one available for continuous testing. Note that kiosks often employ larger monitors, so you'll have to plan your work accordingly.

Broadcast-quality animation for delivery on videotape is among the most demanding of applications. The quality of the images themselves can only be achieved by a few animation programs, although this capability is cropping up more frequently (see Chapter 7, "Animation Tools").

Health Care Kiosk ⌘042

Broadcast quality also means that you' ll have to use the best rendering quality, which will add to rendering time. The high frame rate of video, 30 frames per second (fps), also adds to the development burden, since you' ll have to create many more frames than for the average computer-delivered animation.

You' ll also have to invest in a single-frame recorder—a combination of software and hardware that writes the animation out to tape, one frame at a time. This is necessary because today's desktop computers aren't yet powerful enough to blast out animation at 30 fps. If you do this form of animation only occasionally, you may want to find a service that will do this part of the process for you.

When producing for video, you' ll also need to make sure colors that look fine on the computer screen will read on a TV (or an NTSC) monitor. There is expensive calibration equipment that will ensure this, but if you' re designing for video, you should have an NTSC monitor to check your work every once in a while (see Chapter 17, "Creating Video"). Designers who work in this medium sometimes develop their own test methods to make sure their colors are in the appropriate range. For example, Lynda Weinman uses a simple rule of thumb to make sure that colors are "video" or "NTSC-safe" (meaning they will display correctly in video). When processing an image with fully saturated colors in Photoshop, Weinman will lower either the saturation or brightness of the color by 25%. She finds this works pretty well, although she comments,"what I lose by not having a waveform or vectorscope is that my method is a little conservative, and if I had the scope, I could push it to the limit."

Modeling

Building three-dimensional objects is a process known as *modeling*. Before you animate and render objects, you must define the structure of your 3-D " world"—the shapes and dimensions of objects, and their relationship to one another. Modeling controls also allow you to position and group objects, and define how they will move when animated.

Creating Basic Objects and Shapes

The process of creating real-world models is abetted by the large and versatile collection of predefined shapes and modeling tools offered by most modeling programs. Three-dimensional objects normally start out as *wireframes*, which define their shape in 3-D space. Wireframes, because they lack surfaces, can be quickly manipulated. Some modelers, notably Macromedia's Swivel 3D and MacroModel, and Specular's Infini-D, can do very fast rough or *flat* shading, which sometimes makes it easier to model objects. This type of shading, while too rough for finished work, can help in positioning complex objects, which might otherwise be a sea of wireframes (see Figure 15.3).

TOOLS
Swivel 3D ⌘ 220
MacroModel ⌘ 221

Flat shading is particularly helpful when you are working with more complex elements. In wireframe views, it is sometimes difficult or impossible to tell that

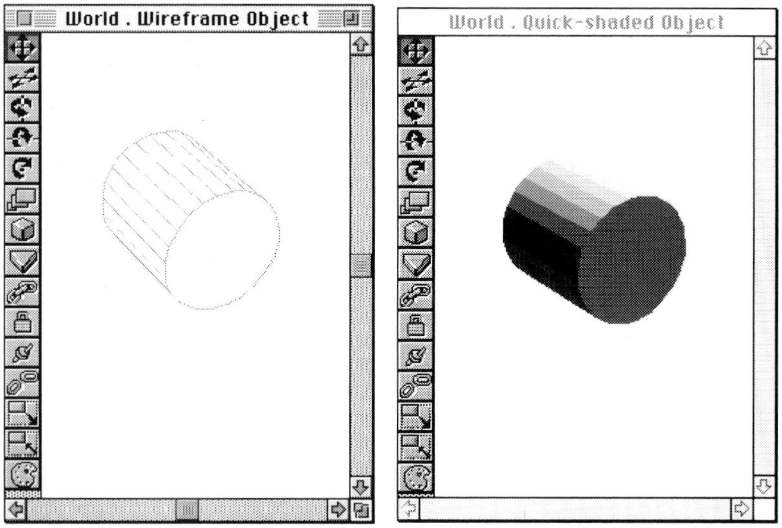

Figure 15.3 Model in wireframe and quick-shaded versions

a wheel on a car is penetrating the body, or that fingers are moving right through a hand. Quick shading can help you visualize better while still keeping screen drawing at an acceptable rate.

Modeling Tools

Modeling in three-dimensions requires a variety of tools to help you represent the array of shapes and structures found in the real world (and some that aren't!). The following is a brief overview of the tools available. Not all modelers have all tools; see Chapter 7, "Animation Tools," for a feature comparison by product.

Cross-Sectional Modeling

This procedure, also called *lofting* or *loafing*, is a simple, general-purpose technique, often overlooked amid the profusion of more exotic modeling methods. You begin by drawing 2-D shapes that will act as cross sections or "ribs" for the 3-D object. Then, the modeler connects the ribs (also known as creating "transitions" or "skinning") to form the object (Figure 15.4).

This is a versatile method and can be used to create any number of free-form shapes. It has the further advantage of being economical in terms of geometry—using fewer polygons to represent a shape in wireframe than do other techniques.

Primitives

Many modeling programs provide simple building blocks, or *primitives*, on which you can base custom shapes created to suit your particular needs (Figure 15.5).

Primitives provide a place to start when modeling objects. But they are also helpful because, since they are a part of the modeling program itself, their code is optimized and they can be represented, manipulated, and stored more efficiently, resulting in quicker screen drawing and faster rendering times.

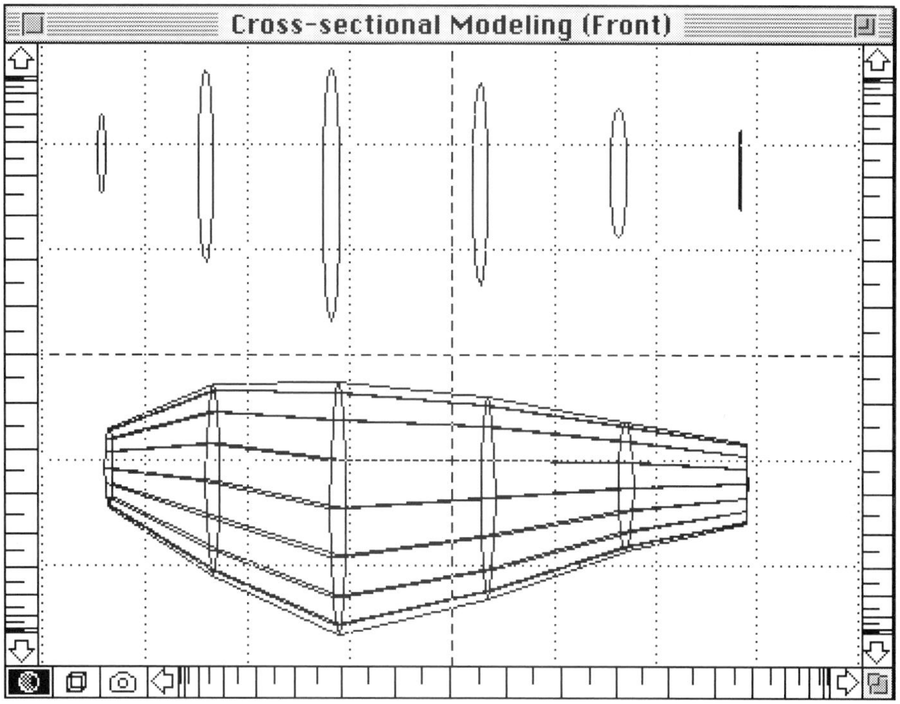

Figure 15.4 Cross-sectional modeling

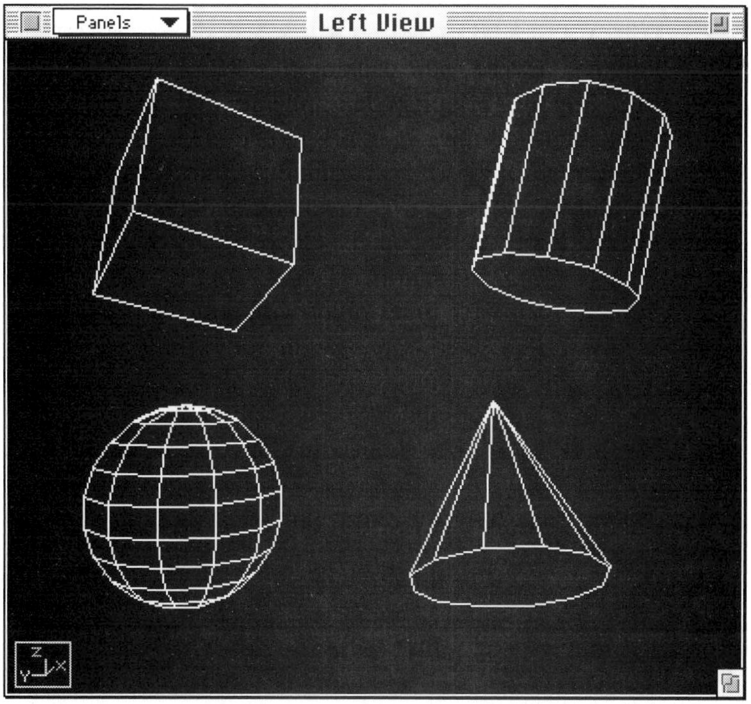

Figure 15.5 Typical modeling primitives

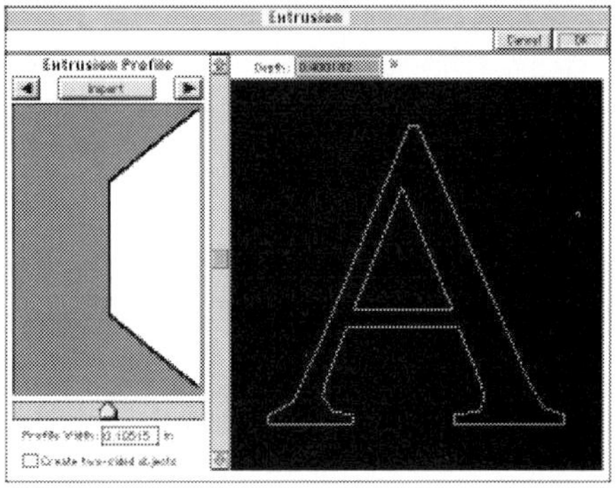

Figure 15.6 Applying a beveled edge to type

Lathe, Extruded, and Free-Form Shapes

In addition to the primitive objects, modeling programs typically include three other types of basic modeling tools: extrude, lathe, and free-form.

Extruding is the process by which you take a 2-D object and push it out, or extrude it into 3-D space. Extrude tools probably are most often used to create 3-D type, but they are also useful for making other shapes. For example, you can use an imported PICT file as a template, trace over it with drawing tools, and then extrude the drawing into a 3-D object.

Extrusion tools generally provide control over various parameters such as extrusion depth; StrataVision even lets you apply a bevel to an extruded object, which yields particularly nice results with beveled type. You can use one of several preset bevels or specify your own (Figure 15.6).

Lathe objects are used to create cylindrical shapes such as glasses, tubes, and pencils—any shape that is symmetrical around a single axis. Lathe objects are surprisingly easy to create, because you draw only the 2-D shape, which the program "spins" around an axis to form the 3-D object (Figure 15.7). Once you have drawn the lathe shape, you can modify the outline by moving the points that define it (Figure 15.8).

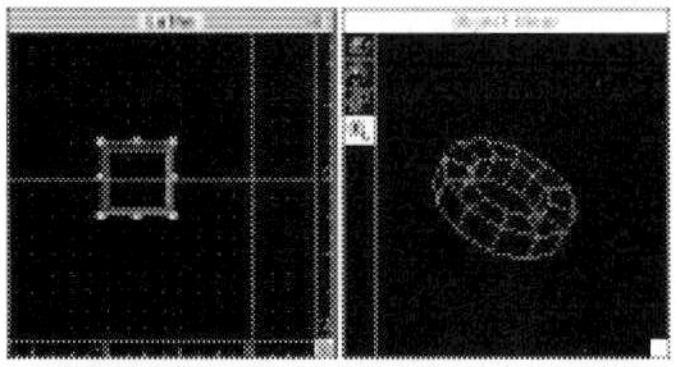

Figure 15.7 Creating a lathe object

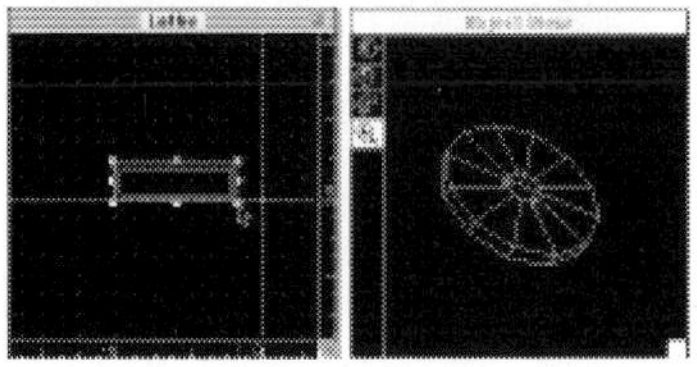

Figure 15.8 Altering the shape of a lathe object

Free-form objects can be created by starting with a free-form primitive (if the modeler you're using has one), or by simply drawing a 2-D shape, which the program will turn into a 3-D shape for you. Free-form objects can be modified by dragging their points as you would with a lathe object. Using free-form tools, you can quickly create odd shapes with complex geometry.

Evolving and Refining Objects and Shapes

As useful as the basic shapes and toolsets are, real-world entities and more intricate models often can be represented only with more sophisticated techniques. Frequently, this means cooking up models from scratch, rather than using predefined shapes. These techniques and tools, while very powerful, generally take more dedication and patience to master; they also can be difficult to control, easily creating extremely odd, unnatural shapes.

Spline-Based Modeling

Spline-based tools are used to create ultrasmooth curves. Until recently, this capability wasn' t even found in some of the highest-end animation programs costing thousands of dollars. It is one measure of the growing maturity of the Mac animation market that there are now a number of low-end products that offer this feature.

Spline curves are especially desirable as the camera moves in on rendered models, where non-spline curves will reveal telltale faceting from close-in views. You can still achieve decent-looking curves with a non-spline modeler, but you'll have to use a lot of polygons to do it—a cumbersome process, and one that will make huge files and increase rendering time.

In Figure 15.9, MacroModel's spline curves were used to create the complex forms that make up the airplane fuselage. Some modelers, like Infini-D, do not themselves create splines, but will import Bezier curves created in Adobe Illustrator and then allow you to change their shape by clicking and dragging the control points.

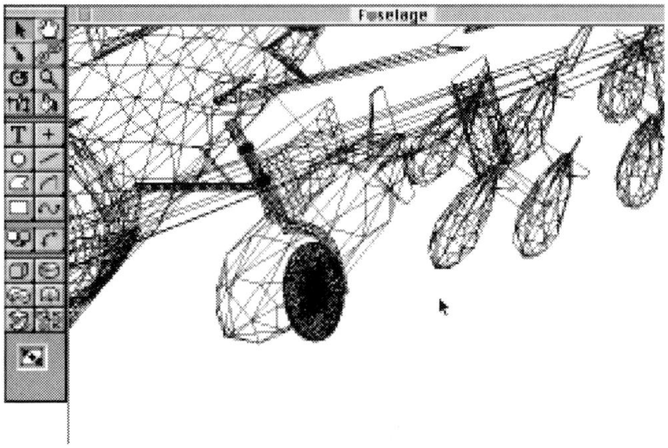

Figure 15.9 Spline-based modeling in MacroModel

Other programs, such as MacroModel, are spline-based modelers, so you can create and adjust spline curves on the spot. If your modeler doesn' t support the creation of splines but will import them, make sure that all of the spline information is retained. Sometimes, information can be lost in the conversion, resulting in splines that are little better than curves created with more traditional techniques.

Most renderers—programs which create the finished 3-D images, complete with shaded surfaces, color, texture, light, and shadow—render only from polygons. That means that unless the renderer you use is specifically designed to handle splines, rather than processing your carefully drawn spline curves it will convert the information to polygons, which may result in the same old faceting.

This is not a concern at all when you use programs that incorporate both modeling and rendering into a single product. However, it but can trip you up if you model in one package and render in another—unless you have the advantage of the compatibility of products made by multimedia giant Macromedia. For example, Three-D, MacroMedia' s renderer, is made to work with MacroModel, and will seamlessly accept and import all modeling information. Generally, though, even spline curves converted to polygonal curves will look smoother than curves originally created with polygons.

Vertex-Level or Mesh Editing

Vertex-level editing is a very precise form of model refinement. It allows you to manipulate control points, or vertices, along the surfaces of a shape. Some programs refer to these editable surface control points as meshes, and the objects themselves as mesh objects. While mesh editing gives you nearly absolute control, it also is a painstaking process, suitable (and tolerable) only for the most exacting of work.

Byte by Byte's Sculpt 3D and 4D offer the most complete vertex-level editing, allowing you to select more than one point at one time. You can then treat these points as separate objects, rotate and resize them, even extrude them into separate features.

Extruding along a Path and Sweeping

These two techniques can produce forms that are sometimes practical, and other times whimsical. To extrude along a path, you begin with a 2-D shape, which is automatically replicated by the modeler (Figure 15.10). This technique is useful for producing uniform architectural features such as moldings.

Sweep is a combination of extruding and lathing, in which you begin with a 2-D shape and use numeric controls to specify the direction, rotation, and increment of the extrusion, which the program then uses to create the object. Using sweep, you can create shapes like bicycle handlebars, snakes, animal horns, or nautilus shells. Figure 15.11 shows a sweep form in StrataVision.

TOOLS StrataVision ⌘226

Drilling is another convenient tool that is unfortunately not often found in

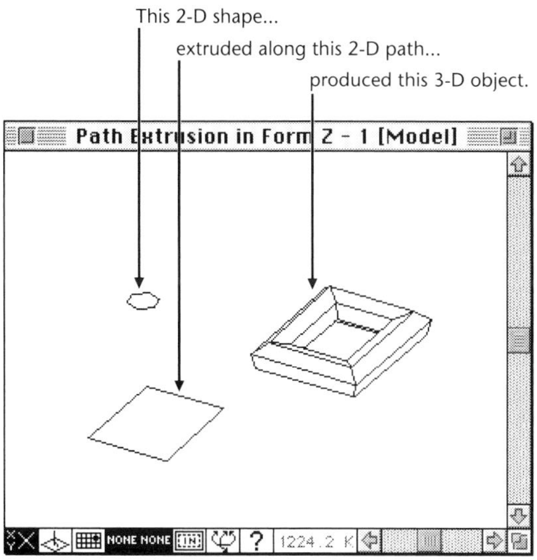

Figure 15.10 Extruding along a path

modeler toolboxes. A 2-D object is used like a bit to carve a hole in a 3-D object, which then contains an actual hole, not simply a facade.

Sculpting with Boolean Operations

Boolean operations are advanced tools that let you use one 3-D object to alter another. You can then use the object created where the two shapes intersect, or either or both of the altered shapes. Figure 15.12 illustrates the Boolean effect. This technique is very useful, and can be used to " sculpt" 3-D objects to create shapes impossible (or very difficult) to achieve any other way. It's also a quick way to create an object that fits another irregularly shaped object perfectly.

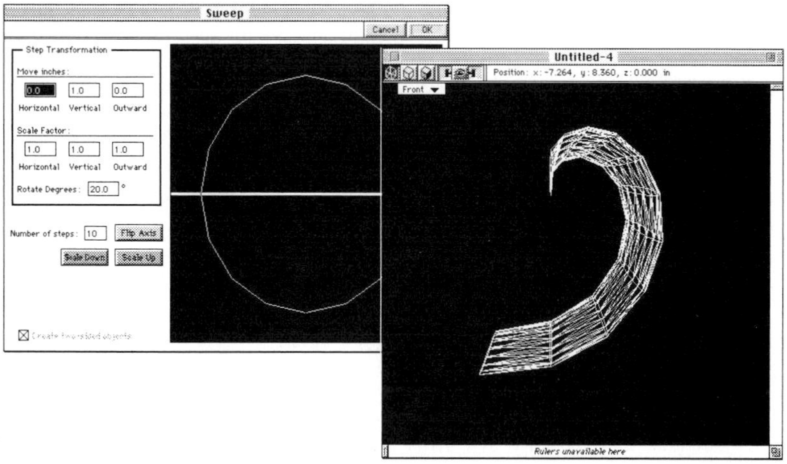

Figure 15.11 Strata' s Sweep control panel

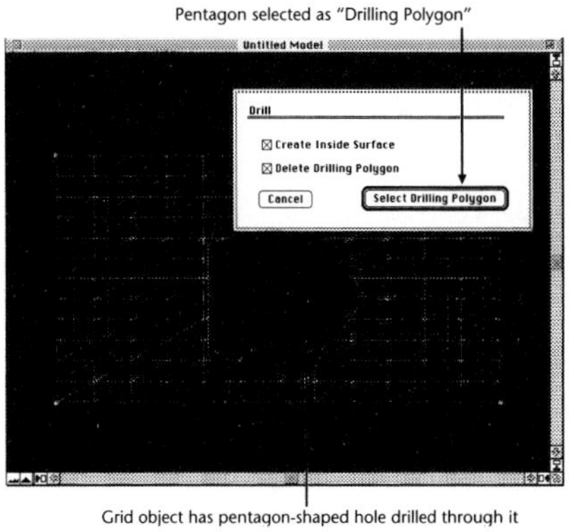

Figure 15.12 The Boolean effect

Working in 3-D Space

The 3-D workspace itself is often called the *3-D world*, in which objects are situated along three axes: X, Y, and Z. When viewing a three-dimensional object from the front, movement left to right is along the X axis, in/out motion is along the Y axis, and up/down motion is along the Z axis (Figure 15.13).

Yoo-hoo…?

Using this coordinate system, you can accurately place objects in space in relation to each other and to the camera, your vantage point on the 3-D world. For precision modeling, these coordinates are essential, and they are also critical to accurate camera positioning and movement.

The concepts of axes and the coordinate system are fundamental to all 3-D animation software, but they may take you a while to get used to. If you were

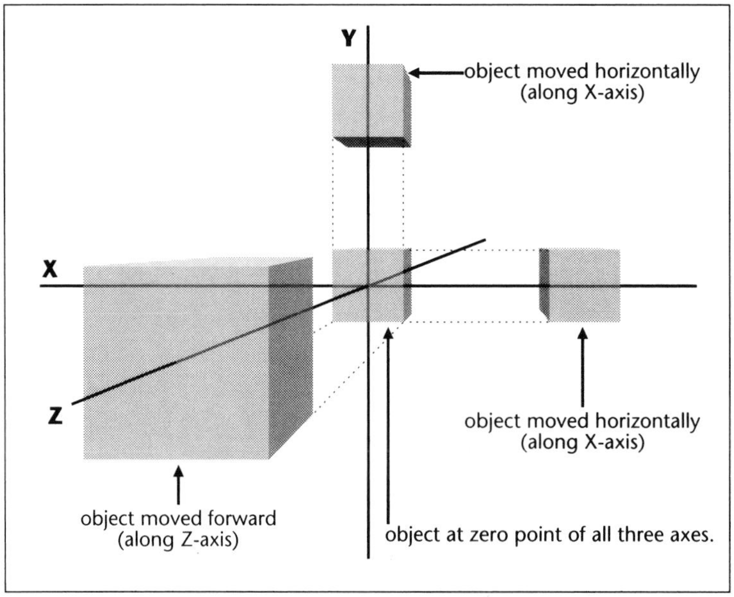

Figure 15.13 X, Y, and Z axes of motion

good at high school geometry and at test questions asking you to guess what diagrams in plain view would look like if they were folded, you'll do fine.

Most programs will show you the position of an object in relation to the center of the world—the place where the X, Y, and Z axes converge. (This is generally the default reference point, but you can alter it.)

If you enter a value for the position of an object on the X axis, the object will move from right to left (in top view). Type a number in the position box for the Y axis, and the object moves in or out. When an object is at the center of the world, the position coordinates are 0,0,0. You also can move the object by clicking and dragging, and the position numbers will dynamically update. Other values will affect an object's orientation in relation to a particular axis. Enter a value in the X axis orientation box, and the object will tilt. The dimension boxes affect the size of an object. Working with a program that has this feature can greatly aid in your understanding of 3-D space.

Programs differ in the way they represent 3-D space, and some help more than others in the visualization process. For example, in World view, Infini-D shows objects in four simultaneous views: top, front, right (or bottom, back, right), and camera. Most modelers require you to enter another mode or view (known variously as the Workshop, Object view, and so on) to make substantive changes to models. While in the World view, you can generally modify objects in very basic ways by resizing, rotating, squashing, stretching, or repositioning.

Look for a modeler that has a few other navigation aids. For example, most modelers let you place an object (or point a camera) anywhere in the 3-D space. But your windows on this space are only narrow views, which might mean that as you move them around, your models will easily disappear from view (in what is known as the *black hole effect*). Modelers that will automatically turn the cameras to an object or move an object without changing its orientation, can be very helpful.

Precise Positioning and Alignment

The coordinate system can be used to align objects precisely . For example, you may want several objects to line up exactly. The fastest and most accurate way to do this is to enter numeric values for the position of the objects. You may want to actually superimpose two objects; in this case, simply use the same position values for both objects.

Sometimes, the perspective views (perspectives have *vanishing points*—objects farther away look smaller) common to 3-D programs can get in the way of precise alignment of two objects. For example, in Figure 15.14, it looks as if the glass is on the table. But actually, it's not, as revealed by the orthographic view (no perspective); (Figure 15.15).

Locks and Linking

Much as you might constrain the movement of drawing tools in a draw program so that, for example, a line comes out exactly straight, you can confine movement, orientation, and size attributes of objects. Locks are very useful in a number of

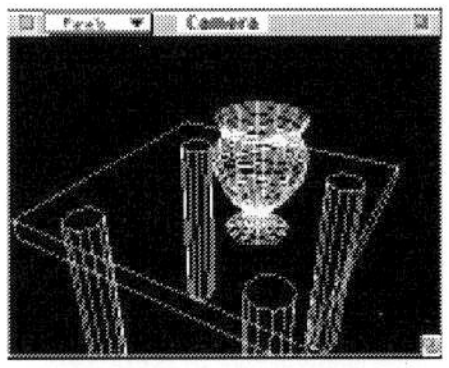

Figure 15.14
Is the glass on the table?

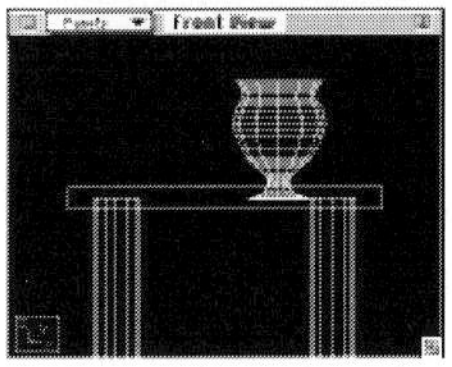

Figure 15.15
Nope.

ways; for instance, when you animate objects, locks on movement and orientation will allow you to create more realistic and consistent motion. Using these constraints, fingers won't bend backwards, trains will stay on their tracks, and planets will revolve around the sun.

Locks can be relative to the world. They also can involve the relationship between objects, so that objects can be grouped as one, for example, to keep together all of the component body parts that make up a figure. When multiple objects are locked or linked, the first is known as the *parent* and the second and any subsequent objects are the *child* or children. These groups of objects are very common to 3-D modeling, and are necessary to the creation of complex forms. Such composite objects are known variously as *hierarchical* models or *object networks*.

Programs that allow a great deal of control over locks and linking, such as Swivel and Infini-D, offer various levels of control. Infini-D, for example, uses free, pivot, position, and full locks. Free locks let you reposition or rotate the child while the parent remains stationary; move the parent, however, and the child will follow. For example, you could use a free lock to position a planet relative to the sun. The planet is free to orbit the sun, but if you reposition the sun the planet will move, too, while still keeping its relative position.

A pivot lock allows you to reposition but not reorient a child independently of the parent. Pivot locks are good for creating specific types of movement, such as the movement of elbow joints, which in the natural world move only along one axis. Specify a position lock and you' ll be able to rotate the child without affecting the parent, but the two will be linked in terms of movement. You might use a position lock to create a telescoping object, so that the components would be able to slide in and out along a single axis only.

A full lock welds two objects in terms of position and orientation. This type of lock is analogous to grouping: you effectively create one composite object. You might use this type of locking to bind the legs of a table to a tabletop, for instance. You can still change the size or surface characteristics of fully locked objects independently of one another. The table would still be manageable as a single unit, but you could apply one surface to the legs and another to the top.

Super 3D has a command called " Seal Vertices" that is very useful when joining objects. Sometimes, objects may look as if they are joined, but they are actually slightly misaligned. This may not be apparent until you add surfaces to the compound object, at which time irregularities due to imperfectly aligned objects may become noticeable. This wastes time, because you' ll have to go and fix the alignment and then rerender. The Seal Vertices command ensures that objects are properly aligned and connected.

Next Year's Model

The tools and primitives described above can help a great deal in creating a geometric description of boxes, cylinders, or coffee cups. However, making convincing people, trees, or cars is more challenging.

You may not want to invest the considerable time necessary to master a modeler, but may prefer to move on to the more gratifying phases of animating and rendering. 3-D clip libraries meet this need by providing sets of prebuilt models that can be used as a basis for an animation, placing them and then rendering and animating them in your own way. (See Appendix B for clip library listings.)

Professional animator Lynda Weinman agrees: " I'm really in favor of [prebuilt models] and I study them myself sometimes for two reasons. First, you don't have to put the effort and time into learning modeling yourself—you can just drop models into your presentation, and—boom—it's done. The other thing is to study how somebody else did it."

While Lynda and other professionals rarely use prebuilt models, such models are, as she points out, very good learning tools. And if you're also tempted to save time and lift a few (but only if you've paid for the clip library!), well, after all, even Picasso said, "Good artists copy, great artists steal."

Animating

Once you've modeled the objects and "players" in your 3-D world, it's time to give them life by animating and rendering them. For the sake of clarity, we've chosen to cover animation and then rendering in this chapter. In reality, however, the processes may be intertwined to some degree. Sometimes animators will render a scene, then animate it, for example. Generally, though, it's best to get basic motions mapped out ahead of rendering, since working with rendered images or wireframes is much slower.

If you are creating 3-D still images, of course, you will move directly from the modeling to the rendering stage.

Motion Studies

Animators usually will start by roughing out movements in a series of motion studies. These are accomplished with objects in wireframe or abbreviated geometry to speed development time. An even quicker way to study potential movements is to substitute *bounding boxes* for models. Bounding boxes are simply cubes with roughly the same dimensions as the models they represent. Because they are very simple forms, bounding boxes are often used to establish the basic movements of objects. Most programs will automatically substitute bounding boxes for complex geometry.

An animator, then, might begin by blocking out movement with bounding boxes to achieve the basic motion desired. Once the essence is established, movement can be refined using the wireframe geometry of the object models. At this stage, objects that possess at least rudimentary features also can be oriented correctly, so that they face the proper direction as the move.

To get a better idea of dimensionality, the animator might next render the wireframes with flat shading, which will give a crude idea of surface and form. Only after the motions have been refined will fully rendered animation be processed and viewed.

Motion Scripting

The process of animating objects is called *motion scripting* or *motion control.* Animation programs offer a wide range of features for effecting motion. (See Chapter 7, "Animation Tools," for a list of features by product.) The basic idea is that you move objects (or cameras) into key positions, and the program takes a snapshot of this setup. Then you move the objects again, and the computer takes another snapshot. These shots are called keyframes.

Once you have identified all of your keyframes, the computer does the rest by *tweening*—calculating the in-between frames. This is analogous to the process used by traditional animators. The animator generally creates the keyframes, and assistant animators (who were known as " in-betweeners" in the early days) then create all the intervening frames; the computer and animation software act as your assistant animators.

Of course, you have many options in creating your keyframes—you aren't limited to movement in space alone. You can resize objects, so that they grow

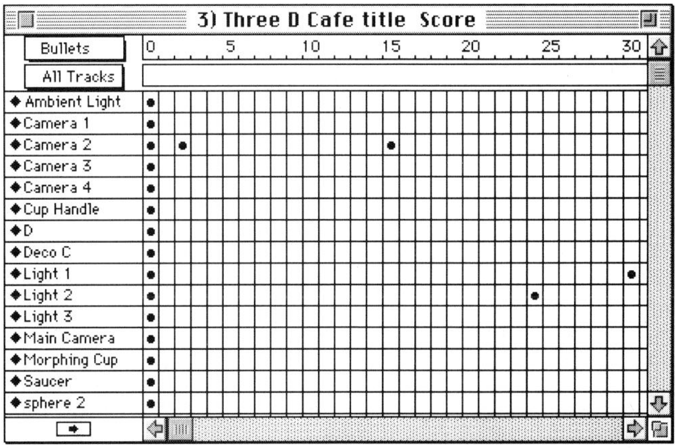

Figure15.16 Three-D's "Score," a time-based visual display

larger or smaller over time; you can reorient them, so that they will move to face a different direction when animated; some programs even allow you to change an object's surface and color over time, or change one object into another.

Time-Based Animation

Macromedia pioneered the idea of the *Score*, which first appeared in its Director 2-D animation and integration program. The Score provides an extremely flexible means by which to control and refine events over time. The Score is also used by Macromedia's rendering and animation package, Three-D, and the concept has been adopted by other animation programs as well. (Infini-D calls its version the *Sequencer.*) Figure 15.16 is an example of what Three-D's score looks like. These time-based visual representations provide enormous control over animation, because they allow you to tweak individual components without affecting any other elements in the overall sequence. If you decide a particular object is moving too slowly, you can adjust the speed of that object alone, while leaving other objects and events untouched.

Suppose you had an object flying around in a circle, an object whose motion you had carefully defined. Let' s say you also wanted that object to change color. You could alter the color without affecting any of the motion attributes associated with the sequence.

In these ways, time-based windows (like the Score and the Sequencer) offer a very flexible and powerful means to tweak and adjust animations down to the individual object. In fact, you can even address parts of an object, such as a person, if the object is made up of component objects.

Refining Movement

While you can get acceptable results simply by dragging objects to create keyframes and then letting the computer fill in the other frames to complete the animation, realistic motion often requires more subtle effects. When objects move in the real world, they accelerate and decelerate gradually, not all at once. This is known as *inertia*, and some animation programs give you control over this effect with parameters called *ease-in* and *ease-out* (Figure 15.17). This effect is particularly useful for camera pans and fly-throughs, which would be noticeably artificial without ease-in/ease-out.

Some programs let you animate objects along a spline-based path, which can also smooth movements to a great degree.

Sophisticated programs like Three-D let you view and tweak motions in graph form. These graphical views, which are available for any animation sequence you've created, offer the ultimate control over motion smoothing. You can tweak the points on the graph to adjust the motion, then replay it to see the results.

Although all of these are convenient and flexible tools, smooth motion can be very difficult to achieve, especially for complex camera fly-throughs. Like everything else in animation, top-quality results are frequently obtainable only through hard work, long hours, and tedious trial and error. For example, San

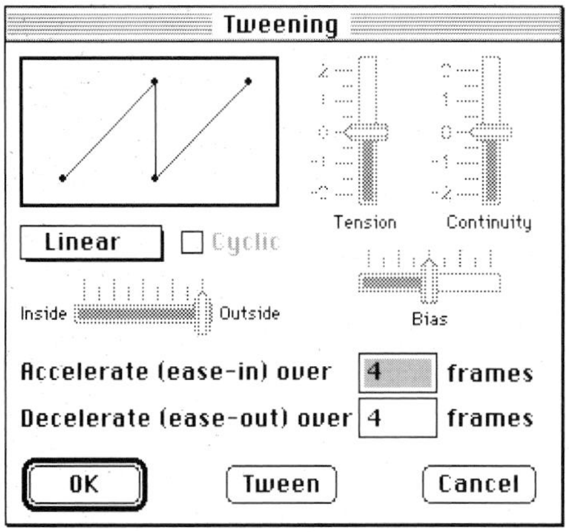

Figure15.17 Smoothing motion with Ease-in/ Ease-out

Francisco animator Donald Grahame inherited a complex 3-D animation project that plays from a record store kiosk to allow customers to listen to CDs before they buy. Even though Grahame discarded most of the work that had already been done, preferring to do his own beautifully designed and rendered scenes, he kept a fluid camera movement that flies through to establish the scene. The previous animator had spent hours perfecting the motion, and Grahame didn' t want to start all over on that.

Interpolating Other Characteristics

Interpolation is another word for the calculations performed by the computer to create in-between frames. Although creating motion, changing the size of objects, and reorienting them are some of the most common animation processes, there are many others, including selection of characteristics like color, shape, and even texture. You might animate these characteristics to change an object's color or texture over time, or even have it change shape altogether. Programs that offer these features make it as easy as animating motion or orientation.

To change an object' s surface characteristics over time, you would simply apply the first surface to the object (see "Rendering," for a complete description of surface characteristics), move the time marker ahead in the timeline, and apply the second texture. When the animation is played back, the first surface will change to the second surface in the allotted time.

Some programs allow you to create animated lighting effects, too, so that you can change the color of a light from one shade to another over time.

Morph ⌘229

One of the most intriguing animated transformations is called *morphing*, in which an object changes shape over time. Morphing was made famous in *Terminator 2*, in which the T-1000 "pseudopod" transformed itself into various human and not-so-human forms. This first use of a digital character—created by computer—has opened the floodgates for computer animation in Hollywood.

Now you see the effect everywhere, but that shouldn' t stop you. Morphing is still a stunning effect, and a lot of fun to play around with. To do it, you simply select or create the first object, create a keyframe, then do the same with the second object. The program will create the necessary in-between frames, and you can play back the animation to watch the transformation.

The Advantages of Being Invisible

Making certain objects invisible is a neat trick that has many uses. For example, you will want to render cameras and lights (which in most programs are simply objects like any others) invisible so that they don' t appear in your final animation. Or, you may not want an object to appear until a given point in time. To do this, you would make it invisible until you want it to show up.

You also can use this technique to conserve disk and memory space when animating moving objects over a static background. You can render the background invisible so that the computer has to animate (and render) only the objects that are actually changing. Later, you can composite the objects with background to create the finished piece. This will save on system resources by having the computer animate and render only what is absolutely necessary.

This is analogous to a major innovation in early film animation. Before the use of celluloid began early in this century, animators had to paint everything—even static backgrounds—for each frame, an incredibly tedious process. *Gertie the Trained Dinosaur* (1908), perhaps the most famous of the first animated films, was done in this way.

With the advent of celluloid, a single background could be placed under a series of cels, saving enormous time and money and freeing talented artists for more challenging undertakings. (Chuck Jones, director of such Warner Bros. classic characters as Bugs Bunny, Wile E. Coyote, and Pepe Le Pew, began his career as a cel washer.)

Making objects invisible also can help with tricky animation effects. Dave Merck, of the Animation Lab at the University of Massachusetts at Amherst, uses the technique to animate a helicopter. First, he creates a small object and links it to the chopper. Then he makes the small object invisible. Next, he creates the blade rotation for the chopper. Finally, he drags the invisible object, which, since it is linked to the helicopter, will move it through space. This creates a separate timeline for the helicopter movement, which doesn' t necessarily have the same period as the blade rotation.

Joe Sparks, acclaimed producer of the *Total Distortion* CD-ROM product, agrees that making objects invisible can be a lifesaver. Sometimes he has animated and rendered a complex scene, only to discover that something is wrong with one of the objects. Rather than start over on the entire scene, he can render the offending object invisible, go back to the original model file for the object and make the necessary modifications. Then, using the scene as a template, Joe deletes everything but the new object,, which leaves it in the correct place for compositing back into the rendered scene.

Taking Advantage of Links and Hierarchies

Hierarchical animation lets you take advantage of locks and links that you set up when modeling objects (see "Locks and Linking," earlier in this chapter). For example, when animating a human form, the arms could be made to sway as the hips move forward. Other possibilities include locking lights to objects, so that as the objects, move, the lights follow. The same relationships can be set up between cameras and objects so that the action is always being followed and will remain in view.

Rendering

Rendering is the process of defining what your objects and scenes will look like. You apply surface characteristics such as color, texture, and reflectivity. You can also control how shadows fall and what they look like. You establish point of view with the camera and select appropriate lenses.

Once you have specified all of these attributes, sit back and relax awhile, because it will take the computer from several minutes to *days* or even *weeks* to render your scene. Just how long it takes depends on the complexity of objects and surfaces, the computer you are using, and the rendering software. Normally, you' ll have done motion tests with bounding boxes and wireframes, and will have test-rendered small patches to get an idea of what the final scene will look like. Still, the rendering process often is misunderstood to be hands-free—you go off to do your laundry, come back, and *voila!,* a complete photorealistic scene is waiting for you.

Reality, as usual, is grittier and less romantic. Animators often will render and rerender half a dozen times, and sometimes much more frequently. And even on the fastest of machines, rendering is like watching paint dry. A Quadra 950 may render at only about twice the speed of your trusty IIci, which doesn't amount to a big difference in the glacial time frames of rendering.

Still, rendering has come a long way, and there are tricks to speed it up; unfortunately, these mostly involve extra hardware or expensive software. We'll cover these alternatives at the end of this section.

Types of Rendering

Most rendering software gives you myriad options for rendering surfaces. The speed of these techniques generally varies with the realism of the surfaces they render. Some programs, such as Swivel, are known for their very rapid flat or even smooth shading, which they can do on-the-fly, greatly aiding in the definition of models and the specification of animation moves. Up the ladder (*way* up the ladder) are ray tracing and radiosity, which bring ultra-realism to computer animations, and for which you pay the price in speed, RAM, and disk space (not to mention playback speed).

Flat Shading

At the bottom of the rendering pecking order is *flat shading,* sometimes called *constant shading,* which is generally used only for rough tests, to get a feel for what models look like with surfaces, or to make sure objects don't intersect when they're not supposed to (which is hard to tell with wireframes).

Flat shading applies the light source to only one point on each face of the model, which results in a faceted appearance, with visible underlying geometry.

Smooth Shading: Gouraud and Phong

These are algorithms (mathematical formulas) that seek to simulate more realistic shading, like the variable shading that characterizes real objects in the natural world. The light is calculated on multiple points on a face, and then smoothly blended to produce an integrated, more naturalistic effect.

Gouraud shading is named after its inventor, Frenchman Henri Gouraud (rhymes with Thoreau, believe it or not). In this technique, the effect of lighting is applied to the vertices of the polygons that make up the face. Values are then interpolated for the intermediate shades, and the result is a smooth effect.

Phong shading is an even more sophisticated formula, developed by Phong Bui-tuong, that calculates shading from multiple points across the entire surface, instead of just the vertices of the component polygons. It is known for its excellent re-creation of specular highlights—the "hot-spots" in a very shiny surface, such as a mirror or a chrome surface.

Ray Tracing and Radiosity

Ray tracing is a computationally intensive shading method that calculates the effects of light sources of many types, including direct illumination, reflections, and *refractions*, (the effects of light passing through transparent substances such as glass and water).

This technique is normally used for 3-D still images, for two reasons. First, it is unbelievably taxing on machine resources, requiring millions of calculations to complete a scene. Second, it is *view-dependent*, because light rays are traced from the light source to the point of view (POV), and vice versa, so any change in the camera angle would mean the entire scene would have to recalculated.

Just as ray tracing calculates the effects of light in a reflective environment, *radiosity* determines the effects of diffuse lighting. Rather than tracing light rays, radiosity computes the light energy in a scene, which may come from other, indirect sources. For example, a light glancing off a wall will cause some bounce light to fall on other objects in a scene.

Unlike ray tracing, radiosity is view-independent, making it suitable for dynamic scenes that may include shifts in the POV. A common application of radiosity is in 3-D architectural renderings which simulate the diffused lighting of building interiors. Because the technique is view-independent, the client can "walk through" the building to get a simulated feel for the space.

For the ultimate in realism, the two techniques can be combined to achieve specular reflections and refractions, and diffuse lighting effects. However, this is not recommended unless you have a water-cooled Cray supercomputer with a couch.

Trade-Offs of Rendering Techniques

As is the case in real life, better quality means more time. No one will argue with the view that ray tracing and radiosity create the best looking and most accurate 3-D imagery, but most desktop computers (and most computer users) are not up to the task. If you' re into photorealism, get a very fast computer (preferably a machine designed to crunch polygons, such as Silicon Graphics workstation,or at the very least, a Quadra 950).

Fortunately, you can achieve very good and even outstanding results with Phong shading, which is what most renderers use to create finished work. Flat and especially Gouraud shading are fine for gauging what a scene will look like, and there are tricks to get some of the effects of the higher-end shading techniques. For example, instead of waiting for calculation of reflections in a shiny object, you can map a tiny version of the scene onto the object' s surface, thus creating a simulated environment map (see below) at huge savings in time and energy.

Just to give an idea of the trade-offs between rendering techniques, we applied a surface to a simple vase. On a Mac II (albeit, not a blazingly fast machine) the vase took about 10 seconds to render with flat shading, around 1 minute to shade with the Gouraud method, and about 10 minutes to render with Phong shading. By then, it was time for bed and we didn' t get a chance to try ray tracing.

Creating Surfaces

The essence of rendering is the application of surfaces to the models you have constructed and animated in your 3-D world. Most renderers supply a bewildering array of surface options—both prefab surfaces included with the program and the means to edit and create your own custom versions.

Surfaces also can be applied in a number of ways, using any of the shading techniques described above, with commensurate differences in quality. Note that subtle effects will be most accurately rendered with Phong shading, ray tracing, or radiosity. Gouraud shading may give only the slightest semblance of the effect, and effects rendered with flat shading probably won' t read at all, except to give some idea of rudimentary characteristics such as color.

There are many ways to create surfaces and textures; the method you use will depend on the particular application and the effect you are trying to achieve.

Working with Surface Libraries

TOOLS

StrataTextures ⌘811-812

Sometimes, the extensive surface libraries included with many renderers will be all you need. For example, Infini-D supplies the list of options shown in Figure 15.18. Note the sphere in the upper right, which gives an idea of the effect of each surface. Most renderers allow you to create your own surfaces by starting with one in the surface library and modifying it, using various controls. StrataVision, for example, displays the dialog box shown in Figure 15.19 for editing preexisting surfaces. Using this dialog box, you can change the characteristics of an existing surface or texture by fiddling with such parameters as ambient fraction, bump amplitude, glow factor, and transparency. A full discourse on these effects is

Figure 15.18 Infini-D's built-in surface characteristics

beyond the scope of this book, but here are a few definitions to whet your appetite. (We just had to find out what "bump amplitude" meant.)

Bump amplitude allows you to set the size of the depressions in a bump texture. Bump maps (see below) are patterns of depressions, such as those on a golf ball, that you can wrap around (map onto) an object.

Ambient fraction is the level of ambient (diffuse) lighting that a given object will reflect, while *glow* will give the illusion that an object is lit from within.

Specular highlight lets you adjust the dot of light reflected in shiny objects.

Texture Mapping

The process of applying surfaces to objects is called *texture-mapping*. You can use the surfaces in surface libraries to do this, or you can create effects such as bumpy surfaces, natural patterns like wood grain and marble, or reflections, by mapping other types of patterns.

Most renderers support a variety of texture-mapping techniques, depending on the type of surface you're creating. One way is to map an image file, such as a PICT or TIFF file created in a paint, image processing, or some other program. Use this type of mapping when you have a specific image you want to use as a surface.

TOOLS

Kai's Power Tools ⌘ 134

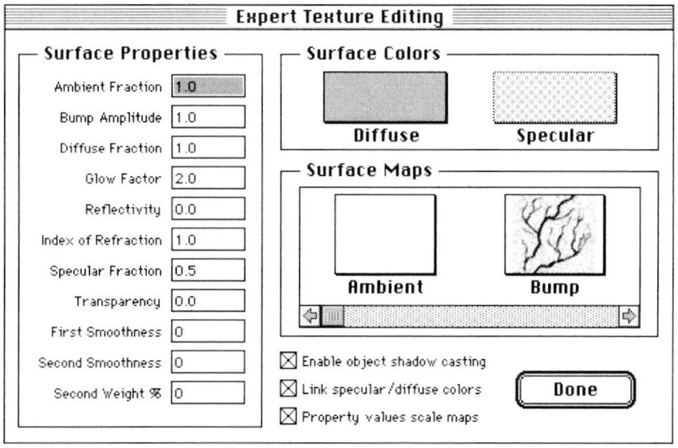

Figure15.19 StrataVision' s Expert Texture Editing dialog box

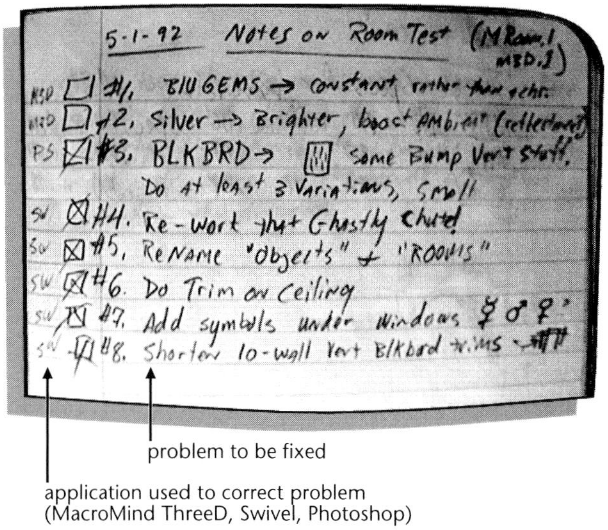

Figure 15.20 **Joe hit on the right processing formula for a *Total Distortion* image.**

TOOLS
Photoshop ⌘ 222

Suppose you want to map a photograph onto an object. To do this, you'd scan the photo into an image processing program like Photoshop or ColorStudio. You could process, filter, or otherwise retouch the image, then import it into the renderer for mapping. This technique is particularly effective for creating realistic effects. Drew Pictures in San Francisco used it extensively to create texture maps of all types for *The Iron Helix*. For example, Photoshop was used to create gritty, oily, scarred textures that were then mapped onto spaceship models using Macromedia Three-D and Electric Image.

Sometimes, it takes quite a while to arrive at the right formula for processing an image. After trial and error, Joe Sparks hit upon the right processing sequence for an image, and recorded it in his project notebook under the legend, "This is It!" (Figure 15.20). Later, when too burned out to do anything else one late night, he'll refer to his notebook and process a bunch of images all at once, using this formula.

External sources for imagery include scanners, with which original art, photographs, and textures may be digitized; image processing programs that can be used both to manipulate scanned imagery and to create it wholesale; paint-and-draw programs, which you can use to create surfaces and backgrounds; and various sorts of cameras, which can be used to bring in both still and motion video. (Consult Chapter 5, "Imaging Tools," for more on the sources for imagery.)

Rendering programs typically offer at least three different ways to project image files onto objects: *bump* mapping, *texture* mapping, and *reflection* mapping (see below for definitions). You can then control how these files are mapped through a dialog box, such as the one from Macromedia's Three-D shown in Figure 15.21. Here, you can control with sliders the blending of object color with texture color, the height of the bumps in a bump map, or the percentage of a reflection color

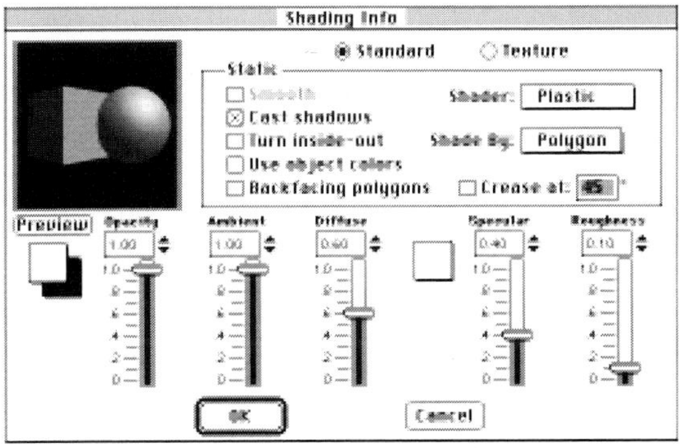

Figure 15.21 Three-D s Shading Info dialog box

that will be added to an object for a reflection map. You also can specify exactly how the image files are wrapped around the object (see *"Mapping Types,"* below).

Textures such as bumps and dents are created with bump mapping. These features are not actually 3-D attributes with real depth; rather, like texture maps, bump maps are image files that are projected onto objects to create the surface. The illusion of dimples, like those found on an orange or a golf ball, is achieved through subtle variations in highlight and shadow.

Because bump mapping doesn't produce actual 3-D features, viewers may notice that large bumps don' t have true dimensionality. For this reason, you may have better luck with smaller bumps, which sustain the illusion more effectively.

The effect of bumps is also heavily influenced by the placement of lights. Low sidelighting will accentuate depressions, for example, while lights placed from above may wash out the texturing (see *"Cameras and Lighting,"* below).

Reflection maps are used to project reflections of the 3-D world onto objects. For example, you might have the reflection of someone's face staring into a crystal ball. Ray tracing (discussed earlier in this chapter) produces the most realistic reflections, but at great cost of time and resources. Because ray tracing actually calculates the path and effects of light (whether they are reflection, refraction, transparency, or shadows), it is highly accurate and can yield gorgeous photorealism. Figure 15.22 makes extensive use of reflection mapping. Because reflection mapping (also called *environment* mapping) involves projection of an image file, images created this way are much quicker to render than ray-traced imagery, and the results are quite good and certainly suitable for most applications.

Mapping Types

When you project a 2-D image on a 3-D object, the program must have a way to identify points on the 2-D image that will correspond with those on the 3-D surface. Renderers commonly furnish four mapping types: orthogonal, spherical, cylindrical, and cubic. When you map a surface, you'll choose the mapping type appropriate to the object: cubic mapping for six-sided cubes, orthogonal for flat objects, and so on. Mapping types apply only to texture and bump maps, since the portion of a reflection map that appears on an object is calculated by the program.

Figure 15.22
A reflection map

Some distortion is inevitable when mapping textures; choosing the correct mapping type for the object you are shading can minimize these irregularities. You also can size texture maps so that their dimensions are similar to those of the 3-D object, which will diminish distortion. Different mapping types produce various " seams," where points of the map meet as they wrap around the object. You can either adjust these so that they meet exactly, or face seams away from the camera during rendering.

Tiling, offered by some renderers, is useful if you rescale or reposition an already mapped texture. Three-D offers Black, Repeat, and Clamp Tiling. If you scale down an image, Black Tiling substitutes black for the area not covered by the texture. Repeat Tiling reproduces the texture in a checkerboard pattern over the surface of the object. Clamp Tiling uses the color of the last pixel on the edge of the pattern's surface to cover the remaining areas of the object.

Instead of creating surfaces by projecting an image file onto objects, procedural maps create surfaces mathematically. These computer-generated surfaces are used to create natural textural patterns like wood grain or marble.

While you could wrap an image file around a broom handle, say, to create the effect of a wooden surface, this surface would be somewhat distorted by the topology—the shape—of the broom handle itself. Instead, you could use a procedural texture to precisely define the color, pattern, plasticity, and other characteristics of the texture. The resulting object will look as if it were actually carved from a hunk of wood, rather than just simulating that surface.

The downside of procedural maps is that you need to fiddle with a number of parameters to get an effect that doesn't look phony or contrived.

Procedural maps can be used to create all sorts of random or chaotic patterns. Infini-D, for example, offers Mandlebrot Map, Julia Map, Tile Map, Noise Map,

Marble Map, Wood Map, Wave Map, and Corrosion Map, among others. Like other types of textures, these special effects maps can be adjusted very flexibly.

Some renderers let you project animated sequences on objects. You could even have a moving object that includes an *animated surface*—maybe a blimp moving across the screen with animated projection or moving text across its surface. With Infini-D, you can even project a QuickTime movie on a surface. (See the CD project XYZ for an example of this effect.)

Cameras and Lighting

You may establish camera angles and fly-throughs while animating, but it is during rendering when movements and surfaces are actually compiled or rendered. When the program renders an image, it does so from a single camera view. If you have multiple cameras for multiple views, scenes are rendered from one camera at a time, meaning you'd have to render each camera sequence separately if you wanted different cuts from one point of view to another. It' s usually easier to make one camera jump from place to place, then render the scene as a whole.

As when placing other objects in relation to one another, determining camera placement is easier in orthogonal view, rather than in the normal perspective views offered by animation programs. Most software allows you to define different camera attributes, such as camera position, orientation, lens type, and focal length.

Camera lens choices range from telephoto, which gives a narrow field of view and magnifies your view, to fish-eye, which shows a wide field of view and makes the scene look farther away. Each type of lens has an associated focal length, or you can create your own custom lenses by specifying a focal length value.

Most renderers offer a number of lighting options, including types of light, intensity, and color.

As you would expect, different types of lights produce various effects. Ambient light is diffuse lighting that doesn' t come from any apparent source. Point lights cast light in all directions, as would a naked light bulb. Spotlights throw directed beams.

You can adjust the beams that lights throw, softening the focus and creating a *penumbra*, or transition from light to dark ("transition" and "roll-off" controls in example above), and also the beam angle (called "cone" in Three-D).

Lighting can greatly enhance the effect of your animation and is a key factor in generating realism and interest in a scene. Aside from basic illumination, many renderers allow you to create lighting effects. For example, you can raise or lower lights as if they were on a dimmer. To do this, you simply set the light' s intensity in one keyframe, and set it at another level in the next keyframe—the program will tween the intermediate values.

You also can assign colors to lights, which will "paint" objects that are illuminated. White lights will not disturb the individual colors of objects, but will simply make them brighter.

Lights can be treated as any other object; they can even be animated so that

Antialiasing and Alpha Channels

Antialiasing is the process by which the edges of images or objects are smoothed so that they blend in with adjacent images or backgrounds. This is done by substituting color values in muted shades that are in the range between the object and background colors. The following is a close-up of an antialiased image:

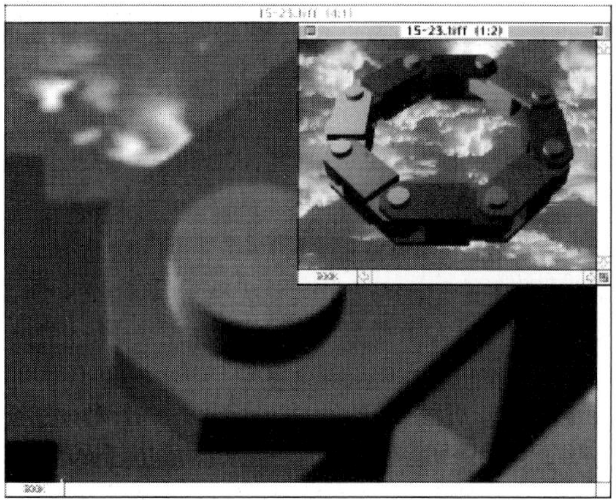

Figure15.23 Antialiased object

Antialiasing is almost a requirement for creating a smooth transition between images and objects, but it does have some drawbacks. Since it requires adjustment of individual pixels, an antialiased image will take longer to render. Also, antialiasing "locks" an image or object to a background, making it difficult to change background attributes, such as color, later .

Luckily, there is another technique that fixes this problem and others. *Alpha channels,* first seen on the desktop in Photoshop (see Chapter 5, "Imaging Tools,") are becoming increasingly important in animation, too. Some animation programs, such as Three-D, Infini-D, and ElectricImage, will automatically create an alpha channel component of a selected object. This alpha channel contains transparency information for the associated object, which the program uses to composite two images together.

Antialiased alpha channels let you combine two images seamlessly. This is convenient, because you can render multiple frames with the same background, and render foreground objects separately. Then, using the alpha channels of the foreground objects, you can composite against the rendered backgrounds. This technique saves rendering time and disk space, since you only render the background once and separately render the objects that change .

Alpha channels have other uses, the most common of which is to mask an object to protect it (or its surrounding background) from effects of a processing or paint effect. For instance, you may want to change a particular color in a surface of an object. If that color also happens to be found in the background, it will get changed, too. On the other

box continued

hand, if the object has an alpha channel, this will prevent any changes from occurring outside the image itself. Alpha channels are also used to composite animation onto a video image, and several animation programs, including ElectricImage and Infini-D, excel at this process.

Most programs do not yet automatically create alpha channels for you; but, says Lynda Weinman, "alpha channels are the way of the future. They're just inevitable—it's got to go in that direction."

As useful as they are, alpha channels, since they are added information, will take up precious RAM and disk space, and naturally, will also slow rendering. So if resources are tight, use alpha channels only when necessary to achieve particular effects.

they follow other objects to create a spotlight effect, or they can dance around, producing moving beams like searchlights. Most renderers also let you decide whether or not lights will cast shadows.

Making the Best of Rendering

Rendering is what the computer does both best and least well. All of the thousands or millions of calculations necessary to render a complex scene, with its varying surfaces, lighting, views, and animation, would be impossible to do without a computer. And, certainly, using a paint program to simply create a 3-D scene—especially an animated one—would be next to impossible.

The Longest Coffee Breaks of Your Life

At the same time, the rendering of very complex animated scenes really pushes desktop machines—even the mighty Quadra—to the very limits of their capabilities. It' s not unusual for a moderately intricate animation to take hours or days to render. We asked Adam Lavine, president of Specular International, makers of Infini-D, how long it would take to render a sophisticated, broadcast-quality, 10-minute animation he was working on; he replied that he hoped it would take *only* a few weeks.

Clearly, something needs to be done about this, and help is fortunately on the way. One of the most promising developments is the advent of *network* or *distributed rendering*. If you are lucky enough to have several Macs—the more, the better—in your work environment, you can use this technique.

Network rendering is a simple idea that works very well. Basically, all you need, aside from the Macs (which have to be connected with LocalTalk or EtherTalk) and your rendering software, is the network rendering software itself, which divides and apportions a rendering job among all the Macs that are available.

The speed advantage achieved by these network renderers is not completely linear; estimates by users indicate that second and subsequent machines devoted to a rendering task will contribute from 50% to 80% of their processing power.

So, a task that took an hour on one Mac would take 33 to 40 minutes with a second machine, and 20 to 30 minutes with the addition of a third.

At least four companies offer network renderers: Specular International (BackBurner), Ray Dream (DreamNet), Pixar (NetRenderMan), and Strata (RenderPro). These programs are covered in Chapter 7, "Animation Tools."

Another way to shorten rendering is to send rendering jobs to a Unix workstation such as the Indigo or NeXT. These workstations are generally more powerful than Macs and can bull their way through rendering jobs. Donald Grahame uses this method, and is quite happy with results. Modeling in Swivel, he exports models in the RenderMan RIB format, which are then transferred to an Indigo via Ethernet, where they are processed with RenderMan and then sent back as bitmaps to the Mac. Asked if there are any disadvantages to this setup, Grahame replies, " Well, I used to organize my life around rendering breaks, using them to return phone calls, shop, or sleep. Now, I find that rendering goes so fast that I end up working for longer stretches, and have to force myself to take a break."

Aside from faster machines, which inevitably will come, the ultimate answer may lie with specialized add-in boards such as Yarc System Corp' s NuSprint RISC board. This card, equipped with a 25MHz RISC processor, runs at speeds of up to 25 Mips and can accelerate rendering up to 25 times over a Mac II.

Final Product

When you have completely modeled, animated, and rendered a scene, it' s time to distribute it. If it is going to be viewed on a computer the considerations are different than if you plan to copy it off to videotape. Some of these, covered at the beginning of this chapter, are expanded on here.

Computer-Based Delivery

PACo Producer ⌘218

The integrity of computer-based playback of animation depends largely on the playback machine itself. A 30 fps animation that plays fine on the Quadra you developed it on may barely make 10 fps on a Mac LC II. For this reason, many animators develop, or at least test, on a target machine for their animations.

You' ll also have to consider whether your animation will be played back from a hard disk or a CD-ROM. If it's coming off CD, the medium's data transfer rate may not be able to keep up with your intended frame rate. CoSA makes a product called PaCo (marketed by Macromedia as QuickPICS) that can help. This product, which is designed primarily to compress animations for faster playback, also has a CD playback simulator that will give you an idea of how fast your animation will play back from a real CD. You also can use PaCo to compress animations so that they can be played back on machines with limited RAM (see Chapter 7, "Animation Tools").

Animators of complex material that includes interactivity often import their finished animations into an integration program like Macromedia Director. Using

Director ⌘ 210

Director, you can create scripts that tell the computer how to behave. For example, a 3-D game would allow you to click buttons to move around a 3-D room. These buttons and the actions they trigger are defined by Director scripts (see *Creating Interactive Multimedia*). Director also includes a utility called Macromedia Accelerator that compiles and accelerates animations to speed them up by as much as five or six times. You also can use Director to "finish" an animation by adding sound, titles, and other refinements.

Copying Animations to Videotape

If you are creating broadcast-quality animations, you'll want to write them to videotape or even videodisc. To do this, you' ll need a fair amount of equipment (if you don't want to take your work to a service bureau). For starters, you' ll need equipment that converts computer data to a video signal, namely an NTSC encoder, and a card that supports video output. A frame-accurate videotape recorder is also necessary.

You'll also need a specialized device called an animation controller. This appliance (generally an add-in card and some software) writes one frame of animation at a time to the VTR, sends a signal to make it back up the tape, then writes out another frame, and so on. The animation controller is necessary because desktop computers are not fast enough to turn out frames of animation in real time.

Craig Weiss of CBS Television in Los Angeles uses a laserdisc recorder instead of a VTR. The higher speed of this device allows him to write about 20 frames per minute, rather than the 3 frames a minute possible with tape. However, laserdisc recorders are still relatively scarce and expensive (about $20,000).

16

Animation Projects

You'll find a varied and interesting group of animation projects on the Power Tools CD. All were designed by experienced animators who are at the top of their field. While the CD details the conceptualization and creation of the projects, we'll give you some project background material in the following pages.

Video Quilt

PROJECTS

Video Quilt ⌘020

Lynda Weinman is an experienced film and video animator who also writes for *New Media, MacWeek, Publish*, and *Step by Step Graphics.* Lynda also finds time to teach animation at the Art Center College for Design, the American Film Institute, and the Center for Creative Imaging.

Deceptively simple in appearance, her *Video Quilt* comprises over 600 individual pieces of art, each separately fashioned, then painstakingly assembled into a coherent whole.

The finished work resembles an infant's blanket, with homespun designs rendered in a palette of muted and soothing shades and accents. The quilt serves as an interface for an interactive training disk used in pre- and postnatal medical clinics. A mouse click on one of the panels—a rocking horse or teddy bear, for instance—and the object moves, and the viewer is whisked to an appropriate section of the demo.

Weinman considers 2-D character animation to be among the most challenging of multimedia undertakings, and though she is pleased with the way *Video Quilt* turned out, she says, "I didn't make any money on it—it was a very difficult project."

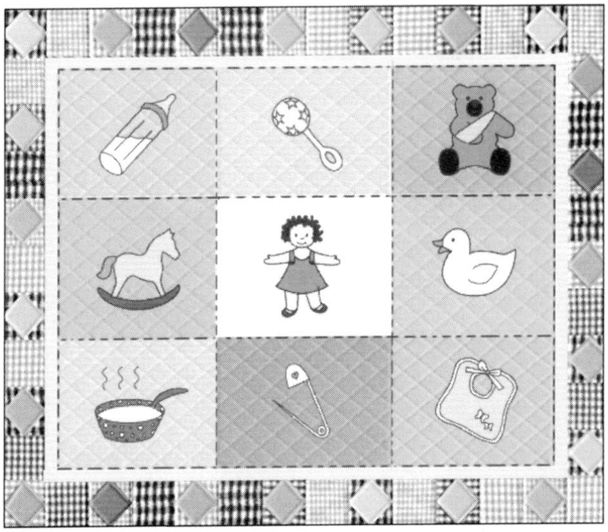

Figure 16.1 A small portion of Lynda Weinman's *Video Quilt*

Special Considerations

TOOLS Director ⌘ 210

One reason for her difficulties with the project had to do with preserving image registration as art was moved between different programs for processing. "I was attempting to do character animation with Illustrator, which is a 2-D art program," says Lynda, "and I used Illustrator's blend function to make each shape move in a particular way. After I had completed all the animation and brought it into Macromedia Director, I found that things didn't register properly—there were slight, shifts of less than a pixel, and it looked awful."

After going back and reexamining her process, Lynda found that the registration problem was caused by her use of the ⌘-V paste command familiar to all Mac users. Lynda learned that if she used the⌘-P paste command instead, her art would be copied to a file in exactly the same position it occupied in the original source file. Although this solved the registration problem, Lynda still had to go back and redo many frames, a painful and time-consuming process.

While this experience may underscore the importance of knowing your tools and technology, Lynda emphasizes that execution usually plays a secondary role in animation projects. "The design process is what takes the most time, so even though I did have to redo all those graphics, it didn't take nearly as long the second time, because I had already mapped out both the aesthetics of the project and the technical execution process."

Tips and Techniques

When Lynda brought her finished art into Director for assembly and animation, she used a technique that she often employs to speed both processing and playback. Each frame of *Video Quilt* had 8 or 9 channels, or layers. When working with these frames in Director, the screen was slow to refresh, because the program had to build all of these layers. To remedy this situation, she exported all the channels of each frame as individual PICTs—so that each frame included all the layers. Then when she brought them back into Director, each frame was a composite of all of its layers.

This technique not only speeds up Director's handling of layered frames, but it also simplifies the cast window—Director's list of all of the frames in a project. Lynda also uses this technique to composite layers when she needs to exceed Director's 24-channel limit.

Lynda exports animation sequences as PICT files rather than in the more compact PICS animation format, because she has had bad experience with the former. She finds that files of over 12Mb—which are common in the world of 24-bit animation—do not save reliably as PICS files, becoming corrupted and unusable.

TOOLS
Photoshop ⌘222

Lynda is also quite taken with both old standby Photoshop and CoSA's new After Effects image processing program (see Chapter 8, "Video Tools," for a review). "If you do a scaling change in Director, it looks like hell," she says, "It either blows up the pixels, or if you zoom down, the image becomes jittery. But Photoshop and After Effects both do subpixel rendering, which makes images look beautiful even when they're scaled up and down."

Tools and Equipment

Lynda uses a Mac IIfx, with an assortment of fixed and removable hard drives, a 24-bit color card, a tape drive for archiving, an NTSC monitor, a video-scanner, and a pressure-sensitive tablet.

NTV Logo

PROJECTS
NTV logo ⌘021

Scott Billups was hired to create a network identity and logo package for Nissan's internal cable station, NTV. Nissan's graphics department had created a design concept, but Nissan executives weren't happy with the results, so they brought in Scott, who has had a long association with the company.

Scott is a systems integration consultant and developer for Sony, Apple, and Silicon Graphics Inc. He is also cochairman of the American Film Institute Media Lab. Over the last 18 years, he has created hundreds of broadcast, industrial, and theatrical projects, and is currently serving as Second Unit Director and Director of Digital Production for the motion picture *The Fantastic Four.*

Special Considerations

Scott is a pioneer in the use of computer tools in video and film production, and he feels that the NTV project is an excellent example of how desktop video makes the process of dealing with corporate productions easier. In conventional video production, client participation is problematic, notes Scott, "because in the traditional process, you don't really have anything to show until it's all done."

For the NTV project, Nissan had a lot of ideas for specific effects his clients wanted to achieve, so the flexibility and participatory nature of computer-based production were very important. "Just the fact that they were kept abreast of the whole production process made them feel they were part of it," he notes.

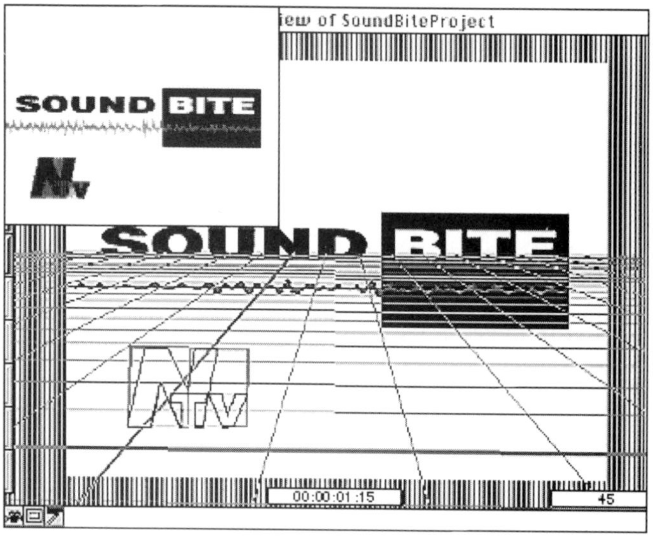

Figure 16.2 NTV Network Identity

An early obstacle stemmed from the original project design, which was done by graphic designers who had specified Pantone colors. "The problem is that most Pantone colors aren't video-safe, so that by the time they get to a video that's been dubbed a few times, they're just flaring all over the place," Scott says. He solved the problem by creating a logo based primarily on black-and-white, with a few added video-safe colors.

Tips and Techniques

Like many desktop video professionals who value Electric Image Incorporated's ElectricImage Animation System for its many high-end animation features, Scott cites one feature as particularly useful: being able to change the playback speed of an animation sequence using only the arrow keys on the keyboard. This makes music syncing easy, because "it allows you to pump up or down the speed until you find a beat that works."

Scott also made good use of the array of filters in Adobe's Photoshop. He treated the "Bite" block with multiple applications of Photoshop's Wave Filters to give the effect of cartoon-like distortion.

Scott also had to make adjustments to account for the differences between the image formats of the computer, where the imagery was created, and video, where the final results would be viewed. "When you view a computer-based image on an NTSC [video] monitor, the images flicker all over the place, and so you run them through Photoshop's video filters, which correct for the differences, resulting in flicker-free images," he notes.

Tools and Equipment

Scott used a Quadra 900 with a cache card that boosts the machine's performance to the level of a Quadra 950. He installed a 24-bit color card, a video card for

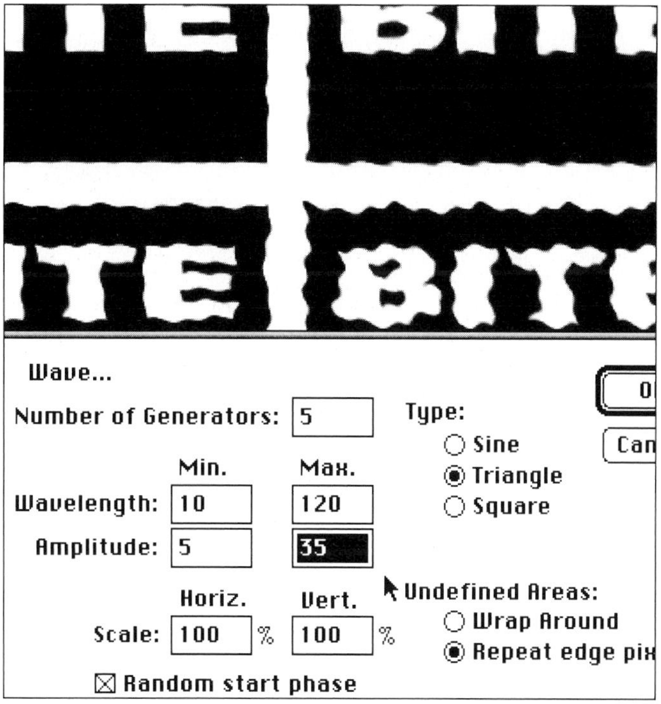

Figure 16.3 Image processing using Photoshop's Wave Filters

piping video frames in and out of the Quadra, and a DigiDesign's AudioMedia board for digitizing sound.

For *compositing* (combining the various elements of the piece), Scott used ADI's MacVAC animation controller. He also used MacVAC to write each frame from the computer to laserdisc, using the Sony LVR 5000 videodisc recorder.

TOOLS

Swivel 3D ⌘220

MacroModel ⌘221

Scott used Photoshop to filter certain elements, as described above, Macromedia's Swivel 3D to model the logo, ElectricImage to animate the model, Macromedia's MacroModel to extrude the model into three dimensions, Macromedia's Director to lay out the timing of the various components, and ElectricImage again for rendering.

The Lawnmower Man

PROJECTS

Lawnmower Man Logo ⌘022

The Lawnmower Man was a 1992 film most notable for its eye-popping, computer-generated imagery. While its jejune plot assured only a fleeting life on the silver screen, and a swift reincarnation at Blockbuster Video, the movie's images were genuinely impressive.

Producer Jack Davis created one modest but effective image on the desktop during his tenure at The Gosney Company. He used Mac graphics and animation tools to design and animate the corporate identity for the film's sinister corporation, Virtual Space Industries.

Figure 16.4 Three views of the Virtual Space Industries logo

The logo consists of a revolving sphere, with a surrounding cube spinning in counter poise. The frames shown in Figure 16.4 give a feeling for the motion, but see the CD for the actual animated logo used in the film.

Jack started by studying sketches of the film's VR equipment—the contraption that you climb into to experience virtual reality. This apparatus, a "kinetic-" or "gyrosphere," allows the subject 360 degrees of free motion along any axis. Jack also examined a prop of the sphere used in the movie.

He also experimented with the idea expressed in Leonardo's famous image, the "Perfect Proportions of Man" (see Figure 16.5). As the concept evolved, he ended up with the circle inside the square. "The idea is that the square is reality and the circle, which is inside, is virtual reality," Jack says. "This sort of blurred the distinction between the two."

Jack notes that the budget for the project was very tight, and the whole film, in fact, was done on a shoestring. Costs were held down by parcelling projects out to a number of small studios, and by creating much of the imagery right on the desktop.

Special Considera-tions

Owing to the tight budget and deadline, desktop technology was a particularly appealing alternative to expensive and time-consuming higher-end tools. Swivel 3D, which was used for the object modeling, was a particular time saver. "Swivel renders an image essentially in real time," says Jack. "So the modeling and rendering tests, as well as choreography, can be done much more quickly than with higher-end systems."

Jack is quick to admit that there are trade-offs in quality: Swivel's quick shading is really only suitable for a rough idea of a rendered model's look, but it gets that job done quite well .(For a brief review of Swivel and its basic features, see Chapter 7, "Animation Tools." See also Chapter 15, "Creating Animation," for a description of fundamental animation concepts such as modeling and rendering.)

Jack describes the project as pretty straightforward, with no particular technical hurdles. Normally, effects such as those in *Lawnmower Man* would be created with film special effects equipment, but they were done, instead, with video and

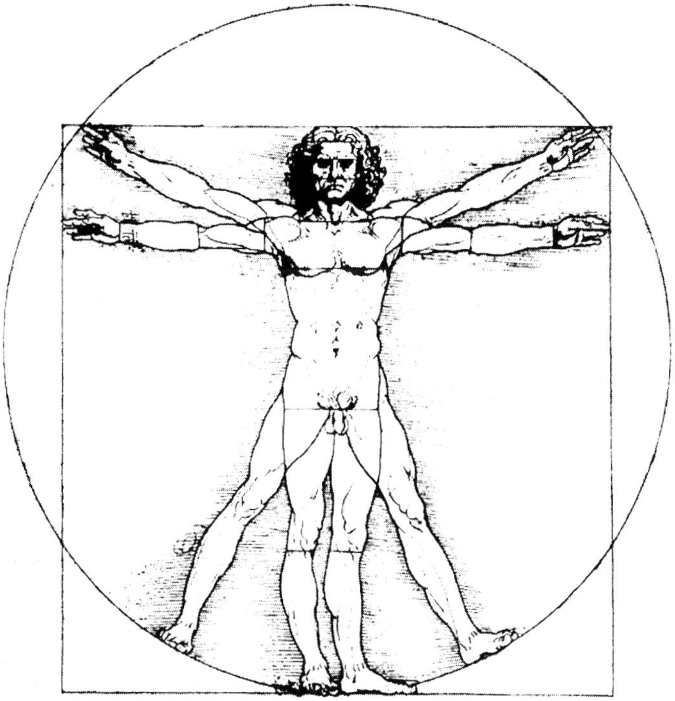

Figure 16.5
Da Vinci's **Perfect Proportions of Man**

desktop tools, due to budget constraints. At one point in the film, Jack's logo is projected on a wall as a six-foot image. The relatively low resolution of the video image was especially apparent at this size, but the filmmakers wanted a grainy look, "or were at least content with it," Jack notes.

Tips and Techniques

Because the logo was completely symmetric, only ¼ revolution had to be animated, which greatly reduced the number of frames (to 20 or less) necessary to create the finished animation. The logo's symmetry actually simplified the entire process, which would have been much more involved for an object that had distinct features visible from different angles.

Jack says that the hardest thing was to get the cube, which was made up of 12 separate objects, to rotate around a common center point. He did this by creating a small, hidden cube in the center of the model (Figure 16.6). Jack then locked the cube and sphere objects to this tiny hidden cube, which does not show up in the final animation. Once linked and locked to the hidden cube, the animated objects could then revolve around a common center point. See the project's step-by-step instructions on the CD for a more detailed explanation. See also Chapter 15, "The Advantages of Being Invisible," for other uses of this technique.

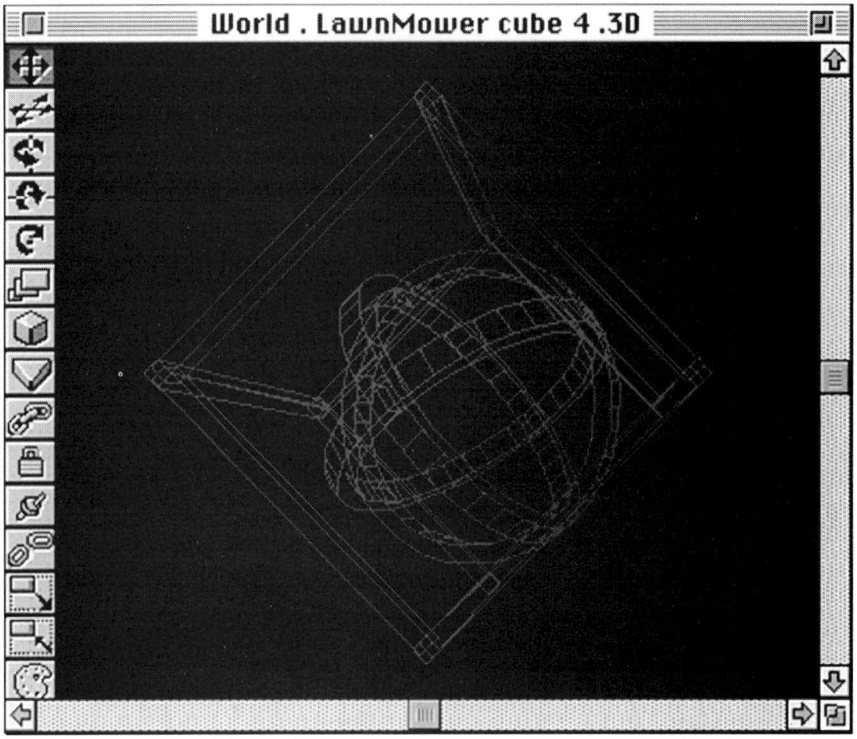

Figure 16.6 Hidden object used for model rotation

Tools and Equipment

Jack used a basic Mac setup that included a Mac IIci with 8Mb RAM and a 100Mb hard drive. He also had a 24-bit color card and a 19" color monitor.

Adobe Illustrator and Photoshop were used to create the original high-contrast logo art, Swivel 3D Professional was used for the modeling and test animation, and Macromedia Three-D was used for rendering and final animation. The whole thing was assembled for playback in Director.

Test Flight

PROJECTS

Test Flight ⌘023

TOOLS

StrataVision ⌘226

When John Odam, a book and graphic designer in Del Mar, California, wanted to experiment with 3-D animation, he turned to Strata Inc.'s StrataVision 3d (for a review of StrataVision 3d, see Chapter 7, "Animation Tools"). Although John had used the program previously and was familiar with 3-D modeling, he wanted to experiment with animating a simple 3-D object for playback as a QuickTime movie.

The project consists of a 3-D airplane flying against a backdrop of clouds. "What fascinates me about 3-D programs is the ability to maneuver in three-dimensional space and time," says John. The project, while uncomplicated, involves many of the considerations all animators face, even in the most involved of undertakings.

John has a traditional commercial art background, starting as a book cover designer in London 25 years ago, after graduating from the Leicester College of

Art. Now with his own firm, John Odam Design Associates of Del Mar, California, John works exclusively using computer design tools, creating nonfiction trade and educational books, from jacket design to inside illustrations and typesetting.

Special Considerations

StrataVision 3d renders in 24-bit color even if you have only an 8-bit color card. That way, you have a high-quality file that can be played back in either mode. Note that this works well for relatively simple projects like *Flight Test*, but can lead to very large files and slow rendering for more complex projects.

Tips and Techniques

John recommends keeping 3-D models simple to speed rendering and reduce the frustration of waiting while models are rendered with surfaces and light. This is especially important for beginners, who may be tempted to build complicated shapes that will render very slowly.

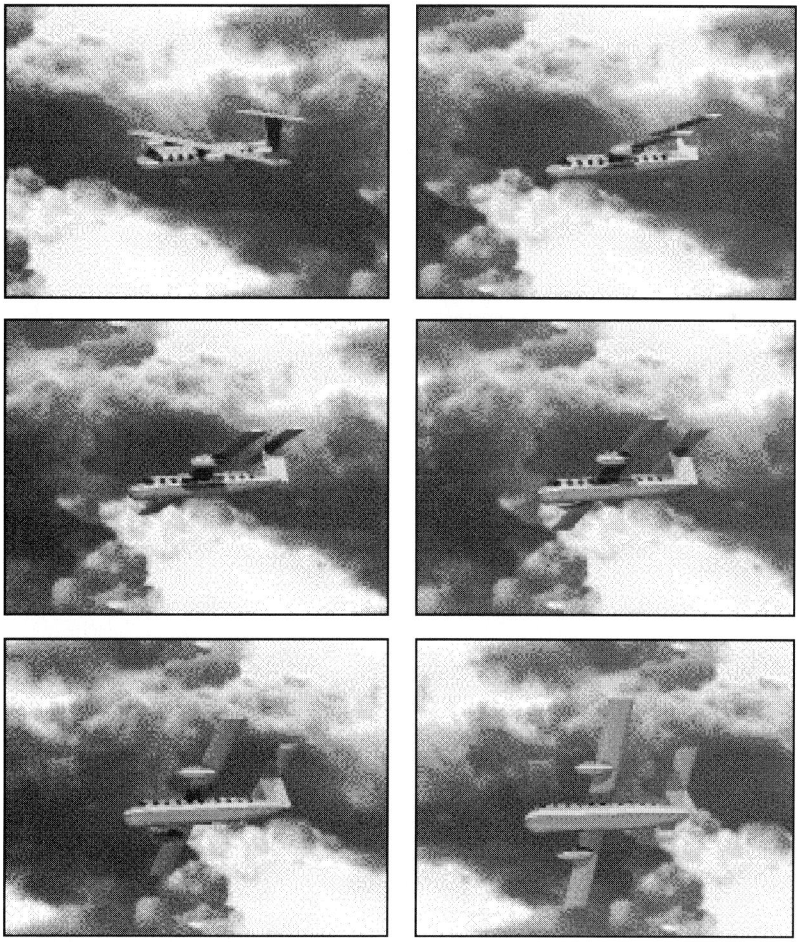

Figure 16.7 Test Flight: The finished model flying through space

"What I found in 3d is that the built-in solids that come with it, the cylinder, cone, and so on, render blindingly fast in comparison to any other kind of shape. So if you can make up a model out of basic primitives and it's convincing enough for your purposes, you'll find it renders quickly—you'll get gratification right away, you won't have to wait all night for results."

To assemble his airplane model, John used only the cylinder, the sphere, and the stretch tool. Figure 16.8 shows the diagram John .used to outline the relationships between the different model elements and how they fit together to form the composite airplane model.

When the model and rendering of the airplane were complete, John set about animating it against a cloud backdrop. Since the cloud background is actually a repeated loop, it's important to carefully adjust the camera angle so that the illusion of movement through fresh territory is maintained.

"If your camera angle is too wide, you start to see a wallpaper of clouds, so that it blows the realism," John says. "The other mistake you can make is to use too narrow a camera angle, too much telephoto, and then the clouds start to break up, you can see the individual pixels. So the scaling of the background in this program is a function of the camera angle."

In order to get the highest-quality results, John normally renders in 24-bit color and saves the results as a PICS animation sequence. He finds that this format is superior to QuickTime, whose compression algorithms sometimes cause banding in subtle shading areas. If you do want to work in QuickTime, you can always convert from the PICS files.

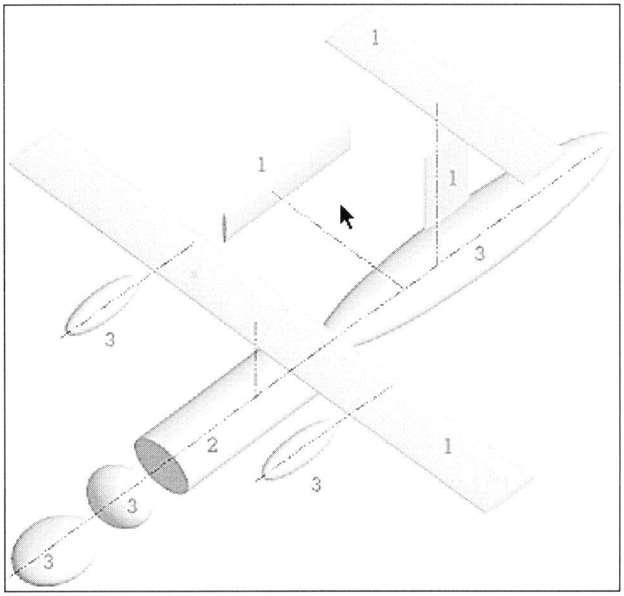

Figure 16.8
The model's composite shapes

Tools and Equipment

Illustrator ⌘223

In addition to StrataVision 3d for the models, rendering, and animation, John used Illustrator and Photoshop to make a texture map of portholes for the plane's windows. His machine was a Mac IIci with a Radius Rocket 25 CPU accelerator and a 24-bit color card (see Chapter 3, "Mac Software and Hardware," for reviews of various Macintosh models, and Chapter 4, "Hardware Peripherals," for a discussion of CPU acceleration and 24-bit video cards).

Robot from The Journeyman Project

Journeyman Project Robot ⌘024

Animators Farshid Almassizadeh, Michel Kripalani, and Dave Flanagan first began discussing ideas for a 3-D game while sitting around a coffee table one night. During subsequent sessions, they began keeping a log of their most promising ideas, and within a short time, they had the basis of *The Journeyman Project.*

Eight months later, the ranks of newly formed Presto Studios had swelled to seven or eight animators, and the founders quit their "real" jobs to devote all of their energies to the project, which, by its completion, was to consume 15,000 hours.

The Journeyman Project, released in 1993, envisions the world in the year 2318. The game begins from your apartment in Caldoria, where you are employed as a member of the Temporal Protectorate, charged with safeguarding history and preserving world peace.

Presto Studios is a San Diego-based team of Macintosh and science fiction enthusiasts, each with a different and complementary area of expertise in media. Currently developing a Japanese version of *Journeyman,* they are planning to publish more of their own work, as well as to serve as a publishing house for other multimedia creators.

Special Considerations

The complexity and demands of *The Journeyman Project* tested many of the limits of currently available 3-D software. "We actually used almost every 3-D package available for the Mac," says Farshid, "because each of them had a feature we needed that the others didn't have."

For example, the team used Specular's Infini-D animation package for rendering and animation, in part because it was one of the few programs that would import the models that were first created in Swivel 3D. "For example, if ElectricImage had that feature, we wouldn't have had to have 10 computers rendering 24 hours a day [because ElectricImage renders much faster than Infini-D]."

Although it was a multidimensional project with many people working simultaneously on different parts of the game, Farshid says the team ran into few project management issues. One reason for this was that, although everyone had his or her specialty, each was versatile enough to pitch in on other aspects when necessary.

Tips and Techniques

Farshid emphasizes that projects as involved and detailed as *Journeyman* require careful planning and organization. For example, the design of *Journeyman* is

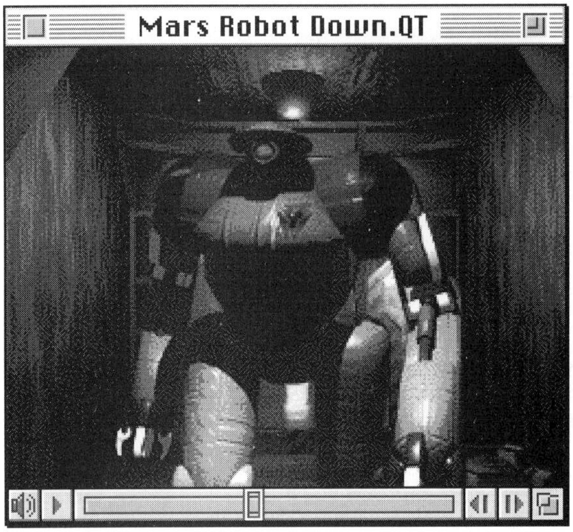

Figure 16.9 Robot from *Journeyman*

nonlinear: Game players have many options at any given juncture. This freedom to explore through interactivity is one of the foundations of multimedia (see Chapter 1, "Multimedia Defined"), but it places great demands on multimedia developers.

Just to keep track of the possible branching at each point in *Journeyman*, the team created and maintained an 8'×10' diagram of all the possible options.

Farshid also points out that the field of 3-D animation is still relatively new, and 3-D products often are created and marketed by small companies that are open and responsive to suggestions by users.

One annoyance was that Infini-D required texture maps to be applied individually to each object in each keyframe. Since *Journeyman* scenes had a dozen or more keyframes with as many as 200 separate objects each, the texture mapping process was almost impossibly time-consuming. When Farshid pointed this out, developers at Specular agreed and promptly modified the program to allow aggregate texture mapping.

Tools and Equipment

Most *Journeyman* animators used Mac IIfx's, while Farshid worked on a Mac II with two Radius Rocket CPU accelerators, 24-bit color card, several medium size hard disks, a removable cartridge drive, and two 13" monitors.

Radius's Rocketshare software was used to turn the Mac into a *multitasking* machine—so that separate programs or rendering tasks could be run simultaneously.

The team used Swivel 3D for the modeling and animation, and then imported the animation keyframes into Infini-D. In this way, Farshid was able to take advantage of the complementary strengths of each program; Swivel was used for its quick modeling and excellent control of hierarchical links—which were necessary for realistic motion; Infini-D recognized and retained all of these links when it imported the Swivel models, and Farshid was able to take advantage of Infini-D's strong rendering options and refined motion control characteristics (for an explanation of basic animation and rendering techniques, see Chapter 15, "Creating Animation"). Macromedia Three-D also was used for some of the complex animation moves.

The Presto team considerably sped up rendering of the many complex 3-D scenes by using Specular International's Backburner software. This network rendering package divides large rendering tasks into smaller pieces, and then parcels them out to any Mac that is available on the network. Some really big jobs took all night to render on 10 different Macs all working at the same time, while the humans on the team caught some much needed rest.

Backburner was particularly valuable for *Journeyman* animators, because many of their scenes had both shadows and objects with individual texture maps—characteristics that greatly increase the number of calculations a computer needs to perform to accurately render such details.

After rendering, various elements of the project were brought together and composited using Photoshop, and the final project was assembled for playback using QuickTime and Director.

17

Creating Video

Desktop video is ushering in a new era of video production, placing more people in the director's chair than ever before. It is opening up exciting and economical new ways of managing video, giving professionals and hobbyists alike the capability of creating and editing their own movies or adding the power of video images to their multimedia productions. Digital video is used in motion picture and television production for storyboarding, retouching shots, and adding impressive but relatively low-cost special effects. Budgets, equipment, personnel, and talent can range from the highest-caliber broadcast quality to making do with what is immediately available.

Unlike traditional video projects requiring large budgets and careful planning, many desktop video productions are realized on shoestring budgets and the plan-as-you-go philosophy. In small productions, a secretary, bookkeeper, accountant, vice president, spouse, child, or friend might be recruited to jump in and help. They may become the leading man or lady, provide voice-over for audio input, make strange sounds for special effects, or be producer, camera person, or any other role required to get the job done on budget and on schedule.

This flexibility is possible due to the forgiving nature of the digital medium, which permits continuous editing and modification throughout a project. However, the ability to continue to make changes after the fact is no substitute for shooting and recording the highest-quality video and sound, which are possible only with proper planning and budgeting. No amount of time using Sound Edit Pro to process the audio will restore a garbled voice or one drowned out by background noise. All the powerful enhancing filters and special effects in Premiere, VideoShop, CoSA After Effects, and VideoFusion combined will not bring back the lost excitement of an event videotaped under poor lighting conditions or with a shakily held camera. The secret to high-quality desktop video is shooting high-quality video in the first place.

The Three Steps of Video Production

The three major steps of video production include preproduction, production, and postproduction (see Figure 17.1). Preproduction represents the planning process, which probably is the most significant stage of the production, as everything else depends on how carefully the stages of production are anticipated. The elements of preproduction include planning, scripting, storyboarding, budgeting, assembling the cast and production team, and determining what equipment will be used.

Most people are familiar with the basics of the production process itself. This is where the production cast and crew assemble together to shoot the raw footage. Effective preproduction planning greatly increases your chances of living through a catastrophe-free production phase.

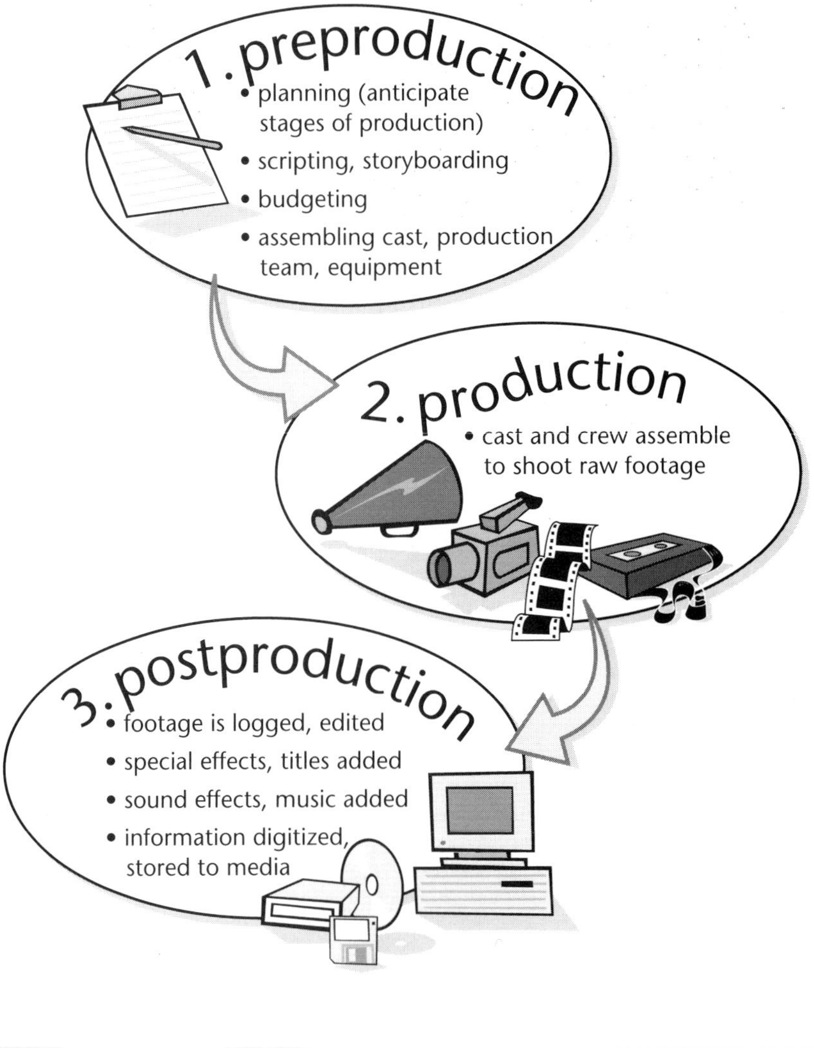

Figure 17.1
The three phases of desktop video production

In postproduction, the filmed or videotaped footage is logged and edited, special effects and titles are inserted, and sound effects and music are added. These basic phases remain the same whether the movie is a major motion picture, an interactive multimedia presentation, or a QuickTime home movie. The primary differences occur in the postproduction phase. If the final product is to be a QuickTime movie, for example, the acquired footage must be digitized into a computer prior to editing, compressed using one of several QuickTime codecs, then either stored on a computer readable medium (hard disk, floppy disk, CD-ROM, etc.) or written out to videotape or film.

QuickTime ⌘ 160

The nature and budgetary constraints of the project dictate whether to utilize traditional video or desktop video production techniques. In general, projects that require full-frame video at 30 frames per second, for transfer to videotape and display on VCRs, often may be less expensive to develop utilizing traditional video production techniques. However, a desktop video production utilizing smaller frame sizes and frame rates can be dramatically less expensive. For example, a consumer 8 mm camcorder, already on hand, might save the cost of renting a high-end ¾ inch video system, and perhaps the fees of a camera operator. In many cases, a marriage of traditional video techniques with the newer desktop video tools may prove to be the best solution.

Preproduction

The importance of proper preproduction planning and budgeting cannot be overstated. Do your homework on this phase and you will be assured that the production will materialize on schedule and that all the pieces will fit together to form a quality work. Since many desktop video productions proceed on a very low budget, the first question to ask is what skills, equipment, talent, and resources are already available to you without incurring additional expenditures. Typically, a color Macintosh with a VideoSpigot card or lower-end RasterOps QuickTime digitizing card, several SyQuest cartridges for storage of clips, and a consumer camcorder may already be available for the project (see Chapter 8, "Video Tools"). The production team may include salaried employees or other persons whose time is available for the project, with no need to pay for professional talent, transportation, or lodging. The storyboard may be put together by a member of the production team, approved by the client, and then a short script written as a plan for the production (see sidebar). Additional costs may nevertheless be incurred for extra SyQuest cartridges, videotape, and necessary props, which should all be included in the budget.

On the other hand, going the economy route may be your undoing—one untalented actor can pull an entire production down to amateur levels. If you can increase your budget to cover a lack of available no-cost personnel, you can juggle the cost versus quality issues of your production.

Which Comes First, Storyboard or Script?

The answer to this question is, "It depends." When a feature or story-based movie is being produced, the script always comes first. It tells the story, describes the characters and scenes, and includes all the dialog. Often, after countless rewrites, the director is finally satisfied with the script and turns it over to a storyboard artist. The storyboard includes one illustration for each shot in the movie. It helps the director and actors visualize the action, and can call attention to potential problems in scene continuity or camera placement.

In a commercial or business movie, the storyboard may come first. The intention may be to sell an idea, present a series of concepts, or train someone to carry out a task. The sequence of ideas and images may be more important than a script. In fact, in this case, there may not even be a script with dialog at all!

One of the most significant factors in determining the cost of a digital video production is the cost of hard disk space, SyQuest drives, DAT tape back-up systems, optical drives, or other means by which to store the megabytes of data that these projects need to have. The purchase of a high-end digital video card that can process 30 frames a second at 640×480 resolution will only increase the amount of storage needed. In the most extreme cases, studios using special equipment to permit QuickTime to do broadcast-quality video require several 2.5 gigabyte (Gb) drives just to hold fifteen minutes of video. Such productions require investments of up to $40,000 for equipment, as compared to the $4000 price tags that are common in the Macintosh world.

Comparative Costs

Before the planning and budgeting process is completed, you should make comparisons between alternative approaches to creating video, in order to determine which one is most cost-effective and best meets the needs of your project. How this is calculated will depend to a large extent on whether you need to purchase or rent equipment, such as computers, hard disks, VCRs, and camcorders, and whether available staff time is allocated to the budget. Needless to say, some projects are more complex than others and require more sophisticated planning and budgeting.

Suppose that you own the Senior Prom Reunion Company, which is in the business of throwing 25th reunion parties for high school classes. You wish to make a promotional video to send to prospective high schools to acquire their business. This could be accomplished by either creating videotape or producing a multimedia CD-ROM. However, your market research shows that most high schools have VCRs but do not have adequate equipment for playing CD-ROMs. The decision is made to produce a videotape, but the question remains whether

Figure 17.2 A High School Reunion QuickTime presentation demonstrates the practice of rephotographing the original senior prom picture with the same partner or a substitute spouse 25 years later.

to use traditional or digital means. You have some existing videotape footage, but additional videotape will have to be shot for the production. Thus, you undertake an analysis to determine the most cost-effective approach.

Creating a videotape using traditional equipment is expensive. Special lighting will be necessary to videotape one of your high school reunion parties, requiring a professional videographer. In addition, two days of postproduction will be necessary to edit together new and existing video, as well as for transitions, titles and special effects. The budget would look something like this:

Budget—Traditional Video

Videographer with camera/lighting for one evening	$1000
Postproduction; two days rent of ¾ editing suite with operator	1500
Total	$2500

This does not include the costs of storyboarding and scripting prior to production, other staff time, videotape duplication after production, or incidentals.

On the other hand, the budget for a *digital* production produced in-house (still requiring a videographer) might look like this:

Budget—Digital Video	
Videographer with camera/lighting for one evening	$1000
High-end 30 frames per second digitizing card	3500
for the Macintosh; comes with editing software	
High-end Macintosh	4000
1.2 gigabyte hard drive	1200
DAT drive	1200
DAT tapes	45
Frame-accurate VCR	2000
Total	$12,945

As you can see, most of the costs are associated with the one-time purchase of capital equipment. If you already have the equipment and can videotape and edit the footage yourself, then the costs of a digital production might actually be less than going the traditional video route. But since our Senior Prom Reunion Company doesn't do multimedia, we're out of luck. The obvious conclusion is that the initial cost of equipment does not justify a digital solution unless the costs can be spread over several projects. Besides, it is likely that the traditional methods will yield a higher-quality video. Even the highest-end Macintosh digitizing boards lose half the information from the original videotape, because at 30 frames per second, they are currently able to digitize only one of the two fields present in every frame of video (see sidebar). While the two fields are very similar, they still are separate images, one-sixtieth of a second apart in time, and each field contains half the information in the videotape.

The digital solution does offer far more flexibility in adding special effects. However, the digital creation of transitions and other special effects takes a great deal of time, and instead of a two-day operation, the estimated time for editing the project is one week. While this can be done in-house, the cost of salaries also has to be figured into the budget. For this particular project, the traditional solution appears to be the most cost-effective.

Now let's imagine that your Senior Prom Reunion Company does multimedia. In fact, one of your primary revenue streams is to offer, for a small and very reasonable fee, a special videotape of the event. You photograph each reunion attendee, then create an animated morph QuickTime movie from the attendees' senior pictures to their current pictures. These morphs are then added to the final videotape in postproduction. Since the ability to produce morphs is not available

Video Fields and Frames

NTSC video actually displays one picture every sixtieth of a second. This is called a video field. It takes two fields to create a complete image or frame, because only every other one of the 525 NTSC horizontal scan lines are displayed at a time. In field one, scan lines 1, 3, 5, 7, etc. are displayed. In field two, scan lines 2, 4, 6, 8, etc. are displayed. This alternating of scan lines is called interleaving. The current crop of digitizing cards captures only one of the two fields. As a result, their image quality is lower than can be achieved through using professional analog video equipment. Undoubtedly, this will change in the near future as new cards are introduced.

through traditional video production houses, the amount of use the equipment will get now may justify the initial expenditures.

One final hypothetical: Let's say you already own a color Macintosh and you want to produce a multimedia presentation, which you can deliver live to the schools. How would that compare to the cost of producing a videotape? In addition to digitized photographs, charts, and graphics, you will incorporate 320×240 QuickTime movies into the presentation. Because the movies will be part of a live presentation and combined with other media, they do not have to stand alone, and due to their small size, professional quality is not essential. Instead of hiring a videographer, a staff member can use your own consumer-grade camcorder. You can use available lighting, or possibly a camera mounted flood. The budget is as follows:

Budget—Live Multimedia Presentation

88M SyQuest drive for storage of QuickTime movies	$550
3 SyQuest cartridges	300
Low-end video digitizing card; comes with editing software	500
8mm videotape	10
Total	$1360

Nothing else is needed except for staff time in which to create the production. Thus, for a business which already has a Macintosh and such basics as a scanner, Photoshop, and Premiere, the digital solution makes sense for a live presentation. Costs after the first production drop to back-up media and video tape. Now, the only major expense is the time it takes for the staff person to create the presentation.

TOOLS Photoshop ⌘ 222

Using Analog Video

For a company doing a great deal of in-house video, another option would be to purchase a computer-assisted, non-digital videotape editing system. This might include, for instance, the FutureVideo A/B roll system (see Figure 17.3), which supports three *prosumer* (low-end industrial) VCRs with computer control capability, a Panasonic switcher modified so that the computer can send it GPI signals for automatic transitions and effects, and the FutureVideo A/B controller with Macintosh software (see Figure 17.3). Such a system is likely to cost under $10,000 and permit in-house analog videotape production at a very low cost with Hi8 or S-VHS quality. The Senior Prom Reunion Company would benefit from this solution if it were going to videotape reunion events on a regular basis. For occasional use of video, the best solution often is to rent equipment and editing time.

Production

Once the initial planning, budgeting, purchasing, scripting, and storyboarding are completed, you're ready to shoot your video. One of the most significant considerations in this phase is the quality of the light. Without light there is darkness, a state in which shooting video is impossible. Light has many qualities, among which is color temperature. This is not the actual temperature of the light bulb, but the hue of the light. Tungsten indoor light bulbs are very "warm" and have an orange tinge to them. Outdoor light is on the "cold" side and has a blue tinge. If light comes from several sources—for instance, daylight through a window, tungsten from a lamp, and the bluish light of a television set—you may

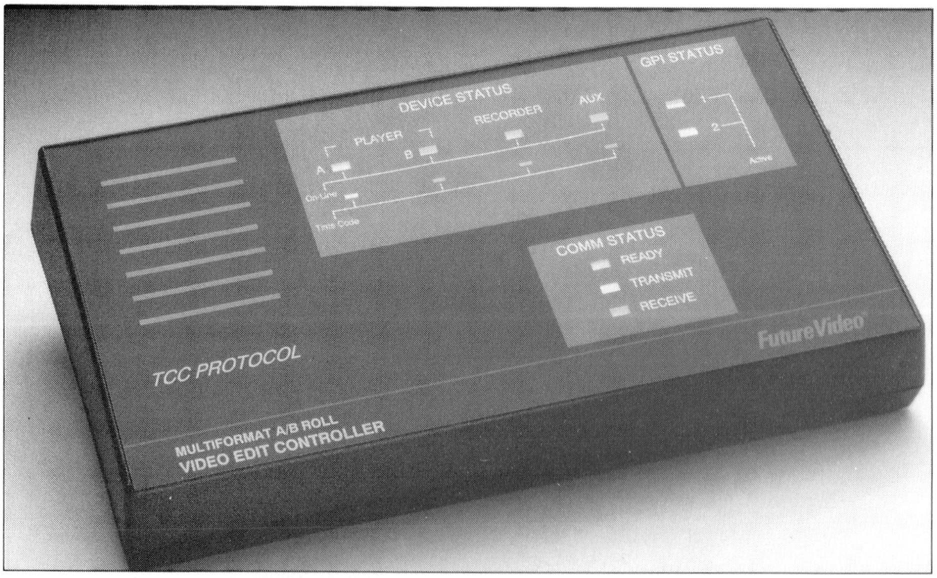

Figure 17.3 FutureVideo A/B roll video edit controller

get strange results. It is difficult to see these colors with the naked eye—humans tend to quickly compensate for the varying hues. But the camera records them to videotape. With professional equipment and older consumer cameras, the color of the light is compensated for through a manual process called white balance. All consumer camcorders have an automatic white balance control, but they also usually have a manual override for unusual lighting conditions (for example, videotaping in a room where all the walls are painted a bright green). The camera is focused on a solid white background, so it fills the frame. This can be a white tee shirt, a white card, or a genuinely white wall. The white balance button is pressed, and the camera calibrates all of the colors so that the chosen area becomes white. Some cameras also permit black balance, which is accomplished by closing the lens as far as possible, putting a lens shade over it, and pressing the black balance button. This assures a good range of contrast from black to white. Since most camcorders display a black-and-white viewfinder image, the only way to confirm that the white balance is set is to attach a monitor or TV to your camcorder's video out.

Video Loves Light and Lots of It

Although today's video manufacturers compete with each other for how little light their camcorders need to operate, the truth of the matter is that the quality of video is dramatically affected in negative ways by low light conditions. Lurking beneath the surface of every video image is noise, which creates an unpleasant grainy effect. When the lights are turned on, video noise runs for cover like exposed cockroaches. Good lighting brings out the subtlety or the brilliance in colors. If your video was shot in poor lighting conditions and has a lot of background noise, the transfer to QuickTime will accentuate everything that is wrong with the image, and leave you with a muddy, grainy look. In addition, when the image is compressed, the codec will not be able to tell the difference between video noise and the image's essential detail. It will faithfully attempt to duplicate the noise in each frame, totally ruining the compression results.

Dealing with Contrast

Video has less capacity than photographic film to handle contrasty situations. Scenes that appear properly lit to the naked eye may, in the final video, look as though they were shot on the moon, with pockets of impenetrable shadows and washed-out highlights. On the other hand, an overcast sky might provide better conditions for shooting than a sunny day. Certain rules of thumb have been used by videographers for years to contend with the light-contrast problem. One of them is the tradition of requiring guests on television to wear a blue shirt instead of a white one: The blue shirt will wash out and look white, whereas a white shirt would be so bright that it may actually appear to glow. Another technique is the use of a neutral density filter which blocks out the highest reflected light from the subject (high gain), allowing shadow areas to become more defined. However, using such a filter requires more overall light.

Shooting Indoors

While lighting complex situations indoors is an art that cannot be mastered in a single day, indoor scenes usually can be shot satisfactorily with existing or natural light. It's probably not a good idea to use a light mounted on the camera. This will cause severe shadows directly behind your actors, creating what looks almost like a double image. Instead, follow the principles of lighting in photography and use two or more artificial lights, a main light on one side, and a less intense fill light on the other. A third, higher light beaming down from the ceiling can reduce unwanted shadows and separate the subject from the background. Since this isn't still photography, don't forget to light the scene to allow for your actors' movement. If the actors move to one side, they shouldn't end up in darkness or in a bright area.

Frame Composition

Although composing a video frame is similar to composing a photograph, motion adds a whole new dimension, and there are a number of simple rules of thumb you can follow for shooting clear, compelling video.

First and foremost, do not hesitate to move in close to your subject. Whereas major motion pictures might show crowd scenes, and the smaller screen of television might emphasize head shots of one or two people, QuickTime movies are sufficiently small to justify focusing on a single object, an individual person, or a particular feature of that individual (i.e., their eyes, hands, etc.).

Traditionally, opening scenes are shot from a distance, followed by a medium shot, and a close-up. Often the transition from long shot to close-up is made with a slow zoom. However, with QuickTime, there are several reasons to avoid zooms. One is that, with disk space being such a precious commodity, the movie may be only a few seconds long, eliminating the usefulness of an opening zoom. You may need to cut more rapidly to the close-up. Another reason is the affect zooming has on temporal compression. Since every part of the image is changing during a zoom, temporal compression (which relies on large parts of the image being the same from frame to frame) will fail, resulting in higher data rates.

Secondly, keep in mind that much of the sense of action and excitement in video is created subliminally as the viewer's eyes follow the motion of the subject matter moving across the screen. Movement can be linear and predictable, or sometimes a total surprise. Just look at any MTV feature segment for a sense of how motion can be used creatively in video.

Continuity of Motion

If, in a scene, a person is walking to the right, that person should continue in the same direction in the next scene. Suddenly reversing a subject's apparent path of motion can confuse the viewer. This will happen when, in professional videographer lingo, the camera "crosses the line" between one shot and the next. The "line" is an invisible one that follows the subject's direction of motion. If the camera is positioned on the other side of the line, it will seem that the subject is moving in the other direction. So, don't let your camera cross the line.

Even if nothing is moving, changes in scene can create the illusion of motion. If a person is looking toward the upper right corner of the frame in the first scene, the next scene might have someone moving from the upper right corner back down to the lower left corner. If you watch shows on television or go to the movies, start to become aware of the motion on the screen, and how it is used to manipulate the viewer's experience.

Simulating Multiple Cameras

When videotaping, a scene should be shot from several different angles to provide the editor with enough material to do an effective job. This is called coverage. Movie makers have developed special techniques for shooting with one camera, as opposed to television studio productions that use live switching between two or three different cameras. The scene is first videotaped using a long shot. This is called the *master shot* and includes full body shots of all the actors, as well as enough of the background to establish the mood of the scene. Next comes medium shots from different angles. If there are two actors in a scene, these might be over-the-shoulder shots—shot from behind and slightly to the side of one actor and catching the second actor full on. Finally, the close-ups are shot, in which the actor's face may fill the frame.

Live interview situations are videotaped in a different manner. You really don't want to ask your subject to repeat himself half a dozen times! One technique that has been around for years in TV journalism is to videotape some of the shots after the interview is finished for cutaways. These shots are taken from behind the subject (so that the subject's face cannot be seen, avoiding potential lip sync problems) and generally show the interviewer asking the questions or nodding her head. Other good cutaways are close-ups of people listening to the interview, a map or some other graphic, or images to illustrate the content of the interview. Thus, a conversation can be edited using shots from several different angles to create the illusion of a second camera. Cutaways are essential to replace unusable footage during the interview, when, for example, the camera jerks, the subject wipes his nose, the phone rings, or simply to cover splices that occur when assembling a story in a nonlinear order.

The Continuum of Sound

When shooting video, the greatest mistake is to let the sound play second fiddle to the image. In multimedia presentations where the image may be small, sound often is more important than the picture in determining the success of the production.

From the wilderness forest to the sand shifting desert to a city's deserted, early morning streets, every place on Earth has background sounds, and the recording of those sounds will dramatically increase the believability and effectiveness of the video. Background sounds are continuous and should be heard throughout the scene.

The reason for capturing continuous sound becomes evident in the editing process. Traditional video productions usually are edited by laying down the sound first, and then editing pictures to fit the sound. Thus, the continuity of the scene is provided by the sound, and the length of the sound track will determine the duration of the video segment.

If, for example, the video consists of an actor talking to the camera in close-up (called a *talking head),* the editor may decide to use 20 seconds of the actor's voice, but only a few seconds of the head. To keep the shot from becoming boring, the editor might cut to shots of the audience, the surrounding environment, or other scenes to illustrate the narrative as the actor's voice is heard in the background.

Recording Spoken Words

If you want to assure that your subject's words are clearly audible, use an appropriate microphone properly placed. All consumer camcorders feature attached microphones, but these may not always be sufficient for your needs. The proximity of the built-in microphone is very close to the lens, so it is possible to pick up the noises made by the zoom lens motor, or the sound of your fingers fumbling to adjust the focus. And if your subject is more than two or three feet away, the camcorder microphone can pick up background noise that may drown out the voice you're trying to record. Any distortions in the audio will be even more noticeable when the sound is converted to the relatively low resolution of 11 kHz or 22 kHz. For the best results, have your subject speak directly into a hand-held or clip-on microphone (positioned several inches away from the mouth), or use a shotgun microphone just out of view of the camera.

Shooting with QuickTime in Mind

When producing a QuickTime movie that will be shown on a computer, the goal is to make the movie look and sound the best it can within the constraints of today's technology. It has to fit on the storage medium you've chosen, it must play in a window large enough to keep the audience's interest, and its sound and video quality should be as good as possible. All of these items directly relate to the amount of data contained within the movie, and how fast that data can be delivered from the disk to the screen. Until computers have unlimited storage and processing speed, trade-offs must be made to get the best results. Here are a series of tips to help you shoot a movie that can then be compressed optimally.

Spatial Compression Tips

You will recall from Chapter 8, "Video Tools," that spatial compression deals with reducing the data within a specific frame.

- Use a solid background—whenever possible, reduce the image detail behind your actors. Large blank areas can be much more easily compressed than areas of great color change. If you are trying to keep the data rate below a certain number, then the Compact Video codec will look for the areas of detail in a frame and give those areas a larger allocation of data. If you also have an actor in the frame, then there may not be enough data left over to provide a good representation of his or her face.

- Solid-colored clothing for actors—unless there is a reason for the actors to wear prints, save the data by having them wear solid colors, or at least clothing with large areas of solid color.
- Use white or black backgrounds—if you can set the white and black levels on your digitizing card so that white is truly white and black is truly black, then any detail in a white or black background will vanish, resulting in the best compression.
- Shoot with bright lights—as mentioned above, low light levels cause video noise, and the codecs can't tell the difference between noise and important information.

Temporal Compression Tips

The goal while shooting with temporal compression in mind is to keep extraneous movement to a minimum, and reduce the number of required key frames (see sidebar on Key Frames). The following tips will improve compression between adjacent frames:

- Use a sandbagged tripod—a hand-held camera will result in every frame being different from the last, making temporal compression impossible. Weigh your tripod down with sandbags or other objects. Bumping the tripod during a shot will create a data spike because adjacent frames will be very different.
- Move the actor, not the tripod—avoid pans, tilts, and zooms. Each of these causes most of the data in the scene to be different in consecutive frames. Instead, cut to different shots to keep things visually interesting. If you want to get closer to the actor, stop the camcorder, zoom in, and then start again. Even better, have the actor walk towards the camcorder. Then only the actor will change and the background will remain constant.
- Shoot in front of a static background—watch out for motion behind the actor, such as a busy street, blowing leaves, etc.

Case Study: "The Engineering Adventure"

The best way to visualize the phases of production is with regard to a particular project. Here we look at the creation of the video portion of "The Engineering Adventure," an interactive program designed to interest minority children in a career in engineering. Produced by Sonni and Ralph Cooper, principals of Creative Enterprises, under a $350,000 grant from the National Science Foundation, it features

Key Frames

Temporal compression uses a *key frame* at the beginning of a sequence of *difference* frames. A key frame is a complete image and does not rely on data from any previous frame. If more than about 90 percent of the scene has changed from the previous image, a key frame is automatically inserted. These are called *natural key frames*. They are usually inserted at the beginning of a scene change, or if there was a camera move. During compression, it's generally a good idea to force a key frame about once a second. If your frame rate is 15 frames per second, then ask for a key frame every 15 frames. This is usually set in the standard QuickTime compression dialog box.

The more key frames a movie has, the larger it will be. So why not just eliminate all of them except for natural key frames? This is fine if you will be playing your movie only in the forward direction. But if you ever need to search for a specific sequence or frame, or need to play the movie backwards (as in the MoviePlayer setting "Looping Back and Forth"), then a lack of key frames will greatly degrade performance. This is because QuickTime must search backwards for the most recent key frame, and then incorporate all subsequent differences until it arrives at the current frame.

short video segments of minority engineers, including African-Americans, Hispanics, and Native Americans, as well as segments showing engineering faculty and students conducting experiments, and visits to manufacturing plants designing the space station.

The Coopers' original budget proposal could not have included anything expressly for desktop video or QuickTime support, because when they wrote it in 1990, QuickTime did not exist. However, by the time the project was underway in 1991, Sonni felt that QuickTime was such an effective vehicle of expression that it had to be included in the project.

The first issue to consider was whether the existing budget could provide the resources for adding video. Although Sonni was not a professional videographer, she previously had observed video production as an actress, and later as a writer on a *Star Trek* production. She had a habit of looking through the camera between scenes to better understand what kind of shot was being taken. Furthermore, she knew about f-stops, focal length, and other technical aspects of video from her experience as a still photographer. Thus, she felt well prepared to shoot the videos she needed.

The only camcorder she had was an 8 mm Canon CCD-F70, which she originally purchased to shoot movies of her children. The budget was sufficient to provide supplies, including several SyQuest cartridges for QuickTime movies storage, a graphic artist, and a programmer who would incorporate the QuickTime movies into the project. In addition, she had already allocated time to generating media for the project. She would have to videotape the subject matter without any additional funds available to pay actors or actresses, professional voices, or other expenses routinely encountered in a production. This turned out to be much easier then she imagined.

She found companies near her business in Long Beach, California for on-location sites. McDonnell Douglas permitted her to tape models of the future American space station, and a nearby water utility allowed her to shoot within their plant. At each location, she obtained the consent of the workers who appeared on the videotape, and complied with all safety regulations, such as the wearing of a hard hat.

In order to videotape engineering experiments without having to hire someone, she worked through organizations of minority engineers who conduct experiments in secondary schools. The experiments already were scheduled, and Sonni Cooper's task was to be there with her camcorder when they took place. She ended up with beautiful live footage of minority students, which was much more effective than anything she could have accomplished on a larger budget with actors and simulated events.

For each shoot, she used the minimal equipment needed to do the job. This lightened her physical burden and increased the likelihood that she would get the shots she wanted. In addition to the camcorder, she brought two extra rechargeable batteries (color coded after each use), a miniature tripod, extra videotape, a still camera, a tape recorder, and an extra microphone, all of which fit into a single camera bag. The still camera was used to obtain higher-resolution images than possible with the camcorder, which were then converted into Macintosh images as part of the multimedia production.

Cooper used the tripod for capturing long narratives by a speaker. She made sure to videotape enough footage so that she could edit around occasional problems with image quality. When it comes to lighting, Sonni carefully avoided backlit scenes, such as shooting against a window, where an unsatisfactory silhouette would be the result.

Sonni is emphatic about sound quality. Nothing can ruin a QuickTime movie more quickly than a garbled audio track. Since the sound can be dubbed using voice-over, the audio does not necessarily have to be shot simultaneously with the video. If an audio segment is slightly too long or too short for a selected video segment, and you do not wish to trim the video segment, the audio can be made slightly longer or shorter using such editing tools as Sound Edit Pro's Tempo command, which can stretch or shrink sound files without raising or lowering the pitch.

TOOLS SoundEdit Pro ⌘ 201

Once all of the video was shot, short QuickTime segments were incorporated into HyperCard. This usually was done indirectly through Macromedia Director by the staff programmer and graphic artist (see Figure 17.4). In Director, the movie was combined with other graphic elements and interactive buttons. The stage in Director was set to the same size as a HyperCard stack, and the Macromedia Player utility was invoked to allow the Director interactive movie to become part of "The Engineering Adventure."

TOOLS Director ⌘ 210

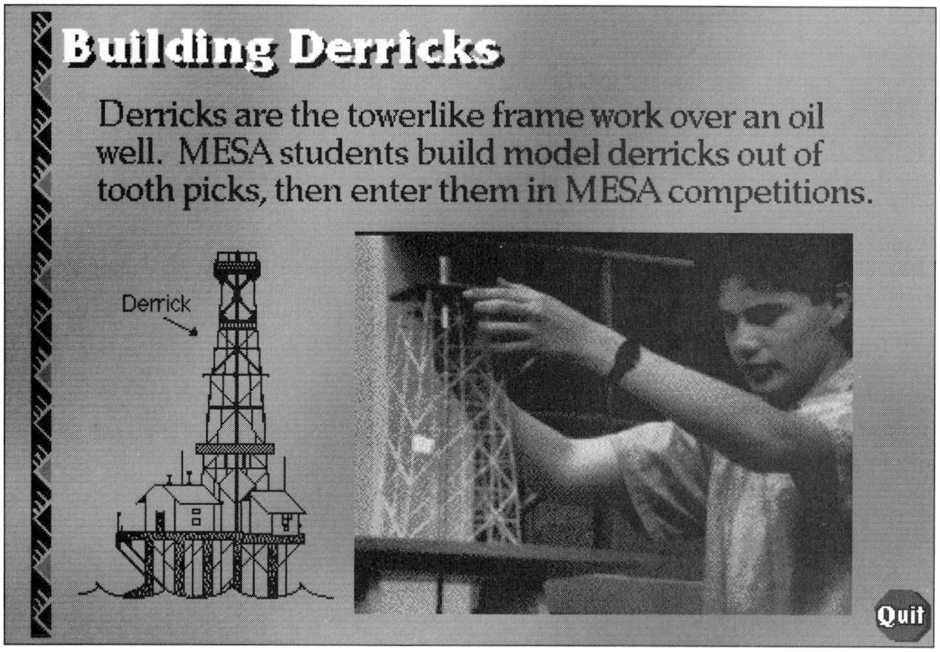

Figure 17.4 QuickTime video integrated into larger Macromedia Director movie the size of a HyperCard stack

Postproduction

Once you've shot your raw footage, you can begin the process of turning it into a finished production. This involves bringing the audio and video into the Mac, and then using digital editing tools to make it conform to your storyboard or intended final presentation.

Logging the Tape

The first step in the editing process is to log each and every videotape that was recorded. The process can be a tedious one, as every significant audio and video segment of the videotape has to be numbered and identified by an accurate written description. To reduce the tedium, use it as an opportunity to think about how each scene could be incorporated into the project.

The purpose of logging the tape is to prevent unnecessary delays in trying to find the right scene while in the process of creative editing, and to provide a reminder of what shots are available. With most consumer VCRs and camcorders, you will have to rely on the tape counter. If you calibrate the counter each time you load a tape by rewinding it to the beginning and then resetting the counter, it should be reasonably accurate. If the counter's numbers represent real time in hours, minutes, seconds, and frames, they may be very similar to other VCRs using a real-time counting system. Such a counter might represent one hour, 20 minutes, 10 seconds, and 18 frames as follows: 1:20:10:18. Other VCR counters use other numbering systems. The important thing to guard against is using a camcorder or VCR with one counting system to log the tape, and then trying to edit the same tape on a unit with a different system. The locations of the segments in your log will no longer match up! Furthermore, since the numbers are just an estimate of tape position, you may have to recalibrate the tape from time to time, especially if you are jogging back and forth quite a bit.

A much better system is available. It is called *timecode*, and consists of identifying frame numbers that are digitally encoded on your videotape. Professional VCRs use the SMPTE timecode system (SMPTE stands for Society of Motion Picture and Television Engineers). Some high-end consumer camcorders and VCRs use Sony's RC (Rewritable Consumer) timecode system. In either case, you can use it to find an exact frame on the tape, even if you change VCRs.

Manual Logging

While many otherwise computer-literate persons are so accustomed to logging by paper and pencil that they stick to the old ways, obvious advantages ensue from enlisting the support of the computer in the logging process. The simplest logging helper would be any word processing program, as the immediate power of word search is available to locate a particular word, phrase or frame number that will then help you find the video or audio segment that you need.

Automated Logging with Software

A more sophisticated logging tool actually provides control of your camcorder or VCR and automatically brings into the computer the correct frame numbers for a given segment (see Chapter 8, "Video Tools," and Sony VISCA sidebar). Products such as AutoLog from Pipeline Digital, VideoToolkit from Abbate Video Inc., or VideoParadise and QT-Paradise from Hatnet, Inc. create small QuickTime thumbnail stills, previews, or entire QuickTime movies of each of the segments that you log. Object-oriented software tools permit the various segments to be placed under categories for future retrieval. Eventually, the process of logging a movie and then editing the segments will be seamless, as the log itself will provide the QuickTime movies for the editing process.

Capturing Only What You Need

Since disk storage will probably be at a premium, it is a good idea to capture only the footage you think you'll need. VideoToolkit from Abbate Video Inc. makes it easy to select only the scenes you need from your log. The program will automatically run through the list and capture a separate QuickTime movie for each shot you request. What makes VideoToolkit especially valuable is its ability to control practically any VCR or camcorder directly from your Macintosh. It comes with a cable that attaches to your modem or printer port, and then plugs into your VCR's or camcorder's Control-L or Control-S port. Even if your machine doesn't have one of these ports, VideoToolkit still can control it with a small infrared module that is included in the package. You will not get frame-accurate control, but for capturing footage, you don't need it. Just follow the instructions and leave enough extra footage at the beginning and end of the scene to ensure that you capture what you want.

Sony's VISCA™ Protocol

Realizing that more control and flexibility was needed in the prosumer market, Sony created VISCA (Video System Control Architecture) as a platform-independent protocol. It allows a personal computer, such as a Macintosh, PC, or Amiga, to control up to seven video devices at once. Sony's Vdeck 1000, a VISCA-compatible Hi8 VCR that was designed as a computer peripheral, can be attached directly to your Macintosh's modem or printer port with a supplied cable. By adding Sony's Vbox CI-1000 to the chain, you can then attach any camcorder or VCR that responds to LANC (or Control-L) or Control-S commands. With multiple VISCA recorders attached to your computer, you can create an analog editing system. Or you can use one of several VISCA-aware applications to automate the capture of QuickTime movies.

Some Macintosh applications that take advantage of the VISCA protocol are:

MediaMaker ⌘215
PROmotion ⌘213

Adobe Premiere

Macromedia MediaMaker

PROmotion from Motion Works International, Inc.

Soft-Edit PRO-750 from The Profusion Group

VideoToolkit from Abbate Video Inc.

VideoParadise and QT-Paradise from Hatnet, Inc.

Digital Video Editing

Premiere ⌘240
VideoShop ⌘242

Editing video is not only the most creative part of making QuickTime movies, but also is an opportunity to clarify, sharpen, and bring into focus the message that the video is designed to communicate. Video editing used to be undertaken only by highly paid professionals working in postproduction studios ("post houses") crammed with millions of dollars worth of equipment. Today, anyone with a few hundred dollars can try his or her hand at video editing, using such software programs as Adobe Premiere, DiVA VideoShop, CoSA After Effects or Video Fusion. In fact, if you own a CD-ROM drive, you can try out the demo versions of several of these products on our enclosed CD-ROM. For a full rundown on the features and functions commonly found in these packages, see Chapter 8, "Video Tools."

We'll now take you through the video editing process by looking at a case study of a CD-ROM project underway at the California Museum of Photography.

In this project, three guest artists were invited to conduct research for their own art projects in the Museum's photography collection, including a quarter-million stereo photographs and glass negatives from the Keystone collection covering virtually every location on the globe. The project received an Artists Forum grant from the National Endowment for the Arts.

One of the artists, Stephen Axelrad, wanted to use the museum's collections as a jump-off point for exploring personal experiences from his own life, and decided to create a multimedia project with the working title "Self Museum." In the mid- and late-1980s, Stephen had exhibited an interactive art exhibition utilizing a multimedia setup based on a PC compatible with a touch screen and videodisc player. He wanted to use some of his previously created material for this new project, and was happy to discover that he could indeed port all the visual imagery and audio directly to QuickTime, with no conversion necessary. Because Stephen primarily relied on audio narrative over still video frames from the computer or videodisc at no more than five frames per second, he was able to use his VideoSpigot board along with the Compact Video compressor to produce a 320×240 pixels movie. Using Director's Lingo scripting language, he found he had far more control over the interactive environment on the Macintosh than he did on the PC when programming in C.

Stephen used Adobe Premiere 2.0 to edit his QuickTime movies. He wanted to edit the video to the existing narrative, so first he placed a video segment containing audio into the editor's timeline. Next, he integrated new video segments to existing footage by cutting and splicing with the razor blade tool among the two video channels. He then added transitions at the beginning and end of each video insert. Finally, he created special effects by placing multiple video segments in the Superimpose channel, which permits moving objects to play on top of the video in the first channel. The Superimpose channel is also used in Premiere to animate titles over a video in another channel after utilizing the built in title editor.

Overview of the Video

In a creative effort to compare his life to a museum of photography, Stephen used a video segment of himself consisting of an extreme close-up of his face and lips while he narrated, "My name is Stephen Axelrad. I am a Museum of Photography. I see through a Camera Obscura all that I know." (He refers to a large Camera Obscura built into the center of the exterior architectural facade of the California Museum of Photography, which makes the building itself resemble a camera, the Camera Obscura acting as the lens.) The Camera Obscura permits persons inside the building to see a large projection of what is going on in the outside world. The video editing challenge in this case was to integrate Stephen's talking head with the museum's facade to re-create the museum in his own image as a composite portrait of himself. The steps he followed to accomplish this are typical of the process of editing QuickTime videos.

Preparing Media Files

All of the media needed to make the movie were converted to the same 320×240 format being used for output of the final QuickTime clip. Still images of the museum's facade and a close-up of the Camera Obscura in the center of the building were resized in Photoshop. Stephen then created a still 320×240 PICT image of his face using ScreenPlay software that comes with the VideoSpigot. The still images of the Museum's facade and Stephen's face and lips were then brought

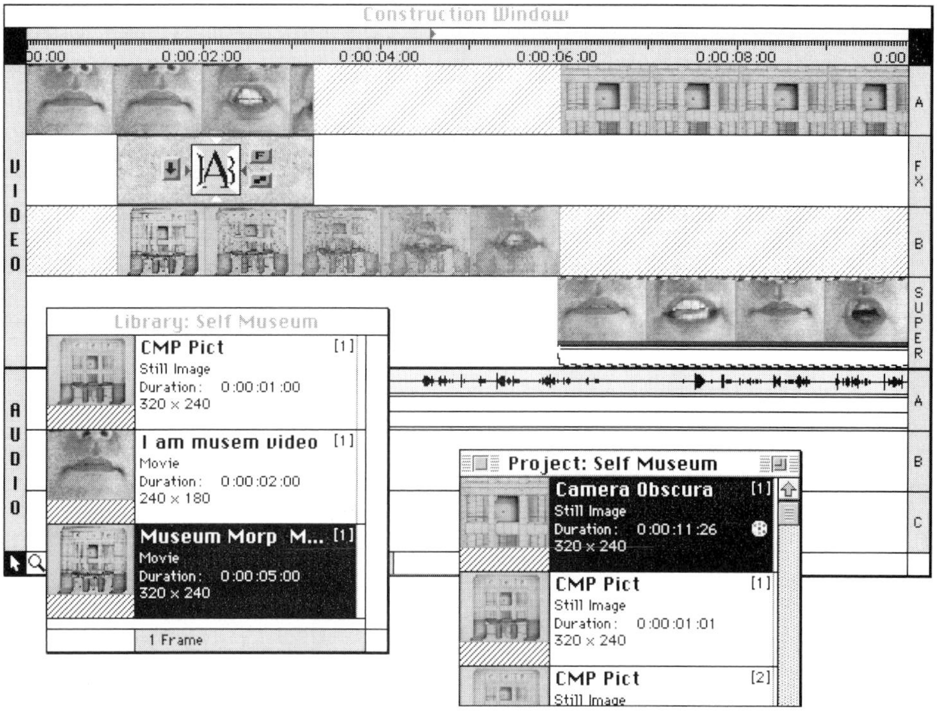

Figure 17.5 Premiere's Construction window with multiple channels occupied by media for the "Self Museum Project"

TOOLS
Morph ⌘229

into Morph, where he created a QuickTime movie in which the museum facade morphs into his face. This QuickTime movie was then edited into the larger production to add multiple levels of convergence between the museum facade and the face.

Setting Up the Project in Premiere

All of the video and audio segments, still images and other material used to make the QuickTime movie were placed in a single folder and then imported into a library window in Premiere. The library was given the name "Self Museum Library" and saved to the same folder on the hard disk. A library contains only one copy of each movie, sound, or image and can be reused in other projects. Although the project window is intended to store media being used for a project, this can create confusion as to which media are actually being used. Each time a video segment is cut with the razor blade tool into a shorter segment, duplicates of the movie appear in the project window and clutter it. Thus, retaining a library file for each project serves the function of clarifying which media files are actually part of the project in progress.

The project window was saved along with the timeline construction window to a file named "Self Museum Project" in the same folder with the other files for the project. Saving all of the work for a particular production in one folder is critical for the simple reason that Premiere utilizes "reference" movies or media, which use pointers to the actual raw clips. Segments do not become contained within a single document until the final movie is made with the "Make Movie" command. If the work were moved to another hard disk, to a SyQuest, or relocated in some other folder, Premiere might not be able to find the media files that are referenced and they would have to be relocated.

Synching Audio to Video

A QuickTime close-up movie of Stephen's face and lips was placed in the first video channel in Premiere. Audio narration was captured using Sound Edit Pro from the original video. To insure the maximum frame rate for the video, Stephen captured the sound in a separate pass from the video. Capturing both together would have provided automatic synchronization, but the additional processing power needed to capture the sound data would have lowered the video frame rate. With an automated capturing system (VideoToolkit, QT-Paradise), the video and audio can be captured separately and then automatically combined by the software.

The next step was to synchronize the separate audio and video tracks. The audio narration was placed in the first sound channel, and a short preview was made to determine the direction the audio needed to be moved to obtain synchronization with the video. Through trial and error and several previews, perfect lip sync was achieved. The "Make Movie" command was used to compile a QuickTime movie to ensure that the preview accurately portrayed the final result. The initial movie used Apple Video compression and the small size of 160×120 pixels as a test, while the final movie was made the larger size of 320×240. While the Apple Video compression isn't effective enough to produce larger window sizes, it can compress video *much* faster than the Compact Video codec.

Video Inserts

While the entire sound track remained intact, much of the original video of Stephen's face and lips was replaced with video inserts in the second video channel or the Superimpose channel, or with other special effects and still images. The morph movie, which was the first video insert, was placed in the second video track. The razor blade tool was used to cut the original video from the first track so that the morph movie could be seen from the second. A preview of this movie showed simple cuts from the movie in the first track to the morph movie in the second track, and then back again to the movie in the first track, which remained in lip-sync with the audio.

Using Transitions

A "Doors" transition was used to go from the artist's face and lips to the morph movie. This transition created a stunning effect as the museum's facade opened up like doors to reveal the morph movie, which itself was in the process of transforming from a museum back into a face, so that the canopy above the museum's own doors morphed onto the lower lip of the artist.

This was an interesting effect, and one of many available to digital directors using video editing software. However, it's important to note that in the real world

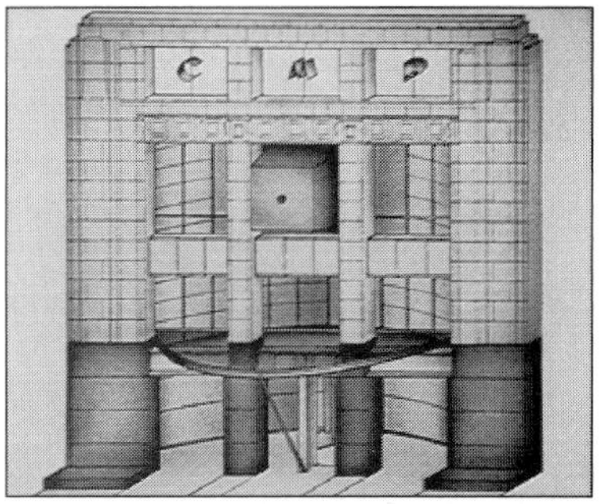

Figure 17.6 Doors transition causes museum's facade to open, revealing a face.

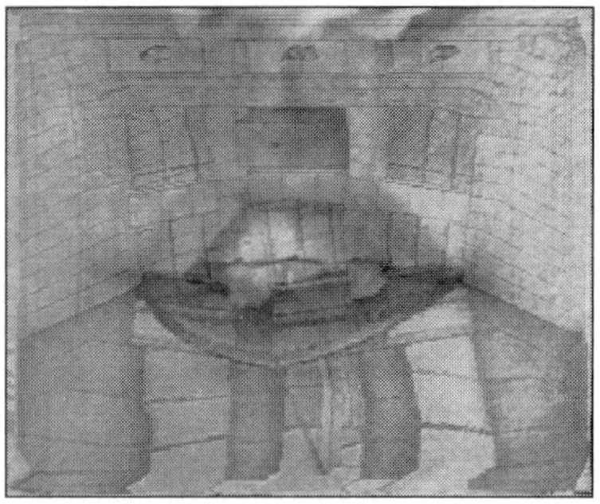

Figure 17.7 The Museum of Photography morphs into the face and lips of the artist.

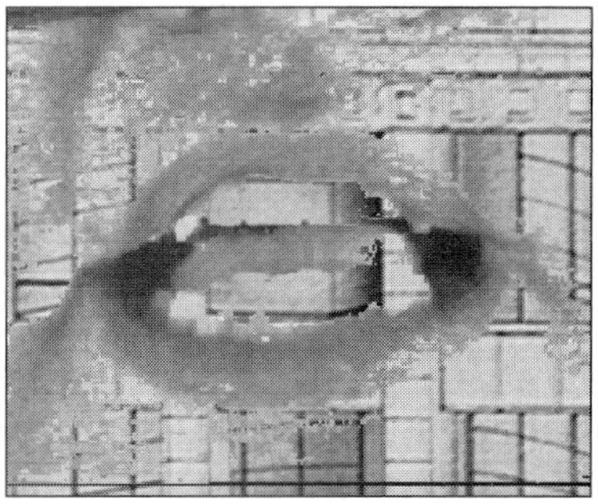

Figure 17.8 The lips in Superimpose channel are overlaid onto the museum's Camera Obscura.

of professional video, the vast majority of transitions are cuts. Dissolves, cross-dissolves, and fades-to-black run a distant second. You have to be careful not to overuse the fancy options, as gratuitous transitions can get quite tiresome to the viewer and can throw off the pace of the story. Feel free to experiment with them, but resist the temptation to use them too often

When applying a transition, consider the sense of motion you want for your scenes. Many transitions are directional, beginning on the far left and proceeding to the far right, or beginning in the top left corner and proceeding to the bottom right corner. Transitions can be used to continue or reverse the motion, maintain the continuity of the scene, or provide contrast in focusing on the differences from one scene to the next. Returning to that person who is looking toward the upper right of the screen, the transition might be a wipe coming from the top right corner. If a person is walking from the left of the screen to the right, a wipe might take place from the left, creating some tension as it slowly catches up with the person and wipes him/her away. Thus, transitions should not be thought of as special effects, but as visual elements that flow from the subject matter of the video.

Using the Superimpose Channel

Following the morph, a segment of the original "talking lips" movie was cut from the first channel and pasted into the special Superimpose channel, so it remained in sync with the underlying audio. A still image of the Camera Obscura was placed in the first video channel to fill the void left when the lips were cut from that channel. In order to create a vision of the lips talking on top of the Camera Obscura, Premiere's transparency effect was used (located under the "Clip" pull-down menu). By means of experimentation, the Key Type "RGB Difference" set to "Similarity = 72" was found to cause everything in the Superimpose channel to disappear, except for the lips, thus resulting in the desired effect.

Wrapping Up

While the QuickTime movies did not fill the screen, Stephen found the extra room was perfect for providing a context in which to view the movies, and to place buttons for interacting with the work.

Once the media were transferred to QuickTime, Stephen used the MovieShop utility (see below) to ensure that the data rate stayed under 90 kilobytes per second, which permits the movie to play from a CD-ROM to just about any color Macintosh. To test the material, he transferred about 14 SyQuest cartridges full of QuickTime movies and computer data to a recordable CD-ROM through a service bureau that charged only $150. This not only provided an opportunity to test the CD-ROM's performance, but also served as an inexpensive storage medium. The test was a complete success. In addition, he had 14 empty SyQuests for continued development of the project, which also was a rousing success and very well received by the museum's administrators and visitors.

Compressing with Compact Video—MovieShop Revisited

After you have completed the editing of your movie, it's time to compress it. In Chapter 8, "Video Tools," we mentioned Apple's MovieShop program (available from APDA on the QuickTime Developer's CD-ROM) and how it can be used to reduce a QuickTime movie's data rate to make it compatible with playback from CD-ROM. Here are the steps to obtain the best results using the Apple Compact Video codec, currently, the most effective QuickTime codec in reducing the overall data rate (though it also takes the longest to do its job).

First, launch MovieShop and press the "Import" button to read in your movie. You can inspect your movie's data rate by selecting the "Play" button.

Next, select the maximum data rate. We mentioned earlier that 90-100K per second is a safe rate for playback from most CD-ROM drives. Choose this rate if you plan to mass distribute your QuickTime movie on CD-ROM. Experiment with higher data rates if you know that your movie will be played only from double-speed CD-ROM drives or from a hard drive.

Under MovieShop's "Preferences" menu, select "Millions of colors" and "Use previous compressed video."

Image size can be changed with "Cropping..." from the "Preferences" menu. If you resize the picture using scaling or cropping, use horizontal and vertical dimensions that are multiples of 4. The Compact Video compressor is optimized for these values. The best size is 240×180 if you are playing back from CD-ROM. You can use 320×240 for movies that have higher data rates (though you may also need the faster Macs to keep up with the frame rate). You'll definitely want to crop if you see noise or jitter along the edges of the video frame.

Remember that sound is data, too. Higher-quality sound requires more information, and may slightly lower the image quality. Choose "Sound..." from the "Preferences" menu if you want to change the sound quality. If you have music in your sound track, you'll probably want it set to 22 kHz. But if you only have voice, choose the "Resample sound to 11 kHz" setting.

Finally, select "Methods..." from the "Preferences" menu to tell MovieShop which compression techniques to apply. The Compact Video compressor automatically takes care of data rate limiting, so turn off all the methods except for items 1 and 8: "1) Compress frame - As frame differenced using the quality settings," and "8) Prefer Natural Key frame - Do not force Key Frame before it." To do this, drag item 8 directly below item 1, and then drag item "18) ONLY DO THOSE ABOVE THIS ITEM," directly below item 8 (see Figure 17.9). Next, click on item 8 and adjust the Forced Key Frame tolerance value in the lower left corner of the window. Use a value that is 1/2 of your key frame rate. If you have key frames every 10 frames, then the value should be 5.

Finally, this note. MovieShop has a bug that causes settings from unused methods to take effect. To override those, select each of the following items and set their values as indicated:

Item 2: Forced key frame—set to 255

Item 3: Natural key frame—set to 1

Item 4: Natural key frame—set to 200

Item 5: Drop duplicate—set to 255

If you have a very large movie to compress, you will want as much processing power as you can get. If you don't have a high-end Macintosh or an accelerator board, see if you can borrow one for the duration of your editing schedule. You also may be able to split your movie into several segments and compress them in parallel on several Macintoshes. Then combine the segments into your final movie.

The Medium Is the Message?

Digital desktop video places communication tools in more hands then ever before. As a result, watching television is no longer the sole domain of the couch potato, but instead has become a place to learn and compare the creative tools of the trade.

While the experts debate whether video is a sign that our culture is declining from one of verbal literacy to visual idiocy, it is nevertheless among the most effective and powerful vehicles for communication, whether for promotion, education, training, or other purposes. Now that power has been placed in your hands through these relatively low-cost, exciting new tools and techniques, it continues a revolution in communication, which began with moveable type half a millennium ago.

It now is possible for anyone to create a multimedia production complete with professional quality digital video. With this immense power to communicate ideas, how will we take advantage of it? Using this medium, stories, which were previously impossible to tell, now can be shared. What will people create when they have grown up with the ability to craft a compelling video production? The answers and the questions will undoubtedly change as the technology and art form mature.

18

Video Projects

Video is one of the most potent elements of multimedia, while creating and editing video is one the most demanding skills required of a producer. In this chapter we'll survey four top-quality video projects: a virtual foray into the sea; a video "poem"; an interactive multimedia novel; and the logo sequence for a television show.

Water Fantasia

Water Fantasia ⌘030

Water Fantasia is a QuickTime movie featuring dreamy sequences that blend and dissolve to the relaxing rhythms of its soundtrack. Watching the movie is sort of like watching an aquarium: You feel drawn into a watery world that is both soothing and engaging. (The underwater segments were in fact shot at an aquarium.)

The work combines creator Don Doerfler's environmental interests with the emerging world of digital video production. Growing up and living near the ocean in Southern California provided both the influences and the material for *Water Fantasia.* In addition to his independent work, Don is a producer at Compton's New Media, where he works on CD-ROM products.

Special Considerations

Don's imagination almost always exceeds what he can actually capture on video, which he cites as a major hurdle in producing *Water Fantasia* or any multimedia project: "No matter how hard you try, you can't get that perfect shot," says Don. "So you're always searching through your tapes looking for that piece that's going to complete your overall visual idea."

The constant challenges are to shoot enough (and the right) material, sort through it all—looking for the right pieces, and reshooting, if possible, to capture those elusive visual ideas.

Figure 18.1
Scene from Don Doerfler's *Water Fantasia*

Technically, Don spent some time making sure the final cut played back acceptably at 15 frames per second. This was a challenge, since for those used to high-quality on-line video, the do-it-in-the-basement look of QuickTime can be something of a letdown. "My favorite misnomer for QuickTime is 'QuickTrash,' how to take a perfectly good video and ruin it," says Don.

QuickTime ⌘ 160

Despite the frustrations of the fledgling digital video tools, Don remains excited about their rapid improvements, and feels you can do good work with existing tools if you're willing to take the time and effort.

Tips and Techniques

Don's visual arts background has helped him in the transition to digital video and multimedia production. His earlier work taught him to visualize and carefully plan before applying brush to canvas or pencil to paper.

The complexities of digital video projects require an equal degree of foresight and planning, says Don. "You need to have certain concepts in mind before you start, especially when you're digitizing video segments—you're going to have a finite amount of space on your disk. So you have to review footage and put together a complete storyboard before you even start."

This planning stage saves time in all phases of video production: It gives a clear idea of what to shoot, saves hard disk space by preventing you from digitizing unnecessary footage, and helps organize the editing and assembly tasks.

On the editing effects side, Don recommends keeping it simple. Programs like Adobe's Premiere offer an assortment of transitional effects such as wipes, dissolves, and fades. While these effects can be fun to experiment with, they can be very distracting to watch. *Water Fantasia* uses only two types of transitions: cuts and dissolves.

Premiere ⌘240

Don adds a few final video tips: "Always use a tripod, never go handheld. And don't use any bad footage. If it's exposed badly, or if it's shaky—no matter how good it is otherwise—don't use it, it'll look terrible. We're all spoiled by watching TV."

Tools and Equipment

As Don notes, no single Mac application does it all when it comes to digital video: "The Mac has all the tools, but they're all in different applications, you have to have at least a half dozen of them to get what you want."

For *Water Fantasia,* Don used the Sony FX510 8mm video camera to shoot video, SuperMac's VideoSpigot card to digitize the video, and Premiere and VideoLake's VideoFusion for editing the digitized segments.

At the center is a Quadra 950 with a 500Mb hard disk, 28Mb of RAM, an Apple 16" color monitor, 24-bit color card, and a 13" NTSC video monitor. A RasterOps Video Expander (an encoder) converts the computer's RGB video to NTSC for output to videotape. Don uses several tape decks, including a Sony EVC40 and a Goldstar GVRA485. A Realistic five-channel stereo mixer for adding several channels of natural sound and music.

Land of Counterpane

As Education Director of the American Film Institute's Apple Lab, Harry Mott works with and teaches digital video, concentrating especially on QuickTime. He created *Land of Counterpane* to show, as he puts it, "what anyone with any color Mac could do with QuickTime."

Land of Counterpane ⌘031

The result is a simple but delicately constructed ode to his son Cameron, accompanied by a restful musical track and a Robert Louis Stevenson poem.

Special Considerations

Although Harry notes that "A year ago, you couldn't dream of the stuff we're doing now" with desktop video tools, he cites those same tools—and sluggish processing times—as a source of frustration. Mastering arcane programs and techniques, waiting for scenes to be rendered, for files to transfer, and for graphics to process are the special challenges of digital video and multimedia in general.

Even though tools are getting easier to use, and machines are getting ever faster, Harry acknowledges that, by and large, these have been incremental improvements. The vast size and complexity of multimedia, and especially digital video, requires machines to be much faster to really make a difference. Harry believes this will happen when Apple and IBM release their PowerPC computers, which use very fast processors. (PowerPC is discussed in Chapter 3, "Mac Software and Hardware.")

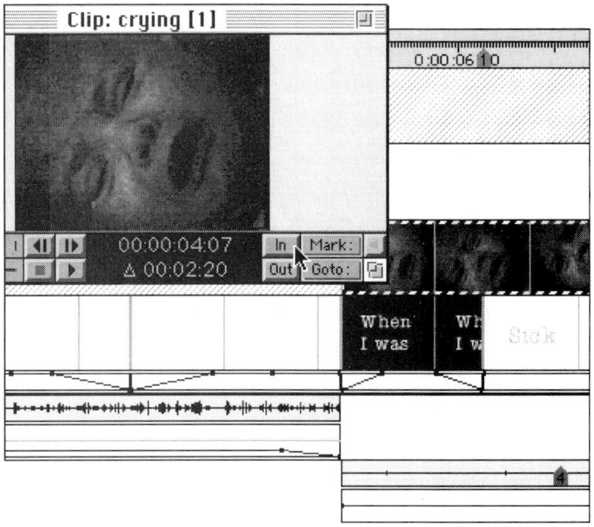

Figure 18.2 Editing Harry Mott's *Land of Counterpane*

Tips and Techniques

Harry has some special advice for those thinking about experimenting with digital video, but who may be put off by the challenges: "Don't wait, do it now. Everything is going to get better, faster, cheaper—maybe next week. Just play and experiment, and make mistakes—that's what the undo key is for."

Harry recommends using Apple's Compact Video QuickTime compressor when creating movies. This ensures that movies will play back smoothly on virtually any Mac. By contrast, says Harry, "if you make a QuickTime movie on a Quadra 950 using Apple Video [another compressor], it will not play smoothly on say an LCIII or even a IIci." Apple bundles the Compact Video compressor with QuickTime.

The downside is that the compression takes awhile to apply to each frame. Although Land of Counterpane is only 1½ minutes long, it took 6 hours to compress on Harry's IIci. Even compressed, the movie is nearly 12Mb in size, which clearly demonstrates the enormous size of digital video files.

Harry also advises that you digitize movies with no compression, and apply compression only when you actually make the movie. This will give you the most compression options later, and ensure that you have the highest quality video stored on disk (since compression can seriously degrade image quality).

Like all seasoned multimedia producers, Harry plans his work carefully, and stresses organization to his students. For example, he keeps titles, animation, video, and still images in their own folders to help him find things and speed the assembly of movies. Perhaps because he's a teacher, Harry's step-by-step guide on the disk is particularly rich in tips and techniques—check it out.

Tools and Equipment

The modest equipment Harry used for *Land of Counterpane* truly shows that equipment need not be a barrier to a thorough exploration of digital video. He used a Mac IIci with 20Mb of RAM and an 80Mb hard drive, the ever popular

VideoSpigot capture card for digitizing video, Macromedia's MacRecorder for digitizing sound, and Premiere for editing the movie.

Madness of Roland

Madness of Roland ⌘032

Chances are, you've never seen anything like *Madness of Roland.* One of the most ambitious QuickTime movies to date, *Roland* is an impressionistic tour de force that its creator Greg Roach calls an "interactive multimedia novel." The story, based on the French legends of Paladin Roland, is told from five different points of view.

The interface, says Greg, is based on the Tarot, "which both represents and allows access to the different points of view—each character is represented by a different Tarot card. It's also predicated on a cubist approach, where different people give you different aspects of events, and eventually, the event will piece itself together for you."

Roland is further enriched by commentary tracks that lend both historical and anachronistic insights into the main narrative. Skillfully blended sound and musical tracks seem to spring organically from the video montages, further enhancing the story.

Greg himself has a background as an artistic director and actor in regional theater, and edits the computer-based video magazine *Hyperbole,* in which *Roland* first appeared.

Special Considerations

Finding a commercial distributor for *Madness of Roland* was among Greg's biggest project challenges. "*Roland* is kind of radical. *Roland* is making some assump-

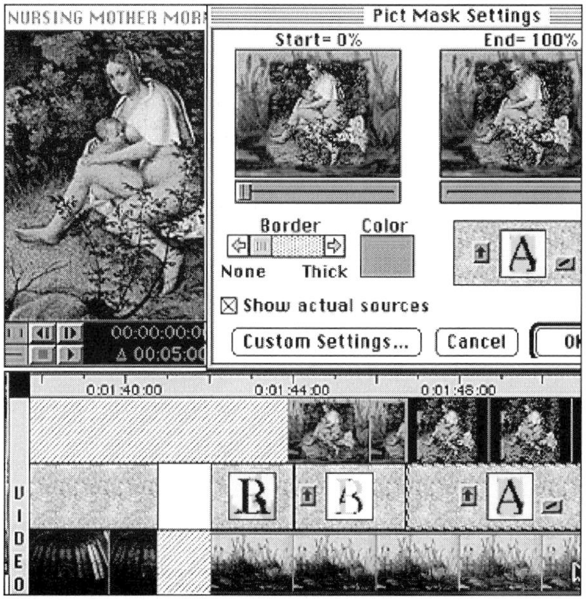

Figure 18.3 Editing *Madness of Roland* using Premiere

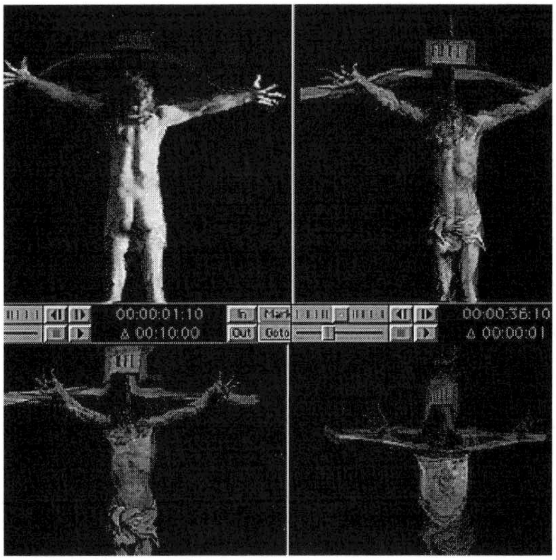

Figure 18.4 ***Roland*** **made effective use of morphing techniques to blend still imagery.**

tions about the nature of interactivity, and what people will be interested in consuming," says Greg.

Among many other elements, *Roland* incorporates many still images, which Greg singles out as another interesting difficulty. Many of these images were morphed to give them an otherworldly sort of motion.

Roland makes extensive use of live actors, a complexity of production might have intimidated many multimedia producers, but which came naturally to Greg, who was trained in the theater.

Still another challenge was optimizing the movie for playback from CD-ROM, which software engineer Mark Arend spent many long hours working on. Rather than leaving it up to the Mac operating system or an application to decide what should be loaded into memory and when, Mark did this memory management himself for each segment.

Although this sort of manipulation is beyond the average weekend interactive programmer, it does make for much more watchable digital video. Unfortunately, notes Greg, not many programmers take the time to optimize playback in this way, "and that, unfortunately, is often very apparent. I've seen beautiful work that is ruined because it's so sluggish. While looking at one CD-ROM recently, I literally fell asleep twice!"

Tips and Techniques

Greg and his team decided early to use QuickTime for all video and audio digitizing and editing, a decision that he says paid off over and over again. "Some of *Roland's* sound and narration files are 30, 40, even 50Mb. We stored even these sound tracks as QuickTime movies, so we didn't have to worry about moving these large segments in and out of memory, or what would happen if you jumped to a different part of *Roland* during a narration sequence," says Greg. "You can come right back and pick up exactly where you left off. The QuickTime architecture handles that for you."

On the technical side, Greg says that you can never have too big a hard disk, and you can never have a fast enough computer for development, especially for digital video. As noted in the *Land of Counterpane* project description earlier in this chapter, compressing video that has been digitized and saved with no compression can be a long haul (this compression process is called *transcoding*).

Greg recommends using the Radius Rocket, which off-loads any computing task to a separate processor, freeing the Mac's internal CPU for other work. (The Rocket is briefly described in Chapter 4's acceleration section.)

A good relationship of hard disk space to project size, says Greg, is 4:1. So if you're producing a 650Mb CD, you'll want about (choke) 2.5 gigabytes of on-line storage space.

Like many experienced multimedia producers, Greg advises digitizing everything—video, audio, still images—at the highest resolution possible. This gives you an archive of high-quality content.

Says Greg, "You can 'down-sample' [reduce file size at the expense of quality] whatever you're going to actually deliver. But then when the next generation of QuickTime comes out, or Macs begin to support on-board hardware compression/decompression, you'll be able to go back and resample that original material and update your product with higher quality versions." The idea is that your content should always be stored at the highest possible quality, so that it can outlive any particular use.

Tools and Equipment

Greg and his team started out using IIci's, but by the end of the two-year-long project, they had switched to much faster Quadra 700's with cache and 24-bit color cards, and two 13" monitors were used for digitizing video one for screen display and one for tools and palettes. Movie Shop and Premiere were used for video editing.

EcoSpies

EcoSpies ⌘ 033

Multimedia wizard Scott Billups was in Japan during the Telly awards, which are given to honor outstanding independent television programs. Scott figured he and his team had "a snowball's chance in hell" of winning an award for *EcoSpies*, so accepted the Japanese engagement rather than attend the award ceremony, which is held in Los Angeles. As it turned out, *EcoSpies*, won the award for best show.

EcoSpies is a pilot (produced by Sam and Sharon Baldoni, directed by Tim Cutt), which you will very likely see in production, thanks in part to the Telly award. Tim wanted to create a hard-hitting, reality-based show about Earth's growing ecological problems. Segments of the show cover toxic pollutants, unsanitary food production, and global eco-terrorism.

Storyboards for the pilot had been created by a graphics firm, but Tim felt their suggestions either missed the mark editorially or would alone eat up the entire $10,000 budget. Desktop production, where one person can perform the job of many, was the only way Tim could get the look he wanted for his budget.

Desktop video pioneer Scott Billups seemed the man for the job. Over the past 18 years, Scott has written, directed, produced, shot, and animated hundreds of broadcast, industrial, and theatrical projects for clients like Reebok, Mattel, Nissan National Geographic Explorer, and KCET-TV.

Using a variety of desktop video tools (see "Tools and Equipment" later in this chapter), Scott created the visual identity for the show.

Special Considerations

Scott's job as production designer was to come up with, as he puts it, "an inexpensive but compelling logo sequence that lent itself to segues, transitions, and 'bumpers,'" the teasers that networks use to keep you watching the show during multiple commercials.

The timing of elements is one of the biggest challenges in creating these sorts of transitions. Matching "stings," which are music or sound effects, with graphic transitions can consume a great deal of time.

Figure18.5
"EcoSpies"

Scott would save the video clips as QuickTime movies and send them to composer Dominic Messinger, who would create music in MIDI format. Scott would then match the music files to the beat of the video transitions, making timing of stings fairly straightforward.

Tips and Techniques

Scott's extensive use of desktop video tools meant that the *EcoSpies* identity could be created much more easily and less expensively than would have been possible with traditional video tools.

Scott cites the timing of animation and video sequences (compositing) as the single most challenging task. Another tough aspect is making things look natural: "The hardest thing in computer graphics is getting them to look organic. It's really easy to make your graphics look slick and metallic. The trend is away from the glitzy, flashy look and toward a more natural appearance," says Scott.

This trend encourages the use of desktop tools, which excel at this organic, photo-montage look. "Desktop tools allow you to sample and combine images instead of simply creating synthetic textures," says Scott.

Tools and Equipment

TOOLS

Director ⌘ 210

Swivel 3D ⌘ 220

MacroModel ⌘ 221

Scott sketched his visualizations using Swivel 3D and Macromedia Director on his Mac IIfx. He exported the rough animations as 320 ×240 PICTs and compressed them into a QuickTime movie using Premiere. Scott created final models with Macromedia's MacroModel, and ElectricImage's MisterFont, rendering them in ElectricImage Animation System. A beta version of CoSA's After Effects image processing software was used to composite live video with animation.

Scott digitized audio tracks with DigiDesign's AudioMedia board. He recorded the video frame by frame to videodisc with Sony's CRV 5000 Laser Videodisc Recorder, Intelligent Resource's VideoExplorer board, and Advanced Digital Imaging's MacVac software.

19

Interface and Interactivity: Bringing It All Together

Interface is the focal point and control center of any multimedia project. It brings the component pieces of text, graphics, sound, animation and videos together into a cohesive whole, and it's the all-critical graphical environment through which a user interacts with them. Creating an elegant and useful interface is where the real art of multimedia production is called to the fore—and it's probably a project's most challenging developmental component.

In this chapter we'll take a close look at the planning and design considerations that go into creating an effective interface, including initial planning and design; the use of text, graphics, sound, animation, and video; and mastering the project. This is not a technical chapter. Rather, it's meant to give you some old fashioned common sense and guidance for developing something that's user-friendly, creative, and useful.

The points we touch on here are meant to start you thinking about ways in which you can creatively enhance the usefulness and enjoyment of your project. After reading this chapter, take a tour through the projects on the Power Tools CD. Their producers have expanded upon these ideas in hundreds of different ways. Hopefully, you'll come up with some creative variations on their techniques and design sensibilities, and so it goes.

Planning a Nonlinear Program

Planning a multimedia presentation means not only gathering all the elements needed but also conceiving a structure and design for the prorgram. Good interface design is extremely important, as it will mean the difference between users scanning the first couple of screens or really poking into the corners of your project. Information flow is important as well, so it might be a good idea to chart your project out on paper, showing the various areas where users can reach out and find data that they might not otherwise encounter. It is the varying levels of interactivity that will ultimately draw users further into your project, hopefully entertaining them enough to keep them there.

Exploit Random Access

Keep in mind that unlike most viewable media, such as television or films, interactive multimedia is a nonlinear medium. Once in the computer, your data is immediately accessible at all times. You can get to the fiftieth screen of your project just as fast as you can get to the second. The random access nature of this technology is what makes it so powerful, and the best multimedia projects take advantage of this fact.

Therefore, "interactive" means that users of your project don't have to necessarily proceed through it in a straight, linear fashion from the first screen to the last. In fact, you can put in buttons allowing them to branch off at any point in the project. Allowing them into places that don't make sense can be a problem as well: If they need one piece of information before proceeding to the next, then plan your project accordingly, making sure that the button to reach item 2 can only be clicked after going through item 1.

Linking: The "Card Metaphor"

All authoring programs will provide some method of linking, which will enable you to create buttons to navigate from one part of your project to another. These links will provide the ability to create a completely interactive environment for the user to explore. Depending on the structure of your project, users can move about freely or in very defined patterns. If it's important that the user learn some basic concepts before giving them complete freedom, it's easy to make the first 5 or 10 screens work in a straight linear fashion. Once the basic concepts have been communicated you can then let the user run wild through audio-visual databases, animated video games or whatever happens to be the content of your project.

Video games are a good example of nonlinear access, as there are often multiple choices as to what can happen to a user. Depending on the user's choice, they may end up going to the next screen, going back to the beginning of the game, or even taking a shortcut to the end. This type of interactivity is what makes multimedia production so exciting.

Many authoring programs also support randomizing. In other words, you can build in functions that will ensure that your project reacts differently each and every time it is run. For example, you can instruct a button to randomly branch to any 1 of 12 different screens when a user clicks on it. Each one of these 12 screens can have buttons that also take random paths, including the possibility of returning to the previous screen.

Avoid Sluggish Performance

One of your most important overall goals should be to achieve a synergy between your hardware and software. With intelligent integration of text, graphics, audio,

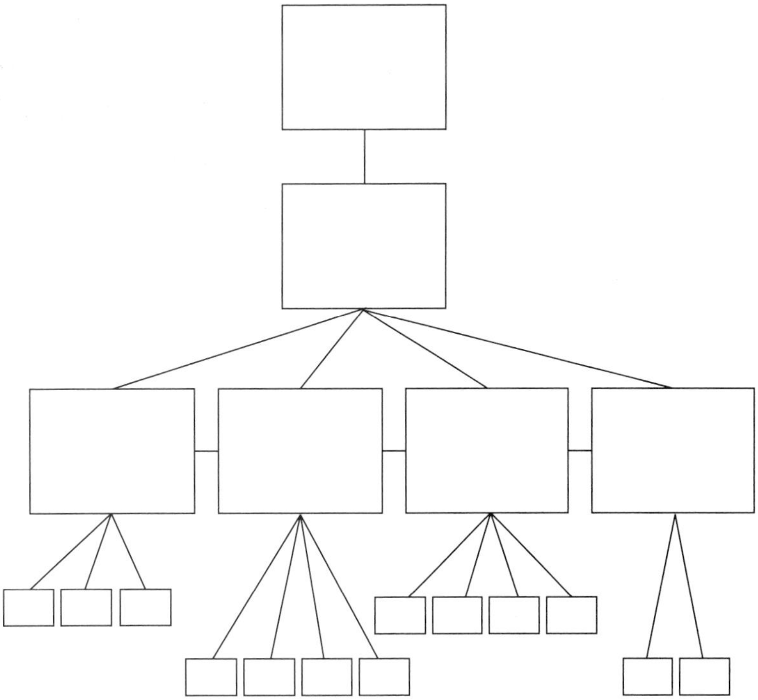

Figure 19.1
It's often useful to create a map that shows the structure of a project and all of its links. A map that shows the relationships between the various sections of a project will allow you to anticipate any dead ends or other difficulties that might be inherent in the structure of your project.

animation, and video, your project should run smoothly and create a lasting impression on users. Unless you take serious precautions to ensure that your hardware can effectively process all the data included in your project, it may run sluggishly, leaving users with a negative impression.

The biggest complaint about interactive media is that it is often just too slow. Make sure that this is not the death of your project. If you have to sacrifice certain things in order to ensure that the overall project runs well, it will be worth it. It may be impossible to make your project run at a blinding pace, but you should at least be considerate of how long it is reasonable to expect the user to wait. There are interactive game CDs on the market that can take a minute or more to load an animation that heralds the next section of the game. This is a surefire killer for most users, as few people have the patience to wait, regardless of how rewarding the animation might be when it finally gets to the screen.

Designing a Clean and Intuitive Interface

By today's standards, a user interface should be extremely intuitive, negating the need for users to follow any written instructions. Proper use of icons, good screen design, logical ordering of content, and a consistent structure are all important concerns when planning a user interface.

Figure 19.2 This is a typical screen layout for a multimedia project.

Be conscious of whether or not your project feels consistent. All the screens should have the same basic design elements, with all the key buttons in a consistent location.

You should also make sure you have enough room to include graphics or text on any given screen. An interface should make sense at a glance, no matter who the user. It should also be intuitive in regard to design sense, button placement, and logical flow of data.

It's important that you offer users an unfettered path through your project. They should be able to intuitively find whatever it is that interests them without having to go through each and every screen or button. They should also be able to navigate through a variety of interactive levels and still find their way back to where they began.

Where possible, you should create extra guidance, as well. For example, some programs will provide dialogue and/or message boxes that inform users of alternate paths or approaches to information. If it's possible for users to hit two buttons on the same screen that don't work together, try and create a warning and some instruction on how they should properly proceed. Some projects include interactive maps that show the levels and sublevels of the project structure, allowing users to change location by referring to the map and clicking on the area they wish to visit.

If help files are included with your project, make them available at all times. This type of guidance and feedback can go a long way toward encouraging users to stick with an interactive project. The more challenging the project is to the user, the more guidance and help you need to offer.

It's also nice to build in rewards for users. If they've completed an entire section of your project, create an animated segue to the next screen. There are lots of

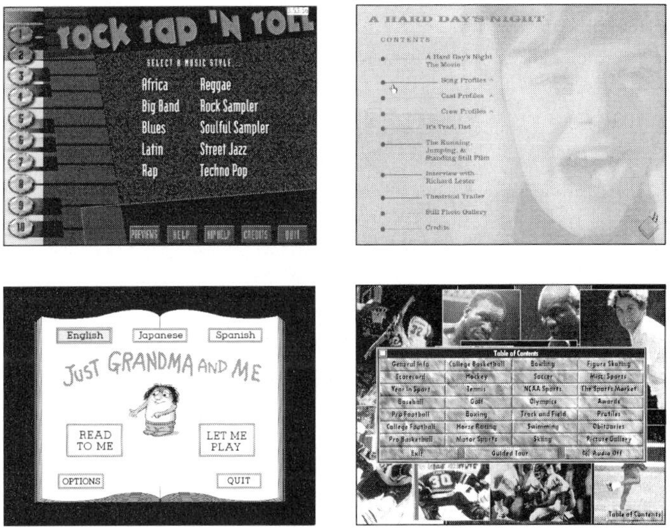

Figure 19.3 Interface designs vary widely, depending on the content and functionality of a project, as these four examples illustrate.

ways to reward users, depending on the nature of your project. Tallying up a current score and assigning it an impressive name is one way. Playing some fanfare music is another. Regardless of the nature of your project, if it asks for users to make their way through lots of data, then you should provide resting spots or other breathers along the way.

Ergonomics

An ergonomically designed interface will offer the user a logical flow between different functions. It should not force users to look all over the place for information and buttons, but rather should maintain consistency in the placement of text, graphics, and navigational tools.

Free navigating through various levels should also be a key feature. For example, if your project has four main areas, each with two or three sublevels, you should give users a means to traverse back and forth easily among the sublevels without having to always return to the top level. If your project demands a lot of text input, then you should offer command-key equivalents for navigating through the various screens as well. This way the user can leave his or her hands on the keyboard, rather than constantly switching from mouse to keyboard and back.

You should also make sure that users can get through your project in a reasonable amount of time, building in shortcuts for those who might wish to skim through various sections.

Using Dynamic Media

Dynamic media refers to any audio, video, and animation clips that are to be used in a project. The use of dynamic media in a multimedia project can add greatly to the impact of your message. There are a variety of ways to integrate animation, audio, and video. They can be used as supportive mechanisms to tell users what kind of progress they have made. They can also be used for establishing an overall tone for your project.

Buttons can be made to glow or pulsate with simple animation tricks, which can heighten the visual impact of your interface. Sound effects to reinforce various choices and actions can also make a project more stimulating. If there are questions in your project, sound effects for yes and no answers are a great means of livening up the presentation, and they make it easier to understand as well.

Annotating key areas of graphics or video clips with simple animations can also help to clarify and emphasize your message. For example, if there is a particular point of interest in a video clip, you can call it to the user's attention by creating graphic overlays or animated arrows.

Make sure you don't include too much dynamic media, as it can lead to other problems. If your project is too heavily laden with animation and video it will tend to slow down, regardless of the system you're working on. Try to spread out the use of video clips and animations. If you need to synchronize a video clip to an animation or sound effect, make sure you test the playback performance on every possible system that will be used to run your project. Don't sacrifice performance for glitz. There's often a middle road that will allow you to incorporate limited video, animation, or audio without losing too much speed.

Assembling Interactive Multimedia Components

Assembling all the components that make up a project involves coordinating hardware, software, and creative resources. Most ambitious projects will involve assembling a team, which could potentially consist of writers, artists, animators, scripting people, and more. Regardless of the size of your team, once you've determined the structure and content of your project, you will need to acquire and prepare all the data that will be incorporated.

Text

If your project relies heavily on text and text fields for disseminating information, make sure that you have a sensible way to handle your data. Generally, you'll assign a writer to provide you with text files that you can then import into your project. You must confirm that the word processor used by the writer can create text files that are compatible with the text importation capabilities of your authoring environment. There are a number of different text formatting models supported by the various word processors, but you can't automatically assume that your writer's format will be compatible. Make sure that imported text comes in cleanly and doesn't have to be fixed up or modified in any way. A text file ready for import should already have line feeds, tab information, and text styles (bold, italics, etc.) in final form.

Conversely, you may need to get text out of your project. If your project requires text input from users, make sure you can access and use the data that is recorded. Apple Events and other similar approaches can allow you to export text entries to databases or other software environments. Name and address fields can be entered in a kiosk and sent directly into a database, but you'll have to know about tab-delimited fields and other particulars about the programs used to ensure smooth communication between applications.

Graphics

Photoshop ⌘222

Almost all projects will involve graphics of some sort, and your authoring program and the type of project you are creating will determine what types of graphics you need. Computer-generated images can always be converted to a format that is compatible with your authoring program (see Chapter 9, "Authoring Tools"), using Adobe Photoshop or a utility specifically designed for file conversions.

The biggest concern you'll probably have in putting together you project is making sure that it runs at a reasonable pace, even with all the graphical overhead. When scanning photographs, it's important to pay attention to the bit-depth of the scanner you use, as there are a multitude of models that record everything from black and white to 32-bit color. Since 8-bit graphics only require one fouth the system performance than that demanded by 32-bit graphics, most people will convert their graphics into 8-bit color before importing them into an authoring environment.

Make sure you scan your graphics at the right resolution as well. Most scanners can scan photos at a resolution of 300 dots per inch, when 72 dpi is all that's generally needed for a project that will be displayed on a screen. For more details on the techniques and hardware for scanning, see Chapter 4, "Hardware Peripherals."

Processing Photos

There are a variety of wonderful graphics tools on the Mac available to aid in the process of fixing and processing images. Adobe Photoshop will enable you to enhance your imported photos in a number of ways. You can cut out key parts of images, colorize black and white photos, add graphic effects to images or highlight key areas of interest. Equally important, programs like Photoshop can be used to change the size and bit-depth of images, so if you need to blow up or reduce images, or convert from color to black and white, an image processing program like Photoshop is more than up to these types of tasks. For more information on Photoshop and other graphics applications, see Chapter 5, "Imaging Tools."

Using CLUTs with 8-bit Graphics

If you use 8-bit graphics it is extremely important that your authoring software is able to import Color Lookup Tables (CLUTs), also known as *custom palettes*, which will allow you to fine-tune the color tint graduations available for your presentation. With custom palettes you should be able to show reasonable quality graphics without sacrificing system performance. Most authoring programs also

TOOLS
Klutz ⌘ 132

allow you to create smooth transitions from one CLUT to another, ensuring that your 8-bit graphics look as good as they can.

The bottom line with using graphics will always be the issue of size and resolution versus system performance. Are your graphics too big? Do they slow your project down excessively? Can you work with 8-bit graphics instead of 24-bit graphics? Does your authoring program support palette transitions, so that you can smoothly shift from one custom palette to the next? It's best to know the answers to these questions *before* scanning and converting 600 photographs, so do your planning and testing ahead of time.

Sound

Sound can be used in a variety of ways to enhance a multmedia project. Introductory fanfares can be added to establish a high-energy mood. Opening animations can be supported with sound effects to add impact. Voice-over announcing can be used to describe or explain what the user is seeing on the screen. The combination of music, sound effects, and voice provide a wide range of audio support for filling out a project and making it that much stronger in the end. The next few sections will give you a rough idea of the ways in which you can use sound in your project. For detailed information, see Chapter 6, "Sound Tools," and Chapter 13, "Producing Sound."

Adding Mood with Music

Music is great for setting the tone or mood of a piece or a section of a project. Used as introductions, transitions, or just as background ambience, music can be a key motivator in getting users in the proper frame of mind. Music can also be used to help establish a different pace. If your project moves from rapid, fast cut video to slow, serene camera moves, use music tracks to complement each section and establish the pace. This will lessen the herky-jerky pace that might exist between two radically different pieces of video.

Music can also create balance in your project. If a needed video segment is moving too slowly, add slightly upbeat music to provide the motivation for viewers to watch the entire segment. If used tastefully, music can do wonders to establish, maintain, and motivate the tempo and pacing of a project. Video producers will often use music to fix a video piece that feels off tempo, and there's no reason why a multimedia producer shouldn't take the same approach.

Sound effects

Sound effects can be one of the most powerful, underlying elements of a project. They can enhance animations by reinforcing key movements. Sound effects can also motivate transitions from one section of a piece to another, and can be employed to let users know they have just completed a section of your project, or that they are about to enter the next section. Buttons can become more tactile when complemented with animation and sound effects. If your project has consistent interface elements, such as multiple-choice questions, try using sound effects for both right and wrong answers. This will enable users to proceed more smoothly through the project, as they'll have the added aural reinforcement to help give them direction.

Voice

Narration is often a key element in multimedia projects. If you have any doubts as to how users will initially percieve your product, add an announcer to your startup screen to clearly define your project's purpose. If there are difficult concepts to explain, use clear, consise graphics or animations coupled with well-timed narrative to make sure the point gets across. Conversely, if there are concepts for which you have no supporting video, graphics, or animation, explain them with an announcer narrative. As with sound effects and music, narration can often be used to "fix" a section that is too slow or not clear enough to users.

As with graphics, there are different hardware and software considerations, depending on the sound quality you need. If standard, 8-bit sound is good enough, then you will have no problems creating sound for your project. Sound can be imported via affordable audio digitizers (Apple includes audio input and microphones with recent machines), and 8-bit sound can be played back on any Mac. Professional quality, 16-bit audio requires a good deal more of a commitment, both in hardware and storage space.

Animation

The ability to play back animation in a project varies greatly among authoring programs. This is due to the wide variety of formats available, including PICS, QuickTime, QuickPICS, Accelerator documents, and Macromedia Director movies. Take a look at Chapter 9, "Authoring Tools," for a rundown on the capabilities of the various programs. Once you've decided which animation format is right for your project, determine the size and color depth that you'll be able to use. Remember, you're balancing quality versus system performance, so be prepared to modify your expecations of glorious, full screen animations in order to ensure that your project runs at a reasonable speed.

Figure 19.4 Multimedia Power Tools comes with a tour guide who appears in the video window with a complete tour of the disc, abbreviated tours, or quick help instructions.

Animation can be applied on a number of levels. You can run entire animated segments, animate foreground elements over a consistent background, and in some cases you can even run animations over imported video.

Animation is often the best tool for explaining advanced concepts. If you need to explain how certain mechanical parts work in conjunction, or how a particular machine is assembled, animation will often be the perfect solution. One of the greatest benefits of animation is that you can alter the material to suit your needs. If your project requires that you explain the movement of planets in the solar system over a fifty-year period, you can easily create a short segment that gets the point across clearly. This is obviously a case where video or still images are not as appropriate as a custom designed animation.

For detailed information on creating and working with animation, see Chapter 7, "3-D and Animation Tools," and Chapter 15, "Creating Animation."

Video

Video is certainly the best visualization tool available, and is often the only way to truly communicate your message. For example, if you're trying to show users the effects of severe weather conditons on certain coastal regions, video footage of storms pounding the coast will have much more effect than an artist's diagram. Again, this will have much more effect than using diagrams or animations. If you're trying to explain different dance steps used in various cultures, video will be easier and more effective to use than any graphic or animation. The visual nature of your project will dicate whether or not you absolutely need video. In many cases, there can be no substitute.

However, using video requires extremely large quantities of memory, and therefore places significant technological demands on your system. Choosing the most sensible approach for you will be determined by the nature of your project. If full-screen video is absolutely essential, you should consider pressing a laser disc. It allows full-screen graphics to be stored and retrieved quite easily. Also, the time it takes to load a full-screen picture off of a laser disc is often much quicker than loading the same image from your hard drive or a CD-ROM. However, be aware that using a laser disc will severly limit your market—there are just not that many players out there compared to CD-ROM drives. A laser disc would be perfect for a project that will be played back in kiosks or in tightly targeted, controlled situations. It would not be appropriate for a mass-market, commercial multimedia project.

From an interface and design point of view, the decision to include video is not so much an aesthetic choice, but rather a content issue. Does your project need video? Although video can be very powerful, you must use it judiciously, based upon your wants and the capacities of your media and playback system. When a beautiful full-screen graphic or animation will suffice, you may want to coinsider using that instead. You can also use short video sequences to make dramatic points or punctuations to deliver quick messages. If you have a longer,

Figure 19.5 The Power Tools CD displays video at 12–15 frames per second (as opposed to the 30 fps of full-motion video) in a moderately sized window. This treatment provides effective video impact at an economical tradeoff with memory, storage, and other factors.

instructional video to tell a complete story, you can use a lower resolution, smaller windowed video. If not, then try to avoid it. Video is the most demanding resource you can have in a multimedia project.

Obviously, if you're producing an interactive music video sampler, you'll need to have video and you should plan accordingly. In other cases, the decision may not be so clear. For example, if you're having a tough time communicating a message clearly, and you think that video might be the answer, make sure you can get the proper video footage to do the job. Shooting your own video can be difficult, and if done poorly will only serve to make your project look shoddy. If you think there is existing footage that will serve your needs, explore the issue of copyrights, since you will most likely want to avoid any legal repercussions of purloining someone else's material. See Chapter 17, "Creating Video," for detailed information on the topic.

Databases

If your project requires searching and referencing large amounts of data, make sure you pick an authoring program that will assist you with this task. Name and address forms, for example, often require 6 to 10 different types of fields, and you'll want users to be able to search each one.

A good example of a multimedia database is LaserReel, an interactive HyperCard stack that searches through a series of laser discs and plays different TV commercials created by different directors. If you enter the search parameters "chocolate bars," "upbeat music," and "bikinis," the program will compile and play a sequence of commercials that have bikini-clad girls dancing around with chocolate bars. The project also allows users to search for different TV directors by name, type of commercial, product category, or a variety of other parameters. This is a great use of a database and multimedia in the same project, and the producers made sure that the database tools in HyperCard were up to the task before investing in serious development time.

Conversely, there will be situations where a large database may require a multimedia front end. Multimedia interfaces are going to be increasingly useful in accessing large databases in the months and years to come.

Inter-applications Communication

Although HyperCard, with its built-in database functions, makes a good starting point for database multimedia, you may be able to address more ambitious projects by working with inter-applications communcation (IAC). Using elements such as Apple Events, IAC allows you to send data from your authoring environment to another program, such as Claris Filemaker, and retrieve information back onto your project screens. This type of approach will generally require some custom programming, so be prepared to invest extra time and resources if you need ambitous database functions.

The Common-sense Factor

Let your project dictate what media you use, and how you use it. Use standard approaches, such as the age-old "form follows function" method of determining what the right approach should be. Ultimately, you want a project that is clearcut and sensible to use. This means picking all the right elements and combining them in an efficient manner. Common sense is often the most important tool you can use in making the right decisions on how to execute any given project.

Designing Screens

Design integrity is one of the most important elements of a good interactive project. To be sure that your project comes across well, make sure you strive for good design. Color composition, font selection, graphic design, and screen layout are all important design considerations. Make sure the layout of the screen reads easily and is able to be browsed quickly. The most important thing is to establish a look and feel immediately and then stick with it. The screen that confronts users when they start your project should establish a natural flow that will make their travels through all subsequent screens enjoyable and unfettered. Regardless of what information you might be trying to pass along, there is no reason it can't be entertaining as well.

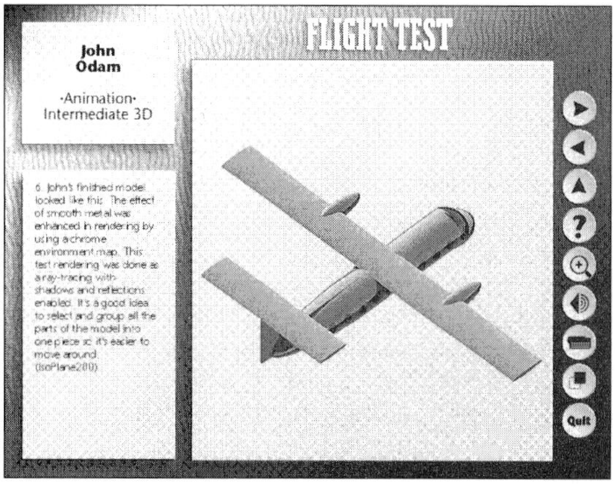

Figure 19.6 This is the interface of the Multimedia Power Tools Sample Projects section.

Backgrounds should have an interesting design with good color composition, yet they should never overpower foreground elements. Buttons should be attractive, large enough, and placed in such a way that they are easy to get to. Good design is often transparent, meaning that users won't even notice your layout because they're too busy devouring the information. This is what you should strive for.

Text

The treatment of text should be carefully considered, as it will make the difference between users breezing through your interface or struggling to read your text information. As with good print design, you'll need to consider things like fonts, point sizes, and character spacing when designing the text layout of your screens. All text should be easily legible, regardless of its importance. Don't make users squint to read tiny text, and don't make all text bold and in capitals. There will be a happy medium that enables users to easily and comfortably browse through your screens. Often, having others test your screen layout and design will be the best method of determining what size and style of text to use.

You will rarely need more than two or three fonts for an entire project. Pick a treatment for headlines, subheads, and body text, and then stick with it. Consistency is probably the most important part of text design. If your first screen starts with 14-point text in a box on the left side of the screen, all subsequent text should 14-point text be in a box on the left side of the screen.

Buttons and Windows

As with text, button and window placement should be intuitive and transparent to the user. Remember that consistency is the most important rule of thumb for designing screen layout. If users have arrow buttons available for navigational purposes, make sure that these buttons remain in the same place at all times. Likewise, window placement should be carefully considered. Do you want the user to see imported video in the same place where he or she reads your text, or do you

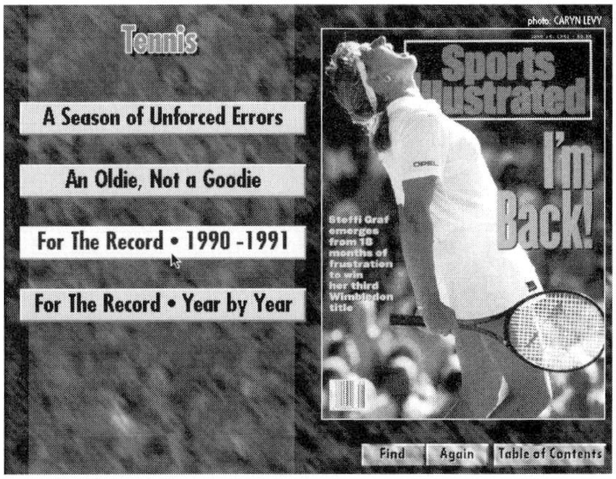

Figure 19.7 Navigational controls should be placed in easy-to-find, easy-to-use locations.

want to have a special location for video segments? Often it's best to have specially designated areas of the screen for different elements. Text will always be in one spot, and video will always be in another. This way, you can have text and video on the screen at the same time. Obviously, different types of data may demand different size windows, so try and accomodate other screen elements when designing your windows. If you need to import a large animation or video clip, try to make sure your buttons and other elements can remain in their original locations.

Building for Quality

Synergy! Consistency! Intuitive! Transparent! Logical! Natural Flow! These are the building blocks of good multimedia. How you bring these elements together will define the quality and ultimate success of your project.

20

Interactive Projects

Interactivity is one of the attributes that makes multimedia what it is. The ability to hop around and explore at will is one of the cornerstones of the new media phenomenon. In this chapter, we'll look at three interesting and very different interactive projects: a new product demo styled as a detective story; a learning tool for medical students; and a touch screen-driven kiosk that describes the facilities of regional hospitals.

PageMaker 5.0 Demo

PageMaker Demo ⌘040

When Aldus Corporation wanted an unusual demo disk to show off a new version of PageMaker, the popular page layout program, they turned to Ikonic, a San Francisco firm specializing in multimedia design.

It sounded like the dream job: "Major software company with deep pockets seeks imaginative, fun approach to creative project." As producer and designer Matthew Fass puts it, "Here was a client asking us to take risks, explore, and be adventurous."

Ikonic's creative team, including Matthew, company president Robert May, and Ann Marie Budrus, didn't let Aldus down: They came up with a disc that cleverly intertwined descriptions of the product's new features with a mystery designed to pique the interests of interactive explorers. (The entire PageMaker demo is on the Power Tools CD.)

Special Considerations

Despite their ambitions and creative freedom, the Ikonic team had to work under one serious constraint: "We wanted to have a lot of graphics and wanted to show off their product," says Matthew. "But it had to be a self running demo that would fit on a single floppy disk."

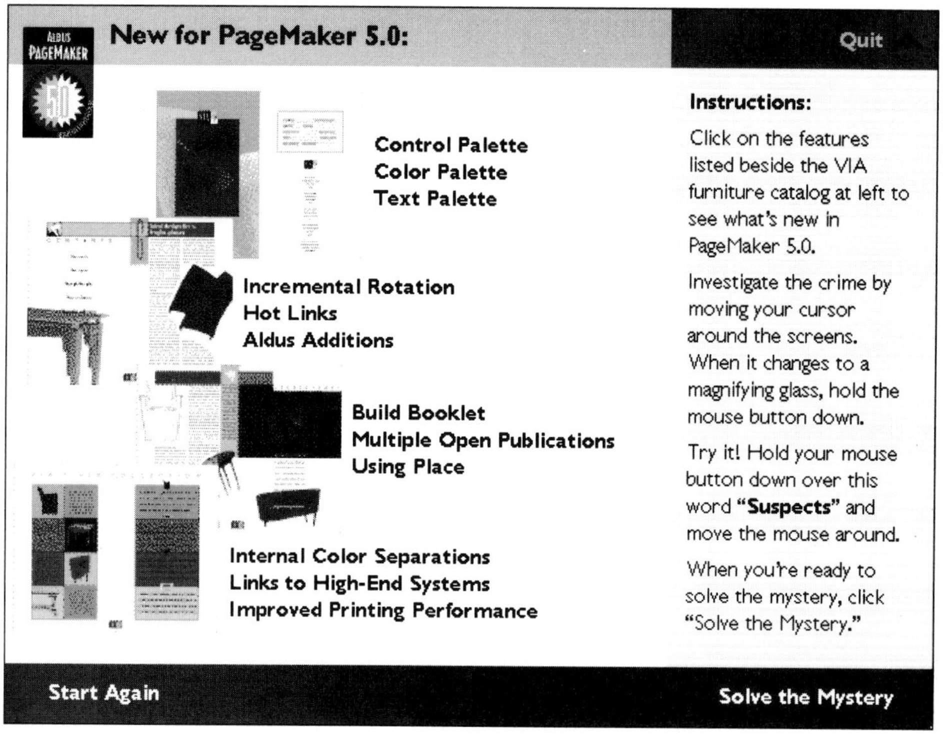

Figure 20.1 Ikonic's *PageMaker* demo disk

DeBabelizer ⌘ 228

Matthew and his team accomplished this by limiting the number of colors to 16, which considerably reduced the demo file size. They used a program called DeBabelizer to optimize the use of the relatively few colors they had to work with, and minimize the color substitution (dithering) that would degrade image quality. "Because we had only 16 colors, and the source images we used had 256 colors [8-bit], or even millions of colors [24-bit], we wanted to optimize the use of those 16 colors in a way that would reduce the dithering pattern," says Matthew.

The team also used DeBabelizer to "lock-in" certain key colors that appeared often, so that those colors would never be dithered. (For a brief description of DeBabelizer, see Chapter 5, "Imaging Tools.")

The Ikonic team did have to go back to the drawing board after presenting the initial design to Aldus. Although the client applauded the overall design and concept, the mystery and the product features were not integrated; it was too easy for users to play the mystery game and skip the product features altogether. As a result of the prototype feedback, Ikonic went back and tweaked the interface so that clues were buried in the feature descriptions.

Tips and Techniques

Matthew echoes the advice of many veteran multimedia producers: "Have your concept down before you start. Do good storyboards and plan well, so that the client and the production people are all thinking along the same lines; otherwise people will get differing ideas about the final outcome."

Director ⌘210

Matthew also warns that interactive programming can be tricky, especially for newcomers. Lingo, which is Macromedia Director's "scripting language," can be tough, "and not as consistent as you'd like it to be. For instance, you can't always find the command that you need," says Matthew. A scripting language is used to write the instructions for a presentation's interactivity—what file the computer is supposed to display when the user clicks a particular icon, and so forth.

A final word of advice: Use an S-Video or Hi-8 video camera when shooting your own video. These formats are higher quality than standard VHS and 8mm cameras and will give you better video source material to start with.

Tools and Equipment

Photoshop ⌘222

The Ikonic team used a Sony Hi-8 video camera to shoot the live video sequences, and a RasterOps 364 video digitizer to bring the video onboard the Mac. DeBabelizer and Photoshop were used for image processing, and Director for the interactivity and final presentation.

MedPics

MedPics ⌘041

As a core part of their studies at the University of California, San Diego (UCSD), medical students take a class called Human Disease. The course comprises both *histology*, the study of the microscopic structure of human tissue, and *pathology*, which is the study of the nature of disease.

A central part of this important course is the review and interpretation of medical images, a challenging task that can tax students even under the best of circumstances; and the circumstances at the School of Medicine's Learning Resource Center (LRC) weren't good. Students using the center to review 35mm slides of medical images found confusing and uneven image annotations. Moreover, slides were available on a limited basis and were often left in a disorganized state.

Fearing that this would cause mediocre performance on the pathology component of the National Board Exams, LRC director Helene Hoffman, Ph.D., and instructional software developer Ann Irwin, M.D., decided to design an interactive computer-based image presentation program. As a result, *MedPics*, is now a successful part of UCSD's medical school curriculum, and is available throughout the campus from workstations linked with Novell's NetWare network operating system. *MedPics* has also generated considerable interest in the worldwide medical community, and has been purchased for use at other universities.

Helene's Ph.D. is in physiology and pharmacology, and she is involved in medical education and the use of computers in education and training. Ann received her M.D. in 1991 and plans to pursue a career in education theory and medical informatics. Helene and Ann were assisted by interactive programmer Michel Kripalani and graphic designer Susan Adornato.

Special Considerations

Helene and Ann's main goal in designing *MedPics* was that the images themselves be of the highest possible quality. The images had to accurately reflect their content, or the project wouldn't win the acceptance of university administration and faculty—support that was necessary for the adoption of the new system. Students would be evaluating images partly to determine what distinguishes normal from abnormal tissue. If resolution wasn't sharp and clean, they would make mistakes (is that a cell mutation or a flipped bit?).

At the same time, the program had to run on the wide range of color monitors on the Macs that were installed at the university. That meant 24-bit color, which would have yielded the highest color fidelity, was out of the question. The team would have to get by with the 256 colors of 8-bit video.

To keep screen transitions smooth and flicker-free, Helene and her team reserved 48 of the 256 for backgrounds, icons, and other interface components. This left 208 colors for the images themselves, ensuring the highest possible image fidelity of 8-bit systems.

While this technique helped the designers achieve their goal of image accuracy and fidelity, 8-bit color has inherent limitations that are impossible to overcome.

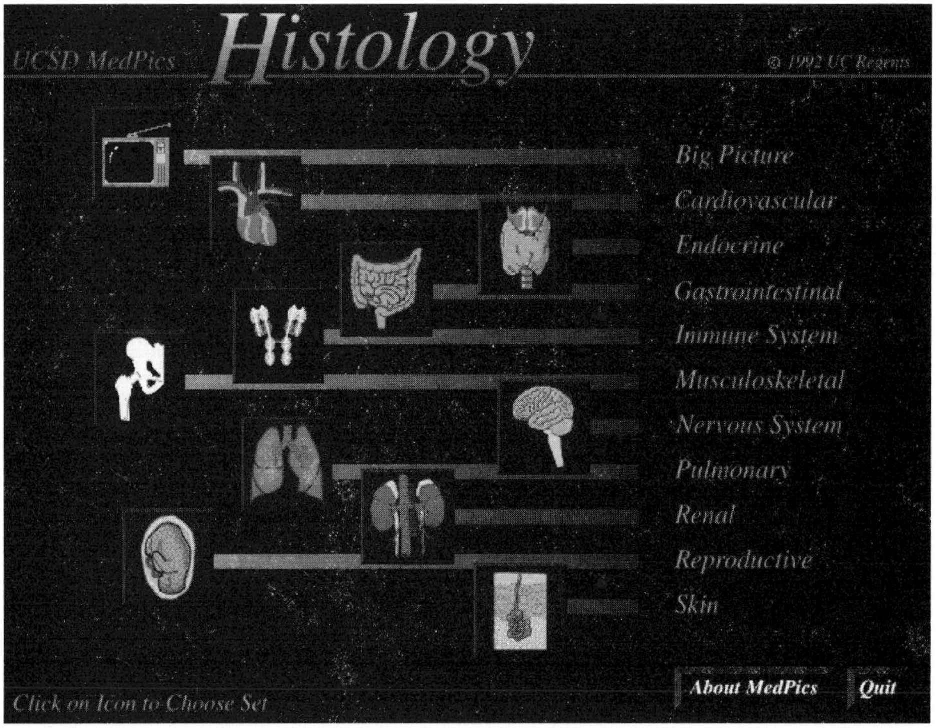

Figure 20.2
***MedPics* interface**

For example, the team would have liked the program to allow students to compare and contrast separate images side by side. This is not possible, however, since you cannot have two index color palettes (one for each image) open at the same time. The position held by gray in one color palette might be occupied by an entirely different color, say purple, in the other.

Tips and Techniques

When asked for some advice for those just beginning to explore interactive system design, Helene offers: "It takes twice as long and costs twice as much as you think at first." Ann agrees, adding, "It's like remodeling your house."

Both advise thorough storyboarding and interactive testing using simple placeholder images to test icon placement, branching, pop-up menus, and other interface and interactive elements before colors and imagery are designed.

The team learned a hard lesson in this respect, because they first designed the look of the program and didn't fully test interactive components before proceeding. This caused difficulty when the developers tried to port *MedPics* to the Windows environment for playback with Director's Windows Player. Elements such as pop-up menus and windows didn't carry over, and the team had to redesign these elements so that *MedPics* would run on both Windows and Mac machines.

Ann offers another tip: "The biggest trap that new interactive designers fall into is to try to incorporate a lot of bells and whistles: too many buttons, links, and visual elements," she said. "Keep it simple, especially on your first project, and you'll have a much easier time."

Tools and Equipment

The *MedPics* team digitized images using a Barneyscan Color Imaging Systems 3515 slide scanner. Photoshop was used for image processing, Aldus SuperCard for graphic overlays, and Director for the interactivity and presentation.

Health Care Kiosk

PROJECTS

Health Care Kiosk ⌘042

The Aesthetics Collection, a San Diego–based multimedia developer, put together an interactive kiosk describing the facilities of local hospitals for a meeting of the Symposium of Health Care Designers. The group's members specialized in all aspects of hospital design, and designer Paul Burgess and the staff of The Aesthetics Collection thought it would be a good showcase for the merits of interactive multimedia kiosks.

"The kiosk showed all the major hospitals in the San Diego area—about 20," says Paul. "It highlighted the services provided by the institutions, their staffs and facilities, their main focus, and their location."

The kiosk allowed viewers to move through the demo by touching the screen and to view descriptive videos accompanied by music. As a result, The Aesthetics Collection has received calls from various hospitals interested in kiosks for their own institutions, which would be used to describe the facilities, provide information, and give directions on finding different areas.

Paul has studied computer science, and both graphic and computer design. He has been authoring with Director for over 5 years, and has worked extensively with 3-D animation tools.

Special Considerations

An experienced interactive programmer and designer, Paul didn't encounter a great deal of technical difficulty with this project. His main challenge was getting the cooperation of all the hospitals.

While many hospitals cooperated, "a lot of them waited to get me their video footage until two days before the demo was to be installed," says Paul. Even though there wasn't a lot of material on each hospital, there were 20 of them, and each video segment had to be digitized, annotated, and edited.

Even with only 6 of the 20 hospitals supplying video segments, and the use of 8-bit instead of 24-bit color (to speed playback), the project still grew to consume over 130Mb, which graphically illustrates the enormous demands of digital video.

One of Paul's pet peeves is that the immediacy of multimedia prompts people to change things at the last minute. "Clients come over and see that all you have to do is click a button to change things," he says. "I'd say projects where the clients come into the office run about three times as long as when you just go to their office and make a presentation."

Tips and Techniques

TOOLS

PlayAIFF ⌘ 100

QuickTime ⌘ 160

Paul says memory was always a constraint. Files had to be kept small so that they could be held in memory, without the computer having to "swap" to disk to find information for display. "People don't like to wait when they're using touch screens and kiosks," notes Paul. "It's got to be pretty much instant."

QuickTime was well suited to this application, because movies can be played directly from disk without delay. Likewise, audio files were stored in the Mac aiff sound file format, so that music did not have to be loaded into memory, but played directly from disk in the same way as the movies did.

By contrast, Director files do have to be loaded into memory, which can produce time lags. For this reason, Paul advises breaking up the interactive portions into small Director files that can be loaded quickly. "If they take longer than 10 or 15 seconds to load," say Paul, "people will walk away."

Aside from a few early crashes, the presentation worked well. Most of these bugaboos were caused by people walking across the carpet and unwittingly zapping the touch screen with a static charge. Once Paul replaced the capacitive resistante touch screen with a pressure membrane model, the problems disappeared.

"Many people are mystified by Director," says Paul, and he recommends taking apart any Director files you can get hold of, which is a great way to learn how to construct your own. Director ships with many demo files that you can "deconstruct."

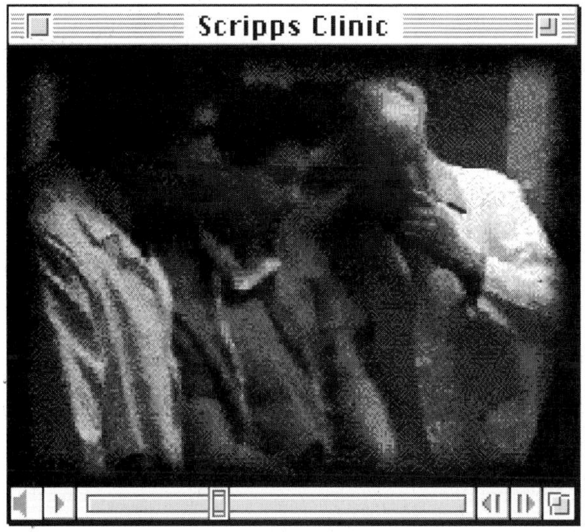

Figure 20.3 Featured QuickTime movies describing the facilities of local hospitals

Tools and Equipment

Paul used a Quadra 950 with 40Mb of RAM and a 500Mb hard drive for both development and play back of the demo. He used QuickTime as the digital video format, and Director to create and present the interactive demo itself.

Part Three

THE POWER TOOLS CD

21

Using the CD-ROM

The *Multimedia Power Tools* CD-ROM included with this package is, on its own, a robust multimedia "title." By this we mean it is a well-rounded interactive multimedia product versus. simply a collection of software supplementing a book. From the beginning, *Multimedia Power Tools* was conceived as an integrated package—*an interactive book.* The Verbum team has taken its experience and resources in digital media design and concentrated them in a disc that provides users with instructional content and usable tools, and also complements the book—covering all the details of multimedia technology, tools, and processes. We've strived to create a disc that is entertaining and easy to use, instructional, and useful for actual multimedia production. We hope it will serve you for a long time to come.

Disc Components

The Power Tools CD-ROM has three primary components:

1. The *disc interface shell,* which includes the interface elements, navigation controls, the program code that controls the disc's functions, and the "top matter" content material (equivalent to a book's front matter) with an introduction, information about how the disc was created, an animated Guided Tour of the disc with a video tour guide, and some general settings controls.
2. The *Sample Projects section,* featuring 15 exemplary multimedia projects presented in a step-by-step "how it was done" format.
3. The *Power Tools section,* containing about 200 megabytes of usable software.

Starting Up the Power Tools CD-ROM

You need a Macintosh with at least 5MB of RAM (preferably 8MB or more for best performance). You will also want to make sure that you have turned off any INITS that might use up that much-needed RAM, and that your color monitor (13" or larger) is set to 256 colors. The Power Tools CD-ROM will work on less-powerful Macintosh systems, but its extensive use of QuickTime movies (digital video clips) and large animations will work best on the faster processors. The disc's hundreds of software files and step-by-step presentations are functional on all color Macintosh models.

Your CD-ROM drive also plays a part in how well the Power Tools QuickTime movies run. If it is an older model with a slower data transfer rate, you may see some performance limitations. Newer double-speed or quad-speed drives offer the best results.

Once you have inserted the CD-ROM into the drive, you will see the "Power Tools CD" icon come up on the Mac screen. Double click to open it, and you will see the various folders that comprise the contents of the CD (see Figure 21.1).

At the top of the window you will see the "Power Tools Startup" icon. This is the interface shell of the CD. The shell is a "Director Projector," a self-running application created with Macromedia Director, the authoring software used to create the Power Tools CD-ROM. It contains the key interface graphics and the code that controls the use of the CD. Double click on the Power Tools Startup icon to launch the Power Tools disc.

The first thing you will see is the Welcome screen (see Figure 21.2), which presents four options:

- **Go:** starts the Power Tools Intro Animation
- **Skip Anim:** bypasses the intro animation and takes you right to the Main Menu

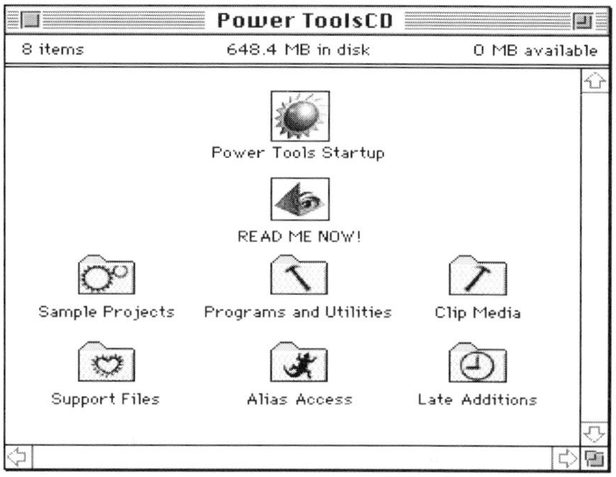

Figure 21.1 The disc is organized into folders for easy access to files. Most users will use the Power Tools CD from the interface shell that is launched by double clicking on the Power Tools Startup icon.

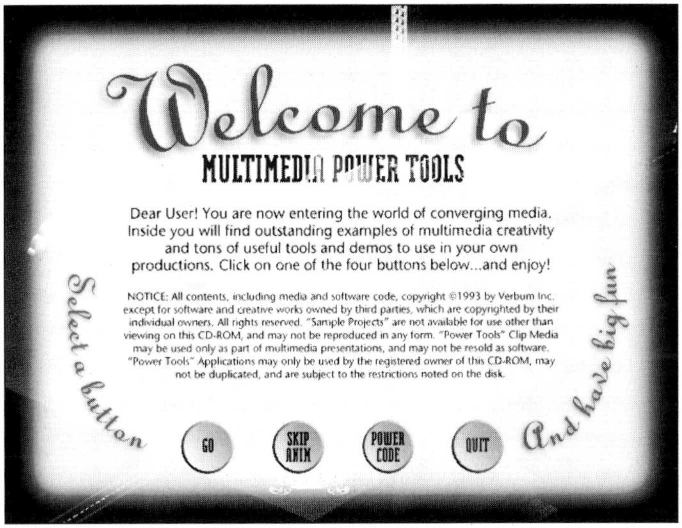

Figure 21.2 The first screen you see when you start the disc is the Welcome screen, from which you can click on Go (to start the Intro Animation of the book's cover illustration), Skip Anim (go straight to the Main Menu), Power Code (bring up a scrolling list of Power Codes), or Quit, to quit the Power Tools shell and return to the desktop.

- **Power Code:** opens the Power Code menu which you can use to go right to a specific point on the disc
- **Quit:** quits the Power Tools CD-ROM and takes you back to the Macintosh desktop

The intro animation was created by John Laney from Glenn Mitsui's book cover illustration. John added 3-D elements and economical (but effective) animations. With a musical score by Christopher Yavelow, this piece is a fine example of simple digital animation created with Macintosh graphics, animation, and music tools. It can be left running as an entertaining "screen saver."

Click anywhere on the screen to go to the Power Tools CD Main Menu (see Figure 21.3). The "transition" animation that leads to the Main Menu was created by Elizabeth Tilles.

The Disc Interface Shell

The CD interface is "flat"—you won't find yourself getting lost as you burrow several levels deep as in some multimedia titles. It is also easy to use, with several features designed to aid users. The primary elements of the interface are: the *video window,* in the upper left, which displays video clips and graphics. The window below it is the *text window,* which provides details on whatever you are viewing, as well as help information on navigating the CD. The large window is the *content window,* which displays graphics, animations, and some interactive works. When you are in the Main Menu (or a submenu for one of the five sections), the content window contains the menu buttons, but its primary use is to display the content of our Sample Projects, and each of the Power Tools. Finally, on the right side of the screen is the *navigation bar*, which you will use to move through the Sample Projects and Power Tools.

Menus and Built-in Help

You can go to the five main sections of the disc by clicking on one of the large buttons in the Main Menu (see Figure 21.3). Note that the two largest buttons for Sample Projects and Power Tools are animated when you are at the "top" level, in the Main Menu. When you click on one of these or one of the other three smaller section buttons, you will call up the submenu buttons for that section, which will appear in the right side of the content window. You can "roll over" on any button in the Main Menu, submenu, or navigation bar to see a description in the text window of what the button will do. This built-in help is available throughout the disc. You don't have to return to the Main Menu to activate other submenus, just click on any of the five buttons. But if you want to get back to the top—with the fun animated buttons—click on the Menu button (the up arrow) in the navigation bar on the right.

Disc Info Section

Disc Info Menu ⌘001

Introduction ⌘006

Credits ⌘007

Production Notes ⌘008

Copyright Info ⌘009

Intro Animation ⌘000

This button brings up buttons for the Introduction, Credits, Production Notes, Publisher/Copyright Info, Intro Animation, and Power Codes (see Figure 21.4).

- **Introduction:** a video by Michael Gosney, complemented with photo illustrations displayed in the content window
- **Credits:** provides buttons for all the contributors to the disc, which will trigger videos and/or text material
- **Production Notes**: brings up a detailed text description of how the CD-ROM was created
- **Publisher/Copyright Info:** provides information on Random House Electronic Publishing and Verbum, Inc., ordering information and copyright notices

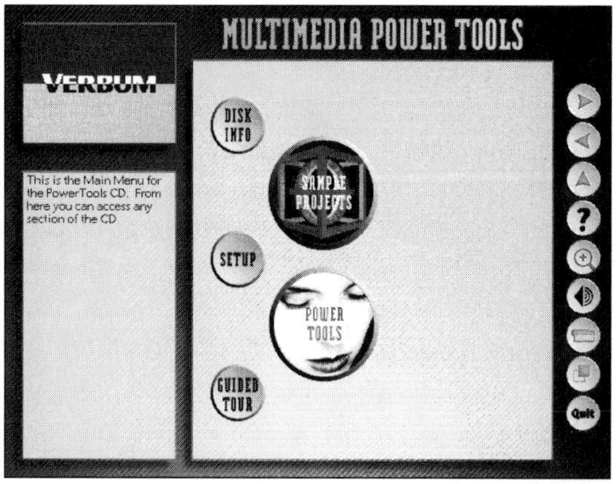

Figure 21.3 The Power Tools CD-ROM interface includes a video window (at upper left) for QuickTime movies, the text window below and the content window in the center.

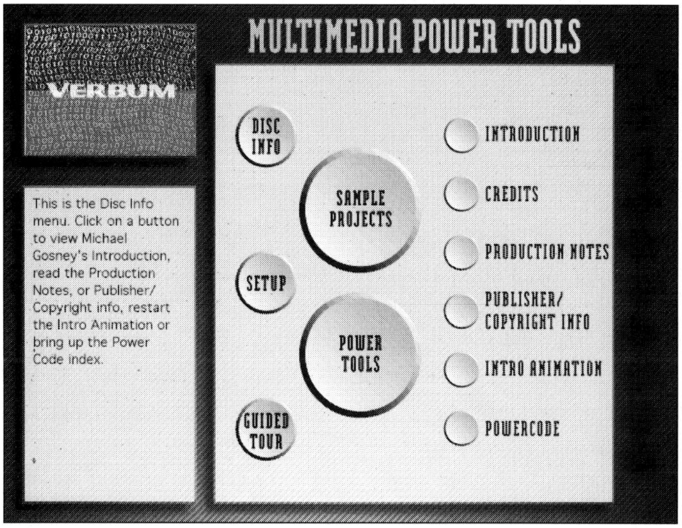

Figure 21.4
In the Disc Info menu you can select Introduction for a video of disc producer Michael Gosney, Credits for video clips of the disc producers and contributors, Production Notes for details on how the disc was made, and Publisher/Copyright for information about the disc, how to order it, etc., and Intro Anim to restart the Intro Animation.

- **Intro Animation:** restarts the animation (from which you can return to the Main Menu, as when you started up, by just clicking the mouse)
- **Power Codes:** brings up a scrolling list of Power Code locations on the disc which will allow instant access to any location (this can also be accessed from the Welcome screen)

Set Up

Set-up Menu ⌘002

This button brings up controls for the following:

- **Producer Videos:** toggles whether the videos should play automatically when you enter a sample project
- **Blendo Mode:** activates hidden buttons and other interesting things in the CD
- **Menu Music:** toggles whether you hear background music in the Main Menu and each of the five submenus

Guided Tour

Guided Tour Menu ⌘003

This displays submenu buttons for *The Compleat Tour*, *Interface Tour*, *Menus Tour*, *Sample Projects Tour* and *Power Tools Tour*. When you click on any of these buttons, Reegan Ray, your tour guide, will appear in the video window and take you through an animated tour of the disc (see Figure 21.5). You can pause the tour anytime by clicking on the video window. You can bypass it completely by clicking on the Next or Previous button.

Navigation Bar

The navigation bar is always available, no matter where you are in the CD-ROM (see Figure 21.6). Some of the buttons will not always function, depending on where you are in the disc. They will be dim in these cases, to let you know they're inactive. Let's review each of the button functions.

Figure 21.5
One of the outstanding features of the CD is the Guided Tour, featuring several minutes of digitally edited video with tour guide Reegan Ray.

Next Button

At the top is the *Next* button, which will turn the page, so to speak, and take you to the next part of the currently displayed sample project, or the next alphabetically organized power tool item.

Previous Button

Beneath the Next button is the *Previous* button. It will take you to the previous part of the currently displayed project or the previous power tool item.

Menu Button

The button with the up arrow is the *Menu* button. It will take you back up to the menu for the section of the CD you are currently viewing and, with a second click, back to the Main Menu.

Help Button

The question mark is the *Help* button. In the Help Mode, the cursor will turn into a question mark allowing you to click on any screen element for an explanation.

Zoom Button

Next is the *Zoom* button. It will perform different functions depending on what is being viewed. If you are viewing a clip media image, you can zoom it to full screen and back. If you're looking at an animation or video, the Zoom button will

Figure 21.6
The Navigation Bar remains consistent everywhere on the disc. Depending on where you are in the disc, buttons are dimmed if they are inactive in that section.

double the video playback size in most cases. The Zoom button will have a plus sign if it is ready to zoom or a minus sign if it is ready to zoom back. If the Zoom button is gray, it won't work for the currently displayed content.

Audio Button

The *Audio* button will allow you to adjust the volume level for the Power Tools CD at any time. Click and drag the pop up volume control.

Print Button

The *Print* button will print any power tool or project screen to your currently selected printer. Make sure you select the appropriate printer before launching the Power Tools CD-ROM.

Copy Button

The *Copy* button will allow you to copy the currently displayed Power Tool to your hard disk. It will not copy Sample Projects.

Quit Button

Finally, *Quit* will exit the Power Tools CD and return to the Macintosh desktop.

The Sample Projects Section

Sample Projects Menu ⌘004

Clicking on the Sample Projects button will bring up the submenu buttons for our project presentations (see Figure 21.7). Note the four categories of Sound, Animation, Video, and Interactive Multimedia. The projects vary widely, and each has a slightly different presentation.

When you choose a project, you'll be taken right to the first screen of the project presentation. Click on the Next button to see a video clip of the project producer in the video window (see Figure 21.8). (You can deactivate the producer videos in the Set Up section so that they do not play when you start the project presentations.) You can then click on the Next button to view a demo of the actual

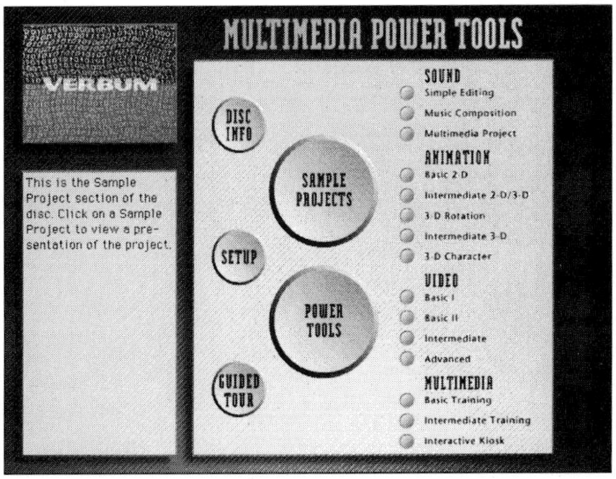

Figure 21.7 The Sample Project menu lists projects by category. Rolling the mouse arrow over a Sample Project button reveals a summary of the project in the text window.

Figure 21.8 Each Sample Project starts with a video clip by the project producer. Clicking on the Next arrow steps you through the project.

project, if available. Click the Next button again to step through the presentation. In addition to the text and graphics, some project presentations include narration, animations, videos, and functional interactive components. You will also find explanations and cues regarding these elements in the text window, along with the ongoing text.

See the book's "Project" chapters for additional backgound information on each of the projects featured on the disk.

The Power Tools Section

Power Tools Menu ⌘005

The other main section on the disc is Power Tools, featuring valuable clip media (animation, video, still images and backgrounds, 3-D graphics, sound effects, and music), and a wide range of applications and utilities for authoring, audio, video, animation, sound, and graphics (see Chapter 22, "Projects and Power Tools on the CD," for complete descriptions). Clicking this button will display buttons for the different categories of Power Tools that are available for viewing and copying (see Figure 21.9).

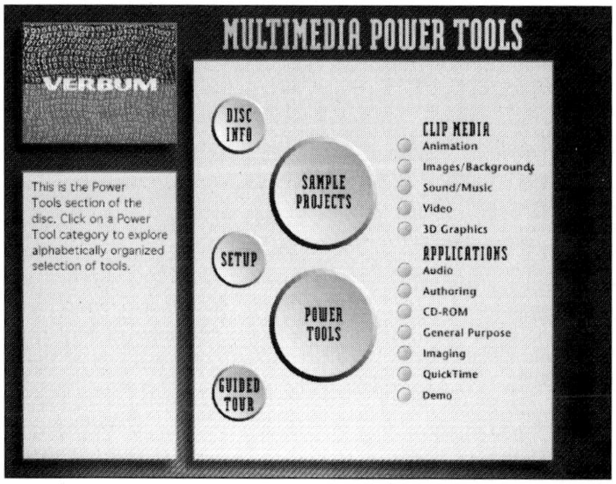

Figure 21.9 The Power Tools menu lists the power tools categories. Clicking on a category brings you to the first power tool (organized alphabetically) in that category.

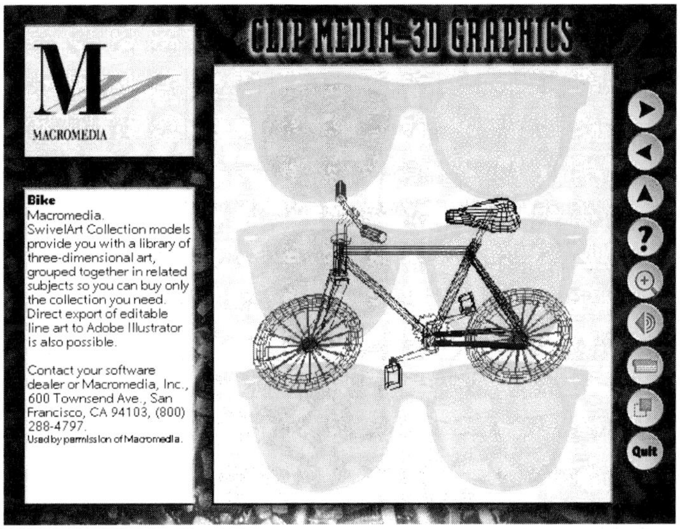

Figure 21.10 Each Power Tool file has a screen with a visual representation of the file and a text description. Clicking on the Zoom button will show a larger image of the file, or increase the size of a video or animation clip. The Copy button will copy the actual file to your hard drive. To see the next Power Tool, hit the Next button.

If you click on a category, you will immediately come to the first Power Tools file in that category (see Figure 21.10). Click on the Next button to step through the alphabetically listed power tools in that category.

The Power Code CD Index

Each "location" on the disc—each project presentation and each Power Tool file—has a three-digit *Power Code.* You will find Power Codes throughout the book in the margins, and a complete list in Appendix B. This unique feature not only provides a useful link between the book and disc content, it is also an additional, highly efficient means of navigating the disc. You can access Power Codes in two ways:

1. When you start up the disc, you can click on the Power Code button on the Welcome Screen (or in the Main Menu under Disc Info) and bring up a scrolling list of the Power Codes. Select the number you want, and you'll be taken immediately to that disc location.
2. At any time you can hold down the Command key and type in the three-digit code to go the the desired location on the disc. Be sure to include any zeros preceeding a number.

Power Tools Quick Access

There is another way to find and access Power Tools files on the disc. When you are in the Power Tools section, you can click on the name of the tool at the top of the text window to bring up a scrolling alphabetical list of Power Tools. "Drag" through the list until you come to the one you want. Release the mouse button and you will be taken immediately to that screen.

Learn, Work—Play!

We hope the Power Tools CD offers plenty of support for all three: *learning* about multimedia, *producing* multimedia, and *having big fun* with multimedia. Whether you are a Mac owner interested in the expanding world of multimedia or an advanced producer—or somewhere in between—you'll find a wealth of resources on the CD.

Engage!

P.S.—Please return your registration card, and give us your feedback!

22

Projects and Power Tools on the CD-ROM

The Power Tools CD-ROM contains 400Mb of interactive tours of critically acclaimed multimedia projects, as well as an unprecedented collection—over 200 megabytes—of valuable multimedia software. This chapter will give you an overview of both categories.

Projects on the CD-ROM

The project presentation section of the CD-ROM is divided into four categories: Sound, Animation, Video, and Interactive Multimedia. Multimedia projects are often fairly complex and these are no exception. You will therefore find a great deal of crossover between categories: The Interactive Multimedia projects often utilize video, Video projects utilize animation, most of the projects feature sound, and so on. However, these step-by-step presentations most often emphasize an instructive portion of the given project, focusing on one particular element or skill. For background information on any of these projects, see the "Project" chapters in the book.

A Wide Range of Exemplary Projects—From Basic to Advanced

In the Sound section, you'll see simple editing demonstrated by *Hip Hop Hits*; music composition demonstrated by our *Multimedia Power Tools* musical theme; and a complete multimedia project, *So You Want to Be a Rock and Roll Star*, that uses innovative interactivity to teach music.

In Animation you can check out basic 2-D animation in *Video Quilt*; an interactive learning project designed for illiterate new mothers; intermediate 2- and 3-D animation with *NTV Logo*, focusing on the creation of a logo for Nissan's corporate television channel; 3-D rotation in the VSI logo from the motion picture *The Lawnmower Man*; 3-D animation in *Flight Test*, a small plane created to fly against a moving background; and finally, 3-D character animation from *The Journeyman Project*, an interactive CD-ROM game.

In the Video section you'll be able to examine video film editing in *Water Fantasia*, a short, artistic exploration of water; basic digital video in *Land of Counterpane;* intermediate digital video in *The Madness of Roland*; an interactive novel, and advanced digital video in *EcoSpies*, a television show.

Under Interactive Multimedia you'll see a basic training program, Aldus PageMaker 5.0's Demo Disk; a curriculum-based training program for second-year medical students in UCSD's *MedPics*; and an interactive kiosk for people seeking information about San Diego's Health Care Community.

Sample Project Summaries

Following are short summaries of each project by category. More detailed information can be found in the "Project" chapters.

Simple Editing: Hip Hop Hits

Hip Hop Hits ⌘011

Mike Salomon's project, *Hip Hop Hits*, is both a demonstration of the original concept of modular audio, which he used to create the Dark Side Productions (a band) song *Straight to the Point* for use in their show, and a stand-alone multimedia demonstration of simple 8-bit sound. It was created by Mike Salomon entirely on a Macintosh IIci equipped with DigiDesign's SoundTools direct-to-disk recording system and a Storage Dimensions 1-gigabyte hard drive. Passport Design's Alchemy program was used to manipulate various individual sound components. This was later recorded on Digital Audio Tape for the band's use. For more details, see Chapter 14, "Sound Projects."

Music Composition: Power Tools Theme

Power Tools Theme ⌘012

Composer, performer, and multimedia producer, Christopher Yavelow demonstrates how he wrote and produced the title screen music for the Multimedia Power Tools CD-ROM. Yavelow's step-by-step project includes QuickTime movies and Macromedia Director animations illustrating the operation of M, an interactive music composition program developed by Intelligent Music, Inc. Using M, Yavelow "conducted" his collection of musical ideas with an on-screen baton, captured the output to Standard MIDI files, and transferred to a Mark of the Unicorn's Performer MIDI sequencer for tweaking. The resulting audio output was recorded at CD-quality using MediaVision's PAS-16 NuBus Card. Alchemy was used to down-sample the soundfile to the 8-bit, 22kHz version for the Power Tools CD-ROM.For more details, see Chapter 14, "Sound Projects."

Multimedia Project: So You Want to Be a Rock and Roll Star

PROJECTS

Rock and Roll Star ⌘013

Steve Rappaport's project explains how he created the sound in his CD-ROM, *So You Want to Be a Rock and Roll Star*. His CD-ROM is all about sound and music; it allows the user to participate in six guitar and keyboard lessons, playing along with tracks from old rock and roll songs. This original idea and its implementation was created and executed by Steve Rappaport, who holds the copyright. He used Macromedia's SoundEdit progam and Passport Designs' Master Tracks Pro 4 program to import, create, process, and edit the sound. The interactivity was created in Macromedia Director. For more details, see Chapter 14, "Sound Projects."

Basic 2D Animation: Video Quilt

PROJECTS

Video Quilt ⌘020

Animator Lynda Weinman was hired by Dr. Mary Anne Sweeney at The University of Texas Medical School to create a Spanish/English laserdisc for women's pre- and post-natal clinics. The disk would be used to educate viewers on infant nutrition, safety, and health care. The clinic serves underprivileged mothers, many of whom are illiterate. The patchwork quilt idea was born out of a desire to create a friendly interface, one that would invite the non-computer user to interact. The University of Texas gave Lynda a rough storyboard describing the icons for the patches on the quilt. From this Lynda created illustrations which she scanned into a Macintosh computer, enhancing, reworking, and finally animating the images. She then added interactivity to create a program that would encourage the user to participate. For more details, see Chapter 16, "Animation Projects."

Intermediate 2-D/3-D Animation: NTV Logo

PROJECTS

NTV Logo ⌘021

Desktop video wizard Scott Billups, a systems integration consultant and developer for Sony, Apple, and Silicon Graphics Inc., and Co-Chairman of the American Film Institute Media Lab, was hired to create a network identity and logo package for Nissan's internal cable station, NTV. Nissan's graphics department had created a design concept, but Nissan executives weren't happy with the results, so they brought in Scott, who has had a long association with the company. Scott gave Nissan what it wanted—and more—using his own unmatched expertise with a number of off-the shelf products, including Macromedia's Swivel 3D [Power Code: Swivel 3D Pro 1.5.7 Demo #220], MacroModel, and Director, as well as Adobe Photoshop for filter effects. For more details, see Chapter 16, "Animation Projects."

3-D Rotation: Lawnmower Man Logo

PROJECTS

Lawnmower Man Logo ⌘022

In 1992, the major motion picture *The Lawnmower Man* required an animated corporate identity for its fictional corporation called Virtual Space Industries (VSI). Graphic artist Jack Davis, working as part of the Gosney Company, Inc., provided the concept and design for the VSI logo. This CD-ROM project is a step-by-step description of the process. Using Macromedia's Swivel 3D, Jack built and animated the VSI Logo. He then imported it into MacroMind 3D and added a bump map, texture map, and shadow-casting light source. Jack's tutorial also contains QuickTime film clips from the movie *The Lawnmower Man*, which is copyrighted by Brett Leonard of Film Light Productions. For more details, see Chapter 16, "Animation Projects."

Intermediate 3-D Animation: Test Flight

Test Flight ⌘023

John Odam of John Odam Design Associates produced this 3-D animation to illustrate the basic process of 3-D animation. Using Strata, Inc.'s StrataVision program, John began assembling the airplane out of simple components: The cylinder, the sphere, and the stretch tool. Once assembled, he applied texture mapping to the airplane to create various surfaces, including a metallic surface finish on the body. Then, using the Animation Palette in StrataVision, he animated the model to simulate a plane fly through. His work in animation and three-dimensional design won him StrataVision's "Oscar" for another, more complex fly through film. For more details, see Chapter 16, "Animation Projects."

3-D Character Animation: Journeyman Project Robot

Journeyman Project Robot ⌘024

The Journeyman Project, an interactive adventure game by Presto Studios on CD-ROM, envisions the world in 2318. The player's job is to safeguard history and current world peace from sabatoge. One of the protaganists is a Robot, which was developed into a three-dimensional character by Presto's lead animator and programmer, Farshid Almassizadeh. Working from sketches, the Presto team created the model out of 17,000 polygons. Farshid then used Macromedia's Swivel 3D to choreograph the model's movements, then imported it into Specular's Infini-D 3D for applying texture maps, final tweaking, and rendering. For more details, see Chapter 16, "Animation Projects."

Basic Video Production: Water Fantasia

Water Fantasia ⌘030

Macintosh Multimedia Artist Don Doerfler created the original concept and design for this digital video project. Water Fantasia explores aquatic environments and their inhabitants through the use of video, audio and the Macintosh computer. Using a Sony FX510 8mm video camera, Don shot three months worth of videotape, which he then logged and used to create storyboards. Once he selected the video clips, he digitized them using a SuperMac Video Spigot board. He then edited and assembled them in Adobe Premiere, creating special effects using Premiere's filters, the FX channel, and transparency settings. Music from Passport Production's "QuickTunes" Vol. 1 CD was added and the entire piece was finally reprinted to video tape. For more details, see Chapter 18, "Video Projects."

Basic Video Production: Land of Counterpane

Land of Counterpane ⌘031

This basic digital video project by Harry Mott, created with video of his three-month-old son, Cameron, and public domain and license-free video, audio, and stills, builds a movie around a poem by Robert Louis Stevenson. In gathering the raw materials, he was careful to respect copyright laws and went to Archive Houses for license-free film and video. He also used license-free music and sound effects on CD-ROMs like *Killer Tracks* and Prosonus' *Music Bytes*. Harry digitized all his material using Digital Film (a digitizing board), and edited, created special effects and assembled in Adobe Premiere, using a Bernoulli drive. *The Land of Counterpane* is 90 seconds long, but it took six hours to "make" the movie using Compact Video compression. For more details, see Chapter 18, "Video Projects."

Intermediate Video Production: The Madness of Roland

Madness of Roland ⌘032

Greg Roach, an interactive artist, designer, and founder of HyperBole studios in Houston, Texas, created an interactive novel on CD-ROM. His project for *Multimedia Power Tools* demonstrates how he created the madness sequence in *The Madness of Roland.* Construction of this sequence was done in Adobe Premiere 2.0. Greg demonstrates how he used Premiere's various special effects filters and transparency settings to combine frames of scanned images (manipulated by Gryphon Software's, Morph) with digitized video and sound to make a movie portraying Roland's decent into madness. For more details, see Chapter 18, "Video Projects."

Advanced Video Production: EcoSpies

EcoSpies ⌘033

Video producer and designer Scott Billups worked with producers Tim Cutt and Sam and Sharon Baldoni to create the graphic design and production for Tim's television pilot, *EcoSpies.* Scott designed the logos, bumpers, and transitional elements of the show, which focuses on ecological concerns. Working on a Macintosh computer, Scott sketched his visualizations using Swivel 3D and MacroMind Director, which he then exported as PICTs and compressed into a QuickTime movie using Adobe Premiere. He created the final models in Macromedia's MacroModel, and ElectricImage's MisterFont, rendering them in ElectricImage Animation System and recording to a Sony Laser Videodisc Recorder. Finally, he inserted Chroma Keys and recorded to a BetaCam SP. For more details, see Chapter 18, "Video Projects."

Basic Training: PageMaker 5.0 Demo

PageMaker 5.0 Demo ⌘040

Designer and producer Matthew Fass of Ikonic Interactive in San Francisco was hired by Aldus to develop an interactive program to demonstrate PageMaker 5.0. Aldus wanted something unusual and fun to use. Matthew suggested an international mystery format with clues buried in screens that highlighted the new features of PageMaker 5.0. Using digitized video and images manipulated in Adobe Photoshop, Matthew and his team assembled and scripted the graphics in Macromedia Director to create an exciting, interactive demo disk. For more details, see Chapter 20, "Interactive Projects."

Intermediate Training: MedPics

MedPics ⌘041

MedPics is an interactive image review and tutorial program developed at the University of California, San Diego (UCSD) School of Medicine by Helene Hoffman, Ph.D., and Ann Irwin, M.D., of the school's Learning Resources Center (LRC). It is copyrighted to the U.C. Regents and administered by the LRC. *MedPics* was designed as a replacement for the traditional slide set review in the second-year Human Disease Course. Helene and Ann used existing slide sets from the Human Disease course during the initial development of *MedPics*, asking faculty to supply slides and technical data. Copyright releases were obtained from contributors, permitting the University to use the image internally and commercially. Helene and Ann built *MedPics* using Photoshop and Director, while

Michel Kripalani of Presto Studios helped them with scripting and creation of the interface. Susan Adanato assisted with the graphic design of the interface. All participants in *MedPics* receive on-screen credit. *MedPics* is available from any color Macintosh computer on the UCSD campus network, including 35 provided by the LRC at 16 locations around campus and affiliated teaching hospitals. For more details, see Chapter 20, "Interactive Projects."

Interactive Kiosk: Health Care Kiosk

Paul Burgess of the San Diego–based The Asthetics Collection scripted this interactive kiosk to provide users with a look at all the major hospitals in San Diego and to allow them to compare the services and staffs. The kiosk presents photos and videos of each hospital. All buttons and screens were developed in Adobe Photoshop using HSC's KAI'S Powertools and Filters. The music is from Killer Tracks Audio CD collection. Using Macromedia Director, Paul scripted the interactivity and created a user-friendly kiosk encompassing many languages and allowing screen adjustment for wheelchair-bound users. The Director coding is copyright-free but the logos and names used in this step-by-step project are copyrighted. For more details, see Chapter 20, "Interactive Projects."

PROJECTS

Health Care Kiosk ⌘042

Learn and Enjoy

Whether you are just curious about multimedia on the Mac and peruse the presentations casually, or you are a practicing professional and take them apart and dig down deep, we hope you learn from the Power Tools Sample Projects. Enjoy the journey!

Power Tools on the CD-ROM

The other portion of the Power Tools CD-ROM is packed with clip media, utilities, and demo applications that you can use immediately. A complete item-by-item review of this material is available in the Power Tools section of the disc, divided into two sections, Clip Media and Programs and Utilities (Applications).

Clip Media

Here you will find a vast collection of photographs, background textures, video clips, animations, sounds, and more—from companies such as Image Bank, Form and Function, Macromedia, Strata, ArtBeats, and 21st Century Media. These files are released for use by owners of the Power Tools CD-ROM. Each file is showcased in a presentation screen. On many of the screens, you can click on the Zoom button to get a full-screen version of images, or trigger video clips and animations. Categories include:

TOOLS

Clip Media Animation ⌘500-575

Images and Backgrounds ⌘600-742

3-D Graphics ⌘800-829

- Animation
- Images and Backgrounds
- 3-D Graphics

Sound/Music ⌘900–993

Video ⌘580–594

- Sound/Music
- Video

Programs and Utilities

This section includes demo versions of most of the multimedia applications available on the Macintosh. These are the latest versions of the actual programs, functional except for one key feature: You can't save work (aw, shucks). But what you can do is open files on the CD (or from other sources) and test drive the programs. You will also find *fully* functional utility programs, for *power* support in your production work. Note that some of these programs are "shareware." If you're not familiar with the concept of shareware, here's how it works—use the utilities and if you like them and you find them useful, register your copy with the creator and send in the suggested shareware fee (usually $10–20). The creators of these utilities have received no payment as part of this project and the price you paid for this CD-ROM does not include their registration fee.

The Programs and Utilities are divided into the following categories:

TOOLS

Audio ⌘100–104

Authoring ⌘110

CD-ROM ⌘120

Imaging ⌘130–134

General ⌘140–153

QuickTime ⌘160–167

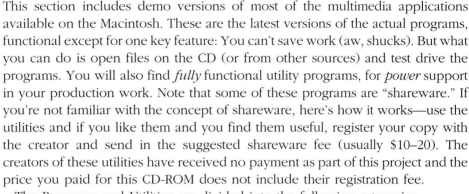

- Audio Tools
- Authoring Tools
- CD-ROM Tools
- Imaging Tools
- General Tools
- QuickTime Tools

Demo programs include Macromedia Director, AuthorWare, Passport Producer, SoundEdit Pro, Animation Works, PACo Producer, Swivel 3D, Adobe PhotoShop, Adobe Illustrator, Adobe Premiere, Videoshop, Stratavision, Capture, Morph, and DeBabelizer. Actual programs include: Apple Quicktime 1.6 Extension and HyperCard XCMDs for movie editing, Adobe Premiere Plug-In Kit, Kai's Power Tools Photoshop filters, and utilities such as Popcorn, Klutz, and Gif Converter,

TOOLS

Demos ⌘200–242

Using the Power Tools

Each item, whether a program or a clip media file, has a one-screen presentation that provides a graphic representation of the item and a text description, plus contact and copyright information. You can click on the Print button in the Navigation Bar to print the screen as a convenient reference on the tool. (See the section following for how to get to the presentation screens.)

You will find the actual Power Tools files in the folders labeled "Programs and Utilities" and "Clip Media" on the CD-ROM. You can copy them to your hard drive by dragging them from the CD-ROM, or you can use the Copy feature in the presentation screen (click on the Copy button and the disc will automatically copy the file to your hard drive).

Access to the Power Tools

Note that throughout the book you will find power codes listing sample projects and power tools, with three-digit codes, in the margins. You can go to a particular tool's presentation screen in several ways:

1. Start the Power Tools CD and when you see the Welcome screen, click on the Power Tools button. This will bring up a scrolling menu of the tools. You can use this feature to find a tool, and go directly to its presentation screen. (You can also access this scrolling menu from the Main Menu by clicking on Disc Info, then hitting the Power Codes button.)
2. Click on "Skip Anim" and when the Main Menu appears, click on the Power Tools icon to go to the first power tool in a category, and then click through the alphabetically listed tools in that category. From any screen you can also click on the name of the tool in the text window to get a pop up scrolling menu of the other tools.
3. From the Main Menu, or anywhere on the disc, simply hold the COMMAND key down and type in the three-digit code, and you will be whisked right to that tool's screen.

For a complete listing of the Power Tools, see Appendix B.

Appendix A: Resources

This comprehensive listing provides the information you need to locate the hundreds of products and services mentioned in the book and on the Power Tools CD-ROM. While this information was the best available at press time, due to the rapidly changing nature of the industry, we cannot guarantee its accuracy.

Product Information

CODE # COMPANY INFO/PRODUCT

3G Graphics, Inc.
114 Second Ave. S., Ste. 104
Edmonds, WA 98020
800-456-0234
Images with Impact!

21st Century Media Photodiscs
2013 4th Avenue, 2nd Floor
Seattle, WA 98121
206-441-9355
CD series

Abbate Video Consultants
83 Main St
Norfolk, MA 02056
508-520-0199
Video Toolkit (CueTrack HyperCard)

Acme Animation Group, Ltd.
40-3010 Newport Parkway
Jersey City, NJ 07310
210-420-6400
ClipProps

Action Plus Software
801-255-0600
Action Plus 5.0
Action Plus Lite
Action Plus 5.0 Network

CODE # COMPANY INFO/PRODUCT

Acuris
125 University Ave, Ste. 125
Palo Alto, CA 95301
415-329-1920
Acuris ClipModel Libraries (for use with ShowPlace)

ADInstruments
2251 Grant Road, Ste. H
Los Altos, CA 94024
415-964-2878
151 *UpdateMaker 1.3.1*

Adobe Systems Incorporated
1585 Charleston Rd.
Mountain View, CA 94039
415-961-4400
800-833-6687
163 *Demo Premiere 2.0 Plugin Developer Kit*
Dimensions
223 *Illustrator 3.0 Demo*
Multiple Master [not yet released]
222 *Photoshop 2.01*
Photoshop 2.5
Photoshop for Windows
240 *Premiere 2.0 Demo*
Type Manager Plus Pack

Advanced Digital Imageing (ADI)
22 Rocky Knoll
Irvine, CA 92715
714-725-0154
MacVAC video animation controller

CODE #	COMPANY INFO/PRODUCT
	Aladdin Systems, Inc
	165 Westridge Dr
	Watsonville, CA 95076
	408-761-6200
162	*Popcorn*
	Aldus Corporation
	411 First Street
	Seattle, WA 98104
	206-343-3502
230	*Aldus Fetch 1.0 Tryout*
	Digital Darkroom
	Fetch
	FreeHand Mac License Pack
	FreeHand 3.1 Windows
	Gallery Effects 1.01
	PageMaker 5.0
	Persuasion 2.12 Mac
	Persuasion License Pack
	PhotoStyler
	SuperCard
	SuperPaint 3.0
	Super 3D
	Texture Art
	Alias Research, Inc.
	Style! Division
	110 Richmond St. E. #500
	Toronto, Ontario, Canada M5C 1P1
	800-447-2542
	Sketch!
	Alphatronix, Inc.
	2300 Englert Dr., Ste. C
	Research Triangle Park, NC 27709
	919-544-0001
	Inspire For Macintosh
	Inspire IIF
	ALsoft, Inc.
	P.O. Box 927
	Spring, TX 77383
	800-257-6381
	MasterJuggler
	Ambrosia
	PO Box 23140
	Rochester, NY 14692
153	*ColorSwitch 1.01*
	APDA (Apple Developer's Association) Apple

CODE #	COMPANY INFO/PRODUCT
	Computers, Inc.
	20525 Mariani Ave., MS 33-G
	Cupertino, CA 95014
	800-282-2732
	QuickTime for Developers CD-ROM
	ResEdit 2.1.1
	Apple Computer Inc.
	20525 Mariani Ave.
	Cupertino, CA 95014
	408-996-1010
	Apple File Exchange
	AppleTalk
	ColorOne Scanner
	Compact Video compressor (bundled with QuickTime)
141	*ExtensionsManager 1.8*
120	*Macintosh CD Setup 4.2*
	Macintosh PC Exchange 1.01
	MIDI Manager PatchBay
161	*Movie Player*
	MovieRecorder (in QuickTime Starter Kit)
	MovieShop for CD-ROM
133	*PICTviewer 1.1*
	QuickDraw GX
	QuickRing
167	*QuickTime 1.6.1 Scrapbook*
160	*QuickTime 1.6.1 Extension*
	QuickTime Developers' CD-ROM:
	MovieShop
	SoundToMovie
	Sound Manager 3.0
	SuperDrive
150	*TeachText 7.1*
152	*VideoSync 1.0*
110	*XCMD's (QuickTime)*
	Argosy Software, Inc.
	133 Spring St., 5th Fl.
	New York, NY 10012
	212-274-1199
	RunPC/Network and Run/PC Remote
	Aris Entertainment
	444 Via Marina, Ste. 811
	Marina del Rey, CA 90292
	310-821-0234
	Media Clip Series
	World View

CODE # COMPANY INFO/PRODUCT

ArtBeats
2611 S. Myrtle Road
Myrtle Creek, OR 97457
503-863-4429
800-444-9392
600–603 *Backgrounds for Multimedia, Vol. 1*
610–615 *Backgrounds for Multimedia, Vol. 2*
Dimensions 1-3
620–623 *Marble and Granite*
Natural Images 1 & 2

Articulate Systems, Inc.
600 W. Cummings Park, Ste. 4500
Woburn, MA 01801
800-443-7077
Voice Impact
Voice Impact Pro (formerly VoiceLink)
Voice Navigator II
Voice Navigator 2.3

Asymmetrix
110 110th Ave. NE
Bellevue, WA 98004
800-448-6543
Multimedia Toolbook

ATTO Technology, Inc.
Baird Research Park
1576 Sweet Home Rd.
Amherst, NY 14228
716-688-4259

Audio Visual Group
398 Columbus Ave., Ste. 355
Boston, MA 02116
617-381-1609
The Multiple Media Tour

AUTO•DES•SYS, Inc.
2011 Riverside Dr.
Columbus, OH 43221
614-488-9777
Form 2

B&B Soundworks
P.O. Box 7828
San Jose, CA 95150
408-241-7986
Musical Instruments & Sound Effects
Resource Libraries

CODE # COMPANY INFO/PRODUCT

Barneyscan Corp.
130 Doolittle Dr. #19
San Leandro, CA 94577
510-562-2480
Color Imaging Systems 3315

Baseline Publishing, Inc.
1770 Moriah Woods Blvd., Ste. 14
Memphis, TN 38117
901-682-9676
Color McCheese

BeachWare
5234 Via Vilarta
San DIego, CA 92124
619-492-9529
MultiWare (for QuickTime)

Bliss Interactive Technologies
6034 W. Courtyard Dr., Ste. 305
Austin, TX 78730
512-338-2458
Resource Library

BMUG
(Berkeley Mac Users Group)
1442A Walnut Street, #62
Berkeley, CA 94709
510-549-2684
BMUG Sound Library
510–514 *TV-ROM*
580–585
980–981

Broderbund Software, Inc.
500 Redwood Blvd.
Novato, CA 94948
800-521-6263
Kid Pix 1.2
Kid Pix Companion

Byte By Byte Corp.
9442 Capital of Texas Hwy. N., Ste. 150
Austin, TX 78759
Sculpt 3D 2.0
Sculpt 4D

CalComp, Inc.
2411 W. La Palma Ave.
Anaheim, CA 92801
800-445-6515, ext. 288
DrawingBoard II
DrawingMaster Plus

CODE #	COMPANY INFO/PRODUCT
	Cameo Interactive, Ltd. 1051 Hamshire St. San Francisco, CA 94110 415-826-1121 *Material Worlds*
	Canon USA, Inc. One Canon Plaza Lake Success, NY 11042 516-488-6700 *8mm CCD-F70 camcorder*
	Cayman Systems, Inc. 26 Landsdowne St. Cambridge, MA 02139 617-494-1999 *networking products*
	CD Folios 6754 Eaton Ave. Canoga Park, CA 91303 800-688-3686
700–703	*Sky, Vol.1 v.2.0*
	CD-ROM Galleries Series, Inc. 512 Gertrude Ave. Aptos, CA 95003 408-685-2715 *Scenic and Nature III CD-ROM*
	Claris Corp. 5201 Patrick Henry Dr. Santa Clara, CA 95052 800-334-3535 *HyperCard 2.1* *MacDraw II 1.1* *MacDraw Pro* *MacPaint 2.0* *MacProject Pro*
	Clement Mok Designs 600 Townsend St., Penthouse San Francisco, CA 94103 415-703-9900 *Wolverine Exterior Design System*
	Coda Music Software 1401 E. 79th St. Minneapolis, MN 55425 800-843-2066 *Finale*
	Colwell, Alexander S., 21222 Marjorie Ave. Torrance, CA 90503 310-540-3806
145	*Notepad++ 1.4*
	Compact Designs, Inc. P.O. Box 8535 Gaithersburg, MD 20898 301-869-3919 *PROclaim! System 7-compatible CD-ROM*
	CompuServe Information Service 5000 Arlington Centre, Blvd. Columbus, OH 43220 800-848-8199 *Online information service for any Macintosh* *Shareware screen grabbers: CAPBUF, GRABBER, TXT2PCX*
	Computer Associates International, Inc. One Computer Associates Plaza Islandia, NY 11788 800-225-5224 *CA-Cricket Presents* *Cricket Draw III*
	Comstock, Inc. The Comstock Building 30 Irvine Pl. New York, NY 10003 212-353-8686 *Desktop Photography Series*
	Connectix Corp. 2655 Campus Dr. San Mateo, CA 94403 800-950-5880 *Maxima 2.0.3* *Virtual 3.0*
	CoSA **(Company of Science and Art)** 14 Imperial Place, Ste. 203 Providence, RI 02903 401-831-2672 *After Effects 3-D program* *PaCo Producer*
218	*PACo Producer 2.0.1 Demo*
	Crystal Graphics 3110 Patrich Henry Santa Clara, CA 95056 408-496-6175 *Topas*

CODE # COMPANY INFO/PRODUCT

D'pix, Inc.
414 W. Fourth Avenue
Columbus, OH 43201
614 - 299-7192
650–656 *FOLIO I Image Library Folio I Print*
Folio 1 Print Pro

DataViz, Inc.
55 Corporate Dr.
Trumbull, CT 06611
800-733-0030
MacLinkPlus series

Dayna Communications
50 S. Main St., 5th Fl.
Salt Lake City, UT 84144
801-531-0600
DOS Mounter 3.0
DOS Mounter Plus

DayStar Digital, Inc.
5556 Atlanta Hwy.
Flowery Branch, GA 30542
800-532-7853
Cache cards
Expansion boards
LT200 Connection card
RAM PowerCard

Dejal Userware
12 Scorpio Pl
Auckland 10, New Zealand
101 *SndConveter Pro 2.0*
102 *SndConverter Lite 1.1*
103 *SndPlayer 2.0*
104 *SndCataloguer 1.1*

Delta Tao Software
760 Howard Ave.
Sunnyvale, CA 94087
408-730-9336
Monet

DeltaPoint, Inc.
2 Harris Ct., Ste. B-1
Monterey, CA 93940
800-367-4334
FreezeFrame

Deneba Software
3305 NW 74th Ave.
Miami, FL 33122
305-596-5644
Canvas 3.0.4
Canvas 3-French

CODE # COMPANY INFO/PRODUCT

Canvas ToolPaks
UltraPaint

Digidesign, Inc.
1360 Willow Rd., Ste. 101
Menlo Park, CA 94025
415-688-0600
Automedia II card
Clip Tunes
MacProteus card
Pro I/0
Pro 5
Pro Tools
Sound Design II
SoundTools
TurboSynth

***Digital Media* Newsletter**
(Seybold Publications)
428 E. Baltimore Pike,
P.O. Box 644
Media, PA 19063
800-325-3830

Discimagery, Inc.
18 E. 16th St.
New York, NY 10003
212-675-8500
Professional Photography Collection

Discovery Systems, International
7001 Discovery Blvd
Dublin, OH 43017
614-761-2000

DiVA Corp.
(Digital Video Applications Corporation)
222 Third St., Ste. 3332
Cambridge, MA 02142
617-491-4147
570–575 *The Image Bank CD Collection*
950–953
VideoShop 1.0
242 *VideoShop 2.0 Demo*
Visual Catalog (VideoShop database)

Dr. T's Music Software
124 Crescent Rd., Ste. 3
Needham, MA 02194
800-989-6434
Interactor
Jam Factory

CODE #	COMPANY INFO/PRODUCT
	M
	MIDI Clips
	MusicMouse
	OvalTune
	UpBeat
	Drew Pictures, Inc.
	315 Franconia St.
	San Francisco, CA 94110
	415-550-7651
	The Iron Helix
	Dubl-Click Software, Inc.
	9316 Deering Ave.
	Chatsworth, CA 91311
	818-700-9525
	WetSet
	Dynamic Graphics, Inc.
	6000 N. Forest Park Dr.
	Peoria, IL 61614
	800-255-8800
	Designer's Club
	Dynaware USA, Inc.
	950 Tower Ln., Ste. 1150, 11th Fl.
	Foster City, CA 94004
	800-445-3962
	Ballade
	E-Machines, Inc.
	9305 SW Gemini Dr.
	Beaverton, OR 97005
	503-646-6699
	ColorLink
	E-mu Systems
	1600 Green Hills Rd.
	P.O. Box 660015
	Scotts Valley, CA 95067
	408-438-1921
	Proteus 1 sample player
	Ear Level Engineering
	21213-B Hawthorne
	Torrance, CA 90509
	213-316-2939
	HyperMIDI 2.0
	Eastman Kodak Co.
	343 State St.
	Rochester, NY 14650
	800-233-1647
	PhotoEdge Photo-CD/MAC

CODE #	COMPANY INFO/PRODUCT
	Picture Exchange
	ProPhoto CD Master
	Photo CD Portfolio
	Photo CD Catalog
	Photo CD Access
	Photo CD Medical
	ShoeBox Image Manager Software
	Educorp
	7434 Trade Street
	San Diego, CA 92121
	619-536-9999
	800-843-9497
740–742	*International Graphics Library*
	Sound/FX CD
	The Sound Machine CD
	Electric Image, Inc.
	117 E. Colorado Blvd., Ste. 300
	Pasadena, CA 91105
	818-577-1627
	ElectricImage Animation System 1.5.1
	Magic
	MisterFont
	Electronic Arts Distribution
	1450 Fashion Island Blvd.
	San Mateo, CA 94404
	800-448-8822
	Studio/32 1.2
	Studio/8 2.0
	Equilibrium Technologies
	475 Gate Five Road, Suite 225
	Sausalito, CA 94965
	415-332-4343
228	*DeBabelizer 1.4 Demo*
	Farallon Computing, Inc.
	1321 Wakarusa Dr., #2010
	Lawrence, KS 66049
	800-998-7761
	HyperSound
	MacRecorder
	PhoneNET Card PC
	SoundEdit
	SoundEdit Pro
	Sound Expansion INIT
	Timbuktu 5.0.1
	FGM, Inc.
	131 Elden St., Ste. 108
	Herndon, VA 22070
	703-478-9881
	PICTure This

CODE # COMPANY INFO/PRODUCT

Fifth Generation Systems, Inc.
10049 N. Rieger Rd.
Baton Rouge, LA 70809
800-766-7283
Suitcase 2.1

FM Waves
70 Derby Ave.
San Francisco, CA 94102
800-497-1234
Graphic News Network

Form and Function
1595 17th Ave.
San Francisco, CA 94122
415-664-4010
520–522 *WraptureReels*
590–594
720–721 *WraptureReels Disc One*
990–993
730–739 *Wraptures Disc One: FineTextures*

Fractal Design Corp.
3355 Spreckels Dr., Ste. F
Aptos, CA 95003
408-688-8800
Fractal Design Painter 2.0
Fractal Design Sketcher 1.0
Fractal Music Generator
Sketcher

The FreeSoft Co.
105 McKinley Rd.
Beaver Falls, PA 15010
412-846-2700
White Knight II telecommunications software

Fusion Data Systems
8920 Business Park Dr., Ste. 350
Austin, TX 78759
512-338-5326
TokaMac II FX 33 accelerator board

FutureVideo
EditLink 3300 Series
FutureVideo A/B controller

FWB Software, Inc.
2040 Polk St., Ste. 215
San Francisco, CA 94109
415-377-1288
Hard Disk Toolkit
Pocket Hammer series

CODE # COMPANY INFO/PRODUCT

Gazelle Systems
305-T N. 500 W.
Provo, UT 84601
810-377-1288
file management software

Gold Disk
20675 S. Western Ave., Ste 120
Torrance, CA 90501
310-320-5080
212 *Animation Works 1.1 Demo*

Golden MIDI Music
330 E. 39th St. #104
New York, NY 10016
212-370-0474
Golden MIDI Sequences

The Grass Valley Group
P.O. Box 1114
Grass Valley, CA 95945
916-478-3800

Gryphon Software Corporation
7220 Trade Street, Suite 120
San Diego, CA 92121
619-536-8815
229 *Morph 1.1 Demo Disk*

GSC Associates
2304 Artesia Blvd., Ste 201
Redondo Beach, CA 92078
310-379-2113
MetaPICT

Gyration, Inc.
12930 Saratoga Ave., Bldg. C
Saratoga, CA 95070
GyroPoint pointing device

HandyKey Corp.
141 Mt. Sinai Ave.
Mt. Sinai, NY 11766
516-474-9405
Twiddler keyboard

Heizer Software
P.O. Box 232019
Pleasant Hill, CA 94523
800-888-7667
Convert It!
HyperCard compilers

CODE # COMPANY INFO/PRODUCT

Hollywood Film Music Library/ Screenmusic International
11684 Ventura Blvd., Suite 850
Studio City, CA 91604
818-760-4123
940–941 *Hollywood Film Music Library*

Hologlyph, Inc.
8100 Ralston Rd., Garden Level
Arvada, CO 80002
800-283-9082
Sound/FX CD Series

Holt, Joe
ALink: ADOBE.JHOLT
148 *Swatch 1.2.2 & 1.7d10*

HSC Software
1661 Lincoln Blvd., Suite #101
Santa Monica, CA 90404
619-536-8815
134 *Kai's Power Tools v.1.0a*

Husom & Rose Photographics
1988 Stanford Avenue
St. Paul, MN 55105
612-699-1858
640–642 *Digital Photographics*

***Hyperbole* magazine**
1412 W. Alabama
Houston, TX 77006
713-529-9696
Hymermedia art, literature and etertainment magazine

HyperMedia Communications Inc.
901 Mariner's Island Blvd., Suite 365
San Mateo, CA 94404
Inside Report on New Media newsletter

The Image Bank
111 Fifth Ave
New York, NY 10003

Image Club Graphics
1902-11th St., SE, Ste. 5
Calgary, Alberta, Canada T2G 3G2
ArtRoom

CODE # COMPANY INFO/PRODUCT

ImageTects
7200 Bollinger Rd., Suite 802
San Jose, CA 95129
408-252-5487
660–664 *ImageCELs*

Impulse Technology
210 Dahlonega St., Ste. 205
Cumming, GA 31030
404-889-8294
33MHz Performance 040 accelerator

Imspace Systems Corporation
4747 Morena Blvd., Suite 360
San Diego, CA 92117
619-272-2600 x4100
224 *Kudo Image Browser 1.0 Demo*
Kudo Image Browser
225 *PICTpocket Demo*

Infogrip
1145 Eugenia Place, Ste. 201
Carpenteria, CA 93013
805-566-1049
The Bat keyboard

Innovation Advertising & Design
41 Mansfield Ave.
Essex Junction, VT 05452
800-255-0562
AdArt series

Inset Systems
71 Commerce Dr.
Brookfield, CT 06804
800-374-6738
HiJaak Pro 2.0

Insignia Solutions, Inc.
526 Clyde Ave.
Mountain View, CA 94043
800-848-7677
AccessPC 2.0

Interactive Media Corp.
P.O. Box 0089
Los Altos, CA 94023
415-948-0745
Special Delivery 1.0

CODE #	COMPANY INFO/PRODUCT
	Iverson, Jeff
	3841 Whispering Way Dr., Ste. 101
	Grand Rapids, MI 49546
	616-949-0346
143	*Gestalt 3.2.1Get Monitors XFCN 1.2*
144	*GetMonitorsXFCN 1.2*
	J.L. Cooper Electronics
	12500 Beatrice St.
	Los Angeles, CA 90066
	310-303-4131
	FadeMaster
	Three-D
	Killer Tracks
	6534 Sunset Blvd.
	Hollywood, CA 90066
	310-306-4131
	Killer Tracks Multimedia Music Library
	Kodak (See Eastman Kodak)
	Kurta
	3007 East Chambers St.
	Phoenix, AZ 85040
	602-276-5533
	Pressure sensitive tablets
	Kurzweil Music Systems (see Young Chang America)
	Leptonics Systems Design Company
	717 East Jerico Turnpike, #321
	Huntington Station, NY 11746
	ALink: LEPTON, CompuServ: 76004,1447
166	*EasyPlay 2.0*
	Letraset USA
	40 Eisenhower Dr.
	Paramus NJ 07653
	800-343-8973
	ColorStudio 1.5 With Shapes
	Fontek
	Phototone Background Image Resource
	Light Source
	17 E. Sir Francis Drake Blvd., Ste. 100
	Larkspur, CA 94939
	415-641-8000
	Ofoto 2.0

CODE #	COMPANY INFO/PRODUCT
	Logitech, Inc.
	6505 Kaiser Dr.
	Fremont, CA 94555
	510-795-0801
	MouseMan
	Loop Software
	P.O. Box 1249
	Menlo Pak, CA 94026
	800-288-7631
	PictureBook+ 1.0
	Mac Media Publications
	5805 West Heimer
	Houston, TX 77057
	713-977-2655
	MIDI Minus One
	Macromedia, Inc.
	600 Townsend Ave.
	San Francisco, CA 94103
	415-252-2250
	800-945-9063
	Action (Mac and Windows versions)
	AuthorWare Professional
214	*AuthorWare Professional 1.7.1 Demo*
540–545	*ClipMedia*
930–935	*ClipMedia, Vol. 1 Samples: Clip Music*
910–919	*ClipMedia, Vol. 1 Samples: Clip Sounds*
	ClipTime
	MacRecorder Sound System Pro
	MacRecorder Voice Digitizer
	Macromedia Director 3.1
210	*Macromedia Director 3.1.1 Demo*
	Macromedia Player
	MacroModel (and MacroModel for Windows)
221	*MacroModel 1.0 Demo*
	Magic 1.1
215	*MediaMaker 1.5 Demo*
	SoundEdit Pro
201	*SoundEdit Pro 2.0*
	SwivelArt
220	*Swivel 3D Pro 2.0.4 Demo*
	Swivel 3D Professional 2.0
	***MacUser* magazine**
	P.O. Box 56986
	Boulder, CO 80322
	800-627-2247
	MCI Mailbox 424-4936

CODE # COMPANY INFO/PRODUCT

MacWeek magazine
(Ziff-Davis Publishing Co.)
1 Park Ave
New York, NY 10016
609-461-2100

Macworld CD Ventures
P.O. Box 105443
Atlanta, GA 30348
800-821-1177, ext. 112

Macworld Communications, Inc.
501 Second St., Ste. 600
San Francisco, CA 94107
415-243-0505
Macworld Interactive
multimedia CD of MACWORLD magazine
MACWORLD magazine

326 **Mainstay**
5311-B Derry Ave.
Agoura Hills, CA 91301
818-991-6540
Capture 4.0
227 *Capture 4.0 Demo*

Mark of the Unicorn, Inc.
222 Third St.
Cambridge, MA 02142
617-576-2760
Digital Performer
Digital WaveBoard
Performer 3.6

Mass Microsystems
810 W. Maude Ave.
Sunnyvale, CA 94086
800-522-7979
QuickImage 24 board

Mathemaesthetics, Inc.
P.O. Box 67-156
Chestnut Hill, MA 02167
617-738-8803
Resourcerer

Maverick Software
11215 Research Blvd #2036
Austin, TX 78759
ALink: Maverick.SFT
146 *PuzzleTime 1.0*
165 *Theater Maker 1.2*

CODE # COMPANY INFO/PRODUCT

MECC
6160 Summit Dr. N.
Minneapolis, MN 55430
800-685-6322
Easy Color Paint

Media in Motion
P.O. Box 170130
San Francisco, CA 94117
415-621-0707
500–505 *Animation on Clips/Business Vol. 1 & 2*
211 *Macromedia Director Training Demo*

Media Vision
3185 Laurelview Ct.
Fremont, CA 94538
800-638-2807
Pro Audio Spectrum (PAS) 16-bit sound board

Media-Pedia Co.
22 Fischer Ave
Wellesley, MA 02181
617-235-5617
Media-Pedia Co. Video Clips

Meridian Data, Inc.
5615 Scotts Valley Dr.
Scotts Valley, CA 95066
800-76-SALES
Personal Scribe CD-ROM

Metatec Discovery Systems
7001 Discovery Blvd.
Dublin, OH 43017
614-761-2000
Best of Photography Series
Nautilus magazine on CD-ROM

Metro ImageBase, Inc.
18623 Ventura Blvd., Ste. 210
Tarzana, CA 91356
800-525-1552
Metro ImageBase Electronic Clip Art

Meyer Software
616 Continental Road
Hatboro, PA 19040
215-675-3890
217 *On the Air Demo 1.0*

CODE # COMPANY INFO/PRODUCT

MicroFrontier, Inc.
3401 101st St., Ste. E
Des Moines, IA 50322
515-270-8109
Color It!

Micrografx
1303 E. Arapaho Rd.
Richardson, TX 75081
800-733-3729
Picture Publisher Mac

MicroNet, Technology, Inc.
20 Mason
Irvine, CA 92718
714-837-6033
Internal Removable 040
Micro/Optical Storage
Micro/Optical Systems

Microsoft Corp.
One Microsoft Way
Redmond, WA 98052
800-426-9400
Microsoft Press:
Windows Multimedia
Authoring and Tools Guide
Multimedia Development Kit (MDK)
Movie Converter (bundled with MDK)
PowerPoint 3.0
Windows 3.1

Microsoft Windows BBS
(Bulletin Board Service)
206-936-6735

Miramar Systems
201 N. Salsipuedes, Ste. 204
Santa Barbara CA 93103
800-862-2526
MacLAN Connect F/P

Mirror Technologies, Inc.
2644 Patton Rd.
Roseville, MN 55113
800-654-5294
Double-Speed CD-ROM
85Mb Mirror Optical Drive

CODE # COMPANY INFO/PRODUCT

Mitchell, Kevin
P. O. Box 803066
Chicago, IL 60680-3066
CompuServ: 74017-3066
131 *Gif Converter, 2.210 & 2.3b2*

Mobius Technologies, Inc.
1125 Atlantic Ave., Ste. 100
Alameda, CA 94501
800-523-7933

Motion Works International, Inc.
1020 Mainland St., Stuite 130
Vancouver, BC V6B 2T4
Canada
604-685-9975
213 *PROMotion 1.0.3 Demo*
900–904 *PrimeTime CD-ROM*
530–536 *PrimeTime I*

Mouse Systems Corp.
47505 Seabridge Dr.
Fremont, CA 94538
510-656-1117
A^3 Mouse

Multi-Ad Services, Inc.
1720 W. Detweiller Dr.
Peoria, IL 61615
309-692-1530
Multi-Ad Search

Multimedia Library, Inc.
37 Washington Square West, Suite 4 D
New York, NY 10011
212-674-1958
960–967 *The Multimedia Library SOUND Series Vol.1*
670–675 *The Multimedia Library IMAGE Series Vol. 1: Russia/China*
680–684 *The Multimedia Library IMAGE Series Vol. 2: South Pacific/Tropical/Calif. Coast*
The Multimedia Library Royalty-Free Series

The Music Bank
P.O. Box 3150
Saratoga, CA 95070
408-867-4756
Stingers CD-ROM disc

***Nautilus* magazine (See Metatec Corp.)**

CODE # COMPANY INFO/PRODUCT

NEC Clip Art 3-D
Collection of 2500+ 1000 24-bit color still images plus ulitity software for altering and rendering models

***New Media* magazine**
(formerly *New Media Age*)
(Hypermedia Publications, Inc.)
901 Mariner's Island Blvd., Ste. 365
San Mateo, CA 94404
415-573-5170

New Video Corp.
1526 Cloverfield Blvd.
Santa Monica, CA 90404
310-449-7000
EyeQ board (digitiser and playback system)

New Visions Technology, Inc.
1149 Sycamore Ln.
Mahwah, NJ 07430
405-523-1639
Indeo codes for QuickTime
Presentation Task Force

Newer Technology
7803 E. Osie , Ste. 105
Wichita, KS 67207
316-685-4904
fx/Overdrive acceleratin option

Newsweek Interactive
(See The Software Toolworks)

Nikon Electronic Imaging
1300 Walt Whitman Rd.
Melville, NY 11747
516-547-4355
ImageAccess

Novell, Inc.
122 East 1799 South
Provo, UT 84606
800-638-9273
NetWare For Macintosh 2.2

Nutmeg Systems
25 South Ave.
New Caanan, CT 06840
800-777-8439
30/8 Color Interface

CODE # COMPANY INFO/PRODUCT

O. Sage Consultants, Inc. (OSC)
7100 Regency Square Blvd., Ste. 136
Houston, TX 77036
713-785-5400
Dyaxis
Metro Deck
A Poke in the Ear With a Sharp Stick
Sound Designer I and II
SoundLab

Olduvai Corp.
7520 Red Rd., Ste. A
South Miami, FL 33142
305-665-4665
SoundClips

Opcode Systems
3641 Haven Dr., Ste. A
Menlo Park, CA 94025
415-369-8131
Audioshop
EZ Vision MIDI *sequencer*
MIDI Play
StudioVision
Vision

Optical Media International
180 Knowles Dr.
Los Gatos, CA
95030
800-347-2664
Desktop Sounds, Volume One CD-ROM

Overpriced Software
P.O. Box 216
Peterborough, NH 03458
603-525-4629
140 *DepthKey 1.5*

Parity Productions
26043 Gushue St.
Hayward, CA 94544
ALink: BERFIELD; CompuServ: 72627,564
147 *Speedometer 3.11*

The Parker Adams Group
MIDI Jukebox

Passport Designs, Inc.
100 Stone Pine Road
Half Moon Bay, CA 94019
415-726-0280

CODE #	COMPANY INFO/PRODUCT
	Alchemy [DISCONTINUED]
	Audio Trax
	HyperMusic
200	*Master Tracks Pro 5 Demo v.5.2*
	MIDI Records (Music Data Division)
	Music Date series
216	*Passport Producer v1.1 Demo*
	QuickTunes
	Trax
	Peripheral Land, Inc. (PLI)
	47421 Bayside Pkwy.
	Fremont, CA 94538
	800-288-8754
	Infinity Removable 88RW44 disk drive
	Personal Training Systems
	828 S. Bascom Ave., Ste.100
	San Jose, CA 95128
	800-832-2499
	Photoshop Basics 2
	Perspect Systems
	5301 Beethoven St., Ste. 155
	Los Angeles, CA 90066
	310-821-7884
	Nexus fx
	PhotoDisc, Inc.
	2013 4th Ave., Suite 200
	Seattle, WA 98121
	800-528-3472
690–699	*PhotoDisc - World Commerce and Travel*
	Pierce Software
	719 Hibiscus Place, Ste. 301
	San Jose, CA 95117
	408-244-6554
	Smoothie 1.02
	Pinnacle Micro
	19 Technology
	Irvine, CA 92718
	800-553-7070
	PMO-650 disk drive
	Pioneer Communications of America, Inc.
	600 E. Crescent Ave.
	Upper Saddle River, NJ 07458
	800-527-3766
	LDV-4400 video disc player

CODE #	COMPANY INFO/PRODUCT
	Pixar
	1001 W. Cutting Blvd.
	Richmond, CA 94804
	800-888-9853
	NetRenderMan
	RenderMan
	Showplace & MacRenderMan 1.3
	Typestry
	Pixel Resources, Inc.
	3020 Business Park Drl, Ste #E
	Norcross, GA 30071
	404-449-4947
	PixelPaint Professional
	Pop Rocket
	181 Downey St.
	San Francisco, CA 94117
	415-731-9112
	Total Distortion
	PressLink
	11800 Sunrise Valley Dr.
	Reston, VA 22094
	On-line service of Knight-Ridder news agency
	Presto Studios
	11066 Red Robin Place
	San Diego, CA 92126
	619-549-9436
920–929	*Hi Rez Vol. 1 Audio for Multimedia*
202	*Hi Rez Audio Demo*
	The Journeyman Project
	Prosonus
	11126 Weddington St.
	N. Hollywood, CA 91601
	MusicBytes
	Q Up Arts
	P.O. Box 1078
	Aptos, CA 95001
	408-376-3511
970–975	*DeskTop Sounds: Sound FX Vol. 1*
	Quanta Press, Inc.
	1313 Fifth St. SE, Ste. 223-A
	Minneapolis, MN 55414
	404-967-2077
	Fresh Arte CD

CODE # COMPANY INFO/PRODUCT

Radius, Inc.
1710 Fortune Dr.
San Jose, CA 95131
800-227-2795
Radius Rocket 33 accelerator
VideoVision video card

RasterOps Corp.
2500 Walsh Ave.
Santa Clara, CA 95051
800-729-2656
24MxTV movie recorder software
24STV board
24XLTV
Colorboard 364
MediaTime
MoviePak (available separately or bundled with Editing Access Suites)
QuickTime digitizing care
VideoExpander

Ray Dream, Inc.
1804 N. Shoreline Blvd.
Mountain View, CA 94043
415-960-0768
addDepth
Raydream Designer 2.04
DreamNet
JAG-Jaggies Are Gone
JAG II

Reactor, Inc.
445 W. Erie St., Ste. 5B
Chicago, IL 60610
312-573-0800
Spaceship Warlock intractive CD-ROM movie

Reed, Chris
3409 Clearview Dr.
San Angelo, TX 76904
915-949-9486
100 *Play AIFF v1.0*

Robbins, Greg
109 Crocker Ave.
Oakland, CA 94610
AOL: JoeS10
142 *Folder Icon Maker 1.1*

CODE # COMPANY INFO/PRODUCT

Roland Digital Group
1961 McGaw Ave.
Irvine, CA 92714
213-685-5141
MT-32 series synthesizer
CM series synthesizer
Sound Brush

Sandhill Arts Publishing Co.
P.O. Box 7298
Menlo Park, CA 94026
800-854-0717
Funny Business (15 EPS cartoons)

Savitar
139 Townsend St., Level M100
San Francisco, CA, 94107
415-243-3030
ScanMatch 1.01 scanner calibration software

Seattle Support Group
415-243-3030
Medley (300+ images in three resolutions)

Shiva Corp.
1 Cambridge Center
Cambridge MA 02142
800-458-3550
NetModem/E

Sigma Designs
47900 Bayside Pkwy.
Fremont, CA 94538
800-845-8086, ext. 230
Power Portrait

Sitka Corp.
950 Marine Village Pkwy.
Alameda, CA 94501
800-445-8677
TOPS FlashCard

The Software Toolworks
60 Leveroni Ct.
Novato, CA
94949
415-883-3000
Newsweek Interactive

CODE # COMPANY INFO/PRODUCT

Software Ventures Corp.
2907 Claremont Ave.
Berkeley, CA 94075
800-336-6477
MicroPhone 1.5
MircoPhone II 4.0
MicroPhone Pro

Sony Corp. of America
3 Paragon Dr.
Montvale, NJ 07645
800-352-7669
BetaCam video system
BVE video editing system
DXC series Hi-8 VCR
EVC40 tape deck
LVR-5000 video disc player
LVS-5000 video disc player
Vbox CI-1000
Vdeck 100
X510 8mm video camera

Spectral Innovations, Inc.
4633 Old Ironsides Dr., Ste. 401
Santa Clara, CA 95054
408-727-1314
MacDSP32CC-MPW

Specular International
P.O. Box 888
Amherst, MA 01004
413-549-7600
Backburner
Infini-D 2.05
Replicas

Spinnaker Software Corp.
201 Broadway, 6th Fl.
Cambridge, MA 02139
800-323-8088
Spinnaker PLUS (Mac and Windows versions)

Stat Media Network
21151 Via Canon
Yorba Linda, CA 92686-6306
714-779-8176
550–553 *Instant Buttons & Controls*

Stein, Lincoln D.
44 Boynton St #3
Boston, MA 02130
617-524-5241
164 *QT Batch Compressor*

CODE # COMPANY INFO/PRODUCT

Steinberg, Bill
156 West 44th St.
New York, NY 10036-4024
212-921-0663
149 *Switch-A-Roo 1.6*
132 *Klutz 1.0*

Steinberg Jones
17700 Raymer St., Ste. 1001
Northridge, CA 91325
415-369-8131
Cubase Audio

Steve Rimmer
c/o Addison Wesley Publishing Co.
One Jacob Way
Reading, MA 10867
800-447-2226
Graphic Workshop (disk with The Graphic File Toolkit: Converting and Using Graphic Files, Addison Wesley, 1992)

Storage Dimensions
1656 McCarthy Blvd.
Milpitas, CA 95035
408-894-1349

Storm Technology, Inc.
1861 Landings Dr.
Mountain View, CA 94043
415-691-6600
130 *PictureDecomPress 2.0.4*

Strata, Inc.
2 West St. George Blvd, Ste. 2100
St. George, UT 84770
801-628-5218
RenderPro
800–802 *StrataShapes*
810–812 *StrataTextures*
Strata Type 3-d 2.0
StrataVision
226 *StrataVision v2.5-A Demo*

CODE #	COMPANY INFO/PRODUCT

SuperMac Technology
485 Potrero Ave.
Sunnyvale, CA 94086
408-245-2202
Digital Film
PixelPaint 2.1
PixelPaint Professional 2.0
Sound Pro
VideoSpigot (with ScreenPlay)
VideoSpigot Pro

Symantec Corp.
10201 Torre Ave.
Cupertino, CA 95014
800-441-7234
More III

Symmetry Software Corp.
8603 E. Royal Palm Rd., #110
Scottsdale, AZ 85258
602-998-9106
Mariah

SyQuest Technology
47071 Bayside Pkwy.
Fremont, CA 94538
800-245-2278
Removable cartridge hard drives
88Mb disk drive (stores QuickTime movies)
105Mb removable disk drive

Systat, Inc.
1800 Sherman Ave.
Evanston, IL 60201
708-864-5670
Systat 5.2

System Technology Corp.
1860 Fern Palm Dr.
Edgewater, FL 32141
800-638-4784

T/Maker
1390 Villa St.
Mountain View, CA 94041
415-962-0195
ClickArt

Tactic Software
Sound Clips

CODE #	COMPANY INFO/PRODUCT

Teach Yourself By Computer Software, Inc.
3400 Monroe Ave.
Rochester, NY 14618
716-381-5450
EduClip Images 1 and 2

TechPool Studios
1463 Warrensville Center Rd.
Cleveland, OH 44121
800-777-8930
Atmosphere Systems (EPS backgrounds)

TechScan
P.O. Box 895
Port Hueneme, CA 93044
805-985-4370
MaxImages A2 (60 TIFF image, 8-bit and 24-bit color and gray-scale)

Tektronix
26600 SW Parkway Ave./Mailstop 63-583
Wilsonville, OR 97070
800-547-8949
Motif Window Manager
Local Client F Kit

Time Arts, Inc.
1425 Corporate Center Pkwy.
Santa Rosa, CA 95407
707-576-7722
Oasis

Timeworks, Inc.
625 Academy Dr.
Northbrook, IL 60062
708-559-1300
Color It 2.0.1

Topas

Toshiba America Information Systems
714-583-3000
Multimedia player
Photo CD compatible drives

Trantor Systems, Ltd.
5415 Randall Pl.
Fremont, CA
94538
510-770-1400
CD-ROM Drivers For Macintosh

CODE #	COMPANY INFO/PRODUCT
	Traveling Software, Inc. 18702 N. Creek Pkwy. Bothell WA 98011 800-343-8080 *LapLink Mac III 3.2* *LapLink Pro*
	Truevision, Inc. 7340 Shadeland Station Indianapolis, IN 46256 800-344-8783 *Bravado 32*
	Tsunami Press 275 Route 18 East Brunswick, NJ 08816 800-448-9815 *The Right Images*
	Turtle Beach Systems P.O. Box 5074 York, PA 17405 800-554-9979 *Wav for Windows*
	UserLand Software 490 California Ave Palo Alto, CA 94306 415-369-6600 *UserLand Frontier 2.0*
	The Valis Group P.O. Box 422 Point Richmond, CA 94807-0422 510-236-4124 *VG Looks* *VG Shaders*
	Vanguard Media *The World of U.S. Manga Corp.*
	Verbum, Inc. P.O. Box 189 Cardiff, CA 92007-0189 619-944-9977 Fax: 619-944-9995 *Blendo Photography 1.0:*
630–639	*Photo Imagery by Craig McClain* *Verbum Interactive*

CODE #	COMPANY INFO/PRODUCT
	VideoFusion, Ltd. 1722 Indian Wood Circle, Ste. H Maumee, OH 43537 800-638-5253 *VideoFusion 1.0.1*
	Videographics Corp. 441 East Erie, Ste. 1804 Chicago, IL 60611 312-642-6652 *Special effects shaders*
	***Videography* magazine** (P.S.N. Publications 2 Park Avenue, Ste. 1820 New York, NT 10016 212-779-1919
	VideoLake (see Video Fusion)
	Vision Software 524 2nd Street San Francisco, CA 94107 800-800-8476
241	*CameraMan 1.0 Demo*
	Visual Information Development, Inc. (VIDI) 16309 Doublegrove St. La Puente, CA 91744 818-918-8834 *Presenter Professional RISC Imaging Node*
	Vividus Corp. 651 Kendall Ave. Palo Alto, CA 94306 415-494-2111 *Cinemation 1.0*
	The Voyager Co. 1351 Pacific Coast Hwy. Santa Monica, CA 90401 800-446-2001 Amanda Stories *AudioStack* *The Louvre, Vols. I-III* *VideoStack* *Voyager Expanded Books*

CODE #	COMPANY INFO/PRODUCT
	Wacom, Inc.
	Park 80 West, Plaza II
	Saddlebrook, NJ 07662
	201-265-4226
	ArtZ tablet
	SD-421-E graphics tablet
	Wayzata Technology, Inc.
	P.O. Box 807
	Grand Rapids, MN 55744
	218-326-0597
	800-735-7321
	Clip art: EPS Professional
	Gallery of Dreams
	Photo Pro
	Procupine Productions/Music Madness
	Sound Library 2000
710–712	*SpaceTime and Art photoBank,*
	Window Painters, Ltd.
	3701 Pennsylvania Ave. S.
	Blumington, MN 55431
	612-881-4212
	SnapPro file conversion software
	WPA Film Lab
	5525 West 159th St.
	Oak Forest, IL 60452
	708-535-1540
	10,000+ hours of film footage
	Young Chang America
	13336 Alondra Blvd.
	Cerritos, CA 90701-2205
	310-926-3200
	Automated Composer Project
	Cybernetic Composer
	Zedcor
	4500 E. Speedway, Ste. 22
	Tucson, AZ 85712
	800-842-4567
	DeskPaint & Desk Draw 3.7
	ZSoft Corp.
	201 Alameda del Prado
	Novato, CA 94049
	415-382-8000
	PC Paintbrush 5+
	PC Paintbrush IV

Project Information

CODE #	COMPANY INFO/PRODUCT
	The Aesthetics Collection
	1060 17th Street
	San Diego, CA 92101
	619-238-1860
042	*Health Care Kiosk*
	Sample Project by Paul Burgess
	Aldus Corporation
	411 First Street
	Seattle, WA 98104
	206-343-3502
040	*Aldus PageMaker 5.0 Demo Disk*
	Sample Project by Matthew Fass
	Billups Communication
	1608 Thayer Ave.
	Los Angeles, CA 90024
	310-474-2229
021	*NTV Logo, EcoSpies*
	Sample Projects by Scott Billups
	Burgess, Paul
	2314 Brookhaven Pass
	Vista, CA 92083
	619-599-9095
042	*Health Care Kiosk*
	Sample Project by Paul Burgess
	Chrysolite Productions
	2811 Whishire Blvd. Ste. 510
	Santa Monica, CA 90403
	310-829-2203
033	*EcoSpies*
	Sample Project by Scott Billups
	Doerfler Design
	4511 Castelar
	San Diego, CA 92107
	619-223-9789
030	*Water Fantasia*
	Sample Project by Don Doerfler
	Gosney Company Inc., The
	2187-C San Elijo Ave.
	Cardiff, CA 92007
	619-944-9977
022	*Lawnmower Man VSI Logo*
	Sample Project by Jack Davis
	Multimedia Power Tools CD-ROM
	and book production

CODE #	COMPANY INFO/PRODUCT
	Horizon 1533 Hunsaker Street Oceanside, CA 92054
011	*Hip Hop Hits* *Sample Project by Mike Salomo n*
	HyperBole Studios 1412 West Alabama Huston, TX 77006 713-529-9696
032	*The Madness of Roland* *Sample Project by Greg Roach*
	Ikonic Interactive 221 Main Stree, Suite 700 San Francisco, CA 94105 415-864-3200
040	*Aldus PageMaker 5.0 Demo Disk* *Sample Project by Matthew Fass*
	Interactive Records 921 Church Street San Francisco, CA 94114 415-285-8650
013	*So You Want to be a Rock & Roll Star* *Sample Project by Steven Rappaport*
	JH Davis Design P.O. Box 262535 San Diego, CA 92196 619-689-4895
022	*Lawnmower Man VSI Logo* *Sample Project by Jack Davis*
	John Odam Design Associates 2163 Cordero Road Del Mar, CA 92014 619-259-8230
023	*Test Flight* *Sample Project by John Odam*
	Mott, Harry 3561 Frances Avenue Los Angeles, CA 90066 310-398-9789
031	*Land of Counterpane* *Sample Project by Harry Mott*

CODE #	COMPANY INFO/PRODUCT
	Presto Studios 11066 Red Robin Place San Diego, CA 92126 619-689-4895
024	*Robot From Journeyman* *Sample Project by Farshid Almassizadeh*
	Salomon, Mike 11835 Sapota Drive Lakeside, CA 92040 619-286-7049
011	*Hip Hop Hits* *Sample Project by Mike Salomon*
	Tim Cutt Productions 2840 N. Beverly Drive Beverly Hills, CA 90210 310-474-2229
033	*EcoSpies* *Sample Project by Scott Billups*
	Tony Retundo Communications 531 South Greenwood Avenue Pasadena, CA 91107 310.719-5231
021	*NTV Logo* *Sample Project by Scott Billups*
	UCSD Medical School 9500 Gilman Drive La Jolla, CA 92093-0661 619-534-3656
041	*MedPics* *Sample Project by Helene Hoffman*
	Univ. of Texas School of Nursing at Galveston 1100 Mechanic, Route J-29 Galveston, TX 77555 409-772-5118
020	*Video Quilt* *Sample Project by Lynda Weinman*
	Weinman, Lynda 618 N. Fredric Street Burbank, CA 91505 818-843-5056
020	*Video Quilt* *Sample Project by Lynda Weinman*

Appendix B: Power Codes List

Outline

Interface Location codes

000 Intro Animation
001 Disc Info Menu
002 Set-up Menu
003 Guided Tour Menu
004 Sample Projects Menu
005 Power Tools Menu
006 Introduction
007 Credits
008 Production Notes
009 Publisher/Copyright Info

Projects

(for exact codes, see Projects)
010–019 Sound
020–029 Animation
030–039 Video
040–049 Interactive Multimedia

Power Tools/Clip Media

(for exact codes, see Power Tools)
500–590 Animation/Video
600–790 Images/Backgrounds
800–890 3-D Graphics
900–990 Sound/Music

Power Tools/Programs & Utilities

(for exact codes, see Power Tools)
100–109 Audio Tools
110–119 Authoring Tools
120–129 CD-ROM Tools
130–139 Imaging Tools
140–159 General Tools
160–179 QuickTime Tools

Demos

(for exact codes, see Demos)
200–209 Audio
210–219 Authoring/Presentation
220–239 Imaging
240–249 QuickTime

Projects

011 PROJECT #1, **Sound**, Simple Editing, Mike Salomon, *Hip Hop Hits*
012 PROJECT #2, **Sound**, Music Composition, Christopher Yavelow, *PowerTools Theme*
013 PROJECT # 3, **Sound**, Multimedia Project, Steve Rappaport, *Rock and Roll Star*
020 PROJECT # 4, **Animation**, Basic 2D, Linda Weinman, *Video Quilt*
021 PROJECT # 5, **Animation**, Intermediate 2D/3D, Scott Billups, *NTV Logo*
022 PROJECT #6, **Animation**, Jack Davis, 3D Rotation, Jack Davis, *Lawnmower Man Logo*
023 PROJECT # 7, **Animation**, Intermediate 3D, John Odam, *Test Flight*
024 PROJECT # 8, **Animation**, 3D Character, Farshid Almassizadeh, *Journeyman Project Robot*
030 PROJECT #9, **Video**, Basic I, Don Doerfler, *Water Fantasia*
031 PROJECT #10, **Video**, Basic II, Harry Mott, *Land of Counterpane*

032 PROJECT #11, **Video**, Intermediate, Greg Roach, *Madness of Roland*
033 PROJECT # 12, **Video**, Advanced, Scott Billups, *EcoSpies*
040 PROJECT #13, **Multimedia**, Basic Training, Matthew Fass, *PageMaker 5.0 Demo*
041 PROJECT #14, **Multimedia**, Intermediate Training, Helene Hoffman, *MedPics*
042 PROJECT #15, **Multimedia**, Interactive Kiosk, Paul Burgess, *Health Care Kiosk*

Power Tools

Clip Media

Animation/Video

500 Media in Motion Animation Clips
- 501 Alarm Clock
- 502 Juke Box
- 503 Ray Gun
- 504 Trumpet
- 505 US Flag

510 TV-ROM
- 511 Clock
- 512 Dr. Seuss Set
- 513 Number Spin Pine
- 514 TV-ROM The Movie

520 WraptureReels
- 521 Terra

530 PrimeTime
- 531 Dart Being Thrown
- 532 Magnifying Glass
- 533 Pen Writing
- 534 Star Twinkling
- 535 Switch Flicking
- 536 TV Strolling

540 ClipMedia
- 541 Arrow
- 542 Chrome
- 543 Globe
- 544 Lock & Key
- 545 Telephone

550 Instant Buttons & Controls
- 551 Brushed Steel
- 552 Button Demo
- 553 QuickTime Stage

570 Image Bank CD Collection
- 571 5 P.M.
- 572 Crusin' 2
- 573 Dollars
- 574 Fast Driving
- 575 Out Of Town

580 TV-ROM
- 581 C&G Video
- 582 Clapping squirrel
- 583 Opening Scan
- 584 The Thinker
- 585 Walk like an Egret

590 WraptureReels
- 591 Beach
- 592 Flames
- 593 Sunset
- 594 ThunderHeads

Images/Backgrounds

600 Backgrounds for Multimedia Vol 1
- 601 Banded Steel
- 602 Currents
- 603 Marble

610 Backgrounds for Multimedia Vol 2
- 611 Bella Rosa
- 612 Palm
- 613 Photo texture
- 614 Sunburst

620 Marble & Granite CD-ROM
- 621 Cherry Blossom
- 622 Jade
- 623 Juparana

630 Blendo Photography I: Photo Imagery by Craig McClain
- 631 Apple
- 632 Bikes
- 633 Building
- 634 Dunes
- 635 FlowerPastel
- 636 San Diego
- 637 Seashore
- 638 The Look
- 639 Utah Mountains

640 Digital Photographics CD-ROM
- 641 Rainbow
- 642 Reflections

650 Folio 1 Image Library
- 651 Bubbles
- 652 Crepe Paper
- 653 Gauze-2
- 654 Marbilized Blue
- 655 Palm Fronds
- 656 Shark

660 ImageCELs
- 661 Brick 9
- 662 Earth
- 663 Pavers
- 664 Trislaur

670 The Multimedia Library IMAGE Series Russia/China
- 671 Chinese Bell temple
- 672 Dragon boat
- 673 Great Wall-2
- 674 Old church-2
- 675 St. Basil's Cathedral-2

680 The Multimedia Library IMAGE Series South Pacific/Tropical/California Coast
- 681 Beach at Sunset
- 682 Costal Scene
- 683 Haleakala Crater-2
- 684 Lava

690 PhotoDisc—World Commerce and Travel
- 691 Aerial Furrows (097)
- 692 Bird Design (039)
- 693 Colored Parasols (059)
- 694 Golden Gate Bridge at Sunset
- 695 Building Steps
- 696 Painted Native
- 697 Pyramids (287)
- 698 Rockpile (013)
- 699 Row of Buddahs (071)

700 CD Folios: Sky, Vol 1 v2.0
- 701 Clouds-3
- 702 Sunset on Mountains-3
- 703 Sunset on Ocean-3

710 SpaceTime and Art
- 711 Jupiter rising-2
- 712 Primordial soup-2

720 WraptureReels Disc One
- 721 Dual Screen

730 Wraptures Disc One: FineTextures
- 731 Fieldstone-2
- 732 Fire-2
- 733 Marble-2
- 734 Marble-Gloss-2
- 735 Mottled-2
- 736 NGC1-2
- 737 NGC2-2
- 738 PaperRag-2
- 739 Ring Nebula-2

740 International Graphics Library
- 741 Liberty3 (USA Images)
- 742 Earth6 (Globes, Earth)

3-D Graphics

800 StrataShapes
- 801 California
- 802 Dice

810 StrataTextures
- 811 Camouflage-Sand
- 812 Stone-Silver Lining

820 Swivel 3D Pro: Sample Models
- 821 Extruded shapes
- 822 Human figures:
- 823 Bike
- 824 Carousel Horse
- 825 Chair
- 826 DIE
- 827 Draft Table
- 828 Fresia
- 829 Macintoshes

Sound/Music

900 PrimeTime I
- 901 Camera
- 902 Champagne
- 903 Light Switch Flicking
- 904 Paintbrush

910 ClipMedia, Vol.1 Samples: ClipSounds
- 911 Button 5
- 912 Camera Shutter
- 913 Car Alarm
- 914 Cartoon Boing
- 915 Cartoon Streak
- 916 Door 2
- 916 Explosion
- 918 Fireworks-Spinners
- 919 Foghorn 2

920 Hi Rez Vol. I Audio for Multimedia
- 921 Celestial Stroll
- 922 Clouds
- 923 Island Panther
- 924 Pouring and Drinking Soda
- 925 Running out of Time
- 926 Short Zipper
- 927 Soothing Dawn
- 928 Water Birth
- 929 Water Drip

930 ClipMedia, Vol. 1 Samples: ClipMusic
- 931 Flying Sorcery
- 932 Light & Easy
- 933 Quick Hits 1
- 934 Robot Bang
- 935 The Harvest

940 Hollywood Film Music Library
- 941 Intro to Hollywood Film Library

950 Image Bank CD Collection
- 951 Light Flute
- 952 New Age 1
- 953 Piano Bar

960 The Multimedia Library SOUND Series Vol. : Music for Multimedia
- 961 Carol of the Bells
- 962 Come Back to Me
- 963 Dulcimer Piece
- 964 Piano Interludes
- 965 Piano Interludes
- 966 Polyrhythms 4
- 967 Polyrhythms 6

970 DeskTop Sounds: Sound FX Vol
- 971 Gregorian Chant C
- 972 Lively Brook
- 973 People Walking
- 974 Rubbed Glass
- 975 Thunder Roll

980 TV-ROM
- 981 Zoo Sound

990 WraptureReels Disc One
- 991 Rolling Thunder
- 992 Mantle Clock
- 993 Seashore

Programs and Utilities

Audio Tools

100 Play AIFF v1.0
101 SndConverter Pro 2.0
102 SndConverter Lite 1.1
103 SndPlayer 2.0
104 SndCataloguer 1.1

Authoring Tools

110 XCMD's
- QuickTime Movie Stack
- QuickTime Edit Movie Stack
- QuickTime Movie Making Stack
- QuickTime PICT Stack

CD-ROM Tools

120 Macintosh CD Setup 4.2

Imaging Tools

130 PictureDecomPress 2.04
131 Gif Converter 2.32b
132 Klutz 1.0
133 PICTviewer 1.1
134 Kai's Power Tools v.1.0a

General Tools

140 DepthKey 1.5
141 ExtensionsManager1.8
142 Folder Icon Maker 1.1
143 Gestalt v3.2.1
144 GetMonitors XFCN v1.2(
145 Notepad++1.4
146 PuzzleTime 1.0
147 Speedometer 3.1.1
148 Swatch v1.2.2, 1.7d10
149 Switch-A-Roo 1.6
150 TeachText 7.0
151 UpdateMaker v1.3.1
152 VideoSync 1.0
153 ColorSwitch 1.0.1

QuickTime Tools

160 QuickTime 1.6.1 Extension
161 MoviePlayer
162 Popcorn 1.0.1
163 Premiere 2.0 Plug-In Kit
164 QT Batch Compressor
165 Theater Maker 1.2
166 EasyPlay 2.0
167 QuickTime 1.6.1 Scrapbook

Demos

Audio

200 MasterTracks Pro 5 Demo
201 SoundEdit Pro 2.0 Demo
202 Hi Rez Audio Demo

Authoring/Presentation

210 Macromedia Director 3.1.1 Demo
211 MacroMind Director Training Demo
212 Animation Works 1.1 Demo
213 PROmotion 1.0 .2 Demo
214 AuthorWare Professional 1.7.1 Demo
215 MediaMaker 1.5 Demo
216 Passport Producer v1.1 Demo
217 On the Air Demo
218 PACo Producer Demo

Imaging

220 Swivel 3D Pro 1.5.7 Demo
221 MacroModel 1.0 Demo
222 Photoshop v2.0.1 Demo
223 Adobe Illustrator 3.0 Demo
224 Kudo Image Browser 1.0 Demo
225 PICTpocket Demo
226 StrataVision v2.5-A Demo
227 Capture 4.0 Demo
228 DeBableizer 1.4 Demo
229 Morph 1.1 Demo
230 Aldus Fetch 1.0 Trial Version Demo

QuickTime

240 Adobe Premiere 2.0 Tryout Demo
241 CameraMan 1.0 Demo
242 VideoShop 2.0 Demo

Appendix C: Copyright Act of 1976

An Act
For the general revision of the Copyright Law, title 17 of the United States
Code, and for other purposes.
Be it enacted by the Senate and House of Representatives of the United States of America in Congress assembled,

TITLE I—GENERAL REVISION OF COPYRIGHT LAW

Sec. 101. Title 17 of the United States Code, entitled "Copyrights," is hereby amended in its entirety to read as follows:

Chapter 1.—Subject Matter and Scope of Copyright

Sec. 115 Scope of exclusive rights in nondramatic musical works: Compulsory license for making and distributing phonorecords.
Sec. 116 Scope of exclusive rights in nondramatic musical works: Public performances by means of coin-operated phonorecord players.
Sec. 117 Scope of exclusive rights: Use in conjunction with computers and similar information systems.
Sec. 118 Scope of exclusive rights: Use of certain works in connnection with noncommercial broadcasting.

Section 101. Definitions

As used in this title, the following terms and their variant forms mean the following:

An "anonymous work" is a work on the copies or phonorecords of which no natural person is identified as author.

"Audio visual works" are works that consist of a series of related images which are intrinsically intended to be shown by the use of machines or devices such as projectors, viewers, or electronic equipment, together with accompanying sounds, if any, regardless of the nature of the material objects, such as films or tapes, in which the works are embodied.

The "best edition" of a work is the edition, published in the United States at any time before the date of deposit, that the Library of Congress determines to be most suitable for its purposes.

A person's "children" are that person's immediate offspring, whether legitimate or not, and any children legally adopted by that person.

A "collective work" is a work formed by the collection and assembling of preexisting materials or of data that are selected, coordinated, or arranged in such a way that the resulting work as a whole constitutes an original work of authorship. The term "compilation" includes collective works.

A "compilation" is a work formed by the collection and assembling of preexisitng materials or of data that are selected, coordinated, or arranged in such a way that the resulting work as a whole constitutes an original work of authorship. The term "compilation" includes collective works.

"Copies" are material objects, other than phonorecords, in which a work is fixed by any method now known or later developed, and from which the work can be perceived, reproduced, or otherwise communicated, either directly or with the aid of a machine or device. The term "copies" includes the material object, other than a phonorecord, in which the work is first fixed.

"Copyright owner," with respect to any one of the exclusive rights comprised in a copyright, refers to the owner of that particular right.

A work is "created" when it is fixed in a copy or phonorecord for the first time; where a work is prepared over a period of time, the portion of it that has been fixed at any particular time constitutes the work as of that time, and where the work has been prepared in different versions, each version constitutes a separate work.

A "derivative work" is a work based upon one or more preexisting works, such as a translation, musical arrangement, dramatization, fictionalization, motion picture version, sound recording, art reproduction, abridgement, condensation, or any other form in which a work may be recast, transformed, or adapted. A work consisting of editorial revisions, annotations, elaborations, or other modifications which, as a whole represent an original work of authorship, is a "derivative work."

A "device," "machine," or "process" is one now known or later developed.

To "display" a work means to show a copy of it, either directly or by means of a film, slide, television image, or any other device or process or, in the case of a motion picture or other audiovisual work, to show individual images nonsequentially.

A work is"fixed" in a tangible medium of expression when its embodiment in a copy or phonorecord, by or under the authority of the author, is sufficiently permanent or stable to permit it to be perceived, reproduced, or otherwise communicated for a period of more than transitory duration. A work consisting of sounds, images, or both, that are being transmitted, is "fixed" for purposes of this title if a fixation of the work is being made simultaneously with its transmission.

The terms "including" and "such as" are illustrative and not limitative.

A "joint work" is a work prepared by two or more authors with the intention that their contributions be merged into inseparable or interdependent parts of a unitary whole.

"Literary works" are works, other than audiovisual works, expressed in words, numbers, or other verbal or numerical symbols or indicia, regardless of the nature of the material objects, such as books, periodicals, manuscripts, phonorecords, film, tapes, disks, or cards, in which they are embodied.

"Motion pictures" are audiovisual works consisting of a series of related images which, when shown in succession, impart an impression of motion, together with accompanying sounds, if any.

"To "perform" a work means to recite, render, play, dance, or act it, either directly or by means of any device or process or, in the case of a motion picture or other audiovisual work, to show its images in any sequence or to make the sounds accompanying it audible.

"Phonorecords" are material objects in which sounds, other than those accompanying a motion picture or other audiovisual work, are fixed by any method now known or later developed, and from which the sounds can be perceived, reproduced, or otherwise communicated, either directly or with the aid of a machine or device. The term "phonorecords" includes the material object in which the sounds are first fixed.

"Pictorial, graphic, and sculptural works" include two-dimensional and three-dimensional works of fine, graphic, and applied art, photographs, prints and art reproductions, maps, globes, charts, technical drawings, diagrams, and models. Such works shall include works of artistic craftsmanship insofar as their form but not their mechanical or utilitarian aspects are concerned; the design of a useful article, as defined in this section, shall be considered a pictorial, graphic, or sculptural work only if, and only to the extent that, such design incorporates pictorial, graphic, or sculptural features that can be identified separately from, and are capable of exisiting independently of, the utilitarian aspects of the article.

A "pseudonymous work" is a work on the copies or phonorecords of which the author is identified under a fictitious name.

"Publication" is the distribution of copies or phonorecords of a work to the public by sale or other transfer of ownership, or by rental, lease, or lending. The offering to distribute copies or phonorecords to a group of persons for purposes of further distribution, public performance, or public display, constitutes publication. A public performance or display of a work does not of itself constitute publication.

To perform or display a work "publicly" means—

(1) to perform or display it at a place open to the public or at any place where a substantial number of persons outside of a normal circle of a family and its social acquaintances is gathered; or

(2) to transmit or otherwise communicate a performance or display of the work to a place specified by clause (1) or to the public, by means of any device or process, whether the memebers of the public capable of receiving the performance or display receive it in the same place or in separate places and at the same time or at different times.

"Sound recordings" are works that result from the fixation of a series of musical, spoken, or other sounds, but not including the sounds accompanying a motion picture or other audiovisual work, regardless of the nature of the material objects, such as disks, tapes, or other phonorecords, in which they are embodied.

"State" includes the District of Columbia and the Commonwealth of Puerto Rico, and any territories to which this title is made applicable by an Act of Congress.

A "transfer of copyright ownership" is an assignment, mortgage, exclusive license, or any other conveyance, alienation, or hypothecation of a copyright or of any of the exclusive rights comprised in a copyright, whether or not it is limited in time or place of effect, but not including a non-exclusive license.

A "transmission program" is a body of material that, as an aggregate, has been produced for the sole purpose of transmission to the public in sequence and as a unit.

To "transmit" a performance or display is to communicate it by any device or process whereby images or sounds are received beyond the place from which they are sent.

The "United States," when used in a geographical sense, comprises the several States, the District of Columbia and the Commonwealth of Puerto Rico, and the organized territories under the jurisdiction of the United States Government.

A "useful article" is an article having an intrinsic utilitarian function that is not merely to portray the appearance of the article or to convey information. An article that is normally a part of a useful article is considered a "useful article."

The author's "widow" or "widower" is the author's surviving spouse under the law of the author's domicile at the time of his or her death, whether or not the spouse has later remarried.

A "work made for hire" is—

(1) a work prepared by an employee within the scope of his or her employment; or

(2) a work specially ordered or commissioned for use as a contribution to a collective work, as a part of a motion picture or other audiovisual work, as a translation, as a supplementary work, as a compilation, as an instructional text, as a test, as answer material for a test, or as an atlas, if the parties expressly agree in a

written instrument signed by them that the work shall be considered a work made for hire. For the purpose of the foregoing sentence, a "supplementary work" is a work prepared for publication as a secondary adjunct to a work by another author for the purpose of introduction, concluding, illustrating, explaining, revising, commenting upon, or assisting in the use of the other work, such as forewords, afterwords, pictorial illustrations, maps, charts, tables, editorial notes, musical arrangements, answer material for tests, biliographies, appendixes, and indexes, and an "instructional text" is a literary, pictorial, or graphic work prepared for publication and with the purpose of use in systematic instructional activities.

A "computer program" is a set of statements or instructions to be used directly or indirectly in a computer in order to bring about a certain result.

Section 102. Subject matter of copyright: In general

(a) Copyright protection subsists, in accordance with this title, in original works of authorship fixed in any tangible medium of expression, now known or later developed, from which they can be perceived, reproduced, or otherwise communicated, either directly or with the aid of a machine or device. Works of authorship include the following categories:

(1) literary works;
(2) musical works, including any accompanying words;
(3) dramatic works, including any accompanying music;
(4) pantomimes and choreographic works;
(5) pictorial, graphic, and sculptural works;
(6) motion picture and other audiovisual works; and
(7) sound recordings.

(b) In no case does copyright protection for an original work of authorship extend to any idea, procedure, process, system, method of operation, concept, principle, or discovery, regardless of the form in which it is described, explained, illustrated, or embodied in such work.

Section 103. Subject matter of copyright: Compilations and derivative works

(a) The subject matter of copyright as specified by section 102 includes compilations and derivative works, but protection for a work employing preexisting material in which copyright subsists does not extend to any part of the work in which such material has been used unlawfully.

(b) The copyright in a compilation or derivative work extends only to the material contributed by the author of such work, as distinguished from the preexisitng material employed in the work, and does not imply any exclusive right in the preexisting material. The copyright in such work is independent of, and does not affect or enlarge the scope, duration, ownership, or subsistence of, any copyright protection in the preexisting material.

Section 104. Subject matter of copyright: National origin

(a) Unpublished Works.—The works specified by sections 102 and 103, while unpublished, are subject to protection under this title without regard to the nationality or domicile of the author.

(b) Published Works.—The works specified by sections 102 and 103, when published, are subject to protection under this title if—

(1) on the date of first publication, one or more of the authors is a national or domiciliary of the United States, or is a national, domiciliary, or sovereign authority of a foreign nation that is a party to a copyright treaty to which the United States is also a

party, or is a stateless person, wherever that person may be domiciled; or

(2) the work is first published in the United States or in a foreign nation that, on the date of first publication, is a party to the Universal Copyright Convention; or

(3) the work is first published by the United States or any of its specialized agencies, or by the Organizations of American States; or

(4) the work comes within the scope of a Presidential proclamation. Whenever the President finds that a particular foreign nation extends, to works by authors who are nationals or domiciliaries of the United States or to works that are first published in the United States, copyright protection on substantially the same basis as that on which the foreign nation extends protection to works of its own nationals and domiciliaries and works first published in that nation, the President may by proclamation extend protection under this title to works of which one or more of the authors is, on the date of first publication, a national domiciliary, or sovereign authority of that nation, or which was first published in that nation. The President may revise, suspend, or revoke any such proclamation or impose any conditions or limitations on protection under a proclamation.

Section 105. Subject matter of copyright: United States Government works

Copyright protection under this title is not available for any work of the United States Government, but the United States Government is not precluded from receiving and holding copyrights transferred to it by assignment, bequest, or otherwise.

Section 106. Exclusive rights in copyrighted works

Subject to sections 107 through 108, the owner of copyright under this title has the exclusive rights to do and to authorize any of the following:

(1) to reproduce the copyrighted work in copies or phonorecords;

(2) to prepare derivative works based upon the copyrighted work;

(3) to distribute copies or phonorecords of the copyrighted work to the public by sale or other transfer of ownership, or by rental, lease, or lending;

(4) in the case of literary, musical, dramatic, and choreographic works, pantomimes, and motion pictures and other audiovisual works, to perform the copyrighted work publicly; and

(5) in the case of literary, musical, dramatic, and choreographic works, pantomimes, and pictorial, graphic, or sculptural works, including the individual images of a motion picture or other audiovisual work, to display the copyrighted work publicly.

Section 107. Limitations on exclusive rights: Fair use

Notwithstanding the provisions of section 106, the fair use of a copyrighted work, including such use by reproduction in copies or phonorecords or by any other means specified by that section, for purposes such as criticism, comment, news reporting, teaching (including multiple copies for classroom use), scholarship, or research, is not an infringement of copyright. In determining whether the use made of a work in any particular case is a fair use the factors to be considered shall include—

(1) the purpose and character of the use, including whether such use is of a commercial nature or is for nonprofit educational purposes;

(2) the nature of the copyrighted work;

(3) the amount and substantiality of the portion used in relation to the copyrighted work as a whole; and

(4) the effect of the use upon the potential market for or value of the copyrighted work.

Section 108. Limitations on exclusive rights: Reproduction by libraries and archives

(a) Notwithstanding the provisions of section 106, it is not an infringement of copyright for a library or archives, or any of its employees acting within the scope of their employment, to reproduce no more than one copy or phonorecord of a work, or to distribute such copy or phonorecord, under the conditions specified by this section, if—

(1) the reproduction or distribution is made without any purpose of direct or indirect commercial advantage;

(2) the collections of the library or archives are (i) open to the public, or (ii) available not only to researchers affiliated with the library or archives or with the institution of which it is a part, but also to other persons doing research in a specialized field; and

(3) the reproduction or distribution of the work includes a notice of copyright.

(b) The rights of reproduction and distribution under this section apply to a copy or phonorecord of an unpublished work duplicated in facsimile form solely for purposes of preservation and security or for deposit for research use in another library or archives of the type described by clause (2) of subsection (a), if the copy or phonorecord reproduced is currently in the collections of the library or archives.

(c) The right of reproduction under this section applies to a copy or phonorecord of a published work duplicated in facsimile form solely for the purpose of replacement of a copy or phonorecord that is damaged, deteriorating, lost, or stolen, if the library or archives has, after a reasonable effort, determined that an unused replacement cannot be obtained at a fair price.

(d) The rights of reproduction and distribution under this section apply to a copy, made from the collection of a library or archives where the user makes his or her request or from that of another library or archives, of no more than one article or other contribution to a copyrighted collection or periodical issue, or to a copy or phonorecord of a small part of any other copyrighted work, if—

(1) the copy or phonorecord becomes the property of the user, and the library or archives has had no notice that the copy or phonorecord would be used for any purpose other than private study, scholarship, or research; and

(2) the library or archives displays prominently, at the place where orders are accepted, and includes on its order form, a warning of copyright in accordance with requirements that the Register of Copyrights shall prescribe by regulation.

(e) The rights of reproduction and distribution under this section apply to the entire work, or to a substantial part of it, made from the collection of a library or archives where the user makes his or her request or from that of another library or archives, if the library or archives has first determined, on the basis of a reasonable investigation, that a copy or phonorecord of the copyrighted work cannot be obtained at a pair price, if—

(1) the copy or phonorecord becomes the property of the user, and the library or archives has had no notice that the copy or phonorecord would be used for any purpose other than private study, scholarship, or research; and

(2) the library or archives displays prominently, at the place where orders are accepted, and includes on its order form a warning of copyright in accordance with requirements that the Register of Copyrights shall prescribe by regulation.

(f) Nothing in this section—

(1) shall be construed to impose liability for copyright infringement upon a library or archives or its employees for the unsupervised use of reproducing equipment located on its premises: Provided, That such equipment displays a notice that the making of a copy may be subject to the copyright law;

(2) excuses a person who uses such reproducing equipment or who requests a copy or phonorecord under subsection (d) from liability for copyright infringement for any such act, or for any later use of such copy or phonorecord, if it exceeds fair use as provided by section 107;

(3) shall be construed to limit the reproduction and distribution by lending of a limited number of copies and excerpts by a library or archives of an audiovisual news program, subject to clauses (1), (2), and (3) of subsection (a); or

(4) in any way affects the right of fair use as provided by section 107, or any contractual obligations assumed at any time by the library or archives when it obtained a copy or phonorecord of a work in its collections.

(g) The rights of reproduction and distribution under this section extend to the isolated and unrelated reproduction or distribution of a single copy or phonorecord of the same material on separate occasions, but do not extend to cases where the library or archives, or its employee—

(1) is aware or has substantial reason to believe that it is engaging in the related or concerted reproduction or distribution of multiple copies or phonorecords of the same material, whether made on one occasion or over a period of time, and whether intended for aggregate use by one or more individuals or for separate use by the individual members of a group; or

(2) engages in the systematic reproduction or distribution of single or multiple copies or phonorecords of material described in subsection (d): Provided, That nothing in this clause prevents a library or archives from participating in interlibrary arrangements that do not have, as their purpose or effect, that the library or archives receiving such copies or phonorecords for distribution does so in such aggregate quantities as to substitute for subscription to or purchase of such work.

(h) The rights of reproduction and distribution under this section do not apply to a musical work, a pictorial, graphic or sculptural work, or a motion picture or other audiovisual owrk other than an audiovisual work dealing with news, except that no such limitation shall apply with respect to rights granted by subsections (b) and (c), or with respect to pictorial or graphic works published as illustrattions, diagrams, or similar adjuncts to works of which copies are reproduced or distribued in accordance with subsections (d) and (e).

(i) Five years from the effective date of this Act, and at five-year intervals thereafter, the Register of Copyrights, after consulting with representatives of authors, book and periodical publishers, and other owners of copyrighted materials, and with representatives of library users and librarians, shall submit to the Congress a report setting forth the extent to which this section has achieved the intended statutory balancing of the rights of creators, and the needs of users. The report should also describe any problems that may have arisen, and present legislative or other recommendations, if warranted.

Section 109. Limitations on exclusive rights: Effect of transfer of particular copy or phonorecord

(a) Notwithstanding the provisions of section 106(3), the owner of a particular copy or phonorecord lawfully made under this title, or any person authorized by such owner, is entitled, without the authority of the copyright owner, to sell or otherwise dispose of the possession of that copy or phonorecord.

(b)(1) Notwithstanding the provisions of subsection (a), unless authorized by the owners of copyright in the sound recording and in the musical works embodied therein, the owner of a particular phonorecord may not, for purposes of direct or indirect commercial advantage, dispose of, or authorize the disposal of, the possession of that phonorecord by rental, lease, or lending, or by any other act or practice in the nature of rental, lease, or lending. Nothing in the preceding sentence shall apply to the rental, lease, or lending of a phonorecord for nonprofit purposes by a nonprofit library or nonprofit educational institution.

(2) Nothing in this subsection shall affect any provision of the antitrust laws. For purposes of the preceding sentence, "antitrust laws" has the meaning given that term in the first section of the Clayton Act and includes section 5 of the Federal Trade Commission Act to the extent that section relates to unfair methods of competition.

(3) Any person who distributes a phonorecord in violation of clause (1) is an infringer of copyright under section 501 of this title and is subject to the remedies set forth in sections 502, 503, 504, 505, and 509. Such violation shall not be a criminal offense under section 506 or cause such person to be subject to the criminal penalties set forth in section 2319 of title 18.

(c) Notwithstanding the provisions of section 106(5), the owner of a particular copy lawfully made under this title, or any person authorized by such owner, is entitled, without the authority of the copyright owner, to display that copy publicly, either directly or by the projection of no more than one image at a time, to viewers present at the place where the copy is located.

(d) The privileges prescribed by subsections (a) and (b) do not, unless authorized by the copyright owner, extend to any person who has acquired possession of the copy or phonorecord from the copyright owner, by rental lease, loan, or otherwise, without acquiring ownership of it.

Section 110. Limitations on exclusive rights: Exemption of certain performances and displays

Notwithstanding the provisions of section 106, the following are not infringements of copyright:

(1) performance or display of a work by instructors or pupils in the course of face-to-face teaching activities of a nonprofit educational institution, in a classroom or similar place devoted to instruction, unless, in the case

of a motion picture or other audiovisual work, the performance, or the display of individual images, is given by means of a copy that was not lawfully made under this title, and that the person responsible for the performance knew or had reason to believe was not lawfully made;

(2) performance of a nondramatic literary or musical work or display of a work, by or in the course of a transmission, if—

(A) the performance or display is a regular part of the systematic instructional activities of a governmental body or a nonprofit educational institution; and

(B) the performance or display is directly related and of material asistance to the teaching content of the transmission; and

(C) the transmission is made primarily for—

(i) reception in classrooms or similar places normally devoted to instruction, or

(ii) reception by persons to whom the transmission is directed because their disabilities or other special circumstances prevent their attendance in classrooms or similar places normally devoted to instruction, or

(iii) reception by officers or employees of governmental bodies as a part of their official duties or employment;

(3) performance of a nondramatic literary or musical work or of a dramatico-musical work of a religious nature, or display of a work, in the course of services at a place of worship or other religious assembly;

(4) performance of a nondramatic literary or musical work otherwise than in a transmission to the public, without any purpose of direct or indirect commercial advantage and without payment of any fee or other compensation for the performance to any of its performers, promoters, or organizers, if—

(A) there is no direct or indirect admission charge; or

(B) the proceeds, after deducting the reasonable costs of producing the performance, are used exclusively for educational, religious, or charitable purposes and not for private financial gain, except where the copyright owner has served notice of objection to the performance under the following conditions;

(i) the notice shall be in writing and signed by the copyright owner or such owner's duly authorized agent; and

(ii) the notice shall be served on the person responsible for the performance at least seven days before the date of the performance, and shall state the reasonas for the objection; and

(iii) the notice shall comply, in form, content, and manner of service, with requirements that the Register of Copyrights shall prescribe by regulation;

(5) communication of a transmission embodying a performance or display of a work by the public reception of the transmission on a single receiving apparatus of a kind commonly used in private homes, unless—

(A) a direct charge is made to see or hear the transmission; or

(B) the transmission thus received is further transmitted to the public;

(6) performance of a nondramatic musical work by a governmental body or a nonprofit agricultural or horticultural organization, in the course of an annual agricultural or horticultural fair or exhibition conducted by such body or organization; the exemption provided by this clause shall extend to any liability for copyright infringement that would otherwise be imposed on such body or organiztaion, under doctrines of vicarious liability or related infringement, for a performance by a concessionnaire, business establishment, or other person at such fair or exhibition, but shall not excuse any such person from liability for the performance;

(7) performances of a nondramatic musical work by a vending establishment open to the public at large without any direct or indirect admission charge, where the sole purpose of the performance is to promote the retail sale of copies or phonorecords of the work, and the performance is not transmitted beyond the place where the establishment is located and is within the immediate area where the sale is occurring;

(8) performance of a nondramatic literary work, by or in the course of a transmission specifically designed for and primarily directed to blind or other handicapped persons who are unable to read normal printed material as a result of their handicap, or deaf or other handicapped persons who are unable to hear the aural signals accompanying a transmission of visual signals, if the performance is made without any purpose of direct or indirect commercial advantage and its transmission is made through the facilities of: (i) a governmental body; or (ii) a noncommercial educational broadcast station (as defined in section 397 of title 47); or (iii) a radio subcarrier authorization (as defined in 47 CFR 73.293—73.295 and 73.593—73.595); or (iv) a cable system (as defined in section 111 (f)).

(9) performance on a single occasion of a dramatic literary work published at least ten years before the date of the performance, by or in the course of a transmission specifically designed for and primarily directed to blind or other handicapped persons who are unable to read normal printed material as a result of their handicap, if the performance is made without any purpose of direct or indirect commercial advantage and

its transmission is made through the facilities of a radio subcarrier authorization referred to in clause (8) (iii), Provided, That the provisions of this clause shall not be applicable to more than one performance of the same work by the same performers or under the auspices of the same organization.

(10) notwithstanding paragraph 4 above, the following is not an infringement of copyright: performance of a nondramatic literary or musical work in the course of a social function which is organized and promoted by a nonprofit veterans' organization or a nonprofit fraternal organization to which the general public is not invited, but not including the invitees of the organizations, if the proceeds from the performance, after deducting the reasonable costs of producing the performance, are used exclusively for charitable purposes and not for financial gain. For purposes of this section the social functions of any college or university fraternity or sorority shall not be included unless the social function is held solely to raise funds for a specific charitable purpose.

Section 111. Limitations on exclusive rights: Secondary transmissions

(a) Certain Secondary Transmissions Exempted.—The secondary transmission of a primary transmission embodying a performance or display of a work is not an infringement of copyright if—

(1) the secondary transmission is is not made by a cable system, and consists entirely of the relaying, but the management of a hotel, apartment house, or similar establishment, of signals transmitted by a broadcast station licensed by the Federal Communications Commission, within the local service area of such station, to the private lodgings of guests or residents of such establishment, and no direct charge is made to see or hear the secondary transmission; or

(2) the secondary transmission is made soley for the purpose and under the conditions specified by clause (2) of section 110; or

(3) the secondary transmission is made by any carrier who has no direct or indirect control over the content or selection of the primary transmission or over the particular recipients of the secondary transmission, and whose activities with respect to the secondary transmission consist solely of providing wires, cables, or other communications channels for the use of others: Provided, That the provisions of this clause extend only to the activities of said carrier with respect to secondary transmissions and do not exempt from liability the activities of others with respect to their own primary or secondary transmissions; or

(4) the secondary transmission is not made by a cable system but is made by a governmental body, or other nonprofit organization, without any purpose of direct or indirect commercial advantage , and without

charge to the recipients of the secondary transmission other than assessments necessary to defray the actual and reasonable costs of maintaining and operating the secondary transmission service.

(b) Secondary Transmission of Primary Transmission to Controlled Group.—Notwithstanding the provisions of subsections (a) and (c), the secondary transmission to the public of a primary transmission embodying a performance or display of a work is actionable as an act of infringement under section 501, and is fully subject to the remedies provided by sections 502 through 506 and 509, if the primary transmission is not made for reception by the public at large but is controlled and limited to reception by particular members of the public: Provided, however, That such secondary transmission is not actionable as an act of infringement if—

(1) the primary transmission is made by a broadcast station licensed by the Federal Communications Commission; and

(2) the carriage of the signals comprising the secondary transmission is required under the rules, regulations, or authorizations of the Federal Communications Commission; and

(3) the signal of the primary transmitter is not altered or changed in any way by the secondary transmitter.

(c) Secondary Transmissions by Cable Systems.—

(1) Subject to the provisions of clauses (2), (3), and (4) of this subsection, secondary transmissions to the public by a cable system of a primary transmission made by a broadcast station licensed by the Federal Communications Commission or by an appropriate governmental authority of Canada or Mexico embodying a performance or display of a work shall be subject to compulsory licensing upon compliance with the requirements of subsection (d) where the carriage of the signals comprising the secondary transmission is permissible under the rules regulations, or authorizations of the Federal Communications Commission.

(2) Notwithstanding the provisions of clause (1) of this subsection, the willful or repeated secondary transmission to the public by a cable system of a primary transmission made by a broadcast station licensed by the Federal Communications Commission or by an appropriate governmental authority of Canada or Mexico and embodying a performance or display of a work is actionable as an act of infringement under section 501, and is fully subject to the remedies provided by sections 502 through 506 and 509, in the following cases:

(A) where the carriage of the signals comprising the secondary transmission is not permissible under the rules, regulations, or authorizations of the Federal Communications Commission; or

(B) where the cable system has not recorded the notice specified by subsection (d) and deposited the statement of account and royalty fee required by subsection (d).

(3) Notwithstanding the provisions of clause (1) of

this subsection and subject to the provisions of subsection (e) of this section, the secondary transmission to the public by a cable system of a primary transmission made by a broadcast station licensed by the Federal Communications Commission or by an appropriate governmental authority of Canada or Mexico and embodying a performance or display of a work is actionable as an act of infringement under section 501, and is fully subject to the remedies provided by sections 502 through 506 and sections 509 and 510, if the content of the particular program in which the performance or display is embodied, or any commercial advertising or station announcements transmitted by the primary transmitter during, or immediately before or after, the transmission of such program, is in any way willfully altered by the cable system through changes, deletions, or additions, except for the alteration, deletion, or substitution of commercial advertisements performed by those engaged in television commercial advertising market research: Provided, That the research company has obtained the prior consent of the advertiser who has purchased the original commercial advertisement, the television station broadcasting that commercial advertisement, and the cable system performing the secondary transmission: And provided further, That such commercial alteration, deletion, or substitution is not performed for the purpose of deriving income from the sale of that commercial time.

(4) Notwithstanding the provisions of clause (1) of this subsection, the secondary transmission to the public by a cable system of a primary transmission made by a broadcast station licensed by an appropriate governmental authority of Canada or Mexico and embodying a performance or display of a work is actionable as an act of infringement under section 501, and is fully subject to the remedies provided by sections 502 through 506 and section 509, if (A) with respect to Canadian signals, the community of the cable system is located more than 150 miles from the United States-Canadian border and is also located south of the forty-second parallel of latitude, or (b) with respect to Mexican signals, the secondary transmissions made by a cable system which received the primary transmission by means other than direct interception of a free space radio wave emitted by such broadcast television station, unless prior to April 15, 1976, such cable system was actually carrying, or was specifically authorized to carry, the signal of such foreign station on the system pursuant to the rules, regulations, or authorizations of the Federal Communications Commision.

(d) Compulsory License for Secondary Transmissions by Cable Systems.—

(1) For any secondary transmission to be subject to compulsory licensing under subsection (c), the cable system shall, at least one month before the date of the

commencement of operations of the cable system or within one hundred and eighty days after the enactment of this Act, whichever is later, and thereafter within thirty days after each occasion on which the ownership or control or the signal carriage complement of the cable system changes, record in the Copyright Office a notice including a statement of the identity and address of the person who owns or operates the secondary transmission service or has power to exercise primary control over it, together with the name and location of the primary transmitter or primary transmitters whose signals are regularly carried by the cable system, and thereafter, from time to time, such further information as the Register of Copyrights, after consultation with the Copyright Royalty Tribunal (if and when the Tribunal has been constituted), shall prescribe by regulation to carry out the purpose of this clause.

(2) A cable system whose secondary transmissions have been subject to compulsory licensing under subsection (c) shall, on a semiannual basis, deposit with the Register of Copyrights, in accordance with requirements that the Register shall, after consultation with the Copyright Royalty Tribunal (if and when the Tribunal has been constituted), prescribe by regulation—

(A) a statement of account, covering the six months next preceding, specifying the number of channels on which the cable system made secondary transmissions to its subscribers, the names and locations of all primary transmitters whose transmissions were further transmitted by the cable system, the total number of subscribers, the gross amounts paid to the cable system for the basic service of providing secondary transmissions of primary broadcast transmitters, and such other data as the Register of Copyrights may, after consultation with the Copyright Royalty Tribunal (if and when the Tribunal has been constituted), from time to time prescribe by regulation. Such statement shall also include a special statement of account covering any nonnetwork television programming that was carried by the cable system in whole or in part beyond the local service area of the primary transmitter, under rules, regulations, or authorizations of the Federal Communications Commission permitting the substitution or addition of signals under certain circumstances, together with logs showing the times, dates, stations, and programs involved in such substituted or added carriage; and

(B) except in the case of a cable system whose royalty is specified in subclause (C) or (D), a total royalty fee for the period covered by the statement, computed on the basis of specified percentages of the gross receipts from subscribers to the cable service during said period for the basic service of providing secondary transmissions of primary broadcast transmitters, as follows:

(i) 0.675 of 1 per centum of such gross receipts for the privilege of further transmitting any nonnetwork programing of a primary transmitter in whole or in part beyond the local service area of such primary transmitter, such amount to be applied against the fee, if any, payable pursuant to paragraphs (ii) through (iv);

(ii) 0.675 of 1 per centum of such gross receipts for the first distant signal equivalent;

(iii) 0.425 of 1 per centum of such gross receipts for each of the second, third, and fourth distant signal equivalents;

(iv) 0.2 of 1 percentum of such gross receipts for the fifth distant signal equivalent and each additional distant signal equivalent thereafter; and

in computing the amounts payable under paragraph (ii) through (iv), above, any fraction of a distant signal equivalent shall be computed at its fractional value and, in the case of any cable system located partly within and partly without the local service area of a primary transmitter, gross receipts shall be limited to those gross receipts derived from subscribers located without the local service area of such primary transmitter; and

(C) if the actual gross receipts paid by subscribers to a cable system for the period covered by the statement for the basic service of providing secondary transmissions of primary broadcast transmitters total $80,000 or less, gross receipts of the cable system for the purpose of this subclause shall be computed by subtracting from such actual gross receipts the amount by which $80,000 exceeds such actual gross receipts, except that in no case shall a cable system's gross receipts be reduced to less than $3,000. The royalty fee payable under this subclause shall be 0.5 of 1 per centum, regardless of the number of distant signal equivalents, if any; and

(D) if the actual receipts paid by subscribers to a cable system for the period covered by the statement, for the basic service of providing secondary transmissions of primary broadcast transmitters, are more than $80,000 but less than $160,000, the royalty fee payable under this subsclause shall be (i) 0.5 of 1 per centum of any gross receipts up to $80,000; and (ii) 1 per centum of any gross receipts in excess of $80,000 but less than $160,000, regardless of the number of distant signal equivalents, if any.

(3) The Register of Copyrights shall receive all fees deposited under this section and, after deducting the reasonable costs incurred by the Copyright Office under

this section, shall deposit the balance in the Treasury of the United States, in such manner as the Secretary of the Treasury directs. All funds held by the Secretary of the Treasury shall be invested in interest-bearing United States securities for later distribution with interest by the Copyright Royalty Tribunal as provided by this title. The Register shall submit to the Copyright Royalty Tribunal, on a semiannual basis, a compilation of all statements of account covering the relevant six-month period provided by clause (2) of this subsection.

(4) The royalty fees thus deposited shall, in accordance with the procedures provided by clause (5), be distributed to those among the following copyright owners who claim that their works were the subject of secondary transmissions by cable systems during the relevant semiannual period:

(A) any such owner whose work was included in a secondary transmission made by a cable system of a nonnetwork television program in whole or in part beyond the local service area of the primary transmitter; and

(B) any such owner whose work was included in a secondary transmission identified in a special statement of account deposited under clause (2)(A); and

(C) any such owner whose work was included in nonnetwork programing consisting exclusively of aural signals carried by a cable system in whole or in part beyond the local service area of the primary transmitter of such programs.

(5) The royalty fees thus deposited shall be distributed in accordance with the following procedures:

(A) During the month of July in each year, every person claiming to be entitled to compulsory license fees for secondary transmissions shall file a claim with the Copyright Royalty Tribunal, in accordance with requirements that the Tribunal shall prescribe by regulation. Notwithstanding any provisions of the antitrust laws, for purposes of this clause any claimants may agree among themselves as to the proportionate division of compulsory licensing fees among them, may lump their claims together and file them jointly or as a single claim, or may designate a common agent to receive payment on their behalf.

(B) After the first day of August of each year, the Copyright Royalty Tribunal shall determine whether there exists a controversy concerning the distribution of royalty fees. If the Tribunal determines that no such controversy exists, it shall, after deducting its reasonable administrative costs under this section, distribute such fees to the copyright owners entitled, or to their designated agents. If the Tribunal finds the existence of a controversy, it shall, pursuant to chapter 8 of this title, conduct a proceeding to determine the distribution of royalty fees.

(C) During the pendency of any proceeding under this subsection, the Copyright Royalty Tribunal shall withhold from distribution an amount sufficient to satisfy all claims with respect to which a controversy exists, but shall have discretion to proceed to distribute any amounts that are not in controversy.

Section 111. Limitations on exclusive rights: Secondary transmission—continued

(e) Nonsimultaneous Secondary Transmissions by Cable Systems.—

(1) Notwithstanding those provisions of the second paragraph of subsection (f) relating to nonsimultaneous secondary transmissions by a cable system, any such transmissions are actionable as an act of infringement under section 501, and are fully subject to the remedies provided by sections 502 through 506 and sections 509 and 510, unless—

(A) the program on the videotape is transmitted no more than one time to the cable system's subscribers; and

(B) the copyrighted program, episode, or motion picture videotape, including the commercials contained within such program, episode, or picture, is transmitted without deletion or editing; and

(C) an owner or officer of the cable system (i) prevents the duplication of the videotape while in the possessin of the system, (ii) prevents unauthorized duplication while in the possession of the facility making the videotape for the system if the system owns or controls the facility, or takes reasonable precautions to prevent such duplication if it does not own or control the facility, (iii) takes adequate precautions to prevent duplication while the tape is being transported, and (iv) subject to clause (2), erases or destroys, or causes the erasure or destruction of, the videotape; and

(D) within forty-five days after the end of each calendar quarter, an owner or officer of the cable system executes an affidavit attesting (i) to the steps and precautions taken to prevent duplication of the videotape, and (ii) subject to clause (2), to the erasure or destruction of all videotapes made or used during such quarter; and

(E) such owner or officer places or causes each such affidavit, and affidavits received pursuant to clause (2)(C), to be placed in a file, open to public inspection, at such system's main office in the community where the transmission is made or in the nearest community where such system maintains an office; and

(F) the nonsimultaneous transmission is one that the cable system would be authorized to transmit under the rules, regulations, and authorizations of the Federal Communications Commission in effect at the time of the nonsimultaneous transmission if the transmission had been made simultaneously, except that this subclause shall not apply to inadvertent or accidental transmissions.

(2) If a cable system transfers to any person a videotape of a program nonsimultaneously transmitted by it, such transfer is actionable as an act of infringement under section 501, and is fully subject to the remedies provided by sections 502 through 506 and 509, except that, pursuant to a written, nonprofit contract providing for the equitable sharing of the costs of such videotape and its transfer, a videotape nonsimultaneously transmitted by it, in accordance with clause (1), may be transferred by one cable system in Alaska to another system in Alaska, by one cable system in Hawaii permitted to make such nonsimultaneous transmissions to another such cable system in Hawaii, or by one cable system in Guam, the Northern Mariana Islands, or the Trust Territory of the Pacific Islands, to another cable system in any of those three territories, if—

(A) each such contract is available for public inspection in the offices of the cable systems involved, and a copy of such contract is filed, within thirty days after such contract is entered into with the Copyright Office (which Office shall make each such contract available for public inspection); and

(B) the cable system to which the videotape is transferred complies with clause (1) (A), (B), (C) (i), (iii), and (iv), and (D) through (F); and

(C) such system provides a copy of the affidavit required to be made in accordance with clause (1) (D) to each cable system making a previous nonsimultaneous transmission of the same videotape.

(3) This subsection shall not be construed to supersede the exclusivity protection provisions of any existing agreement, or any such agreement hereafter entered into, between a cable system and a television broadcast station in the area in which the cable system is located, or a network with which such station is affiliated.

(4) As used in this subsection, the term "videotape", and each of its variant forms, means the reproduction of the images and sounds of a program or programs broadcast by a television broadcast station licensed by the Federal Communications Commission, regardless of the nature of the material objects, such as tapes or films, in which the reproduction is embodied.

(f) Definitions.— As used in this section, the following terms and their variant forms mean the following:

A "primary transmission" is a transmission made to the public by the transmitting facility whose signals are being received and further transmittd by the secondary transmission service, regardless of where or when the performance or display was first transmitted.

A "secondary transmission" is the further

transmitting of a primary transmission simultaneously with the primary transmission, or nonsimultaneously with the primary transmission if by a "cable system" not located in whole or in part within the boundary of the forty-eight contiguous States, Hawaii, or Puerto Rico: Provided however, That a nonsimultaneous further transmission by a cable system located in Hawaii of a primary transmission shall be deemed to be a secondary transmission if the carriage of the television broadcast signal comprising such further transmission is permissible under the rules, regulations, or authorizatons of the Federal Communications Commission.

A "cable system" is a facility, located in any State, Territory, Trust Territory, or Possession, that in whole or in part receives signals transmitted or programs broadcast by one or more television broadcast stations licensed by the Federal Communications Commission, and makes secondary transmissions of such signals or programs by wires, cables, or other communications channels to subscribing members of the public who pay for such service. For purposes of determining the royalty fee under subsection (d) (2), two or more cable systems in contiguous communities under common ownership or control or operating from one head-end shall be considered as one system.

The "local service area of a primary transmitter", in the case of a television broadcast station, comprises the area in which such station is entitled to insist upon its signal being retransmitted by a cable system pursuant to the rules, regulations, and authorizations of the Federal Communications Commission in effect on April 15, 1976, or in the case of a television broadcast station licensed by an appropriate governmental authority of Canada or Mexico, the area in which it would be entitled to insist upon its signal being retransmitted it it were a television broadcast station subject to such rules, regulations, and authorizations. The "local service area of a primary transmitter", in the case of a radio broadcast station, comprises the primary service area of such station, pursuant to the rules and regulations of the Federal Communications Commission.

A "distant signal equivalent" is the value assigned to the secondary transmission of any nonnetwork television programing carried by a cable system in whole or in part beyond the local service area of the primary transmitter of such programing. It is computed by assigning a value of one to each independent station and a value of one-quarter to each network station and noncommercial educational station for the nonnetwork programing so carried pursuant to the rules, regulations, and authorizations of the Federal Communications Commission. The foregoing values for independent, network, and noncommercial educational stations are subject, however, to the following exceptions and limitations. Where the rules and regulations of the Federal Communications Commission require a cable system to omit the further transmission of a particular program and such rules and regulations also permit the substitution of another program embodying a performance or display of a work in place of the omitted transmission, or where such rules and regulations in effect on the date of enactment of this Act permit a cable system, at its election, to effect such deletion and substitution of a nonlive program or to carry additional programs not transmitted by primary transmitters within whose local service area the cable system is located, no value shall be assigned for the substituted or additional program; where the rules, regulations, or authorizations of the Federal Communications Commission in effect on the date of enactment of this Act permit a cable system, at its election, to omit the further transmission of a particular program and such rules, regulations, or authorizations also permit the substitution of another program embodying a performance or display of a work in place of the omitted transmission, the value assigned for the substituted or additional program shall be, in the case of a live program, the value of one full distant signal equivalent multiplied by a fraction that has as its numerator the number of days in the year in which such substitution occurs and as its denominator the number of days in the year. In the case of a station carried pursuant to the late-night or specialty programing rules of the Federal Communications Commission, or a station carried on a part-time basis where full-time or speciality programing rules of the Federal Communications Commission, or a station carried on a part-time basis where full-time carriage is not possible because the cable system lacks the activated channel capacity to retransmit on a full-time basis all signals which it is authorized to carry, the values for independent, network, and noncommercial educational stations set forth above, as the case may be, shall be multiplied by a fraction which is equal to the ratio of the broadcast hours of such station carried by the cable system to the total broadcast hours of the station.

A "network station" is a television broadcast station that is owned or operated by, or affiliated with, one or more of the television networks in the United States providing nationwide transmissions, and that transmits a substantial part of the programing supplied by such networks for a substantial part of that station's typical broadcast day.

An "independent station" is a commercial television broadcat station other than a network station.

A "noncommercial educational station" is a television station that is a noncommercial educational broadcast station as defined in section 397 of title 47.

Section 112. Limitations on exclusive rights: Ephemeral recordings

(a) Notwithstanding the provisions of section 106, and except in the case of a motion picture or other audiovisual work, it is not an infringement of copyright for a transmitting organization entitled to transmit to the public a performance or display of a work, under a license or transfer of the copyright or under the limitations on exclusive rights in sound recordings specified by section 114(a), to make no more than one copy or phonorecord of a particular transmission program embodying the performance or display, if—

(1) the copy or phonorecord is retained and used solely by the transmitting organization that made it, and no further copies or phonorecords are reproduced from it; and

(2) the copy or phonorecord is used solely for the transmitting organization's own transmissions within its local service area, or for purposes of archival preservation or security; and

(3) unless preserved exclusively for archival purposes, the copy or phonorecord is destroyed within six months from the date the transmission program was first transmitted to the public.

(b) Notwithstanding the provisions of section 106, it is not an infringement of copyright for a governmental body or other nonprofit organization entitled to transmit a performance or display of a work, under section 110(2) or under the limitations on exclusive rights in sound recordings specified by section 114(a), to make no more than thirty copies or phonorecords of a particular transmission program embodying the peformance or display, if—

(1) no further copies or phonorecords are reproduced from the copies or phonorecords made under this clause; and

(2) except for one copy or phonorecord that may be preserved exclusively for archival purposes, the copies or phonorecords are destroyed within seven years from the date the transmission program was first transmitted to the public.

(c) Notwithstanding the provisions of section 106, it is not an infringement of copyright for a governmental body or other nonprofit organization to make for distribution no more than one copy or phonorecord, for each transmitting organization specified in clause (2) of this subsection, of a particular transmission program embodying a performance of a nondramatic musical work of a religious nature, or of a sound recording of such a musical work, if—

(1) there is no direct or indirect charge for making or distributing any such copies or phonorecords; and

(2) none of such copies or phonorecords is used for any performance other than a single transmission to the public by a transmitting organization entitled to transmit to the public a performance of the work under a license or transfer of the copyright; and

(3) except for one copy or phonorecord that may be preserved exclusively for archival purposes, the copies or phonorecords are all destroyed within one year from the date the transmission program was first transmitted to the public.

(d) Notwithstanding the provisions of section 106, it is not an infringement of copyright for a governmental body or other nonprofit organization entitled to transmit a performance of a work under section 110(8) to make no more than ten copies or phonorecords combodying the performance, or to permit the use of any such copy or phonorecord by any governmental body or nonprofit organization entitled to transmit a performance of a work under section 110(8), if—

(1) any such copy or phonorecord is retained and used solely by the organization that made it, or by a governmental body or nonprofit organization entitled to transmit a performance of a work under section 110(8),

and no further copies or phonorecords are reproduced from it; and

(2) any such copy or phonorecord is used solely for transmissions authorized under section 110(8), or for purposes of archival preservation or security; and

(3) the governmental body or nonprofit organization permitting any use of any such copy or phonorecord by any governmental body or nonprofit organization under this subsection does not make any charge for such use.

(e) The transmission program embodied in a copy or phonorecord made under this section is not subject to protection as a derivative work under this title except with the express consent of the owners of copyright in the preexisting works employed in the program.

Section 113. Scope of exclusive rights in pictorial,graphic, and sculptural works

(a) Subject to the provisions of subsections (b) and (c) of this section, the exclusive right to reproduce a copyrighted pictorial, graphic, or sculptural work in copies under section 106 includes the right to reproduce the work in or on any kind of article, whether useful or otherwise.

(b) This title does not afford, to the owner of copyright in a work that portrays a useful article as such, any greater or lesser rights with respect to the making, distribution, or display of the useful article so portrayed than those afforded to such works under the law, whether title 17 or the common law or statutes of a State, in effect on December 31, 1977, as held applicable and construed by a court in an action brought under this title.

(c) In the case of a work lawfully reproduced in useful articles that have been offered for sale or other distribution to the public, copyright does not include any right to prevent the making, distribution, or display of pictures or photographs of such articles in connection with advertisements or commentaries related to the distribution or display of such articles, or in connection with news reports.

Section 114. Scope of exclusive rights in sound recordings

(a) The exclusive rights of the owner of copyright in a sound recording are limited to the rights specified by clauses (1), (2), and (3) of section 106, and do not include any right of performance under section 106(4).

(b) The exclusive right of the owner of copyright in a sound recording under clause (1) of section 106 is limited to the right to duplicate the sound recording in the form of phonorecords, or of copies of motion pictures and other audiovisual works, that directly or indirectly recapture the actual sounds fixed in the recording. The exclusive right of the owner of copyright in a sound recording under clause (2) of section 106 is limited to the right to prepare a derivative work in which the actual sounds fixed in the sound recording are rearranged, remixed, or otherwise altered in sequence or quality. The exclusive rights of the owner of copyright in a sound recording under clauses (1) and (2) of section 106 do not extend to the making or duplication of another sound recording that consists entirely of an independent fixation of other sounds, even though such sounds imitate or simulate those in the copyrighted sound recording. The exclusive rights of the owner of copyright in a sound recording under clauses (1), (2), and (3) of section 106 do not apply to sound recordings included in educational television and radio programs (as defined in section 397 of title 47) distriubted or transmitted by or through public broadcasting entities (as defined by section 118(g)): Provided, That copies or phonorecords of said programs are not commercially distributed by or through public broadcasting entities to the general public.

(c) This section does not limit or impair the exclusive right to perform publicly, by means of a phonorecord, any of the works specified by section 106(4).

(d) On January 3, 1978, the Register of Copyrights, after consulting with representatives of owners of copyrighted materials, representatives of the broadcasting, recording, motion picture, entertainment industries, and arts organizations, representatives of organized labor and performers of copyrighted materials, shall submit to the Congress a report setting forth recommendations as to whether this section should be amended to provide for performers and copyright owners of copyrighted material any performance rights in such material. The report should describe the status of such rights in foreign countries, the views of major interested parties, and specific legislative or other recommendations, if any.

Section 115. Scope of exclusive rights in nondramatic musical works:

Compulsory license for making and distributing phonorecords

In the case of nondramatic musical works, the exclusive rights provided by clauses (1) and (3) of section 106, to make and to distribute phonorecords of such works, are subject to compulsory licensing under the conditions specified by this section.

(a) Availability and Scope of Compulsory License.—

(1) When phonorecords of a nondramatic musical work have been distributed to the public in the United States under the authority of the copyright owner, any other person may, by complying with the provisions of this section, obtain a compulsory license to make and distribute phonorecords of the work. A person may obtain a compulsory license only if his or her primary purpose in making phonorecords is to distribute them to the public for private use. A person may not obtain a compulsory license for use of the work in the making of phonorecords duplicating a sound recording fixed by another, unless: (i) such sound recording was fixed lawfully; and (ii) the making of the phonorecording or, if the sound recording was fixed before February 15, 1972, by any person who fixed the sound recording pursuant to an express license from the owner of the copyright in the musical work or pursuant to a valid compulsory license for use of such work in a sound recording.

(2) A compulsory license includes the privilege of making a musical arrangement of the work to the extent necessary to conform it to the style or manner of interpretation of the performance involved, but the arrangement shall not change the basic melody or fundamental character of the work, and shall not be subject to protection as a derivative work under this title, except with the express consent of the copyright owner.

(b) Notice of Intention To Obtain Compulsory License.—

(1) Any person who wishes to obtain a compulsory license under this section shall, before or within thirty days after making, and before distributing any phonorecords of the work, serve notice of intention to do so on the copyright owner. If the registration or other public records of the Copyright Office do not identify the copyright owner and include an address at which notice can be served, it shall be sufficient to file the notice of intention in the Copyright Office. The notice shall comply, in form, content, and manner of service, with requirements that the Register of Copyrights shall prescribe by regulation.

(2) Failue to serve or file the notice required by clause (1) forecloses the possibility of a compulsory license and, in the absence of a negotiated license, renders the making and distribution of phonorecords actionable as acts of infringement under section 501 and fully subject to the remedies provided by sections 502 through 506 and 509.

(c) Royalty Payable Under Compulsory License.—

(1) To be entitled to receive royalties under a compulsory license, the copyright owner must be identified in the registration or other public records of the Copyright Office. The owner is entitled to royalties for phonorecords made and distributed after being so identified, but is not entitled to recover for any phonorecords previously made and distributed.

(2) Except as provided by clause (1), the royalty under a compulsory license shall be payable for every phonorecord made and distributed in accordance with the license. For this purpose, a phonorecord is considered "distributed" if the person exercising the compulsory license has voluntarily and permanently parted with its possession. With respect to each work embodied in the phonorecord, the royalty shall be either two and three-fourths cents, or one-half of one cent per minute of playing time or fraction thereof, whichever amount is larger.

(3) A compulsory license under this section includes the right of the maker of a phonorecord of a nondramatic musical work under subsection (a)(1) to distribute or authorize distribution of such phonorecord by rental, lease, or lending (or by acts or practices in the nature of rental, lease, or lending). In addition to any royalty payable under clause (2) and chapter 8 of this title, a royalty shall be payable by the compulsory licensee for every act of distribution of a phonorecord by or in the nature of rental, lease, or lending, by or under the authority of the compulsory licensee. With respect to each nondramatic musical work embodied in the phonorecord, the royalty shall be a proportion of the revenue received by the compulsory licensee from every such act of distribution of the phonorecord under this clause equal to the proportion of the revenue received by the compulsory licensee from distribution of the phonorecord under clause (2) that is payable by a compulsory licensee under that clause and under chapter 8. The Register of Copyrights shall issue regulations to carry out the purpose of this clause.

(4) Royalty payments shall be made on or before the twentieth day of each month and shall include all royalties for the month next preceding. Each monthly payment shall be made under oath and shall comply with requirements that the Register of Copyrights shall prescribe by regulation. The Register shall also prescribe regulations under which detailed cumulative annual statements of account, certified by a certified public accountant, shall be filed for every compulsory license under this section. The regulations covering both the monthly and the annual statements of account shall prescribe the form, content, and manner of certification with respect to the number of records made and the number of records distributed.

(5) If the copyright owner does not receive the

monthly payment and the monthly and annual statements of account when due, the owner may give written notice to the licensee that, unless the default is remedied within thirty days from the date of the notice, the compulsory license will be automatically terminated. Such termination renders either the making or the distribution, or both, of all phonorecords for which the royalty has not been paid, actionable as acts of infringement under section 501 through 506 and 509.

Section 116. Scope of exclusive rights in nondramatic musical works: Public performance by means of coin-operated phonorecord players

(a) Limitation on Exclusive Right.—In the case of a nondramatic musical work embodied in a phonorecord, the exclusive right under clause (4) of section 106 to perform the work publicly by means of a coin-operated phonorecord player is limited as follows:

(1) The proprietor of the establishment in which the public performance takes place is not liable for infringement with respect to such public performance unless—

(A) such proprietor is the operator of the phonorecord player; or

(B) such proprietor refuses or fails, within one month after receipt by registered or certified mail of a request, at a time during which the certificate required by clause (1)(C) of subsection (b) is not affixed to the phonorecord player, by the copyright owner, to make full disclosure, by registered or certified mail, of the identity of the operator of the phonorecord player.

(2) The operator of the coin-operated phonorecord player may obtain a compulsory license to perform the work publicly on that phonorecord player by filing the application, affixing the certificate, and paying the royalties provided by subsection (b).

(b) Recordation of Coin-Operated Phonorecord Player, Affixation of Certificate, and Royalty Payable Under Compulsory License.—

(1) Any operator who wishes to obtain a compulsory license for the public performance of works on a coin-operated phonorecord player shall fulfill the following requirements:

(A) Before or within one month after such performances are made available on a particular phonorecord player, and during the month of January in each succeeding year that such performances are made available on that particular phonorecord player, the operator shall file in the Copyright Office, in accordance with requirements that the Register of Copyrights, after consultation with the Copyright Royalty Tribunal (if and when the Tribunal has been constituted), shall prescribe by regulation, an application containing the name and address of the operator of the phonorecord player and the manufacturer and serial number or other explicit identification of the phonorecord player, and deposit with the Register of Copyrights a royalty fee for the current calendar year of $8 for that particular phonorecord player. If such performances are made available on a particular phonorecord player for the first time after July 1 of any year, the royalty fee to be deposited for the remainder of that year shall be $4.

(B) Within twenty days of receipt of an application and a royalty fee pursuant to subclause (A), the Register of Copyrights shall issue to the applicant a certificate for the phonorecord player.

(C) On or before March 1 of the year in which the certificate prescribed by subclause (B) of this clause is issued, or within ten days after the date of issue of the certificate, the operator shall affix to the particular phonorecord player, in a position where it can be readily examined by the public, the certificate, issued by the Register of Copyrights under subclause (B), of the latest application made by such operator under subclause (A) of this clause with respect to that phonorecord player.

(2) Failure to file the application, to affix the certificate, or to pay the royalty required by clause (1) of this subsection renders the public performance actionable as an act of infringement under section 501 and fully subject to the remedies provided by sections 502 through 506 and 509.

(c) Distribution of Royalties.—

(1) The Register of Copyrights shall receive all fees deposited under this section and, after deducting the reasonable costs incurred by the Copyright Office under this section, shall deposit the balance in the Treasury of the United States, in such manner as the Secretary of the Treasury directs. All funds held by the Secretary of the Treasury shall be invested in interest-bearing United States securities for later distribution with interest by the Copyright Royalty Tribunal as provided by this title. The Register shall submit to the Copyright Royalty Tribunal, on an annual basis, a detailed statement of account covering all fees received for the relevant period provided by subsection (b).

(2) During the month of January in each year, every person claiming to be entitled to compulsory license fees under this section for performances during the preceding twelve-month period shall file a claim with the Copyright Royalty Tribunal, in accordance with requirements that the Tribunal shall prescribe by regulation. Such claim shall include an agreement to accept as final, except as provided in section 810 of this title, the determination of the Copyright Royalty Tribunal in any controversy concerning the distribution of royalty fees deposited under subclause (A) of subsection (b)(1) of this section to which the claimant is

a party. Notwithstanding any provisions of the antitrust laws, for purposes of this subsection any claimants may agree among themselves as to the proportionate division of compulsory licensing fees among them, may lump their claims together and file them jointly or as a single claim, or may designate a common agent to receive payment on their behalf.

(3) After the first day of October of each year, the Copyright Royalty Tribunal shall determine whether there exists a controversy concerning the distribution of royalty fees deposited under subclause (A) of subsection (b)(1). If the Tribunal determines that no such controversy exists, it shall, after deducting its reasonable administrative costs under this section, distribute such fees to the copyright owners entitled, or to their designated agents. If it finds that such a controversy exists, it shall, pursuant to chapter 8 of this title, conduct a proceeding to determine the distribution of royalty fees.

(4) The fees to be distributed shall be divided as follows:

(A) to every copyright owner not affiliated with a performing rights society, the pro rata share of the fees to be distributed to which such copyright owner proves entitlement.

(B) to the performing rights societies, the remainder of the fees to be distributed in such pro rata shares as they shall by agreement stipulate among themselves,or, if they fail to agree, the pro rata share to which such performing rights societies prove entitlement.

(C) during the pendency of any proceeding under this section, the Copyright Royalty Tribunal shall withhold from distribution an amount sufficient to satisfy all claims with respect to which a controversy exists, but shall have discretion to proceed to distribute any amounts that are not in controversy.

(5) The Copyright Royalty Tribunal shall promulgate regulations unde which persons who can reasonably be expected to have claims may, during the year in which performances take place, without expense to or harassment of operators or proprietors of establishments in which phonorecord players are located, have such access to such establishments and to the phonorecord players located therein and such opportunity to obtain information with respect thereto as may be reasonably necessary to determine, by sampling procedures or otherwise, the proportion of contribution of the musical works of each such person to the earnings of the phonorecord players for which fees shall have been deposited. Any person who alleges that he or she has been denied the access permitted under the regulations prescribed by the Copyright Royalty Tribunal may bring an action in the United States

District Court for the District of Columbia for the cancellation of the compulsory license of the phonorecord player to which such access has been denied, and the court shall have the power to declare the compulsory license thereof invalid from the date of issue thereof.

(d) Criminal Penalties.—Any person who knowingly makes a false representation of a material fact in an application filed under clause (1)(A) of subsection (b), or who knowingly alters a certificate issued under clause (1)(B) of subsection (b) or knowingly affixes such a certificate to a phonorecord player other than the one it covers, shall be fined not more than $2,500.

(e) Definitions.—As used in this section, the following terms and their variant forms mean the following:

(1) A "coin-operated phonorecord player" is a machine or device that—

(A) is employed solely for the performance of nondramatic musical works by means of phonorecords upon being activated by insertion of coins, currency, tokens, or other monetary units or their equivalent;

(B) is located in an establishment making no direct or indirect charge for admission;

(C) is accompanied by a list of the titles of all the musical works available for performance on it, which list is affixed to the phonorecord player or posted in the establishment in a prominent position where it can be readily examined by the public; and

(D) affords a choice of works available for performance and permits the choice to be made by the patrons of the establishment in which it is located.

(2) An "operator" is any person who, alone or jointly with others:

(A) owns a coin-operated phonorecord player; or

(B) has the power to make a coin-operated phonorecord player available for placement in an establishment for purposes of public performance; or

(C) has the power to exercise primary control over the selection of the musical works made available for public performance on a coin-operated phonorecord player.

(3) A "performing rights society" is an association or corporation that licenses the public performance of nondramatic musical works on behalf of the copyright owners, such as the American Society of Composers, Authors and Publishers, Broadcast Music, Inc., and SESAC, Inc.

Section 117. Limitations on exclusive rights: Computer programs

Notwithstanding the provisions of section 106, it is not an infringement for the owner of a copy of a computer program to make or authorize the making of another copy or adaptation of that computer program provided:

(1) that such a new copy or adaptation is created as an essential step in the utilization of the computer program in conjunction with a machine and that it is used in no other manner, or

(2) that such new copy or adaptation is for archival purposes only and that all archival copies are destroyed in the event that continued possession of the computer program should cease to be rightful.

Any exact copies prepared in accordance with the provisions of this section may be leased, sold, or otherwise transferred, along with the copy from which such copies were prepared, only as part of the lease, sale, or other transfer of all rights in the program. Adaptations so prepared may be transferred only with the authorization of the copyright owner.

Section 118. Scope of exclusive rights: Use of certain works in connection with noncommercial broadcasting

(a) The exclusive rights provided by section 106 shall, with respect to works specified by subsection (b) and the activities specified by subsection (d), be subject to the conditions and limitations prescribed by this section.

(b) Not later than thirty days after the Copyright Royalty Tribunal has been constituted in accordance with section 802, the Chairman of the Tribunal shall cause notice to be published in the Federal Register of the initiation of proceedings for the purpose of determining reasonable terms and rates of royalty payments for the activities specified by subsection (d) with respect to published nondramatic musical works and published pictorial, graphic, and sculptural works during a period beginning as provided in clause (3) of this subsection and ending on December 13, 1982. Copyright owners and public broadcasting entities shall negotiate in good faith and cooperate fully with the Tribunal in an effort to reach reasonable and expeditious results. Notwithstanding any provision of the antitrust laws, any owners of copyright in works specified by this subsection and any public broadcasting entitites, respectively, may negotiate and agree upon division of fees paid among various copyright owners, and may designate common agents to negotiate, agree to, pay, or receive payments.

(1) Any owner of copyright in a work specified in this subsection or any public broadcasting entity may, within one hundred and twenty days after publication of the notice specified in this subsection, submit to the Copyright Royalty Tribunal proposed licenses covering such activities with respect to such works. The Copyright Royalty Tribunal shall proceed on the basis of the proposals submitted to it as well as any other relevant information. The Copyright Royalty Tribunal shall permit any interested party to submit information relevant to such proceedings.

(2) License agreements voluntarily negotiated at any time between one or more copyright owners and one or more public broadcasting entities shall be given effect in lieu of any determination by the Tribunal: Provided, That copies of such agreements are filed in the Copyright Office within thirty days of execution in accordance with regulations that the Register of Copyrights shall prescribe.

(3) Within six months, but not earlier than one hundred and twenty days, from the date of publication of the notice specified in this subsection the Copyright Royalty Tribunal shall make a determination and publish in the Federal Register a schedule of rates and terms which, subject to clause (2) of this subsection, shall be binding on all owners of copyright in works specified by this subsection and public broadcasting entitities, regardless of whether or not such copyright owners and public broadcasting entities have submitted proposals to the Tribunal. In establishing such rates and terms the Copyright Royalty Tribunal may consider the rates for comparable circumstances under voluntary license agreements negotiated as provided in clause (2)

of this subsection. The Copyright Royalty Tribunal shall also establish requirements by which copyright owners may receive reasonable notice of the use of their works under this section, and under which records of such use shall be kept by public broadcasting entities.

(4) With respect to the period beginning on the effective date of this title and ending on the date of publication of such rates and terms, this title shall not afford to owners of copyright or public broadcasting entities any greater or lesser rights with respect to the activities specified in subsection (d) as applied to works specified in this subsection than those afforded under the law in effect on December 31, 1977, as held applicable and construed by a court in an action brought under this title.

(c) The initial procedure specified in subsection (b) shall be repeated and concluded between June 30 and December 31, 1982, and at five-year intervals thereafter, in accordance with regulations that the Copyright Royalty Tribunal shall prescribe.

(d) Subject to the transitional provisions of subsection (b)(4), and to the terms of any voluntary license agreements that have been negotiated as provided by subsection (b)(2), a public broadcasting entity may upon compliance with the provisions of this section, including the rates and terms established by the Copyright Royalty Tribunal under subsection (b)(3), engage in the following activities with respect to published nondramatic musical works and published pictorial, graphic, and sculptural works:

(1) performance or display of a work by or in the course of a transmission made by a noncommercial educational broadcast station referred to in subsection (g); and

(2) production of a transmission program, reproduction of copies or phonorecords of such a transmission program, and distribution of such copies or phonorecords, where such production, reproduction, or distribution is made by a nonprofit institution or organization solely for the purpose of transmissions specified in clause (1); and

(3) the making of reproductions by a governmental body or a nonprofit institution of a transmission program simultaneously with its transmission as specified in clause (1), and the performance or display of the contents of such program under the conditions specified by clause (1) of section 110, but only if the reproductions are used for performances or displays for a period of no more than seven days from the date of the transmission specified in clause (1), and are destroyed before or at the end of such period. No person supplying, in accordance with clause (2), a reproduction of a transmission program to governmental bodies or nonprofit institutions under this clause shall have any liability as a result of failure of such body or institution to destroy such reproduction: Provided, That it shall have notified such body or institution of the requirement for such destruction pursuant to this clause: And provided further, That if such body or institution itself fails to destroy such reproduction it shall be deemed to have infringed.

(e) Except as expressly provided in this subsection, this section shall have no applicability to works other than those specified in subsection (b).

(1) Owners of copyright in nondramatic literary works and public broadcasting entities may, during the course of voluntary negotiations, agree among themselves, respectively, as to the terms and rates of royalty payments without liability under the antitrust laws. Any such terms and rates of royalty payments shall be effective upon filing in the Copyright Office, in accordance with regulations that the Register of Copyrights shall prescribe.

(2) On January 3, 1980, the Register of Copyrights, after consulting with authors and other owners of copyright in nondramatic literary works and their representatives, and with public broadcasting entities and their representatives, shall submit to the Congress a report setting forth the extent to which voluntary licensing arrangements have been reached with respect to the use of nondramatic literary works by such broadcast stations. The report should also describe any problems that may have arisen, and present legislative or other recommendations, if warranted.

(f) Nothing in this section shall be construed to permit, beyond the limits of fair use as provided by section 107, the unauthorized dramatization of a nondramatic musical work, the production of a transmission program drawn to any substantial extent from a published compilation of pictorial, graphic, or sculptural works, or the unauthorized use of any portion of an audiovisual work.

(g) As used in this section, the term "public broadcasting entity" means a noncommercial educational broadcast station as defined in section 397 of title 47 and any nonprofit institution or organization engaged in the activities described in clause (2) of subsection (d).

Chapter 2.—Copyright Ownership and Transfer

Sec. 201 Ownership of copyright.
Sec. 202 Ownership of copyright as distinct from ownership of material object.
Sec. 203 Termination of transfers and licenses granted by the author.
Sec. 204 Execution of transfers of copyright ownership.
Sec. 205 Recordation of transfers and other documents.

Section 201. Ownership of copyright

(a) Initial Ownership.—Copyright in a work protected under this title vests initially in the author or authors of the work. The authors of a joint work are coowners of copyright in the work.

(b) Works Made for Hire.—In the case of a work made for hire, the employer or other person for whom the work was prepared is considered the author for purposes of this title, and, unless the parties have expressly agreed otherwise in a written instrument signed by them, owns all of the rights comprised in the copyright.

(c) Contributions to Collective Works.—Copyright in each separate contribution to a collective work is distinct from copyright in the collective work as a whole, and vests initially in the author of the contribution. In the absence of an express transfer of the copyright or of any rights under it, the owner of copyright in the collective work is presumed to have acquired only the privilege of reproducing and distributing the contribution as part of that particular collective work, and revision of that collective work, and any later collective work in the same series.

(d) Transfer of Ownership.—

(1) The ownership of a copyright may be transferred in whole or in part by any means of conveyance or by

operation of law, and may be bequeathed by will or pass as personal property by the applicable laws of intestate succession.

(2) Any of the exclusive rights comprised in a copyright, including any subdivision of any of the rights specified by section 106, may be transferred as provided by clause (1) and owned separately. The owner of any particular exclusive right is entitled, to the extent of that right, to all of the protection and remedies accorded to the copyright owner by this title.

(e) Involuntary Transfer.—When an individual author's ownership of a copyright, or of any of the exclusive rights under a copyright, has not previously been transferred voluntarily by that individual author, no action by any governmental body or other official or organization purporting to seize, expropriate, transfer, or exercise rights of ownership with respect to the copyright, or any of the exclusive rights under a copyright, shall be given effect under this title, except as provided under title 11.

Section 202. Ownership of copyright as distinct from ownership of material object

Ownership of a copyright, or of any of the exclusive rights under a copyright, is distinct from ownership of any material object in which the work is embodied. Transfer of ownership of any material object, including the copy or phonorecord in which the work is first fixed, does not of itself convey any rights in the copyrighted work embodied in the object; nor, in the absence of an agreement, does transfer of ownership of a copyright or of any exclusive rights under a copyright convey property rights in any material object.

Section 203. Termination of transfers and licenses granted by the author

(a) Conditions for Termination.—In the case of any work other than a work made for hire, the exclusive or nonexclusive grant of a transfer or license of copyright or of any right under a copyright, executed by the author on or after January 1, 1978, otherwise than by will, is subject to termination under the following conditions:

(1) In the case of a grant executed by one author, termination of the grant may be effected by that author or, if the author is dead, by the person or persons who, under clause (2) of this subsection, own and are entitled to exercise a total of more than one-half of that author's termination interest. In the case of a grant executed by two or more authors of a joint work, termination of the grant may be effected by a majority of the authors who executed it; if any of such authors is dead, the termination interest of any such author may be exercised as a unit by the person or persons who, under clause (2) of this subsection, own and are entitled to exercise a total of more than one-half of that author's interest.

(2) Where an author is dead, his or her termination interest is owned, and may be exercised, by his widow or her widower and his or her children or grandchildren as follows:

(A) the widow or widower owns the author's entire termination interest unless there are any surviving children or grandchildren of the author, in which case the widow or widower owns one-half of the author's interest;

(B) the author's surviving children, and the surviving children of any dead child of the author, own the author's entire termination interest unless there is a widow or widower, in which case the ownership of one-half of the author's interest is divided among them;

(C) the rights of the author's children and grandchildren are in all cases divided among them and exercised on a per stirpes basis according to the number of such author's children represented; the share of the children of a dead child in a termination interest can be exercised only by the action of a majority of them.

(3) Termination of the grant may be effected at any time during a period of five years beginning at the end of thirty-five years from the date of execution of the grant; or, if the grant covers the right of publication of the work, the period begins at the end of thirty-five years from the date of publication of the work under the grant or at the end of forty years from the date of execution of the grant, whichever term ends earlier.

(4) The termination shall be effected by serving an advance notice in writing, signed by the number and proportion of owners of termination interests required under clauses (1) and (2) of this subsection, or by their duly authorized agents, upon the grantee or the grantee's successor in title.

(A) The notice shall state the effective date of the termination, which shall fall within the five-year period specified by clause (3) of this subsection, and the notice shall be served not less than two or more than ten years before that date. A copy of the notice shall be recorded in the Copyright Office before the effective date of termination, as a condition to its taking effect.

(B) The notice shall comply, in form, content, and manner of service, with requirements that the Register of Copyrights shall prescribe by regulation.

(5) Termination of the grant may be effected notwithstanding any agreement to the contrary, including an agreement to make a will or to make any future grant.

(b) Effect of Termination.—Upon the effective date of termination, all rights under this title that were covered by the terminated grants revert to the author, authors, and other persons owning termination interests under clauses (1) and (2) of subsection (a), including those owners who did not join in signing the notice of termination under clause (4) of subsection (a), but with the following limitations:

(1) A derivative work prepared under authority of the grant before its termination may continue to be utilized under the terms of the grant after its termination, but this privilege does not extend to the preparation after the termination of other derivative works based upon the copyrighted work covered by the terminated grant.

(2) The future rights that will revert upon termination of the grant become vested on the date the notice of termination has been served as provided by clause (4) of subsection (a). The rights vest in the author, authors, and other persons named in, and in the

proportionate shares provided by, clauses (1) and (2) of subsection (a).

(3) Subject to the provisions of clause (4) of this subsection, a further grant, or agreement to make a further grant, of any right covered by a terminated grant is valid only if it is signed by the same number and proportion of the owners, in whom the right has vested under clause (2) of this subsection, as are required to terminate the grant under clauses (1) and (2) of subsection (a). Such further grant or agreement is effective with respect to all of the persons in whom the right it covers has vested under clause (2) of this subsection, including those who did not join in signing it. If any person dies after rights under a terminated grant have vested in him or her, that person's legal representatives, legatees, or heirs at law represent him or her for purposes of this clause.

(4) A further grant, or agreement to make a further grant, of any right covered by a terminated grant is valid only if it is made after the effective date of the termination. As an exception, however, an agreement for such a further grant may be made between the persons provided by clause (3) of this subsection and the original grantee or such grantee's successor in title, after the notice of termination has been served as provided by clause (4) of subsection (a).

(5) Termination of a grant under this section affects only those rights covered by the grants that arise under this title, and in no way affects rights arising under any other Federal, State, or foreign laws.

(6) Unless and until termination is effected under this section, the grant, if it does not provide otherwise, continues in effect for the term of copyright provided by this title.

Section 204. Execution of transfers of copyright ownership

(a) A transfer of copyright ownership, other than by operation of law, is not valid unless an instrument of conveyance, or a note or memorandum of the transfer, is in writing and signed by the owner of the rights conveyed or such owner's duly authorized agent.

(b) A certificate of acknowledgement is not required for the validity of a transfer, but is prima facie evidence of the execution of the transfer if—

(1) in the case of a transfer executed in the United States, the certificate is issued by a person authorized to administer oaths within the United States; or

(2) in the case of a transfer executed in a foreign country, the certificate is issued by a diplomatic or consular officer of the United States, or by a person authorized to administer oaths whose authority is proved by a certificate of such an officer.

Section 205. Recordation of transfers and other documents

(a) Conditions for Recordation.—Any transfer of copyright ownership or other document pertaining to a copyright may be recorded in the Copyright Office if the document filed for recordation bears the actual signature of the person who executed it, or if it is accompanied by a sworn or official certification that it is a true copy of the original, signed document.

(b) Certificate of Recordation.—The Register of Copyrights shall, upon receipt of a document as provided by subsection (a) and of the fee provided by section 708, record the document and return it with a certificate of recordation.

(c) Recordation as Constructive Notice.—Recordation of a document in the Copyright Office gives all persons constructive notice of the facts stated in the recorded document, but only if—

(1) the document, or material attached to it, specifically identifies the work to which it pertains so that, after the document is indexed by the Register of Copyrights, it would be revealed by a reasonable search under the title or registration number of the work; and

(2) registration has been made for the work.

(d) Recordation as Prerequisite to Infringement Suit.—No person claiming by virtue of a transfer to be the owner of copyright or of any exclusive right under a copyright is entitled to institute an infringement action under this title until the instrument of transfer under which such person claims has been recorded in the Copyright Office, but suit may be instituted after such recordation on a cause of action that arose before recordation.

(e) Priority Between Conflicting Transfers.—As between two conflicting transfers, the one executed first prevails if it is recorded, in the manner required to give constructive notice under subsection (c), within one month after its execution in the United States or within two months after its execution outside the United States, or at any time before recordation in such manner of the later transfer. Otherwise the later transfer prevails if recorded first in such manner, and if taken in good faith, for valuable consideration or on the basis of a binding promise to pay royalties, and without notice of the earlier transfer.

(f) Priority Between Conflicting Transfer of Ownership and Nonexclusive License.—A nonexclusive license, whether recorded or not, prevails over a conflicting transfer of copyright ownership if the license is evidenced by a written instrument signed by the owner of the rights licensed or such owner's duly authorized agent, and if—

(1) the license was taken before execution of the transfer; or

(2) the license was taken in good faith before recordation of the transfer and without notice of it.

Chapter 3.—Duration of Copyright

Section 301. Preemption with respect to other laws

(a) On and after January 1, 1978, all legal or equitable rights that are equivalent to any of the exclusive rights within the general scope of copyright as specified by section 106 in works of authorship that are fixed in a tangible medium of expression and come within the subject matter of copyright as specified by sections 102 and 103, whether created before or after that date and whether published or unpublished, are governed exclusively by this title. Thereafter, no person is entitled to any such right or equivalent right in any such work under the common law or statutes of any state.

(b) Nothing in this title annuls or limits any rights or remedies under the common law or statutes of any State with respect to—

(1) subject matter that does not come within the subject matter of copyright as specified by sections 102 and 103, including works of authorship not fixed in any tangible medium of expression; or

(2) any cause of action arising from undertakings commenced before January 1, 1978; or

(3) activities violating legal or equitable rights that are not equivalent to any of the exclusive rights within the general scope of copyright as specified by section 106.

(c) With respect to sound recordings fixed before February 15, 1972, any rights or remedies under the common law or statutes of any State shall not be annulled or limited by this title until February 15, 2047. The preemptive provisions of subsection (a) shall apply to any such rights and remedies pertaining to any cause of action arising from undertakings commenced on and after February 15, 2047. Notwithstanding the provisions of section 303, no sound recording fixed before February 15, 1972, shall be subject to copyright under this title before, on, or after February 15, 2047.

(d) Nothing in this title annuls or limits any rights or remedies under any other Federal statute.

Section 302. Duration of copyright: Works created on or after January 1, 1978

(a) In General.—Copyright in a work created on or after January 1, 1978, subsists from its creation and, except as provided by the following subsections, endures for a term consisting of the life of the author and fifty years after the author's death.

(b) Joint Works.—In the case of a joint work prepared by two or more authors who did not work for hire, the copyright endures for a term consisting of the life of the last surviving author and fifty years after such last suviving author's death.

(c) Anonymous Works, Pseudonymous Works, and Works Made for Hire.—In the case of an anonymous work, a pseudonymous work, or a work made for hire, the copyright endures for a term of seventy-five years from the year of its first publication, or a term of one hundred years from the year of its creation, whichever expires first. If, before the end of such term, the identity of one or more of the authors of an anonymous or pseudonymous work is revealed in the records of a registration made for that work under subsections (a) or (d) of section 408, or in the records provided by this subsection, the coyright in the work endures for the term specified by subsection (a) or (b), based on the life of the author or authors whose identity has been revealed. Any person having an interest in the copyright in an anonymous or pseudonymous work may at any time record, in records to be maintained by the Copyright Office for that purpose, a statement identifying one or more authors of the work; the statement shall also identify the person filing it, the nature of that person's interest, the source of the information recorded, and the particular work affected, and shall comply in form and content with requirements that the Register of Copyrights shall prescribe by regulation.

(d) Records Relating to Death of Authors.—Any person having an interest in a copyright may at any time record in the Copyright Office a statement of the date of death of the author of the copyrighted work, or a statement that the author is still living on a particular date. The statement shall identify the person filing it, the nature of that person's interest, and the source of the information recorded, and shall comply in form and content with requirements that the Register of Copyrights shall prescribe by regulation. The Register shall maintain current records of information relating to the death of authors of copyrighted works, based on such recorded statements and, to the extent the Register considers practicable, on data contained in any of the records of the Copyright Office or in other reference sources.

(e) Presumption as to Author's Death.—After a period of seventy-five years from the year of first publication of a work, or a period of one hundred years from the year of its creation, whichever expires first, any person who obtains from the Copyright Office a certified report that the records provided by subsection (d) disclose nothing to indicate that the author of the work is living, or died less than fifty years before, is entitled to the benefit of a presumption that the author has been dead for at least fifty years. Reliance in good faith upon this presumption shall be a complete defense to any action for infringement under this title.

Section 303. Duration of copyright: Works created but not published or copyrighted before January 1, 1978

Copyright in a work created before January 1, 1978, but not theretofore in the public domain or copyrighted, subsists from January 1, 1978, and endures for the term provided by section 302. In no case, however, shall the term of copyright in such a work expire before December 31, 2002; and, if the work is published on or before December 31, 2002, the term of copyright shall not expire before December 31, 2027.

Section 304. Duration of copyright: Subsisting copyrights

(a) Copyrights in Their First Term on January 1, 1978.—Any copyright, the first term of which is subsisting on January 1, 1978, shall endure for twenty-eight years from the date it was originally secured: Provided, That in the case of any posthumous work or of any periodical, cyclopedic, or other composite work upon which the copyright was originally secured by the proprietor thereof, or of any work copyrighted by a corporate body (otherwise than an assignee or licensee of the individual author) or by an employer for whom such work is made for hire, the proprietor of such copyright shall be entitled to a renewal and extension of the copyright in such work for the further term of forty-seven years when application for such renewal and extension shall have been made to the Copyright Office and duly registered therein within one year prior to the expiration of the original term of copyright: And provided further, That in the case of any other copyrighted work, including a contribution by an individual author to a periodical or to a cyclopedic or other composite work, the author of such work, if still living, or the widow, widower, or children of the author, if the author be not living, or if such author, widow, widower, or children be not living, then the author's executors, or in the absence of a will, his or her next of kin shall be entitled to a renewal and extension of the copyright in such work for a further term of forty-seven years when application for such renewal and extension shall have been made to the Copyright Office and duly registered therein within one year prior to the expiration of the original term of copyright: And provided further, That in default of the registration of such applicaton for renewal and extension, the copyright in any work shall terminate at the expiration of twenty-eight years from the date copyright was originally secured.

(b) Copyrights in Their Renewal Term or Registered for Renewal Before January 1, 1978.—The duration of any copyright, the renewal term of which is subsisting at any time between december 31 1976 and December 31, 1977, inclusive, or for which renewal registration is made between December 31, 1976, and December 31, 1977, inclusive, is extended to endure for a term of seventy-five years from the date copyright was originally secured.

(c) Termination of Transfers and Licenses Covering Extended Renewal Term.—In the case of any copyright subsisting in either its first or renewal term on January 1, 1978, other than a copyright in a work made for hire, the exclusive or nonexclusive grant of a transfer or license of the renewal copyright or any right under it, executed before January 1, 1978, by any of the persons designated by the second proviso of subsection (a) of this section, otherwise than by will, is subject to termination under the following conditions:

(1) In the case of a grant executed by a person or persons other than the author, termination of the grant may be effected by the surviving person or persons who executed it. In the case of a grant executed by one or more of the authors of the work, termination of the grant may be effected, to the extent of a particular author's share in the ownership of the renewal copyright, by the author who executed it or, if such author is dead, by the person or persons who, under clause (2) of this subsection, own and are entitled to exercise a total of more than one-half of that author's termination interest.

(2) Where an author is dead, his or her termination interest is owned, and may be exercised, by his widow or her widower and his or her children or grandchildren as follows:

(A) the widow or widower owns the author's entire termination interest unless there are any surviving children or grandchildren of the author, in which case the widow or widower owns one-half of the author's interest;

(B) the author's surviving children, and the surviving children of any dead of the author, own the author's entire termination interest unless there is a widow or widower, in which case the ownership of one-half of the author's interest is divided among them;

(C) the rights of the author's children and grandchildren are in all cases divided among them and exercised on a per stirpes basis according to the number of such author's children represented; the share of the children of a dead child in a termination interest can be exercised only by the action of a majority of them.

(3) Termination of the grant may be effected at any time during a period of five years beginning at the end of fifty-six years from the date copyright was originally secured, or beginning on January 1, 1978, whichever is later.

(4) The termination shall be effected by serving an advance notice in writing upon the grantee or the

grantee's successor in title. In the case of a grant executed by a person or persons other than the author, the notice shall be signed by all of those entitled to terminate the grant under clause (1) of this subsection, or by their duly authorized agents. In the case of a grant executed by one or more of the authors of the work, the notice as to any one author's share shall be signed by that author or his or her duly authorized agent or, if that author is dead, by the number and proportion of the owners of his or her termination interest required under clauses (1) and (2) of this subsection, or by their duly authorized agents.

(A) The notice shall state the effective date of the termination, which shall fall within the five-year period specified by clause (3) of this subsection, and the notice shall be served not less than two or more than ten years before that date. A copy of the notice shall be recorded in the Copyright Office before the effective date of termination, as a condition to its taking effect.

(B) The notice shall comply, inform, content, and manner of service, with requirements that the Register of Copyrights shall prescribe by regulation.

(5) Termination of the grant may be effected notwithstanding any agreement to the contrary, including an agreement to make a will or to make any future grant.

(6) In the case of a grant executed by a person or persons other than the author, all rights under this title that were covered by the terminated grant revert, upon the effective date of termination, to all of those entitled to terminate the grant under clause (1) of this subsection. In the case of a grant executed by one or more of the authors of the work, all of a particular author's rights under this title that were covered by the terminated grant revert, upon the effective date of termination, to that author or, if that author is dead, to the persons owning his or her termination interest under clause (2) of this subsection, including those owners who did not join in signing the notice of termination under clause (4) of this subsection. In all cases the reversion of rights is subject to the following limitations:

(A) A derivative work prepared under authority of the grant before its termiation may continue to be utilized under the terms of the grant after its termination, but this privilege does not extend to the preparation after the termination of other derivative works based upon the copyrighted work covered by the terminated grant.

(B) The future rights that will revert upon termination of the grant become vested on the date the notice of termination has been served as provided by clause (4) of this subsection.

(C) Where the author's rights revert to two or more persons under clause (2) of this subsection, they shall vest in those persons in the proportionate shares provided by that clause. In such a case, and subject to the provisions of subclause (D) of this clause, a further grant, or agreement to make a further grant, of a particular author's share with respect to any right covered by a terminated grant is valid only if it is signed by the same number and proportion of the owners, in whom the right has vested under this clause, as are required to terminate the grant under clause (2) of this subsection. Such further grant or agreement is effective with respect to all of the persons in whom the right it covers has vested under this subclause, including those who did not join in signing it. If any person dies after rights under a terminated grant have vested in him or her, that person's legal representatives, legatees, or heirs at law represent him or her for purposes of this subclause.

(D) A further grant, or agreement to make a further grant, of any right covered by a terminated grant is valid only if it is made after the effective date of the termination. As an exception, however, an agreement for such a further grant may be made between the author or any of the persons provided by the first sentence of clause (6) of this subsection, or between the persons provided by subclause (C) of this clause, and the original grantee or such grantee's successor in title, after the notice of termination has been served as provided by clause (4) of this subsection.

(E) Termination of a grant under this subsection affects only those rights covered by the grant that arise under this title, and in no way affect rights arising under any other Federal, State, or foreign laws.

(F) Unless and until termination is effected under this subsection, the grant, if it does not provide otherwise, continues in effect for the remainder of the extended renewal term.

Section 305. Duration of copyright: Terminal date

All terms of copyright provided by sections 302 through 304 run to the end of the calendar year in which they would otherwise expire.

Chapter 4.—Copyright Notice, Deposit, and Registration

Sec. 401 Notice of copyright: Visually perceptible copies.
Sec. 402 Notice of copyright: Phonorecords of sound recordings.
Sec. 403 Notice of copyright: Publications incorporating United States Government works.

Section 401. Notice of copyright: Visually perceptible copies

(a) General Requirement.—Whenever a work protected under this title is published in the United States or elsewhere by authority of the copyright owner, a notice of copyright as provided by this section shall be placed on all publicly distributed copies from which the work can be visually perceived, either directly or with the aid of a machine or device.

(b) Form of Notice.—The notice appearing on the copies shall consist of the following three elements:

(1) the symbol © (the letter C in a circle), or the word "Copyright", or the abbreviation "Copr."; and

(2) the year of first publication of the work; in the case of compilations or derivative works incorporating previously published material, the year date of first publication of the compilation or derivative work is sufficient. The year date may be omitted where a pictorial, graphic, or sculptural work, with accompanying text matter, if any, is reproduced in or on greeting cards, postcards, stationery, jewelry, dolls, toys, or any useful articles; and

(3) the name of the owner of copyright in the work, or an abbreviation by which the name can be recognized, or a generally known alternative designation of the owner.

(c) Position of Notice.—The notice shall be affixed to the copies in such manner and location as to give reasonable notice of the claim of copyright. The Register of Copyrights shall prescribe by regulation, as examples, specific methods of affixation and positions of the notice on various types of works that will satisfy this requirment, but these specifications shall not be considered exhaustive.

Section 402. Notice of copyright: Phonorecords of sound recordings

(a) General Requirement.—Whenever a sound recording protected under this title is published in the United States or elsewhere by authority of the copyright owner, a notice of copyright as provided by this section shall be placed on all publicly distributed phonorecords of the sound recording.

(b) Form of Notice.—The notice appearing on the phonorecords shall consist of the following three elements:

(1) the symbol p [statutory text shows the letter p in a circle] (the letter P in a circle); and

(2) the year of first publication of the sound recording; and

(3) the name of the owner of copyright in the sound recording, or an abbreviation by which the name can be recognized, or a generally known alternative designation of the owner; if the producer of the sound recording is named on the phonorecord labels or containers, and if no other name appears in conjunction with the notice, the producer's name shall be considered a part of the notice.

(c) Position of Notice.—The notice shall be placed on the surface of the phonorecord, or on the phonorecord label or container, in such manner and location as to give reasonable notice of the claim of copyright.

Section 403. Notice of copyright: Publications incorporating United States Government works

Whenever a work is published in copies or phonorecords consisting preponderantly of one or more works of the United States Government, the notice of copyright provided by sections 401 or 402 shall also include a statement identifying, either affirmatively or negatively, those portions of the copies or phonorecords embodying any work or works protected under this title.

Section 404. Notice of copyright: Contributions to collective works

(a) A separate contribution to a collective work may bear its own notice of copyright, as provided by sections 401 through 403. However, a single notice applicable to the collective work as a whole is sufficient to satisfy the requirements of sections 401 through 403 with respect to the separate contributions it contains (not including advertisements inserted on behalf of persons other than the owner of copyright in the collective work), regardless of the ownership of copyright in the contributions and whether or not they have been previously published.

(b) Where the person named in a single notice applicable to a collective work as a whole is not the owner of copyright in a separate contribution that does not bear its own notice, the case is governed by the provisions of section 406 (a)

Section 405. Notice of copyright: Omission of notice

(a) Effect of Omission on Copyright.—The omisson of the copyright notice prescribed by sections 401 through 403 from copies or phonorecords publicly distributed by authority of the copyright owner does not invalidate the copyright in a work if—

(1) the notice has been omitted from no more than a relatively small number of copies or phonorecords distributed to the public; or

(2) registration for the work has been made before or is made within five years after the publication without notice, and a reasonable effort is made to add notice to all copies or phonorecords that are distributed to the public in the United States after the omission has been discovered; or

(3) the notice has been omitted in violation of an express requirement in writing that, as a condition of the copyright owner's authorization of the public distribution of copies or phonorecords, they bear the prescribed notice.

(b) Effect of Omission on Innocent Infringers.—Any person who innocently infringes a copyright, in reliance upon an authorized copy or phonorecord from which the copyright notice has been omitted, incurs no liability for actual or statutory damages under section 504 for any infringing acts committed before receiving actual notice that registration for the work has been made under section 408, if such person proves that he or she was misled by the omission of notice. In a suit for infringement in such a case the court may allow or disallow recovery of any of the infringer's profits attributable to the infringement, and may enjoin the continuation of the infringing undertaking or may require, as a condition or permitting the continuation of the infringing undertaking, that the infringer pay the copyright owner a reasonable license fee in an amount and on terms fixed by the court.

(c) Removal of Notice.—Protection under this title is not affected by the removal, destruction, or obliteration of the notice, without the authorization of the copyright owner, from any publicly distributed copies or phonorecords.

Section 406. Notice of copyright: Error in name or date

(a) Error in Name.—Where the person named in the copyright notice on copies or phonorecords publicly distributed by authority of the copyright owner is not the owner of copyright, the validity and ownership of the copyright are not affected. In such a case, however, any person who innocently begins an undertaking that infringes the copyright has a complete defense to any action for such infringement if such person proves that he or she was misled by the notice and began the undertaking in good faith under a purported transfer or license from the person named therein, unless before the undertaking was begun—

(1) registration for the work has been made in the name of the owner of copyright; or

(2) a document executed by the person named in the notice and showing the ownership of the copyright had been recorded.

The person named in the notice is liable to account to the copyright owner for all receipts from transfers or licenses purportedly made under the coyright by the person named in the notice.

(b) Error in Date.—When the year date in the notice on copies or phonorecords distribued by authority of the copyright owner is earlier than the year in which publication first occurred, any period computed from the year of first publication under section 302 is to be computed from the year in the notice. Where the year date is more than one year later than the year in which publication first ocurred, the work is considered to have been published without any notice and is governed by the provisions of section 405.

(c) Omisson of Name or Date.—Where copies or phonorecords publicly distributed by authority of the copyright owner contain no name or no date that could reasonably be considered a part of the notice, the work is considered to have been published without any notice and is governed by the provisions of section 405.

Section 407. Deposit of copies or phonorecords for Library of Congress

(a) Except as provided by subsection (c), and subject to the provisions of subsection (e), the owner of copyright or of the exclusive right of publication in a work published with notice of copyright in the United States shall deposit, within three months after the date of such publication—

(1) two complete copies of the best edition; or

(2) if the work is a sound recording, two complete phonorecords of the best edition, together with any printed or other visually perceptible material published with such phonorecords.

Neither the deposit requirements of this subsection nor the acquisition provisions of subsection (e) are conditions of copyright protection.

(b) The required copies or phonorecords shall be deposited in the Copyright Office for the use or disposition of the Library of Congress. The Register of Copyrights shall, when requested by the depositor and upon payment of the fee prescribed by section 708, issue a receipt for the deposit.

(c) The Register of Copyrights may by regulation exempt any categories of material from the deposit requirements of this section, or require deposit of only one copy or phonorecord with respect to any categories. Such regulations shall provide either for complete exemption from the deposit requirements of this section, or for alternative forms of deposit aimed at providing a satisfactory archival record of a work without imposing practical or financial hardships on the depositor, where the individual author is the owner of copyright in a pictorial, graphic, or sculptural work and (i) less than five copies of the work have been published, or (ii) the work has been published in a limited edition consisting of numbered copies, the monetary value of which would make the mandatory deposit of two copies of the best edition of the work burdensome, unfair, or unreasonable.

(d) At any time after publication of a work as provided by subsection (a), the Register of Copyrights may make written demand for the required deposit on any of the persons obligated to make the deposit under subsection (a). Unless deposit is made within three months after the demand is received, the person or persons on whom the demand was made are liable—

(1) to a fine of not more than $250 for each work; and

(2) to pay into a specially designated fund in the Library of Congress the total retail price of the copies or phonorecords demanded, or, if no retail price has been fixed, the reasonable cost of the Library of Congress of acquiring them; and

(3) to pay a fine of $2,500, in addition to any fine or liability imposed under clauses (1) and (2), if such person willfully or repeatedly fails or refuses to comply with such a demand.

(e) With respect to transmission programs that have been fixed and transmitted to the public in the United States but have not been published, the Register of Copyrights shall, after consulting with the Librarian of Congress and other interested organizations and officials, establish regulations governing the acquisition, through deposit or otherwise, of copies or phonorecords of such programs for the collections of the Library of Congress.

(1) The Librarian of Congress shall be permitted,

under the standards and conditions set forth in such regulations, to make a fixation of a transmission program directly from a transmission to the public, and to reproduce one copy or phonorecord from such fixation for archival purposes.

(2) Such regulations shall also provide standards and procedures by which the Register of Copyrights may make written demand, upon the owner of the right of transmission in the United States, for the deposit of a copy or phonorecord of a specific transmission program. Such deposit may, at the option of the owner of the right of transmission in the United States, be accomplished by gift, by loan for purposes of reproduction, or by sale at a price not to exceed the cost of reproducing and supplying the copy or phonorecord. The regulations established under this clause shall provide reasonable periods of not less than three months for compliance with a demand, and shall allow for extensions of such periods and adjustments in the scope of the demand or the methods for fulfilling it, as reasonably warranted by the circumstances. Willful failure or refusal to comply with the conditions prescribed by such regulations shall subject the owner of the right of transmission in the United States to liability for an amount, not to exceed the cost of reproducing and supplying the copy or phonorecord in question, to be paid into a specially designated fund in the Library of Congress.

(3) Nothing in this subsection shall be construed to require the making or retention, for purposes of deposit, of any copy or phonorecord of an unpublished transmission program, the transmission of which occurs before the receipt of a specific written demand as provided by clause (2).

(4) No activity undertaken in compliance with regulations prescribed under clauses (1) or (2) of this subsection shall result in liability if intended solely to assist in the acquisition of copies or phonorecords under this subsection.

Section 408. Copyright registration in general

(a) Registration Permissive.—At any time during the subsistence of copyright in any published or unublished work, the owner of copyright or of any exclusive right in the work may obtain registration of the copyright claim by delivering to the Copyright Office the deposit specified by this section, together with the application and fee specified by sections 409 and 708. Subject to the provisions of section 405(a), such registration is not a condition of copyright protection.

(b) Deposit for Copyright Registration.—Except as provided by subsection (c), the material deposited for registration shall include—

(1) in the case of an unpublished work, one complete copy or phonorecord;

(2) in the case of a published work, two complete copies or phonorecords of the best edition;

(3) in the case of a work first published outside the United States, one complete copy or phonorecord as so published;

(4) in the case of a contribution to a collective work, one complete copy or phonorecord of the best edition of the collective work.

Copies or phonorecords deposited for the Library of Congress under section 407 may be used to satisfy the deposit provisions of this section, if they are accompanied by the prescribed application and fee, and by any additional identifying material that the Register may, by regulation require. The Register shall also prescribe regulations establishing requirements under which copies or phonorecords acquired for the Library of Congress under subsection (e) of section 407, otherwise than by deposit, may be used to satisfy the deposit provisions of this section.

(c) Administrative Classification and Optional Deposit.—

(1) The Register of Copyrights is authorized to specify by regulation the administrative classes into which works are to be placed for purposes of deposit and registration, and the nature of the copies or phonorecords to be deposited in the various classes specified. The regulations may require or permit, for particular classes, the deposit of identifying material instead of copies or phonorecords, the deposit of only one copy or phonorecord where two would normally be required, or a single registration for a group of related works. This administrative classification of works has no significance with respect to the subject matter of copyright or the exclusive rights provided by this title.

(2) Without prejudice to the general authority provided under clause (1), the Register of Copyrights shall establish regulations specifically permitting a single registration for a group of works by the same individual author, all first published as contributions to periodicals, including newspapers, within a twelve-month period, on the basis of a single deposit, application, and registration fee, under all of the following conditions—

(A) if each of the works as first published bore a separate copyright notice, and the name of the owner of copyright in the work, or an abbreviation by which the name can be recognized, or a generally known alternative designation of the owner was the same in each notice; and

(B) if the deposit consists of one copy of the entire issue of the periodical, or of the entire section in the case of a newspaper, in which each contribution was first published; and

(C) if the application identifies each work separately, including the periodical containing it and its date of first publication.

(3) As an alternative to separate renewal registrations under subsection (a) of section 304, a single renewal registration may be made for a group of works by the same individual author, all first published as contributions to periodicals, including newspapers, upon the filing of a single application and fee, under all of the following conditions:

(A) the renewal claimant or claimants, and the basis of claim or claims under section 304(a), is the same for each of the works; and

(B) the works were all copyrighted upon their first publication, either through separate copyright notice and registration or by virtue of a general copyright notice in the periodical issue as a whole; and

(C) the renewal application and fee are received not more than twenty-eight or less than twenty-seven years after the thirty-first day of December of the calendar year in which all of the works were first published; and

(D) the renewal application identifies each work separately, including the periodical containing it and its date of first publication.

(d) Corrections and Amplifications.—The Register may also establish, by regulation, formal procedures for the filing of an applicaton for supplementary registration, to correct an error in a copyright registration or to amplify the information given in a registration. Such application shall be accompanied by the fee provided by section 708, and shall clearly identify the registration to be corrected or amplified. The information contained in a supplementary registration augments but does not supersede that contained in the earlier registration.

(e) Published Edition of Previously Registered Work.—Registration for the first published edition of a work previously registered in unpublished form may be made even though the work as published is substantially the same as the unpublished version.

Section 409. Application for copyright registration

The application for copyright registration shall be made on a form prescribed by the Register of Copyrights and shall include—

(1) the name and address of the copyright claimant;

(2) in the case of a work other than an anonymous or pseudonymous work, the name and nationality or domicile of the author or authors, and, if one or more of the authors is dead, the dates of their deaths;

(3) if the work is anonymous or pseudonymous, the nationality or domicile of the author or authors;

(4) in the case of a work made for hire, a statement to this effect;

(5) if the copyright claimant is not the author, a brief statement of how the claimant obtained ownership of the copyright;

(6) the title of the work, together with any previous or alternative titles under which the work can be identified;

(7) the year in which creation of the work was completed;

(8) if the work has been published, the date and nation of its first publication;

(9) in the case of a compilation or derivative work, an identification of any preexisting work or works that it is based on or incorporates, and a brief, general statement of the additional material covered by the copyright claim being registered;

(10) in the case of a published work containing material of which copies are required by section 601 to be manufactured in the United States, the names of the persons or organizations who performed the processes specified by subsection (c) of section 601 with respect to that material, and the places where those processes were performed; and

(11) any other information regarded by the Register of Copyrights as bearing upon the preparation or identification of the work or the existence, ownership, or duration of the copyright.

Section 410. Registration of claim and issuance of certificate

(a) When, after examination, the Register of Copyrights determines that, in accordance with the provisions of this title, the material deposited constitutes copyrightable subject matter and that the other legal and formal requirements of this title have been met, the Register shall register the claim and issue to the applicant a certificate of registration under the seal of the Copyright Office. The certificate shall contain the information given in the application, together with the number and effective date of the registration.

(b) In any case in which the Register of Copyrights determines that, in accordance with the provisions of this title, the material deposited does not constitute copyrightable subject matter or that the claim is invalid for any other reason, the Register shall refuse registration and shall notify the applicant in writing of the reasons for such refusal.

(c) In any judicial proceedings the certificate of a registration made before or within five years after first publication of the work shall constitute prima facie evidence of the validity of the copyright and of the facts stated in the certificate. The evidentiary weight to be accorded the certificate of a registration made thereafter shall be within the discretion of the court.

(d) The effective date of a copyright registration is the day on which an application, deposit, and fee, which are later determined by the Register of Copyrights or by a court of competent jurisdiction to be acceptable for registration, have all been received in the Copyright Office.

Section 411. Registration as prerequisite to infringement suit

(a) Subject to the provisions of subsection (b), no action for infringement of the copyright in any work shall be instituted until registration of the copyright claim has been made in accordance with this title. In any case, however, where the deposit, application, and fee required for registration have been delivered to the Copyright Office in proper form and registration has been refused, the applicant is entitled to institute an action for infringement if notice thereof, with a copy of the complaint, is served on the Register of Copyrights. The Register may, at his or her option, become a party to the action with respect to the issue of registrability of the copyright claim by entering an appearance within sixty days after such service, but the Register's failure to become a party shall not deprive the court of jurisdiction to determine that issue.

(b) In the case of a work consisting of sounds, images, or both, the first fixation of which is made simultaneously with its transmission, the copyright owner may, either before or after such fixation takes place, institute an action for infringement under section 501, fully subject to the remedies provided by sections 502 through 506 and sections 509 and 510, if, in accordance with requirements that the Register of Copyrights shall prescribe by regulation, the copyright owner—

(1) serves notice upon the infringer, not less than ten or more than thirty days before such fixation, identifying the work and the specific time and source of its first transmission, and declaring an intention to secure copyright in the work; and

(2) makes registration for the work within three months after its first transmission.

Section 412. Registration as prerequisite to certain remedies for infringement

In any action under this title, other than an action instituted under section 411(b), no award of statutory damages or of attorney's fees, as provided by sections 504 and 505, shall be made for—

(1) any infringement of copyright in an unpublished work commenced before the effective date of its registration; or

(2) any infringement of copyright commenced after first publication of the work and before the effective date of its registration, unless such registration is made within three months after the first publication of the work.

Chapter 5.—Copyright Infringement and Remedies

Section 501. Infringement of Copyright

(a) Anyone who violates any of the exclusive rights of the copyright owner as provided by sections 106 through 118, or who imports copies or phonorecords into the United States in violation of section 602, is an infringer of the copyright.

(b) The legal or beneficial owner of an exclusive right under a copyright is entitled, subject to the requirements of sections 205(d) and 411, to institute an action for any infringement of that particular right committed while he or she is the owner of it. The court may require such owner to serve written notice of the action with a copy of the complaint upon any person shown, by the records of the Copyright Office or otherwise, to have or claim an interest in the copyright, and shall require that such notice be served upon any person whose interest is likely to be affected by a decision in the case. The court may require the joinder, and shall permit the intervention, of any person having or claiming an interest in the copyright.

(c) For any secondary transmission by a cable system that embodies a performance or a display of a work which is actionable as an act of infringement under subsection (c) of section 111, a television broadcast station holding a copyright or other license to transmit or perform the same version of that work shall, for purposes of subsection (b) of this section, be treated as a legal or beneficial owner if such secondary transmission occurs within the local service area of that television station.

(d) For any secondary transmission by a cable system that is actionable as an act of infringement pursuant to section 111(c)(3), the following shall also have standing to sue: (i) the primary transmitter whose transmission has been altered by the cable system; and (ii) any broadcast station within whose local service area the secondary transmission occurs.

Section 502. Remedies for infringement: Injunctions

(a) Any court having jurisdiction of a civil action arising under this title may, subject to the provisions of section 1498 of title 28, grant temporary and final injunctions on such terms as it may deem reasonable to prevent or restrain infringement of a copyright.

(b) Any such injunction may be served anywhere in the United States on the person enjoined; it shall be operative throughout the United States and shall be enforceable, by proceedings in contempt or otherwise, by any United States court having jurisdiction of that person. The clerk of the court granting the injunction shall, when requested by any other court in which enforcement of the injunction is sought, transmit promptly to the other court a certified copy of all the papers in the case on file in such clerk's office.

Section 503. Remedies for infringement: Impounding and disposition of infringing articles

(a) At any time while an action under this title is pending, the court may order the impounding, on such terms as it may deem reasonable, of all copies or phonorecords claimed to have been made or used in violation of the copyright owner's exclusive rights, and of all plates, molds, matrices, masters, tapes, film negatives, or other articles by means of which such copies or phonorecords may be reproduced.

(b) As part of a final judgment or decree, the court may order the destruction or other reasonable disposition of all copies or phonorecords found to have been made or used in violation of the copyright owner's exclusive rights, and of all plates, molds, matrices, masters, tapes, film negatives, or other articles by means of which such copies or phonorecords may be reproduced.

Section 504. Remedies for infringement: Damages and profits

(a) In General.—Except as otherwise provided by this title, an infringer of copyright is liabile for either—

(1) the copyright owner's actual damages and any additional profits of the infringer, as provided by subsection (b); or

(2) statutory damages, as provided by subsection (c).

(b) Actual Damages and Profits.—The copyright owner is entitled to recover the actual damages suffered by him or her as a result of the infringement, and any profits of the infringer that are attributable to the infringement and are not taken into account in computing the actual damages. In establishing the infringer's profits, the copyright owner is required to present proof only of the infringer's gross revenue, and the infringer is required to prove his or her deductible expenses and the elements of profit attributable to factors other than the copyrighted work.

(c) Statutory Damages.—

(1) Except as provided by clause (2) of this subsection, the copyright owner may elect, at any time before final judgment is rendered, to recover, instead of actual damages and profits, an award of statutory damages for all infringements involved in the action, with respect to any one work, for which any one infringer is liable individually, or for which any two or more infringers are liable jointly and severally, in a sum of not less than $250 or more than $10,000 as the court considers just. For the purposes of this subsection, all the parts of a compilation or derivative work constitute one work.

(2) In a case where the copyright owner sustains the burden of proving, and the court finds, that infringement was committed willfully, the court in its discretion may increase the award of statutory damages to a sum of not more than $50,000. In a case where the infringer sustains the burden of proving, and the court finds, that such infringer was not aware and had no reason to believe that his or her acts constituted an infringement of copyright, the court it its discretion may reduce the award of statutory damages to a sum of not less than $100. The court shall remit statutory damages in any case where an infringer believed and had reasonable grounds for believing that his or her use of the copyrighted work was a fair use under section 107, if the infringer was: (i) an employee or agent of a nonprofit educational instiution, library, or archives acting within the scope of his or her employment who, or such institution, library, or archives itself, which infringed by reproducing the work in copies or phonorecords; or (ii) a public broadcasting entity which or a person who, as a regular part of the nonprofit activities of a public infringed by performing a published nondramatic literary work or by reproducing a transmission program embodying a performance of such a work.

Section 505. Remedies for infringement: Costs and attorney's fees

In any civil action under this title, the court in its discretion may allow the recovery of full costs by or against any party other than the United States or an officer thereof. Except as otherwise provided in this title, the court may also award a reasonable attorney's fee to the prevailing party as part of the costs.

Section 506. Criminal offenses

(a) Criminal Infringement.—Any person who infringes a copyright willfully and for purposes of commercial advantage or private financial gain shall be punished as provided in section 2319 of title 18.

(b) Forfeiture and Destruction.—When any person is convicted of any violation of subsection (a), the court in its judgment of conviction shall, in addition to the penalty therein prescribed, order the forfeiture and destruction or other disposition of all infringing copies or phonorecords and all implements, devices, or equipment used in the manufacture of such infringing copies or phonorecords.

(c) Fraudulent Copyright Notice.—Any person who, with fraudulent intent, places on any article a notice of copyright or words of the same purport that such person knows to be false, or who, with fraudulent intent, publicly distributes or imports for public distribution any article bearing such notice or words that such person knows to be false, shall be fined not more than $2,500.

(d) Any person who, with fraudulent intent, removes or alters any notice of copyright appearing on a copy of a copyrighted work shall be fined not more than $2,500.

(e) False Representation.—Any person who knowingly makes a false representation of a material fact in the application for copyright registration provided for by section 409, or in any written statement filed in connection with the application, shall be fined not more than $2,500.

Section 507. Limitations on actions

(a) Criminal Proceedings.—No criminal proceeding shall be maintained under the provisions of this title unless it is commenced within three years after the cause of action arose.

(b) Civil Actions.—No civil action shall be maintained under the provisions of this title unless it is commenced within three years after the claim accrued.

Section 508. Notification of filing and determination of actions

(a) Within one month after the filing of any action under this title, the clerks of the courts of the United States shall send written notification to the Register of Copyrights setting forth, as far as is shown by the papers filed in the court, the names and addresses of the parties and the title, author, and registration number of each work involved in the action. If any other copyrighted work is later included in the action by amendment, answer, or other pleading, the clerk shall also send a notification concerning it to the Register within one month after the pleading is filed.

(b) Within one month after any final order or judgment is issued in the case, the clerk of the court shall notify the Register of it, sending with the notification a copy of the order or judgment together with the written opinion, if any, of the court.

(c) Upon receiving the notifications specified in this section, the Register shall make them a part of the public records of the Copyright Office.

Section 509. Seizure and forfeiture

(a) All copies or phonorecords manufactured, reproduced, distributed, sold, or otherwise used, intended for use, or possessed with intent to use in violation of section 506(a), and all plates, molds, matrices, masters, tapes, film negatives, or other articles by means of which such copies or phonorecords may be reproduced, and all electronic, mechanical, or other devices for manufacturing, reproducing, or assembling such copies or phonorecords may be seized and forfeited to the United States.

(b) The applicable procedures relating to (i) the seizure, summary and judicial forfeiture, and condemnation of vessels, vehicles, merchandise, and baggage for violations of the customs laws contained in title 19, (ii) the disposition of such vessels, vehicles, merchandise, and baggage or the proceeds from the sale thereof, (iii) the remission or mitigation of such forfeiture, (iv) the compromise of claims, and (v) the award of compensation to informers in respect of such forfeitures, shall apply to seizures and forfeitures incurred, or alleged to have been incurred, under the provisions of this section, insofar as applicable and not inconsistent with the provisions of this section; except that such duties as are imposed upon any officer or employee of the Treasury Department or any other person with respect to the seizure and forfeiture of vessels, vehicles, merchandise; and baggage under the provisions of the customs laws contained in title 19 shall be performed with respect to seizure and forfeiture of all articles described in subsection (a) by such officers, agents, or other persons as may be authorized or designated for that purpose by the Attorney General.

Section 510. Remedies for alteration of programing by cable systems

(a) In any action filed pursuant to section 111(c)(3), the following remedies shall be available:

(1) Where an action is brought by a party identified

in subsections (b) or (c) of section 501, the remedies provided by sections 502 through 505, and the remedy provided by subsection (b) of this section; and

(2) When an action is brought by a party identified in subsection (d) of section 501, the remedies provided by sections 502 and 505, together with any actual damages suffered by such party as a result of the infringement, and the remedy provided by subsection (b) of this section.

(b) In any action filed pursuant to section 111(c)(3), the court may decree that, for a period not to exceed thirty days, the cable system shall be deprived of the benefit of a compulsory license for one or more distant signals carried by such cable system.

Chapter 6.—Manufacturing Requirements and Importation

Sec. 601 Manufacture, importation, and public distribution of certain copies.
Sec. 602 Infringing importation of copies or phonorecords.
Sec. 603 Importation prohibitions: Enforcement and disposition of ex-excluded articles.

Section 601. Manufacture, Importation and Public Distribution of Certain Copies

(a) Prior to July 1, 1986, and except as provided by subsection (b), the importation into or public distribution in the United States of copies of a work consisting preponderantly of nondramtic literary material that is in the English language and is protected under this title is prohibited unless the portions consisting of such material have been manufactured in the United States or Canada.

(b) The provisions of subsection (a) do not apply—

(1) where, on the date when importation is sought or public distribution in the United States is made, the author of any substantial part of such material is neither a national nor a domiciliary of the United States or, if such author is a national of the United States, he or she has been domiciled outside the United States for a continuous period of at least one year immediately preceding that date; in the case of a work made for hire, the exemption provided by this clause does not apply unless a substantial part of the work was prepared for an employer or other person who is not a national or domiciliary of the United States or a domestic corporation or enterprise;

(2) where the United States Customs Service is presented with an import statement issued under the seal of the Copyright Office, in which case a total of no more than two thousand copies of any one such work shall be allowed entry; the import statement shall be issued upon request to the copyright owner or to a person designated by such owner at the time of registration for the work under section 408 or at any time thereafter;

(3) where importation is sought under the authority or for the use, other than in schools, of the Government of the United States or of any State or political subdivision of a State;

(4) where importation, for use and not for sale, is sought—

(A) by any person with respect to no more than one copy of any work at any one time;

(B) by any person arriving from outside the United States, with respect to copies forming part of such person's personal baggage; or

(C) by an organization operated for scholarly, educational, or religious purposes and not for private gain, with respect to copies intended to form a part of its library;

(5) where the copies are reproduced in raised characters for the use of the blind; or

(6) where, in addition to copies imported under clauses (3) and (4) of this subsection, no more than two thousand copies of any one such work, which have not been manufactured in the United States or Canada, are publicly distributed in the United States; or

(7) where, on the date when importation is sought or public distribution in the United States is made—

(A) the author of any substantial part of such material is an individual and receives compensation for the transfer or license of the right to distribute the work in the United States; and

(B) the first publication of the work has previously taken place outside the United States under a transfer or license granted by such author to a transferee or licensee who was not a national or domiciliary of the United States or a domestic corporation or enterprise; and

(C) there has been no publication of an authorized edition of the work of which the copies were manufactured in the United States; and

(D) the copies were reproduced under a transfer or license granted by such author or by the transferee or licensee of the right of first publication as mentioned in subclause (B), and the transferee or the licensee of the right of reproduction was not a national or domiciliary of the United States or a domestic corporation or enterprise.

(c) The requirement of this section that copies be manufactured in the United States or Canada is satisfied if—

(1) in the case where the copies are printed directly from type that has been set, or directly from plates made from such type, the setting of the type and the making of the plates have been performed in the United States or Canada; or

(2) in the case where the making of plates by a lithographic or photoengraving process is a final or intermediate step preceding the printing of the copies, the making of the plates has been performed in the United States or Canada; and

(3) in any case, the printing or other final process of producing multiple copies and any binding of the copies have been performed in the United States or Canada.

(d) Importation or public distribution of copies in violation of this section does not invalidate protection for a work under this title. However, in any civil action or criminal proceeding for infringement of the exclusive rights to reproduce and distribute copies of the work, the infringer has a complete defense with respect to all of the nondramatic literary material comprised in the work and any other parts of the work in which the exclusive rights to reproduce and distribute copies are owned by the same person who owns such exclusive rights in the nondramatic literary material, if the infringer proves—

(1) that copies of the work have been imported into or publicly distributed in the United States in violation of this section by or with the authority of the owner of such exclusive rights; and

(2) that the infringing copies were manufactured in the United States or Canada in accordance with the provisions of subsection (c); and

(3) that the infringement was commenced before the effective date of registration for an authorized edition of the work, the copies of which have been manufactured in the United States or Canada in accordance with the provisions of subsection (c).

(e) In any action for infringement of the exclusive rights to reproduce and distribute copies of a work containing material required by this section to be manufactured in the United States or Canada, the copyright owner shall set forth in the complaint the names of the persons or organizations who performed the processes specified by subsection (c) with respect to that material, and the places where those processes were performed.

Section 602. Infringing importation of copies or phonorecords

(a) Importation into the United States, without the authority of the owner of copyright under this title, of copies or phonorecords of a work that have been acquired outside the United States is an infringement of the exclusive right to distribute copies or phonorecords under section 106, actionable under section 501. This subsection does not apply to—

(1) importation of copies or phonorecords under the authority or for the use of the Government of the United States or of any State or political subdivision of a State, but not including copies or phonorecords for use in schools, or copies of any audiovisual work imported for purposes other than archival use;

(2) importation, for the private use of the importer and not for distribution, by any person with respect to no more than one copy or phonorecord of any one work at any one time, or by any person arriving from outside the United States with respect to copies or phonorecords forming part of such peson's personal baggage; or

(3) importation by or for an organization operated for scholarly, educational, or religious purposes and not for private gain, with respect to no more than one copy of an audiovisual work solely for its archival purposes, and no more than five copies or phonorecords of any other work for its library lending or archival purposes, unless the importation of such copies or phonorecords is part of an activity consisting of systematic reproduction or distribution, engaged in by such organization in violation of the provisions of section 108(g)(2).

(b) In a case where the making of the copies or phonorecords would have constituted an infringement of copyright if this title had been applicable, their importation is prohibited. In a case where the copies or phonorecords were lawfuly made, the United States Customs Service has no authority to prevent their importatin unless the provisions of section 601 are applicable. In either case, the Secretary of the Treasury is authorized to prescribe, by regulation, a procedure under which any person claiming an interest in the copyright in a particular work may, upon payment of a specified fee, be entitled to notification by the Customs Service of the importation of articles that appear to be copies or phonorecords of the work.

Section 603. Importation prohibitions: Enforcement anddisposition of excluded articles

(a) The Secretary of the Treasury and the United States Postal Service shall separately or jointly make regulations for the enforcement of the provisions of this title prohibiting importation.

(b) These regulations may require, as a condition for the exclusion of articles under section 602—

(1) that the person seeking exclusion obtain a court order enjoining importation of the articles; or

(2) that the person seeking exclusion furnish proof, of a specified nature and in accordance with prescribed procedures, that the copyright in which such person claims an interest is valid and that the importation would violate the prohibiton in section 602; the person seeking exclusion may also be required to post a surety bond for any injury that may result if the detention or exclusion of the articles proves to be unjustified.

(c) Articles imported in violation of the importation prohibitions of this title are subject to seizure and forfeiture in the same manner as property imported in violation of the customs revenue laws. Forfeited articles shall be destroyed as directed by the Secretary of the Treasury or the court, as the case may be; however, the articles may be returned to the country of export whenever it is shown to the satisfaction of the Secretary of the Treasury that the importer had no reasonable grounds for believing that his or her acts constituted a violation of law.

Chapter 7.—Copyright Office

Sec. 701 The Copyright Office: General responsibilities and organization.
Sec. 702 Copyright Office regulations.
Sec. 703 Effective date of actions in Copyright Office.
Sec. 704 Retention and disposition of articles deposited in Copyright Office.
Sec. 705 Copyright Office records: Preparation, maintenance, public inspection, and searching.
Sec. 706 Copies of Copyright Office records.
Sec. 707 Copyright Office forms and publications.
Sec. 708 Copyright Office fees.
Sec. 709 Delay in delivery caused by disruption of postal or other services.
Sec. 710 Reproduction for use of the blind and physically handicapped: voluntary licensing forms and procedures.

Section 701. The Copyright Office: General Responsibilities and Organization

(a) All administrative functions and duties under this title, except as otherwise specified, are the responsibility of the Register of Copyrights as director of the Copyright Office of the Library of Congress. The Register of Copyrights, together with the subordinate officers and employees of the Copyright Office, shall be appointed by the Librarian of Congress, and shall act under the Librarian's general direction and supervision.

(b) The Register of Copyrights shall adopt a seal to be used on and after January 1, 1978, to authenticate all certified documents issued by the Copyright Office.

(c) The Register of Copyrights shall make an annual report to the Librarian of Congress of the work and accomplishments of the Copyright Office during the previous fiscal year. The annual report of the Register of Copyrights shall be published separately and as a part of the annual report of the Librarian of Congress.

(d) Except as provided by section 706(b) and the regulations issued thereunder, all actions taken by the Register of Copyrights under this title are subject to the provisions of the Administrative Procedure Act of June 11, 1946, as amended (c. 324, 60 Stat. 237, title 5, United States Code, Chapter 5, Subchapter II and Chapter 7).

Section 702. Copyright Office regulations

The Register of Copyrights is authorized to establish regulations not inconsistent with law for the administration of the functions and duties made the responsibility of the Register under this title. All regulations established by the Register under this title are subject to the approval of the Librarian of Congress.

Section 703. Effective date of actions in Copyright Office

In any case in which time limits are prescribed under this title for the performance of an action in the Copyright Office, and in which the last day of the prescribed period falls on a Saturday, Sunday, holiday, or other nonbusiness day within the District of Columbia or the Federal Government, the action may be taken on the next succeeding business day, and is effective as of the date when the period expired.

Section 704. Retention and disposition of articles

deposited in Copyright Office

(a) Upon their deposit in the Copyright Office under sections 407 and 408, all copies, phonorecords, and identifying material, including those deposited in connection with claims that have been refused registration, are the property of the United States Government.

(b) In the case of published works, all copies, phonorecords, and identifying material deposited are available to the Library of Congress for its collections, or for exchange or transfer to any other library. In the case of unpublished works, the Library is entitled, under regulations that the Register of Copyrights shall prescribe, to select any deposits for its collections or for transfer to the National Archives of the United States or to a Federal records center, as defined in section 2901 of title 44.

(c) The Register of Copyrights is authorized, for specific or general categories of works, to make a facsimile reproduction of all or any part of the material deposited under section 408, and to make such reproduction a part of the Copyright Office records of the registration, before transferring such material to the Library of Congress as provided by subsection (b), or before destroying or otherwise disposing of such material as provided by subsection (d).

(d) Deposits not selected by the Library under subsection (b), or identifying portions or reproductions of them, shall be retained under the control of the Copyright Office, including retention in government storage facilities, for the longest period considered practicable and desirable by the Register of Copyrights and the Librarian of Congress. After that period it is within the joint discretion of the Register and the Librarian to order their destruction or other disposition; but, in the case of unpublished works, no deposit shall be knowingly or intentionally destroyed or otherwise disposed of during its term of copyright unless a facsimile reproduction of the entire deposit has been made a part of the Copyright Office records as provided by subsection (c).

(e) The depositor of copies, phonorecords, or identifying material under section 408, or the copyright owner of record, may request retention, under the control of the Copyright Office, of one or more of such articles for the full term of copyright in the work. The Register of Copyrights shall prescribe, by regulation, the conditions under which such requests are to be made and granted, and shall fix the fee to be charged under section 708(a)(11) if the request is granted.

Section 705. Copyright Office records: Preparation, maintenance, public inspection, and searching

(a) The Register of Copyrights shall provide and keep in the Copyright Office records of all deposits, registrations, recordations, and other actions taken under this title, and shall prepare indexes of all such records.

(b) Such records and indexes, as well as the articles deposited in connection with completed copyright registrations and retained under the control of the Copyright Office, shall be open to public inspection.

(c) Upon request and payment of the fee specified by section 708, the Copyright Office shall make a search of its public records, indexes, and deposits, and shall furnish a report of the information they disclose with respect to any particular deposits, registrations, or recorded documents.

Section 706. Copies of Copyright Office records

(a) Copies may be made of any public records or indexes of the Copyright Office; additional certificates of copyright registration and copies of any public records or indexes may be furnished upon request and payment of the fees specified by section 708.

(b) Copies or reproductions of deposited articles retained under the control of the Copyright Office shall be authorized or furnished only under the conditions specified by the Copyright Office regulations.

Section 707. Copyright Office forms and publications

(a) Catalog of Copyright Entries.—The Register of Copyrights shall compile and publish at periodic intervals catalogs of all copyright registrations. These catalogs shall be divided into parts in accordance with the various classes of works, and the Register has discretion to determine, on the basis of practicability and usefulness, the form and frequency of publication of each particular part.

(b) Other Publications.—The Register shall furnish, free of charge upon request, application forms for copyright registration and general informational material in connection with the functions of the Copyright Office. The Register also has the authority to publish compilations of information, bibliographies, and other material he or she considers to be of value to the public.

(c) Distribution of Publications.—All publications of the Copyright Office shall be furnished to depository libraries as specified under section 1905 of title 44, and, aside from those furnished free of charge, shall be offered for sale to the public at prices based on the cost of reproduction and distribution.

Section 708. Copyright Office fees

(a) The following fees shall be paid to the Register of Copyrights:

(1) on filing each application for registration of a copyright claim or a supplementary registration under section 408, including the issuance of a certificate of registration if registration is made, $10;

(2) on filing each application for registration of a claim to renewal of a subsisting copyright in its first term under section 304(a), including the issuance of a certificate of registration if registration is made, $6;

(3) for the issuance of a receipt for a deposit under section 407, $2;

(4) for the recordation, as provided by section 205, of a transfer of copyright ownership or other document of six pages or less, covering no more than one title, $10; for each page over six and each title over one, 50 cents additional;

(5) for the filing, under section 115(b), of a notice of intention to make phonorecords, $6;

(6) for the recordation, under section 302(c), of a statement revealing the identity of an author of an anonymous or pseudonymous work, or for the recordation, under section 302(d), of a statement relating to the death of an author, $10 for a document of six pages or less, covering no more than one title; for each page over six and for each title over one, $1 additional;

(7) for the issuance, under section 601, of an import statement, $3;

(8) for the issuance, under section 706, of an additional certificate of registration, $4;

(9) for the issuance of any other certification, $4; the Register of Copyrights has discretion, on the basis of their cost, to fix the fees for preparing copies of Copyright Office records, whether they are to be certified or not;

(10) for the making and reporting of a search as provided by section 705, and for any related services, $10 for each hour or fraction of an hour consumed;

(11) for any other special services requiring a substantial amount of time or expense, such fees as the

Register of Copyrights may fix on the basis of the cost of providing the service.

(b) The fees prescribed by or under this section are applicable to the United States Government and any of its agencies, employees, or officers, but the Register of Copyrights has discretion to waive the requirement of this subsection in occasional or isolated cases involving relatively small amounts.

(c) All fees received under this section shall be deposited by the Register of Copyrights in the Treasury of the United States and shall be credited to the appropriation for necessary expenses of the Copyright Office. The Register may, in accordance with regulations that he or she shall prescribe, refund any sum paid by mistake or in excess of the fee required by this section.

Section 709. Delay in delivery caused by disruption of postal or other services

In any case in which the Register of Copyrights determines, on the basis of such evidence as the Register may by regulation require, that a deposit, application, fee, or any other material to be delivered to the Copyright Office by a particular date, would have been received in the Copyright Office in due time except for a general disruption or suspension of postal or other transportation or communications services, the actual receipt of such material in the Copyright Office within one month after the date on which the Register determines that the disruption or suspension of such services has terminated, shall be considered timely.

Section 710. Reproduction for use of the blind and physically handicapped: Voluntary licensing forms and procedures

The Register of Copyrights shall, after consultation with the Chief of the Division for the Blind and Physically Handicapped and other appropriate officials of the Library of Congress, establish by regulation standardized forms and procedures by which, at the time applications covering certain specified categories of nondramatic literary works are submitted for registration under section 408 of this title, the copyright owner may voluntarily grant to the Library of Congress a license to reproduce the copyrighted work by means of Braille or similar tactile symbols, or by fixation of a reading of the work in a phonorecord, or both, and to distribute the resulting copies or phonorecords solely for the use of the blind and physiclaly handicapped and under limited conditions to be specified in the standardized forms.

Chapter 8.—Copyright Royalty Tribunal

Section 801. Copyright Royalty Tribunal: Establishment and Purpose

(a) There is hereby created an independent Copyright Royalty Tribunal in the legislative branch.

(b) Subject to the provisions of this chapter, the purposes of the Tribunal shall be—

(1) to make determinations concerning the adjustment of reasonable copyright royalty rates as provided in sections 115 and 116, and to make determinations as to reasonable terms and rates of royalty payments as provided in section 118. The rates applicable under sections 115 and 116 shall be calculated to achieve the following objectives:

(A) To maximize the availability of creative works to the public;

(B) To afford the copyright owner a fair return for his creative work and the copyright user a fair income under existing economic conditions;

(C) To reflect the relative roles of the copyright owner and the copyright user in the product made available to the public with respect to relative creative contribution, technological contribution, capital investment, cost, risk, and contribution to the opening of new markets for creative expression and media for their communication;

(D) To minimize any disruptive impact on the structure of the industries involved and on generally prevailing industry practices.

(2) to make determinations concerning the adjustment of the copyright royalty in section 111 solely in accordance with the following provisions:

(A) The rates established by section 111(d)(2)(B) may be adjusted to reflect (i) national monetary inflation or deflation or (ii) changes in the average rates charged cable subscribers for the basic service of providing secondary transmissions to maintain the real constant dollar level of the royalty fee per subscriber which existed as of the date of enactment of this Act: Provided, That if the average rates charged cable system subscribers for the basic service of providing secondary transmissions are changed so that the average rates exceed national monetary inflation, no change in the rates established by section 111(d)(2)(B) shall be permitted: And provided further, That no increase in the royalty fee shall be permitted based on any reduction in the average number of distant signal equivalents per subscriber. The Commission may consider all factors relating to the maintenance of such level of payments including, as an extenuating factor, whether the cable industry has been restrained by subscriber rate regulating authorities from increasing the rates for the basic service of providing secondary transmissions.

(B) In the event that the rules and regulations of the Federal Communications Commission are amended at any time after April 15, 1976, to permit the carriage by cable systems of additional television broadcast signals beyond the local service area of the primary transmitters of such signals, the royalty rates established by section 111(d)(1)(B) may be adjusted to insure that the rates for the additional distant signal equivalents resulting from such carriage are reasonable in the light of the changes effected by the amendment to such rules and regulations. In determining the reasonableness of rates proposed following an amendment of Federal Communications Commission rules and regulations, the Copyright Royalty Tribunal shall consider, among other factors, the economic impact on copyright owners and users: Provided, That no adjustment in royalty rates shall be made under this subclause with respect to any distant signal equivalent or fraction thereof represented by (i) carriage of any signal permitted under the rules and regulations of the Federal Communications Commission in effect on April 15, 1976, or the carriage of a signal of the same type (that is, independent, network, or noncommercial educational) substituted for such permitted signal, or (ii) a television broadcast signal first carried after April 15, 1976 pursuant to an individual waiver of the rules and regulations of the Federal Communications Commission, as such rules and regulations were in effect April 15, 1976.

(C) In the event of any change in the rules and regulations of the Federal Communication Commission with respect to syndicated and sports program exclusivity after April 15, 1976, the rates established by section 111(d)(1)(B) may be adjusted to assure that such rates are reasonable in light of the charges to such rules and regulations, but any such adjustment shall apply only to the affected television broadcast signals carried on those systems affected by the change.

(D) The gross receipts limitations established by section 111(d)(1)(C) and (D) shall be adjusted to reflect national monetary inflation or deflation or changes in the average rates charged cable system subscribers for the basic service of providing secondary transmissions to maintain the real constant dollar value of the exemption provided by such section; and the royalty rate specified therein shall not be subject to adjustment; and

(3) to distribute fees deposted with the Register of Copyrights under sections 111 and 116, and to determine, in cases where controversy exists, the distribution of such fees.

(c) As soon as possible after the date of enactment of this Act, and no later than six months following such date, the President shall publish a notice announcing the initial appointments provided in section 802, and shall designate an order of seniority among the initially-appointed commissioners for purposes of section 802(b).

Section 802. Membership of the Tribunal

(a) The Tribunal shall be composed of five commissioners appointed by the President with the advice and consent of the Senate for a term of seven years each; of the first five members appointed, three shall be designated to serve for seven years from the date of the notice specified in section 801(c), and two shall be designated to serve for five years from such date, respectively. Commissioners shall be compensated at the highest rate now or hereafter prescribe [sic] for grade 18 of the General Schedule pay rates (5 U.S.C. 5332).

(b) Upon convening the commissioners shall elect a chairman from among the commissoners appointed for a full seven-year term. Such chairman shall serve for a term of one year. Thereafter, the most senior commissioner who has not previously served as chairman shall serve as chairman for a period of one year, except that, if all commissioners have served a full term as chairman, the most senior commissioner who has served the least number of terms as chairman shall be designated as chairman.

(c) Any vacancy in the Tribunal shall not affect its powers and shall be filled, for the unexpired term of the appointment, in the same manner as the original appointment was made.

Section 803. Procedures of the Tribunal

(a) The Tribunal shall adopt regulations, not inconsistent with law, governing its procedure and methods of operation. Except as otherwise provided in this chapter, the Tribunal shall be subject to the provisions of the Administrative Procedure Act of June 11, 1946, as amended (c.324, 60 Stat. 237, Title 5, United States Code, Chapter 5, Subchapter II and Chapter 7).

(b) Every final determination of the Tribunal shall be published in the Federal Register. It shall state in detail the criteria that the Tribunal determined to be applicable to the particular proceeding, the various facts that it found relevant to its determination in that proceeding, and the specific reasons for its determination.

Section 804. Institution and conclusion of proceedings

(a) With respect to proceedings under section 801(b)(1) concerning the adjustment of royalty rates as provided in sections 115 and 116, and with respect to proceedings under section 801(b)(2)(A) and (D)—

(1) on January 1, 1980, the Chairman of the Tribunal shall cause to be published in the Federal Register notice of commencement of proceedings under this chapter; and

(2) during the calendar years specified in the following schedule, any owner or user of a copyrighted work whose royalty rates are specified by this title, or by a rate established by the Tribunal, may file a petition with the Tribunal declaring that the petitioner requests an adjustment of the rate. The Tribunal shall make a determination as to whether the applicant has a significant interest in the royalty rate in which an adjustment is requested. If the Tribunal determines that the petition has a significant interest, the Chairman shall cause notice of this determination, with the reasons therefor, to be published in the Federal Register, together with notice of commencement of proceedings under this chapter.

(A) In proceedings under section 901(b)(2)(A) and (D), such petition may be filed during 1985 and in each subsequent tenth calendar year.

(B) In proceedings under section 801(b)(1) concerning the adjustment of royalty rates as provided in section 115, such petition may be filed in 1987 and in each subsequent tenth calendar year.

(C) In proceedings under section 801(b)(1) concerning the adjustment of royalty rates under section 116, such petition may be filed in 1990 and in each subsequent tenth calendar year.

(b) With respect to proceedings under subclause (B) or (C) of section 801(b)(2), following an event described in either of those subsections, any owner or user of a copyrighted work whose royalty rates are specified by section 111, or by a rate established by the Tribunal, may, within twelve months, file a petition with the tribunal declaring that the petitioner requests an adjustment of the rate. In this event the Tribunal shall proceed as in subsection (a)(2), above. Any change in royalty rates made by the Tribunal pursuant to this subsection may be reconsidered in 1980, 1985, and each fifth calendar year thereafter, in accordance with the provisions in section 801 (b)(2)(B) or (C), as the case may be.

(c) With respect to proceedings under section 801(b)(1), concerning the determination of reasonable terms and rates of royalty payments as provided in section 118, the Tribunal shall proceed when and as provided by that section.

(d) With respect to proceedings under section 801(b)(3), concerning the distribution of royalty fees in certain circumstances under sections 111 or 116, the Chairman of the Tribunal shall, upon determination by the Tribunal that a controversy exists concerning such distribution, cause to be published in the Federal Register notice of commencement of proceedings under this chapter.

(e) All proceedings under this chapter shall be initiated without delay following publication of the notice specified in this section, and the Tribunal shall render its final decision in any such proceeding within one year from the date of such publication.

Section 805. Staff of the Tribunal

(a) The Tribunal is authorized to appoint and fix the compensation of such employees as may be necessary to carry out the provisions of this Chapter, and to prescribe their functions and duties.

(b) The Tribunal may procure temporary and intermittent services to the same extent as is authorized by section 3109 of title 5.

Section 806. Administrative support of the Tribunal

(a) The Library of Congress shall provide the Tribunal with necessary administrative services, including those related to budgeting, accounting, financial reporting, travel, personnel, and procurement. The Tribunal shall pay the Library for such services, either in advance or by reimbursement from the funds of the Tribunal, at amounts to be agreed upon between the Librarian and the Tribunal.

(b) The Library of Congress is authorized to disburse funds for the Tribunal, under regulations prescribed jointly by the Librarian of Congress and the Tribunal and approved by the Comptroller General. Such regulations shall establish requirements and procedures under which every voucher certified for payment by the Library of Congress under this chapter shall be supported with a certification by a duly authorized officer or employee of the Tribunal, and shall prescribe the responsibilities and accountability of said officers and employees of the Tribunal with respect to such certifications.

Section 807. Deduction of costs of proceedings

Before any funds are distributed pursuant to a final decision in a proceeding involving distribution of royalty fees, the Tribunal shall assess the reasonable costs of such proceeding.

Section 808. Reports

In addition to its publication of the reports of all final determinations as provided in section 803(b), the Tribunal shall make an annual report to the President and the Congress concerning the Tribunal's work during the preceding fiscal year, including a detailed fiscal statement of account.

Section 809. Effective date of final determinations

Any final determination by the Tribunal under this chapter shall become effective thirty days following its publication in the Federal Register as provided in section 803(b), unless prior to that time an appeal has been filed pursuant to section 810, to vacate, modify, or correct such determination, and notice of such appeal has been served on all parties who appeared before the Tribunal in the proceeding in question. Where the proceeding involves the distribution of royalty fees under sections 111 or 116, the Tribunal shall, upon the expiration of such thirty-day period, distribute any royalty fees not subject to an appeal filed pursuant to section 810.

Section 810. Judicial review

Any final decision of the Tribunal in a proceeding under section 801(b) may be appealed to the United States Court of Appeals, within thirty days after its publication in the Federal Register by an aggrieved party. The judicial review of the decision shall be had, in accordance with chapter 7 of title 5, on the basis of the record before the Tribunal. No court shall have jurisidiction to review a final decision of the Tribunal except as provided in this section.

Chapter 9.—Protection of Semiconductor Chip Products

Section 901. Definitions

(a) As used in this chapter—

(1) a "semiconductor chip product" is the final or intermediate form of any product—

(A) having two or more layers of metallic, insulating, or semiconductor material, deposited or otherwise placed on, or etched away or otherwise removed from, a piece of semiconductor material in accordance with a predetermined pattern; and

(B) intended to perform electronic circuitry functions;

(2) a "mask work" is a series of related images, however, fixed or encoded—

(A) having or representing the predetermined, three-dimensional pattern of metallic, insulating, or semiconductor material present or removed from the layers of a semiconductor chip product; and

(B) in which series the relation of the images to one another is that each image has the pattern of the surface of one form of the semiconductor chip product;

(3) a mask work is "fixed" in a semiconductor chip product when its embodiment in the product is sufficiently permanent or stable to permit the mask work to be perceived or reproduced from the product for a period of more than transitory duration;

(4) "distribute" means to sell, or to lease, bail, or otherwise transfer, or to offer to sell, lease, bail, or otherwise transfer.

(5) to "commercially exploit" a mask work is to distribute to the public for commercial purposes a semiconductor chip product embodying the mask work; except that such term includes an offer to sell or

transfer a semiconductor chip product only when the offer is in writing and occurs after the mask work is fixed in the semiconductor chip product;

(6) the "owner" of a mask work is the person who created the mask work, the legal representative of that person if that person is deceased or under a legal incapacity, or a party to whom all the rights under this chapter of such person or representative are transferred in accordance with section 903(b); except that, in the case of a work made within the scope of a person's employment, the owner is the employer for whom the person created the mask work or a party to whom all the rights under this chapter of the employer are transferred in accordance with section 903(b);

(7) an "innocent purchaser" is a person who purchases a semiconductor chip product in good faith and without having notice of protection with respect to the semiconductor chip product;

(8) having "notice of protection" means having actual knowledge that, or reasonable grounds to believe that, a mask work is protected under this chapter; and

(9) an "infringing semiconductor chip product" is a semiconductor chip product which is made, imported, or distributed in violation of the exclusive rights of the owner of a mask work under this chapter.

(b) For purposes of this chapter, the distribution or importation of a product incorporating a semiconductor chip product as a part thereof is a distribution or importation of that semiconductor chip product.

Section 902. Subject matter of protection

(a)(1) Subject to the provisions of subsection (b), a mask work fixed in a semiconductor chip product, by or under the authority of the owner of the mask work, is eligible for protection under this chapter if—

(A) on the date on which the mask work is registered under section 908, or is first commercially exploited anywhere in the world, whichever occurs first, the owner of the mask work is (i) a national or domiciliary of the United States, (ii) a national, domiciliary, or soverign authority of a foreign nation that is a party to a treaty affording protection to mask works to which the United States is also a party, or (iii) a stateless person, wherever that person may be domiciled;

(B) the mask work is first commercially exploited in the United States; or

(C) the mask work comes within the scope of a Presidential proclamation issued under paragraph (2).

(2) Whenever the President finds that a foreign nation extends, to mask works of owners who are nationals or domiciliaries of the United States protection (A) on substantially the same basis as that on which the foreign nation extends protection to mask works of its own nationals and domiciliaries and mask works first

commercially exploited in that nation, or (B) on substantially the same basis as provided in this chapter, the President may by proclamation extend protection under this chapter to mask works (i) of owners who are, on the date on which the mask works are registered under section 908, or the date on which the mask works are first commercially exploited anywhere in the world, whichever occurs first, nationals, domiciliaries, or sovereign authorities of that nation, or (ii) which are first commercially exploited in that nation. The President may revise, suspend, or revoke any such proclamation or impose any conditions or limitations on protection extended under any such proclamation.

(b) Protection under this chapter shall not be available for a mask work that—

(1) is not original; or

(2) consists of designs that are staple, commonplace, or familiar in the semiconductor industry, or variations of such designs, combined in a way that, considered as a whole, is not original.

(c) In no case does protection under this chapter for a mask work extend to any idea, procedure, process, system, method of operation, concept, principle, or discovery, regardless of the form in which it is described, explained, illustrated, or embodies in such work.

Section 903. Ownership, transfer, licensing, and recordation

(a) The exclusive rights in a mask work subject to protection under this chapter belong to the owner of the mask work.

(b) The owner of the exclusive rights in a mask work may transfer all of those rights, or license all or less than all of those rights, by any written instrument signed by such owner or a duly authorized agent of the owner. Such rights may be transferred or licensed by operation of law, may be bequeathed by will, and may pass as personal property by the applicable laws of intestate succession.

(c)(1) Any document pertaining to a mask work may be recorded in the Copyright Office if the document filed for recordation bears the actual signature of the person who executed it, or if it is accompanied by a sworn or official certification that it is a true copy of the original, signed document. The Register of Copyrights shall, upon receipt of the document and the fee specified pursuant to section 908(d), record the document and return it with a certificate of recordation. The recordation of any transfer or license under this paragraph gives all persons constructive notice of the facts stated in the recorded document concerning the transfer or license.

(2) In any case in which conflicting transfers of the exclusive rights in a mask work are made, the transfer first executed shall be void as against a subsequent transfer which is made for a valuable consideration and without notice of the first transfer, unless the first transfer is recorded in accordance with paragraph (1) within three months after the date on which it is executed, but in no case later than the day before the date of such subsequent transfer.

(d) Mask works prepared by an officer or employee of the United States Government as part of that person's official duties are not protected under this chapter, but the United States Government is not precluded from receiving and holding exclusive rights in mask works transferred to the Government under subsection (b).

Section 904. Duration of protection

(a) The protection provided for a mask work under this chapter shall commence on the date on which the mask work is registered under section 908, or the date on which the mask work is first commercially exploited anywhere in the world, whichever comes first.

(b) Subject to subsection (c) and the provisions of this chapter, the protection provided under this chapter to a mask work shall end ten years after the date on which such protection commences under subsection (a).

(c) All terms of protection provided in this section shall run to the end of the calendar year in which they would otherwise expire.

Section 905. Exclusive rights in mask works

The owner of a mask work provided protection under this chapter has the exclusive rights to do and to authorize any of the following:

(1) to reproduce the mask work by optical, electronic, or any other means;

(2) to import or distribute a semiconductor chip product in which the mask work is embodied; and

(3) to induce or knowingly to cause another person to do any of the acts described in paragraphs (1) and (2).

Section 906. Limitation on exclusive rights: reverse engineering; first sale

(a) Notwithstanding the provisions of section 905, it is not an infringement of the exclusive rights of the owner of a mask work for—

(1) a person to reproduce the mask work solely for the purpose of teaching, analyzing, or evaluating the concepts or techniques embodied in the mask work or the circuitry, logic flow, or organization of components used in the mask work; or

(2) a person who performs the analysis or evaluation described in paragraph (1) to incorporate the results of such conduct in an original mask work which is made to be distributed.

(b) Notwithstanding the provisions of section 905(2), the owner of a particular semiconductor chip product made by the owner of the mask work, or by any person authorized by the owner of the mask work, may import, distribute, or otherwise dispose of or use, but not reproduce, that particular semiconductor chip product without the authority of the owner of the mask work.

Section 907. Limitation on exclusive rights: innocent infrinement

(a) Notwithstanding any other provision of this chapter, an innocent purchaser or an infringing semiconductor chip product—

(1) shall incur no liability under this chapter with respect to the importation or distribution of units of the infringing semiconductor chip product that occurs before the innocent purchaser has notice of protection with respect to the mask work embodied in the semiconductor chip product; and

(2) shall be liable only for a reasonable royalty on each unit of the infringing semiconductor chip product that the innocent purchaser imports or distributes after having notice of protection with respect to the mask work embodied in the semiconductor chip product.

(b) The amount of the royalty referred to in subsection (a)(2) shall be determined by the court in a civil action for infringement unless the parties resolve the issue by voluntary negotiation, mediation, or binding arbitration.

(c) The immunity of an innocent purchaser from liability referred to in subsection (a)(1) and the limitation of remedies with respect to an innocent purchaser referred to in subsection (a)(2) shall extend to any person who directly or indirectly purchases an infringing semiconductor chip product from an innocent purchaser.

(d) The provisions of subsections (a), (b), and (c) apply only with respect to those units of an infringing semiconductor chip product that an innocent purchaser purchased before having notice of protection with respect to the mask work embodied in the semiconductor chip product.

Section 908. Registration of claims of protection

(a) The owner of a mask work may apply to the Register of Copyrights for registration of a claim of protection in a mask work. Protection of a mask work under this chapter shall terminate if application for registration of a claim of protection in the mask work is not made as provided in this chapter within two years after the date on which the mask work is first commercially exploited anywhere in the world.

(b) The Register of Copyrights shall be responsible for all administrative functions and duties under this chapter. Except for section 708, the provisions of chapter 7 of this title relating to the general responsibilities, organization, regulatory authority, actions, records, and publications of the Copyright Office shall apply to this chapter, except that the Register of Copyright may make such changes as may be necesary in applying those provisions to this chapter.

(c) The application for registration of a mask work shall be made on a form prescribed by the Register of Copyrights. Such form may require any information regarded by the Register as bearing upon the preparation or identification of the mask work, the existence or duration of protection of the mask work under this chapter, or ownership of the mask work. The application shall be accompanied by the fee set pursuant to subsection (d) and the identifying material specified pursuant to such subsection.

(d) The Register of Copyrights shall by regulation set reasonable fees for the filing of applications to register claims of protection in the administration of this chapter or the rights under this chapter, taking into consideration the cost of providing those services, the benefits of a public record, and statutory fee schedules under this title. The Register shall also specify the identifying material to be deposited in connection with the claim for registration.

(e) If the Register of Copyrights, after examining an application for registration, determines, in accordance with the provisions of this chapter, that the application relates to a mask work which is entitled to protection under this chapter, then the Register shall register the claim of protection and issue to the applicant a certificate of registration of the claim of protection under the seal of the Copyright Office, the effective date of registration of a claim of protection shall be the date on which an application, deposit of identifying material, and fee, which are determined by the Register of Copyrights or by a court of competent jurisdiction to be acceptable for registration of the claim, have all been received in the Copyright Office.

(f) In any action for infringement under this chapter, the certificate of registration of a mask work shall constitute prima facie evidence (1) of the facts stated in the certificate, and (2) that the applicant issued the certificate has met, the requirements of this chapter, and the regulations issued under this chapter, with respect to the registration of claims.

(g) Any applicant for registration under this section who is dissatisfied with the refusal of the Register of Copyrights to issue a certificate of registration under this section may seek judicial review of that refusal by bringing an action for such review in an appropriate United States district court not later than sixty days after the refusal. The provisions of chapter 7 of title 5 shall apply to such judicial review. The failure of the Register of Copyrights to issue a certificate of registration within four months after an application for registration is filed shall be deemed to be a refusal to issue a certificate of registration for purposes of this subsection and section 910(b)(2), except that, upon a showing of good cause, the district court may shorten such four-month period.

Section 909. Mask work notice

(a) The owner of a mask work provided protection under this chapter may affix notice to the mask work, and to masks and semiconductor chip products embodying the mask work, in such manner and location as to give reasonable notice of such protection. The Register of Copyrights shall prescribe by regulation, as examples, specific methods of affixation and positions of notice for purposes of this section, but these specifications shall not be considered exhaustive. The affixation of such notice is not a condition of protection under this chapter, but shall constitute prima facie evidence of notice of protection.

(b) The notice referred to in subsection (a) shall consist of—

(1) the words "mask work", the symbol *M*, or the symbol [statutory text shows an M enclosed in a circle] (the letter M in a circle); and

(2) the name of the owner or owners of the mask work or an abbreviation by which the name is recognized or is generally known.

Section 910. Enforcement of exclusive rights

(a) Except as otherwise provided in this chapter, any person who violates any of the exclusive rights of the owner of a mask work under this chapter, by conduct in or affecting commerce, shall be liable as an infringer of such rights.

(b)(1) The owner of a mask work protected under this chapter, or the exclusive licensee of all rights under this chapter with respect to the mask work, shall, after a certificate of registration of a claim of protection in that mask work has been issued under section 908, be entitled to institute a civil action for any infringement with respect to the mask work which is committed after the commencement of protection of the mask work under section 904(a).

(2) In any case in which an application for registration of a claim of protection in a mask work and the required deposit of identifying material and fee have been received in the Copyright Office in proper form and registration of the mask work has been refused, the applicant is entitled to institute a civil action for infringement under this chapter with respect to the mask work if notice of the action, together with a copy of the complaint, is served on the Register of Copyrights, in accordance with the Federal Rules of Civil Procedure. The Register may, at his or her option, become a party to the action with respect to the issue of whether the claim of protection is eligible for registration by entering an appearance within sixty days after such service, but the failure of the Register to become a party to the action shall not deprive the court of jurisdiction to determine that issue.

(c)(1) The Secretary of the Treasury and the United States Postal Service shall separately or jointly issue regulations for the enforcement of the rights set forth in section 905 with respect to importation. These regulations may require; as a condition for the exclusion of articles from the United States, that the person seeking exclusion take any one or more of the following action:

(A) Obtain a court order enjoining, or an order of the International Trade Commission under section 337 of the Tariff Act of 1930 excluding, importation of the articles.

(B) Furnish proof that the mask work involved is protected under this chapter and that the importation of the articles would infringe the rights in the mask work under this chapter.

(C) Post a surety bond for any injury that may result if the detention or exclusion of the articles proves to be unjustified.

(2) Articles imported in violation of the rights set forth in section 905 are subject to seizure and forfeiture in the same manner as property imported in violation of the customs laws. Any such forfeited articles shall be destroyed as directed by the Secretary of the Treasury or the court, as the case may be, except that the articles may be returned to the country of export whenever it is shown to the satisfaction of the Secretary of the Treasury that the importer had no reasonable grounds for believing that his or her acts constituted a violation of the law.

Section 911. Civil Actions

(a) Any court having jurisdiction of a civil action arising under this chapter may grant temporary restraining orders, preliminary injunctions, and permanent injunctions on such terms as the court may deem reasonable to prevent or restrain infringement of the exclusive rights in a mask work under this chapter.

(b) Upon finding an infringer liable, to a person entitled under section 910(b)(1) to institute a civil action, for an infringement of any exclusive right under this chapter, the court shall award such person actual damages suffered by the person as a result of the infringement. The court shall also award such person the infringer's profits that are attributable to the infringement and are not taken into account in computing the award of actual damages. In establishing the infringer's profits, such person is required to present proof only if the infringer is required to prove his or her deductible expenses and the elements of profit attributable to factors other than the mask work.

(c) At any time before final judgment is rendered, a person entitled to institute a civil action for infringement may elect, instead of actual damages and profits as provided by subsection (b), an award of statutory damages for all infringements involved in the action, with respect to any one mask work for which any two or more infringers are liable jointly and severally, in an amount not more than $250,000 as the court considers just.

(d) An action for infringement under this chapter shall be barred unless the action is commenced within three years after the claim accrues.

(e)(1) At any time while an action for infringement of the exclusive rights in a mask work under this chapter is pending, the court may order the impounding, on such terms as it may deem reasonable, of all semiconductor chip products, and any drawings, tapes, masks, or other products by means of which such products may be reproduced, that are claimed to have been made, imported, or used in violation of those exclusive rights. Insofar as practicable, applications for orders under this paragraph shall be heard and determined in the same manner as an application for a temporary restraining order or preliminary injunction.

(2) As part of a final judgment or decree, the court may order the destruction or other disposition of any infringing semiconductor chips products, and any masks, tapes, or other articles by means of which such products may be reproduced.

(f) In any civil action arising under this chapter, the court in its discretion may allow the recovery of full costs, including reasonable attorneys' fees, to the prevailing party.

Section 912. Relation to other laws

(a) Nothing in this chapter shall affect any right or remedy held by any person under chapters 1 through 8 of this title, or under title 35.

(b) Except as provided in section 908(b) of this title, references to "this title" or "Title 17" in chapters 1 though 8 of this title shall be deemed not to apply to this chapter.

(c) The provisions of this chapter shall preempt the laws of any State to the extent those laws provide any rights or remedies with respect to a mask work which are equivalent to those rights or remedies provided by this chapter, except that such preemption shall be effective only with respect to actions filed on or after January 1, 1986.

(d) The provisions of sections 1338, 1400(a) and 1498(b) and (c) of title 28 shall apply with respect to exclusive rights in mask works under this chapter.

(e) Nothwithstanding subsection (c), nothing in this chapter shall detract from any rights of a mask work owner, whether under Federal law (exclusive of this chapter) or under the common law or the statutes of a State, heretofore or hereafter declared or enacted, with respect to any mask work first commercially exploited before July 1, 1983.

Section 913. Transitional provisions

(a) No application for registration under section 908 may be filed, and no civil action under section 910 or other enforcement proceeding under this chapter may be instituted, until sixty days after the date of the enactment of this chapter.

(b) No monetary relief under section 911 may be granted with respect to any conduct that occurred before the date of the enactment of this chapter, except as provided in subsection (d).

(c) Subject to subsection (a), the provisions of this chapter apply to all mask works that are first commercially exploited or are registered under this chapter, or both, on or after the date of the enactment of this chapter.

(d)(1) Subject to subsection (a), protection is available under this chapter to any mask work that was first commercially exploited on or after July 1, 1983, and before the date of the enactment of this chapter, if a claim of protection in the mask work is registered in the Copyright Office before July 1, 1985, under section 908.

(2) In the case of any mask work described in paragraph (1) that is provided protection under this chapter, infringing semiconductor chip product units manufactured before the date of the enactment of this chapter may, without liability under sections 910 and 911, be imported into or distributed in the United States, or both, until two years after the date of registration of the mask work under section 908, but only if the importer or distributor, as the case may be, first pays or offers to pay the reasonable royalty referred to in section 907(a)(2) to the mask work owner, on all such units imported or distributed, or both, after the date of the enactment of this chapter.

(3) In the event that a person imports or distributes infringing semiconductor chip product units described in paragraph (2) of this subsection without first paying or offering to pay the reasonable royalty specified in such paragraph, or if the person refuses or fails to make such payment, the mask work owner shall be entitled to the relief provided in subsections 910 and 911.

Section 914. International transitional provisions

(a) Notwithstanding the conditions set forth in subparagraphs (A) and (C) of section 902(a)(1) with respect to the availability of protection under this chapter to nationals, domiciliaries, and sovereign authorities of a foreign nation, the Secretary of Commerce may, upon the petition of any person, or upon the Secretary's own motion, issue an order extending protection under this chapter to such foreign nationals, domiciliaries, and sovereign authorities if the Secretary finds—

(1) that the foreign nation is making good faith efforts and reasonable progress toward—

(A) entering into a treaty described in section 902(a)(1)(A); or

(B) enacting legislation that would be in compliance with subparagraphs (A) or (B) of section 902(a)(2); and

(2) that the nationals, domiciliaries, and sovereign authorities of the foreign nation, and persons controlled by them, are not engaged in the misappropriation, or unauthorized distribution or commercial exploitation, of mask works; and

(3) that issuing the order would promote the

purposes of this chapter and international comity with respect to the protection of mask works.

(b) While an order under subsection (a) is in effect with respect to a foreign nation, no application for registration of a claim for protection in a mask work under this chapter may be denied solely because the owner of the mask work is a national, domiciliary, or sovereign authority of that foreign nation, or solely becausee the mask work was first commercially exploited in that foreign nation.

(c) Any order issued by the Secretary of Commerce under subsection (a) shall be effective for such period as the Secretary designates in the order, except that no such order may be effective after the date on which the authority of the Secretaryof Commerce terminates under subsection (e). The effective date of any such order shall also be designated in the order. In the case of an order issued upon the petition of a person, such effective date may be no earlier than the date on which the Secretary receives such petition.

(d)(1) Any order issued under this section shall terminate if—

(A) the Secretary of Commerce finds that any of the conditions set forth in paragraphs (1), (2), and (3) of subsection (a) no longer exist; or

(B) mask works of nationals, domiciliaries, and sovereign authorities of that foreign nation or mask works first commercially exploited in that foreign nation become eligible for protection under subparagraphs (A) or (C) of section 902(a)(1).

(2) Upon the termination or expiration of an order issued under this section, registrations of claims of protection in mask works made pursuant to that order shall remain valid for the period specified in section 904.

(e) The authority of the Secretaryof Commerce under this section shall commence on the date of the enactment of this chapter, and shall terminate on July 1, 1991.

(f)(1) The Secretary of Commerce shall promptly notify the Register of Copyrights and the Committees on the Judiciary of the Senate and the House of Representatives of the issuance or termination of any order under this section, together with a statement of the reasons for such action. The Secretary shall also publish such notification and statement of reasons in the Federal Register.

(2) Two years after the date of the enactment of this chapter, the Secretary of Commerce, in consultation with the Register of Copyrights, shall transmit to the Committees of the Judiciary of the Senate and the House of Representatives a report on the actions taken under this section and on the current status of international recognition of mask work protection. The report shall include such recommendations for modifications of the protection accorded under this chapter to mask works owned by nationals, domiciliaries, or sovereign authorities of foreign nations as the Secretary, in consultation with the Register of Copyright, considers would promote the purposes of this chapter and international comity with respect to mask work protection.

Not later than July 1, 1990, the Secretary of Commerce, in consultation with the Register of Copyrights, shall transmit to the Committees on the Judiciary of the Senate and the House of Representatives a report updating the matters contained in the report transmitted under the preceding sentence.

*Section 1 of Public Law 100-159, 101 Stat. 899 (Nov. 9, 1987), is a follows:

(a) Findings.—The Congress finds that—

(1) Section 914 of title 17, United States Code, which authorizes the Secretary of Commerce to issue orders extending interim protection under chapter 9 of title17, United States Code, to mask works fixed in semiconductor chip products and originating in foreign countries that are making good faith efforts and reasonable progress toward providing protection, by treaty or legislation, to mask works of United States nationals, has resulted in substantial and positive legislative developments in foreign countries regarding protection of mask works;

(2) the Secretary of Commerce has determined that most of the industrialized countries of the world are eligible for orders affording interim protection under section 914 of title 17, United States Code;

(3) the World Intellectual Property Organization has commenced meetings to draft an international convention regarding the protection of integrated electronic circuits;

(4) these bilateral and multilateral developments are encouraging steps toward improving international protection of mask works in a consistent and harmonious manner; and

(5) it is inherent in section 902 of title 17, United States Code, that the President has the authority to revise, suspend, or revoke, as well as issue, proclamations extending mask work protection to nationals, domiciliaries, and sovereign authorities of other countries if conditions warrant.

(b) Purposes.—The purposes of this act are—

(1) to extend the period within which the Secretary of commerce may grant interim protective orders under section 914 of title 17, United States Code, to continue this incentive for the bilateral and multilateral protection of mask works; and

(2) to codify the President's existing authority to revoke, suspend, or limit the protection extended to mask works of foreign entities in nations that extend mask work protection to United States nationals.

TRANSITIONAL AND SUPPLEMENTARY PROVISIONS

Section 102
Section 103
Section 104
Section 105
Section 106
Section 107
Section 108
Section 109

Section 110
Section 111
Section 112
Section 113
Section 114
Section 115

Transitional and Supplementary Provisions
Section 102

This Act becomes effective on January 1, 1978, except as otherwise expressly provided by this Act, including provisions of the first section of this Act. The provisions of sections 118.304(b), and chapter 8 of title 17, as amended by the first section of this Act, take effect upon enactment of this Act.

Transitional and Supplementary Provisions
Section 103

This Act does not provide copyright protection for any work that goes into the public domain before January 1, 1978. The exclusive rights, as provided by section 106 of title 17 as amended by the first section of this Act, to reproduce a work in phonorecords and to distribute phonorecords of the work, do not extend to any nondramatic musical work copyrighted before July 1, 1909.

Transitional and Supplementary Provisions
Section 104

All proclamations issued by the President under section 1(e) or 9(b) of title 17 as it existed on December 31, 1977, or under previous copyright statutes of the United States, shall continue in force until terminated, suspended, or revised by the President.

Transitional and Supplementary Provisions
Section 105

(a)(1) Section 505 of title 44 is amended to read as follows:

"§ 505. Sale of duplicate plates

"The Public Printer shall sell, under regulations of the Joint Committee on Printing to persons who may apply, additional or duplicate stereotype or electrotype plates from which a Government publication is printed, at a price not to exceed the cost of composition, the metal, and making to the Government, plus 10 per centum, and the full amount of the price shall be paid when the order is filed.".

(2) The item relating to section 505 in the sectional analysis at the beginning of chapter 5 of title 44, is amended to read as follows: "505. Sale of duplicate plates.".

(b) Section 2113 of title 44 is amended to read as follows:

"§ 2113. Limitation on liability

"When letters and other intellectual productions (exclusive of patented material, published works under copyright protection, and unpublished works for which copyright registration has been made) come into the custody or possession of the Administrator of General

Services, the United States or its agents are not liable for infringement of copyright or analogous rights arising out of use of the materials for display, inspection, research, reproduction, or other purposes.".

(c) In section 1498(b) of title 28, the phrase "section 101(b) of title 17" is amended to read "section 504(c) of title 17".

(d) Section 543(a)(4) of the Internal Revenue Code of 1954, as amended, is amended by striking out "(other than by reason of section 2 or 6 thereof)".

(e) Section 3202(a) of title 39 is amended by striking out clause (5). Section 3206 of title 39 is amended by deleting the words "subsections (b) and (c)" and inserting
"subsection (b) in subsection (a), and by deleting subsection (c). Section 3206(d) is renumbered (c).

(f) Subsection (a) of section 290(e) of title 15 is amended by deleting the phrase "section 8" and inserting in lieu thereof the phrase "section 105".

(g) Section 131 of title 2 is amended by deleting the phrase "deposit to secure copyright," and inserting in lieu thereof the phrase "acquisition of material under the copyright law.".

Transitional and Supplementary Provisions
Section 106

In an case where, before January 1, 1978, a person has lawfuly made parts of instruments serving to reproduce mechanically a copyrighted work under the compulsory license provisions of section 1(e) of title 17 as it existed on December 31, 1977, such person may continue to make and distribute such parts embodying the same mechanical reproduction without obtaining a new compulsory license under the tems of section 115 of title 17 as amended by the first section of this Act. However, such parts made on or after January 1, 1978, constitute phonorecords and are otherwise subject to the provisions of said section 115.

Transitional and Supplementary Provisions
Section 107

In the case of any work in which an ad interim copyright is subsisting or is capable of being secured on December 31, 1977, under section 22 of title 17 as it existed on that date, copyright protection is hereby extended to endure for the term or terms provided by section 304 of title 17 as amended by the first section of this Act.

Transitional and Supplementary Provisions
Section 108

The notice provisions of sections 401 through 403 of title 17 as amended by the first section of this Act apply to all copies or phonorecords publicly distributed on or after January 1, 1978. However, in the case of a work published before January 1, 1978, compliance with the notice provisions of title 17 either as it existed on December 31, 1977, or as amended by the first section of this Act, is adequate with respect to copies publicly distributed after December 31, 1977.

Transitional and Supplementary Provisions
Section 109

The registration of claims to copyright for which the required deposit, application, and fee were received in the Copyright Office before January 1, 1978, and the recordation of assignments of copyright or other instruments received in the Copyright Office before January 1, 1978, shall be made in accordance with title 17 as it existed on December 31, 1977.

Transitional and Supplementary Provisions
Section 110

The demand and penalty provisions of section 14 of title 17 as it existed on December 31, 1977, apply to any work in which copyright has been secured by publication with notice of copyright on or before that date, but any deposit and registration made after that date in response to a demand under that section shall be made in accordance with the provisions of title 17 as amended by the first section of this Act.

Transitional and Supplementary Provisions
Section 111

Section 2318 of title 18 of the United States Code is amended to read as follows:

"§ 2318. Transportation, sale or receipt of phonograph records bearing forged or counterfeit labels

"(a) Whoever knowingly and with fraudulent intent transports, causes to be transported, receives, sells, or offers for sale in interstate or foreign commerce any phonograph record, disk, wire, tape, film, or other article on which sounds are recorded, to which or upon which is stamped, pasted, or affixed any forged or counterfeited label, knowing the label to have been falsely made, forged, or counterfeited shall be fined not more than $10,000 or imprisoned for not more than one year, or both, for the first such offense and shall be fined not more than $25,000 or imprisoned for not more than two years, or both, for any subsequent offense.

"(b) When any person is convicted of any violation of subsection (a), the court in its judgment of conviction shall, in addition to the penalty therein prescribed, order the forfeiture and destruction or other disposition of all counterfeit labels and all articles to which counterfeit labels have been affixed or which were intended to have had such labels affixed.".

"(c) Except to the extent they are inconsistent with the provisions of this title, all provisions of section 509, title 17, United States Code, are applicable to violations of subsection (a).".

Transitional and Supplementary Provisions
Section 112

All causes of action that arose under title 17 before January 1, 1978, shall be governed by title 17 as it existed when the cause of action arose.

Transitional and Supplementary Provisions
Section 113

(a) The Librarian of Congress (hereinafter referred to as the "Librarian") shall establish and maintain in the Library of Congress a library to be known as the American Television and Radio Archives (hereinafter referred to as the "Archives). The purpose of the Archives shall be to preserve a permanent record of the television and radio programs which are the heritage of the people of the United States and to provide access to such programs to historians and scholars without encouraging or causing copyright infringement.

(1) The Librarian, after consultation with interested organizations and individuals, shall determine and place in the Archives such copies and phonorecords of television and radio programs transmitted to the public in the United States and in other countries which are of present or potential public or cultural interest, historical significance, cognitive value, or otherwise worthy of preservation, including copies and phonorecords of published and unpublished transmission programs—

(A) acquired in accordance with sections 407 and 408 of title 17 as amended by the first section of this Act, and

(B) transferred from the existing collections of the Library of Congress; and

(C) given to or exchanged with the Archives by other libraries, archives, organizations, and individuals; and

(D) purchased from the owner thereof.

(2) The Librarian shall maintain and publish appropriate catalogs and indexes of the collections of the Archives, and shall make such collections available for study and research under conditions prescribed under this section.

(b) Notwithstanding the provisions of section 106 of title 17 as amended by the first section of this Act, the Librarian is authorized with respect to a transmission program which consists of a regularly scheduled newscast or on-the-spot coverage of news events and, under standards and conditions that the Librarian shall prescribe by regulation—

(1) to reproduce a fixation of such a program, in the same or another tangible form, for the purposes of preservation or security or for distribution under the conditions of clause (3) of this subsection; and

(2) to compile, without abridgment or any other editing, portions of such fixations according to subject matter, and to reproduce such compilations for the purpose of clause (1) of this subsection; and

(3) to distribute a reproduction made under clause (1) or (2) of this subsection—

(A) by loan to a person engaged in research; and

(B) for deposit in a library or archives which meets the requirements of section 108(a) of title 17 as amended by the first section of this Act, in either case for use only in research and not for further reproduction or performance.

(c) The Librarian or any employee of the Library who is acting under the authority of this section shall not be liable in any action for copyright infringement committed by any other person unless the Librarian or such employee knowingly participated in the act of infringement committed by such person. Nothing in this section shall be construed to excuse or limit liability under title 17 as amended by the first section of this Act for any act not authorized by that title or this section, or for any act performed by a person not authorized to act under that title or this section.

(d) This section may be cited as the "American Television and Radio Archives Act".

Transitional and Supplementary Provisions
Section 114

There are hereby authorized to be appropriated such funds as may be necessary to carry out the purposes of this act.

Transitional and Supplementary Provisions
Section 115

If any provision of title 17, as amended by the first section of this Act, is declared unconstitutional, the validity of the remainder of this title is not affected.

Appendix D: Product Copyright List

All *Power Tools* clip media, *Power Tools* application programs/Demos, and *Power Tools* Sample Projects are included in *Multimedia Power Tools* Book/CD-ROM.by permission of their respective copyright holders. All brand or product names are trademarks or registered trademarks of their respective holders.

Adobe Illustrator® 3.0 Demo; Adobe Systems, Incorporated; Adobe Illustrator is a trademark of Adobe Systems Incorportated, which may be registered in certain jurisdictions. Adobe Illustrator © 1987-91 Adobe Systems Incorporated. All rights reserved.

Adobe Photoshop™ v2.0.1 Demo; Adobe Systems, Incorporated; Adobe Photoshop is a trademark of Adobe Systems Incorporated which may be registered in certain jurisdictions. Adobe Photoshop © 1989-91 Adobe Systems Incorporated. All rights reserved.

Adobe Premiere© 2.0 Plug-In Developer Kit; Adobe Systems, Incorporated; Adobe Premiere 2.0 Plug-in Developer Kit is a trademark of Adobe Systems Incorporated which may be registered in certain jusrisdictions. Adobe Premiere © 1991-1992 Adobe Systems Incorporated. All rights reserved.

Adobe Premiere™ 2.0 Plug-in Developer Kit; Adobe Systems, Incorporated; Adobe Premiere is a trademark of Adobe Systems Incorporated which mauy be registered in certain jusrisdictions. Adobe Premiere © 1991-92 Adobe Systems Incorporated. All rights reserved.

Adobe Premiere™ 2.0 Tryout Demo; Adobe Systems, Incorporated; Adobe Premiere is a trademark of Adobe Systems Incorporated which may be registered in certain jusrisdictions. Adobe Premiere © 1991-92 Adobe Systems Incorporated. All rights reserved.

Aldus® Fetch™ 1.0 Trial Version; Aldus® Corporation; Aldus Fetch 1.0 is a trademark of Aldus Corporation and is © 1992 Aldus Corporation.

Animation Works ™ 1.1 Demo; Gold Disk®, Inc.; Animation works 1.1 is © 1992 by Gold Disk, Incorporated.

Authorware® Professional 1.7.1 Demo; Macromedia, Incorporated; Authorware is a registered trademark and Authorware Professional is a trademark of Macromedia, Inc. Used by permission of Macromedia.

Backgrounds for Multimedia, Volumes 1 & 2; ArtBeats®; This software package (*Multimedia Power Tools* Book/CD-ROM) contains art originated and owned by ARTBEATS and is provided for the purchaser of this package only. © 1993 ARTBEATS, Box 1287, Myrtle Creek, OR 97457 (503) 863-4429.

Blendo™ Photography I: Photo Imagery by Craig McClain; Verbum®, Inc.; Blendo™ and Verbum® are trademarks of Verbum, Inc.. Blendo Photography I is © 1993 Craig McClain and Verbum Inc.

CameraMan™ 1.1 Demo; Vision Software; CameraMan is © 1991, 1992, 1992, Vision Software. All rights reserved. CameraMan is a trademark of Vision software, Santa Clara, USA.

Capture™ 4.0 Demo; Mainstay; Capture v.4.0 is © 1988-91 by Yves Lempereur.

CD Folios: Sky, Vol 1 v2.0; CD Folios; CD Folios: Sky, Vol, 1 v2.0 - Pre press is © 1993 CD Folios.

ClipMedia™; Macromedia, Inc.; ClipMedia is a trademark of Macaromedia, Inc. Used by permission of Macromedia.

ColorSwitch 1.0.1; Ambrosia, Andrew Welch; ColorSwitch is © 1992 Andrew Welch.

DeBableizer® 1.4 Demo; Equilibrium TechnologieS; DeBabelizer is © 1992, 1993 Equilibrium. All rights reserved. DeBabelizer is a registered trademark of Equilibrium.

DepthKey 1.5; Overpriced Software; DeptKey 1.5 is © 1990-1992, Overpriced Software. All rights reserved.

DeskTop Sounds: Sound FX Vol 1; Q Up Arts/Optical Media International; DeskTop Sounds is © (P) 1989-1993 Optical Media International. All rights reserved.

Digital Photographics CD-ROM™; Husom & Rose Photographics; Digital Photographics CD-ROM is © 1993 Husom and Rose Photographics

EasyPlay™ 2.0; Leptonics Systems Design Company; EasyPlay 2.0 is © 1993 Leptonics Systems Design Company. All rights reserved.

Extensions Manager 1.8; Apple Computer, Inc.; Extensions Manager 1.8 is © 1993 Random House Electronic Publishing and its licensors. All rights reserved. RANDOM HOUSE ELECTRONIC PUBLISHING'S LICENSOR(S) MAKES NO WARRANTIES, EXPRESS OR IMPLIED, INCLUDING WITHOUT LIMITATION THE IMPLIED WARRANTIES OF MERCHANTABILITY AND FITNESS FOR A PARTICULAR PURPOSE, REGARDING THE SOFTWARE. RANDOM HOUSE ELECTRONIC PUBLISHING'S LICENSOR(S) DOES NOT WARRANT, GUARANTEE OR MAKE ANY PRPRESENTATIONS REGARDING THE USE OR THE RESULTS OF THE USE OF THE SOFTWARE IN TERMS OF ITS CORRECTNESS, ACCURACY, RELIABILITY, CURRENTNESS OR OTHERWISE. THE SOFWARE IS ASSUMED BY YOU. THE EXCLUSION OF IMPLIED WARRANTIES IS NOT PERMITTED BY SOME JURISDICTIONS. THE ABOVE EXCLUSION MAY NOT APPLY TO YOU. IN NO EVENT WILL RANDOM HOUSE ELECTRONIC PUBLISHING'S LICENSOR(S), AND THEIR DIRECTORS, OFFICERS, EMPLOYEES OF AGENTS (COLLECTIVELY RANDOM HOUSE ELECTRONIC PUBLISHING'S LICENSOR) BE LIABLE TO YOU FOR ANY CONSEQUENTIAL, INCIDENTAL OR INDIRECT DAMAGES (INCLUDING DAMAGES FOR LOSS OF BUSINESS PROFITS, BUSINESS INTERRUPTION, LOSS OF BUSINESS INFORMATION, AND THE LIKE) ARISING OUT OF THE USE OR INABILITY TO USE THE SOFTWARE EVEN IF RANDOM HOUSE ELECTRONIC PUBLISHING'S LICENSOR HAS BEEN ADVISED OF THE POSSIBILITY OF SUCH DAMAGES. BECAUSE SOME JURISDICTIONS DO NOT ALLOW THE EXCLUSION OR LIMITATION OF LIABILITY FOR CONSEQUENTIAL OR INCIDENTAL DAMAGES, THE ABOVE LIMITATIONS MAY NOT APPLY TO YOU. Random House Electronic Publishing's Licensor's liability to you for actual damages from any cause whatsoever, and regardless of the form of the action (whether in contract, tort (including negligence), product liability or otherwise), will be limited to $50.

Folder Icon Maker 1.1; Gregory M. Robbins; Folder Icon Maker 1.1 software and documentation is © 1991, 1992 Gregory M. Robbins

FOLIO I Image Library; D'Pix™, Incorporated; FOLIO I Image Library is © 1991 D'pix, Incorporated. Due to space limitations of this CD-ROM, some image resolutions may have been reduced. FOLIO I images are offered in two resolutions: 3192 x 2394 pixels and 900 x 675 pixels and are available in PICT or TIFF formats.

From Alice to Ocean; Against All Odds Productions: From Alice to Ocean is © 1992 Against All Odds Productions. Photographs © Rick Smolan. Text from "Tracks" © 1980. Robyn Davidson. "Tracks" audio © 1987 LBP Audio Books. Portions of video © 1992, Globe TV. Interface design, artwork, and programming © 1992 Magnum Design.

Gestalt v3.2.1; Jeffrey Donald Iverson; Gestalt v3.2.1 is © 1993 Jeffrey Donald Iverson.

GetMonitors XFCN v1.2; Jeffrey Donald Iverson; GetMonitors XFCN v1.2 is © 1993 by Jeffrey Donald Iverson.

GIFConverter 2.32b; Kevin A. Mitchell; GIFConverter is © 1991-1993 by Kevin A. Mitchell. All rights reserved.

Hi Rez Vol. I Audio for Multimedia; Presto Studios; Hi Rez Vol. I Audio for Multimedia is © (P) 1992, Hi Rez Audio. All rights reserved.

Hollywood Film Music Library; Hollywood Film Music Library, a division of Screenmusic International, Incorporated; Hollywood Film Music Library is © (P) 1992, Screenmusic International. All rights reserved.

Image Bank CD Collection, Footage Vol. 1; DiVA™ Corporation/The Image Bank, Inc; Image Bank CD Collection, Footage Vol. 1 is © 1992 Image Bank, Inc. and DiVA Corporation.

ImageCELs®; ImageTects™; ImageCELs is a registered trademark and IMAGETECTS is a trademark ImageTects in the USA and other countries. ImageCELs is © 1993 IMAGETECTS. All rights reserved.

Instant Buttons & Controls v1.0 and #2 Sampler Disk; Stat Media™ Network; Instant Buttons & Controls v1.0 and #2 Sampler Disk are registered trademarks of Stat™ Media and are © 1992.

International Graphics Library; Educorp; International Graphics Library is © 1990 Gazelle Technologies, Inc. and CASCOM, Inc.

Kai's POWER TOOLS™ v.1.0a: Glass Lens Bright Filter, Pixel Storm Filter, Hue Protected Noise/Maximum Filter, Sharpen Intensity Filter, Gradient Designer Filter; HSC Software; Kai's POWER TOOLS is a registered trademark of Harvard Systems Corporation and is © 1992 Harvard Systems Corporation. All rights reserved

Klutz 1.0; Bill Steinberg; Klutz 1.0 is © 1987, 1988 Bill Steinberg. All rights reserved.

Kudo® Image Browser 1.0 Demo; Imspace™ Systems Corporation; Kudo Image Browser 1.0 Demo is © 1993 Imspace Systems Corporation and its licensors.

Macintosh CD Setup 4.0.2; Apple Computer, Inc.; Macintosh CD Setup 4.0.2 is © 1993 Random House Electronic Publishing and its licensors. All rights reserved. (See product named *Extensions Manager 1.8* for Random House Electronic Publishing's and Apple Computer's warranty disclaimer and other disclaimers.)

Macromedia Director™ 3.1.1 Demo; Macromedia, Incorporated; Macromedia Director 3.1.1 Demo is a trademark of Macromedia, Incorporated. Used by permission of Macromedia, Incorporated.

MacroModel™ 1.0 Demo; Macromedia, Incorporated; MacroModel 1.0 Demo is a registered trademark of Macromedia, Inc. Used by permission of Macromedia.

Marble and Granite CD-ROM; ArtBeats®; Marble and Granite CD-ROM is originated and owned by ARTBEATS and is provided for the purchaser of this package only and is © 1993 ARTBEATS.

MasterTracks Pro™ 5 Demo v5.2; Passport Designs, Incorporated; MasterTracks Pro 5 Demo v5.2 is published and created by Passport Designs of Half Moon Bay, CA, and is © 1992 Passport Designs, Incorporated. All rights reserved.

Media in Motion™ Animation Clips/ Business Vol, 1 & 2; Media in Motion™; Media in Motion Animation Clips are © 1991-1992 Media in Motion. All rights reserved worldwide.

Media in Motion™ Interactive Training for Macromind® Director™ 3.0 & 3.1 Demo; Media in Motion™; Interactive training for Macromind Director 3.0 & 3.1 is © 1991,1992 Media in Motion. All rights reserved worldwide.

MediaMaker™ 1.5 Demo; Macromedia,Incorporated; MediaMaker is a trademark of Macromedia, Incorporated. Used by permission of Macromedia, Incorporated.

Morph™ 1.1 Demo; Gryphon™ Software; Incorporated Morph 1.1 Demo is © 1992. All rights reserved.

Notepad++1.4 , 1.4J, 1.4SC; Alexander S. Colwell; Notepad++1.4 , 1.4J, 1.4SC are © 1988-1992 Alexander S. Colwell. All rights reserved.

On the Air™ Demo; Meyer Software; On the Air Demo is © 1991 Meyer Software. All rights reserved.

PACo™ Producer Demo 2.0.1 and **PACo Animation Demo;** Company of Science and Art, CoSA™; PACo Producer Demo 2.0.1 and Animation Demo is © March 1992. All rights reserved.

Passport Producer™ v1.1 Demo; Passport Design; Passport Producer v1.1 Demo is published and created by Passport Designs of Half Moon Bay, CA, and is © 1992 Passport Designs, Incorporated. All rights reserved.

PhotoDisc™ - World Commerce and Travel; PhotoDisc, Inc.; PhotoDisc-World Commerce and Travel is © 1993 Tom Hughes. All rights reserved.

PICTpocket™ Demo; Imspace Systems™ Corporation; PICTpocket is © 1993 Imspace Systems Corporation and its licensors.

PictureDecomPress™ 2.04; Storm Technology, Incorporated; PictureDecomPress 2.04 is © 1992 Storm Technology, Incorporated. All rights reserved.

PICTviewer 1.1; Apple Computer, Inc.; PICTviewer 1.1 is © 1993 Random House Electronic Publishing and its licensors. All rights reserved. (See product named *Extensions Manager 1.6* for Random House Electronic Publishing's and licensor's warranty disclaimer and other disclaimers.)

PlayAIFF v1.0; Chris Reed; PlayAIFF v1.0 is © 1991 Chris Reed. No commercial use without permission.

Popcorn™ 1.0.1; Aladdin Systems, Incorporated; Popcorn is by Leonard Rosenthol and is © 1992, Aladdin Systems, Incorporated.

PrimeTime I CD-ROM; Motion Works International, Incorporated; PrimeTime I CD-ROM is a trademark of Motion Works International, Incorporated and is © 1990-1992 Motion Works Internationa, Incorporated. All rights reserved.

PROmotion 1.0 .2 Demo; Motion Works International, Incorporated; PROmotion 1.0.3 Demo is a trademark of Motion Works International, Incorporated and is © 1990-1992 Motion Works Internationa, Incorporated. All rights reserved.

PuzzleTime 1.0; Maverick Software; PuzzleTime 1.0 is a trademark of Mark Adams/Maverick Software. Used by permission.

QT Batch Compressor v1.0; Lincoln D. Stein; QT Batch Compressor v1.0 is © 1992 Lincoln D. Stein.

QuickTime™ 1.6.1 Package: QuickTime™ Extension, MoviePlayer, Scrapbook.; Apple Computer, Inc.; QuickTime and the QuickTime Logo are trademarks of Apple Computer, Inc. and are used under license, © 1993 Random House Electronic Publishing and its licensors. All rights reserved. (See product named *Extensions Manager 1.8* for Random House Electronic Publishing's and Apple Computer's warranty disclaimer and other disclaimers.)

SndCataloguer 1.1; Dejal Userware™; Dejal Userware is a privately owned company operated by David Lambert. The software is distributed under the Shareware system.

SndConverter Lite 1.1; Dejal Userware™; Dejal Userware is a privately owned company operated by David Lambert. The software is distributed under the Shareware system.

SndConverter Pro 2.0; Dejal Userware™; Dejal Userware is a privately owned company operated by David Lambert. The software is distributed under the Shareware system.

SndPlayer 2.0; Dejal Userware™; Dejal Userware is a privately owned company operated by David Lambert. The software is distributed under the Shareware system.

SoundEdit™ Pro™ 2.0 Demo; Macromedia, Incorporated; SoundEdit Pro 2.0 is a trademark of Macromedia, Incorporated. Used by permission of Macromedia.

SpaceTime and Art; Wayzata Technology, Incorporated; SpaceTime and Art is © A/PIX VISions and Wayzata Technology, Incorporated.

Speedometer 3.1.1; Parity Productions; Speedometer 3.1.1 is © 1992 Scott Berfield. All rights reserved.

StrataVision™ v2.5-A Demo; Strata, Incorporated; StrataVision™ v2.5-A is © 1989-1992 Strata, Incorporated. All rights reserved.

Switch-A-Roo™ 1.6; Bill Steinberg; Switch-A-Roo; 1.6 is © 1987-1990 by Bill Steinberg.

Swivel 3D Pro™: Sample Models; Macromedia, Incorporated; Swivel3D Pro Sample Models are trademarks of VPL Research, Inc. Used by permission of Macromedia.

Swivel 3D™ Professional v2.4.0 Demo; Macromedia, Incorporated; Swivel 3D and Swivel 3D Professional are trademarks of VPL Research, Incorporated.

System Watch (Swatch) v1.2.2, 1.7d10; Joe Holt; System Watch (Swatch) v1.2.2, 1.7d10 is © 1991 Joe Holt.

TeachText 7.1; Apple Computer, Inc.; TeachText 7.0 is © 1993 Random House Electronic Publishing and its licensors. All rights reserved. (See product named *Extensions Manager 1.8* for Random House Electronic Publishing's and Apple Computer's warranty disclaimer and other disclaimers.)

The Multimedia Library IMAGE Series Vol. 1: Russia/China; The Multimedia Library, Incorporated; The Multimedia Library IMAGE Series, Vol. 1: Russia/China is © 1992 The Multimedia Library, Incorporated.

The Multimedia Library IMAGE Series Vol. 2: South Pacific/Tropical/California Coast; The Multimedia Library, Incorporated; The Multimedia Library IMAGE Series Vol. 2: South Pacific/Tropical/California Coast is © 1992 The Multimedia Library, Incorporated.

The Multimedia Library SOUND Series, Vol. 1: Music For Multimedia; The Multimedia Library, Incorporated; The Multimedia Library SOUND Series, Vol. 1: Music For Multimedia is © 1992 The Multimedia Library, Incorporated.

Theater Maker 1.2; Maverick Software; Theater Maker 1.2 is a trademark of Mark Adams/Maverick Software. Used by permission.

TV-ROM™; BMUG Incorporated Software; TV-ROM and BMUG are trademarks of BMUG Incorporated Software. TV-ROM is © 1992 BMUG Incorporated.

UpdateMaker v1.3.1; ADInstruments; UpdateMaker v1.3.1 was conceived and created by Michael ™ Hamel, a singularly clever chap, © 1993. MacApp® 2.0 assisted in the birth.

VideoShop® 2.0 Demo; DiVA™ Coproration; VideoShop 2.0 is © 1993 DiVA Corporation.

VideoSync 1.0; Apple Computer, Inc.; VideoSync 1.0 is © 1993 Random House Electronic Publishing and its licensors. All rights reserved. (See product named *Extensions Manager 1.8* for Random House Electronic Publishing's and Apple Computer's warranty disclaimer and other disclaimers.)

WraptureReels™ Disc One; Form and Function; WraptureReels Disc One and its contents are © 1992 Form and Function. All rights not expressed are reserved.

Wraptures™ Disc One: FineTextures; Form and Function; Wraptures Disc One and its contents are © 1992 Form and Function. All rights not expressed are reserved.

XCMD's: QuickTime™ Movie Stack, QuickTime™ Edit Movie Stack, QuickTime™ Movie Making Stack, QuickTime™ PICT Stack.; Apple Computer, Inc.; XCMD's are © 1993 Random House Electronic Publishing and its licensors. All rights reserved. (See product named *Extensions Manager 1.8* for Random House Electronic Publishing's and Apple Computer's warranty disclaimer and other disclaimers.)

Glossary

Compiled by Steve Rosenthal

4:2:2: international standard for digital videotape and production equipment. The numbers refer to the ratio of the sampling rates used for turning components of the analog video signal into a digital signal. Also known as CCIR 601, which is the recommendation of the international standards body that set up the format.

8-bit color: said of display systems that allocate 8 bits of memory to each pixel and therefore can show up to 256 different colors at a time.

8-bit sound: sound boards and other digital sound systems that record or play back sound using 8 bits of resolution for each digital sample. The result is fidelity slightly better than normal AM radio.

16-bit adapter: an add-on board that can exchange 16 bits of data at a time with the computer's processor or memory. However, for a sound, video or other I/O board this does not necessarily mean it uses 16 bits of data for each pixel or sample.

16-bit color: said of display systems that allocate 5 bits of memory each for red, blue components of each pixel and 6 bits to the green hues. Such an arrangement can show up to therefore can show up to 65.536 different colors at a time.

16-bit sound: audio that is created or digitized using 16 bits of information (and thus over 64,000 levels) for each sample. This is the standard used for audio Compact Discs.

24-bit color: video systems that allocate 24 bits of data to each point in an image. Usually, the bits are allocated as 8 bits each for the three additive primary colors (red, green and blue). That provides up to 16.8 million colors possibilities.

9660: short for ISO 9660, a standard format adopted by the International Standards Organization for CD-ROM discs intended for use with diverse computer systems. Most drives now come with software to read ISO 9660 discs.

A/B editing: creating an edited result by combining inputs from two or more sources.

ActionMedia II: a Intel trademark for a video capture card that uses the firm's Digital Video Interactive (DVI) technology.

active lines: the number of horizontal sweeps across the screen in a video display that represent picture information rather than those used for timing or data. In the standard 525-line NTSC system used for television in the U.S., there are about 490 active lines.

adaptive differential pulse code modulation (ADPCM): a type of digital encoding used for audio signals that continuously alters the meaning of the codes to best represent the range of the signal.

A/D converter (ADC): a circuit or unit that produces digital codes corresponding to a sample or series of samples of an analog input.

additive color mixing: producing colors by mixing colors of light rather than by mixing pigments. If the additive primary colors are mixed in equal proportions, the result is white.

additive synthesis: in the creation of sound by computers or electronic instruments, creating a composite waveform by summing the signals from multiple sources.

alpha channel: in video and computer graphics, an extra signal, bit or set of bits used to control special effects such as transparency and overlay.

analog RGB: video systems that send images in separate signal lines for the red, green, and blue information and encode each signal as a proportional voltage rather than as digital bits.

analog video: a signal that represents video image information directly by changes in signal size or timing, rather than encoding the information as digital number values.

animation: a video or film sequence that provides the illusion of motion by presenting a succession of slightly different drawn or artificially-constructed images.

anti-alias: to smooth over sharp or small jagged edges to create more pleasing images or reduce the effects of limitations in signal capture or storage.

aspect ratio: the ratio of the width to the height of an image, screen, or medium. Standard VGA screens for the PC or external screens for the Macintosh are 640:480 or 4:3, as is broadcast television. Most slide and movie film formats use other aspect ratios.

assemble: referring to editing, a style in which sequences are placed one after another without a continuing reference signal. While requiring less preparation than insert editing (which places sequences on top of an existing image or reference track), the result is likely to have small errors in timing.

asymmetrical compression: as applied to video or audio data, methods for squeezing the data for storage or transmission that take a different (usually larger) amount of time or resources to compress the data than to de-compress it.

attenuate: to reduce the level of a signal, especially to do so deliberately to fit the level of a signal to the needs of an input.

Audio-Video Interleaved (AVI): the file format Microsoft specifies for Video for Windows. As its name implies, it intersperses blocks of audio information within the stream of digitized video frames.

authoring system: 1) the hardware and software used to create a multimedia project, but not necessarily needed for playback. 2) a programming environment designed to help users create computer-aided instruction (CAI) lessons.

bitmapped: referring to video displays and other graphic output, a system where each possible dot of the display is controlled independently by one or more corresponding bits in memory.

BNC: a common round connector used with coaxial cable. It is pushed on, then locked with a quarter twist.

boolean: 1) referring to the system of logic that deals only in true and false values plus the combinations made up of those values and the operators "and," "or," and "not." 2) a variable that can only take on a true or false value.

broadband: said of a communications link that provides a large enough bandwidth (range of frequencies) to accommodate several independent channels.

broadcast quality: a common term for video images good enough to be used on broadcast television. There is no precise standard that fully defines this level, so interpretation varies with the circumstances.

browser: a program, system, or mode used to help the user look through a body of information. Most commonly, browsers show some kind of overview or summary, allowing the user to zoom in for a more detailed view.

buyout music: music that is sold with a license that permits it to be used in specified types of productions without further royalty payments.

caddy: a plastic carrier used with many popular CD-ROM drives to hold the disc while it is inserted in the drive and to protect the disc while it is not in use.

CD (Compact Disc): a popular format for optical discs originally developed by Philips and Sony for music and now used for data and video as well.

CD-DA: an abbreviation for "Compact Disc Digital Audio," the standard format for compact discs and players used for mass-market music applications. Also known as "Red Book" for the informal name of the standard that defines the format.

CD-I: an abbreviation for "Compact Disc Digital Interactive," a standard for CDs containing combinations of sound, images, and computer instructions and for players specially constructed for these discs. Also known as Green Book for the document that defines the format.

CD-PROM: a proposed acronym (pronounced see-dee-promm) for "Compact Disc Programmable Read-Only Memory," proposed term for optical discs that can be written on by special recorders and read back on any standard CD-ROM reader.

CD-ROM: an acronym (pronounced see-dee-romm) for Compact Disc read-only memory, a type of optical data disk that uses the same basic technology as the popular CD audio disks to store computer data. Although the standard CD-ROM drive can only read data (the data is permanently stamped on the disc during manufacturing), disks are inexpensive to make, and each can hold up to about 600 megabytes of data.

CD-ROM Extensions: a set of routines that connect the MS-DOS or PC-DOS operating systems to the driver routines for specific models of CD-ROM players. The extensions allow MS-DOS machines to read CD-ROM discs in the ISO 9660 and High Sierra formats.

CD-ROM upgrade kit: a complete combination of CD-ROM drive, interface board, software and cables needed to connect a CD drive to a particular type of personal computer.

CD-ROM XA: an abbreviation for "Compact Disc Read-Only Memory Extended Architecture," a format developed by Microsoft and others that adds compressed interleaved sound and graphics to the basic CD-ROM format.

CDTV: an abbreviation for Commodore Dynamic Total Vision, an interactive multimedia system designed for the home that uses programs on specially-formatted CD-ROM discs.

CD-WO: an abbreviation for a "Compact Disc Write Once," a term for optical discs that can be written on by special recorders and read back on any standard CD-ROM reader.

chrominance (chroma): the color component of a signal or image.

chroma key: a color-based video matting (overlay) system that drops all areas of a selected color (usually blue) out of the foreground image, and substitutes instead the corresponding areas of a second image.

Chyron: a popular brand of video character generators. The name is often used loosely in the video industry to indicate any character generator or the resulting lettering.

CMYK: a color model based on the cyan (C), magenta (M), yellow (Y) and black (K) inks used in color printing The first three inks are used to form all the available colors using subtractive color mixing, while the black is used to change tones or define edges.

coaxial cable (coax): a type of wire that surrounds a central conductor with an insulating layer and a foil shield or wire braid. This arrangement provides high bandwidth and good protection again signal interference or radiation.

color bars: a standard video test signal that uses blocks of solid colors made up of the three primary colors and their combinations. The most commonly used version was developed by the Society of Motion Picture and Television Engineers (SMPTE), and is consequently called "SMPTE bars."

color model: a method of representing the color of colored items, usually by their components as specified along at least three dimensions. Common models include RGB (using red, green, and blue light), HLS (hue, lightness, and saturation), HSV (hue, saturation, and value) and CYMK (using the common printing colors of cyan, yellow, magenta, and black).

Compact Disc (CD): 1) the standard developed by Sony and Philips for distributing music and other information on plastic optical discs. 2) a plastic disc formatted according to these standards.

Compact Disc Interactive (CD-I): a standard both for CDs containing combinations of sound, images, and computer instructions and for players specially constructed for these discs. Also known as Green Book for the informal name of the standard that defines the format.

Compact Video: the original name of the video compression method developed by SuperMac now called CinePak.

component: 1) referring to video signals, a format that keeps color and brightness (luminance) information as two or more separate signals rather than combining them in one composite signal. Popular component formats include Betacam, MII, D1, and SVHS. 2). in the Apple operating system, a software object that provides services to clients.

composite: 1) as applied to video, a signal that contains more than one type of information, such as picture and timing, or monochrome and color. 2) in image-creation software and systems, several items that are treated together as one object or given one name. 3). in multimedia and information storage systems, said of items that contain data of more than one type or format or that are made up of references to multiple documents.

compression: the translation of data to a more compact form for storage or transmission (after which it can be restored to normal form).

control track: 1) on many video recording formats, a separate track that carries pulses used to set the timing and align the tape with the recording and playback heads. 2) a simple type of video positioning that relies on counting pulses on the tape rather than reading exact location information.

courseware: originally the term referred to the software containing actual lesson material for computerized instructional systems. Now, the term is often used more generically for educational software, audiovisual aids and sometimes even textbooks.

cuts only: as applied to video editing, a system that can create a finished piece only out of sequences of separate clips, but cannot overlay or mix signals. The usual contrast is with "online" systems, although they are not strictly corresponding choices.

D-1: a format for recording component video signals (in which color and brightness information are carried on separate signals) in digital form developed by SMPTE.

D-2: a format for recording composite video signals (in which color and brightness information are carried within the same signal) in digital form developed by SMPTE.

decimate: to throw out selected portions of a signal to reduce the amount that has to be encoded or compressed. It is a usual step in most types of lossey compression. Decimation is the most common form of subsampling.

device driver: a special section of computer code that translates the more general commands from an operating system or user programs into the exact code needed by a specific peripheral device.

device-independent bitmap (DIB): a Microsoft Windows format for 256-color bitmapped graphics.

digital compositing: combining images in digital form rather than as analog signals. Digital compositing allows all the features of computer image processing to be applied to video or graphic arts images.

digital signal processor (DSP): a specialized computer chip designed to perform speedy and complex operations on signals representing waveforms. Most DSPs include some type of parallel processing-capability.

digital-to-analog converter (DAC): a circuit or module that changes a digital value to a corresponding continuous signal such as a current or voltage.

digital video: signals that represent moving pictures (with or without sound) as a series of number values rather than as a smoothly varying signal.

Digital Video Interactive (DVI): a set of hardware and software products for compressing and decompressing video images sold by Intel Corp. The system offers both a real-time form (RTV) offering near-VHS quality and a more detailed version (PLV) that requires more extensive processing.

dither: to place small dots of black, white or color in an area of an image to soften an edge, to visually smooth a jagged line, or to simulate a shade or tone.

DMA: an abbreviation for "direct memory access," the transfer of data to and from memory without routing through the central processing unit (CPU) chip.

downsampling: to reduce the amount of data in a file or stream by selecting only parts of the original information.

drop frame: a type of time code for video sequences that periodically skips a code to take into account the small difference between the nominal 60 frames per second (fps) and actual 59.57 fps rate of NTSC-format video. Over an hour, 108 codes are dropped.

dub: 1) to make a copy of a video or audio sequence or program. 2) the copy so made. 3) to copy a new audio section into an existing video or film sequence.

edit controller: a device or system that sends the instructions to video (or audio) recording or playback devices to position them at the right points and set the modes needed to assemble an edited production.

edit decision list (EDL): a list of points where cuts or special effects should be made. An edit decision list can be created on an off-line system or a personal computer-based editing system for later assembly on an on-line system.

envelope: referring to sound or video signals, the shape of the waveform that makes up a sound. Two notes of the same basic pitch will sound very different if they have different envelopes.

Extended Graphics Architecture (XGA): a video display standard introduced by IBM in 1990 that provides for 256 colors at 1024 by 768 pixels or 65 thousand colors at 640 by 480 pixels. The original IBM version only supported interlaced displays.

extrude: a video effect that seemingly gives three dimensions to a two dimensional object by generating solid objects outward from two-dimensional lines and shapes.

fidelity: closeness of the received signal to the original. In most audio and video formats, there is a trade-off between fidelity and maximum storage capacity.

field: for a video signal, a set of lines produced in one sweep down the screen. For interlaced video, it takes two such fields to make a frame (complete image).

field rate: the number of fields transmitted per second.

fill: in video production, a supplementary light used to soften shadows and bring out the background missed by the key light.
2) in graphics, a color or pattern occupying a defined region 3) to place color or pattern in a region.

filter: a partially-transparent material that passes (or blocks) light of a particular color or orientation. 2) an electronic circuit or unit that passes (or blocks) signals of a particular type or frequency. 3) more loosely, any circuit or device that shapes or conditions a signal. That includes so-called anti-aliasing, deflickering and sharpening filters.

flanging: an audio effect that creates a "wow-wow" effect by echoing different frequencies at a changing rate.

flash digitizer: A device that turns an analog signal such as a video input into digital form through a rapid direct parallel process instead of through a longer sequential process. Flash digitizers are used in some video frame grabbers for fast image conversions.

flat: 1) as applied to images in general, ones with low contrast. 2) as applied to the shading of objects in image creation software, shading that uses a uniform color and brightness for each polygon (small region) rather than varying the shading at edges or across the polygon.

flicker: 1) perceived rapid variations in image brightness caused by insufficiently rapid screen refresh rates 2) rapid variations in an interlaced image caused by differences in the image presented in each field.

flying erase head: an erase head that rotates along with the recording heads in a helical scan video recorder, and consequently can erase a single video line at a time. This allows new segments to be added after previously recorded segments without creating a visible glitch between them.

FM synthesis: a method of creating sounds or musical tones by directly manipulating the frequency (number of cycles per second) of the audio signal. Most simple computer music systems use this method.

FMV: an abbreviation for full motion video.

fractal: 1) an image or object that can be constructed using an iterative mathematical formula. 2) compression techniques that use these mathematical formulas to represent images.

frame: 1) a complete video image (which in an interlaced system such as the NTSC format used for television is made of 2 fields). 2)
in computerized instruction, usually taken as the material shown at one time on screen. But with greater use of animation and interactive screens, the term is also used to mean a logical sequence of images treated as a unit in the instructional design.

frame accurate: said of video editing, record, and playback systems that can locate and act on video images exactly at a specified single picture image. Most professional video equipment is frame accurate, but consumer products can find only approximate locations.

frame buffer: 1) an area of memory used hold a complete video image. 2) a video adapter that includes enough memory to hold an entire image.

frame grabber: a circuit or card that can capture and digitize a single video frame.

frame rate: for a video image or movie, the number of complete images shown per second.

full motion video (FMV): video presented at the standard frame rate (number of images per second) normally used for broadcasting in that area. In the U.S. and Japan, FMV is usually considered 30 frames per second, while in Europe it's 25 frames per second.

General MIDI: A standard configuration for MIDI digital music systems that assigns popular instruments and sounds to specified channels.

general-purpose controller: as applied to MIDI systems, a device that can be assigned by the user to regulate various other devices and instruments.

generation: for an image or copy, the number of reproduction steps from the original (which is the first generation). In general, higher generation numbers are likely to be less sharp.

genlock: 1) short for "synchronization generator lock," a feature of some video systems that allows them to set their timing to match an outside signal. Genlock is needed to overlay or mix two video signals.
2) more loosely, a computer display adapter that includes such a circuit and can overlay computer graphics on external video.

Green Book: an informal name for the standard developed by Sony and Philips for CD-I (Compact Disc Interactive) discs and players.

header: 1) as applied to CD-ROM discs, a section of four bytes at the start of data sectors that indicates the type of information in the sector. 2) a set of pins on a circuit board where a connector will be connected. Most common are duals, right angle or in-line. 3) the prefix part of a message in data communication giving address and control information.

Hi8: a Sony trademark for a variation on the 8mm videotape format that adds extended fidelity for the luminance (brightness) detail and separated video (S-video) outputs.

High Sierra format (HSF): a format for CD-ROM disks that can be read on different types of computers. It has largely been supplanted for new discs by the related ISO 9660 format.

hybrid: for a CD-ROM, one that contains tracks in more than one format.

hypermedia: a system or document that presents multiple pathways that the user can select and follow, rather than simply follow from beginning to end. It may include text, graphics, sound and other types of data.

hypertext: a system or document that provides multiple pathways through a collection of text that the user can select and follow, rather than simply presenting material from beginning to end.

in-betweening or tweening: a mode or function in computer animation programs that draws the needed intermediate images to create simulated motion between two given points.

Indeo: Intel's new trademark for products that apply the firm's DVI technology to desktop and digital video systems.

indexed color: a color system that uses information from the user or from programs as a pointer to a table of output colors, rather than specifying the color directly.

infotainment: programs that deliver informational elements while presenting the appearance of entertainment.

insert edit: referring to video editing, a style where new sequences are laid down on top of an existing continuous control track. While requiring more preparation than assemble editing (which places sequences one after each other), the result is likely to have fewer errors in timing.

Interactive Multimedia Association (IMA): a trade association of producers of interactive multimedia equipment headquartered in Arlington, Virginia. It used to be called the Interactive Video Industry Association (IVIA).

interactive video: 1) the integration of video and computer technologies in which a video program (moving pictures and voice tracks) and computer programs run together so that the user's choices or actions affect the program outcome. 2) the linking of a videodisc or videotape player to a computer, allowing selections from the video program to be shown under computer control.

Interactive Video Industry (Association (IVIA): the previous name for an organization of multimedia equipment makers now known as the Interactive Multimedia Association (IMA).

interformat editing: in video production, editing from a source sequence on one format (type of videotape or recording mode) to a result in another format. It is often done to combine the advantages of portable small formats for taping with larger formats for editing.

interframe compression: methods for reducing the size of a video stream or file that use information about the similarities between successive video frames. Interframe recording tends to be more compact than intraframe coding, but requires more complex systems for compression or editing.

interlaced: for video signals and displays, ones that paint each image in two passes (fields) down the screen, with the first pass creating the odd lines and the second the even lines. This reduces bandwidth for transmitted video, but causes flicker in computer graphics.

interleaved audio: a method of recording blocks of digital data interspersed with blocks of audio information on a compact disc or other medium.

International Interactive Communications Society (IICS): an organization of producers of interactive multimedia projects, headquartered in Washington, D.C..

interpolated frame: in the MPEG standard for encoding video signals, a single video image recreated by the received based on applying averaging or smoothing operations to preceding and following frames.

intraframe compression: methods for reducing the size of a video stream or file that make use of the information within each frame but not the similarities between successive frames.

ISO 9660: a standard format adopted by the International Standards Organization for CD-ROM discs intended for use with diverse computer systems. Most drives now come with software to read ISO 9660 discs.

jewel box: the clear hard plastic case that many CDs come in.

jog: in a video editing system, to change position in a video clip by a single frame or small number of frames.

JPEG: 1) an acronym (pronounced jay-pegg) for "Joint Photographic Experts Group", an industry committee that developed a compression standard originally intended for still images. 2) more informally, the compression standard developed by that group.

jukebox: a optical or magnetic storage unit that holds multiple discs that can be selected and automatically loaded into the play or record station.

key: 1) in an animation sequence or video edit, short for keyframe (an image used as a starting, ending or reference point). 2). in lighting for video, film, or photography, short for keylight, the principal (and usually brightest) light illuminating the main subject. 3) to switch between two or more video sources, based on a control signal. 4) the control signal used to switch between two or more video sources. 5).an image whose color or brightness as each point is used to determine the switching between two or more video signals.

keyer: a piece of video equipment that seemingly superimposes two or more images by quickly switching among inputs during the individual scans across a screen that make up a video image. This allows a weather forecaster to appear to be standing in front of a map, or a newscaster to appear to be in front of an electronic background.

keyframe: in animation or video editing, an image used as a starting, ending or reference point

Knowledge Navigator: an imaginary future product presented in an Apple Computer video as an example of where personal computing could be heading. The notepad-sized device combines a color flat-screen display, voice input, an on-screen software agent, integrated voice and video mail, and calendar software.

LaserDisc: a trademark of Pioneer Electronics for its line of videodiscs and players.

Level 1: 1) in referring to a multimedia PC, one equipped for the initial Microsoft Multimedia PC (MPC) specifications. 2) as applied to a videodisc system, the common industry designation for one that supports only direct controls such as start and stop, rather than complete computer-controlled interaction or programmability.

Level 2 or Level II: as applied to videodisc system, the common industry designation for one that supports some interaction through an internal processor, but not full control by an external computer. A Level II system can read a data program from audio channel 2 of the videodisc, but can't normally record user responses.

Level 3 or Level III: as applied to a videodisc system, the common industry designation for one that supports interactive use, computer connections, and the recording of user responses. Macintosh-computer-controlled systems are usually configured as Level III systems.

Level 4 or Level IV: as applied to a videodisc system, one that supports interactivity but gets its data program from information encoded in video portion of the signal from the videodisc rather than from an audio track or computer connection.

Level A: in the CD-I format, a method of recording audio that offers fidelity comparable to that of standard CD audio but compresses the data to use only about half as much space on disc.

Level B: in the CD-I and CD-ROM XA compact disc formats, a method of recording audio that offers medium fidelity but that is somewhat compressed compared with full-fidelity audio. Level B uses 4-bit sampling at 37.8 kHz for an effective bandwidth of 17 kHz. Level B mono requires 1 out of every 8 sectors on the disc, while stereo requires 1 in 4.

Level C: in the CD-I and CD-ROM XA compact disc formats, a method of recording audio that offers fidelity sufficient for speech but that is highly compressed compared with full-fidelity audio. Level C uses 4-bit sampling at 18.9 kHz for an effective bandwidth of 8.5 kHz. Level C mono requires 1 out of every 16 sectors on the disc, while stereo requires 1 in 8.

linear audio: a method of recording audio on videotape that uses a separate track along the length of the tape. This method generally provides lower fidelity, but allows the audio to be edited separately from the video.

linear editing: video editing methods where you have to shuttle the tape back and forth to get from a clip at the beginning of the source reel to one at the end.

line in: an input on a audio or video system that expects a pre-amplifier-level signal (typically 100 mV to 1V).

line level: in audio connections, a signal that ranges up to approximately 1 volt for full signal. This is likely to be the output of a preamplifier rather than the direct signal from a microphone.

line out: an output on a audio or video system that provides a pre-amplifier-level signal (typically 100 mV to 1V) for connection to other equipment

link: 1) a connection between nodes or items of information in a hypermedia system. 2) a connection between network nodes.

longitudinal time code (LTC): a time signal placed in one of the tracks that run the length of a videotape. On some recorders, one of the audio tracks must be used for the LTC, while others provide a special time code track. The code is normally the SMPTE Time Code. LTC can only be read while the tape is moving.

loop through: on a video on MIDI connection, an output connector that provides the signal received on a corresponding input.

lossey compression: compression methods that produce files that decompress to provide only an approximate copy of the original data. These approaches usually provide larger compression ratios than lossless methods, and are used primarily for images or sounds where every bit of data isn't essential to provide a useful representation.

lossless compression: compression methods that produce files that decompress to provide an exact copy of the original data. These approaches usually provide smaller compression ratios than lossey methods, and are used primarily for programs or text files where every bit of data is essential.

luminance: the brightness or intensity of an image or signal, particularly the brightness without regard to color.

luminance bandwidth: the range of frequency representing brightness (and therefore the amount of shape detail) that a system can record or transmit. In many video formats, it is greater than the chroma (color) bandwidth.

luminance key: a signal used to switch between two or more video images based on the brightness (luminance) of a signal.

machine-independent: 1) software designed to work on more than one type or model of computer. 2) software that offers similar performance or output even when run on different types or models of machines.

Media Control Interface (MCI): a platform-independent set of commands and structures that define how a program can interact with multimedia devices and resources. It was defined by Microsoft as part of the firm's multimedia specification.

media independent: said of a project or program that will produce the same sound and/or images when played back from different format systems—such as a training program designed to work either on videodisc or on videotape.

mic level or microphone level: a high-sensitivity audio input intended for low signal-strength inputs such as those provided by microphones rather than the more powerful signals provided by amplifiers.

MIDI: an acronym (pronounced middee) for Musical Instrument Digital Interface, an industry-standard connection for digital control of musical instruments and devices.

Mode 1: for CD-ROM disks, a format that adds a 3rd level of error correction for each block, leaving 2048 bytes for data.

Mode 2: for CD-ROM disks, a format that uses only the error-correction facilities of the underlying Red Book layer for each block, leaving 2352 bytes for data.

morph: 1) to change one image into another by moving corresponding elements rather than by cross-fading. 2) a graphics program published by Gryphon Software in both Mac and Windows versions that produces such changes.

motion blur: a blending or streaking effect deliberately added to images to simulate the appearance of moving objects.

motion choreography: in animation and computer graphics, determining the displacement (change in position) of each object over time.

motion video: the type of video image produced by a camera, rather than still video, animation or computer graphics.

MPEG: 1) an acronym (pronounced emm-pegg) for "Moving Pictures Experts Group", an industry committee that is developing a set of compression standards for moving images that use interframe compression (frame differencing) as well as compression within frames 2) informally, the first standard developed by the group.

MPEG 1: a form of the MPEG compression method optimized for data rates in the 1 to 1.5 megabit/sec range, such as the transfer rate of CD-ROM drives and T-1 communications links.

MPEG 2 or MPEG II: a form of the MPEG compression method optimized for data rates above 5 megabit/sec rate and intended for applications such as broadcast video and medical imaging.

MS-DOS CD-ROM Extensions: a set of routines that connect the MS-DOS or PC-DOS operating system to the driver routines for specific models of CD-ROM players. The extensions allow MS-DOS machines to read CD-ROM discs of the ISO 9660 and High Sierra format.

Multimedia Extensions: a set of routines and specifications for running multimedia programs with Microsoft Corp.'s Windows 3.0 operating environment. Their functions were absorbed into Windows 3.1.

Multimedia Windows: an informal term for Microsoft's Windows operating environment along with the company's Multimedia Extensions running on the appropriate hardware.

MultiSpin: a trademark of NEC Technologies Inc. for the firm's line of dual-speed CD-ROM drives that transfer data at both 150 KB/s (kilobytes per second) and 300 KBs). The first model was introduced in 1992.

MultiSync: 1) a registered trademark of NEC Technologies, Inc. for the firm's line of monitors designed to work with a wide range of video input frequencies and formats. 2) commonly but improperly used to refer to any multifrequency monitor.

narration: dialog or commentary by someone outside the frame (visible scene) in a film or video, or that is not synchronized with the action or visible speech.

narrowcast: 1) to aim a program at a small but defined portion of the potential audience. 2) a program so aimed.

National Television Standards Committee: a common misnomer for the National Television Systems Committee (NTSC), the industry group that formulated the standards for American (U.S.) color television.

National Television Systems Committee (NTSC): the industry group that formulated the standards for American (U.S.) color television.

noninterlaced: said of video systems that create images by painting each horizontal line across the screen in succession rather than painting alternate sets of lines in two sweeps down the screen (which is called interlaced scan). Also called progressive scan.

nonlinear editing: video editing methods that record the source clips on hard disk, allowing you to jump directly to any clip without having to shuttle through any clips that came before or after.

off-line: 1) as applied to video editing, a system than can only make an edit decision list (EDL) or simple edits (recordings) such as cuts, rather than one that can perform a full range of editing and video effects. 2) to edit a program using such a system

On-line: 1) as applied to video editing, a complete system that can perform edits (make recordings) and add special effects. On-line systems are expensive, so rough edits or edit decision lists (EDLs) are commonly done on less costly off-line systems.

Orange Book: 1) the informal name for the document that defines the standards for write-once CD discs 2) discs or tracks written with that format

overdub: 1) to add a signal or channel to existing material. 2) particularly to add a new layer or channel to existing audio material.

overlay: to show one video image positioned on top of another. To overlay two video signals, they must be synchronized to the same timing signal (genlocked). 2) especially in video images, to show text on top of a picture.

oversampling: to read data at a higher rate than normal to produce more accurate values or to make it easier to filter the results.

overscan: for a video system, a mode in which the image is made slightly larger than the face of screen, ensuring the image fills the whole screen. This is the normal mode for television-style video, but most computer systems use underscan instead.

pan: 1) in video and film, to rotate the camera horizontally 2) in computer graphics, to move in a specified direction along the plane of an image, maintaining the same scale and orientation 3) in a MIDI (computerized music) system, a controller that shifts the position of a voice between the right and left stereo channels.

phase alternate line (PAL): the format for color television signals used in West Germany, England, Holland, and several other countries. PAL uses an interlaced format with 50 fields and 25 frames per second, and 625 lines per screen.

Photo CD: a format developed by Kodak for storing compressed still images (and accompanying sound) on CD-ROM discs. The format can be used both as a means of storing and delivering snapshots to view on home players and for delivering clip art and photos for use with computer-based systems.

pickup: 1. a microphone. 2. a non-acoustic transducer intended to emit an electronic signal corresponding to the sound produced by a musical instrument. 3. in video or film production, a shot or sequence recorded after the main sequence and used in editing either to add interest during editing or to cover flaws.

PICT: the standard file format used to pass images back and forth between Macintosh applications and the main format used by the Clipboard. PICT files consist of collections of the Macintosh QuickDraw routines needed to create the image.

picture depth: the amount of storage allocated per picture element, usually expressed either in bits or in the number of colors (or shades) that can be represented by that number of bits. Common values include 1-bit (black and white), 8-bit (256 colors) and 24-bit (millions of colors).

picture element (pixel): the smallest part of a picture that can be addressed or changed in a digital image.

post: short for post-production, the steps in producing a film, video or multimedia project that take place after any live filming or construction of the basic images.

posterize: to transform an image to a more stark form by rounding all tonal values to a small number of possible values.

premaster: in the production of a compact disc, record, or videodisc, to format the data into the special logical configuration needed on the master. This might include adding error correction and location information on digital recordings.

processor audio: sound, music, or speech created by data that has been routed through or created in the normal digital pathways of a computer system and played back under the control of the computer, rather than sound that is merely encoded in digital form for playback using standard digital-to-analog circuits.

progressive scan: video systems that create images by painting each horizontal line across the screen in succession rather than painting alternate sets of lines in two sweeps down the screen (which is called interlaced scan).

prosumer: a neologism (made-up word) for a market niche for products in the intersection between professional and consumer markets. It is often used for video gear that is below the usual broadcast grade but above what most people would buy for home use.

public access: 1) referring to public or private television and radio systems, the provision of time for independent program producers to air their work. Many cable TV systems are required to provide a certain level of public access as part of their franchise agreements. 2) referring to multimedia systems, ones intended for use by the general public or by a wide variety of customers or visitors. Most feature touchscreens or other simple inputs.

pulse code modulation (PCM): The representation of analog signals as discrete pulses of digital information.

QuickTime (QT): 1) Apple Computer's architecture for working with time-based data types such as sounds and video. 2) the Extension program for the Macintosh Operating System used to add the ability to work with time-based media. 3) used loosely for the QuickTime Movie Format, a data format defined by Apple Computer for digital presentations that can include sound, animation and video images.

ray tracing: a technique for creating graphic images by calculating where each ray (small point) of light that reaches the viewer would have come from and what objects would have altered it

RCA connector: the common connector used for most back-panel audio connections and for some types of video. It uses relatively low-cost push-on male and female connectors consisting of an inner connector within a concentric ring about 8 mm in diameter that forms the outer connector. Also commonly called a "phono connector" because of its frequent use on phonographs.

Red Book: 1) the common name for the book that lists the standards for Compact Disc audio as specified by Sony and Philips, the developers of this format. 2) on a mixed mode disc, audio tracks formatted according to this standard.

refresh rate: the number of times per second that a video display system redraws the image on screen. Rates below about 75 images per second can cause flicker, depending on the image size, lighting and image content.

rehearse: during editing, to see what the results of an edit step would look like without actually recording the result; also called "preview" on most systems.

render: to draw an image as it would appear in final form rather than as a schematic or blueprint.

retrieval engine: a program or section of code to be embedded in other programs that finds and presents data in large data collections. Retrieval engines are commonly used to provide faster and easier access to the large stores of data on CD-ROM discs.

RGB: 1). as applied to video systems, short for red green and blue, three color signals that can between them create a complete video image. Most computer graphics systems use this tri-color approach. Early models of the IBM PC uses TTL RGB, which allows the color signals to take on only a few discrete values. Most computers now use analog RGB, which allows the color signals to take on a continous range values 2) as a color model, a method of representing all colors as the combination of red, green and blue light that would create that color. 3) a characterization of video systems that work with picture information carried on three signal (red, green blue) lines rather than combined in a single line (composite color).

RGB analog: a characterization of video systems that work with video signals carried on three signal lines in continuos (analog) form. This is the type of video used by the IBM VGA video system, the Apple Macintosh II line and by most other high-end personal computers.

rich text: 1) text that has additional embedded information regarding formatting or structuring. For example, text with italics or a document with an outline format. 2) specifically Rich Text Format (RTF), a format developed by Microsoft to exchange text with styles and formatting using only normal alphanumeric symbols.

Rock Ridge Interchange Protocol (RRIP): a proposed extension of the ISO 9660 standards for CD-ROM discs to handle files in the POSIX format.

RS-170A: a recommended standard (RS) of the Electronics Industries Association that specifies color video signals for the common "NTSC" format used for broadcast and most consumer video products in the United States and Japan.

safe area: in a video image, the portion that will be visible after transmission and reception on the average receiver or monitor. The outer 10% to 20% of the image is usually considered unsafe because it may be hidden behind a bezel (frame) on the receiver.

sampled sound: sound that has been captured in digital form from an acoustic or electrical waveform rather than synthesized (created) by a computer system.

saturated: said of areas or images that have a strong color (chroma) component. They're harder to reproduce in most types of broadcast video.

scalable: as applied to video or sound playback technologies, ones that allow the same data to create output over a range of quality levels, with better reception systems automatically generating higher quality levels.

scan line: one of the horizontal sweeps across the screen that makes up a video image.

scanning frequency: 1) usually meaning the horizontal scanning frequency, the number of horizontal sweeps across the screen per second used to form a video image 2) the vertical scanning frequency, the number of sweeps down the screen used to form a video image

score: 1) the written form of a piece of music. 2) the process of writing down a composition in a form suitable for reading and playing. 3) in MacroMedia's animation programs, the diagrammatic representation of an animation sequence (a movie).

seek time: The time required to locate specific data on a disk. On average it includes the time necessary to move the read head to the correct track and the time for the disk to rotate half the way around.

sequencer: 1) a computer or controller that issues instructions to programmable musical instruments. 2) software that lets the user compose and edit music.

serial VTR: a videotape recorder (VTR) that can be controlled over a single-channel control wire such as the normal RS-232 or RS-422 connections used between computers and modems.

sfx: in audio work, a common abbreviation for "sound effects."

shot: a single continuous run of film or tape.

SMPTE: (pronounced "simm-tee") an abbreviation for "Society of Motion Picture and Television Engineers," a group that, among other efforts, defined a time-coding system used on almost all professional videotape and film. SMPTE is based in White Plains, NY.

snd: a standard resource format for sounds on the Macintosh.

spatial resolution: in video systems, the number of lines or dots that make up each image. When not otherwise specified, the word "resolution" by itself is presumed to mean spatial resolution, rather than color or time resolution.

special effects generator (SEG): a video signal–processing device that changes the way one or more images appear on the video screen.

spline: a type of curve used in many graphics programs to create smooth motion paths.

split edit: in video or film production, an edit (switch to a new input) of just the audio or just the video, leaving the other of these elements continuing from the previous source.

sprite: a graphics object that can be moved around the screen as a unit.

Standard MIDI File (SMF): a format for placing the data from a MIDI data stream in a file that can be used with many music applications.

step time: in MIDI recording, recording event by event for later playback at full speed instead of recording at full (real-time) speed.

still store: a large-capacity optical or magnetic disc that is used to store a number of single video images for use in editing or broadcast.

storyboard: 1) to produce a set of images representing the flow of a video or film project 2) a mounted collection of images produced for that purpose.

subsample: to throw out selected portions of a signal to reduce the amount that has to be encoded or compressed. It is a usual step in most types of lossey compression. The most common technique is decimation.

sustained transfer rate: for a CD-ROM disc, the number of bytes per second the drive can supply when reading a clip much longer than its built-in buffer.

S-video: short for separated video, formats such as S-VHS and Hi8 that keep the brightness and color (luminance and chroma) as separate signals. Also called Y/C video.

symmetrical compression: as applied to video or audio data, methods for squeezing the data for storage or transmission that take an equal amount of time and resources to compress the data as to de-compress it.

sync: as applied to video signals, the portion of the signal or a separate signal that carries the overall timing information.

synthesized sound: sound that is created based on a series of parameters rather than replayed from recorded samples.

synthesizer: 1) a musical instrument, module or circuit that creates and shapes sounds electronically according to changeable settings. Along with providing a choice of such basic sound qualities as pitch, loudness ,and duration, most synthesizers allow the user to alter the tonal qualities of each note. 2) particularly, a module or instrument that responds to MIDI commands and produces the requested audio output.

TARGA: an image format defined by Truevision, originally for that company's line of TARGA videographics interface cards. It is now used as an exchange format by many other image-creation and editing programs.

temporal redundancy: signal data that duplicates information found at an earlier or later time in the signal.

timbre: the character of a sound, determined by the overtones.

timebase corrector or time base corrector (TBC): a unit that resets the timing portion of a video signal to the standard values for a specified video format. TBCs are often used to clean up the output from computer video boards or from videocassette recorders (VCRs) before broadcast or further recording.

time code: 1) in video production, an electronic marking of elapsed time placed on a tape to facilitate editing. 2) specifically, the SMPTE time signals as defined by the Society of Motion Picture and Television Engineers. The code consists of 4 sets of numbers representing hour, minute, second and frame, in the format hh:mm:ss:ff.

title: in publishing, a single volume or set of volumes sold as a set under the same name. Often used in discussions of the number of titles available in different electronic formats.

true color: 1) color systems in which the color information in the image is used directly to create the output color rather than as an index to a table of colors in a palette. 2) said of color systems that have enough available colors to make the choices seem continuous to the human eye. In most cases, this is considered to be 24-bit color (about 16 million available colors).

tween: in animation and graphics, to automatically create an interpolated image between two set images. Tweening speeds up the creation of animated sequences by letting the user define only the keyframe images and letting the computer fill in the ones in between.

UHF: 1) short for "ultra-high frequency, " the radio frequency from 300 to 3,000 MHz. 2) Also used more specifically to indicate the TV broadcast band located in this range. In the United States, UHF channels 14 through 83 occupy the range from 470 MHz to 890 MHz.

Ultimatte: a brand name for a type of chroma key system used to overlay multiple video images. The Ultimatte system also transfers the luminance (brightness) image of the dropout color, allowing shadows to be transferred into the composite image.

Ultimedia: IBM's brand name for its multimedia hardware and software products. It is supposed to suggest "the ultimate in multimedia."

U-matic: a trademark for Sony Corporation's 3/4-inch video systems, including tape, recorders and players. The first U-matic units were delivered in 1971. It is a composite format, with moderate resolution.

unbalanced: said of signal channels in which the information is carried as the signal on a single wire referenced to ground.
underscan: as applied to video images, set to fill less than the full screen (and thus making the edges of the image visible). Although the normal mode for computer images, this mode is used in traditional video only for checking signal quality.

validation: in computerized instruction, trying the lesson out on a group of students to check that it proceeds the way it is intended to.

value: when speaking of color, the degree of lightness or darkness.

variable frequency monitor: a video monitor that can accommodate a range of horizontal and vertical input frequencies, and thus work with signals from a variety of sources. Usually, the range includes several common computer video formats or several broadcast standards.

vector graphic: images and drawings made up of lines and other geometric elements rather than out of individual dots.

vectorscope: a television test instrument that shows a video signal in a circular form with the displacement around the circle indicating the timing of that portion relative to signal reference points. It is widely used to check and adjust the color component of the signal.

vertical blanking interval (VBI): the portion of the video signal during which the picture information is suppressed at the end of the field. It is provided to allow the scanning beam in a CRT to return from the bottom to the top of the picture. In the standard NTSC video format, it includes the first 21 horizontal lines of each field.

vertical interval switching: changing between two video signals during the vertical blanking interval at the end of a scan down the screen so that there is no visible glitch in the output signal.

vertical interval time code (VITC): a digital time signal placed in a portion of the video signal normally used for the interval between images. Once recorded, it cannot be changed or edited without re-recording the accompanying video signal, but it can be read in slow scan or pause modes.

VHS: an abbreviation for "Video Home System," a trademark for the 1/2-inch consumer videotape format developed by Matsushita and JVC and now widely used for consumer videotape recorders.

videodisc: a standard format for 12-inch optical discs that carry analog video signals.

Video Electronics Standards Association (VESA): an industry trade group formed to codify the software interface to advanced video cards, and now active as well in the definition of one type of local bus.

videographic: loosely speaking, a term for computer video systems and subsystems that produce signals compatible with standard noncomputer video. In the United States, this usually means units that support output in the NTSC format.

video overlay: 1) the combining of two or more video signals to get one resulting video output. 2) in particular, the placement of computer-generated video over standard video, including the placement of lettering (titles) by dedicated titling systems. Video overlay requires special hardware (including a unit called a genlock) to synchronize the input video signals.

video RAM (VRAM): memory chips or systems engineered for use with video displays, particularly those built with a dual data ports to allow the video information to be read out without interfering with and reading and writing of data through the primary port. 2) a section of main memory used to store data for display.

video server: a computer or program that delivers video sequences over a network.

videotext: a text-based information service that distributes information over video links or displays the result on a video display. Videotext services can be distributed through cable or any other television system, or by sending signals over telephone lines to a computer that can draw the images locally.

video wall: a large display made up of multiple monitors with synchronized programming.

visualization: in computer graphics, techniques that let the computer present graphics images or charts of phenomena that would not normally be visible. Visualization is becoming an important tool in many fields of science and engineering.

voxel: a volume element, the three-dimensional equivalent to the picture element (pixel); it is the smallest region that can be represented in a volumetric imaging system.

VU meter: (volume unit meter) an indicator of audio signal strength. Most VU meters are set to indicate 0 dB as the maximum undistorted signal level, with markings that show a red zone for levels above that.

walk-through: 1) in film and video production, a rehearsal done without cameras. 2) a simulated trip through a computerized architectural model, especially one where the viewer can interactively navigate a path through the model.

waveform monitor: a video test instrument that shows the shape of the video signal graphed over a selected interval of time, rather than the video picture itself.

wavelet: an exotic mathematical technique that's recently been applied as a means for compressing images.

wavetable synthesis: music and sounds produced by adding together samples of recorded sounds rather than using completely artificial synthesized sound.

white balance: the adjustment of a camera or other video source so that a white object will produce the correct signal for white. Most consumer video cameras have automatic white-balance circuits.

white level: in a video signal, the signal level corresponding the brightest possible white value. Because of the way the signal is encoded, in most video formats it is actually the minimum voltage.

XA: short for "Extended Architecture", an addition to the format for CD-ROM optical data discs that adds provisions for storing and playing back interleaved sound and graphics. See CD-ROM XA for more details.

XGA: an abbreviation for Extended Graphics Architecture, a video display standard introduced by IBM in 1990 that provides for 256 colors at 1024 by 768 pixels or 65 thousand colors at 640 by 480 pixels. The original IBM version only supported interlaced displays.

Y/C: A type of component video signal found in S-VHS, Hi-8mm and 3/4" SP video formats that separates a signal's brightness (luminance) and color (chrominance) information to maintain better picture quality. This is an intermediate step in image resolution between standard video (composite) and component video.

Yellow Book: 1) an informal name for the documents defining the standards for the CD-ROM format developed by Philips and Sony. 2) data tracks in this format.

YUV: a type of video encoding that allocates full bandwidth to the intensity (Y) channel and 1/2 bandwidth to the color information (UV).

zoom: 1) to change the size of the area selected for viewing or display to provide either a more detailed view or more of an overview. 2) for a camera shot, to change the magnification of the lens and thus change the width of the shot and its apparent closeness.

Index